D1565444

THE ARCHEOLOGY OF

WORLD RELIGIONS

THE ARCHEOLOGY

OF

WORLD RELIGIONS

The Background of
Primitivism, Zoroastrianism,
Hinduism, Jainism, Buddhism,
Confucianism, Taoism,
Shinto, Islam, and Sikhism

BY JACK FINEGAN

PRINCETON, NEW JERSEY
PRINCETON UNIVERSITY PRESS
1952

Printed in the United States of America
by Princeton University Press, Princeton, New Jersey

To Mildred

Preface

THERE are many living religions in the world today. In addition to the more prominent systems of belief and practice cherished by groups which have long recorded histories or political or numerical importance, there are the numerous forms of faith found among preliterate peoples in various parts of the earth. If the latter may be dealt with collectively under the heading of "primitivism" the major religions of the present world are at least twelve. They are Buddhism, Christianity, Confucianism, Hinduism, Islam, Jainism, Judaism, Primitivism, Shinto, Sikhism, Taoism, and Zoroastrianism.

The archeological background of the Hebrew and Christian faiths was the subject of my *Light from the Ancient Past* (Princeton University Press, 1946), and it is the purpose of the present book to give a similar account relative to the ten others.

In a study primarily archeological it is clear that the chief concern will be with the early history of the religions, rather than with their recent and contemporary aspects. A beginning of the entire inquiry will be made with Primitivism. Pertaining as the adjective primitive does to that which is earliest in time, this subject directs our attention to the first discernible evidences of religion, back in the mists of man's prehistory; but synonymous as the same adjective is with aboriginal, it also points to the faiths of native peoples still on earth today. Many of these may have been in existence for a very long time and even have had a history as long as that of men of literate cultures, but the facts that this history has not been recorded in writing and that these people have lived in relative isolation from advancing civilization, suggest that among them religion may be at least relatively simple and archaic. It will not be assumed in advance that the contemporary beliefs of such folks correspond with those of prehistoric men, but if similarities are actually observed they will be pointed out. Thus two glimpses will be had of Primitivism, one in prehistoric times, the other in the life of present-day preliterate peoples.

We shall then deal with the other religions, in an order suggested by both geographical and chronological considerations. As far as geography is concerned, the study will take us eastward from Iran to India, China and Japan, then westward to Arabia and back once more to India. Each of these lands will be described briefly when we first come to it. In regard to chronology, it is of course often difficult or impossible to assign exact dates to the lives of the founders of religions or to crucial events in the history of religions. Evidence will be presented on such questions, however, and the order in which the various religions are considered will reflect at least to some extent the relative times of their emergence in world history. In each major geographical area the rise of human culture will be traced from the earliest times; in each religion the history of the faith will be followed from its origin to the point where its most distinctive emphases have come into view. Considerations of space as well as the archeological interest preclude any attempt to carry the history farther than such point as this. Inevitably the limitation means that a great many developments cannot be touched at all. In the case of Buddhism, for example, a relatively full story is told of its rise in India but to its later spread through many other lands only very brief references are made.

The archeological interest also determines the fact that attention is focused throughout upon the ancient monuments and documents of the various religions. The actual objects and manuscripts which archeology brings to light provide materials of tangible and fascinating sort for understanding the nature of the religions which produced them. Through the ancient writings and the monuments which are often far older than any written records, the religion speaks with its own authentic voice.

In order to make these fundamental materials known in as direct a way as possible, extensive quotations are given from the texts, and many of the monuments are reproduced in photographs. The work is based upon my own travel around the world, gathering of material from museums, libraries and other sources in Asia, Europe and America, and consultation of the literature cited. Except for books appearing in the List of Abbreviations, each work is listed fully upon its first mention.

I wish to express deep appreciation to various members of the staff of Princeton University Press, and especially to Miss Margot Cutter, Fine Arts Editor, for many courtesies.

JACK FINEGAN

Pacific School of Religion
Berkeley, California

Acknowledgments

SOURCES of photographs and quotations are given in the List of Illustrations and in the footnotes. In addition to these acknowledgments, appreciation is also expressed to the following for permission to make reproductions of pictures: to the American Council of Learned Societies, Washington, for Fig. 133; to the Director General of Archaeology in India, New Delhi, for Figs. 54, 61 and 65; to Ludwig Bachhofer for Figs. 89, 91, 92, 93, 94, 95, 96, 97, 99, 100 and 101; to Ernest Benn Limited, London, for Fig. 59; to the Bobbs Merrill Company, Indianapolis, for Fig. 187; to the Trustees of the British Museum, London, for Fig. 33; to W. Norman Brown for Figs. 82, 83, 84, 85, 86 and 87; to Avery Brundage for Fig. 141; to the Syndics of the Cambridge University Press for Fig. 115; to the Carnegie Institution of Washington for Fig. 46; to the Chicago Natural History Museum for Fig. 149; to the Clarendon Press, Oxford, for Fig. 238; to the Columbia University Library, New York, for Fig. 220; to Mrs. A. K. Coomaraswamy for Figs. 55, 56, 57, 62, 63, 64, 67, 72 and 113; to the John Day Company, Inc., New York, for Fig. 143; to Faber and Faber Limited, London, for Fig. 16; to the Freer Gallery of Art, Washington, for Figs. 82 and 83; to Librairie Orientaliste Paul Geuthner, Paris, for Figs. 154, 158, 159, 162, 211 and 219; to George G. Harrap and Company Limited, London, for Fig. 183; to Harvard University Press, Cambridge, for Fig. 129; to the late Ernst E. Herzfeld for Figs. 23, 32, 41 and 42; to the High Commissioner for India, London, for Fig. 128; to the Institut de Paleontologie Humaine, Paris, for Figs. 11, 12 and 13; to the Macmillan Company, New York, for Fig. 136; to the Matson Photo Service, Jerusalem, for Fig. 227; to the Museum of Navajo Ceremonial Art, Santa Fe, for Fig. 19; to the National Geological Survey of China, Nanking, for Figs. 137 and 138; to the National Museum, Stockholm, for Figs. 180, 184, 185 and 186; to the New York Public Library for Fig. 208; to Martinus Nijhoff, The Hague, for Figs. 124, 125 and 126; to Oxford University Press, London, for Figs. 37, 39, 40, 44, 45, 243, 244 and 250; to Oxford University Press, New York, for Fig. 23; to Pantheon Books Inc., New York, for Figs. 148 and 176; to Arthur Upham Pope for Figs. 37, 39, 40, 44, 45, 243, 244 and 250; to Presses Universitaires de France, Paris, for Fig. 237; to Princeton University Press, Princeton, for Fig. 131; to Routledge and Kegan Paul Ltd., London, for Fig. 136; to the Society

[ix]

of Antiquaries of London for Figs. 209 and 210; to the Society for Promoting Christian Knowledge, London, for Fig. 164; and to Van Oest, Les Editions d'Art et d'Histoire, Paris, for Figs. 110, 118, 167, 202, 205 and 206.

Certain material reproduced in this book, namely, seven pictures, three figures, two plates, and the reproduction of the first page of a preface of a work (in Japanese), which material is specifically identified in the acknowledgments in the List of Illustrations, was taken from six German works and two Japanese works, originally published in Germany and Japan, respectively. The German and Japanese interests in the United States copyrights in these works were vested in the Attorney General of the United States in 1950, pursuant to law. The works involved and the particular material taken therefrom are listed below. The use of this material in the present book is by permission of the Attorney General of the United States under License No. JA-1482.

1. William Cohn, *Buddha in der Kunst des Ostens.* Leipzig: Klinkhardt & Biermann, 1925. "Copyright 1924 by Klinkhardt & Biermann, Leipzig."
   (1) Picture on page 5, with title on page 4 (for my Fig. 102)
   (2) Picture on page 101, with title on page 100 (for my Fig. 132)
2. Ernst Diez, *Die Kunst Indiens.* Wildpark-Potsdam: Akademische Verlagsgesellschaft Athenaion M.B.H., 1925.
   (1) Figure 136, on page 115 (for my Fig. 105)
3. P. Andreas Eckardt, *Geschichte der koreanischen Kunst.* Leipzig: Karl W. Hiersemann, 1929. "Copyright 1929 by Karl W. Hiersemann, Leipzig."
   (1) Figure 178 on Plate LXII (for my Fig. 130)
4. Otto Fischer, *Die Kunst Indiens, Chinas und Japans.* Propyläen-Kunstgeschichte, IV. 2d ed. Berlin: Propyläen-Verlag, 1928. "Copyright 1928 by Propyläen-Verlag, G.M.B.H., in Berlin."
   (1) Picture on page 168 (for my Fig. 104)
   (2) Picture on page 247 (for my Fig. 77)
5. Helmuth von Glasenapp, *Die Literaturen Indiens von ihren Anfängen bis zur Gegenwart.* In Oskar Walzel, ed., Handbuch der Literatur-Wissenschaft. Wildpark-Potsdam: Akademische Verlagsgesellschaft Athenaion M.B.H., 1929. "Copyright 1929 by

Akademische Verlagsgesellschaft Athenaion M.B.H., Wildpark-Potsdam."

(1) Figure 26 on page 51 (for my Fig. 50)

6. Heinrich Glück and Ernst Diez, *Die Kunst des Islam*. Propyläen-Kunstgeschichte, v. 3d ed. Berlin: Propyläen-Verlag, 1925. "Copyright 1925 by Der Propyläen-Verlag G.M.B.H., Berlin."

(1) Picture on page 186 (for my Fig. 241)

(2) Picture between pages 188 and 189 (for my Fig. 242)

(3) Picture on page 338 (for my Fig. 252)

7. Mizoguchi, Teijiro and Eikyu Matsuoka, eds., *Nihon Emakimono Shusei*. Tokyo: Yuzankaku, 1929.

(1) Vol. iii, Plate 64 (for my Fig. 193)

(2) Vol. iv, Plate 10 (for my Fig. 192)

8. Uematsu, Yasushi and Tatso Otsuka, annotators, *Kojiki Zenshaku*. Tokyo: Fukyusha-shoten, 1935.

(1) Facsimile in Japanese language of first page of Preface (for my Fig. 188)

Contents

CONTENTS

III. *HINDUISM*

CONTENTS

Page

V. BUDDHISM

Page

VI. CONFUCIANISM

VII. TAOISM

VIII. *SHINTO*

IX. *ISLAM*

X. *SIKHISM*

List of Illustrations

[xix]

[xx]

[xxiii]

[xxiv]

[xxvi]

[xxviii]

[xxix]

LIST OF ILLUSTRATIONS

[xxxi]

[xxxii]

LIST OF MAPS

LIST OF ABBREVIATIONS

AJA *American Journal of Archaeology.*
ARAB Daniel D. Luckenbill, *Ancient Records of Assyria and Babylonia.* 2 vols. 1926-27.
ARE James H. Breasted, *Ancient Records of Egypt.* 5 vols. 1906-07.
BASOR *Bulletin* of the American Schools of Oriental Research.
BEIS Ludwig Bachhofer, *Early Indian Sculpture.* 2 vols. 1929.
CAH J. B. Bury, S. A. Cook, F. E. Adcock, M. P. Charlesworth and N. H. Baynes, eds., *The Cambridge Ancient History.* 12 vols. and 5 vols. of plates. 1923-39.
CBC Herrlee G. Creel, *The Birth of China, A Study of the Formative Period of Chinese Civilization.* 1937.
CEMA K. A. C. Creswell, *Early Muslim Architecture, Umayyads, Early 'Abbāsids and Ṭūlūnids.* Part I, *Umayyads,* A.D. 622-750 (1932); Part II, *Early 'Abbāsids, Umayyads of Cordova, Aghlabids, Ṭūlūnids, and Samānids,* A.D. 751-905 (1940).
CHI E. J. Rapson, Wolseley Haig, Richard Burn and H. H. Dodwell, *The Cambridge History of India.* 6 vols. 1922-37.
CHIIA Ananda K. Coomaraswamy, *History of Indian and Indonesian Art.* 1927.

CRW Carl Clemen and others, *Religions of the World, Their Nature and Their History.* tr. A. K. Dallas. 1931.
CSECC Herrlee G. Creel, *Studies in Early Chinese Culture,* First Series (American Council of Learned Societies Studies in Chinese and Related Civilizations, 3). 1937.
CSHI H. H. Dodwell, ed., *The Cambridge Shorter History of India.* 1934.
EB *The Encyclopaedia Britannica.* 14th ed. 24 vols. 1929.
EI M. Th. Houtsma and others, eds., *The Encyclopaedia of Islām, A Dictionary of the Geography, Ethnography and Biography of the Muhammadan Peoples.* 5 vols. 1913-38.
FAH Nabih Amin Faris, ed., *The Arab Heritage.* 1944.
FHCP Fung Yu-lan, *A History of Chinese Philosophy,* I, *The Period of the Philosophers (From the Beginnings to circa 100 B.C.).* tr. Derk Bodde. 1937.
FLP Jack Finegan, *Light from the Ancient Past, The Archeological Background of the Hebrew-Christian Religion.* 1946.
GCBD Herbert A. Giles, *A Chinese Biographical Dictionary.* 1898.
GCE René Grousset, *The Civilizations of the East.* tr.

[xxxix]

Catherine A. Phillips. I, *The Near and Middle East*. 1931; II, *India*. 1931; III, *China*. 1934; IV, *Japan*. 1934.

GJ   Helmuth von Glasenapp, *Der Jainismus, Eine indische Erlösungsreligion* (Kultur und Weltanschauung, Eine Sammlung von Einzeldarstellungen). 1925.

HERE   James Hastings, ed., *Encyclopaedia of Religion and Ethics*. 12 vols. 1910-22.

HHA   Philip K. Hitti, *History of the Arabs*. 2d ed. 1940.

JAOS   *Journal of the American Oriental Society*.

JGRMW   Edward J. Jurji, ed., *The Great Religions of the Modern World, Confucianism, Taoism, Hinduism, Buddhism, Shintoism, Islam, Judaism, Eastern Orthodoxy, Roman Catholicism, Protestantism*. 1946.

JNES   *Journal of Near Eastern Studies*.

LCL   *The Loeb Classical Library*.

MASI   *Memoirs of the Archaeological Survey of India*.

MHR   George Foot Moore, *History of Religions* (International Theological Library). I, *China, Japan, Egypt, Babylonia, Assyria, India, Persia, Greece,*

Rome. rev. ed. 1920; II, *Judaism, Christianity, Mohammedanism*. 1919.

MPEW   Charles A. Moore, ed., *Philosophy—East and West*. 1946.

OIC   *Oriental Institute Communications*.

PSPA   Arthur Upham Pope, ed., *A Survey of Persian Art from Prehistoric Times to the Present*. 6 vols. 1938-39.

REJH   *Early Japanese History* (c.40 B.C.-A.D. 1167). 2 vols. Part A by Robert K. Reischauer; Part B by Jean Reischauer and Robert K. Reischauer. (Princeton University: School of Public and International Affairs). 1937.

SAOC   *Studies in Ancient Oriental Civilization*. Oriental Institute.

SBE   F. Max Müller, ed., *The Sacred Books of the East Translated by Various Oriental Scholars*. 50 vols. 1885-1910.

SJSCH   G. B. Sansom, *Japan, A Short Cultural History*. rev. ed. 1943.

SLR   Alfred Bertholet and Edvard Lehmann, eds., *Lehrbuch der Religionsgeschichte, begründet von Chantepie de la Saussaye*. 2 vols. 4th ed. 1925.

THE ARCHEOLOGY OF

WORLD RELIGIONS

CHAPTER I

Primitivism

THE account of world religions opens in prehistoric times. Archeological evidences, shortly to be described, attest the existence of religion at the dawn of human history. Among the simplest folk yet to be found on earth, too, there is religion. The faith witnessed to by the remains of prehistoric periods and that encountered among peoples far from civilization today may not be the same. Indeed there are many different configurations of belief and practice among contemporary preliterate groups, and there may have been many likewise among the men of prehistoric ages. In the two areas of exploration, therefore, we are confronted by a multiplicity of forms of faith. Nevertheless, despite this recognized diversity, the realms of ancient prehistory and contemporary preliterate life have this much in common, that they are the two places accessible to our investigation which are the farthest removed from the advances of civilization. In the earliest human times before civilization had hardly begun, and in the remotest regions where it has scarcely yet penetrated, we may reasonably expect to find a relatively simple and untutored kind of religious expression which has been largely superseded in the circles of civilization. To this we may properly give the name of Primitivism, since that which is primitive is what is first (*primus*) or earliest, and, by a ready extension of meaning, what is aboriginal or native. The number of persons living on the level of "primitivism" in religion is commonly estimated at about 175,000,-000.[1]

In actual practice, as anthropologists have studied preliterate peoples they have found not only that there are unmistakable evidences of religion among every folk of whom full ethnographic records have been made, but that in the midst of all the manifold data there are at least a few very widespread agreements.[2] Furthermore, some of

[1] For the statistical estimate of this and the other religions, which in every case is only approximate, see John Clark Archer, *Faiths Men Live By*. 1934, p. 2. Revised figures in latest printing.
[2] Ruth Benedict in Franz Boas, ed., *General Anthropology*. 1938, p.628. For scientific methods of ethnographic research among native peoples see, for example, Bronislaw Malinowski, *Argonauts of the Western Pacific*. 1922, pp.4-25.

the basic attitudes and ideas thus attested provide helpful clues for the interpretation of some of the findings made by archeologists working in the field of prehistory. Several of these fundamental ways of feeling, thinking and acting will now be described.

1. CHARACTERISTICS OF PRIMITIVE RELIGION

IT IS everywhere observable among preliterate peoples that some of their attitudes and activities are of the sort which we would describe as belonging to the realms of common sense or science and some as belonging to the areas of magic or religion.

COMMON SENSE AND SCIENCE

By common sense is generally meant the way of thought and body of opinions held about ordinary things by ordinary men. The ideas characteristic of common sense are usually based upon what can readily be seen in one's surroundings, or they are derived by inference from such observations. Preliterate people certainly employ common sense. They guide their lives to a considerable extent by what they have learned in everyday experience, and they deal with much of their environment in accordance with the obvious behavior which it manifests.

Science constitutes a system of concepts and techniques which has developed out of the common-sense approach to the world. Like common sense, science is based upon experience, but its observations are more methodical, its reasoning more rigorously logical, and its techniques more highly developed. At least the rudiments of science are also to be found among many preliterate peoples. Such a procedure, for example, as the chipping of a flint to produce a cutting edge, or the tilling of the soil to make a garden, exhibits to a degree the empirical basis and elaborated technique characteristic of scientific method.[3]

MAGIC AND RELIGION

When we speak of magic we have reference to ideas and practices which relate to more mysterious aspects of the environment. Visible objects still play a large part in magical procedures, of course, but instead of being taken at their face value and employed for workaday purposes they are now regarded as the bearers of invisible potencies and manipulated as agencies for the accomplishment of ends which are not attainable by common sense techniques. That much of the life of preliterate peoples is permeated by beliefs and occupied by activities which must be classified as magical is well known. As a single example, a practice of the aborigines of Central Australia may

[3] Bronislaw Malinowski, *Coral Gardens and Their Magic, A Study of the Methods of Tilling the Soil and of Agricultural Rites in the Trobriand Islands.* 1935, I, p.77.

[5]

be cited. Believing that the pearl shell contains the concentrated "essence" of water, they will suck out this "essence" and spit it into the sky in order that the drops may cause rain clouds to form.[4] The distinction between this practice and, for example, the use of a shell as an ornament in everyday life is perfectly clear and there is no doubt but that the ceremony just described must be recognized as belonging to the realm of magic.

Religion, for its part, also has to do with something more than the obvious surface of things. Like magic, it is oriented toward unseen forces. The forces are not necessarily the same as those with which magic is concerned, nor is the attitude of the person engaged in an act of religion necessarily similar to that of the practitioner of magic. Nevertheless, in religion as in magic, although perhaps in quite a different way, there is an attempt to relate life to a dimension of existence other than that with which common sense and science are concerned. What this something more is may be defined differently in different cultures, and the attitudes and acts judged appropriate in relation to it may likewise vary widely. It remains true that throughout all the ramifications of feelings, conceptions and practices there is an orientation toward a plus factor in existence. Whether this plus factor is apprehended and dealt with as fearsome or mysterious or wonderful or awe-inspiring or as possessing yet other attributes does not matter at this point; what we are here concerned to establish is that religion, like magic, represents a relationship of man to an aspect of the universe, real or imaginary, which is different from that with which common sense and science are habitually concerned.

Since religion and magic agree in their orientation toward aspects of the universe which transcend those dealt with by common-sense and scientific methods, how are they themselves to be distinguished from one another? In the case of the relationship of common sense and science it was suggested that the latter might be regarded as developing out of the former. The theory has not lacked for supporters that in a somewhat similar way religion arose out of magic. Thus Sir James G. Frazer maintained that the age of magic preceded the age of religion.[5] This supposition is not verified, however, by actual observation. Magic and religion are coexistent and even almost inextricably interwoven in too many instances to make it possible to

[4] Charles P. Mountford in *The National Geographic Magazine.* 89 (1946), p.101.
[5] See e.g. James G. Frazer, *Totemica—A Supplement to Totemism and Exogamy.* 1937, p.257.

believe that the one was the predecessor and the root of the other.[6] The distinction between magic and religion does not consist in the temporal priority of the one over the other. Rather, if it is to be found at all, the distinction must be sought in the nature of the two systems of ideas and practices.

Here it must be said that the drawing of a sharp dividing line is not always possible. There are practices which it is difficult to classify with confidence on one side of such a line or the other. On the whole, however, there are some broad differences in methods and attitudes which often appear. The tendency is for magic to be more mechanical in procedure and coercive in intent, religion more personal and supplicatory.[7] A characteristic act in the practice of magic, for example, is to prepare an object or medicine so that it will be charged with special potency, and then to manipulate it so that the potency will work effectively toward the desired end. All must be done in accordance with very precise rules, and it is believed that if the practitioner knows these rules and follows them accurately the effect will not fail to be secured. At this point there is a similarity between magic and science, in that both depend upon a knowledge of the laws involved in a given procedure, and assume that if man's knowledge is sufficient and his procedure flawless he can constrain the forces with which he is working to accomplish what he wishes. Nevertheless, magic remains unmistakably different from science, in that it professes to manipulate forces of a more mysterious sort than those with which science deals. Religion, for its part, often addresses itself to more mysterious forces of the universe not so much with the intent to constrain them by mechanical manipulations as to gain a favorable relationship to them by the establishment of such attitudes as those of submission and dependence and the performance of such acts as those of propitiation and petition. Of course, even a prayer may be uttered with a belief in the automatic efficacy of the pronunciation of certain syllables or in the compulsive effect of a sufficient number of repetitions, and thus the line of demarcation often remains indistinct between magic and religion.

THE NATURAL AND THE SUPERNATURAL

In the attempt, then, to classify ways of feeling, thinking and act-

[6] Bronislaw Malinowski, *A Scientific Theory of Culture and Other Essays.* 1944, pp.196-201.
[7] Bronislaw Malinowski in Joseph Needham, ed., *Science, Religion and Reality.* 1925, pp.71f.,81.

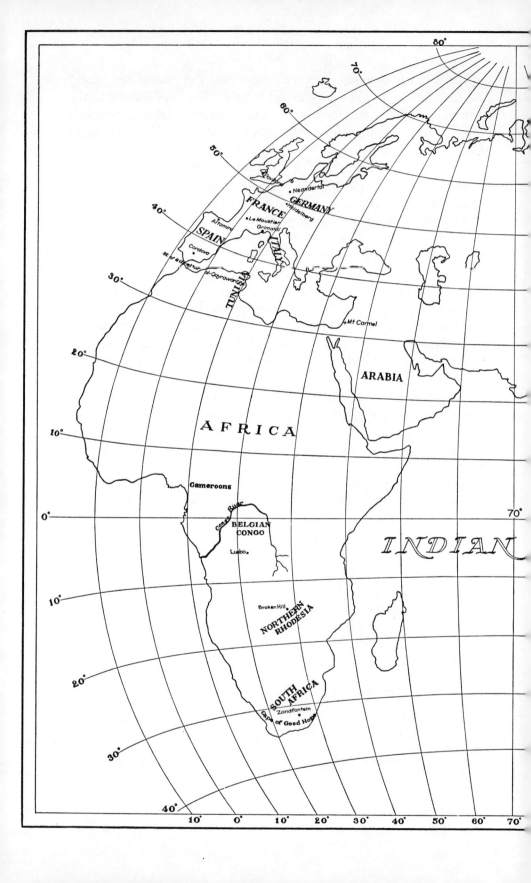

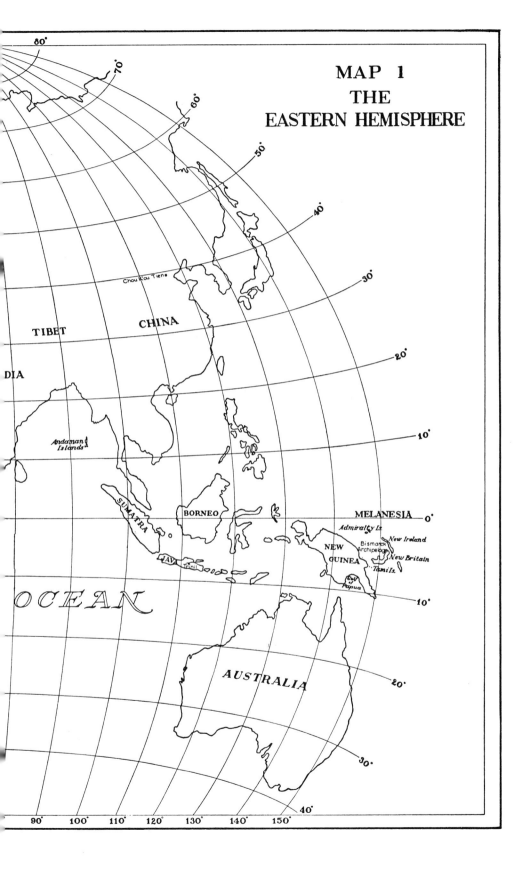

MAP 1
THE
EASTERN HEMISPHERE

ing encountered among preliterate people we have put together the things of common sense and science, and the things of magic and religion. Between common sense and science we have made a distinction, and likewise between magic and religion; nevertheless the first two have a discernible degree of affinity with each other and so, too, do the last two. Is it possible to give a name to the areas with which common sense and science, on the one side, and magic and religion, on the other, are concerned? In the English language the words most conveniently and frequently used to designate the two spheres are the natural and the supernatural. By the natural is meant the realm of everyday affairs, by the supernatural the realm that is more marvelous and mysterious, the "extra dimension"[8] of the universe.

While the employment of these terms is convenient and seems necessary, their use is not intended to suggest that preliterate man draws the line between the natural and the supernatural at the same place that a man of our own culture might, nor indeed that preliterate man himself always draws the dividing line consistently or clearly. Rather, the impingement of the supernatural in both time and space may be apprehended in varying ways in primitive thought. At one time a native's attention may be given quite exclusively to an undertaking in the workaday world, and at another every energy be devoted to a procedure related to the domain of the more mysterious; but again concern may be evident with both realms at one and the same time, as, for example, when the tilling of the tangible soil is accompanied by the performance of rites directed toward the forces believed to govern fertility. Likewise, a given object may on one occasion excite no particular interest whatever, but on another be treated as if it had been invested with the most remarkable attributes. Nevertheless, despite the fluidity or inchoateness of concepts, the difference is usually unmistakable between the attitudes and dealings which have to do with the natural and those which have to do with the supernatural. From this point on, we shall be concerned primarily with the realm of the supernatural.

DYNAMISM AND ANIMISM

It is clear that the realm of the supernatural is apprehended as having a bearing upon the life of man, and that both magic and religion are concerned with adjusting man's life effectively and satis-

[8] Benedict in Boas, ed., *General Anthropology*, p.631.

factorily to the forces that are operative in that realm. When we inquire as to what specific conceptions prevail about these supernatural forces, we find, of course, a great variety of ideas. Broadly speaking, however, they all fall within two general groups. A convincing explanation, moreover, has been advanced by Ruth Benedict to account for the rise of precisely these two types of thought. As she has pointed out,[9] what preliterate man evidently has done has been to extend to the area of the supernatural what he has learned in dealing with the natural. Here in everyday life man has to do both with impersonal things and with other persons. In both the impersonal and the personal he encounters qualities and forces which affect him. Even impersonal things exhibit attributes and manifest powers. A stone is hard and heavy; a river flows and the wind blows. Other persons make an impact upon him with their will and emotions. Even so, in the realm of the supernatural it may be supposed either that the operative forces are of an impersonal sort, or that they are comparable to the intentions and drives of man himself. Thus, to illustrate the one type of supposition, a particular stone may not only possess the attributes of hardness and weight but also have the quality of supernatural power pertaining to it, and thus be an amulet of peculiar potency. And, to give an example of the other type of supposition, a tree may fall upon an unfortunate individual because it hates him and wishes to kill him.

To the first mode of thought, which conceives the supernatural as operating in terms of impersonal forces, we may give the designation dynamism. This word is derived from the Greek δύναμις, meaning "power," and in the present sense has been introduced and employed notably by Alfred Bertholet.[10] Dynamism means belief in and relationship to supernatural power, conceived of as impersonal, immanent and pervasive, a force which may be encountered anywhere in the universe, a quality which may inhere in anything.

To the second way of thinking, which personalizes the forces of the supernatural world, the name animism is applicable. This term comes from the Latin *anima*, which basically means "breath" or "breath of life," and therefore also has the connotation of "soul" or "spirit." In the sense in which it is here used, the designation was brought into currency by the writings of Edward B. Tylor.[11] It con-

[9] In Boas, ed., *General Anthropology*, pp.631f.
[10] Alfred Bertholet, *Das Dynamistische im Alten Testament*. 1926, p.6; Van der Leeuw in RGG IV, cols.1366-1368.
[11] Edward B. Tylor, *Primitive Culture*. 1st ed. 1871; 6th ed. 1920, I, pp.425f.

[11]

notes belief in and relationship to supernatural powers insofar as they are thought of in terms of personal will and understood to exist in the form of spirits.

Of the two manners of thought just described, the impersonal might logically be supposed to have preceded the personal, and it has been said of what we have called dynamism that it "seems to be the first clearly formed religious idea."[12] In actual observation, however, dynamism and animism so often appear side by side, and indeed are so often inextricably interwoven, that it is perhaps safer not to attempt to attribute priority either to the one or to the other. Without hesitation, however, we may state that they are both extremely early and extremely widespread aspects of religion.

Concrete illustration of dynamism may be found in many places. One of its most characteristic and well-known formulations occurs in Melanesia. Here there is a widespread belief in a power which, while it may originate in a spirit or be manifest in a person, is essentially an impersonal potency and may equally well be effective in inanimate objects. The name of this power is *mana*. Robert H. Codrington has written about it and its significance in Melanesian religion as follows: "The religion of the Melanesians consists, as far as belief goes, in the persuasion that there is a supernatural power about belonging to the region of the unseen; and, as far as practice goes, in the use of means of getting this power turned to their own benefit. The notion of a Supreme Being is altogether foreign to them, or indeed of any being occupying a very elevated place in their world. . . . There is a belief in a force altogether distinct from physical power, which acts in all kinds of ways for good and evil, and which it is of the greatest advantage to possess or control. This is Mana. . . . It is a power or influence, not physical, and in a way supernatural; but it shows itself in physical force, or in any kind of power or excellence which a man possesses. This Mana is not fixed in anything, and can be conveyed in almost anything; but spirits, whether disembodied souls or supernatural beings, have it and can impart it; and it essentially belongs to personal beings to originate it, though it may act through the medium of water, or a stone, or a bone. All Melanesian religion consists, in fact, in getting this Mana for one's self, or getting it used for one's benefit—all religion, that is, as far as religious practices go, prayers and sacrifices."[13]

[12] A. Campbell Garnett, *God In Us.* 1945, p.100.
[13] R. H. Codrington, *The Melanesians, Studies in Their Anthropology and Folk-*

Looking elsewhere, we find that in Africa the Bantu people have a very strong belief in a sort of universal energy or potency. This is an intangible, all-pervasive something which is immanent in and flows through all things, but which comes to a focus in special objects. It can be used for either good or evil, and at all times it must be approached and employed with circumspection. The religion of the Bantu, according to Edwin W. Smith, "consists very largely in getting this power to work for his benefit and in avoiding that which would bring him into violent and harmful contact with it."[14]

In America a similar concept is met with among many families of Indians. The Algonquins believe in a great power which permeates all things and orders all happenings. This is known as *manitou*.[15] The Iroquois explain all the activities of life and nature as due to an immanent, impersonal energy which they call *orenda*.[16] The Sioux think that a mysterious, superhuman power pervades the world and manifests itself in both fortunate and unfortunate happenings. Its name is *wakanda*.[17]

In Australia the aboriginal Arunta believe in a supernatural power which seems always to work in a harmful way, and which may be employed for the accomplishment of evil. They give the name *arungquilta* both to this evil influence itself and to an object in which it is supposed to reside.[18]

While in the last instance the supernatural power appears to be altogether evil and dangerous, in the other cases it is clearly capable of doing good as well as working harm. Likewise, while it might be supposed that the impersonal nature of the dynamistic power would render it specially amenable to the relatively mechanical procedures of magic rather than to those of religion, the foregoing illustrations have made it plain that this type of belief functions perfectly well as

Lore. 1891, p.118 n.1. Cf. Codrington in HERE VIII, p.530; R. R. Marett, *The Threshold of Religion.* 2d ed. 1914, pp.99-121; and in HERE VIII, pp.375-380; Nathan Söderblom, *Das Werden des Gottesglaubens, Untersuchungen über die Anfänge der Religion.* 2d ed. 1926, p.27.

[14] E. W. Smith, *The Religion of Lower Races as Illustrated by the African Bantu.* 1923, p.10.

[15] Clark Wissler, *Indians of the United States* (The American Museum of Natural History Science Series, I). 1940, pp.103f.

[16] J. N. B. Hewitt in *Report of the Bureau of American Ethnology.* 43 (1925-26), p.608 n.3.

[17] Alice C. Fletcher and Francis La Flesche in *Report of the Bureau of American Ethnology.* 27 (1905-06), pp.597f. (for the Omaha tribe of the Siouan family); Edwin T. Denig, *ibid.*, 46 (1928-29), pp.486f. (for the Assiniboin).

[18] Baldwin Spencer and F. J. Gillen, *The Arunta, A Study of a Stone Age People.* 1927, II, p.414 n.1.

a basis not only for magic but also for religion. The purposes and feelings with which men approach the unseen power are varied. The attitudes exhibited run the gamut all the way from fear to trust. If it is possible to name one attitude as most characteristic of all, it is perhaps that of awe, in which fear and trust are commingled, and in which there is a strange compulsion not to flee from the unseen power but to draw near to it.[19]

To give illustrations of animism is almost unnecessary, it is so widespread and well known.[20] Animism peoples the world with spirits, and their number is legion. Any object whatsoever may have its individual soul, and free spirits may be anywhere and everywhere. The Bantu of Africa think that spirits dwell in springs, rivers and lakes, in rocks and piles of stone, in trees, caves and hills.[21] The Arunta of Australia have a firm belief in the existence of spirits, which are thought to live in trees and rocks, to prowl about especially at night, to travel long distances rapidly and easily, and to be capable of both cruel and beneficent deeds.[22]

In man's response to the spirits there is the same ambivalence which appeared in his relation to the dynamistic power. He is both repelled and attracted, both made fearful and moved to trust. Fear of the spirits may seem to predominate, as in this description of the Guiana native given by a traveler in that land: "His whole world swarms with beings. He is surrounded by a host of them, possibly harmful. It is therefore not wonderful that the Indian fears to be without his fellow, fears even to move beyond the light of his campfire, and when obliged to do so, carries a fire-brand with him, that he may have a chance of seeing the beings among whom he moves."[23] Yet the possible availability of superhuman assistance from the spirits may lead to a sense not so much of fear as of dependence and confidence. Similarly, it goes without saying that both the practices of magic and the procedures of religion are employed with relation to the spirits.

Such, then, are the two great ways of thought about the super-

[19] Karl Beth, *Religion und Magie bei den Naturvölkern*. 1914, p.125; John Murphy, *Lamps of Anthropology* (Publications of the University of Manchester, cclxxxi). 1943, pp.38-49.
[20] George W. Gilmore, *Animism*. 1919.
[21] W. C. Willoughby, *Nature-Worship and Taboo, Further Studies in "The Soul of the Bantu."* 1932, pp.1-118.
[22] Spencer and Gillen, *The Arunta*, ii, pp.421-428.
[23] E. F. Im Thurn, *Among the Indians of Guiana*. 1883. Quoted by Gilmore, *Animism*, p.99.

natural which we distinguish as dynamism and animism. Yet, as we have already said, the two are not always in fact sharply separated. In Melanesia, as we have seen, the ultimate source of *mana* is usually supposed to be a ghost or spirit, and there, too, it is correct to say both that a man has *mana* and that a spirit is *mana*.[24] Among a number of the Bantu tribes the word *mulungu* is applied to the vague, impersonal power in which they believe, but the same word is also used to designate all the spirits of the dead.[25]

THE SOUL AND ITS SURVIVAL

Thus far, then, we have described belief in, and a sense of relationship to, supernatural power or powers as a major characteristic of primitive religion. A widely encountered aspect of primitivism must now be mentioned. This is belief in the human soul and in its survival after death, together with the feelings and attitudes and practices that accompany such belief. While this may be a matter in which very diverse conceptions appear and which is correspondingly difficult to deal with, it is at the same time a matter which is unmistakably prominent in the thought and life of a great many nonliterate peoples.

A single example will illustrate one sort of practice which is widely encountered. The Bantu inter the deceased. It is their custom to wrap the corpse in skins and blankets and place it in an excavated grave. Then the members of the family kneel around the opening in the earth and place upon the body such things as a calabash of milk, a pipe and tobacco, and seeds. Finally they bid the deceased one farewell with some such words as these: "Good-bye! Do not forget us! See, we have given you tobacco to smoke and food to eat! A good journey to you! Tell old friends who died before you that you left us living well."[26]

Elsewhere in the world many forms other than that just cited are found for the disposal of the body of the deceased. The corpse is sometimes deposited in the jungle, exposed on a platform in a tree, placed in a hut, committed to the waters of a river or the sea, or cremated. Where a grave is employed it may be located beneath the hut in which the deceased lived, or in the enclosure for the cattle, or out in the forest away from the village. It may be sunk deep in the earth, or left shallow and covered with a pile of boughs, a mound

[24] Marett in HERE VIII, p.376.   [25] E. Sidney Hartland in HERE II, p.365.
[26] Smith, *The Religion of Lower Races as Illustrated by the African Bantu*, p.29.

of earth, or a heap of stones. The body is often placed in a crouching position, or flexed and laid on one side in the grave. In some cases the position may have been determined by the binding of the corpse; again these may have been considered natural attitudes of rest.[27]

Throughout the world it is customary to place food and property in or upon the grave. Sometimes the objects left at the grave are broken or burned, the principle involved evidently being that the things themselves must be "killed" in order to go with and be of service to the dead. Animals are also slaughtered that they may continue to be available to their deceased owner, and until recent times the custom has existed in some parts of the earth of slaying wives, slaves or other dependents, that they may accompany their dead master into the other world. The severity of some of these customs has often been mitigated and the economy of property and life promoted by the substitution in the grave of models for the actual objects, of figures for the slaughtered animals, and of statuettes for the slain persons.[28]

The wide variety of beliefs entertained concerning the state of the dead seems to have included the idea that the deceased person lived on in the grave in bodily form. At any rate the apprehension sometimes appears that the dead may come forth in the body from the grave, and the opinion is frequently found that the ghost or soul lingers for a time at the place of burial. Most generally, the principle of life which animates the body is considered to be the soul, and the soul is regarded as separable from the body and capable of living on after it.

Fundamentally, the soul is the life of the body, and as such it may be identified with the blood, the heart, the breath, the shadow, the name, or with light or fire. The separability of the soul from the body may have been suggested even in life by experiences in dreams, unconsciousness and illness. In death the separation of the soul from the body is sometimes thought of as attended by great difficulty and as requiring considerable time for its complete fulfillment.[29]

After death the soul is often expected to survive indefinitely or forever, but again it may be thought that it will live on for only a limited time until it reaches a final end in a second or third death. The place of life after death is variously supposed to be in caves,

[27] E. Sidney Hartland in HERE IV, pp.420-426.
[28] *ibid.*, pp.428-431.
[29] H. B. Alexander in HERE XI, pp.725-731.

hills or rocks, in a distant forest, valley or mountain, in a subterranean region, in a land near where the sun rises or sets, in the sky, or among the stars. In other cases the lot of the soul is imagined to be that of rebirth in human form or transmigration into animal form. Often the state of the dead is expected to be similar to earthly life, but again it is anticipated that it will be much happier, or it is believed that it will vary in accordance with the status or character of the person, or the circumstances of his death, or the conditions of his burial.[30]

For illustrations of these beliefs we may adduce examples from among the Melanesians and the American Indians. On one of the Melanesian islands a lake fills the crater of an ancient volcano. To this lake the dead man's soul is believed to make its way after it has quitted its former habitation. Sometimes men notice recent footprints on the mountain path which leads thither, and they go down to the villages to ask who has died and just gone up that way. Near the lake is a volcanic vent by which the soul is supposed to descend to the abode of the dead. In the nether world there are trees and houses, it is thought, and the deceased live a happy life, free from pain and sickness.[31]

Among the American Indians, those of the Thompson River think that the land of departed souls is in the underground, toward the sunset. It is reached by a long track, at the end of which is a large lodge with doors at the east and west, and a double row of fires extending throughout its length. When the spirit reaches this place, he finds his deceased relatives assembled there, talking, laughing and singing. They welcome him warmly, and he finds a land of abundant grass and flowers and perfumed air, and enters among a people who are joyful and happy.[32]

Since primitive man seems usually to think of the dead as living unseen by mortal eye and with a certain independence of everyday limitations, he can also easily assume that the deceased possess some power which the living man does not have. This power may be expected to bring help to the living in such pursuits as hunting, fishing or agriculture, or it may be thought to bring harm in the form of famine, sickness or death. Therefore the attitude toward the dead may be that of trust, or of fear, or a mingling of both. Hence there

[30] J. A. MacCulloch in HERE XI, pp.817-828.
[31] Codrington, *The Melanesians, Studies in Their Anthropology and Folk-Lore,* pp.285f.
[32] MacCulloch in HERE XI, p.822.

may arise various practices of sacrifice, propitiation and ancestor worship, in which the purpose is to obtain the assistance of the departed spirits, or to ward off their malevolent influence.[33]

However ramified and variegated the customs and conceptions concerning the dead, basic to them all is the belief in the continuance of the personality beyond death. So widely encountered is this fundamental idea that Émile Durkheim has not hesitated to say that "the idea of the soul seems to have been contemporaneous with humanity itself";[34] and Sir James G. Frazer has spoken of belief in the immortality of the soul, in the sense of the indefinite persistence of personality after death, as "remarkably widespread and persistent among mankind from the earliest times down to the present."[35]

We have now noted two major aspects of primitive religion: on the one hand, the belief in supernatural power or powers, together with the attitudes and practices connected therewith; on the other, the belief in the soul and its survival of death, together with the feelings and procedures related to that conception. In fact, these two ideas seem to approach the status of universal beliefs as nearly as anything that can be found in the entire realm of primitive religion. Analyzing primitive beliefs and customs from the standpoint of anthropology, Bronislaw Malinowski points to the basic nature and universal extension of these beliefs in the following words: "Two affirmations preside over every ritual act, every rule of conduct, and every belief. There is the affirmation of the existence of powers sympathetic to man. . . . This is the belief in Providence. . . . The second belief is that beyond the brief span of natural life there is compensation in another existence. . . . In their deepest foundations, as well as in their final consequences, the two beliefs in Providence and Immortality are not independent of one another. . . . The unity of religion in substance, form and function is to be found everywhere. Religious development consists probably in the growing predominance of the ethical principle and in the increasing fusion of the two factors of all belief, the sense of Providence and the faith in Immortality."[36]

[33] James G. Frazer, *The Fear of the Dead in Primitive Religion.* 1933; Paul Radin, *Primitive Religion, Its Nature and Origin.* 1937, pp.221-227.

[34] Émile Durkheim, *The Elementary Forms of the Religious Life.* tr. Joseph W. Swain. 1915, p. 240.

[35] Frazer, *The Fear of the Dead in Primitive Religion,* p.6.

[36] Bronislaw Malinowski, *An Anthropological Analysis of Primitive Beliefs and Conduct with Special Reference to the Fundamental Problems of Religion and Ethics* (Rid-

OTHER IDEAS

Around the two basic ideas just presented cluster many subsidiary concepts. Of the most widely encountered of these, a very few may now be mentioned. The conception of taboo is a frequent concomitant of dynamistic and animistic belief.[37] The term is derived from the Polynesian *tabu* or *tapu*, and means something which is marked off, or not to be lightly approached. Anything which partakes of superhuman force, or anything connected with a spirit, may be taboo. Objects, plants, animals, persons, places and activities all may upon occasion fall within this category of the sacred or prohibited. A state of taboo may be inherent in something or in somebody, as in a mother or baby, a warrior on a campaign, a stranger, king or priest, a sick or dead person, a sacred place or object, a time, number or name. Taboo may also be imposed by a superior authority, as when a chief or priest declares some act or place to be forbidden; and it may likewise be acquired by contact with an object or person already tabooed. The entire system is easily capable, therefore, of building up into a very complex body of compulsions and restraints. It is understandable that in such a set of taboos fear may be a prominent motive. Nevertheless, something of the same ambivalence already noted in the entire relationship of man to supernatural power or powers may also appear here. That which is marked off because of its connection with the supernatural is certainly dangerous but it may also be potentially helpful. Therefore the attitude of shrinking away from what may cause evil may be balanced at least in part by the mood of interest in and approach to what may bring good. And, as R. R. Marett says, "fear tempered with wonder and submissiveness, and thus transmuted into reverence, is the forerunner of love."[38]

Closely related to taboo, and like it an expression of dynamistic and animistic belief, is fetishism. A fetish is a visible medium of the supernatural power or powers. It is generally a material object in which *mana* or a spirit dwells either temporarily or permanently. It may be a natural thing, such as an unusual stone, or a manufactured instrument or a strange concoction. In West Africa, for example, one fetish was simply a mixture of clay and various roots in an earthen

---

dell Memorial Lectures 1934-1935, University of Durham). 1936, pp.60f. Quoted by permission of the publishers, Oxford University Press, London.

[37] James G. Frazer, *The Golden Bough, A Study in Magic and Religion.* 3d ed. 1911. Part II, *Taboo and the Perils of the Soul*; Hutton Webster, *Taboo, A Sociological Study.* 1942.

[38] In HERE XII, p.183.

pot. Another was a household broom which had been brought by the medicine man into contact with every sort of tabooed object, and before which he had uttered every forbidden name which might not ordinarily be spoken aloud. Thus the broom itself was invested with concentrated taboo, and became a fetish. By its nature a fetish lends itself to the manipulations of magic, yet it may also be a symbol and an object useful in the practices of religion.[39]

Another conception which appears in nonliterate society is that of totemism. Here a group of kindred people is regarded as related to a species of natural objects, usually animals or plants.[40] The term comes from the Indians of America, and the totemic organization of society appears in many other places too, notably including Australia. The Arunta of Australia believe that every individual has a special relationship to some animal or plant. His ancestors are often supposed to have been transformed into human beings out of this animal or plant, and by birth he himself was introduced into the totem group which bears its name and uses its symbol.[41] A possible explanation of totemism relates it to a dynamistic background. The men of the clan, the emblems of the totem, and the individuals of the totemic species, it may be supposed, all share in and are animated by a common principle or force comparable to *mana*. "This is what the totem really consists in," writes Émile Durkheim, "it is only the material form under which the imagination represents this immaterial substance, this energy diffused through all sorts of heterogeneous things, which alone is the real object of the cult."[42]

Reference must also be made to the idea of "high gods." Whether this conception arose through the personifying of *mana*, as might be supposed in the light of our previous discussion, whether it is always an importation due to missionary or other influence which is no longer traceable, as some observers believe, or whether it is evidence of the existence of an original monotheism, as has been argued notably by Wilhelm Schmidt,[43] is not yet clear. At any event, the idea,

[39] W. G. Aston in HERE v, p.896; Wilson D. Wallis, *Religion in Primitive Society.* 1939, p.33; William Howells, *The Heathens, Primitive Man and His Religions.* 1948, pp.59f.

[40] James G. Frazer, *Totemism and Exogamy.* 1910, IV, pp.3f.

[41] Spencer and Gillen, *The Arunta*, I, p.67; Frazer, *Totemica*, p.252.

[42] Émile Durkheim, *The Elementary Forms of the Religious Life.* tr. Joseph W. Swain. 1915, p.189.

[43] Wilhelm Schmidt, *Der Ursprung der Gottesidee, Eine historische-kritische und positive Studie.* 4 vols. 1912-33; *The Origin and Growth of Religion, Facts and Theories.* tr. H. J. Rose. 1931; *High Gods in North America.* 1933; *Primitive Revelation.* tr. Joseph J. Baierl. 1939.

although conspicuously lacking in some places, is indubitably present in others. Thus among the Melanesians there is reported to be no thought whatsoever of a Supreme Being,[44] but among the Bantu there is stated to exist a belief in a personal Being, who is the Creator of all things.[45] This deity is associated with the sky, and thought of as the determiner of all human destiny. For the practical purposes of everyday religion, however, attention remains centered on the spirits and on *mana*, while this deity for the most part occupies a place only on the fringe of consciousness. Similar ideas of one Supreme Being, who is Creator, Lord or Father, occur also among a number of other preliterate peoples in Africa, Australia, America and the Arctic regions.

PRIMITIVE ART

Many of the ideas and practices which are a part of primitivism are such as to encourage the employment and fabrication of sacred objects. These may be of the crudest, such as the pot of roots and clay which was a West African fetish; or they may exemplify the application of no little technical skill and artistic ability. Those which we will adduce in illustration are ones in the making of which at least some artistic effort is evident.

Among the widely varied sorts of objects found in primitive religious art, three are specially prominent, namely fetishes, masks and ancestral images. Fetishes or charms, being the dwelling places of supernatural power or powers, are often manufactured with elaborate ceremonial procedure and no little artistic labor. Two examples of such charms will be presented. The first (Fig. 1) is a war charm, twenty-four inches high and decorated with frigate bird feathers. It came from the Admiralty Islands, and is now in the collections of the American Museum of Natural History in New York City. The second (Fig. 2) is also a fighting charm. It is not quite twelve inches high, is made of cocoanut fiber and adorned with feathers, shells and seeds. It was made on the Gulf of Papua, New Guinea, and belongs to the collections of the Buffalo Museum of Science in Buffalo, New York.

The mask is another kind of artistic object which may represent a spirit or serve as a concentration point for spiritual power.[46] As

[44] Codrington, *The Melanesians,* p.118 n.1.
[45] Smith, *The Religion of Lower Races as Illustrated by the African Bantu,* pp.54-61.
[46] Eckart von Sydow, *Die Kunst der Naturvölker und der Vorzeit* (Propyläen-Kunstgeschichte, I). 2d ed. 1927, pp.32-36.

[21]

practiced for example on the Gulf of Papua, New Guinea, the making of such masks is strictly governed by taboos and surrounded by ritualistic procedures. Years may be required for the completion of the work, and when the masks are at last ready they are brought forth before all the people in ceremonial dances. Each mask is named after some spirit who figures in Papuan mythology, and the use of the objects is one of the chief means of perpetuating the mythical and totemistic ideas which prevail. The masks are generally made of bark-cloth stretched over cane and palm-wood frames, and painted with various designs.[47] In Fig. 3 we show an elaborate example of a bird mask, seventy-two inches high, from the Papuan Gulf, and in Fig. 4 a group of other smaller masks also from New Guinea. All are now in the Newark Museum, Newark, New Jersey.

The making of such masks is done in many other places too. We will turn for further illustration only to Borneo and West Africa. The mask pictured in Fig. 5 is from Borneo. It is of wood, painted. That in Fig. 6 is from the Cameroons, West Africa. It is of brass, with ornamented headdress, heavy eyebrows, filed incisors, and chin beard. Both of these masks are now in the American Museum of Natural History, New York City.

The importance in primitive religion of the worship of ancestors and of the dead explains the prominence of ancestral images among the works of primitive art.[48] The making of an image of this sort is usually done ceremonially, and in case it is so constructed that this is possible magical substances may be placed within it in order to assure that it will be the bearer of supernatural powers. As a potent fetish it may be employed for such purposes as to drive off enemies or to cure sickness. The making of such ancestral figures must have played a large role in the development of cult images and idols in general, and it is by no means always certain when a statuette should be specifically described as an ancestral image or just called a cult figure. The images shown in Figs. 7 and 8 are probably to be identified as ancestral figures. Both are from New Zealand, and are now in the M. H. de Young Memorial Museum, San Francisco. Mention may also be made here of the colossal stone idols of Easter Island (Rapa Nui), which in origin may have been conceived as ancestral images. They were cut out of the tufa of the crater of the volcano

---

[47] Ralph Linton, Paul S. Wingert, and René D'Harnoncourt, *Arts of the South Seas.* 1946, pp.96-98.

[48] Von Sydow, *Die Kunst der Naturvölker und der Vorzeit*, pp.37-42.

Rano-raraku, on the slopes of which they still stand looking out to sea. Shown in Fig. 9, they are probably the most powerful of all known expressions of primitive art.[49]

Certain outstanding characteristics found in primitive religion have now been described in general terms. Necessary as such a generalized treatment is in order to provide initial familiarity with basic concepts, it constitutes only an introduction to the further task of studying specific cultural groups with the purpose of comprehending the configurations of belief distinctive of each.[50] The remainder of this chapter will be devoted to an account of the religions of prehistoric man and of several groups of preliterate people today. While the relative scantiness of archeological remains from the very ancient past makes it impossible to reconstruct full pictures of the practice of religion at that time, there is at least enough to provide definite glimpses of the kind of faith which then existed. Among various folk living on a preliterate level today, there is abundant opportunity for observing different and developed configurations of religious belief and practice.

[49] *ibid.*, p.41; Linton, Wingert and D'Harnoncourt, *Arts of the South Seas*, pp.44-46; cf. Thor Heyerdahl, *Kon-Tiki, Across the Pacific by Raft.* 1950, pp.176-185.
[50] Ruth Benedict, *Patterns of Culture.* 1934, pp.xiii,49f.

2. THE RELIGION OF PREHISTORIC MAN

As WE look back into the remoteness of prehistoric antiquity, it is not possible to discern any absolute beginning of religion. Rather, religion may be said to be as old as man himself. As R. R. Marett puts it: "The principle that everything must have a beginning does not seem to apply to any of the major institutions of mankind—to family, tribe and state, to government and law, to morality and fine art, and finally, and above all, to religion. In every case alike, if we work backwards from the present, traces of them persist until they fade out together precisely at the point at which Man himself fades out also."[51]

THE DIMENSIONS OF PREHISTORY

Man and his religion are at least dimly within the focus of our vision as far back as in the Old Stone Age. Speaking of the stratified rock formations which comprise the outer covering, perhaps fifty miles thick, of our planet, geologists distinguish four principal rock systems or periods, namely the Primary, Secondary, Tertiary and Quaternary. From the standpoint of the plant and animal fossils imbedded in these rocks, four successive eras are recognized, to which are given the names Eozoic (dawn life), Paleozoic (ancient life), Mesozoic (middle life), and Cenozoic (recent life). The Cenozoic era has numerous subdivisions, of which the last two are the Pleistocene and the Holocene. The Pleistocene epoch was that in which "most of the new" or present-day animals were in existence, and the Holocene is that in which "all of the new" or present-day fauna are known. The Quaternary rock period includes both the Pleistocene and the Holocene epochs of life.

In relation to climate, the Pleistocene was the epoch of the Ice Age. Within this period there were four major times when the great glaciers crept down out of the north, and three intervening occasions when they withdrew again. Since the advancing ice sheets also brought more abundant rainfall, the glacial and interglacial periods were correlated with pluvial and interpluvial phases of climate. When the last great ice sheets retreated, the transition was made to the Holocene or recent epoch in which the climate became much as it is at present.

[51] R. R. Marett, *Head, Heart and Hands in Human Evolution.* 1935, p.81. Quoted by permission of the publishers, Hutchinson and Company, Ltd., London.

1. War Charm from the
Admiralty Islands

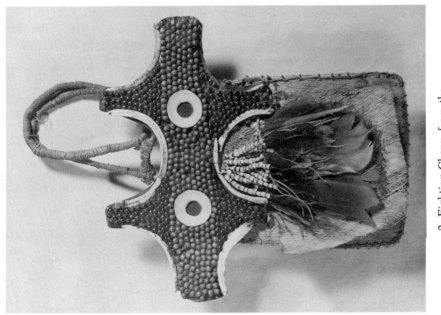

2. Fighting Charm from the
Gulf of Papua

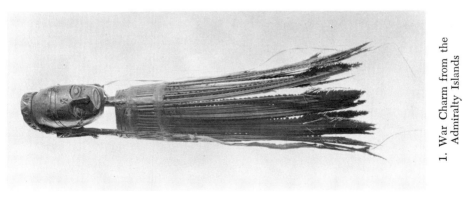

3. Bird Mask from the
Gulf of Papua

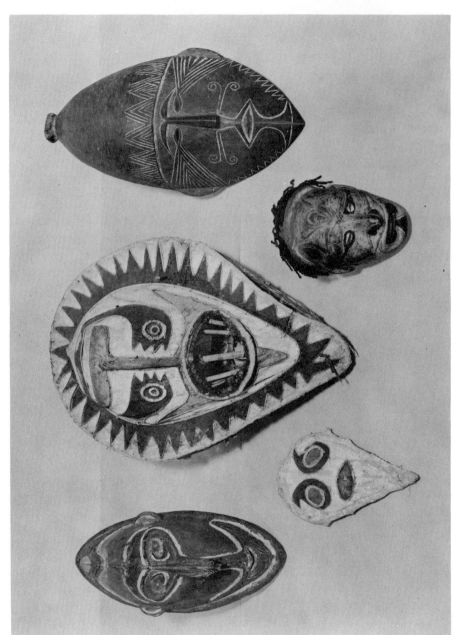

4. Masks from New Guinea

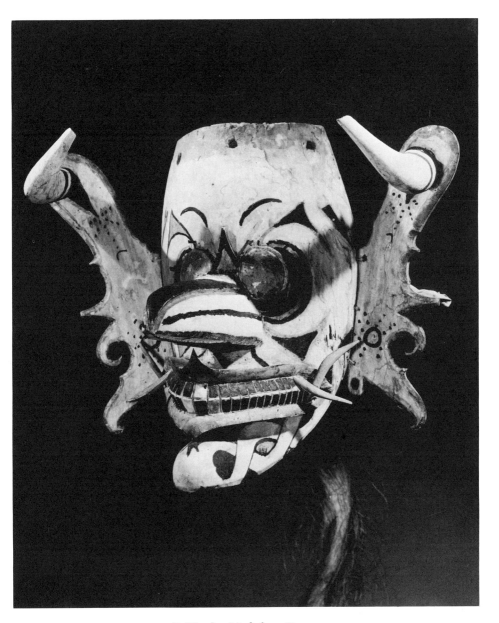

5. Wooden Mask from Borneo

6. Brass Mask from the Cameroons

7. Ancestral Figure from New Zealand   8. Ancestral Figure from New Zealand

9. Colossal Stone Images on Easter Island

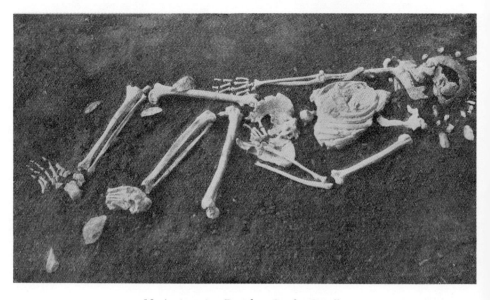

10. Aurignacian Burial at Combe-Capelle

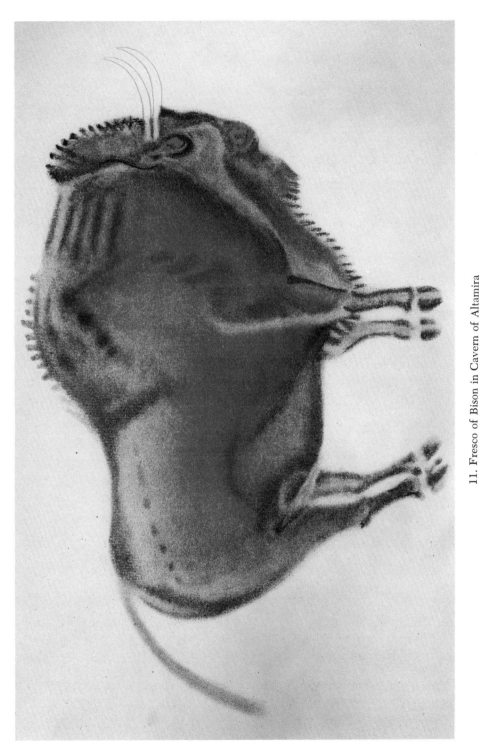

11. Fresco of Bison in Cavern of Altamira

12. Engraving of Rhinoceros in Cave of Les Combarelles

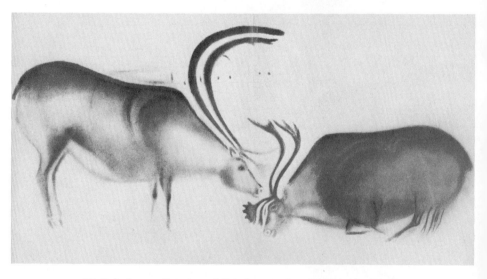

13. Polychrome Painting of Reindeer in Cave of Font-de-Gaume

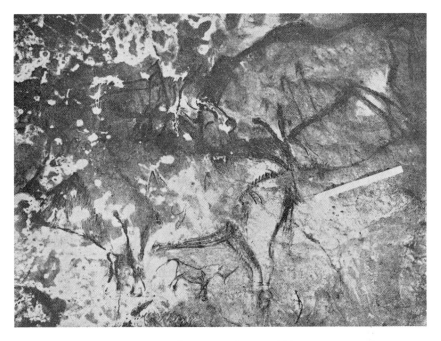

14. Painted Bison in Cavern of Niaux

15. Statue of Bison in Grotto of Tuc d'Audoubert

16. Bison Charging Hunter, Painting in Cave of Lascaux

17. Bushman Painting in South Africa

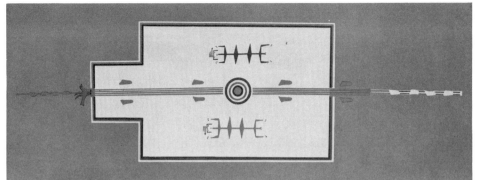

19. Navaho Sand Painting

18. Navaho Singers

20. Mescalero Apache Masked Dancers and Shaman

21. Governor and Women of Zuñi

As far as human life and culture are concerned, the Pleistocene corresponds approximately to the Paleolithic or Old Stone Age, a period which in Europe is customarily subdivided into Pre-Chellean, Chellean, Acheulian, Mousterian, Aurignacian, Solutrean and Magdalenian epochs. The Holocene is the period of modern man, and includes the Mesolithic, Neolithic, Chalcolithic, Bronze and Iron Ages. We have to do here with the Pleistocene epoch and the Paleolithic Age.

Estimates of geological time are based chiefly upon the counting of varves, which are the annual deposits of sediment left by the melting of the retreating ice sheets; upon observation of the extent to which uranium in the rocks has been transformed into lead in the very slow course of its radioactive disintegration; and upon comparison with astronomical results in the study of solar radiation. By such methods of investigation it is now calculated that the duration of the Pleistocene epoch was something like 600,000 years.[52] It lasted, of course, until the Holocene epoch, which began some ten thousand years ago. Thus the Pleistocene epoch and the Paleolithic Age have occupied over ninety-eight per cent of the total time span of human culture, leaving less than the last two per cent of the time to be filled by the Mesolithic, Neolithic, Bronze and Iron Ages combined.[53]

HOMO NEANDERTALENSIS

The appearance of man upon earth probably fell within the Pleistocene epoch. Fossil remains of anthropoid creatures are found first. These include the skeletal remains of *Pithecanthropus erectus*, the "erect ape man," discovered near Trinil, Java, in 1891 by Eugène Dubois, and *Sinanthropus pekinensis*, the "Chinese man of Peking," unearthed in 1927 and afterward by Gunnar Andersson near Chou K'ou Tien, forty miles from Peiping, China. Both belong probably to the Middle Pleistocene epoch (around 400,000 years ago), and both are considered "hominids," that is extremely early members of the great family now represented on earth by the genus *Homo*, or mankind.[54]

[52] Frederick E. Zeuner, *Dating the Past, An Introduction to Geochronology*. 1946, pp.144f.; Carey Croneis and William C. Krumbein, *Down to Earth, An Introduction to Geology*. 1936, pp.294-297,444.

[53] William Howells, *Mankind So Far* (The American Museum of Natural History Series, v). 1944, pp.120f.

[54] Franz Weidenreich, *Giant Early Man from Java and South China* (Anthropological Papers of the American Museum of Natural History, XL, 1). 1945; *The Skull of Sinanthropus Pekinensis* (Palaeontologia Sinica, N. S. D., 10. Whole Series, 127). 1943;

Elsewhere in the world, probably including Europe, at least equally primitive forms must have existed. In the east it is possible to trace the line of development from *Pithecanthropus erectus* through *Homo soloensis* (found at Ngandong on the Solo River six miles from Trinil, Java), to fossil forms and modern primitive types in Australia; and from *Sinanthropus pekinensis* to modern Mongoloid groups which have comparable physical characteristics. In the west a like development may be presumed to have taken place antecedent to the appearance of the relatively advanced types of which we will now speak.

For our purposes it will suffice to tell of *Homo heidelbergensis* and *Homo neandertalensis*. "Heidelberg man" is known only insofar as inferences are possible from an unquestionably human jaw discovered at Mauer, near Heidelberg, Germany, in 1907.[55] His date was perhaps in the Second Interglacial Period.[56] "Neandertal man" is more fully revealed by modern discovery. The first fossil human skeleton so designated was found in the Neander valley, not far from Düsseldorf, Germany, in 1857, and since that time skeletal remains of a similar type have been found elsewhere in Europe all the way from Russia and Yugoslavia to Belgium, France, Italy and Gibraltar. Other remains also related, but less closely, have been unearthed at points as far distant as Mount Carmel, Palestine (*Paleoanthropus palestinensis*) and Broken Hill, Northern Rhodesia (*Homo rhodesiensis*).

The date of Neandertal man in Europe was probably during the Third Interglacial and Fourth Glacial Periods, or perhaps from 100,-000 to 50,000 years ago. In its cultural aspects this epoch is known in Europe as the Mousterian. The name is derived from the village of Le Moustier, France, near which numerous flint implements of characteristic kind were found.[57]

Primitive as he was, *Homo neandertalensis* was indeed a human being, and probably in the direct line of evolution leading to *Homo sapiens*. In physique, Neandertal man was heavily built and of great strength, while his low, broad skull contained a brain as large or a

---

and *Apes, Giants and Man.* 1946; Hellmut de Terra in *The Scientific Monthly.* 51 (July-Dec. 1940), pp.112-124; Robert J. Braidwood in JNES 6 (1947), pp.30-42.

[55] For geographical details, particularly European sites not shown on our Map I, see the maps in Henry F. Osborn, *Men of the Old Stone Age, Their Environment, Life and Art.* 2d ed. 1915; and *The National Geographic Magazine.* 94 (1948), p.774.

[56] James H. McGregor in Boas, ed., *General Anthropology*, p.60.

[57] George G. MacCurdy, *The Coming of Man.* 1932, pp.35,51f.; Howells, *Mankind So Far*, p.165.

little larger than that of modern man. His flint tools were skillfully edged, and included scrapers, cleavers, drills and knives. He had fire, as even *Sinanthropus pekinensis* before him had had, and he lived on the cold-weather animals of the time.[58]

For the story we have to tell, however, the immensely significant fact is that Neandertal man had at least some conception and practice which may properly be termed religious. The evidence appears in the burials of the Mousterian Age. Previous to this time there is no indication of the practice of burial. The extant skeletal remains were generally found lying in the bed of a stream or lake, and if they were in a cave there was no sign of interment with care. Nor was interment unanimously practiced by Neandertal man, there being no trace of any burial, for example, in connection with the important Mousterian remains discovered at La Quina, France.

But at a number of other notable Mousterian sites, Neandertal man was found to have buried the dead with care. At Le Moustier the skeleton of a Neandertal youth of about sixteen years of age was unearthed. The body had been placed in a rock shelter in the side of a cliff. The right arm was bent so that the right side of the skull rested on it. The left arm was extended, and lying near the bones of the left hand were a beautiful stone cleaver and a scraper. Many other flint artifacts were immediately about. In similar fashion at La Ferrassie several adults and children were buried in a rock shelter, and stone tools were placed at their hands. Also at La Chapelle-aux-Saints a skeleton of the Mousterian epoch was found interred, together with beautifully made implements, in a rectangular burial pit which had been sunk in the floor of a cave.[59]

This burial of the dead with care which is so marked a feature of the Mousterian epoch is, to be sure, capable of various interpretations. It may be supposed that we have here evidence of natural affection. The bodies were placed with a certain tenderness, we may think, in the position of one asleep, and familiar implements were put near by. But it has also been argued that it was fear which accounted for such treatment of the dead. Perhaps the manner of burial and the placing of gifts in the grave show an intent to restrain and appease the deceased. It is not impossible, indeed, that both motives were at work. However that may be, one fact is unmistakable. Man believed in life after death. He thought that the departed would

[58] Howells, *Mankind So Far*, pp.148,164-170.
[59] George G. MacCurdy, *Human Origins*. 1924, I, pp.359-362.

continue to lead a life at least to some extent comparable to that lived here. In that life there would be need to have objects and implements like those which had been of service here. If fear of the dead entered the picture, then living man evidently believed in the possibility of a continued relationship in which the deceased might do him harm if not propitiated. All of this is sometimes called the "cult of the dead"; certainly it reveals attitudes, ideas and practices which must properly be designated religious.[60]

HOMO SAPIENS

The successor of *Homo neandertalensis* was *Homo sapiens*. This is "man the wise," the species which today inhabits the earth and not infrequently belies its anthropological designation by its actual behavior. The date of appearance of *Homo sapiens* is about the beginning of the Upper Paleolithic or most recent period of the Old Stone Age, say fifty thousand years ago.[61]

Carmel man (*Paleoanthropus palestinensis*) may have been an intermediate or transitional type,[62] Rhodesian man (*Homo rhodesiensis*) displays features which suggest the *sapiens* species,[63] and Solo man (*Homo soloensis*) has been called "the oldest at present known representative of *Homo sapiens fossilis*."[64] Fossil *Homo sapiens* is also represented by Wadjak man (*Homo wadjakensis*) in Java, and by the Upper Chou K'ou Tien cave types in China.[65] But it is Cro-Magnon man in Europe of whom we have the fullest knowledge and through whom we can best picture the life of prehistoric "man the wise."

Cro-Magnon is French patois for "great hole," and is the name of a rock shelter at the village of Les Eyzies, France. Parts of five skeletons were uncovered here in 1868, and became the type specimens of the race to which the name Cro-Magnon is given. Similar remains have been found at numerous other locations in western Europe.

As revealed by his skeletal remains, Cro-Magnon man was tall of stature and had a prominent chin and high forehead. Both physically and mentally he was much like the succeeding races of Mesolithic

[60] G.-H. Luquet, *The Art and Religion of Fossil Man.* tr. by J. Townsend Russell. 1930, pp.151-179.
[61] Lewis G. Westgate in *The Scientific Monthly.* 51 (July-Dec. 1940), p.157.
[62] J. Philip Hyatt in *The Journal of Bible and Religion.* 12 (1944), pp.235f.
[63] McGregor in Boas, ed., *General Anthropology*, pp.87f.
[64] W. F. F. Oppenoorth in George G. MacCurdy, ed., *Early Man.* 1937, p.359.
[65] De Terra in *The Scientific Monthly.* 51 (July-Dec. 1940), p.124.

and Neolithic times, which in turn were closely similar to modern races of men.[66]

The culture of Cro-Magnon man passed through three stages, known as Aurignacian, Solutrean and Magdalenian, and taken as a whole was much in advance of that of Neandertal man. Many kinds of stone instruments were manufactured, and the technique of chipping flint was developed to the highest degree in the entire Paleolithic Period. Other materials such as ivory, bone and reindeer horn were also employed extensively in the making of such things as needles, javelin points and harpoons.

Like Neandertal man, Cro-Magnon man lived in rock shelters and caves, and there buried his dead. Typical burials of the Aurignacian epoch have been found at Paviland in Wales, where the skeleton was deeply stained with red ocher and accompanied by implements and ornaments; at Grimaldi on the Italian frontier, where among others a man, young woman and youth were interred with a covering of red ocher, and an old woman and a young man were buried beneath a flagstone supported by two upright stones to protect their skulls; and at Combe-Capelle in France, where the skeleton of a tall man was surrounded by flints and shells. A burial of the Solutrean epoch was discovered at Klause in Bavaria, where the body was surrounded by a mass of powdered ocher. Magdalenian interments were found in France at the Laugerie-Basse rock shelter near Les Eyzies, where perforated shells remained at the forehead, elbows, knees and feet of the skeleton; and at Les Hoteaux, where again the body had been enveloped in powdered ocher and accompanied by various implements.[67]

A photograph of the Aurignacian burial at Combe-Capelle, mentioned in the preceding paragraph, is reproduced in Fig. 10.[68] There it may be seen that small shells, some perforated, had been placed about the head, and flint implements near the head, right arm, right leg and left foot.

Generally speaking, then, Cro-Magnon burials were comparable to those of Neandertal man, but showed certain advances. The richer culture of the period provided finer tools and weapons for the dead than were previously available, as well as numerous personal ornaments, including necklaces and other adornments made of such ma-

[66] MacCurdy, The Coming of Man, p.41.
[67] MacCurdy, Human Origins, I, pp.380-405.
[68] H. Klaatsch and O. Hauser in Praehistorische Zeitschrift. 1 (1909-10), p.276, Fig. 2.

terials as perforated shells and animal teeth. A prominent feature was the strewing of many of the graves with red ocher, but the significance of the practice is not known. One hypothesis is that the red color was intended to represent the blood, and that the application of the ocher was therefore meant to convey life-giving qualities to the corpse.[69] Whatever the correct solution of this particular problem, the total evidence leaves no doubt that Cro-Magnon man, like the Neandertal before him, believed in some kind of continuing and real existence beyond death.

PREHISTORIC ART

The love of ornament revealed in objects like necklaces found in Cro-Magnon graves was only one aspect of an extensive interest in art, which notably characterizes this period. As far as is now known, the first appearance of the fine arts in prehistory was during the Aurignacian epoch. Sculpture, drawing and painting were all included.

In part it was tools and weapons which were decorated with engravings; again fragments of stone, bone, ivory and horn were carved into various shapes; and also figurines and statuettes were produced. Prominent among the figurines and statuettes is a whole series of sculptured figures of women, dating from the Aurignacian epoch, and giving exaggerated and even grotesque emphasis to the female characteristics. A probable explanation of these is that they were employed within the framework of dynamistic and magical belief, where like was thought to have the power to produce like, and where such representations consequently could be expected to be powerful aids to fertility.[70]

The first discovery of Paleolithic paintings was a dramatic event. This was in 1879, when Don Marcelino de Sautuola was investigating the cave of Altamira not far from Santander in northern Spain. While he searched for relics of ancient man in the floor deposits of the vestibule, his small daughter, María, aged five, went under the low roof of the cave. Looking upward, she cried out, "Toros!" (bulls). When her father came he saw that the painting of a bison was on the ceiling. Upon closer examination, extensive frescoes were discovered and it was found that a large group of animals was depicted, includ-

[69] CRW p. 5; Phyllis Ackerman in Vergilius Ferm, ed., *Forgotten Religions*. 1950, pp.3f.

[70] William F. Albright, *From the Stone Age to Christianity*. 1940, p.92.

ing not only the bison but also the hind, the horse, the wild boar and others.[71]

One of the paintings at Altamira is shown in Fig. 11, as reproduced by the Abbé Breuil.[72] The animal is a bison, of an extinct species, with long slender horns. The ancient artist has evidently portrayed his subject with the greatest faithfulness.

This discovery was greeted with skepticism and was soon almost forgotten by the world. Then in 1895 a farmer, digging in a field south of Les Eyzies in the Dordogne region of France, found a hitherto unknown passage leading into the rock. A boy crawled into the hole with a candle and upon emerging declared that the walls of the tunnel were covered with pictures of wild animals. Thus was discovered the grotto of La Mouthe, where the scholar Émile Rivière soon confirmed the existence of prehistoric engravings. These were crude and only in part painted, but many different animals were recognizable, including the bison, horse, reindeer, mammoth and ibex. Edouard Piette, a magistrate who pursued the subject of prehistoric art as an avocation, connected the newly found pictures with those of Altamira and thus gave a new impetus to the study of the whole subject. While Piette was at the time almost seventy years of age, his work was continued by a pupil who attained the highest distinction in the field. This was l'Abbé Henri Breuil, who became Professor at the Institute of Human Palaeontology in Paris.[73]

In 1901, Breuil, Capitan and Peyrony studied more engravings and paintings in the caves of Les Combarelles and Font de Gaume, both also in the vicinity of Les Eyzies. The cavern of Combarelles is a low narrow winding tunnel extending underground for seven hundred and twenty feet. Its drawings begin about three hundred and fifty feet from the entrance and extend to the end of the passage, some of the finest being in a small chamber just before an extremely constricted place. Some three hundred pictures have been counted, and among them appear representations of the bison, horse, reindeer, mammoth, ibex, stag, rhinoceros, lion and wolf, as well as of men both masked and unmasked.[74]

[71] Émile Cartailhac and Henri Breuil, *La Caverne d'Altamira à Santillane près Santander (Espagne)*. Peintures et gravures murales des cavernes paléolithiques. 1906.

[72] *ibid.*, Pl. xxiii.

[73] M. C. Burkitt, *Prehistory, A Study of Early Cultures in Europe and the Mediterranean Basin*. 2d ed. 1925, pp.13,249; Osborn, *Men of the Old Stone Age*, pp.392f.

[74] L. Capitan, H. Breuil and D. Peyrony, *Les Combarelles aux Eyzies (Dordogne)*. Peintures et gravures murales des cavernes paléolithiques. 1924.

Fig. 12 is a photograph of one of these engravings in the cave of Les Combarelles.[75] The animal is a rhinoceros, and the head and horns are portrayed with special effectiveness. A later drawing, turned at right angles and cut across the withers of the pachyderm, is of the head of a hind.

The cave of Font-de-Gaume opens high on the side of a valley and extends back into the hill for nearly five hundred feet. Far back within the cave, almost half of the distance from the entrance to the end, there is a very narrow passage now called the Rubicon. Beyond this is the Grande Galerie des Fresques, where relatively smooth, concave surfaces provided unusually favorable opportunities for murals. Here there are both simple drawings and fine polychrome paintings. Great processions of bison, reindeer and mammoths appear, while pictures of the horse, rhinoceros and wild boar are also found. Even in a narrow fissure at the extreme end of the cavern, known as the Diverticule Final, there are engravings of the lion and horse and paintings of the rhinoceros. Also on the walls are certain schematic drawings now designated as tectiforms. These are more or less in tent form and are believed to represent shelters or dwellings of some kind.[76]

One of the polychrome paintings at Font-de-Gaume is selected for illustration here (Fig. 13). The reproduction is by the Abbé Breuil.[77] Two reindeer face each other, their horns rising in splendid curves.

In 1906 the great cavern of Niaux became known with its impressive array of prehistoric pictures. The cave is in the Ariège region of southern France, on the slopes of the Pyrenees not far from Tarascon. With its entrance high on the sloping side of a river valley, this grotto extends almost horizontally into the mountain for a distance of forty-two hundred feet. In the year mentioned, a French officer, Commandant Molard, retired from the Engineers, was surveying this cave with his two sons, Paul and Jules. Far back in the cave, Paul, who had been reporting surveying measurements, suddenly exclaimed, "Drawings!" The pictures thus first noticed by any modern observer were found to include a splendid series of black paintings of bison and horses, as well as engravings of the ibex, the chamois, the ox and two trout. There are also various signs including

---

[75] *ibid.*, Pl. xxv.

[76] L. Capitan and H. Breuil, *La Caverne de Font-de-Gaume aux Eyzies* (*Dordogne*). Peintures et gravures murales des cavernes paléolithiques. 1910.

[77] *ibid.*, Pl. xxviii.

dots and tectiforms and outlines which look like clubs and arrows. In some cases the bison are shown with arrows in their sides, and in the case of the figure of a bison drawn upon the ground, engraved arrows are directed toward small cavities in the floor evidently intended to be taken for wounds.[78]

Fig. 14 is a representation from the so-called Black Salon in the Niaux cave.[79] Depicted are two bison, with black and red arrows in their sides; and also a small horse. The white marker was inserted to provide a reference scale, and is itself about sixteen inches long.

In 1912 another notable cavern on the northern slope of the Pyrenees in the Ariège district of France was explored. This was the Tuc d'Audoubert, which was first entered in modern times by the Comte de Bégouen and his three sons, Max, Jacques and Louis. Since a subterranean river flowed out of the cave, it was necessary to use a small boat in order to gain access to the inner recesses of the grotto. Then, leaving the boat, a veritable labyrinth of corridors and chambers was negotiated on foot and by climbing and crawling. Many engravings, some with splashes of color, were found. They represented the hind, horse, reindeer and bison. In an upper cave, which it was very difficult to enter, were clay statues of two bison, a male following a female. The figures were placed against a rock, and where the sides of the animals leaned against this rock they were not modeled. Otherwise, however, they were excellently sculptured. Each figure was about two feet in length. Despite some cracks, the state of preservation was remarkable, due to the perpetual dampness of the cave, free however from running water.[80]

The foremost of the two clay bison is shown in Fig. 15.[81] The work of the prehistoric artist has been executed with realism and a keen sense of observation. Although the figure is made to lean up against the rock, it is executed in such high relief that the ears and curved horns stand out as if on a fully detached statue. The treatment of the eye, with a small hole marking the pupil, the nostrils, mane and beard, is also noteworthy.

Only two years later, near the Tuc d'Audoubert, the Bégouen boys went down a vertical shaft and found themselves in yet another cave. Named by their father in their honor, Trois Frères, this cave, too,

---

[78] E. Cartailhac and H. Breuil in *L'anthropologie*. 19 (1908), pp.15-46.

[79] *ibid.*, p.27, Fig. 10.

[80] Bégouen in *Académie des Inscriptions et Belles-Lettres, Comptes rendus.* 1912, pp.532-538.

[81] *ibid.*, Pl. II following p.532.

was adorned with numerous pictures. On the walls were the figures not only of the bison, reindeer, horse, mammoth, rhinoceros, lion and bear, but also of birds something like owls, and of a man wearing stag's antlers on his head, and a tail, presumably a prehistoric sorcerer.[82]

In 1922 the previously unknown cave of Montespan, in the district of Haute Garonne, west and somewhat north of the region in which the caverns of Tuc d'Audoubert and Trois Frères were found, was discovered and explored by Norbert Casteret. While once probably dry, a subterranean stream was now flowing here through an underground tunnel two miles in length. When the grotto was first entered by Casteret, a water-filled siphon blocked the way completely at one point, but was passed through by swimming. Within, rich discoveries awaited the explorer, including some fifty engravings of animals and thirty specimens of modeling in clay. Many of the engravings were in a sloping tortuous passage. They pictured the horse, bison, stag, reindeer, hind, hyena, ibex, chamois and wild ass. In many cases the animals were represented as wounded. The clay sculptures included statues of a bear and two large lions or tigers, as well as relief models of horses. The clay bear was of particular interest. It was a headless statue, three and one half feet in length and two feet in height. Fallen between the front paws of the statue was an actual bear's skull, suggesting that at one time a real bear's head had surmounted the model. The sides of the figure were scarred with the marks of more than thirty blows from spears or arrows.[83]

The most remarkable cave of all, as it is generally recognized to be, was discovered in 1940.[84] This is the cave of Lascaux, above the village of Montignac, in the Dordogne. The discovery was made by a seventeen-year-old youth of Montignac, Marcel Ravidat, and three companions. Indeed it was their dog that was truly responsible for the find, for this animal accidentally fell into a hole hidden by bushes. Seeking to retrieve the pet, Ravidat descended into what seemed a natural well but actually gave access to a large cavern. Here, in the subterranean recesses of a grotto which had long been sealed up by a cave-in, were the finest and best preserved prehistoric paintings yet found. A veritable cavalcade of animal figures, four hundred in

[82] Burkitt, Prehistory, pp.257f.; José Pijoán, El arte prehistórico europeo (Cossío-Pijoán, Historia general del arte, vi). 1934. pp.113f.
[83] Norbert Casteret in The National Geographic Magazine. 46 (1924), pp.123-152.
[84] Life. Feb. 24, 1947, pp.62-69; Norbert Casteret in The National Geographic Magazine. 94 (1948), pp.771-794; Fernand Windels, The Lascaux Cave Paintings. 1949.

number, painted in red and black colors that are still fresh and vivid, appears upon the walls and ceilings. Bison, rhinoceroses, bears, stags, antelopes, cattle, deer and horses, and occasionally men as well, are seen. Many of the animals are depicted in more than life-size, as for example a gigantic black bull eighteen feet long. Some of the animals, including a red horse and a black bison, are pierced in vital places with arrows. In one picture a barred rectangle may represent a trap; in another, there is a stampede of horses, one of which is falling backward over a cliff or into a trap. At the bottom of a very narrow rock well are paintings of a rhinoceros, and of a bison the flanks of which have been torn by the spear of a hunter. The enormous beast has turned to charge the hunter, and the latter, pictured with a long body and birdlike head, is falling over back-ward with his arms flung out on either side (Fig. 16).

In addition to such finds as these already described on the main-land of Europe, other discoveries of prehistoric engravings and paint-ings have been made all the way from Scandinavia to South Africa.[85]

As far as chronological sequence is concerned in the mural art of Cro-Magnon man in Europe, four chief phases of development are distinguished.[86] The first corresponds with the Lower Aurignacian Period, and characteristically includes rude, deeply incised animal figures, ordinarily shown in absolute profile with only a single fore-leg and a single hind leg. Examples are to be found at Altamira, La Mouthe, Les Combarelles and Font-de-Gaume. The second is Upper Aurignacian in date, and is marked by the combination of engraving with painting. The figures are now far more lifelike. Altamira, La Mouthe, Les Combarelles and Font-de-Gaume again all provide il-lustrations. The third phase is that of Lower Magdalenian times. Here the animal outlines are generally incised deeply but are fol-lowed by light contour lines. In the painting, shading is practiced and color is sometimes used almost to excess. Early Magdalenian engravings and paintings are found at Altamira, Les Combarelles, Font-de-Gaume, Niaux, Tuc d'Audoubert and Montespan. Animal sculpture also appears, as notably illustrated by the bison of Tuc d'Audoubert. The fourth and climactic phase in the development of Paleolithic art was reached in the Upper Magdalenian Period. In

[85] Leo Frobenius and Douglas C. Fox, *Prehistoric Rock Pictures in Europe and Africa*. 1937; Frederick R. Wulsin, *The Prehistoric Archaeology of Northwest Africa* (Papers of the Peabody Museum of American Archaeology and Ethnology, Harvard University, xix, 1). 1941, pp.114-137.

[86] cf. Osborn, *Men of the Old Stone Age*, p.395.

the drawings we now witness a perfection of animal outlines and an attention to detail which extends even to the employment of fine lines to indicate the hair. In the paintings, brilliant polychromes are produced which are truly magnificent. Splendid examples are to be seen on the famous ceiling at Altamira and on the walls of Font-de-Gaume and Lascaux. Here, too, there are human representations, of which one of the most remarkable is that of the disguised man with the stag's antlers and tail in the cave of Trois Frères.

By what methods were these remarkable pictures made in the recesses of these subterranean caverns? Some kind of illumination was obviously necessary, and it is surmised that this was furnished by small stone lamps. A lamp of this sort was found, for example, in the Magdalenian layer of the cave of La Mouthe. Bits of carbonized matter remaining on it suggested that an animal fat had fed its wick. The wick itself might have been of moss. The incised drawings, often involving extremely fine lines, must have been executed with various types of flint graving tools. The painting was presumably done most often with some sort of brush, although for some of the work it appears as if the fingers were used directly, while again there are examples which suggest that the paint was applied in a powdered form through a blowtube such as a hollow bone. The paint itself was probably made of ocher, oxide of manganese and other mineral materials, which were ground up and mixed with animal oils or fats.[87]

More important for our inquiry is the question as to the purpose which was served by the execution of these paintings and other works of art in the caves of the Paleolithic Period. It should be made plain that the interiors of the caves were not the places of habitation of Cro-Magnon man. We know little about where and how these people lived, although the tectiforms already mentioned have been believed to represent their huts or hide-covered shelters. In the mouths of the caves, also, deposits have been uncovered containing implements and traces of fire, suggesting human residence. But back in the caves there are no evidences of permanent habitation, nor would the deep interiors have provided satisfactory or safe places for living. Not only were the subterranean recesses generally uncomfortable for human dwelling, they also offered the dangerous possibility that the men within would be trapped by enemies, men or beasts, occupying the entrance. Nevertheless, it was into these inner reaches of the caves, and even into chambers and fissures which

[87] Osborn, *Men of the Old Stone Age*, pp.401,415; Burkitt, *Prehistory*, pp.205f.

were most extremely difficult of access, that the prehistoric artists went to accomplish their works.

It seems impossible, therefore, to give a satisfactory explanation of the art of the caves in terms of esthetic impulse alone. Without question many of the paintings and other works of art have a high value as measured by artistic criteria. The prehistoric artist certainly observed the animal life about him with extreme care and reproduced it with a vivid realism. In the creation of such fine images as he produced he may well have taken pleasure of an esthetic sort. Some of the pictures may have been intended to serve a purely decorative purpose. But if this were the only motive involved, why were many of the works put in such almost inaccessible places?

Furthermore, we note that the animals most frequently represented were precisely those upon which prehistoric man was chiefly dependent for his food and livelihood. They are most often shown as near at hand, which is the way they would have appeared to the Paleolithic hunter who had to contend with them at relatively close quarters. In some cases there seems to be an emphasis upon the fertility of the animals; often, as we have seen, they are shown with wounds, with darts or arrows hanging from their sides, or with clubs placed about them or traps near them.

Even a cautious evaluation of these facts leads to the conclusion that the raison d'être of this art included elements beyond the esthetic. In part at least, particularly where the figures are in relatively inaccessible places and where wounded animals are shown, the work must have been done because it was thought it would exercise some potent influence. The purpose was undoubtedly that of wielding power over the animals whose capture was desired. To portray the animal was to give the hunter some control over it, and to show the weapons with which it was attacked was to heighten the efficacy of those arms in the actual chase. The power of the representation extended to the thing represented. And some relation to this dynamistic and magical play of force was as necessary as life itself to prehistoric man.[88]

---

[88] Beth, *Religion und Magie bei den Naturvölkern*, pp.111-115; Ernest A. Parkyn, *An Introduction to the Study of Prehistoric Art*. 1915, pp.118f.; G. Renard, *Life and Work in Prehistoric Times*. tr. R. T. Clark. 1929, p.171; Miles C. Burkitt in EB II, pp.240f.; Luquet, *The Art and Religion of Fossil Man*, pp.96-113: Albright, *From the Stone Age to Christianity*, p.93; Max Raphael, *Prehistoric Cave Paintings* (The Bollingen Series, IV). 1945.

3. THE RELIGION OF PRELITERATE MAN

WE TURN now from religion as we have glimpsed it in prehistoric times to religion as it may be seen among preliterate peoples of the present. Brief descriptions will be given of several contemporary preliterate groups, in which at least certain highlights will appear of the configurations of religious and magical belief and practice prevailing among them. The groups selected for mention will be the Congo Pygmies, Bushmen, Andaman Islanders, Azande, Navaho, Chiricahua and Mescalero Apache, and Zuñi Pueblo Indians. At least the first three of these groups are among the rudest peoples on the globe.[89] All of them have been the object of scientifically dependable studies and publications, upon which we shall draw for the very short narratives which can be given here.

CONGO PYGMIES

The Pygmies are a dwarf folk living in equatorial Africa. Under five feet in height, they have skins which are dark, yet lighter than those of true Negroes, and are usually classified among the Negrito peoples, otherwise represented elsewhere in Africa and also in Oceania.

Among the Pygmies a practice has been seen by a modern observer which is strikingly parallel in significance to the dynamistic meaning which we have inferred for the cave art of the Old Stone Age. In the two hundredth century B.C., prehistoric man was painting pictures of the animals he wished to catch, and showing them with darts piercing their sides. In the twentieth century A.D., Professor Leo Frobenius of the *Forschungsinstitut für Kulturmorphologie* (Research Institute for the Morphology of Civilization) at Frankfort-on-the-Main was traveling in the Congo. In the jungle district near Luebo his expedition was guided for a time by three men and a woman who belonged to a hunting tribe of Pygmies. "One afternoon," relates Professor Frobenius, "finding our larder rather depleted, I asked one of them to shoot me an antelope, surely an easy job for such an expert hunter. He and his fellows looked at me in astonishment and then burst out with the answer that, yes, they'd do it gladly, but that it was naturally out of the question for that day since no preparations had been made. After a long palaver they declared themselves ready

[89] Robert H. Lowie, *Primitive Religion.* 1925, p.124.

to make these at sunrise. Then they went off as though searching for a good site and finally settled on a high place on a near-by hill."

"As I was eager to learn what their preparations consisted of," continues Frobenius, "I left camp before dawn and crept through the bush to the open place which they had sought out the night before. The pygmies appeared in the twilight, the woman with them. The men crouched on the ground, plucked a small square free of weeds and smoothed it over with their hands. One of them then drew something in the cleared space with his forefinger, while his companions murmured some kind of formula or incantation. Then a waiting silence. The sun rose on the horizon. One of the men, an arrow on his bowstring, took his place beside the square. A few minutes later the rays of the sun fell on the drawing at his feet. In that same second the woman stretched out her arms to the sun, shouting words I did not understand, the man shot his arrow and the woman cried out again. Then the three men bounded off through the bush while the woman stood for a few minutes and then went slowly towards our camp. As she disappeared I came forward and, looking down at the smoothed square of sand, saw the drawing of an antelope four hands long. From the antelope's neck protruded the pygmy's arrow. . . . That afternoon the hunters appeared with a fine 'buschbock,' an arrow in its throat."[90]

For the purpose of our study, it suffices to point out the remarkable correspondence in conception between this practice in the heart of contemporary Africa and the cave paintings of prehistoric man in Europe. Whether the agreement is evidence only of comparable ways of thought, or proves an actual cultural continuity, is not here of great importance. The latter possibility, however, certainly exists. In earlier times the Straits of Gibraltar probably had not been formed, and Europe was more intimately connected with Africa than now. As was thus geographically possible, and as is suggested by the existence in various parts of Africa of prehistoric rock pictures comparable to those of Spain and France, one culture doubtless then overspread the regions both to the north and the south of the Mediterranean lake. When the last ice sheet retreated and northern Africa turned into a desert, the African branch of this culture naturally moved southward into the moist interior. Thus it is understandable

[90] Frobenius and Fox, *Prehistoric Rock Pictures in Europe and Africa*, pp.22f. Quoted by permission of the publishers, The Museum of Modern Art, New York.

that, as Frobenius states, "that which existed once in Europe lives on among its epigones in Africa today."

BUSHMEN

The Bushmen of South Africa are also a Negrito people, small in stature, living normally as nomadic hunters. Rude as their existence is, they have a decided artistic sense and possess a wealth of folklore.

Their chief artistic expression has been in the form of rock paintings which are found scattered all over South Africa. More permanent than the sand drawing of the Pygmies just described, these pictures are like that one and like the cave pictures of prehistoric man[91] in that their subjects are most often the animals which are objects of the chase. The animals represented include antelopes, elephants, boars, leopards and lions, and the portrayals are usually very realistic. Since the hunting of these animals is often depicted, it may be believed that the pictures have more than a purely artistic significance, and, like those we have discussed already, were intended to bring success in the actual hunt.

One example of the Bushmen paintings is reproduced in Fig. 17 from a copy made by M. Helen Tongue. This picture is in a cave at Zandfontein, Cape of Good Hope. The animal is a fearsome hippopotamus, and is charging into a trap while under attack by natives. This method of hunting large game is, of course, well known among the Bushmen.[92]

The extensive folklore of the Bushman was made available for scientific study only through the learning by western scholars of the guttural, clicking language of these people and the recording from the lips of various narrators of the stories which had hitherto been told only orally. The collection of Bushman folklore which was made in this manner and published by Dr. Wilhelm H. I. Bleek and Miss Lucy C. Lloyd contains descriptions of wild animals and their habits, accounts of Bushman customs and practices, myths, legends, fables and poetry.[93]

The sample selected for presentation here is a myth called The

[91] For comparison of prehistoric man and the Bushman see Burkitt, *Prehistory*, pp.306f.

[92] *Bushman Paintings Copied by M. Helen Tongue.* 1909, p.13, Pl. IV. For these paintings see also *Rock-Paintings in South Africa from Parts of the Eastern Province and Orange Free State, Copied by George William Stow, with an Introduction and Descriptive Notes by Dorothea F. Bleek.* 1930; Herbert Kühn, *Die Kunst der Primitiven.* 1923, pp.31-39.

[93] W. H. I. Bleek and L. C. Lloyd, *Specimens of Bushman Folklore.* 1911.

Origin of Death.[94] This takes the form of a story about the Moon and the Hare. The hare, it appears, was at one time a human being but came to have his present animal form as a result of the happenings recited in the present story.

It occurred, the narrative begins, that the hare's mother died. He thereupon lamented grievously and declared emphatically "that he would not be silent, for his mother would not again living return; for his mother was altogether dead. Therefore, he would cry greatly for his mother."

To this the Moon replied that he should cease to cry, for his mother was not altogether dead; she would indeed again living return. Despite this, the hare maintained his stubborn belief that his mother was irrevocably lost, and contradicted all the assurances given by the Moon. At that the Moon became angry and struck the hare with his fist, cleaving the hare's mouth. Then he pronounced this curse: "This person . . . his mouth shall altogether be like this, even when he is a hare; he shall always bear a scar on his mouth; he shall spring away, he shall doubling come back. The dogs shall chase him; they shall, when they have caught him, they shall grasping tear him to pieces, he shall altogether die."

Not only was the hare thus made to assume permanently his animal form and become subject to death; the curse of death was also placed upon all men. The Moon continued: "And they who are men, they shall altogether dying go away, when they die."

One vestige of its former human status remains with the hare, according to Bushman belief. This is a certain small part of the flesh of the animal which is still human flesh, and consequently is scrupulously avoided when the rest of the hare is eaten.

As for man himself, he remembers his lost estate sadly and blames his subjection to death upon the deed of the hare. "The hare's doings," says the Bushman, "are those on account of which the Moon cursed us; that we should altogether die." The original intention of the Moon had been that man should be like itself, seeming to die indeed but then coming back again alive. "For I," said the Moon, "when I am dead, I again living return. I had intended that ye who are men, ye should also resemble me and do the things that I do; that I do not altogether dying go away." If only the hare had assented to the Moon's suggestion and said, "Yes, my mother lies sleeping; she will presently arise," then "we who are people, we

94 ibid., pp.57-65.

should have resembled the Moon; for the Moon had formerly said that we should not altogether die."

When the new moon first becomes visible, the Bushman addresses to it this prayer: "Take my face yonder! . . . Thou shalt give me thy face—with which thou, when thou hast died, thou dost again living return; when we did not perceive thee, thou dost against lying down come—that I may also resemble thee. For, the joy yonder, thou dost always possess it yonder, that is that thou art wont again to return alive, when we did not perceive thee. . . . Thou didst formerly say that we should also again return alive when we died."

Thus it is that the passing of the moon through its successive phases suggests to the Bushman not only the transition from life to death but also from death to life again. To pass from life to death he knows is now his lot. To go from death to renewed life he believes once was possible and wistfully hopes and prays may yet again become his privilege.

ANDAMAN ISLANDERS

The Andaman Islands lie in the Bay of Bengal between India and the Malay Peninsula. The inhabitants are also a Negrito people, short and black-skinned, with frizzly hair. Anthropological researches were carried out among this folk by A. R. Brown in 1906-1908 and were published more recently.[95] From the detailed information here provided about their social organization, customs and beliefs, myths and legends, we select for condensed report certain materials concerning their belief in spiritual beings.[96]

The Andaman Islanders believe in a large number of supernatural beings. These may be divided into two classes. The first is that of the spirits which inhabit the jungle and the sea and are thought to be the ghosts of human beings. Whenever a man or woman of the Andamans dies, he or she becomes one of these spirits. In the mythology of the Islands there is reference to the remote ancestors of the Andamanese people, and these are believed to be spirits now, too. They are thought of as occupying positions of prominence among the other ghosts, and are called "big" spirits.

All of these spirits are under ordinary circumstances invisible. From time to time the report is heard, however, that a human being has seen them. When described, they are often spoken of as being

---

[95] A. R. Brown, *The Andaman Islanders, A Study in Social Anthropology.* 1922.
[96] *ibid.*, pp.136-166.

light skinned and having long hair and beards, in all of which features they contrast with the Andamanese themselves. Their bodies are thought to be small, their arms and legs extraordinarily long. On the whole, the impression they make is that of grotesqueness and ugliness. They are believed to carry lights, and sometimes men see these without glimpsing the spirits themselves.

The spirits have their own villages or camps in the forest and in the sea. Their customary sustenance is the flesh of dead men and women. The spirits of the jungle devour the bodies of those who are buried in the earth; the spirits of the sea consume those who are drowned or lost there.

It is evident that the spirits are fearful beings. Men wandering in the jungle by themselves run the danger of being taken captive by the spirits. It is said that when this happens, if the individual shows fear he is slain but if he manifests bravery is released after a period of detention. In the latter case, the man himself is henceforth endowed with magical powers. Aside from such individuals as have had experiences of this kind through which they have become friends of the spirits, men do well to avoid every contact with these beings. It is they who cause sickness and death resulting therefrom. Danger from the spirits is greater at night than in the day, greater when one is alone than when in company, greater when one is in a strange region than when in the precincts of home.

The second class of supernatural beings is that of the spirits associated with the heavenly bodies, with thunder and lightning, and with the monsoons. The sun and moon, it is usually held, are wife and husband respectively, and the stars are their children. One tribe believes that upon occasion the moon turns himself into a pig and comes down to earth in that form. All the tribes hold that when the moon rises in the early evening, he will be extremely angry if he sees any fire or bright light. Therefore fires and lights are extinguished or dimmed for a time at moonrising.

Thunder and lightning are also personal beings. Lightning lives in the sky and produces the familiar phenomenon associated with himself by shaking his foot. Thunder lives there too, and makes his great rumbling noise by rolling a stone about over the sky.

Of the monsoons, the chief ones to affect the Andamans are the northeast and the southwest. These, too, are personified, the northeast wind being known as Biliku, the southwest as Tarai. The entire year is divided between these two beings, the Tarai season being the period of usually four or five months while the southwest monsoon is blowing; the Biliku season being the remainder of the year including not only the stormy season of October and November but also the cold season of December to February and the hot season of March and April.

Biliku and Tarai are often considered wife and husband; again they are said to have been friends who experienced an estrangement. The tale told by one tribe is this: "Once upon a time Puluga (Biliku) and Daria (Tarai) were great friends, but they quarreled. Puluga said that he was the bigger (more important). Daria said that he was. So now they are always quarreling. Puluga sends the wind for one period. Then Daria sends his wind."

When bad weather comes it is because Biliku or Tarai has been angered. Three actions by men are specially offensive to these beings: (1) burning or melting beeswax; (2) killing a cicada or making a noise, particularly chopping or banging wood, during the time in the morning or evening when the cicada is singing; (3) using certain foods including specified kinds of yams and edible roots. Actually the special seasons of the year for honey, for cicadas and for the yams and roots, are when stormy weather is beginning; hence the conclusion in the native mind that deeds in connection with these things are responsible for causing anger to the beings who control the weather. Thus it is clear that Biliku and Tarai are personifications of natural forces, and the myths and customs associated with them are expressions of the social value of natural phenomena.[97]

AZANDE

The Azande are a Negroid people who live in the southern Sudan, on the divide between the Nile and the Congo Rivers. Extensive ethnological researches were conducted in Zandeland in 1926 and following by Dr. E. E. Evans-Pritchard, and his detailed account of Zande witchcraft will provide the basis for the following short sketch.[98]

Witchcraft occupies a place of dominant importance in the configuration of belief and practice characteristic of the Azande. It is ubiquitous. It plays a part in agriculture, hunting and fishing, in domestic and communal life, in law, morals and religion. In any

[97] *ibid.*, pp.351-376.
[98] E. E. Evans-Pritchard, *Witchcraft, Oracles and Magic among the Azande.* 1937.

realm, an unfortunate event will probably be attributed to witch-craft.

The Azande have a perfectly good understanding of the normal sequences of events which we describe as cause and effect. But the particular conditions in any chain of causation which bring an individual into relation to natural happenings in such a manner that he sustains injury, are due, it is most often believed, to witchcraft. Thus when a Zande boy struck his foot against a small stump of wood in the center of a path in the bush, and the wound became infected and caused him much pain and inconvenience, he declared that it was the result of witchcraft. With the argument that it was not witchcraft which had placed the stump of wood in his path, since it had grown there naturally, he was entirely willing to agree. But to him the proof that witchcraft was involved lay in the fact that, whereas he had been as careful as ever to watch for obstructions, he had actually struck the stump; and whereas such a wound ordinarily heals quickly, this one had festered and become very painful. These unfortunate circumstances in a chain of happenings otherwise not out of the ordinary were the proof, to his mind, that witchcraft had been involved.

What, then, is witchcraft? It is evident that it is a normal thing in everyday life, just as normal as the misfortunes which constantly plague the steps of any native. Perfectly familiar as it is, witchcraft still has about it something peculiar. Men know that it exists and that it accomplishes evil, but the way in which it works eludes their understanding. They have a feeling about it rather than any clear-cut comprehension of it. In their feeling concerning it there is a sense of a mysterious hidden side, an inherent power, a soul of the thing. When witchcraft causes death, as it constantly does according to Zande thought, it is the soul of witchcraft which goes forth by night and devours the soul of its victim.

Suprasensible as it is, the power of witchcraft emanates from a tangible substance. This substance exists in the bodies of persons who are witches. Witchcraft-substance is inherited by a child from its parent, and grows more and more powerful as the person grows older. The individual may be unaware of his endowment, or even if aware of it may not make use of it. If others, however, suspect him of being a witch, upon his death an autopsy may be performed to discover whether witchcraft-substance is present. Those who are skilled in such matters are able at once to recognize the mysterious substance if they see it in the body of the deceased.

It is much more important, however, to be able to recognize a witch while he is still alive, for then it may be possible to avert his evil machinations or take vengeance on him for them. The ways in which witches may be identified are chiefly through oracles. Of these, the poison oracle is the most important. So important is it, indeed, that it is probably the most cherished of all Zande institutions of any kind.

In typical employment, the poison oracle works as follows. A death takes place. This, to the Azande, is never a purely natural happening. Natural causes may be and doubtless are involved, but the peculiar concatenation of them is obviously, to the Zande mind, due to the operation of witchcraft. It is therefore incumbent upon the kinsfolk of the deceased to ascertain the witch who is responsible for this murder, and to avenge upon him the death of the relative. In earlier days the vengeance might take the form of the slaughter of the witch, particularly if he were known to have committed several such murders. Today the duty of vengeance may be considered fulfilled if compensation is obtained from the witch, or if magical processes are instituted which lead to his death through the working of such mystical forces as he himself has unleashed.

But how can it be found out who the guilty witch is? This can be accomplished best of all by the poison oracle. Known as *benge,* the oracular poison is a red powder made, under strictest ceremonial conditions, from a forest creeper and mixed with water to form a paste. So reverentially is it treated, there is little doubt that *benge* possesses a supernatural dynamism. The employment of the poison as an oracle consists essentially in the administering of it to fowls and the observation of the results.

The usual place for consulting the oracle is in some secluded spot in the bush, and the normal time is from about eight to nine o'clock in the morning. Any male may conduct the séance, but it is usually done by a married householder who enjoys sufficient prosperity to have available the necessary fowls. Women are quite debarred, and normally neither operate the oracle nor consult it.

Ordinarily two chickens are used, and two consecutive tests are carried out. For the first test the poison oracle may be addressed somewhat as follows:

Poison oracle, poison oracle, if it is Bazugba who killed Bafuka, let this chicken die, if it is not he, let the chicken live.

After this the operator administers a dose of poison to the fowl, and all who are participating in the séance watch closely to see if it will die or survive. After the answer has been obtained, the second test is conducted. This must corroborate the first, otherwise the verdict is invalid. Also it is customary for the question in the second test to be framed in such a way as to require opposite behavior on the part of the second chicken in order to give agreement with the first. That is, if a fowl dies in the first test, then another fowl must live through the second test, and if a fowl survives the first ordeal then another must perish in the second, for the judgment to be accepted as valid. Thus, in the hypothetical case we are using for illustration, where we may suppose the first chicken died, the address introducing the second test might run like this:

The poison oracle has declared Bazugba guilty by slaying the fowl. If its declaration is true let it spare this second fowl.

If, then, the second fowl lives after being given the poison, the verdict is valid, and Bazugba is indubitably guilty.

While we have illustrated the use of the poison oracle in relation to the ascertainment of a witch's guilt for the death of a person, which is perhaps the most important single legal problem in Zandeland, the same oracle is also employed to obtain answers to questions about a great variety of other matters of significance to individuals and society. Typical situations occasioning consultation of the poison oracle are: before the marriage of a daughter; in the sickness of any member of the family; to discover the agent responsible for any misfortune; in cases of sorcery, adultery, or disloyalty to a prince; before long journeys; before hunting.

Other oracles are also employed, however, although none has as great an authority as that just described. Next in esteem is the termites oracle, and since it does not involve the possible sacrifice of chickens, it is more readily available to the poor man. The procedure is to find a termite mound and insert into it two branches of different trees. The next day the interrogator gets his answer by observing which branch the termites have eaten. Yet somewhat lower in authority, but used most widely of all because of ease and expeditiousness of operation, is the rubbing-board oracle. The rubbing-board is something like a miniature table with a tail, and with a separate lid having a vertical handle. The operator sits on the ground and steadies the board by holding his right foot on its tail. Holding the handle of the lid between his thumb and first finger, he jerks the lid backward and forward. Prior to use, the table has been made ready by placing on its surface plant juices or grated wood, and during the operation the lid is dipped from time to time into a gourd of water. The oracle answers the questions which are put to it by sliding back and forth smoothly or by sticking in place firmly, the two responses corresponding to "No" and "Yes" respectively.

Oracles, therefore, constitute the first and most distinctive means by which the Azande cope with witchcraft. By oracles it is determined who has injured or is about to injure another by witchcraft, and whether or not witchcraft threatens a projected undertaking. The second thing of importance in dealing with omnipresent witchcraft is magic. By magic men can guard themselves against witchcraft and destroy it. The main purpose of magic is to combat the mystical forces of witchcraft. When a man dies, the cause is, as we have seen, witchcraft, and vengeance-magic provides a way of dealing with the ascertained culprit. When a man falls sick, witchcraft is attacked by the making of magic. Likewise the other misfortunes of life may be dealt with by the practices of magic.

The third channel through which the Azande are able to contend against the dangers of witchcraft is provided by the witch doctor. He serves both as diviner and as magician. As a diviner he exposes witches in their nefarious deeds; as a magician he performs the rituals which thwart them in their evil undertakings. Such is the threefold structure of defense which is erected in Zandeland against the perils of witchcraft by which man is so constantly surrounded.

NAVAHOS

The Navaho and Apache Indians belong to the southern branch of that extensive linguistic family of North American Indians known as Athapascan, the Pacific branch of which is found in California and Oregon, the northern in Canada and Alaska. Encountered first by the Spaniards near a Tewa pueblo called *Navahú*, or "great fields," the Navahos, as they thus came to be known, live now on a reservation occupying parts of Colorado, Utah, Arizona and New Mexico. A file of Navaho singers is shown in Fig. 18.

The Navaho people believe in the supernatural as a realm of power and of danger.[99] In order to influence the forces of the supernatural

[99] Clyde Kluckhohn and Dorothea Leighton, *The Navaho*. 1946, p.121.

[48]

and thereby affect the course of human events, various techniques have been elaborated. Of these some are socially approved and some socially disapproved. The two classes of procedures will be illustrated by reference to ceremonies and witchcraft respectively.

Navaho religious ceremonies follow for the most part a single general pattern. Ordinarily they center around a patient, perhaps a person who is actually sick, perhaps one who has been frightened by a dream. They are conducted at and in the hogan or dwelling of the patient, and are in the charge of a medicine man who is assisted by various helpers. Before a medicine man can give a healing ceremony he must have had the same conducted on his own behalf, and needless to say must have mastered all the intricate details of procedure and accompanying songs as well as the myth material basic to the ceremony.

Originally each ceremony was of nine days' duration, although now many are conducted more briefly. The first days of the ceremony have to do with cleansing from evil. At the outset the hogan is blessed and then various procedures are employed for cleansing the patient, such as sweat baths for the body and passing through a series of hoops to mark the shedding of the old personality. Herbs are infused, the patient's body painted, and prayers uttered as dictated by the medicine man. On the sixth day of a nine-day ceremony, after the patient has again been ceremonially bathed in the morning, the sand paintings begin.

The art of sand painting, also called dry painting and not unknown elsewhere in the world, has been carried to a very high degree of perfection by the Navahos. The actual work of the sand painting is done by relatives or friends of the patient and by other assistants, but under the immediate direction of the medicine man. Pieces of white, red, and yellow sandstone are ground to make the colors; charcoal is used for black, and blue is made by mixing charcoal and white sand. Instead of mineral colors, cornmeal, pollens and powdered flowers or plants may also be used for the various colors; but the background is still usually of sand and the method of work the same, hence the term sand painting still applies.

The sand or other material is taken up by the painter in his hand, a small amount at a time, and poured out on the background area, beginning at the center and working out toward the edges. The rate of flow and consequent thickness of line is controlled by letting the material escape from beneath the thumb and through the nearly closed joint of the index finger. A high degree of precision is attained by skilled workers.

The stylized figures and symbols which are wrought out in the sand painting have to do with the myth which underlies the ceremony. The course of man's life and the supernatural powers which play about it are vividly portrayed. A series of such sand paintings, depicting successive phases of the myth, may be executed on successive days, each painting being destroyed in turn to make way for the next. Indeed the life of the painting, painstakingly executed though it is, is in any event not long. In climactic parts of the ceremony the patient is caused to sit on the sand painting, and the medicine man takes his place on it, too.

One ceremony is the Hozhonji, or Blessing Chant. This blessing is conceived in terms of an appeasement and control of the supernatural powers, and of an achievement of right relationship between the individual and the universe. When this is accomplished, the person enjoys blessing or happiness.

The mythical materials employed in the Blessing Chant are from the Navaho Creation Myth, or Story of the Emergence. This myth was narrated to Mary C. Wheelwright, who recorded it in permanent form,[100] by Hasteen Klah, an aged and honored Navaho medicine man living at Nava, halfway between Gallup and Shiprock. The story begins in the dark First World, where were Begochiddy, the blue-eyed and yellow haired great god; Hashjeshjin, the fire god, son of the Fire and a Comet; Etsay-hashkeh, the Coyote Man; Asheen-as-sun, the Salt Woman; and Etsay-hasteen and Estsa-assun, First Man and First Woman, the prototypes of the human beings on this earth. All of these went upward to the Second World which is the blue world. There Begochiddy created twin men and twin women, only to have them destroyed by Hashjeshjin. From their bodies, however, Begochiddy created new twins, the Ethkay-nah-ashi, and breathed his spirit into them. In the yellow Third World, to which the powers later ascended, Begochiddy made many things, mountains, water, animals, birds, fishes, and the first four men and four women. Taking a bamboo and breathing through the Ethkay-nah-ashi, he gave life to all that he had created. There was no sun or moon in this world but the mountains gave plenty of light. Here the first marriage took place, and the first misunderstanding and sin. When big storms and

[100] *Navajo Creation Myth, The Story of the Emergence,* by Hasteen Klah, recorded by Mary C. Wheelwright. Navajo Religion Series, I. 1942.

hot waters poured upon this world, all the creatures went up a rapidly growing bamboo to reach the white Fourth World, which is this present world.

The waters from the lower world kept threatening to overwhelm the Fourth World. The reason lay in the fact that Coyote had stolen a baby from the lower world, and when this was discovered and the baby returned there, the waters ceased to rise toward this world and ever after remained at a constant level. Gathering his people together in a sweat house, Begochiddy led a conference on the creation of the new world. He and the other powers there planned the mountains, the sun, moon and stars, and the months. In each case, as the work of creation proceeded, the spirit of the thing about to be created was made first. When all was ready, these spirits went into the places where they belonged. The universe did not begin to move, however, until the first person, called Etsay-dassalini, died. Then, the first time the sun crossed the sky it was too near the earth and was too hot; not until its fourth crossing was it in exactly the right spot where it has stayed ever since.

Finally the powers began to make a new kind of human being. Distinct from Hahjeenah-dinneh, The-People-Who-Came-Up, the new people were called Anlthtahn-nah-olyah, meaning Created-from-Everything. The feet and ankles of the new man were made of soil of the earth, his legs of lightning, his knees of white shell and his body of white and yellow corn. His heart was of obsidian and his breath was the white wind. They made animals, too. When the newly-made people arose they ate some white corn, for although they were made of corn it was good for them to eat it, and the Navahos live on corn even until now.

Thus was ended the creating of human beings and creatures, and Begochiddy was glad and laughing, it is said, when he had finished the creation.

One of the sand paintings of the Blessing Chant is shown in Fig. 19.[101] This is from the ceremony as conducted by Hasteen Klah, and the sand painting was recorded by Franc J. Newcomb. The background was of sand, the colored designs of corn meal, pollen and powdered flowers or plants. At the bottom of the illustration is a rainbow path, leading from the east, with white footsteps on it. This is man's path from the unknown. The white oblong is enclosed with four lines, black, blue, yellow and white, signifying the four worlds

---

[101] *ibid.*, Set 1, First Sand Painting.

through which man made his ascent, as told in the Creation Myth. Near the center, the circular figure represents the place of emergence, through which mankind came out into the present fourth, white world. In the making of this figure the ground is first colored all black, the blue is placed over that, then the yellow and finally the white. Thus the painter symbolically passes through the four worlds. On either side are the insect figures of the mythical Messenger Fly, Dontso, while at the top is the blue bird of happiness. Approaching the center, the path of man and his footsteps are made of yellow pollen, signifying prayer, blessing and fertility.

Turning from the socially approved religious ceremonies of the Navahos to the socially disapproved techniques of relationship to supernatural powers, we encounter witchcraft. Although a subject only reluctantly discussed by most Navahos, through long acquaintance Clyde Kluckhohn has gathered extensive data relating to witchcraft among these people.[102]

Four distinct types of malevolent activity in relation to the supernatural are recognizable and may be referred to as Witchery, Sorcery, Wizardry and Frenzy Witchcraft. It is Witchery which is most often mentioned. According to the stories on this subject, both men and women may become witches, the profession most often being learned from a parent or other relative, the initiation requiring the killing of a near relative. The witches are said to constitute a group and to hold meetings in a cave by night, presided over by a chief witch. Naked save for masks, beads and jewelry, they sit in a circle surrounded by baskets of human flesh. The evil counterpart of a religious ceremonial is conducted, with songs and sand paintings. Going forth upon their nefarious missions, the witches roam at great speed, clothed in skins of the wolf, coyote or other animals. Having made a powdered poison from the flesh of corpses, they drop it through the smokehole of their victim's hogan or blow it into his face from a furrowed stick. The poison at once causes fainting, lockjaw or a swollen tongue, and from the ensuing illness there is no recovery since in such a case the usual curing rituals are ineffective.

Ceremonial knowledge does give an advance protection against the attacks of witches, however, and certain small sand or pollen paintings are made by family members for the same purpose. The most potent protection of all is gall medicine, made from the gall of the

[102] Clyde Kluckhohn, *Navaho Witchcraft* (Papers of the Peabody Museum of American Archaeology and Ethnology, Harvard University, xxii, 2). 1944.

eagle, bear, mountain lion and skunk. This acts, it is believed, as an immediate antidote to the fainting caused by corpse poison, and is kept in most Navaho homes and carried by many Navahos when traveling or going into crowds.

After a person has fallen ill from Witchery the most effective cure consists in finding the witch and extracting, by questioning or by force, a confession. Capital punishment is said to have been visited not infrequently upon witches. Specific prayer ceremonials and chants also are designated for the cure of victims of witchcraft.

Sorcery is practiced by obtaining a part of the victim's clothing or hair or nails and uttering spells over it; or by making an image of the one to be attacked and "killing" or "torturing" this effigy. Wizardry is believed to depend upon the injection of some foreign particle such as a stone or bit of bone or ashes into the body of the victim. The shooting of such projectiles is accomplished by an incantation. Frenzy Witchcraft is essentially a love magic, involving the use of medicines made out of certain plants, especially including Datura or Jimson weed.

As Kluckhohn has shown, the Navaho belief in witchcraft has created a veritable pageant of everything that is most evil in society and has provided in the supposed witches an object upon which anxieties may be focused and against which animosities may be released.

CHIRICAHUA AND MESCALERO APACHES

The Chiricahua and Mescalero tribes of Apache Indians live together on the Mescalero Reservation in southern New Mexico. It is their common belief that a mighty force pervades the universe and works through natural phenomena to reach man.[103] This supernatural power may be conducted through anything and it may come to anybody. The sun, the lightning, the bear, the snake, the owl, the coyote, all these and other things may be the channels through which power communicates with human beings. There is no restriction on those to whom the communication may come. Any man or woman may upon occasion have "something speak to him." The message, whether it comes as a vision in a dream or as a word reaching an individual in the midst of a crowd, is always highly individual, meant for the person to whom it is addressed alone. Thus Bear may appear in a vision to a man, offering him power to cure bear sickness. The latter

[103] Morris E. Opler in *American Anthropologist.* New Series 37 (1935), pp. 65-70.

illness is incurred when a person has an unfortunate contact with a bear, as for example upon being frightened by one. The man to whom the curing power is offered is free to accept it or reject it. Indeed a considerable palaver may take place on the subject, Bear stating that he has studied this individual carefully and singled him out as the proper recipient of the gift, the man suggesting that others might be better qualified for it than he. If the man does accept, then he is given directions for the conduct of a ceremony through which power will be effective to the end specified.

The same general pattern is discernible in all the ceremonies. There is at first a ceremonial smoking, then a casting of pollen in the four directions, then prayer, and then the singing of a set of songs. The proper actions, prayers and songs of the particular ceremony having been made known to the individual recipient, he is henceforth their custodian. If any man should attempt to perform a ceremony to which he has not been granted the supernatural right, it would be fatal. If it is in accord with the wishes of his power, the owner of a ceremony may, however, transmit it to another. Usually this is from an older person to a younger, with the intent that the ceremony not be lost upon the death of the former. If the ceremony is handed down to another member of the same family, there is no fee; if it is transmitted outside the family, the payment of a fee is necessary. It is possible for the custodian of a ceremony to employ it privately on behalf of his own family, or also to use it for others. In the latter case, certain gifts are asked in return for the service, for which an extensive demand may develop.

There is a certain ambivalence about the supernatural power. It may bring benefit or work harm. It may be manipulated malevolently by a sorcerer or employed benevolently by a shaman, in either case to the accomplishment of extraordinary ends. Wonderful as it is, the power always remains dangerous. Especially if it is employed with notable success over a long period of time, it is apt to demand in payment the life of the one who has used it, or of a near relative of his. If consent is given to the latter sacrifice, for example, the relative will soon fall in battle or be destroyed by an accident.

In some ceremonies, masked dancers play an important part. Like the other ceremonies, these too originate in personal experiences with the supernatural. One Chiricahua shaman received such a ceremony in the following way. A spirit told him to go into a certain mountain. Led by a clown, he passed through four stone doors, some guarded by snakes and mountain lions. Within, an old man who controlled the whole mountain asked him what kind of power he wanted. To show the various ceremonies which were available, many Indians, dressed in buckskin, and Mountain People came in, dancing, followed by all kinds of birds, snakes and animals. Recognizing the Mountain Spirits to be the leading personages, the man chose them. For four days he stayed on in the mountain, learning the ceremony they had to impart. At last the old man of the mountain told him, "You may go home and use the ceremony according to what the Mountain People want you to do." From that time on, whenever the shaman held his ceremony, the Mountain People sent messages to him. When he wanted to know how to cure a man, they would come and tell him.[104]

In the case of such a ceremony, the masked dancers impersonate the Mountain People. The costuming and painting of the dancers is done under the immediate direction of the shaman, and to the accompaniment of full ritual details. During the painting the shaman beats upon his drum and sings songs about the Mountain People, their holy home, and the protection which may be expected from them against sickness and danger. The costume of the dancer includes high moccasins and a buckskin shirt, colored yellow. The arms and upper part of the body are painted with designs in black, white, yellow and blue colors. On the head a buckskin mask is worn, surmounted by a superstructure of painted wooden slats, while in each hand a sharp painted stick is carried. The dancing, angular and spectacular, is carried out around a blazing fire. No one confuses the masked men with the Mountain People themselves; it is clearly understood that they are only their impersonators. Nevertheless, through the ceremony the mighty power of these spirits is brought to bear upon the affairs of men.[105]

A photograph of two Mescalero Apache masked dancers together with a shaman is reproduced in Fig. 20.

Turning to the mythology of the Apaches, it will be readily understood that in it the Mountain People, whom we have just met, play an important part. They are described in various legends as protectors of the tribal territory. An even more important role, perhaps, is assumed by White Painted Woman and her son, Child of the Water. The latter is the Apache culture hero, and his exploits in the conquest

---

[104] Morris E. Opler, *An Apache Life-Way, The Economic, Social, and Religious Institutions of the Chiricahua Indians.* 1941, pp.269-272.
[105] *ibid.*, pp.100-115.

of numerous monsters provide the mythological background for much ritual. Still more popular, no doubt, is the character named Coyote, whose escapades are the subject of an entire cycle of accounts. Always a prankster, Coyote appears at the beginning of his travels and adventures with the characteristics of a human being, but at the end loses the ability of speech and assumes the appearance and manifests the traits of the animal whose name he bears. Actually, Coyote is not so much either an individual beast or human being, as a type; he has been called a self-portrait of the Apache character and a satire upon its weaknesses. While to their audience the stories about Coyote are entertaining in and of themselves, they also provide, through their narrative of the misdeeds of the chief character and his subsequent embarrassments, a certain amount of moral teaching. Also the Coyote cycle has been utilized as a vehicle for an account of the creation, a matter with which Child of the Water and White Painted Woman also are concerned.

As told by the Mescalero Apache, the story of Coyote and the Creation has been recorded by Harry Hoijer, during researches conducted from 1930 to 1934. His principal informant for this and other mythological materials of the Mescalero was a member of the tribe named Charles Smith. Ethnological notes have been provided by Morris Edward Opler.[106]

Coyote, the episode begins, informed his family that he was going away. When they expressed displeasure at being left alone so often, Coyote explained that he was learning as he traveled about, and that he would doubtless bring back something good from the new journey. He would go, he declared, to the Frog people, who were of high repute. The journey involved the crossing of broad rivers, deep canyons and high mountains, but was facilitated by directions kindly vouchsafed him both by birds and by a bear en route. Like Coyote, these animals manifested human qualities and spoke one universal language. Meanwhile, however, Coyote was taken possession of by Child of the Water, the culture hero of the Mescalero, who henceforth talked and worked through him. Through Coyote, Child of the Water made known that the things of earth were to be changed. When Coyote comes and speaks to the animals they will lose their

---

[106] Harry Hoijer, *Chiricahua and Mescalero Apache Texts*, with ethnological notes by Morris Edward Opler. The University of Chicago Publications in Anthropology, Linguistic Series. 1938, pp.170-181,217-219.

human attributes and common language; they will become as they have remained ever since:

Earth! Now, for some reason, that which lies upon your surface, those who live upon your surface, [and] those animate beings who exist upon your surface, none of them disappearing, will all be transformed in a place similar to this one which he will make somewhere. The people to whom I am going, on the very day that I come to them, will become like those in that place. Then, when they have spoken to me and I have spoken to them, from that moment on, they, their words and their bodies by means of which they customarily move about on the surface of the earth, will change. I will not have heard them.

Coyote arrived finally at a region where were four small mountains, with four cliffs. Under the cliffs, in turn, were four lakes, and on the east side of the uppermost lake were four rivers which flowed into it. On the farthest river bank on the uppermost clump of tule was a black rock. There sat the Frog chief.

As Coyote stopped before him, the change took place which had already been predicted. "The Frog chief was transformed exactly as [Coyote] had said he would be transformed. Right at that moment he became an ordinary frog. [Coyote] was unable to talk to him at all. And therefore he did not talk to him. [The frog] jumped away from him into the water."

"So that one was the first of all living creatures to be transformed," the account continues. "From this time on, everyone that [Coyote] looks at, whoever it is, will be changed in this way. He walked about sadly. He looked at the water. He also tried in vain to speak."

Then the work of creation proceeded. The voice of Child of the Water spoke to Coyote, putting into his mind the names of many plants. As he thought of these things, they were created. " 'Tule, spike rush, sedge, slender tule, carrizo, water cress, white violet, asphodel, side oats grama, blue-eyed grass, [and] everything, though it does not [now] exist, of whatever sort that grows in the water will be created,' [the voice] said to Coyote. [The voice] made him think only of these things. From here [Coyote] went on. 'And right now all the varieties of grass on the earth's surface: grama grass, false flax, big blue-stem grass, buffalo grass, corn grass, wild violet, salt grass, black grama grass, red columbine, wild barley, side oats grama, big blue-stem grass, and blue grass. Whether or not I've been heard to name all the varieties, let all of the other kinds come with [those I have named] also.' All of them were created."

These and many other plants and trees were named and created, and then the voice of Child of the Water addressed them: "All kinds of people, all people, will repeatedly make use of you in some good way."

After that, hills and mountains were made. "Then Coyote looked about everywhere. Whatever he thought of became so. 'Let green hills extend upward everywhere,' he, thinking, thought so. Beautiful hills with all sorts of green plants growing on them came into existence. Big mountains also arose everywhere."

Then Coyote thought about all kinds of snakes, lizards and rodents, all varieties of antelope, deer, bear and mountain lions, and all varieties of birds both small and large, and as he thought about them they were created.

At last, Coyote himself was caused to change in condition and appearance, just as he had been the instrument through whom the other plants and animals had been transformed. "Now I have become very tired. He has made me in the form of a man. Therefore, I shall make my body small. [So will change] my ears, my nose, my eyes, my body hair, [and] my teeth. My legs will be four, my tail will be bushy, I shall howl and bark, my feet will be bunched, and I shall close up my arms and my hands. Coyote is no more. Now I will return as coyote the animal [to] my wife [and] my children. Wherever I go, wherever I live, I will sleep well everywhere. Only all varieties of meat will be my food and I will drink only water. I will howl."

Once again the mysterious voice spoke, and this time Coyote challenged: "Who is this person who is speaking to me again? Now, come before me!"

At that juncture a roar of thunder was heard from inside a cloud. "A rainbow had come down on both sides from inside the cloud. He who was its power came down. The whole earth began to shake. . . . The being who had just come, he of whom one could certainly not say that he was an evil man, had come down. He stood facing [Coyote]. 'Now, since you do not want to be human, you may go away. Humankind will do to you whatever they will. They will give you troubles that do not exist for human beings.' At this point, Coyote trotted away. There stood Child of the Water."

Child of the Water was now heard to opine that much was still lacking in creation. Forthwith, therefore, he proceeded to further acts of creation. "The voices of all sorts of birds that do not [now] exist will be heard singing and making a noise," he declared. "People made in my image will follow me. . . . There will be lightning . . .

water will rain down. Let it come!" said Child of the Water. "Everything happened just so."

Still there was something wrong. Mankind was subject to disease. "Since disease will be among them," said Child of the Water, "make something that will cure it that they can prepare. I ask my mother for this." Thereupon White Painted Woman, the mother of Child of the Water, came to him and spoke as follows: "You will make for them all sorts of herbs, all of which will cure [diseases]. Some they will boil, some they will chew, some they will paint on, some they will customarily burn for their smoke, some they will drink, [and] they will breathe the vapors of some. There will be names for these things. They will be called medicines. They will make them for whatever purpose they want. These medicinal herbs will be called 'medicines which are holy.'"

At this point in the story there follows a detailed inventory of medicinal herbs and sacred rocks and mineral substances, together with enumeration of ceremonial gestures and practices which accompany the employment of these substances for the purpose of curing disease.

Child of the Water then spoke again and uttered a final, solemn word of adjuration, promise and warning to his creation. "Now then, there is nothing more of value to me that I can set down on the surface of the earth for you. You are my people, my children. I am right here. Think about me. I have done everything for you. Now I shall put you all together. Even if you speak in many different ways, I shall do so for you. Thereby, I have given you a chance [to live together peaceably (?)]. You will do whatever you like with your minds. In spite of that, there will be difficulties everywhere. I have made witches and disease to live among you."

And the episode of creation comes to a conclusion with a description of the dispersion of human beings over the earth and their division into peoples and tribes.

ZUÑIS

Even before the Navaho and Apache tribes came in from the north, the Pueblo Indians were living in the great American southwest. Themselves the successors of the yet earlier Basket Makers, the early Pueblo people lived in the cliff dwellings and semicircular valley cities the ruins of which are still so impressive in the valley of the San Juan. Prior to the advent of the Spaniards in the sixteenth cen-

tury, the cliff dwellings and semicircular citadels had been abandoned and their inhabitants had settled in the pueblos which are still
occupied in the Rio Grande valley and the deserts of New Mexico
and Arizona.

The configuration of religious belief and practice distinctive of the
Pueblo Indians may be described as a ceremonious collectivism.
Whereas the Apaches emphasize the vision or dream experience of
the individual shaman and the Navahos are not free from a tendency
toward the violent and the frenzied, the people of the pueblos characteristically make their approach to the supernatural through group
rituals marked by the greatest formality and sobriety. For concrete
illustration, we turn to the Zuñi Pueblo and the kachina cult.

Zuñi Pueblo was first viewed from afar by Friar Marcos de Niza
in 1539. Back in Mexico, his glowing account of the great city which
he had seen led to the expedition of Coronado. A procession of present-day women of Zuñi led by the governor of the Pueblo is shown
in Fig. 21. For modern research in the religion of Zuñi we will turn
to the works of Ruth L. Bunzel and Ruth Benedict.[107]

To the Zuñi people the entire world appears animate. All matter
is alive and has a spiritual essence. Sun and earth, clouds and rain,
trees and plants of corn, all are living beings. Thus the Zuñi prays:

> When our earth mother is replete with living waters,
> When spring comes,
> The source of our flesh,
> All the different kinds of corn,
> We shall lay to rest in the ground.
> With their earth mother's living waters,
> They will be made into new beings.
> Coming out standing into the daylight
> Of their sun father,
> Calling for rain,
> To all sides they will stretch out their hands.
> Then from wherever the rain makers stay quietly
> They will send forth their misty breath;
> Their massed clouds filled with water will come out to sit
>   down with us;
> Far from their homes,

[107] Ruth L. Bunzel in *Forty-Seventh Annual Report of the Bureau of American
Ethnology to the Secretary of the Smithsonian Institution 1929-1930*. 1932, pp.467-
1086; Benedict, *Patterns of Culture*, pp.57-129. For Zuñi mythology also see Ruth
Benedict in *Columbia University Contributions to Anthropology*, xxi. 2 vols. 1935.
cf. also Frank Waters, *Masked Gods, Navaho and Pueblo Ceremonialism*. 1950,
pp.277-280.

With outstretched hands of water they will embrace the corn,
Stepping down to caress them with their fresh waters,
With their fine rain caressing the earth,
With their heavy rain caressing the earth,
And yonder, wherever the roads of the rain makers come forth,
Torrents will rush forth,
Silt will rush forth,
Mountains will be washed out,
Logs will be washed down,
Yonder all the mossy mountains
Will drip with water.
The clay-lined hollows of our earth mother
Will overflow with water,
From all the lakes
Will rise the cries of the children of the rain makers,
In all the lakes
There will be joyous dancing—
Desiring that it should be thus,
I send forth my prayers.[108]

Of this animated universe man is an integral and harmonious part. In it he is not the master but only one being among many, an equal with the rabbit, the deer and the corn plant. In order that his hunting or his agriculture may go well, the Zuñi must therefore request the aid of the supernatural and perform with punctilious accuracy the ceremonies by which his own life is kept in proper relationship with the spiritual forces about him. Granted exactitude and precision in the conduct of the ritual, the desired results must automatically follow.

There are no less than six esoteric cults in existence, each devoted to the worship of a special supernatural being or group of supernatural beings, each possessing a secret body of ritual knowledge, and each bound to the preservation and performance of certain distinctive ceremonies. To the work of these cults a large part of the collective effort of the people of Zuñi is devoted. The cults are those of the sun, of the water spirits, of the kachinas, of the kachina priests (related to but distinct from the foregoing), of the war gods, and of the beast gods respectively.

The kachina cult is widespread among almost all the Pueblos, but has developed most richly among the Hopi and the Zuñi. Its fundamental elements include belief in the existence of a large group of supernatural beings, the kachinas, who live in a lake and are identi-

---

[108] Bunzel in *Forty-Seventh Annual Report of the Bureau of American Ethnology,* p.484.

fied with clouds and rain as well as with the dead; the practice of the impersonation of these supernaturals by masked dancers; the initiation of all the men of the community into the cult and the custom of ceremonial whipping as a part of the initiation; the extreme sanctity of the masks, which can cause death to the careless wearer; and the complete identification of the one wearing the mask with the supernatural being who is thereby represented.

According to their myth of origin, the Zuñi people were long ago searching for the middle land where they might dwell in peace. Having to cross a stream, the first group of women were horrified to see their children turn into water snakes, turtles and frogs. The mothers cried out and dropped them into the water. Later the twin heroes of the Zuñis went back to see what had become of the children. They found them dwelling happily at the bottom of a lake. They had been transformed into kachinas, that is, supernaturals. They were adorned with beads and feathers, and they spent their days happily in dancing and singing.

To their parents the kachinas sent word that only one day's journey remained to reach the middle land, and that they themselves would stay at the lake forever in order to be near them and be able to help them in time of need. Thus the kachinas addressed the twin heroes: "You will tell our parents, Do not worry. We have not perished. In order to remain thus forever we stay here. To Itiwana but one day's travel remains. Therefore we stay near by. When our world grows old and the waters are exhausted and the seeds are exhausted, none of you will go back to the place of your first beginning. Whenever the waters are exhausted and the seeds are exhausted you will send us prayer sticks. Yonder at the place of our first beginning with them we shall bend over to speak to them. Thus there will not fail to be waters. Therefore we shall stay quietly near by."[109]

Pitying the loneliness of their people, the kachinas used to come often to Zuñi and dance for them. But every time they went away they took someone with them, that is, someone died. Therefore they decided not to come any more in person. They told the people to make headdresses and costumes like their own, and to imitate their dances. When the people did that, the kachinas were with them in spirit and everybody was happy.[110]

In the kachina ceremony, the dancers wear leather masks adorned with eagle feathers and spruce boughs. Their faces and bodies are

[109] *ibid.*, p.597.   [110] *ibid.*, p.607.

painted, and they usually wear a kilt and moccasins. From the back of their belt a fox skin is suspended, and numerous necklaces of white shell, turquoise and coral are worn. A small package of seeds is placed in the belt, gourd rattles are carried in the right hand, and spruce in the left.

Thus accoutered and wearing the mask of the kachina, the impersonator becomes the very supernatural being he represents. The mask is the corporeal substance of the kachina, and in putting it on the man assumes the personality of the god. As the entire company of dancers executes its precisely ordered and synchronized steps, to the rhythmic and melodic accompaniment of drum and song, it is the kachinas themselves who are joyously dancing in the midst of their people. They will not fail to visit them thereafter in life-giving rain.

Here is a portion of one of the prayers in the kachina cult. It is prayed by the impersonator of Pautiwa, the latter being the kachina chief at the lake village of the kachinas. In address to this supernatural, he is referred to by the double name, Kawulia Pautiwa. The one praying refers at the outset of our quotation to his assumption of the personality of the god in the putting on of his mask. The plume wands which he mentions are the staves of office made by the priests and covered with sacred paint.

Representing my father,
Kawulia Pautiwa,
I assumed his person.
Carrying his waters,
His seeds,
And carrying my fathers' perfect plume wands,
I made my road come hither.
I offered my fathers plume wands. . . .
I prayed that throughout the country of the Corn priests
Our earth mother might be wrapped
In four layers of green blanket,
That the land might be full of moss,
Full of flowers
Full of corn pollen. . . .
Then far off to his own country
My father
Made his road go forth
Carrying my fathers' plume wands,
Carrying his prayer meal,
I made his road go forth.
Far off at the place of the first beginning

Touching them with my plume wands,
With all the others he will hold discourse.
Our fathers will take hold of our plume wands.
Then in that way
Their long life,
Their old age,
They will grant to us.
That our roads may reach to where the life-giving road of our
    sun father comes out,
That we may finish our roads—
This they will grant us.
This day in accordance with whatever you wished,
Whatever you wished when you appointed me,
I have fulfilled your thoughts.
With thoughts in harmony
May we live together.
For even while I call myself poor,
Somewhere far off
Is one who is my father.
Beseeching the breath of the divine one,
Kawulia Pautiwa,
His life-giving breath,
His breath of old age,
His breath of waters,
His breath of seeds,
His breath of riches,
His breath of fecundity,
His breath of power,
His breath of strong spirit,
His breath of all good fortune whatsoever,
Asking for his breath
And into my warm body drawing his breath,
I add to your breath
That happily you may always live.
To this end, my fathers,
My children:
May you be blessed with light.[111]

[111] *ibid.*, pp.699-701.

CHAPTER II

Zoroastrianism

THE homeland of Zoroastrianism was on the great Iranian plateau which stretches from the valley of the Indus on the east to that of the Tigris on the west. The eastern portion of this plateau is occupied by Baluchistan and Afghanistan, and the western by Iran. Iran, with which we are chiefly concerned, lies between the Caspian Sea on the north and the Persian Gulf on the south, and extends from the edge of the Tigris valley on the west to boundaries along the Tejen River or the Hari Rud (as it is known in its upper course), the Helmand swamps and the Talab River on the east.

There are also mighty mountain ramparts on most sides of the land. Curving south of the Caspian Sea is the Elburz range, whose Mount Demavend (Fig. 22) attains a height of about 18,600 feet and is the loftiest Asian mountain west of the Himalayas. In the extreme northwest beyond Lake Urmia is the massif of Ararat, with the highest peak known as Great Ararat rising to some 16,916 feet. On the west are the Zagros Mountains, while yet other ranges alternate with deserts in the south and east.

In this mountain-buttressed upland of Iran the chief cities are situated at considerable elevations, Isfahan and Kerman being over five thousand feet high, Tabriz over four thousand, and Meshed and Teheran over three thousand. In the center of the country there is a great desert, generally known as the Lut, the elevation of which is about two thousand feet.

1. EARLY IRAN

THE CASPIANS

THE life of man on the Iranian plateau began in early prehistoric times. The discovery of three human skeletons of the Old Stone Age in Hotu Cave near the southern Caspian shore has recently been announced by the Iranian Expedition of the University Museum of the University of Pennsylvania. The remains are reported to have been found in gravel of the last Glacial Period, but to resemble Cro-Magnon rather than Neandertal man and definitely to represent *Homo sapiens*. With the skeletons were large numbers of flint tools.[1]

Dwelling like their Paleolithic predecessors in the general region of the Caspian Sea and hence commonly designated as Caspians, the inhabitants of Iran in the Neolithic Age presumably lived long in a hunting stage of existence and then eventually developed the practice of farming. At any rate in the fifth millennium B.C., at the end of the Neolithic Period, a sedentary population was settled in large villages the maintenance of which would hardly have been possible without agriculture.

One of these villages was excavated by Professor Ernst E. Herzfeld in 1928 and 1931 at a small mound about two miles from Persepolis. The buildings were of stamped earth, and constituted a continuous agglomeration of rooms and courts suggesting that the community lived in clans. Numerous stone, flint and clay implements and instruments were found, but weapons of warfare were almost nonexistent. There were many human figurines of clay which were probably idols. The female ones may have represented a mother goddess. The making and decorating of pottery provided the chief avenue of artistic expression, and both unpainted and painted pottery was found in abundance. The painted pottery exhibits a great variety of designs, including symbols, geometrical patterns, animal representations, and, rarely, human figures. On a spherical vase a great ibex, an animal which still abounds in the rocks around the plain of Persepolis, is painted in profile. Its horns, as its most characteristic feature, are exaggerated in size and pictured as sweeping back in splendid curves. On the bowl shown in Fig. 24 a thrice-repeated triangle provides the background for a figure in human form. The body is shown in a front view, the feet are turned outward, and the heavy forearms and five-fingered hands are raised. The head is small, and it is difficult to tell whether it is human or animal. Perhaps it is an animal head, and the entire figure may well represent a demon.[2]

Similar fine pottery, displaying a yet more sophisticated art, was also found in the lowest levels at the famous site of Susa on the plains of Elam just west of the Iranian plateau proper. Susa was probably founded about 4000 B.C., and its inhabitants had implements not only of obsidian but also of copper, and thus had already entered the

[1] *Life.* May 21, 1951, pp.113-116; *Science News Letter.* Nov. 24, 1951, p.325.
[2] Ernst E. Herzfeld, *Iran in the Ancient East.* 1941, pp.9-62, Pl. v,lower.

Chalcolithic Age. It is thought probable that the first discovery in the Middle East of the use of metal was made by the Caspians. At any rate their lofty plateau contains an abundance of mineral deposits, and at its numerous Bronze Age sites, dating from around 3000 to 1000 B.C., a wealth of metal objects has been recovered. Of these the famous bronze bits, rings, weapons and ornaments found in Luristan in western Persia, dating probably from the second millennium to the Assyrian Period, may be specially mentioned.[3]

Other important prehistoric sites in Iran include Tepe Giyan, Tepe Hissar and Turang Tepe. Tepe Giyan is in central Iran near Nehavend, and has been excavated by G. Contenau and R. Ghirshman.[4] Its pottery appears to be approximately contemporary with the early levels at Susa, and features among other motifs an ibex painted in a style clearly descended from the representation found on the pottery at the mound near Persepolis.

Tepe Hissar is in the north near Damghan, and has been excavated by Dr. Erich F. Schmidt.[5] This site seems to have been occupied from about 3500 to 1200 B.C., and then not again until the time of the Sasanians. Painted pottery, copper pins, needles and daggers, beads, stamp seals, and animal figurines probably used for purposes of sympathetic magic, were characteristic finds at Tepe Hissar. The painted pottery was decorated with geometric and animal figures. An example from the second phase of the lowest stratum (Hissar I, c.3500-c.2800 B.C.) may be seen in the chalice pictured in Fig. 25, which is now in the Archaeological Museum at Teheran. At the top is a feline, perhaps a leopard, which is apparently stalking an ibex from behind a rock.

Turang Tepe or "Pheasant Mound" is also in northern Iran, about twelve miles northeast of Astarabad or Gurgan. The site is shown in Fig. 23 where the truncated, partly conical, partly pyramidal shape of the main mound may be clearly seen. Test excavations have been made here by Frederick R. Wulsin,[6] and the findings have revealed

[3] André Godard, Les bronzes du Luristan (Ars Asiatica, xvii). 1931; René Dussaud in PSPA I, pp.254-277; Ernst Herzfeld and Sir Arthur Keith in PSPA I, pp.46-51.
[4] G. Contenau and R. Ghirshman, Fouilles du Tépé-Giyan près de Néhavend 1931 et 1932. 1935.
[5] Erich F. Schmidt, Excavations at Tepe Hissar, Damghan. 1937; M. Rogers Warren in PSPA I, pp.151-162.
[6] Frederick R. Wulsin in Supplement to the Bulletin of the American Institute for Persian Art and Archaeology. ii, 1 bis (March 1932); and in PSPA I, pp.163-167. For related discoveries at Shah Tepe, see T. J. Arne in Acta Archaeologica, 6 (1935), pp.1-48.

a Bronze Age culture of considerable importance, dating probably around 2200 to 1200 B.C. The numerous graves contained offerings, usually of pottery, but also of stone, bronze or copper, silver and lead. The most plentiful pottery was a burnished gray ware. A number of human figurines were likewise unearthed, prominent among which were representations of a goddess of fertility.[7]

From the end of the Stone Age to the end of the Bronze Age, then, the peoples of the Iranian plateau remained mostly at the stage of village life. To the west of the plateau the city of Susa of course continued its development, and a series of Elamite kingdoms came into existence there, most of which were, however, under the domination of Mesopotamia. Likewise in the northwestern part of the plateau around Lake Urmia the transition from village to urban life was made relatively early, and by the beginning of the first millennium B.C. the kingdoms of Man and Urartu (Biblical Minni and Ararat, Jeremiah 51:27) were developing into importance. It was the Aryan immigration, however, which introduced a distinctively new period of cultural development on the Iranian plateau proper, and resulted in the foundation of the large and famous cities like Ecbatana, Pasargadae and Persepolis.[8]

THE ARYANS

It was probably around or shortly after the middle of the second millennium B.C. that the Aryans first entered Iran. Those who came at this time seem to have passed on through the land. One large body went eastward into the Indus valley to take a thenceforward prominent place in the history of India. Others pressed into western Asia where they left their mark in the name of the sun god Surya, who was worshiped among the non-Aryan Kassites; and in the names of the gods Mitra, Varuna, Indra and the Nasatyas (the Twins), which appear in Hittite records from Mitanni.[9] Somewhat later, perhaps toward the end of the second millennium B.C.,[10] other Aryans came into Iran and settled permanently in the land. From them the country derived its name of Airyana or Iran, meaning "the [land] of the Aryans," a designation to which the Persian government officially returned in 1935.[11]

---

[7] Phyllis Ackerman in PSPA I, pp.198f.,212f.   [8] PSPA I, pp.52,61f.

[9] Arthur Christensen, Die Iranier (in Walter Otto, ed., Handbuch der Altertumswissenschaft, III, i, 3, 3, 1). 1933, p.209; V. Gordon Childe, The Aryans, A Study of Indo-European Origins (The History of Civilization). 1926, p.13.

[10] William F. Albright in BASOR 106 (Apr. 1947), p.19.

[11] Ernst E. Herzfeld, Archaeological History of Iran. 1935, p.8; PSPA I, pp.42,60.

The names of the gods just mentioned are well known also in India, and thus it is shown that the western Aryans shared a common linguistic and religious background with those who went eastward. An outstanding feature of that common heritage in religion was the worship of the great powers of nature, while even the titles which were applied to the deities were the same in the west and the east. In the course of time, however, an interesting differentiation in usage took place between Iran and India. In India the Aryans called their gods *devas* and *asuras*, but soon came to look upon the *devas* as good gods and upon the *asuras* as evil demons. In Iran the Aryans used the same two words, save that the "s" of India was "h" in their language and thus *asura* became *ahura*. The differentiation between the *devas* and the *ahuras*, moreover, was carried out in diametrical opposition. In Iran the *devas* became for the most part the evil spirits. Thus, for example, Indra was a prominent and beneficent deity in India but appears in Iran as a demon.[12] Only a few of the good gods of India, such as Mitra (Mithra) and Soma (Haoma), were the objects of equal reverence in Iran. The *ahuras*, on the other hand, were not demons as in India but "lords" or "masters" who became the real gods of Iran.[13]

The two main tribes of Aryans to settle in Iran were the Amadai (Medes) and the Parsua (Persians). Both are mentioned for the first time in the inscriptions of Shalmaneser III about 836 B.C., and they appear regularly thereafter in the annals of the Assyrian kings. Shalmaneser III writes, for example: "I received the gifts of 27 kings of the land of Parsua. From Parsua I departed. To the lands of . . . and of the Medes . . . I descended."[14]

THE MEDES

The Medes settled toward the northwestern part of the plateau and eventually occupied three provinces known as Media Magna, now Iraq-i-ajam; Media Atropatene, modern Azerbaijan; and Media Rhagiana, around present-day Teheran. The one great natural route from Mesopotamia to the Caspian plateau runs across the Zagros Mountains and through the heart of the country occupied by the Medes, and it is not surprising to learn that for centuries they suffered conquest and the exaction of tribute by the Assyrian kings.[15]

[12] HERE XII, p.604; cf. A. Christensen, *Essai sur la démonologie iranienne.* 1941.
[13] Goetz, *Epochen der indischen Kultur,* pp.27f.
[14] ARAB I, §581.
[15] Percy Sykes, *A History of Persia.* 3d ed. 1930, I, pp.115-119.

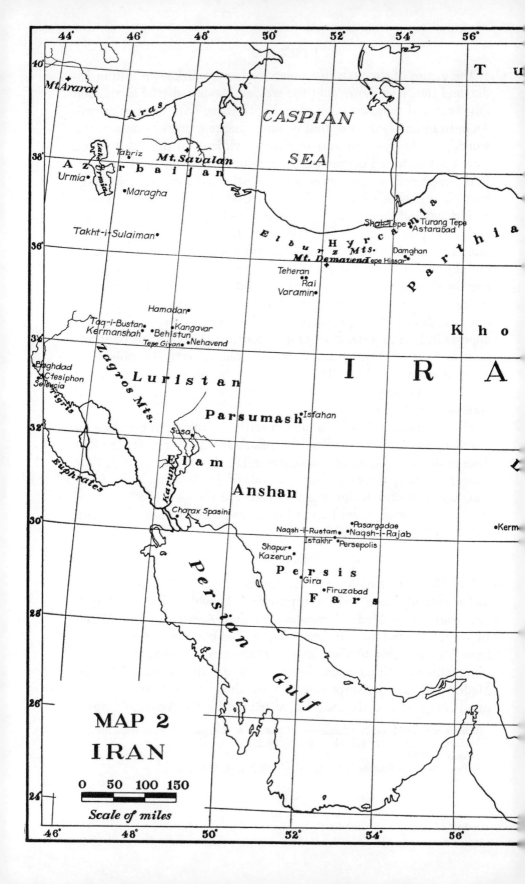

MAP 2

IRAN

0   50   100 150

Scale of miles

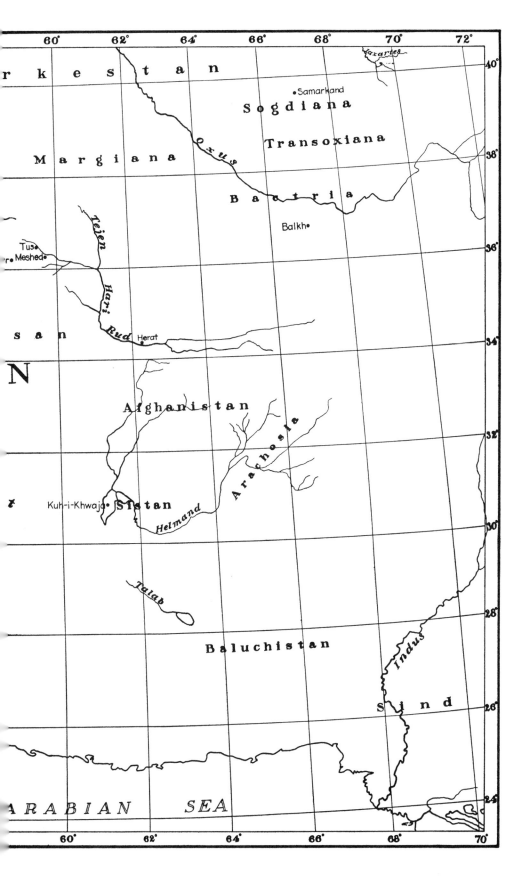

For at least a brief time, however, the Medes had a great empire. According to Herodotus (c.484-425 B.C.), the founder of their royal dynasty was a certain Deioces, whom the Greek historian called "a clever man."[16] The capital of Deioces was at Hagmatana, "the meeting place of many roads," a city which the Greeks knew as Ecbatana and which is now Hamadan. His kingdom appears to figure in the inscriptions of Sargon II (721-705 B.C.) under the name Bit-Daiukki, "House of Deioces."[17]

Daiukku or Deioces was succeeded by his son Fravartish, the Phraortes of the Greeks, and he in turn by his son Uvakhshatra or Cyaxares (625-585 B.C.). By this time the Medes were strong enough to war successfully against their Assyrian enemies, and in cooperation with Nabopolassar of Babylon and with the king of the Scythians, Cyaxares took and destroyed Nineveh in 612 B.C. Cyaxares' son and successor, Ishtuvegu or Astyages (585-550 B.C.) enjoyed a long and luxurious reign, but in the end was dethroned by Cyrus, as dominance among the Iranian peoples passed from the Medes to the Persians.[18]

[16] I, 96-103. tr. A. D. Godley, LCL (1920-24), I, pp.127-135.
[17] ARAB I, §23.
[18] René Grousset in PSPA I, p.63.

2. THE ACHAEMENID PERIOD, c.700-331 B.C.

THE PERSIANS

THE Persians had gone on to the southern part of the Iranian plateau and settled not far from the Elamite land Anshan or Anzan in a region which they called Parsumash or Parsamash in memory of their homeland, Parsua. Around 700 B.C. their leader was Hakhamanish or Achaemenes, from whom the kings of the Achaemenid dynasty traced their descent. Chishpish or Teispes his son extended the Persian domain to include an area east of Anshan and north of the Persian Gulf which became known as Parsa (Fars) or Persian land. After the death of Teispes, his son Cyrus I (c.640-c.600) succeeded to the throne of Parsumash, and his other son Ariaramna (c.640-c.615 B.C.) ruled in Parsa.

The kings who followed Cyrus I in Parsumash were Cambyses I (c.600-c.559 B.C.), Cyrus II the Great (c.559-530 B.C.) and Cambyses II (530-522 B.C.). As is well known, Cyrus the Great was one of the outstanding rulers of all history. Hitherto the Persians had been subservient to the Medes, but Cyrus took Ecbatana without difficulty, and from that time on Parsa was the first ranking satrapy in the land, Media the second, and Elam the third. Thereafter Cyrus extended his conquests from Asia Minor and Babylon to eastern Iran. Everywhere he proceeded with a deep understanding of men, and manifested a humane attitude which contrasted most favorably with that of other ancient oriental conquerors. His capital and eventually his tomb were at Pasargadae[19] in the land of Parsa.

When Cambyses II died the new empire almost broke up. Many of the recently annexed provinces revolted, and a Magian named Gaumata pretended to be the younger brother of Cambyses (who actually had been murdered) and attempted to usurp the throne. Then the Persian line descended from Ariaramna reentered the picture in prominence. Ariaramna had been succeeded by Arsames, whose son was Hystaspes (Vishtaspa), and whose grandson was Darius I the Great (522-486 B.C.). It was Darius who became the deliverer of the imperiled empire. As was imperishably recorded on the massive Rock of Behistun (Fig. 26), Darius seized and slew Gaumata and suppressed all rebellion. He subsequently completed a reorganization of his holdings into twenty satrapies, and administered with great efficiency and wisdom an empire which extended from

[19] cf. Ernst Herzfeld, *Archaeologische Mitteilungen aus Iran.* I (1929), pp.4-16.

Egypt and Macedonia to southern Russia and the Indus valley. His capital was at Persepolis (Fig. 27) and his tomb at Naqsh-i-Rustam (Fig. 28). After Darius I the rulers of Persia were Xerxes (486-465 B.C.), Artaxerxes I Longimanus (465-423 B.C.), Darius II (423-404 B.C.), Artaxerxes II Mnemon (404-359), Artaxerxes III Ochus (359-338), Arses (338-335), and Darius III (335-331). Then the Achaemenid empire was destroyed by Alexander the Great.[20]

[20] For more details of this history and for archeological monuments at Ecbatana, Pasargadae, Persepolis, Susa, Behistun and Naqsh-i-Rustam see FLP pp.192-205; A. T. Olmstead, *History of the Persian Empire [Achaemenid Period]*. 1948.

3. ZOROASTER AND THE RISE OF ZOROASTRIANISM

ZOROASTER[21] lived not later than the period to which our swift historical survey has now brought us, and at this point we turn therefore to consideration of the prophet and his religion. First it is necessary to give a brief account of the most important written sources, the scriptures of Zoroastrianism.

THE ZOROASTRIAN SCRIPTURES

The authoritative religious writings of the Zoroastrian religion are known as the Avesta. This word may mean "the original text" in contrast with the Zand (Zend) or "commentary" which was later attached to it, thus giving rise to the term Zend-Avesta. These scriptures comprised in their entirety no less than twenty-one treatises known as Nasks,[22] but of these many have now been lost. The chief portions still extant are the following: (1) the Yasna, a liturgical work; (2) the Gathas, included in the Yasna, but written in verse and containing the teachings of Zoroaster; (3) the Visparad, invocations addressed to "all the lords"; (4) the Yashts, hymns of praise; and (5) the Vendidad, a priestly code of purifications and penalties.[23] In addition, there are a number of minor texts and fragments. As to date, the Gathas may well be contemporary with Zoroaster himself, while the composition and redaction of the remaining portions of the Avesta may have extended down into the fourth century A.D. The language in which the Avesta is written is commonly referred to as "Avestan." It is an ancient Iranian language to which Old Persian, Middle Persian and Modern Persian are related. Sanskrit and "Avestan" are very similar, and these two languages together with their respective linguistic relatives form the Indo-Iranian or Aryan family of Indo-European languages. The language of the Gathas seems older than that of the rest of the Avesta, and may be said to bear to the Younger Avestan somewhat the same relation as the Vedic language in India does to the classical Sanskrit.[24]

In later times a version of the Avesta was made in Pahlavi, a form of the Middle Persian language. This version was composed perhaps

[21] Zoroaster is the Greek form of the name which appears in Avestan as Zarathushtra, in Pahlavi as Zaratusht, and in modern Persian as Zaradusht or Zardusht.

[22] Dinkard III, 8. SBE XXXVII, p.6.

[23] These works and additional fragments are translated by James Darmesteter and L. H. Mills in SBE IV, XXIII, XXXI.

[24] A. V. Williams Jackson in HERE II, p.270.

in the fourth century A.D. and revised in the sixth.[25] It not only provided a translation or paraphrase of the text, but also gave at many points an explanatory commentary. In addition to this, an extensive literature dealing with religious subjects also came into existence in the Pahlavi language. At least fifty-five works are known, of which the most important are: (1) the Bundahish or "original creation," dealing with cosmogony, mythology and history; (2) the Dinkard or "acts of religion," relating to religious doctrines, customs, traditions, history and literature; (3) the Dadistan-i Dinik or "religious opinions" of the high priest Manushkihar in response to ninety-two questions; (4) the Epistles of the same Manushkihar; (5) the Selections of Zad-sparam, written by the younger brother of Manushkihar; (6) the Shayast la-shayast or "the proper and improper," a miscellaneous compilation of laws and customs concerning sin and impurity; (7) the Dinai-i Mainog-i Khirad or "opinions of the Spirit of Wisdom" in reply to sixty-two inquiries on miscellaneous religious subjects; (8) the Shikand-gumanik Vijar or "doubt-dispelling explanation," in defense of the Zoroastrian solution of the problem of evil as opposed to Jewish, Christian, Manichean, and Muslim theories; (9) the Arda-Viraf Namak or Book of Arda-Viraf, who describes his visit to heaven and hell while in a trance.[26] Manushkihar, the author of the Dadistan-i Dinik, is known from a note in one of his epistles[27] to have lived around A.D. 881, and a ninth century date is probable for most of the Pahlavi works which have just been listed.[28]

In Fig. 29 we show a facsimile of a single leaf of the Bundahish, written probably in the first half of the fourteenth century and now in the University Library of Copenhagen. Fig. 30 reproduces a page of the Arda-Viraf Namak from a more extensive codex dating probably in the latter half of the fourteenth century and preserved in the same library.[29]

[25] E. W. West in SBE XLVII, p.xvii.

[26] For English translations of these books in whole or in part see E. W. West in SBE V, XVIII, XXIV, XXXVII, XLVII; and Martin Haug and E. W. West, *The Book of Arda Viraf, The Pahlavi Text Prepared by Destur Hoshangji Jamaspji Asa, Revised and Collated with Further MSS., with an English Translation and Introduction, and an Appendix Containing the Texts and Translations of the Gosht-i Fryano, and Hadokht-Nask.* 1872.

[27] Epistle III, 21. SBE XVIII, p.365.

[28] Edward G. Browne, *A Literary History of Persia from the Earliest Times until Firdawsí.* 1902, pp.7f.,105-107.

[29] *Codices Avestici et Pahlavici Bibliothecae Universitatis Hafniensis*, I, *The Pahlavi Codices K20 and K20b, Containing Ardâgh Virâz-Nâmagh, Bundahishn etc., Published in Facsimile by the University Library of Copenhagen, with an Introduction by Arthur Christensen.* 1931, pp.10f.,15.

THE DATE OF ZOROASTER

Although there is little doubt that Zoroaster was an actual historical personage, the date of his life is uncertain. Three chief periods have been suggested for him. The first is at a time earlier than 6000 B.C. This was the date generally accepted by the ancient Greeks. Xanthus the Lydian (c.450 B.C.) was quoted by Diogenes Laertius (A.D. c.230) as stating that there were six thousand years between Zoroaster and the invasion of Xerxes (c.480 B.C.). Hermodorus, a disciple of Plato (c.427-347 B.C.) was also quoted by Diogenes as putting Zoroaster five thousand years before the taking of Troy, an event traditionally dated about 1200 B.C. Eudoxus (c.365 B.C.) was said by Pliny the Elder (A.D. 23-79) to have placed the life of Zoroaster six thousand years before the death of Plato, and to have had in this assertion the support of Aristotle (384-322 B.C.). Hermippus (c.200 B.C.) was also cited by Pliny as dating Zoroaster five thousand years before the Trojan War. Plutarch (A.D. c.46-c.120) gave the same date of five thousand years before the Trojan War.[30] Such an extremely early date is scarcely credible, and as a matter of fact the Greek tradition rested perhaps upon a misunderstanding of the Zoroastrian belief concerning the preexistence of Zoroaster's spiritual body. According to the Dinkard,[31] the spiritual body of the prophet was framed together six millenniums before Zoroaster was born on earth, and this could easily have accounted for the rise of the idea among the Greeks that Zoroaster had lived at that remote time.[32]

A second period proposed for Zoroaster is around the tenth or ninth centuries B.C. Among those who support such a date are historians of the highest eminence, and it may well prove to be correct.[33] According to a variant reading in the text of Diogenes, Xanthus placed Zoroaster six hundred years before Xerxes, which would give a date a little earlier than 1000 B.C. This textual reading is perhaps less likely to be correct, however, than the one already cited with the figure of six thousand years, which is in agreement with the prevail-

---

[30] Carl Clemen, *Fontes historiae religionis Persicae* (Fontes historiae religionum ex auctoribus Graecis et Latinis collectos subsidiis Societatis Rhenanae Promovendis Litteris, edidit Carolus Clemen, Fasciculus I). 1920, pp.74,42,48.

[31] VII, 15f. SBE XLVII, pp.21f., cf. xxviii,xl.

[32] cf. esp. É. Benveniste, *The Persian Religion According to the Chief Greek Texts.* 1929, pp.15f.

[33] Eduard Meyer, *Ursprung und Anfänge des Christentums.* II (1921), p.58; CRW p.142; Maneckji Nusservanji Dhalla, *History of Zoroastrianism.* 1938, p.xxxi; Albright in BASOR 106 (Apr. 1947), p.19; Arthur Christensen in *Acta Orientalia.* 4 (1926), pp.90f. (he subsequently changed his position).

ing Greek tradition.[34] Other evidence of greater weight pointing back to as early as around 1000 B.C. is to be found in the fact that the Gathas are at about the same stage of linguistic development as the most ancient Vedic hymns in India.

A third epoch in which Zoroaster may have lived is the Achaemenid Period. It, too, is favored by most eminent historians. We consider this period to be the most likely, but we also believe the tenth or ninth century date to be a very strong possibility. Several approaches lead to the Achaemenid Period, although they result in considerable variation in precise dates. One is a literary study of the Yashts which finds traces in them of a Zoroastrian reworking of earlier hymns, and surmises that the Zoroastrian reformation took place around 650-600 B.C.[35] Another is an investigation of the relationships of the Achaemenid kings to the Zoroastrian religion; including the possible connection of the father of Darius with Zoroaster. One survey of this evidence concludes that Zoroaster lived from 559 to 522 or after.[36] Some facts in this field will be set forth in later sections of our own chapter. Yet another line of inquiry turns to the chronology embodied in the Zoroastrian theory of the ages of the world as given in the Bundahish. This theory is admittedly a theological and eschatological construction; nevertheless it is not impossible that it preserves some memory of when Zoroaster lived, and was made to accord with some facts in history. Despite the difficulties and ambiguities inherent in it, this theory will now be set forth briefly, both because it contains information of possible value on the date of Zoroaster and because it is of intrinsic interest for an understanding of Zoroastrian thought.

The theory of world-ages appears prominently in the Bundahish and other writings. While the Bundahish probably belongs to the ninth century A.D. it no doubt draws upon much earlier sources. As a matter of fact the idea of the ages of the world must be as old as the fifth century B.C., since belief in the preexistence of Zoroaster's spiritual body six thousand years before his birth on earth is a part of the

---

[34] James H. Moulton, *Early Zoroastrianism* (The Hibbert Lectures, Second Series). 1913, p.412.

[35] Christensen, *Die Iranier*, pp.214f.; based on his *Les Kayanides* (Det Kgl. Danske Videnskabernes Selskab. Historisk-filologiske Meddelelser, XIX, 2). 1931.

[36] Johannes Hertel, *Die Zeit Zoroasters* (Indo-iranische Quellen und Forschungen, 1). 1924, pp.21,47. Historians of the first rank who accept substantially this dating include C. F. Lehmann-Haupt in Jal Dastur Cursetji Pavry, ed., *Oriental Studies in Honour of Cursetji Erachji Pavry.* 1933, pp.251-280; and Olmstead, *History of the Persian Empire*, p.94; in *Review of Religion.* 4 (1939), pp.3f.

theory and since this belief had evidently become known among the Greeks by the time of Xanthus.

A concise statement of the theory may be found in Chapter xxxiv of the Bundahish,[37] and the account which follows is based primarily upon this chapter along with supplementary references in other chapters of the Bundahish and in other Zoroastrian books. Bundahish xxxiv begins with the statement that "Time was for twelve thousand years." These twelve thousand years which comprise the total extent of all time are then divided into four periods of three thousand years each. The first period of three thousand years "was the duration of the spiritual state, where the creatures were unthinking, unmoving, and intangible." Comparing Bundahish i, 8 (sbe v, p.5), we gather that it is meant that at this time the *fravashis* or spiritual prototypes of later creatures were already in existence.

The second period of three thousand years "was the duration of Gayomard, with the ox, in the world." Gayomard was the primeval man, who with the primeval ox lived undisturbed during this trimillennium. According to Dinkard vii, ii, 15f. (sbe xlvii, pp.21f.), the spiritual body of Zoroaster was framed together by the archangels at the beginning of this period; and according to Bundahish i, 22; iii, 1 (sbe v, pp.8f.,15), the evil spirit remained in impotent confusion throughout the entire three thousand years.

When the third period of three thousand years began, "the adversary rushed in, and Gayomard lived thirty years in tribulation." In Bundahish iii, 21-23 (sbe v, pp.18f.) we are told that the evil spirit was assisted by a thousand demons in his attack on Gayomard, and that during the thirty years of his existence in duress Gayomard declared, "Although the destroyer has come, mankind will be all of my race; and this one thing is good, when they perform duty and good works." The sole-created Gayomard then passed away, but from his seed grew up Mashya and Mashyoi (also called Marhaya and Marhiyoih), the first human pair, who became the progenitors of mankind (Bundahish xv. sbe v, pp.52-59; Dadistan-i Dinik xxxvii, 82. sbe xviii, p.105). Among their descendants were Hoshyang, considered to have been founder of the first Iranian dynasty (Bundahish xv, 28. sbe v, p.58), and Takhmorup and Yim, kings who also appear in the Shah Namah of Firdausi as Tahmuras and Jamshed (cf. Bundahish xxxi, 1-3. sbe v, p.130). The dynasties of these kings filled out the first thousand years of this third trimillennium.

[37] sbe v, pp.149-151.

Throughout the second thousand years of this period Dahak held sway, the reference evidently being to a foreign dynasty personified as a single king. During the first half of the third thousand years the dynasty of Fredun (Feridun in the Shah Namah) ruled, and then the second five hundred years was occupied with the following reigns: Manushkihar,[38] 120 years; Zob, 5 years; Kai-Kabad, 15 years; Kai-Kaus, "till he went to the sky,"[39] 75 years, and 75 years after that, altogether 150 years"; Kai-Khusrov, 60 years; Kai-Lorasp, 120 years; Kai-Vishtasp, "till the coming of the religion, 30 years."[40]

Thus we are brought up to the beginning of the fourth trimillennium, which was inaugurated by "the coming of the religion," that is to say by the founding of Zoroastrianism. This last period of three thousand years extends yet, of course, far into the future, but its first thousand years and slightly more are covered by the chronological notices which bring Chapter xxxiv of the Bundahish to a conclusion. These notices fall into two groups: first a rather detailed list of kings or dynasties from Kai Vishtasp to Alexander "the Ruman";[41] then summary statements mentioning the Ashkanians or Arsacids who ruled for two hundred and eighty-four years, Ardashir and the Sasanians who ruled for four hundred and sixty years, and the Arabs to whom sovereignty finally passed.

Returning to the detailed list which extends from Kai-Vishtasp, the last Kayanid, to Alexander, we find that Kai-Vishtasp is said to have still held sway for ninety years after "the coming of the religion," and then to have been followed by four more rulers, apparently Achaemenids, prior to Alexander the Great. The names and years of these five kings who ruled between "the coming of the religion" and the time of Alexander the Great may be tabulated as follows:[42]

[38] This Manushkihar, a descendant of Fredun (Bundahish xxxi, 9-12. sbe v, pp.133f.) and an ancestor of Zoroaster (Bundahish, xxxii, 1f. sbe v, pp.140f.), is of course not to be confused with Manushkihar, author of the Dadistan-i Dinik and of several epistles.

[39] The reference is to the legendary attempt of Kai-Kaus to fly in a machine lifted by four eagles, each attracted upward by meat set on a spear above its head. This is narrated in the Shah Namah, 411f. tr. Warner and Warner, ii, pp.103f.; cf. *The Sacred Books and Early Literature of the East*, vii, pp.329f.

[40] The series of kings whose names begin with Kai forms a dynasty known as the Kaianid or Kayanid. cf. Clément Huart, *Ancient Persia and Iranian Civilization* (The History of Civilization). tr. M. R. Dobie. 1927, p.210.

[41] Alexander the Great was called "the Ruman" in Zoroastrian tradition because he came from Greek provinces which later were a part of the eastern Roman empire.

[42] cf. J. Hertel, *Achaemeniden und Kayaniden, Ein Beitrag zur Geschichte Irans* (Indo-iranische Quellen und Forschungen, 5). 1924, pp.16f. Vohuman is equated with

Kai-Vishtasp	90
Vohuman	112
Humai	30
Darai	12
Darai son of Darai	14
	258

A reign of fourteen years is then ascribed to Alexander "the Ruman," and since he died in 323 B.C. this chronology would seem to indicate 595 B.C. for the founding of Zoroastrianism.

Before accepting this figure, however, comparison must be made with certain other statements, and possible revision introduced. In the Book of Arda-Viraf and in the Selections of Zad-sparam it is said that Zoroastrianism remained in purity for three hundred years until Alexander the Great came to Iran and destroyed the monarchy.[43] The passage in question in the Book of Arda-Viraf stands at the opening of the work and reads as follows:

They say that once upon a time the pious Zaratusht [Zoroaster] made the religion which he had received current in the world; and tfll the completion of 300 years the religion was in purity and men were without doubts. But afterward the accursed evil-spirit, the wicked one, in order to make men doubtful of this religion, instigated the accursed Alexander the Ruman, who was dwelling in Egypt, so that he came to the country of Iran with severe cruelty and war and devastation; he also slew the ruler of Iran, and destroyed the metropolis and empire, and made them desolate.

And this religion, namely, all the Avesta and Zand, written upon prepared cowskins, and with gold ink, was deposited in the archives in Stakhar Papakan [Persepolis]; and the hostility of the evil-destined, wicked Ashemok, the evil-doer, brought onward Alexander the Ruman, who was dwelling in Egypt, and he burnt them up. And he killed several desturs and judges and herbads and mobads and upholders of the religion,[44] and the competent and wise of the country of Iran. And he cast hatred and strife, one with the other, amongst the nobles and householders of the country of Iran; and self-destroyed, he fled to hell.[45]

"Artahshatar" (Ardashir) in Bahman Yasht II, 17 (SBE V, pp.198f.) and Bundahish XXXI, 30 (SBE V, p.137). This must be Artaxerxes I. Darius (Darai) I Hystaspes is made the father of Darius III Codomanus. The list is thus incomplete. It is doubtful whether Kai-Vishtasp is connected with the others. cf. Christensen, Les Kayanides.

[43] West in SBE XLVII, p.xxviii; cf. A. V. Williams Jackson, Zoroaster, The Prophet of Ancient Iran. 1898, pp.159,176.

[44] These are various grades of the Zoroastrian priesthood. The destur is the high priest. The judge is also of high rank, but is distinguished from the destur. The herbad is one who has completed his theological studies. The mobad is a herbad who is chiefly engaged in the performance of ceremonies. The upholder of the religion is a student of the Avesta.

[45] I, 1-11. Haug and West, The Book of Arda Viraf, pp.141-143.

The statement in the Selections of Zad-sparam says of Zoroastrianism that "it exists day and night till the three-hundredth year. Afterward the religion is disturbed and the monarchy is contested."[46]

These references in the Book of Arda-Viraf and the Selections of Zad-sparam may be explained and dismissed as giving only a round number for the period of time which appears more precisely in the Bundahish as totaling 258 years.

Significantly enough, the exact figure of 258 years appears explicitly in another document. This is The Chronology of Ancient Nations, which was written in A.D. 1000 by the Muslim scholar al-Biruni. In discussing Zoroastrian chronology, al-Biruni says, "From his [Zoroaster's] appearance till the beginning of the Era of Alexander, they count 258 years."[47]

It appears that al-Biruni and the author of the Bundahish drew upon similar but not identical sources. Both give 258 years from Zoroaster to Alexander the Great, but in the Bundahish the 258 years bring us to a point fourteen years before the death of Alexander, while with al-Biruni the terminus ad quem is "the beginning of the Era of Alexander." Since in the Bundahish the figure of 258 years has been worked into a chronological scheme which is on the whole artificial and mystical, we may prefer the testimony of al-Biruni and believe that the original Zoroastrian tradition dated Zoroaster 258 years before the Era of Alexander.

Al-Biruni thought that the Era of Alexander began with Alexander's attack on Persia in the twenty-sixth year of his life (331 B.C.), but since he also says that this was the era employed by the Jews and Greeks for more than a thousand years,[48] it could in actuality have been the same as the Seleucid Era, which was the first real era in history and which prevailed for so long in western Asia.[49] In that case, since the Seleucid Era began in 312-311 B.C., the appearance of Zoroaster would be dated in 570 B.C.

We may suppose that by the "appearance" of Zoroaster, al-Biruni meant the birth of the prophet. On the other hand, the Dinkard (VII, viii, 51. SBE XLVII, p.105) reckons the first century of Zoroastrianism from the spiritual "conference" of Zoroaster which took place

---

[46] XXIII, 11f. SBE XLVII, p.166.

[47] p.14. C. Edward Sachau, ed., *The Chronology of Ancient Nations, An English Version of the Arabic Text of the Athâr-ul-Bâkiya of Albîrûnî, or "Vestiges of the Past,"* Collected and Reduced to Writing by the Author in A.H. 390-1, A.D. 1000. 1879, p.17.

[48] p.28. ed. Sachau, pp.32f.

[49] Eduard Meyer, *Geschichte des Altertums.* I, i (2d ed. 1907), p.239.

when the prophet was thirty years old, and it is of course possible that this was the terminus a quo. If we accept the former hypothesis, we come at the conclusion of this line of chronological calculation to the year 570 B.C. as the date of the birth of Zoroaster.[50]

This date is here set forth, it must be remembered, not as an assured fact but only as a possibility which is to be considered seriously and which has back of it the line of reasoning we have just traced. Since it does give us a precise, though hypothetical, date, it may be of interest to indicate the other chronological points in Zoroaster's life which would follow from it if we continue to accept Zoroastrian tradition. The Dinkard states not only that Zoroaster was thirty years old at his "conference," but also that he was forty-two years old when Vishtasp was converted, and seventy-seven years old at the time of his death (vii, v, 1. SBE XLVII, pp.73f.). Counting from a birth date of 570 B.C., the "conference" would have taken place in 540 B.C., the conversion of Vishtasp in 528 B.C., and the prophet's death in 493 B.C.

VISHTASPA

As we have seen, a certain Vishtasp or Vishtaspa is named in Zoroastrian traditions as ruler at the time when Zoroaster lived, and his conversion in the forty-second year of the prophet's life was of much importance for the establishment of the new faith.

The name Vishtaspa is philologically the same as Hystaspes,[51] the name of the father of Darius I the Great (522-486 B.C.). This Hystaspes is known to us both from Herodotus and from Persian inscriptions. Herodotus says that "Hystaspes son of Arsames was an Achaemenid, and Darius was the oldest of his sons."[52] Darius declares in his own inscriptions, "I am Darius, great king, king of kings, king of lands, son of Hystaspes, the Achaemenid";[53] and Xerxes writes as

[50] Ernst Herzfeld, *Archaeologische Mitteilungen aus Iran.* ii (1930), pp.39-47; in Pavry, ed., *Oriental Studies in Honour of Cursetji Erachji Pavry,* pp.132-136; and *Zoroaster and His World.* 1947, i, pp.1-30. For a severe criticism of this view see H. S. Nyberg, *Die Religionen des alten Iran* (Mitteilungen der Vorderasiatisch-Aegyptischen Gesellschaft [E. V.], 43). German tr. by H. H. Schaeder. 1938, pp.31-36. Nyberg himself concludes (pp.44f.) that it is impossible to determine the date of Zoroaster, except to say that he lived sometime before 485 B.C. For reviews of Herzfeld's *Zoroaster and His World* see Richard N. Frye in *Harvard Journal of Asiatic Studies.* 10 (1947), pp.440-448; Arthur D. Nock in AJA 53 (1949), pp.272-285.

[51] L. W. King and R. C. Thompson, *The Sculptures and Inscription of Darius the Great on the Rock of Behistûn in Persia.* 1907, p.lxi.

[52] i, 209.

[53] F. H. Weissbach, *Die Keilinschriften der Achämeniden.* 1911, pp.80f.; cf. King and Thompson, *The Sculptures and Inscription of Darius the Great on the Rock of Behistûn in Persia,* pp.1,84,85,93,152,159.

follows in an inscription recently discovered at Persepolis: "Says Xerxes the king: My father [is] Darius, Darius' father was one named Vishtaspa, Vishtaspa's father was one named Rshama. Vishtaspa as well as Rshama, both were alive when Ahuramazda, as was his will, made Darius my father king over this earth."[54]

The approximate dates of Hystaspes' life may be estimated from information provided by Ctesias and Herodotus. Ctesias was a fifth century B.C. Greek physician who was at the Persian court and who wrote a history called *Persica* which was preserved in abridged form in the *Bibliotheca* of Photius, the ninth century A.D. patriarch of Constantinople. According to Ctesias-Photius, Darius was seventy-two years old when he died (486 B.C.),[55] and thus would have been born in 558 B.C. This is in general agreement with Herodotus,[56] who says that Darius was around twenty years of age in the year Cyrus the Great died (530 B.C.). Since his oldest son Darius was born about 558 B.C., it may be estimated that Hystaspes himself was born around 580 B.C. Ctesias also tells that Hystaspes died by accident when he went to view the tomb of Darius, which that king had prepared in advance of his own death.[57] The death of Hystaspes, we may therefore estimate, took place around 500 B.C.[58]

While Hystaspes was never king in the sense of "great king," it is probable that he ruled the provinces of Bactria and Hyrcania under Cyrus the Great,[59] and the Behistun inscription shows that he suppressed rebellion in Parthia and Hyrcania under Darius the Great.[60] The Arab historian Masudi (d. A.D. c.956) states that his residence was in Balkh, which was the ancient Bactra, the capital of Bactria.[61]

If Zoroaster lived around 570-493 B.C., it would be possible to identify the Vishtaspa whom he converted with this Hystaspes, the father

[54] Ernst E. Herzfeld, *A New Inscription of Xerxes from Persepolis* (SAOC, 5). 1932, p.4.

[55] §50 (19). John Gilmore, *The Fragments of the Persika of Ktesias.* 1888, p.152. Ctesias wrongly says that Darius reigned thirty-one years instead of thirty-six.

[56] I, 209.

[57] §46 (15). ed. Gilmore, p.150.

[58] Herzfeld, *Archaeologische Mitteilungen aus Iran.* I (1929), p.123.

[59] C. F. Lehmann-Haupt in Paulys *Real-Encyclopädie der classischen Altertumswissenschaft*, ed. Georg Wissowa, Wilhelm Kroll and Kurt Witte. Zweite Reihe, II, 1 (1921), col. 85; and in Pavry, *Oriental Studies in Honour of Cursetji Erachji Pavry*, pp.252,261,268.

[60] King and Thompson, *The Sculptures and Inscription of Darius the Great on the Rock of Behistûn in Persia*, pp.40-43,125-127,184-186.

[61] Abū-l Ḥasan ʿAlī ibn Ḥusain ibn ʿAlī ul-Masʿūdī, *Murūj udh-Dhahab wa Maʿādin ul-Jawāhir*, XXI. tr. C. Barbier de Meynard and Pavet de Courteille, *Les Prairies d'Or.* 1861-77, II (2d printing, 1914), p.123.

of Darius the Great. This is nothing new but was already done by the Roman historian Ammianus Marcellinus (A.D. c.360), who said in speaking of Media, of the Magi and of magic or "holy rites": "To this science, derived from the secret lore of the Chaldeans, in ages long past the Bactrian Zoroaster made many contributions, and after him the wise king Hystaspes, the father of Darius."[62] If, on the other hand, Zoroaster lived at quite a different time, say around 1000 B.C., the identification would of course be impossible. The fact that it is possible when a date around 570-493 B.C. is assigned to Zoroaster lends some strength to the hypothesis of the later date.

THE LIFE OF ZOROASTER

Where Zoroaster lived is almost as uncertain as when. The two chief possibilities are the northeast and the northwest of Iran. Favoring the northeast are the facts that Ammianus Marcellinus called Zoroaster a Bactrian, that Vishtaspa-Hystaspes ruled in Bactria and Hyrcania, and that the geographical allusions of the Avesta give prominence to eastern Iran.[63] On the other hand the language of the Gathas has been identified as a dialect of northwestern Iran,[64] and in both Zoroastrian and Arabic traditions there are references indicating that Zoroaster was born in that region. Several of these passages may be cited:

Chapter xx of the Bundahish contains a list and description of rivers in which we read: "The Daraja River is in Airan-vej, on the bank of which was the dwelling of Porushasp, the father of Zaratusht" (xx, 32. SBE v, p.82). A little later in the same book it is explicitly stated that Zoroaster was born at this place: "The Daraja River is the chief of exalted rivers, for the dwelling of the father of Zaratusht was on its banks, and Zaratusht was born there" (xxiv, 15; SBE v, p.89). Finally it is stated that "Airan-vej is in the direction of Ataro-patakan" or Azerbaijan (xxix, 12. SBE v, p.120). While any specific identification of the Daraja River is hypothetical, this sequence of passages clearly reflects the opinion that the native place of Zoroaster was in Azerbaijan.

Arab sources also state that Zoroaster came from Azerbaijan, and point specifically to the district of Shiz and the city of Urumiah (Ur-

[62] *History.* XXIII, vi, 32. tr. John C. Rolfe, LCL (1935-39) II, p.367. cf. Hertel, *Die Zeit Zoroasters*, p.21.

[63] Jackson, *Zoroaster, The Prophet of Ancient Iran*, p.218; cf. Christensen, *Die Iranier*, p.214.

[64] Grousset in PSPA I, p.68.

miah, or Urmia, now called Rizaiyeh). Yaqut, who compiled a large geography about A.D. 1224, says under the heading, Shiz: "A district of Azerbaijan. . . . It is believed that this is the native land of Zaradusht, the prophet of the fire worshipers. The chief place of the district is Urmiah"; and under the heading, Urmiah: "It is claimed that this is the city of Zaradusht and that it was founded by the fire worshipers."[65] Ibn Hurdadhbah (A.D. c.816) likewise speaks of "Urmia, the city of Zaradusht and . . . Shiz, in which last city there is the fire temple Adharjushnas, which is held in high esteem by the Magians."[66]

The Selections of Zad-sparam (XVI, 12. SBE XLVII, p.147) point to a different city for the origin of Zoroaster, and state that "Zaratusht arose from Ragh," meaning the ancient city of Ravy, Rhages, or Rai ('Ράγαι), whose ruins are near modern Teheran. A proposed explanation to reconcile the discrepancy is that the mother of Zoroaster came from this place. In the Dinkard (VII, ii, 9f. SBE XLVII, p.20) she is represented as coming to Porushasp from another district than that in which the latter lived, and the Arab writer Shahrastani (A.D. 1086-1153), who lived in Khorasan, states explicitly in regard to Zoroaster, "His father was from Azerbaijan and his mother, whose name was Dughdu, was from Rai."[67]

Perhaps a reconciliation can also be effected between the views which place Zoroaster in the northwest and in the northeast of Iran respectively, by supposing that he was indeed born in the northwest but later lived and worked in the northeast. An explicit statement to this effect is made by al-Biruni and will be quoted a little later.

As has appeared in the references already given, the traditional name of Zoroaster's father was Porushasp. In Chapter XXXII of the Bundahish (SBE V, pp.140f.) the genealogy of the prophet is traced on back to Manushkihar (cf. above p. 80). From this genealogy we need here only note that one of the ancestors was Spitaman, and that from him the family designation of Spitama was derived. According to the same source (SBE V, pp.142-144), Zoroaster himself was married to three wives and had several sons and daughters.

[65] C. Barbier de Meynard, *Dictionnaire géographique, historique et littéraire de la Perse et des contrées adjacentes extrait du Mo'djem el-Bouldan de Yaqout, et complète a l'aide de documents arabes et persans pur la plupart inédits.* 1861, pp.367,26.

[66] Quoted by Richard J. H. Gottheil in *Classical Studies in Honour of Henry Drisler.* 1894, p.44.

[67] I, ii, 2, ch.1, §3. Theodor Haarbrücker, *Abu-'l-Fath' Muh'ammad asch-Schahrastâni's Religionspartheien und Philosophen-Schulen zum ersten Male vollständig aus dem Arabischen übersetzt und mit erklärenden Anmerkungen versehen.* 1850-51, I, p.280. Bundahish XXXII, 10 (SBE V, p.144) gives Dughda as the name of Zoroaster's mother.

The first spiritual "conference" of Zoroaster is described both in the Dinkard (vii, iii, 51-62. sbe xlvii, pp.47-50) and in Chapter xxxi of the Selections of Zad-sparam (sbe xlvii, pp.154-159). Following the latter and fuller source, we learn that at the age of thirty Zoroaster crossed the Daiti River and on the far bank met the archangel Vohu Manah or Good Thought. Vohu Manah asked Zoroaster, "Who mayest thou be, and from whom of them mayest thou be? also what is mostly thy desire, and the endeavor in thy existence?" Zoroaster replied, "I am Zaratusht of the Spitamas; among the existences righteousness is more my desire, and my wish is that I may become aware of the will of the sacred beings, and may practice so much righteousness as they exhibit to me in the pure existence." Upon this reply, Vohu Manah led Zoroaster "to an assembly of the spirits," and "when he came within twenty-four feet of the archangels, he then did not see his own shadow on the ground, on account of the great brilliancy of the archangels." Zoroaster cried, "Homage to Auharmazd,"[68] and "went forward and sat down in the seat of the inquirers." Ahura Mazda then instructed Zoroaster in the doctrines of the pure religion.

Other revelations are said to have continued to come to Zoroaster during a span of ten years, and then at the end of this period he won his first convert, his own cousin Maidhyo-maungha or Medyomah. As is stated in the Selections of Zad-sparam (xxiii, 1. sbe xlvii, p.163): "On the completion of revelation, that is, at the end of the ten years, Medyomah, son of Arastai, became faithful to Zaratusht." At this time the prophet said despondently, "In ten years only one man has been attracted by me" (*ibid.*, xxiii, 2).

It was two years longer before Zoroaster won his great victory with the conversion of the ruler Vishtaspa. It is said that Zoroaster departed "alone, by the advice and command of Auharmazd, to the residence of Vishtasp," and that when he met the king "he invited Vishtasp to the religion of Auharmazd" (Dinkard vii, iv, 65f. sbe xlvii, pp.64f.). Before the conversion of the king was completed, Zoroaster experienced a "terrible combat with evil" in which he himself suffered imprisonment and was involved "in controversy about the religion with the famous learned of the realm" (Dinkard vii, iv, 69,73. sbe xlvii, pp.65-67). The king was at last won to the faith, however, and his conversion marked the beginning of the triumph of Zoroastrianism throughout the land. As the author of the Dinkard

---

[68] The supreme god is known as Ahura Mazda in the Avesta, as Auharmazd in the Pahlavi literature, and as Ormazd or Hormuzd in later Persian.

says, if Vishtaspa and the people of that time had not accepted the religion announced by Zoroaster, "it would not have reached unto us" (VII, iv, 63. SBE XLVII, p.64).

A concise summary, covering the essential facts thus far and suggesting the later course of events, is found in the writings of the Muslim author, al-Biruni (A.D. c.973-c.1048): "Zarathustra went forth from Adharbaijan [Azerbaijan] and preached Magism in Balkh [Bactra]. His doctrines came into favor with King Gushtasp [Vishtaspa], and his son Isfendiyad spread the new faith both in east and west, both by force and by treaties. He founded fire temples throughout his whole empire, from the frontiers of China to those of the Greek empire. The succeeding kings made their religion [i.e., Zoroastrianism] the obligatory state religion for Persis and Iraq."[69]

Vishtaspa's son Isfendiyad (Isfendiar or Asfandiyar), who is called Spento-data in Avestan and Spend-dad in Pahlavi (i.e. Darius, according to Herzfeld), played an important part in the spreading of the faith, as stated by al-Biruni. In particular he was the great hero of the holy wars which the Zoroastrians had to fight against invading Turanians. His part in achieving the victory in these conflicts, through which the faith of Zoroaster was established on a firm foundation, is narrated in stirring detail in the Shah Namah or Book of Kings, the epic history of Persia composed by Firdausi (A.D. c.940-c.1020).[70]

In these wars, however, Zoroaster himself is said to have lost his life. According to the Shah Namah, this was when the Turanians stormed Balkh and destroyed the Zoroastrian temple Nush Azar. We read:

> The host reached Balkh, the world was wrecked with sack
> And slaughter. Making for the Fane of Fire (Nush Azar),
> For hall and palace decked with gold, they gave
> Them and the Zandavasta to the flames.
> The fane had eighty priests, God's worshippers,
> And all before the Fire the Turkmans slew,
> And swept that cult away. The Fire, that erst
> Zarduhsht had litten, of their blood did die;
> Who slew that priest himself I know not I.[71]

[69] India I, 10. ed. Sachau, I, p.21. cf. below p.179.

[70] tr. Arthur G. Warner and Edmond Warner, The Sháhnáma of Firdausi Done into English (Trübner's Oriental Series. 9 vols. 1905-15). vol. v. Part of the account (1495-1553. tr. Warner and Warner, v, pp.30-87) in the Shah Namah concerning Zoroaster, Gushtasp and Isfendiar was derived according to Firdausi from his predecessor Dakiki.

[71] 1559. tr. Warner and Warner, v, p.92.

22. Air View of Mount Demavend above the Plain of Ravy

23. Air View of Turang Tepe

24. Painted Pottery Bowl from the Early Mound near Persepolis

25. Painted Pottery Chalice from Tepe Hissar

26. Air View of the Rock of Behistun

27. Air View of Persepolis

28. Air View of the Burial Place of the Achaemenid Kings at Naqsh-i-Rustam

30. A Page of the Arda-Viraf Namak in Codex K20

29. A Page of the Bundahish in Codex K20b

31. Clay Tablet with Inscription of Darius I the Great

32. Symbol of Ahura Mazda on the Rock of Behistun

Gardner, use of tight-
papes -

34. Air View of the City Mound of Istakhr

33. Carving above the Tomb of Artaxerxes III at Persepolis

35. The Ancient City of Gur in the Valley of Modern Firuzabad

36. The Ruins of the Palace of Ardashir I at Firuzabad

37. The Investiture of Ardashir I by Hormuzd, as Carved at Naqsh-i-Rustam

38. The Site of the City of Shapur

39. The Investiture of Bahram I by Hormuzd, a Rock Relief at Shapur

40. The Investiture of Narseh by Anahita, a Rock Relief at Naqsh-i-Rustam

41. Taq-i-Bustan

42. The Investiture of Ardashir II by Hormuzd and Mithra, at Taq-i-Bustan

43. Takht-i-Sulaiman, the Site of Ancient Shiz

44. Chosroes II on the Steed Shabdez, at Taq-i-Bustan

45. The Investiture of Chosroes II by Hormuzd and Anahita, at Taq-i-Bustan

The same story is repeated a little later, and it is also told how a messenger carried to the absent Vishtaspa the news of the fall of the city, of the death of Lohrasp, the father of Vishtaspa, and of the slaying of the Master, by whom Zoroaster is meant:

> The Turkmans
> Have slain at Balkh Luhrasp, the king of kings,
> And turned our days to gloom and bitterness,
> Proceeded thence to Nush Azar and there
> Beheaded both Zarduhsht and all the archmages,
> Quenched in whose blood the radiant Fire expired.[72]

In Zoroastrian traditions the very name of the murderer of their prophet is given. In the Dinkard (v, iii, 2. sbe xlvii, p.126) the killing of Zoroaster is ascribed to Bradro-resh the Tur, and in the Dadistan-i Dinik (lxxii, 8. sbe xviii, p.218) Tur-i Bradar-vakhsh is mentioned, "by whom the best of men [i.e. Zoroaster] was put to death." Also the exact day of Zoroaster's death is recorded in the Selections of Zad-sparam (xxiii, 9. sbe xlvii, p.165): "In the forty-seventh year Zaratusht passes away, who attains 77 years and 40 days in the month Ardavahisto on the day Khur." This was the eleventh day of the second month of the Zoroastrian year.

THE GATHAS

For an understanding of the original teachings of Zoroaster we are dependent upon the Gathas.[73] The Gathas are five in number, containing seventeen hymns in all, and are now found as a part of the Yasna. Each Gatha is named after its opening words.

As revealed in the Gathas, Zoroaster's religion was a development of the ancient *asura-ahura* conceptions, with two characteristic features: first a strong tendency toward monotheism, and second an avowed but not fully elucidated dualism. The supreme god is called Ahura Mazda, meaning the Lord, the All-knowing One. In origin Ahura Mazda is probably identical with the ancient Varuna, and he appears now as a universal being who is the creator and sustainer of the world of good. Although Mazda is the Ahura par excellence, there are also other divine beings among whom the higher ones also are occasionally called Ahuras. These other divine beings are sometimes said to be sons and daughters of Mazda, or are spoken of as created by him, but soon come to be treated as personified qualities

[72] 1559f. tr. Warner and Warner, v, p.93.
[73] Christensen, *Die Iranier*, pp.221-227.

of his nature. Six of these are called Amesha Spentas or Immortal Beneficent Ones. They are: Vohu Manah or Good Thought, Asha Vahishta or Best Righteousness (Right), Khshathra Vairya or Wished-for Dominion, Spenta Armaiti or Holy Piety, Haurvatat or Welfare, and Ameretat or Immortality. Along with the foregoing there is sometimes counted as a seventh, Spenta Mainyu or Holy Spirit, who is probably the same as Mazda himself in his character as opponent of the spirit of evil. Yet other spiritual beings include Sraosha or Obedience, Ashi or Reward, and the strange figure of the Ox-soul which evidently represents the realm of animal life as entrusted to the diligent husbandman.

Over against the good world of the Ahuras stands the evil world of the Devas. As the idea of Asha or Righteousness makes clear the essence of the world of good, so the conception of the Druj or Lie, in the sense of antagonism to religious truth and order, expresses the nature of the world of evil. Sometimes the Druj or Lie appears personified as a feminine demon. Other spiritual personalities of the evil world include Aeshma or Fury, Aka Manah or Evil Thought who opposes Vohu Manah or Good Thought, and Angra Mainyu (Ahriman) or Evil Spirit who contends against Spenta Mainyu or Holy Spirit.

As long as this cosmic conflict continues man must choose his side and take his part in the struggle. By good thoughts, good deeds and good words, man assists the cause of Ahura Mazda. As George Foot Moore put it, "There is no place for saints who flee from the world; the saint is he who overcomes the evil in the world."[74]

A dualism of good and evil thus appears clearly in the Gathas. It is, however, a dualism which is limited in time, and the ultimate triumph of Ahura Mazda and of good is definitely envisaged. At death every soul must approach the Cinvat Bridge or Bridge of the Separator. There the righteous pass over to blessedness while the adherents of the Lie are turned back to punishment. At the end of the world, moreover, there will be a fiery test of all things when a flood of molten metal is poured out in which all evil will be burned up, but the good be left unharmed.

We may now turn directly to the Gathic texts.[75] The first Gatha is called Ahunavaiti, and consists of seven hymns found in Chapters

[74] MHR I, p.394.
[75] For translations of the Gathas see L. H. Mills, SBE XXXI, pp.1-194; James H. Moulton, *Early Zoroastrianism*, pp.343-390; and *Early Religious Poetry of Persia* (The Cambridge Manuals of Science and Literature). 1911, pp.80-118. Quotations here are from the translation by Moulton in *Early Zoroastrianism*.

28 to 34 of the Yasna. It opens with this prayer of Zoroaster (Yasna 28:1-4,7):

With outspread hands in petition for that help, O Mazda, first of all things I will pray for the works of the holy spirit, O thou the Right, whereby I may please the will of Good Thought and the Ox-soul.

I who would serve you, O Mazda Ahura and Good Thought—do ye give through the Right the blessings of both worlds, the bodily and that of Thought, which set the faithful in felicity.

I who would praise you, as never before, Right, and Good Thought, and Mazda Ahura, and those for whom Piety makes an imperishable Dominion grow; come ye to my help at my call.

I who have set my heart on watching over the soul, in union with Good Thought, and as knowing the rewards of Mazda Ahura for our works, will, while I have power and strength, teach men to seek after Right. . . .

Grant, O thou the Right, the reward, the blessings of Good Thought; O Piety, give our desire to Vishtaspa and to me; O thou, Mazda and Sovran, grant that your Prophet may perform the word of hearing.

The second hymn (Yasna 29) consists of a dialogue in heaven, in which the Ox-soul complains that the cattle on earth are treated with violence, and in which Vohu Manah names Zarathushtra Spitama to protect them. The Ox-soul however laments, "That I must be content with the ineffectual word of an impotent man for my protector." Zoroaster then prays earnestly for strength for his task, and the Ox-soul is satisfied and says, "O Ahura, now is help ours."

The third hymn is one of the central expositions of the creed of the prophet. It runs as follows (Yasna 30):

Now will I proclaim to those who will hear the things that the understanding man should remember. . . .

Hear with your ears the best things; look upon them with clear-seeing thought, for decision between the two Beliefs, each man for himself before the Great Consummation. . . .

Now the two primal Spirits, who revealed themselves in vision as Twins, are the Better and the Bad in thought and word and action. And between these two the wise once chose aright, the foolish not so.

And when these twain spirits came together in the beginning, they established Life and Not-Life, and that at the last the Worst Existence shall be to the followers of the Lie, but the Best Thought to him that follows Right.

Of these twain Spirits he that followed the Lie chose doing the worst things; the holiest Spirit chose Right, he that clothes him with the massy heavens as a garment. So likewise they that are fain to please Ahura Mazda by dutiful actions.

Between these twain the demons also chose not aright, for infatuation came upon them as they took counsel together, so that they chose the

[91]

Worst Thought. Then they rushed together to Violence, that they might enfeeble the world of man.

And to him [mankind] came Dominion, Good Thought, and Right; and Piety gave continued life of their bodies and indestructibility, so that by thy retributions through the [molten] metal he may gain the prize over those others.

So when there cometh the punishment of these evil ones, then, O Mazda, at thy command shall Good Thought establish the Dominion in the Consummation, for those who deliver the Lie, O Ahura, into the hands of Right.

So may we be those that make this world advance! O Mazda, and ye other Ahuras, gather together the Assembly, and thou too the Right, that thoughts may meet where Wisdom is at home.

Then truly on the Lie shall come the destruction of delight; but they that get them good name shall be partakers in the promised reward in the fair abode of Good Thought, of Mazda, and of Right.

If, O ye mortals, ye mark those commandments that Mazda hath ordained—of happiness and pain, the long punishment for the liars, and blessings for the righteous—then hereafter shall ye have bliss.

The long fourth hymn contains the following exalted passage (Yasna 31:7f.), in which the idea of the opening sentence has been compared to the thought of the two parts of the nineteenth Psalm and to the saying of Immanuel Kant about the starry heavens above and the moral law within.[76]

He that in the beginning thus thought, "Let the blessed realms be filled with lights," he it is that by his wisdom created Right. Those realms that the Best Thought shall possess thou dost prosper, Mazda, by thy spirit, which, O Ahura, is ever the same.

I conceived of thee, O Mazda, in my thought that thou, the First, art also the Last—that thou art Father of Good Thought, for thus I apprehended thee with mine eye—that thou didst truly create Right, and art the Lord to judge the actions of life.

The fifth hymn (Yasna 32) is a dialogue in which Zoroaster denounces the Devas; and the sixth contains the saying (Yasna 33:14), "As an offering Zarathushtra brings the life of his own body," which has been compared with Romans 12:1. The seventh hymn contains the words (Yasna 34:4), "Of thy Fire, O Ahura, that is mighty through Right, promised and powerful, we desire that it may be for the faithful man with manifested delight, but for the enemy with visible torment"; and then concludes with the supplication (Yasna 34:15), "O Mazda, make known to me the best teachings and actions, these, O Good Thought, and, O Right, the due of praise.

[76] Moulton, *Early Religious Poetry of Persia*, p.85.

Through your Dominion, O Ahura, assure us that mankind shall be capable according to thy will."

The second Gatha is called Ushtavaiti and contains four hymns (Yasna 43-46). We quote from the passage in which the prophet muses on the mystery of nature (Yasna 44:3-5,7):

This I ask thee, tell me truly, Ahura. Who is by generation the Father of Right, at the first? Who determined the path of sun and stars? Who is it by whom the moon waxes and wanes again? This, O Mazda, and yet more, I am fain to know.

This I ask thee, tell me truly, Ahura. Who upheld the earth beneath and the firmament from falling? Who the waters and the plants? Who yoked swiftness to winds and clouds? Who is, O Mazda, creator of Good Thought?

This I ask thee, tell me truly, Ahura. What artist made light and darkness? What artist made sleep and waking? Who made morning, noon, and night, that call the understanding man to his duty? . . .

This I ask thee, tell me truly, Ahura. Who created together with Dominion the precious Piety? Who made by wisdom the son obedient to his father? I strive to recognize by these things thee, O Mazda, creator of all things through the holy spirit.

The third Gatha (Yasna 47-50) is known as Spenta Mainyu since it opens with the name of the Holy Spirit:

By his holy Spirit and by Best Thought, deed, and word, in accordance with Right, Mazda Ahura with Dominion and Piety shall give us Welfare and Immortality.

This verse appears to be a sort of Zoroastrian creed, including as it does mention of all seven of the Amesha Spentas together with Ahura Mazda.

The fourth and fifth Gathas contain but a single hymn each. In the fourth, named Vohu Khshathra, we read of "Ahura Mazda, who through his Dominion appoints what is better than good to him that is attentive to his will, but what is worse than evil to him that obeys him not, at the last end of life" (Yasna 51:6). In the fifth, called Vahishto Ishti, it is stated (Yasna 53:1): "The best possession known is that of Zarathushtra Spitama, which is that Mazda Ahura will give him through the Right the glories of blessed life unto all time, and likewise to them that practise and learn the words and actions of his Good Religion."

ACHAEMENID INSCRIPTIONS

Since Zoroaster lived not later than the Achaemenid Period and perhaps at the very height of that period, it will be of interest now

[93]

to inquire whether any reflection of his religion appears in the inscriptions of the Achaemenid kings.

It is possible, as we have seen, to identify the Vishtaspa whom Zoroaster converted with Hystaspes. Since the latter exercised authority under Cyrus II the Great, it may be further supposed that Cyrus had some knowledge of the prophet and perhaps even manifested a favorable attitude toward the new religious teaching.[77] For this supposition there is, however, no direct inscriptional evidence. In his Akkadian cylinder inscription telling of the fall of Babylon (539 B.C.) Cyrus mentions Marduk, chief god of that city,[78] and according to the Old Testament he spoke of Yahweh in his proclamation concerning the rebuilding of the Jewish temple.[79] In view of the diplomatic purpose of Cyrus, these references are natural and do not contradict the hypothesis of acquaintance by Cyrus with Zoroastrianism or even espousal of it. That hypothesis remains at present, therefore, without positive proof or disproof.

Darius I the Great (522-486 B.C.) also makes reference to the deity worshiped by the Jews as "the God of heaven" in his decree furthering the rebuilding of their temple,[80] and in the Behistun inscription mentions "the other gods, [all] that there are."[81] Nevertheless almost all of his inscriptions emphasize his devotion to Ahura Mazda. In the great trilingual inscription on the Rock of Behistun Darius tells how he put down the widespread revolt initiated by Gaumata. He begins with mention of himself and his lineage, and then acknowledges that it is "by the grace of Ahuramazda" that he is king over the twenty-three provinces of the Persian empire. Coming to the account of the revolt, he introduces it with the statement that "the Lie multiplied in the land." Telling of his suppression of the rebellion he says first of all, "I prayed to Ahuramazda; Ahuramazda brought me help."[82] Throughout the inscription he speaks constantly of "the grace of Ahuramazda" and ascribes his victory and his possession of the kingdom to the help of that god.[83] So continuous is the emphasis upon the help of Ahura Mazda and so explicit is the reference to the connection of the revolutionists with the Lie, that it seems possible

[77] Lehmann-Haupt in Pavry, *Oriental Studies in Honour of Cursetji Erachji Pavry*, p.279.

[78] F. H. Weissbach, *Die Keilinschriften der Achämeniden*. 1911, pp.2f.; FLP p.191.

[79] II Chronicles 36:23 = Ezra 1:2.

[80] Ezra 6:6-12.

[81] King and Thompson, *The Sculptures and Inscription of Darius the Great on the Rock of Behistûn in Persia*, p.71.

[82] *ibid*., pp.3,7,11.   [83] *ibid*., p.3, etc.

to suppose that Zoroastrianism was at that time the newly adopted national religion and that the Magians were representatives of the old faith of "the Lie," whose rebellion had been motivated at least in part by religious reasons.[84]

After the Behistun inscription, the next longest inscription of Darius I is that on his tomb at Naqsh-i-Rustam. Here the great king presents not only a statement of some of his achievements but also an evaluation of his own character. In it all Darius acknowledges the favor of Ahura Mazda through which he has received his endowments. Darius says:

A great god is Ahuramazda, who created this excellent work which is seen, who created happiness for man, who bestowed wisdom and activity upon Darius the king.

Says Darius the king: By the favor of Ahuramazda I am of such a sort that I am a friend to right, I am not a friend to wrong; it is not my desire that the weak man should have wrong done to him by the mighty; nor is that my desire, that the mighty man should have wrong done to him by the weak.

What is right, that is my desire. I am not a friend to the man who is a Lie-follower. I am not hot-tempered. What things develop in my anger, I hold firmly under control by my will-power. I am firmly ruling over my own [impulses].

The man who co-operates, him according to his co-operative action, thus him do I reward. Who does harm, him according to the damage thus I punish. It is not my desire that a man should do harm; nor indeed is that my desire, if he should do harm, he should not be punished. . . .

Of such a sort is my understanding and my command: when what has been done by me thou shalt see or hear of, both in the city and in the war-camp, this is my activity over my will-power and my understanding.

This indeed is my activity: as far as my body has the strength, as a battle-fighter I am a good battle-fighter. . . .

Trained am I both with hands and with feet. As a horseman I am a good horseman. As a bowman I am a good bowman both afoot and on horse-back. As a spearman I am a good spearman both afoot and on horseback.

And the [physical] skillfulnesses which Ahuramazda has bestowed upon me and I have had the strength to use them—by the favor of Ahuramazda, what has been done by me I have done it with those skillfulnesses which Ahuramazda has bestowed upon me.[85]

[84] Ernst Herzfeld in *Revue de l'histoire des religions*. 1936, pp.21f.; H. R. Hall, *The Ancient History of the Near East from the Earliest Times to the Battle of Salamis.* 7th ed. 1927, p.556; and in CAH III, p.313; Lehmann-Haupt in Pavry, *Oriental Studies in Honour of Cursetji Erachji Pavry*, pp.253,271f. Benveniste, *The Persian Religion According to the Chief Greek Texts*, denied that Zoroastrianism ever became the religion of the Achaemenids. Christensen, *Die Iranier*, p.215 favors that position.
[85] Roland G. Kent in JNES 4 (1945), pp.41f.

The third longest inscription we have from Darius concerns his construction of a palace at Susa, a work of about 517-516 B.C. As the words of Darius show, the palace was completed while his father Hystaspes was still living. Like the records just mentioned and like most of the Achaemenid inscriptions, this, too, is written in Old Persian, Elamite and Akkadian. The reverse side of the beautiful but damaged baked clay tablet containing the Old Persian inscription is shown in Fig. 31. It need not be quoted at length since it is largely concerned with details of the work and workers on the palace, but we may note that it begins, "A great god is Ahuramazda, who has created that heaven, who has created man, who has created good things for man, who has made Darius king, sole king of many, sole commander of many. I am Darius, great king, king of kings, king of lands, king of this earth, son of Hystaspes, the Achaemenid"; and that it concludes, "King Darius says: By the grace of Ahuramazda I constructed a magnificent [palace] in Susa. May Ahuramazda protect me and my . . . my father and my country against injury."[86]

As in the case of the palace at Susa so, too, in the case of the canal which Darius constructed from the Nile River to the Red Sea, the king gave praise to Ahura Mazda in his commemorative inscription:

A great god [is] Ahuramazda, who created yonder sky, who this earth created, who created man, who created welfare for man, who made Darius king, who bestowed upon Darius the King the kingdom, great, rich in horses, rich in men. I [am] Darius the Great King, King of Kings, King of countries containing all [kinds of] men, King in this great earth far and wide, son of Hystaspes, an Achaemenian. Saith Darius the King: I am a Persian; from Persia I seized Egypt; I ordered this canal to dig, from the river by name Nile, which flows in Egypt, to the sea which goes from Persia. Afterwards this canal was dug thus as I commanded, and ships went from Egypt through this canal to Persia thus as was my desire.[87]

From the numerous other inscriptions of the same king we quote one more: "I am Darius, great king, king of kings, king of lands, son of Hystaspes, the Achaemenid. King Darius says: Mine is Ahuramazda, Ahuramazda I reverence! May Ahuramazda bring me help!"[88]

---

[86] V. Scheil, *Inscriptions des Achéménides à Suse* (Mémoires de la Mission Archéologique de Perse, XXI). 1929, pp.17,21, Pl. IX; J. M. Unvala in PSPA I, p.339; Herzfeld in *Archaeologische Mitteilungen aus Iran.* 3 (1931), pp.29-124; Roland G. Kent in JAOS 51 (1931), pp.189-240.

[87] Roland G. Kent in JNES 1 (1942), p.419.

[88] Scheil, *Inscriptions des Achéménides à Suse*, p.50; cf. F. H. Weissbach in *Archiv für Orientforschung, Internationale Zeitschrift für die Wissenschaft vom Vorderen Orient.* 7 (1931-32), p.45.

Like Darius his father, Xerxes (486-465 B.C.) also regularly begins his inscriptions with some such affirmation as, "A great god [is] Ahuramazda, who created this earth, who created yonder heaven, who created man, who created good things for man, who made Xerxes king, sole king of many, sole commander of many," and frequently refers to "the grace of Ahuramazda" through which he has been able to accomplish what he has done.[89]

In a long inscription of Xerxes discovered at Persepolis, it is revealed that he, too, had to contend with uprisings, and that in part at least these took place in lands where previously the Devas were worshiped. Xerxes states, "Then by Ahuramazda's will of such temples of the Daivas I sapped the foundations, and I ordained: the Daivas shall not be worshiped. Where the Daivas had been worshiped before, there I worshiped Ahuramazda with Arta the exalted; and whatever else had been done wrongfully, that I righted. This which I did, I did it all by the will of Ahuramazda; Ahuramazda helped me until I had completed the task." Xerxes then includes in the same inscription this exhortation: "Thou who art of an after age, if thou thinkest, 'I wish to be happy in life, and in death I wish to belong to Arta,' abide in those laws which Ahuramazda has established and worship Ahuramazda together with Arta the exalted. The man who abides in the laws which Ahuramazda has established and worships Ahuramazda together with Arta the exalted, that one shall be happy in life, and in death he shall belong to Arta." Finally the king concludes with the supplication, "May Ahuramazda guard from evil me and my house and this land. This I implore of Ahuramazda; this may Ahuramazda grant me."[90]

It may be noted that Arta, who is mentioned so prominently along with Ahura Mazda in the foregoing passages, is probably the same as Asha or Right. The name of Xerxes (Persian, Khshayarsha) himself is probably related to the Avestan Khshathra or Dominion, and his son's name, Artaxerxes, corresponds to Asha Khshathra and means, "One whose Dominion is according to Right."[91]

Like his predecessors, Artaxerxes I Longimanus (465-423 B.C.) says in an inscription at Persepolis:

[89] F. H. Weissbach, *Die Keilinschriften der Achämeniden*. 1911, p.107; Unvala in PSPA I, pp.342f.
[90] Erich F. Schmidt, *The Treasury of Persepolis and Other Discoveries in the Homeland of the Achaemenians*. OIC 21 (1939), pp.14f.
[91] Moulton, *Early Zoroastrianism*, p.109.

A great god is Ahuramazda, who created this earth, who created yonder sky, who created man, who created happiness for man, who made Artaxerxes king, one king of many, one lord of many.

I [am] Artaxerxes the Great King, King of Kings, King of Countries containing all [kinds of] men, King in this great earth far and wide, son of Xerxes the King, grandson of Darius, an Achaemenian.

Saith Artaxerxes the Great King: By the favor of Ahuramazda, this palace Xerxes the King, my father, previously [built]; afterwards I built [it to completion]. Me may Ahuramazda along with the gods protect, and my kingdom, and what was built by me.[92]

When we come to Artaxerxes II Mnemon (404-359 B.C.), we find new elements entering the inscriptions. Concerning his reconstruction of the Apadana or Hall of Columns built by Darius I at Susa, he states:

Says Artaxerxes, great king, king of kings, king of lands, king of this earth . . . : This hall of columns (*apadana*) Darius [I] my great-grand-father[92a] had constructed. Later on, during the reign of my grandfather Artaxerxes [I] had burnt it down. By the grace of Ahuramazda, and Anahita, and Mithra, I reconstructed this hall of columns. May Ahuramazda, Anahita and Mithra protect me from all injury, and may they neither injure nor destroy this [hall of columns] which I have constructed.[93]

We observe that Anahita and Mithra are now mentioned along with Ahura Mazda as if they formed a triad of deities. The goddess Anahita appears also in the Yashts. In the fifth or Aban Yasht (SBE XXIII, pp.52-84), which means the Yasht of the Waters, there is a long hymn of praise in her honor. Here she is called Ardvi Sura Anahita, meaning the High, Powerful, Undefiled, and is described as a river-goddess and bringer of fertility. At the opening of the Yasht (v, i, 3) she seems to be a spring-fed river itself, which pours down from a western mountain to the earth-surrounding ocean: "Ahura Mazda spake unto Spitama Zarathushtra, saying: 'Offer up a sacrifice, O Spitama Zarathushtra! unto this spring of mine, Ardvi Sura Anahita, the wide-expanding and health-giving, who hates the Devas and obeys the laws of Ahura, who is worthy of sacrifice in the material world, worthy of prayer in the material world; the life-increasing and holy, the herd-increasing and holy, the fold-increasing and holy, the wealth-increasing and holy, the country-increasing and

[92] Roland G. Kent in JNES 4 (1945), p.230.

[92a] Literally "father of the father of my father"—an unprecise way of referring to one who was really his great-great-grandfather, since the sequence of kings was Darius I, Xerxes, Artaxerxes I, Darius II, Artaxerxes II.

[93] Weissbach, *Die Keilinschriften der Achämeniden*, pp.123-125; Unvala in PSPA I, p.344.

holy. . . . The large river, known afar, that is as large as the whole of the waters that run along the earth; that runs powerfully from the height Hukairya down to the sea Vouru-Kasha.'"

At the end of the same Yasht (v, 126), however, the mystical river is fully personified, and Anahita appears "in the shape of a maid, fair of body, most strong, tall-formed, high-girded, pure, nobly born of a glorious race."

Anahita later became widely known abroad, and was assimilated with goddesses like Ma, Cybele, Ishtar and Aphrodite.[94]

Mithra is the same as Mitra, the sky god who appears in the Vedic literature of India. In the Avesta, Mithra is the object of worship and praise throughout the long tenth or Mihir Yasht (SBE xxiii, pp.119-158). In this Yasht he appears as a god of light, closely connected but not yet identical with the sun. He is the one "who first of the heavenly gods reaches over the Hara,[95] before the undying, swift-horsed sun; who, foremost in a golden array, takes hold of the beautiful summits, and from thence looks over the abode of the Aryans with a beneficent eye" (Yasht x, 13). He is also the great protagonist of the good, who drives forward in his chariot to smite the forces of evil (Yasht x, 124f.,130,133-135):

With his arms lifted up toward Immortality, Mithra, the lord of wide pastures, drives forward from the shining Garo-nmana [Paradise], in a beautiful chariot that drives on, ever-swift, adorned with all sorts of ornaments, and made of gold. Four stallions draw that chariot, all of the same white color, living on heavenly food and undying. The hoofs of their fore-feet are shod with gold, the hoofs of their hind-feet are shod with silver; all are yoked to the same pole. . . . On a side of the chariot of Mithra, the lord of wide pastures, stand a thousand spears well-made and sharp-piercing. They go through the heavenly space, they fall through the heavenly space upon the skulls of the Devas. . . . After he has smitten the Devas, after he has smitten down the men who lied unto Mithra, Mithra, the lord of wide pastures, drives forward. . . . Angra Mainyu, who is all death, flees away in fear. . . . O, may we never fall across the rush of Mithra, the lord of wide pastures, when in anger! May Mithra, the lord of wide pastures, never smite us in his anger; he who stands up upon this earth as the strongest of all gods, the most valiant of all gods, the most energetic of all gods, the swiftest of all gods, the most fiend-smiting of all gods, he, Mithra, the lord of wide pastures.

Later Mithra was identified with the Semitic sun god, Shamash, and his worship spread into the west, where as *deus Sol invictus Mithras*

[94] Franz Cumont, *The Oriental Religions in Roman Paganism.* 1911, pp.54,65,146.
[95] The mountain where the sun rises.

he was prominently known throughout the Roman empire in the early centuries of the Christian era.[96]

As in the inscriptions of Artaxerxes II, so, too, in those of Artaxerxes III Ochus (359-338 B.C.), Mithra is linked with Ahura Mazda. In his building inscriptions this king says: "May Ahura Mazda and Mithra protect from all evil that which I have constructed"; "May Ahura Mazda and god Mithra protect me and this country and that which has been constructed by me."[97]

Because of the prominence of Anahita and Mithra in these last inscriptions we may conclude that, from the time of Artaxerxes II on, the old Iranian nature religion, as advocated no doubt by the Magians, was regaining its strength and finding an increasingly large place within the framework of Zoroastrianism.[98]

ACHAEMENID ARCHITECTURE AND SCULPTURE

We may now ask whether there are any marks of the Zoroastrian religion in the architectural and sculptural monuments of the Achaemenid Period. A well-known statement of Herodotus[99] might lead us to expect a complete lack of anything of this sort. The Greek historian declared that the Persians had no images of the gods, no temples and no altars, and that they considered the use of such things to be a sign of folly. When they worshiped, he said, they went up on the summits of the loftiest mountains and sacrificed to Jupiter, meaning the firmament, and to the sun and moon, to the earth, to fire, to water and to the winds. On the other hand we have the explicit statement of Darius the Great in the Behistun inscription: "The temples which Gaumata, the Magian, had destroyed I restored for the people."[100] The solution of the apparent contradiction probably lies in the fact that Herodotus was describing the old popular cult which was practiced on the high hills beneath the open

[96] Franz Cumont, *The Mysteries of Mithra.* 2d ed. tr. Thomas J. McCormack, 1903; H. Stuart Jones in HERE VIII, pp.752-759.

[97] Scheil, *Inscriptions des Achéménides à Suse*, p.100; Weissbach, *Die Keilinschriften der Achämeniden*, p.129; Unvala in PSPA I, p.345.

[98] Herzfeld, *Archaeological History of Iran*, p.40. Magian influence is probably also to be recognized in the eventual adoption by Zoroastrianism of the practice of exposure of the bodies of the dead, a custom of the Magi which is attested by Herodotus (I, 140) and Strabo (*Geography*, xv, iii, 20). Moulton, *Early Zoroastrianism*, pp.202-204; Benveniste, *Les mages dans l'ancien Iran.* 1938.

[99] I, 131.

[100] King and Thompson, *The Sculptures and Inscription of Darius the Great on the Rock of Behistûn in Persia*, p.13.

sky, while with the adoption of Zoroastrianism by the Achaemenid kings and under their patronage actual temples were erected.[101]

The characteristic temple of Zoroastrianism was the fire sanctuary. Fire was a natural symbol of Ahura Mazda, who was expected to destroy the wicked in a flood of molten metal at the end of the world (cf. pp. 90,92); and in the Vendidad (VIII, 80 [246]. SBE IV, p.112) fire was personified as the son of Ahura Mazda. According to Arab writers like Shahrastani,[102] there were places of fire worship in Iran even before the time of Zoroaster, but the prophet built new fire temples and so did Vishtaspa and other Zoroastrian kings. Actually we now know that the veneration of fire goes back to the earliest times in Central Asia. Archeological excavation in Khorezm, in the delta of the Amu Darya (Oxus) east of the Caspian Sea, has uncovered the communal houses of a neolithic people of the fourth and third millenniums B.C. In the center of each house was a sacred hearth in which a fire was kept burning continuously; and thus we have a primitive anticipation of the inextinguishable fires of the later faith.[103]

It is possible that such a fire temple of the Achaemenid Period is to be recognized in the famous Ka'bah-i-Zardusht ("Cube of Zoroaster") at Naqsh-i-Rustam. This is a rectangular stone structure in the shape of a sort of tower house. It stands in front of the cliff at Naqsh-i-Rustam, directly over against the rock-hewn tomb of Darius I the Great, and may be clearly seen in the photograph of that place in Fig. 28. One interpretation of the building is that it is a tomb of Achaemenid times, possibly of Zoroaster as its popular designation would suggest, or more probably of some Achaemenid king.[104] In 1936, however, some excavation was done around the lower part of the structure, and a hitherto unknown Pahlavi inscription of thirty-four lines was uncovered. Decipherment of the inscription[105] finds that it was written in the third century A.D. and has to do with the enthronement of a Sasanian monarch. Mention is also explicitly made of the fire of Anahita, and the supposition is thereby raised that at least in Sasanian times the building was a fire temple. As the great

[101] Ernst Diez, *Iranische Kunst.* 1944, p.59.
[102] I, ii, 2, ch.1. tr. Haarbrücker, pp.298f.
[103] V. Altman in JAOS 67 (1947), p.83.
[104] Herzfeld, *Archaeological History of Iran*, pp.35,37,60; *Iran in the Ancient East*, p.213.
[105] Martin Sprengling in *The American Journal of Semitic Languages and Literatures.* 53 (Oct. 1936-July 1937), pp.126-144; A. T. Olmstead in *Classical Philology.* 37 (1942), pp.241-262,398-420; cf. R. Ghirshman in *Syria.* 24 (1944-45), pp.174-193.

temple near the capital it was the sacred center for the crowning of the kings, and also probably the place where the crown jewels were stored.

If the immediately foregoing interpretation is correct, then perhaps the Ka'bah-i-Zardusht was a fire temple from the very beginning. Its location agrees with this, for it is so placed that the shadows of the cliffs would prevent the sun from entering the door and falling upon the sacred fire, a provision which is in accord with Zoroastrian usage. Since the structure is directly opposite the tomb of Darius the Great it may have been erected by that ruler.[106]

Turning now to the tomb of Darius itself, we find that its façade is a cruciform recess in the face of the cliff.[107] The doorway opening into the inner chamber is in the long horizontal panel, while in the panel above there is a large sculptured picture. This shows a platform supported by twenty-eight men arranged in two rows and doubtless representing the countries of the Persian empire. On this platform there is a pedestal of three steps on which the king is standing. In his left hand he holds a bow, while his right hand is uplifted toward an altar on which a fire is burning. Above, hovers a symbolic winged figure, concerning which we will shortly say more, while in the upper right hand corner is also a crescent moon shown upon a full moon disk.[108]

The description just given is also applicable to the tombs of the successors of Darius, for they were patterned in both plan and sculptures after the grave of this great king. Those of Xerxes (486-465 B.C.), Artaxerxes I (465-423), and Darius II (423-404) are in the same cliff at Naqsh-i-Rustam, while those of Artaxerxes II Mnemon (404-359) and Artaxerxes III Ochus (359-338), and the unfinished tomb of Darius III Codomannus (335-331) are in the rocks near Persepolis.[109] The sculptured panel of the grave of Artaxerxes III at Persepolis, corresponding in detail to that of the tomb of Darius the Great, is pictured in Fig. 33.[110]

The winged symbol which occupies the place of honor in these panels appears frequently in other Achaemenid sculptures. It is used

---

[106] Diez, *Iranische Kunst*, p.61.   [107] FLP Fig. 91.

[108] F. H. Weissbach in *Berichte über die Verhandlungen der Konigl. Sächsischen Gesellschaft der Wissenschaften zu Leipzig*. Philologisch-historische Klasse. 62 (1910), p.4.

[109] Friedrich Sarre, *Die Kunst des alten Persien* (in William Cohn, ed., Die Kunst des Ostens, v). 1923, p.14.

[110] Friedrich Sarre and Ernst Herzfeld, *Iranische Felsreliefs, Aufnahmen und Untersuchungen von Denkmälern aus alt- und mittelpersischer Zeit*. 1910, Fig. 5.

at Persepolis, for example, on the eastern gate of the Tripylon above the figures of Darius I and Xerxes;[111] on the palace of Xerxes;[112] and on the Hall of One Hundred Columns.[113] It is also prominent on the sculptured panel at the Rock of Behistun, from which place we reproduce the close-up photograph in Fig. 32.[114]

The symbol consists essentially of a winged ring or disk from which an anthropomorphic form arises, attired in robe and tiara like a king. At Behistun the headdress is cylindrical and is surmounted by a solar disk with eight rays.[115] The lower part of the body ends in feathers which spread out beneath the disk, while scrolls depend on either side. One hand is extended as if in blessing, and the other holds forth an object like a ring.[116]

This type of representation probably came originally from Egypt, where the winged sun disk appears as early as the Middle Kingdom and is frequent in the time of the New Kingdom. From Egypt it had made its way by the middle of the second millennium B.C. also to Assyria, where ere long the feathered tail became a characteristic part of the composition. Typical examples appear on the monuments of Tukulti-Ninurta II (890-884 B.C.), Ashur-nasir-pal II (883-859 B.C.), and Shalmaneser III (858-824 B.C.). This symbol in Assyria is usually taken to represent the national god Ashur, but it is also possible that it may have stood for Ninurta.[117]

In Persia on the Achaemenid monuments of which we have just been speaking there is no doubt that the winged symbol represents the god Ahura Mazda, of whom the kings so frequently speak in their accompanying inscriptions. Hovering over the royal figures, the symbol expresses the divine protection of that deity for which prayer is so earnestly made.

As far as actual images or idols of the deities are concerned, we have an interesting statement by Berossos, who was a priest of Marduk at Babylon in the time of Antiochus I (281-261 B.C.), and who was quoted on this point by Clement of Alexandria (A.D. c.200) in

[111] FLP Fig. 93.
[112] PSPA IV, Pl. 86,C; Sarre and Herzfeld, *Iranische Felsreliefs*, Pl. XXIII.
[113] PSPA IV, Pl. 89,B; Sarre and Herzfeld, *Iranische Felsreliefs*, Pl. XXV.
[114] King and Thompson, *The Sculptures and Inscription of Darius the Great on the Rock of Behistûn in Persia*, Pl. VIII.
[115] *ibid.*, pp.xxii-xxiii.
[116] Georges Perrot and Charles Chipiez, *Histoire de l'art dans l'antiquité.* V (1890), pp.813f.
[117] Birger Pering in *Archiv für Orientforschung, Internationale Zeitschrift für die Wissenschaft vom Vorderen Orient.* 8 (1932-33), pp.281-296.

his *Exhortation to the Greeks*.[118] According to Berossos, idolatry was introduced by Artaxerxes II (404-359 B.C.), who set up images of Anahita in various cities, a fact which we can well credit remembering the prominence of the mention of the goddess in the inscriptions of this king. The passage runs as follows: "It was not, however, till many ages had passed that they began to worship statues in human form, as Berosus shows in his third book of *Chaldaean History*; for this custom was introduced by Artaxerxes the son of Darius and father of Ochus, who was the first to set up the statue of Aphrodite Anaitis in Babylon, Susa and Ecbatana, and to enjoin this worship upon Persians and Bactrians, upon Damascus and Sardis." Such idols of Anahita as Berossos mentions are not now extant, but we do have representations of this goddess from the Achaemenid Period on gold intaglio seals. There Anahita is shown richly costumed, wearing a crown or a high headdress, and holding a flower and wreath, or a branch and bird.[119]

[118] v. tr. G. W. Butterworth, LCL (1919), pp.147-149.
[119] Ackerman in PSPA I, p.214; IV, Pl. 124,w,y.

4. ALEXANDER THE GREAT AND THE SELEUCID KINGS, 331-c.250 B.C.

ALEXANDER the Great conquered Persia in 331 B.C. He did such damage to Zoroastrianism that in the traditions of the religion he was ever after remembered as "the accursed Sikander (or Iskander)." In an act evidently intended to symbolize the end of Achaemenid power, Alexander burned the royal capital at Persepolis, and in this conflagration an original copy of the Zoroastrian scriptures perished. In a brief notice the Dinkard (v, iii, 4. SBE XLVII, p.127) states that the Avesta and Zand were written upon oxhides with gold, "and kept in the royal treasury," and in a fuller passage in the last chapter of the third book (SBE XXXVII, p.xxxi) declares that it was Kai-Vishtasp who commanded the Zoroastrian scriptures to be written down, and that "he ordered them to deliver the original to the treasury of Shapigan, and to distribute copies provided. And, after that, he sends a copy to the fortress of documents, to keep the information also there. And during the ruin that happened to the country of Iran, and in the monarchy, owing to the evil-destined villain Alexander, that which was in the fortress of documents came to be burnt, and that in the treasury of Shapigan into the hands of the Arumans, and was translated by him even into the Greek language, as information which was connected with the ancients."

The "fortress of documents" just mentioned in the Dinkard, where one copy of the Zoroastrian writings was kept, must have been at Persepolis, since this copy is said to have been burnt by Alexander. It will be remembered (p.81) that the Book of Arda Viraf also states that the Avesta and Zand were written with gold ink on prepared cowskins, deposited in the archives at Stakhar Papakan, and there burned by Alexander. Likewise the Arab historian Tabari (A.D. 838-923) and Tha'alibi (A.D. 961-1038) record that an original copy of the Zoroastrian scriptures was kept at Persepolis. Speaking of Bishtasp or Vishtaspa, Tabari writes: "It is said that he built in Persia the city of Pasa or Fasa, and in India and other places temples for the fires, and placed over them the fire priests. . . . Zaradusht, the son of Aspiman, appeared in the thirtieth year of his reign. He laid claim to the gift of prophecy. Now he wished that the king should receive his faith; but he refused. But afterward he believed in him and accepted that to which Zaradusht had invited him. He brought the king part of a book, which he claimed to be an inspiration. It was written upon the hides of twelve thousand oxen—the writing cut into the hide and covered with gold. Bishtasp sent this to a place in Istakhr called Darbisht."[120] On Tabari's authority, Tha'alibi says that Zoroaster's book was written on twelve thousand cowhides and deposited "in the citadel of Istakhr."[121] Istakhr, it may be explained, was the name of the later capital which replaced Persepolis. The actual site of Istakhr is about three miles from Persepolis, and the city mound is shown in an air view in Fig. 34.

The "treasury of Shapigan," mentioned in the Dinkard as the repository of another copy of the Zoroastrian scriptures, may have been in Samarkand. A ninth century Pahlavi treatise called Shatroiha-i-Airan or "The Cities of Iran" states that Samarkand was founded by Kai-Kaus and completed by his son Siavakhsh, and that a splendid fire temple was built there by his grandson Kai-Khusrov. Then the treatise continues: "In the end, Zoroaster brought the religion and by the order of king Vishtasp wrote 1,200 chapters of religious writings on golden tablets and deposited them in the treasury of that fire temple. At last the accursed Sikander [Alexander] burnt and threw into the river the [collection of the] religious writings of seven kings."[122] We know that Samarkand, anciently called Maracanda, was destroyed by Alexander the Great in 329 B.C., but the statement of the present treatise that Alexander burned the Zoroastrian books here too, may be due to a confusion with what happened at Persepolis. As we have seen, the Dinkard only claims that at the treasury of Shapigan the books fell into the hands of the Arumans, that is the Greeks from what was later a part of the Roman empire, and that they had translations of them made into Greek.

Although Alexander the Great was remembered by the Zoroastrians as an archenemy of their faith, our understanding of his purposes in general would lead us to suppose that he really desired not to destroy any single religion but rather to cause all the religions of both east and west to be mingled in the united world of which he dreamed.[123] As an illustration of the outworking of this Hellenistic idea which Alexander so powerfully furthered, we may cite the temple which, after his conquest, was built at the foot of the terrace of

[120] Quoted by Gottheil in *Classical Studies in Honour of Henry Drisler*, p.37.

[121] H. Zotenberg, *Histoire des rois des Perses par Aboû Mansoûr 'Abd al-Malik ibn Mohammad ibn Ismà'il al-Tha'âlibî, Texte arabe publié et traduit*. 1900, p.257.

[122] Jivanji Jamshedji Modi, *Asiatic Papers, Papers Read before the Bombay Branch of the Royal Asiatic Society*. 1 (1905), p.153.

[123] cf. W. W. Tarn in CAH VI, pp.434-437.

Persepolis. This was used for the worship of the old gods of Persia, but now their names were written in Greek: Zeus Megistos for Ahura Mazda; Apollo and Helios in the place of Mithra; and Artemis and Queen Athena instead of Anahita.[124]

Alexander's successors in the east were the Seleucids,[125] whose cultural and religious interests were also thoroughly Hellenistic. Among the cities which they founded and which were centers of Hellenistic influence were Seleucia on the Tigris, which was founded by Seleucus I Nicator (312-281 B.C.) shortly after the beginning of his official reign in 312 B.C.; and Hecatompylos, the "Town of a Hundred Gates," a city in Parthia the exact site of which has not yet been located.[126]

As we shall see later (p.142), Seleucus I sent his ambassador Megasthenes to the court of Chandragupta Maurya, and in the next century or two Greek influence bore rather strongly upon India. Indeed from there it even made itself felt in farthest East Asia.[127] The Seleucids, however, turned their interests more and more away from the east and toward the west. Their capital was first at Babylon, then at Seleucia on the Tigris, and finally at Antioch in Syria.[128] In the east their possessions soon fell into the hands of the Greco-Bactrians and the Parthians.

It was around 250 B.C. that a satrap of Bactria named Diodotus rebelled and was able to establish a Greco-Bactrian kingdom which included Bactria, Sogdiana and Margiana, and which later was extended to Arachosia, the Indus and the Punjab. This kingdom endured until around 135 B.C.,[129] when it gave way to nomadic invaders from central Asia, the Sakas who passed on to settle in Sistan (which derived its name from them) and Sind. In India, however, Greek rulers maintained themselves longer, and of these the best known was Menander (Milinda), who may be dated in the first century B.C.[130]

---

[124] Herzfeld, *Iran in the Ancient East*, p.274.

[125] Edwyn R. Bevan, *The House of Seleucus*. 2 vols. 1902.

[126] Erich F. Schmidt, *Flights Over Ancient Cities of Iran* (Special Publication of the Oriental Institute of the University of Chicago). 1940, pp.34f.

[127] Christensen, *Die Iranier*, p.303.

[128] Huart, *Ancient Persia and Iranian Civilization*, pp.103f.

[129] The kings were: Diodotus I, c.250-c.240; Diodotus II, c.240-c.225; Euthydemos of Magnesia, c.225-c.200; Demetrios, c.200-c.175; Eukradites, c.175-c.165; Heliokles Dikaios, c.160-c.135. Grousset in PSPA I, p.70; W. W. Tarn, *The Greeks in Bactria and India*. 1938.

[130] Christensen, *Die Iranier*, pp.303f.

[107]

5. THE PARTHIAN PERIOD, c. 250 B.C.-A.D. c.229

ARSACES

THE success of the Greco-Bactrians encouraged the Parthians also to rise against the Seleucids. The Parthians were a people who had come into northern Iran, and whose leader at this time was Arsaces, whom the Roman historian Trogus Pompeius (A.D. c.10) described as "a man of uncertain origin but of undisputed bravery."[131] Arsaces was joined in the leadership of the revolt by his brother Tiridates, and the two brothers became the first two kings of the Parthian dynasty, Arsaces being on the throne c. 250-c.248 B.C. and Tiridates I following him c.248-c.211 B.C. The Parthian era is taken as beginning in 247 B.C. All the successors of Arsaces used his name as a title,[132] and the Arsacid dynasty comprised in all some thirty-nine kings who reigned until A.D. c.229.[133]

By progressive steps, and particularly through the successful campaigns of Mithradates I (c.171-138/137 B.C.), most of Persia and Mesopotamia now came into the hands of the Parthians. Early in the first century B.C., prior to the coming of the Yueh-chi, Parthian power was also for a time extended into India. The ruling dynasty there is often called "Pahlava" to distinguish it from the contemporary royal family of Parthia.[134] The greatest of the Pahlava kings was Gondophares. In the west the Parthians came into conflict with the Romans, and carried on intermittent warfare for some three hundred years.

After the achievements of Mithradates I the Arsacid rulers, although really foreigners, set themselves up as heirs of the Achaeme-

[131] As quoted in the abridgement of his work by the later Roman historian, Justin, XLI, 4. tr. John S. Watson, *Justin, Cornelius Nepos, and Eutropius*. 1876, p.275.

[132] Justin XLI, 5. tr. Watson, p.276.

[133] These kings were: Arsaces, c.250-c.248; Tiridates I, c.248-c.211; Artabanus I, c.211-c.191; Priapatius, c.191-c.176; Phraates I, c.176-c.171; Mithradates I, c.171-138/137; Phraates II, 138/137-c.128; Artabanus II, c.128-124/123; Mithradates II, c.123-88/87; Gotarzes I, 91-81/80; Orodes I, 80-76/75; Sinatruces, 76/75-70 or 69; Phraates III, 70 or 69-58/57; Mithradates III, 58/57-55; Orodes II, c.57-37/36; Pacorus I, died in 38; Phraates IV, c.38-2; Tiridates II, c.30-c.25; Phraataces (Phraates V), 2 B.C.-A.D. 4; Orodes III, A.D. 4-c.6/7; Vonones I, 7/8-12; Artabanus III, 12-c.38; Tiridates III, c.36; Cinnamus, c.37; Gotarzes II, c.38-51; Vardanes, c.39-47/48; Vonones II, c.51; Vologases I, 51/52-79/80; Pacorus II, 78-115/116?; Artabanus IV, 80-81; Osroes, c.109/110-128/129; Parthamaspates, c.117; Vologases II, 105/106?-147; Mithradates IV, 128/129?-147?; Vologases III, 148-192; Vologases IV, 191-207/208; Vologases V, 207/208-222/223; Artabanus V, c.213-227; Artavasdes, c.227-228/229?. Neilson C. Debevoise, *A Political History of Parthia*. 1938, p.270; Richard A. Parker and Waldo H. Dubberstein, *Babylonian Chronology 626 B.C.-A.D. 45*. SAOC 24, 1942, p.22.

[134] Debevoise, *A Political History of Parthia*, p.65.

nids, and took the old title "king of kings."[135] At first their capital was at Hecatompylos, but in the first half of the second century B.C. they transferred the seat of their rule to Ctesiphon, a city which they built on the left bank of the Tigris opposite Seleucia.[136] The official Parthian language was Pahlavi, which is Persian written in Aramaic characters.[137]

The spirit of Hellenism still prevailed in this time. On their coins the Arsacid kings regularly called themselves "Philhellenes,"[138] and in religion they were doubtless broadly eclectic. Despite the damage it had suffered under Alexander, and the syncretistic influences to which it had been exposed under the Seleucids, the religion of Zoroaster yet lived on, however, and in the Parthian Period seems gradually to have regained some of its strength.

Isidore of Charax, a Greek author who probably lived in Charax Spasini at the head of the Persian Gulf around the end of the first century B.C., says that Arsaces, doubtless meaning the first ruler of that name, was proclaimed king in the city of Asaak, and that "an everlasting fire is guarded there."[139] The mention of the fire at this city is doubtless an indication of the existence of Zoroastrianism in the Parthian territory at the time. Isidore of Charax also attests the worship of Anahita, for in connection with Ecbatana he mentions "a temple, sacred to Anaitis," and says, "they sacrifice there always."[140] The ruins of this very temple are believed to have been discovered at Kangavar, which is some distance from Hamadan or the ancient Ecbatana. The structure found here was built of stone, and had an enormous columnar hall over six hundred and sixty feet square, portions of some of the columns of which are still standing.[141]

Mithra, likewise, was prominent in the Parthian Period. Mithradates I was the first of several Arsacid monarchs whose name honored this god, and the tenth Yasht in praise of Mithra (p.99) is believed to date from the last years of his reign.[142]

---

[135] Grousset in PSPA I, p.72.
[136] Maximilian Streck, *Seleucia und Ktesiphon* (in *Der alte Orient*, 16 [1916-17], 3/4). 1917, pp.17f.
[137] Debevoise, *A Political History of Parthia*, pp.xxvi,27.
[138] E. T. Newell in PSPA I, pp.475-492.
[139] Wilfred H. Schoff, *Parthian Stations by Isidore of Charax, An Account of the Overland Trade Route between the Levant and India in the First Century B.C., The Greek Text, with a Translation and Commentary*. 1914. §11, p.9.
[140] *ibid.*, §6, p.7.
[141] Oscar Reuther in PSPA I, p.413.
[142] A. T. Olmstead in JAOS 56 (1936), p.253 n.40; Debevoise, *A Political History of Parthia*, p.27.

Mithradates II (c.123-88/87 B.C.), "to whom," as Trogus Pompeius wrote, "his achievements procured the surname of Great; for . . . he carried on many wars, with great bravery, against his neighbors, and added many provinces to the Parthian kingdom,"[143] and Gotarzes II (A.D. c.38-51) have left us two badly damaged carvings on the Rock of Behistun near the monument of Darius I. In the first, Mithradates is seen with three officials including "Gotarzes, the satrap of satraps," who as Gotarzes I (91-81/80 B.C.) became his co-regent and successor; and in the second, "Gotarzes, the son of Gew," or Gotarzes II, is charging an enemy, while a winged Victory hovers overhead to crown him with a wreath.[144]

VOLOGASES I

Vologases I (A.D. 51/52-79/80) is of special interest to us because he is probably the king called Valkhash in Dinkard iv, 24 (SBE XXXVII, p.413).[145] This passage reads: "Valkhash, descendant of Ashkan, in each district, just as he had come forth, ordered the careful preservation, and making of memoranda for the royal city, of the Avesta and Zand as it had purely come unto them, and also of whatever instruction, due to it, had remained written about, as well as deliverable by the tongue through a high-priest, in a scattered state in the country of Iran, owing to the ravages and devastation of Alexander and the cavalry and infantry of the Arumans."[146] According to this statement, then, Vologases I was responsible for first undertaking to have the remnants of the scattered Zoroastrian scriptures gathered together again. It is entirely credible to picture the king in this role, especially inasmuch as his brother Tiridates is definitely known to have been a Zoroastrian. Tacitus (A.D. c.55-c.117) says that Tiridates was a priest,[147] and Pliny (A.D. 23-79) calls him a Magian and relates that he was so scrupulous in the observance of the regulations of his faith that on a journey to Rome he went all the way by land in order to avoid defiling the sea.[148]

[143] Justin XLII, 2. tr. Watson, p.278.

[144] Ernst E. Herzfeld, *Am Tor von Asien, Felsdenkmale aus Irans Heldenzeit.* 1920, pp.39f.

[145] Neilson C. Debevoise in *The American Journal of Semitic Languages and Literatures.* 47 (1930-31), p.81.

[146] cf. also Dinkard VII, 3 (SBE XLVII, p.82): "Even after the devastation which happened owing to Alexander, those who were rulers after him brought back much to the collection from a scattered state; and there are some who have ordered the keeping of it in the treasury of Shapan."

[147] *Annals* xv, 24. tr. John Jackson, LCL (1931-37) IV, p.253.

[148] *Natural History* xxx, 6. tr. John Bostock and H. T. Riley (Bohn's Classical Library), v (1856), p.428.

KUH-I-KHWAJA

While relatively few Parthian ruins are yet known on the Iranian plateau proper, there is an interesting and impressive monument of the first century A.D. in the east in Sistan which should be mentioned before leaving this period. This is at the Kuh-i-Khwaja, the "Mount of the Lord," where a broad flat-topped hill stands in a lake. The place may well have been sacred in very ancient times,[149] and it has even been surmised that it was here that Vishtaspa gave a safe refuge to Zoroaster against Gaumata.[150] On the southern slope of the mount are the ruins of a palace and temple, probably dating in their original form from the first century A.D. and then having been restored in the third century. The palace was built around a large court, while the temple stood upon a higher platform. The temple had an inner room with a cupola over it supported on four corner-piers, and around this inner room ran a narrow closed passageway. There was also a monumental entrance. In the room under the cupola the foundation of a stone fire altar was still preserved and the altar itself was fallen not far away. Such, then, was a first century fire temple.

As for the palace, the walls of many of its rooms were originally painted. Besides ornamental compositions, there was a scene on the back wall of the gallery showing a king and queen standing under something like a canopy, and there was a representation on the window wall of the gallery of a series of gods. The gods were portrayed in Greek style and with Greek garments, but their emblems and attributes are half Greek and half oriental. One wears a winged helmet. In purely Greek art there would have been two wings and the god would have been Hermes. Here there are three wings and the god is Vrthragna, a deity of the sun and of war, closely associated with Mithra, and fully described in his ten avatars in the fourteenth or Bahram Yasht (sbe xxiii, pp.231-248). Another god holds a trident, which in Greek symbolism would indicate Poseidon; here it is the mark of Śiva, the god of India. It was thus a far-reaching syncretism which prevailed at this place, in which Zoroastrianism was mingled with elements from both Greece and India.[151]

[149] Phyllis Ackerman in pspa i, pp.874-877.
[150] Herzfeld, *Archaeological History of Iran*, p.62.
[151] Herzfeld, *Archaeological History of Iran*, pp.58-74; *Iran in the Ancient East*, pp.291-297.

6. THE SASANIAN PERIOD, A.D. c.229-651

THE revolt which put an end to the empire of the Parthians began in the province of Fars, or, as the Greeks called it, Persis. Here at the beginning of the third century A.D. the Sasanian family rose to power. Their name was derived from a certain Sasan, who had been a priest in the fire temple of Anahita at Istakhr.[152] In this city, Ardashir, son of Papak, son of Sasan, was recognized as king. Under his leadership the rebellion against the authority of the Parthians went forward swiftly. In the fighting which broke out, the Parthian king Vologases V was evidently killed (A.D. c.222/223), and about A.D. 227 Artabanus V also suffered defeat and death. The Parthian forces fled to the mountains and endeavored to continue the struggle under Artavasdes, but he, too, was finally captured and executed in Ctesiphon (A.D. c.229). Ardashir I thereby became master of all Iran, and the empire which he founded, endured until the victory of the Arabs in A.D. 651.[153]

Throughout most of its history the Sasanian empire was engaged in conflict with the Roman and the Byzantine empires. This was a continuation of the Greco-Persian and the Roman-Parthian wars, and was mutually destructive to both the east and the west. Nevertheless, under the Sasanian kings Persia enjoyed a period of great cultural brilliance and made outstanding achievements in architecture, sculpture, painting, metalwork and textiles. The Sasanian capitals were at Istakhr and Ctesiphon.[154]

ARDASHIR I

Ardashir I assumed the title, "King of the kings of the Iranians," and as this suggests the rise of the Sasanian empire represented a revival of national Iranian or Persian feeling. For this reason the

---

[152] Schmidt, *Flights over Ancient Cities of Iran*, p.12.

[153] The Sasanid kings were: Ardashir I, c.229-241; Shapur I, 241-272; Hormuzd I, 272-273; Bahram I, 273-276; Bahram II, 276-293; Bahram III, 293; Narseh (Narses), 293-302; Hormuzd II, 302-310; Shapur II, 310-379; Ardashir II, 379-383; Shapur III, 383-388; Bahram IV, 388-399; Yazdegerd I, 399-420; Bahram V Gor, 420-438; Yazdegerd II, 438-457; Hormuzd III, 457-459; Peroz, 459-484; Balash, 484-488; Kavadh I, 488-531; Djamasp, 496-498; Chosroes (Khusrov or Khusrau) I Anushirvan, 531-579; Hormuzd IV, 579-590; Chosroes II Parvez, 590-628; Bahram VI Cobin, Bistam, 590-596; Kavadh II Sheroe, 628; Ardashir III, 628-630; Shahrbaraz, 630; Boran and others, 630-632; Yazdegerd III, 632-651. Theodor Nöldeke, *Geschichte der Perser und Araber zur Zeit der Sasaniden, aus der arabischen Chronik des Tabari übersetzt und mit ausführlichen Erläuterungen und Ergänzungen versehn.* 1879, p.435; Eduard Meyer in EB XVII, p.583.

[154] Grousset in PSPA I, p.74.

empire is also known as Neo-Persian, and its kings consciously and vigorously continued the traditions of their Achaemenid predecessors. In this reawakening of Iranian sentiment the Zoroastrian faith played an important part. Ardashir I took the designation "Mazdayasnian," and the Mazdean cult became the religion of state.[155]

According to the Dinkard (IV, 25f. SBE XXXVII, p.414), the first two Sasanian kings, Ardashir I and Shapur I, were responsible for carrying forward the collection of the Zoroastrian writings which Vologases I had begun: "That Artakhshatar [Ardashir I], king of kings, who was son of Papak, summoned Tosar, and also all that scattered instruction, as true authority, to the capital; Tosar having arrived, him alone he approved, and, dismissing the rest of the high-priests, he also gave this command, namely: 'For us every other exposition of the Mazda-worshiping religion becomes removed, because even now there is no information or knowledge of it below.' Shahpuhar [Shapur I], king of kings and son of Artakhshatar, again brought together also the writings which were distinct from religion, about the investigation of medicine and astronomy, time, place, and quality, creation, existence, and destruction, the submission of a wild beast, evidence, and other records and resources that were scattered among the Hindus, and in Arum[156] and other lands; and he ordered their collocation again with the Avesta, and the presentation of a correct copy of each to the treasury of Shapigan; and the settlement of all the erring upon the Mazda-worshiping religion, for proper consideration, was effected."

FIRUZABAD

As one of the first marks of his defiance of the Parthians, Ardashir I had built in southern Fars the city of Ardashir-Khurra ("Ardashir's Glory") or Gur, which is now known as Firuzabad. As may be seen in the air view in Fig. 35, the city was surrounded with great circular defenses which are about three-quarters of a mile in diameter. Exactly in the center of the circle one structure still remains standing above ground. This is a tapering pyramidal tower, on which traces of steep stairways can still be seen. It is thought that this may have been a tower to bear the everlasting fire of the Zoroastrian faith.[157]

At the edge of the Firuzabad valley are the impressive, domed

---

[155] Eduard Meyer in EB XVII, p.580; Arthur Christensen, *L'Iran sous les Sassanides.* 1936, p.136.
[156] The eastern empire of the Romans.
[157] Schmidt, *Flights over Ancient Cities of Iran,* p.20.

ruins of the palace of Ardashir I, as shown in the air view in Fig. 36.[158] Not far away, where a rocky gorge opens into the plain of Firuzabad, is a rock carving symbolizing the victory of Ardashir I over the Arsacids.[159] Three tournaments are shown between three pairs of horsemen. At the right Ardashir I is engaged in combat with Artabanus V; in the center his son Shapur is slaying the vizier of Artabanus; and at the left a page of Ardashir is dragging an antagonist from the saddle. Yet farther up the gorge a second rock sculpture portrays the divine investiture of Ardashir I.[160] The same theme is also the subject of rock carvings of Ardashir I at Naqsh-i-Rajab[161] and Naqsh-i-Rustam. Of the three scenes of investiture just mentioned, that at Naqsh-i-Rustam is the finest and is probably the masterpiece of early Sasanian rock sculpture. A photograph of this monument is shown in Fig. 37.[162] Here Ardashir and the god Hormuzd, as Ahura Mazda was now called, face each other on horseback, and the king receives from the god the ribboned circlet which was the symbol of power. The composition is in perfect symmetry. The flowing cloak of the god is balanced by the figure of an attendant behind the king, and the prostrate form of the evil being Ahriman beneath the steed of Hormuzd is matched by the body of Artabanus V under the horse of Ardashir. The portrayal of the enemy as fallen beneath the feet of the conqueror is a frequent motif in the Sasanian rock reliefs, and evidently has a magical import, the desire being to make the triumph permanent.[163] In this aspect, then, these reliefs may be compared with the rock pictures of prehistoric and primitive man. An inscription in three languages, Arsacidan and Sasanian Pahlavi and Greek, accompanies the investiture scene and reads: "This represents the servant of Hormuzd, the divine Ardashir, king of kings of Iran, scion of a divine family, son of the divine Papak, of the kings."[164]

SHAPUR I

Shapur I (A.D. 241-272) was the son of Ardashir I, and he did a number of things which paralleled the work of his father. As we have seen (p.113), the Dinkard states that he, too, was interested in the

---

[158] Sarre and Herzfeld, *Iranische Felsreliefs*, p.128.

[159] Herzfeld, *Iran in the Ancient East*, Pl. CIX.

[160] *ibid.*, Pl. CVIII,upper.   [161] *ibid.*, Pl. XVIII,lower.   [162] PSPA IV, Pl. 154,A.

[163] Herzfeld, *Archaeological History of Iran*, pp.81f.,84,86; *Am Tor von Asien*, p.154 n.102.

[164] Friedrich Sarre in PSPA I, p.594.

collecting of the Zoroastrian writings. Like his father also he built a new city. It was located some distance southwest of Istakhr, and bore the king's own name, Shapur.[165] As shown in the air view in Fig. 38, the site is between a curving river and a broad, deep moat which appears in the upper part of the picture. At the left on a rocky spur is the citadel of the town. Yet farther to the left where the stream flows out of a rocky gorge are a number of rock sculptures some of which belong to Shapur I and some to his successors.[166] They include representations of the victory of Shapur I over the Roman emperor Valerian (A.D. 260), a scene which Shapur portrayed repeatedly and of which the finest example is at Naqsh-i-Rustam.[167] Shapur I further followed the pattern set by his father in that he had his own investiture by Hormuzd represented in a rock sculpture at Naqsh-i-Rajab which is very similar to that of Ardashir I at Naqsh-i-Rustam.[168]

Bahram I, who was the younger son of Shapur I and who reigned A.D. 273-276, likewise followed the example of his father and grandfather in the portrayal of his investiture. At Shapur there is a fine panel (Fig. 39) which is almost a copy of the sculptures of Ardashir I and Shapur I. The king, at the right, receives the symbol of authority from Hormuzd, at the left. Both king and god are mounted upon horses which are sculptured with superior artistic skill.[169]

It was during the reigns of Shapur I, Hormuzd I and Bahram I that the remarkable prophet Mani lived and worked. His teachings, which were a combination of Mazdean, Jewish, Christian, Gnostic and Buddhist elements, were first promulgated in public on the coronation day of Shapur I, and met with some favor on the part of that monarch. The Zoroastrian priests opposed him strongly, however, and he soon went into a long exile during which he preached in the Far East. Returning with royal favor under Hormuzd I, he was soon thereafter (A.D. c.274) given up to a horrible death at the hands of the Mazdean clergy by Bahram I.[170]

Going on to the time of King Narseh (A.D. 293-302), we find at Naqsh-i-Rustam an investiture scene (Fig. 40) where all the partici-

[165] Georges Salles and R. Ghirshman in *Revue des arts asiatiques*. 10 (1936), pp.117-129; 12 (1938), pp.12-19.
[166] Sarre and Herzfeld, *Iranische Felsreliefs*, pp.213-223.
[167] FLP p.198.
[168] Sarre and Herzfeld, *Iranische Felsreliefs*, p.97.
[169] Sarre in PSPA I, p.597.
[170] A. V. Williams Jackson, *Researches in Manichaeism with Special Reference to the Turfan Fragments*. 1932, p.6.

pants are standing and where Narseh, in the center, receives the symbol of authority from the goddess Anahita, at the right. The figure at the left is that of an attendant.[171]

TAQ-I-BUSTAN

Thus far in Sasanian history the most important rock sculptures have been at Naqsh-i-Rustam and Shapur, but by the last part of the fourth century A.D. yet a third place came into prominence. This was at Taq-i-Bustan near Kermanshah. Here springs pour forth from a great rocky hill into what is now an artificial lake (Fig. 41).[172] At the right near the modern building is a rock panel with a relief of Ardashir II (A.D. 379-383). This may be seen in greater detail in Fig. 42.[173] The king stands in the center and receives in outstretched hand the usual emblem of authority which is extended to him by the god Hormuzd. Participating in the investiture, at the left, is the god Mithra, distinguished by the radiant sun rays. Mithra stands upon a lotus, a motif probably reflecting influence from India, while Ardashir II and Hormuzd tread upon the prostrate form of an enemy.

Some distance to the left of this relief is a small grotto which was probably constructed by Shapur III (A.D. 383-388) to serve as a resting place from the hunt. It was adorned by the same king with figures of himself and of Shapur II, and with inscriptions describing both of them as "Mazda-worshiping" kings. The much larger grotto to the left is the Taq-i-Bustan or "Grotto of the Garden" proper, which gives its name to the entire place. Since it probably dates from two centuries later under Chosroes II Parvez it will be mentioned again below in its chronological order (p.119).[174]

SHIZ

Bahram V Gor reigned from A.D. 420 to 438. The Arab historian Tabari tells how, early in his reign, Bahram Gor fought victoriously against the Turanians. On his way home the king passed through Azerbaijan, and sent to the fire temple in Shiz the treasures he had taken from the Turanian leader, as well as the latter's queen herself whom he made to serve as a priestess in that temple. Tabari's account reads: "Bahram's route, on returning from that campaign, lay

[171] Sarre and Herzfeld, *Iranische Felsreliefs*, pp.84-88.
[172] Herzfeld, *Am Tor von Asien*, Pl. xxviii.
[173] *ibid.*, Pl. xxix.   [174] *ibid.*, pp.57-71.

through Azerbaijan. Accordingly he sent to the fire temple in Shiz the rubies and other jewels which were in the crown of the [vanquished] Khakan, and also his own sword, inlaid with pearls and jewels, as well as many other ornaments. The Khatun, the wife of the Khakan, he made a servant in the temple."[175] Ibn Hurdadhbah, it will be remembered (p.86), also referred to "the fire temple Adharjushnas" in the city of Shiz; and in the geography of Yaqut there is furthermore an extended description of the same city and fire temple. The passage in Yaqut, which cites the poet Mis'ar ibn Muhalhal (A.D. c.940) and another unnamed author, runs as follows: "Here is what Mis'ar ibn Muhalhal says about Shiz: 'This town is situated . . . in the midst of mountains containing mines of gold, quicksilver, lead, silver, orpiment, and amethysts. . . . Walls enclose the city, and at the center of it is a lake whose depth is not known. . . . I sounded it to a depth of more than 14,000 cubits, without the plumb line coming to a rest. . . . There is also at Shiz a fire temple, which is for the inhabitants the object of great veneration. From it are lighted all the sacred fires of the Gabars from the East to the West. The dome is surmounted by a silver crescent, which is considered a talisman, and which many rulers have tried in vain to remove from its foundation. One of the remarkable things in regard to the temple is that the fire has been kept burning in it for 700 years, and has not left any ashes and has not gone out once.' Yaqut, the humble author of this book, adds: 'This whole story comes from Abu Dulaf Mis'ar ibn Muhalhal, the poet, and I cannot be responsible for its authenticity, for he tells things which are exaggerated and untrue. I have simply transcribed it as I found it. Allah knows the truth.' Another author states that at Shiz there is the fire temple of Adharakhsh which is highly celebrated among the Magians, and that it was customary for the kings of Persia, when they ascended the throne, to make a pilgrimage thither on foot. The inhabitants of Maragha call the place Gazna."[176]

In the passages just quoted the fire temple at Shiz was called Adharakhsh or Adharjushnas. This is evidently the same as the Atur Gushnasp (Gushasp) which is mentioned in the Bundahish (xvii, 7. SBE v, p.63) as one of the famous fires of Zoroastrianism.[177] It is ex-

---

[175] Nöldeke, *Geschichte der Perser und Araber zur Zeit der Sasaniden, aus der arabischen Chronik des Tabari*, p.104, cf. pp.100,102.

[176] de Meynard, *Dictionnaire géographique, historique et littéraire de la Perse et des contrées adjacentes extrait du Mo'djem el-Bouldan de Yaqout*, pp.367-370; A. V. Williams Jackson, *Persia Past and Present*, pp.132f.

[177] Jackson, *Zoroaster, The Prophet of Ancient Iran*, p.100.

tremely interesting that the site of the city of Shiz and the ruins of the fire temple of Atur Gushnasp have been identified with much probability. Shiz was located, it is believed, at the place now called Takht-i-Sulaiman or "Throne of Solomon." This site, with its well-preserved city wall, and the lake within the city, is shown in an air view in Fig. 43. Also visible to the left of the lake are the ruins of the ancient, domed fire temple.[178]

A vizier of Bahram V Gor named Mihrnarseh is said by Tabari to have built four villages in the valley of Gira and to have provided each with a fire temple.[179] The ruins of four fire temples, two large and two small, have actually been found in the Gira valley, which is between Firuzabad and Kazerun, and their identification with those founded by Mihrnarseh is most probable. In each case the central part of the temple consists of a square room roofed with a dome. Around this room runs a corridor which is roofed on the sides with vaults and at the corners with four small domes. The architectural plan is perfectly symmetrical, and appears to be a development from the simple, corridor-surrounded, square room of the fire temple at Kuh-i-Khwaja (p.111).[180]

Under Kavadh I (A.D. 488-531), the leader of a Manichean sect, Mazdak, preached a doctrine of radical communism and nonviolence, but suffered death together with many of his followers at the hands of Kavadh's son, Chosroes.[181] Chosroes or Khusrau I, surnamed Anushirvan ("of the Immortal Soul"), reigned from A.D. 531 to 579, and was one of the most illustrious of the Sasanian monarchs. He conducted economic reforms, and manifested a spirit of free thought and liberalism in religion. In his time orthodox Zoroastrianism suffered decadence.[182]

CHOSROES II PARVEZ

Chosroes II, who received the name of Parvez ("the Victorious"), reigned from A.D. 590 to 628. He was famed for the splendor of his

[178] Christensen, *L'Iran sous les Sassanides*, p.161; Schmidt, *Flights over Ancient Cities of Iran*, p.73, Pl. 89.

[179] Nöldeke, *Geschichte der Perser und Araber zur Zeit der Sasaniden, aus der arabischen Chronik des Tabari übersetzt*, pp.111f.

[180] Herzfeld, *Archaeological History of Iran*, pp.91-93; Ugo Monneret de Villard in *Bulletin of the American Institute for Persian Art and Archaeology.* 4 (1935-36), p.176.

[181] Arthur Christensen in *Det. Kgl. Danske Videnskabernes Selskab. Historish-filologiske Meddelelser.* IX, 6 (1925).

[182] Christensen, *L'Iran sous les Sassanides*, p.429.

oriental court, and legend busied itself with his remarkable possessions which included a rich golden throne, a very swift Roman horse
called Shabdez, and a large and beautifully ornamented carpet
known as "the Spring of Chosroes" which was spread in the palace
at Ctesiphon and gave the illusion of spring even in the midst of
winter.[183]

It was probably in the time of Chosroes II that the large grotto
at Taq-i-Bustan was constructed (p.116). The walls of this grotto
are covered with sculptures. On the side walls are fine, lively scenes
of boar and deer hunting. On the back wall there are two scenes. In
the lower panel, sculptured in very high relief, is a colossal figure of
Chosroes II on his famous horse Shabdez (Fig. 44);[184] in the upper
panel is an investiture scene where Chosroes II stands between Hormuzd at the right and Anahita at the left, both of whom are extending to him the symbols of authority (Fig. 45).[185]

Beneath the outward splendor of the reign of Chosroes II, however, Persia was growing weaker. In the last years of this king's reign
the East Roman emperor Heraclius (A.D. 610-641) successfully invaded Persia and burned the fire temple at Shiz, or Ganzaca as the
Byzantines called it.[186] Thereafter, virtual anarchy ensued and various kings and pretenders followed one another. The last Sasanid king
was Yazdegerd III who occupied the throne from A.D. 632 to 651.
In the year of his coronation the first Arab cohorts entered Persia,
and in A.D. 651 Yazdegerd III was assassinated and the entire land
fell to the Muslims.

While the official Muslim policy was that of toleration of Zoroastrianism,[187] there was actual persecution and controversy,[188] and the
Dinkard (SBE XXXVII, p.xxxi) speaks of "the ruin and devastation that
came from the Arabs." Under these circumstances the ancient Persian faith gradually almost disappeared from the land.

Only a remnant of Zoroastrians remained in Iran. Known as the Gabars, they number today less than ten thousand.[189] The others made
their way in the seventh and eighth centuries to India, where, as the
descendants and survivors of the ancient Persians, they are called the

[183] Jivanji Jamshedji Modi, *Asiatic Papers.* 4 (1929), pp.19-45.
[184] PSPA IV, Pl. 161,A.
[185] PSPA IV, Pl. 160,B; Herzfeld, *Am Tor von Asien*, pp.71-103.
[186] Georgius Cedrenus (A.D. c.1100), *Historiarum Compendium.* I, 721f. (Jacques
Paul Migne, *Patrologiae cursus completus. . . . Series Graeca.* 121 [1894], cols. 789f.).
[187] C. H. Becker in EI, I, p.1051.
[188] Eduard Meyer in EB XVII, p.586.
[189] D. Menant in HERE VI, pp.147-156.

Parsis.[190] Settling largely on the western coast, particularly in Bombay, they formed a distinct community which now contains some one hundred thousand persons. It was among the Parsis that Anquetil du Perron in the eighteenth century found and learned to read the ancient manuscripts of the Avesta, and thus inaugurated the modern western study of the religion of Zoroaster.[191]

[190] D. Menant in HERE IX, pp.640-650. For their funeral customs see also Nathan Söderblom and Louis H. Gray in HERE IV, pp.502-505; Jackson, *Persia Past and Present*, pp.387-400; Jivanji Jamshedji Modi, *The Funeral Ceremonies of the Parsees, Their Origin and Explanation*. 3d ed. 1923.

[191] Robert W. Rogers, *A History of Ancient Persia, from Its Earliest Beginnings to the Death of Alexander the Great*. 1929, pp.28-30; John W. Waterhouse, *Zoroastrianism*, pp.42f.

CHAPTER III

Hinduism

HINDUISM is the inclusive name for the native religion and social system of India, a faith and society to which some 245,-000,000 persons belong.

The words Hinduism and Hindu as well as India are derived ultimately from the Sanskrit *sindhu* meaning river, a term which was applied preeminently to the Indus River. The corresponding Persian form of the Sanskrit word was *hindu,* and the Achaemenian kings designated the area beside the Indus as Hinduka. The Greeks used forms based on Persian usage but in borrowing them omitted the *h* and made such words as Indos and India. While the former was the name of the river, the latter was applied to the whole country. Our names come from the Greek by way of Latin.

The land occupied by the nations of India and Pakistan is a vast quadrangle extending from the rampart of the Himalayas to a point only eight degrees from the equator. From east to west across its greatest breadth it stretches for some two thousand miles, and from north to south its length is nearly the same. Three regions distinguish themselves within the land. The first is that of the stupendous mountain wall which curves like a scimitar along the northern frontier. The peaks of the Himalayas and the adjacent Karakoram range are the highest in the world, and separate the subcontinent from the remainder of Asia with a formidable barrier. The wall of mountains continues in the extreme northwest with the Hindu Kush, and runs down all the way to the sea with such subsidiary but not insignificant ranges as the Sulaiman, named for the Biblical Solomon.[1] Here, however, there are ways through, and the Kabul River, and the Khyber, Bolan and other passes, provide gateways between India and Afghanistan.

The second division of the land is made up of the plains which curve across the north from the Arabian Sea to the Bay of Bengal. These flat and fertile regions are traversed by three important river systems. The first is that of the Indus. Its main sources are north of the Himalayas and it flows through Kashmir, then curves to the

---

[1] The legend is that Solomon visited India to marry Balkis, and returning tarried on these hills to allow his bride to look back on her beloved land. EB XXI, p.536.

southwest and empties at last into the Arabian Sea below Karachi. The Indus has five main tributaries, the Jhelum, Chenab, Ravi, Beas, and Sutlej, and the region traversed by the rivers is known as the Punjab or "five waters." The alluvial plain built up and watered by the Indus in the last three hundred and fifty miles of its journey to the sea is called Sind.

The Ganges forms the second river system. With its numerous tributaries, it drains the whole southern slope of the Himalayas. So level are the plains it flows across on its way to the sea, that nearly a thousand miles from its mouth it is only five hundred feet above sea level. The third system is the Brahmaputra (Son of Brahma), which rises beyond the Himalayas not far from the sources of the Indus but flows in the opposite direction, crossing southern Tibet under the name of the Tsangpo or "purifier," then pouring through mountain gorges and finally coming down across Assam to join the Ganges and flow with it into the Bay of Bengal.

The third main geographical division is the plateau which covers most of the southern or peninsular part of the land and is known as the Deccan. On the east and west this tableland falls off toward the coasts in hills and slopes known as the Eastern and Western Ghats.

As elsewhere in the world, so also in India prehistoric man made his appearance within the Pleistocene epoch. The stone tools of his Paleolithic culture are found all the way from Madras in the southeast to the Punjab in the northwest.[2] A group of hand axes and other implements from Paleolithic times which were found in the Soan valley in the Punjab is shown in Fig. 46.[3] Neolithic tools also are found at various places, and the discovery of the Late Stone Age sites at Sukkur and Rohri on the lower Indus in Upper Sind is particularly important. These sites are near Mohenjo-daro, which is one of the chief places where remains of India's first known civilization are found, and suggest that that civilization was the result of an indigenous development as well as of influence from abroad.[4]

[2] H. de Terra and T. T. Paterson, *Studies on the Ice Age in India and Associated Human Cultures* (Carnegie Institution of Washington Publication No. 493). 1939, pp.301-312,327-330; Hallam L. Movius, Jr., *Early Man and Pleistocene Stratigraphy in Southern and Eastern Asia* (Papers of the Peabody Museum of American Archaeology and Ethnology, Harvard University, XIX, 3). 1944, Fig. 45, p.105; V. D. Krishnaswami in *Ancient India, Bulletin of the Archaeological Survey of India.* 3 (Jan. 1947), pp.11-57.

[3] De Terra and Paterson, *Studies on the Ice Age in India and Associated Human Cultures,* Pl. XXXI.

[4] *ibid.,* pp.331-336.

1. THE PRE-ARYAN PERIOD

THE civilization just referred to emerged in the Chalcolithic Age, when the use of stone for implements was gradually being supplanted by the employment of metals, and continued in the Bronze Age. At the same time civilization was also advancing notably in the valleys of the Tigris and Euphrates and of the Nile, and there is clear evidence of the cultural interrelationship of all three areas.[5] While the Indian civilization was thus related to a wider Afrasian culture, it was nevertheless a particular focus of that culture and had its own distinctive character. Its most important known centers were at Harappa, Mohenjo-daro and Chanhu-daro, and it probably flourished from about 2500 to about 1500 B.C.[6]

HARAPPA, MOHENJO-DARO AND CHANHU-DARO

From the area of its general distribution this is often called the Indus valley civilization;[7] from the type site where its distinctive elements were first recognized it is more precisely designated the Harappa civilization. Harappa is on the Ravi River in the Punjab, fifteen miles southwest of Montgomery, and its mounds have long been a prominent landmark.[8] In 1853 and 1856 the site was visited by Alexander Cunningham, who became the first director general of the Archaeological Survey of India. In the twenties and thirties of the present century, eleven years of intensive explorations were conducted here;[9] again in 1946 another season of work was devoted to further excavation.[10]

Mohenjo-daro, "the Place of the Dead," is four hundred miles from Harappa, on the lower Indus, twenty-five miles south of Larkana in Sind. In 1922 Mr. R. D. Banerji was studying a second century Buddhist stupa which stands at this place, and discovered that

[5] FLP pp.19,75.

[6] For other prehistoric sites and their cultural sequences see W. Norman Brown in JAOS Supplement 4 (1939), pp.35f.; Stuart Piggot in *Ancient India*. 1 (Jan. 1946), pp.8-26; and *Prehistoric India to 1000 B.C.* 1950.

[7] Ernest Mackay, *Early Indus Civilization*. 2d ed. rev. by Dorothy Mackay. 1948.

[8] *India's Past, A Survey of Her Literatures, Religions, Languages and Antiquities*. 1927, p.9.

[9] Madho Sarup Vats, in *Annual Bibliography of Indian Archaeology* (Kern Institute—Leyden). 12 (1937), pp.1-9; and *Excavations at Harappā, Being an Account of Archaeological Excavations at Harappā Carried Out between the Years 1920-21 and 1933-34. 2 vols. 1940.

[10] R. E. M. Wheeler in *Ancient India*. 3 (Jan. 1947), pp.58-130.

beneath the ground was a buried ancient city.[11] In that and the following years the site was extensively and carefully excavated, although the subterranean water level had risen to such a point that it was no longer possible to reach the lowest strata.[12]

Chanhu-daro too, is in the lower Indus valley, eighty miles south of Mohenjo-daro. Once directly on the river, the site is now twelve miles from it, the Indus having shifted its course that far to the west. In 1931 Mr. N. G. Majumdar examined the mounds at this place and recognized their ancient date and importance. In 1935-1936 excavations were conducted there by the first American Archaeological Expedition to India.[13]

Harappa and Mohenjo-daro were large cities, Chanhu-daro a much smaller town, but all three represent what was essentially a complex urban civilization. The cities were well built and carefully planned; there must have been a strong central government.[14]

At Mohenjo-daro the main street was thirty-three feet in width, and all the streets ran due north and south or east and west, intersecting at right angles. The houses of the ordinary townspeople were extraordinarily commodious and substantial. Usually built of burnt brick, many had excellent bathrooms, as well as elaborate drainage systems and rubbish chutes for the disposal of refuse. The most prominent public buildings were a large bath at Mohenjo-daro and a great granary at Harappa. No large palaces or temples were found.

Both agriculture and trade were sources of wealth. Wheat, barley and the date palm were cultivated. The short-horned bull, humped zebu or Brahmany bull, elephant, buffalo, camel, sheep, pig and dog were domesticated. Interchange of goods may have extended indirectly to Burma or China on the east; it certainly reached to Mesopotamia on the west.[15]

Copper and bronze were employed for weapons and utensils, while

[11] John Cumming, ed., *Revealing India's Past, A Co-operative Record of Archaeological Conservation and Exploration in India and Beyond, by Twenty-two Authorities, British, Indian and Continental.* 1939, pp.99f.

[12] John Marshall, ed., *Mohenjo-daro and the Indus Civilization, Being an Official Account of Archaeological Excavations at Mohenjo-daro Carried Out by the Government of India between the Years 1922 and 1927.* 3 vols. 1931; E. J. H. Mackay, *Further Excavations at Mohenjo-daro, Being an Official Account of Archaeological Excavations at Mohenjo-daro Carried Out by the Government of India between the Years 1927 and 1931.* 2 vols. 1937-38.

[13] E. J. H. Mackay, *Chanhu-daro Excavations 1935-36* (American Oriental Series, 20). 1943.

[14] V. Gordon Childe, *What Happened in History.* 1942. p.120.

[15] V. Gordon Childe, *New Light on the Most Ancient East.* 1935, p.210.

gold and silver were used for ornaments, as were also amazonite, lapis lazuli, ivory and shells. Fine pottery was made on a fast wheel and often decorated very beautifully, black painting on a red slip being perhaps most characteristic. Several examples of painted pottery from Mohenjo-daro are shown in Fig. 47.[16]

That a high degree of proficiency was attained in sculpturing is indicated by a number of finds. The finest piece of statuary unearthed at Mohenjo-daro is pictured in Fig. 48.[17] It is a steatite statue now seven inches high, possibly representing one of the ancient inhabitants of the city. The figure is shown with an elaborately decorated shawl over the left shoulder and under the right arm. A short beard and close-cut mustache are worn, and the hair is parted in the middle. The eyes are narrow and straight, and the nose prominent and well formed. Several other facial types are reflected by other statuettes and figurines found at Mohenjo-daro. One, with thick lips and coarse nose, has been said to be comparable to the surviving aboriginal tribes of south India, and another is claimed to be Mongoloid in character.[18]

Among the most numerous and distinctive products of art were the seals. These were of both the cylinder and the stamp variety. The latter, consisting of square tablets of steatite with a boss on the back and engraving on the face, is by far the more common. These vary in size from about one-half inch square to two and one-half inches square. They have a perforated boss on the back which suggests that they may have been carried as amulets. The intaglio engravings are very beautifully executed. They usually show some animal such as the "unicorn," bull, zebu, elephant, rhinoceros, tiger, buffalo, crocodile, antelope, or a hybrid creature, and also have a brief inscription in a pictographic script. This script has not yet been deciphered.

RELIGION OF THE PRE-ARYANS

From the archeological remains of the Harappa civilization it is possible to learn something of the religion which prevailed in this pre-Aryan period. A very large number of human figurines has been unearthed at Harappa, Mohenjo-daro and Chanhu-daro, the majority of which are female. Some of these, like the figure of a woman kneading dough or holding a dish of cakes in her arms, may have been

[16] Marshall, ed., *Mohenjo-daro and the Indus Civilization*, III, Pl. LXXXVII.
[17] *ibid.*, III, Pl. XCVIII,3.
[18] Childe, *New Light on the Most Ancient East*, pp.208f.

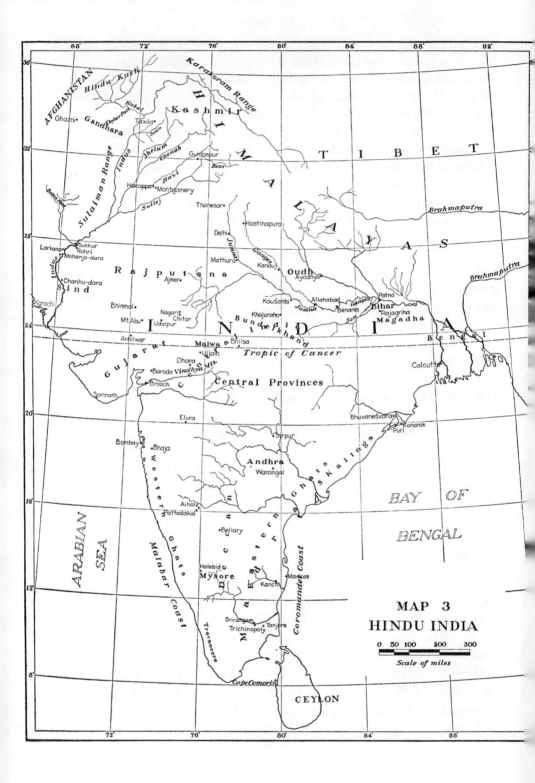

68°   72°   76°   80°   84°   88°   92°

36°

AFGHANISTAN
Hindu Kush
Ghazni• Gandhara
Kabul
Khyber Pass
Taxila•
Karakoram Range
Kashmir
H   I   M   A   L   A   Y   A   S
T   I   B   E   T

32°
Sulaiman Range
Indus
Jhelum
Soan
Chenab
Gurdaspur•
Beas
Ravi
Harappa•
•Montgomery
Sutlej
Thanesar•
Brahmaputra

28°
Larkana•
Sukkur
Rohri•
Mohenjo-daro•
Chanhu-daro•
Sind
Karachi•
Indus
Rajputana
Ajmer•
Delhi•
Mathura•
•Hastinapura
Jumna
Ganges
Kanauj•
Oudh
Ayodhya•
Brahmaputra

24°
Babul River
Bhinmal•
Nagari•
Mt.Abu•
Chitor
•Udaipur
I   N   D
Kauśambi•
Khajuraho•
Bundelkhand
Jumna
Allahabad
Benares•
Ganges
Son
Patna•
Bihar
Rajagriha
Magadha
I   A
Bengal

Anhilwar•
Gujarat
Malwa•
Ujjain•
•Bhilsa
Tropic of Cancer
Calcutta•

20°
Somnath•
Dhara•
•Baroda
Vindhya Mts.
Broach•
Central Provinces
Elura•
Bhuvanesvara•
Puri•
Konarak

Bombay•
•Bhaja
Sirpur•
Andhra
Warangal•
Kalinga
BAY   OF

16°
ARABIAN
SEA
Western Ghats
Malabar Coast
Aihole•
Pattadakal•
•Bellary
Eastern Ghats
Coromandel Coast
BENGAL

12°
Halebid⊙
Mysore
Kanchi•
Deccan
•Madras
Srirangam•
•Tanjore
Trichinopoly•
MAP   3
HINDU INDIA
0   50 100   200   300
Scale of miles

8°
Travancore
Cape Comorin•
CEYLON

72°   76°   80°   84°   88°

toys or dolls for children. Others, however, holding children or obviously pregnant, may have been intended as aids toward procuring offspring; while many which were standing, almost nude figures, comparable to similar objects found in Mesopotamia, Palestine and Egypt, must have been effigies of a mother goddess. Such figurines are a link, then, between the dynamistic statuettes of the Old Stone Age (p.30) and the legion village goddesses to which many people in India still look as the authoresses of fertility and the givers of life and all things. They may also foreshadow the form of worship known in historic Hinduism as Śaktism. Here the object of veneration is a personification of the female energy (śakti).

In addition to the mother goddess, a male god was also an object of worship. A striking portrayal of this deity appears on the roughly carved seal shown in Fig. 49, which was uncovered at Mohenjo-daro.[19] A three-faced personage is seated on a low platform, with his legs bent double beneath him, and feet placed heel to heel with toes turned down. His extended arms are encased in bangles, and more ornaments cover his chest. His head is crowned with a tall headdress from which long horns project. At his right hand are an elephant and a tiger, at his left a rhinoceros and a buffalo, and beneath the throne are two deer. At the top of the seal is an inscription of seven characters.

The identification of this personage as the prototype of Śiva, one of the supreme deities in later Hinduism, is a plausible guess. His three faces accord with the representation of Śiva as often having three, four or five faces, and usually three eyes supposed to denote insight into the past, present and future. His posture is that of a yogi, and Śiva is regarded as the typical ascetic and prince of all yogis. He is accompanied by wild animals, and Śiva is called the lord of beasts. His horned headdress is comparable to the trisul or trident later used as royal insignia, a religious symbol in early Buddhist sculpture, and often specially associated in Hinduism with Śiva.

There appears to have been much animism in the religion of the early Indus civilization, and there is evidence for the worship of trees and animals, as well as for cults of baetylic and phallic stones. But the figure just considered may also show that the conception of higher deities in personal form already existed. If both a mother goddess and a prototypal Śiva were worshiped, then the people of the Indus valley had already advanced from dynamistic and ani-

---

[19] Marshall, ed., *Mohenjo-daro and the Indus Civilization*, I, Pl. XII,17.

mistic foundations to the creation of distinctive aspects of India's historical polytheism. "Their religion," says Sir John Marshall, speaking of the Indus peoples, "is so characteristically Indian as hardly to be distinguishable from still living Hinduism or at least from that aspect of it which is bound up with animism and the cults of Śiva and the Mother Goddess—still the two most potent forces in popular worship."[20] It is also interesting that in this ancient civilization there appear symbols, such as the swastika, which likewise have a religious significance in historic India.

[20] *ibid.*, I, p.vii.

2. THE VEDIC PERIOD

IT WAS probably in the second half of the second millennium, sometime between 1500 and 1200 B.C., that a new people poured into India. They were the Aryans, who came from the northwest and settled in the Punjab, whence they later moved on eastward. Their language belongs to the same family as that embracing Greek, Latin, Celtic, Teutonic and Slavic. Our knowledge concerning them comes from the Vedas, which are collections of ancient religious hymns and other writings.[21] The language of these compositions is simply called Vedic, and is an early type of the Sanskrit language which was given its classical formulation by the Hindu grammarians, especially Panini in probably the fourth century B.C. The word *veda* is a Sanskrit noun meaning "knowledge,"[22] and is applied to these works as the preeminent compilation of religious knowledge.

THE FOUR VEDAS

In its wider use the word Veda includes a very large number of texts—hymns, exegesis, liturgy, speculation—and in its narrower usage the term refers particularly to the four Vedas. Of these the Rig-Veda is the oldest and most important.[23] It comprises over a thousand hymns to the gods, arranged in ten books called *mandalas* or circles. Six of these are known as family books, and are ascribed to different families of *rishis* or inspired poets. Fig. 50 shows the opening hymn to Agni in a manuscript of the Rig-Veda belonging to the Preussische Staatsbibliothek in Berlin.[24] The Yajur-Veda contains formulas in verse and prose with exegesis for use in the ritual of worship.[25] The Sama-Veda presents hymns for chanting often

[21] For this and other literature of India see Arthur A. Macdonell, *A History of Sanskrit Literature*. 1900; M. Winternitz, *Geschichte der indischen Litteratur* (Die Litteraturen des Ostens in Einzeldarstellungen). 3 vols. (I, 2d ed.), 1907-20; Helmuth von Glasenapp, *Die Literaturen Indiens von ihren Anfängen bis zur Gegenwart* (Handbuch der Literaturwissenschaft). 1929.

[22] It is derived from the root *vid*, "know," which is akin to the roots in Greek οἶδα, Latin *videre*, German *wissen*, and archaic English *wit*, "to know."

[23] tr. Ralph T. H. Griffith, *The Hymns of the Rigveda, Translated with a Popular Commentary*. 4 vols. 1896f. 3d ed. 2 vols. 1920-26. There are complete German translations by H. Grassmann (1876f.) and A. Ludwig (1876ff.). Selected hymns are translated by F. Max Müller in SBE XXXII and by Hermann Oldenberg in SBE XLVI.

[24] Von Glasenapp, *Die Literaturen Indiens von ihren Anfängen bis zur Gegenwart*, Fig. 26.

[25] tr. Ralph T. H. Griffith, *The Texts of the White Yajurveda, Translated with a Popular Commentary*. 1899.

accompanied by musical notations.[26] The Atharva-Veda is made up of hymns and magical charms.[27] The hymns of the Rig-Veda are generally believed to go back to the time from about 1500 to 1000 B.C.,[28] and they come down to us in a text which has been transmitted without substantial variation at least since the sixth or fifth century B.C., when the authors of the so-called Pratisakhya conducted important critical researches.[29] In this connection it must be remembered that it was long the custom to transmit the sacred texts by memorization and recital. Interesting illustrations occur later, when two pupils of the poet Valmiki recited the twenty-four thousand stanzas of the Ramayana in twenty-five days;[30] and when S. Pandit edited the Atharva-Veda using reciters of the text as well as manuscripts.

The geographical allusions which they contain make it evident that the hymns of the Rig-Veda were composed in India, and in particular there are many references to the rivers of the Indus system. The people of whom we learn in the Rig-Veda name themselves Aryas, from the Sanskrit *arya*, meaning "noble." They are in conflict with dark-skinned, flat-nosed inhabitants of the land, whom they call Dasas, using the word (*dasa*) which in Sanskrit came to mean "slave." The Dasas are presumably to be identified with speakers of Dravidian languages, some of whose descendants are possibly the submerged stratum in the north and a large mass of the population in the south of India, where Dravidian languages are current. If, as is also presumable, the Dasas were once among the inhabitants of Mohenjo-daro and Harappa, they had a background of higher civilization than would be suspected from the character of the references to them in the Rig-Veda.[31]

The Aryans themselves appear still to have been a pastoral people, whose wealth was derived mainly from their cattle and their agriculture. They were organized in tribes, each ruled by its king.

[26] tr. Ralph T. H. Griffith, *The Hymns of the Samaveda, Translated with a Popular Commentary.* 1907.

[27] tr. Ralph T. H. Griffith, *The Hymns of the Atharva-veda, Translated with a Popular Commentary.* 2 vols. 1895-96; Maurice Bloomfield in SBE XLII.

[28] CSHI p.6; cf. von Glasenapp, *Die Literaturen Indiens von ihren Anfängen bis zur Gegenwart,* p.47.

[29] F. Max Müller in SBE XXXII, pp.xliv-xlv.

[30] Ramayana VII. tr. Romesh C. Dutt, *The Ramayana and the Mahabharata Condensed into English Verse* (Everyman's Library, 403). 1910, pp 171-176.

[31] Hermann Goetz, *Epochen der indischen Kultur.* 1929, pp.24-28.

RELIGION OF THE VEDAS

As revealed in the Vedas,[32] the religion of the Aryans emphasized a worship of natural phenomena, particularly the sky and the powers associated with it. The deities are in the main conceived as human, but as A. Berriedale Keith remarks, "it is seldom difficult to doubt that the anthropomorphic forms but faintly veil phenomena of nature."[33] The name for the gods appears in Sanskrit as *deva*, meaning the "heavenly one," a word which is closely related to the Latin *deus*.[34] Another designation for deity in the Rig-Veda is *asura*, but in the Yajur-Veda, the Atharva-Veda and the subsequent Vedic literature the *asuras* have become the enemies of the gods and are thought of as evil spirits or demons.[35]

The gods are usually stated to be thirty-three in number and are ideally divided into three groups of eleven each, distributed in sky, atmosphere and earth.[36] Among these deities are the following:

Varuna, probably originally a sky god and possibly related to the Greek Ouranos or "Heaven," is the sustainer of the natural order and the upholder of the moral law. The prayers to him are the most exalted in the entire Rig-Veda.

> Varuna, true to holy law, sits down among his people; he,
> Most wise, sits there to govern all.
>
> From thence perceiving, he beholds all wondrous things,
>   both what hath been
> And what hereafter will be done.
>
> Varuna, hear this call of mine, be gracious unto us this day,
> Longing for help I cry to thee.
>
> Thou, O wise god, art lord of all, thou art the king
>   of earth and heaven;
> Hear, as thou goest on thy way.[37]

Other deities of the celestial regions are Mitra, the frequent companion of Varuna, and identical with the Persian Mithra; Dyaus, the bright sky, whose name is the same as the Greek Zeus; Surya, the sun, etymologically related to the Greek Helios; and Ushas, the goddess of the dawn, who is the Greek Eos. Possibly also a sun god in

---

[32] A. Berriedale Keith, *The Religion and Philosophy of the Veda and Upanishads* (Harvard Oriental Series, 31, 32). 2 vols. 1925.

[33] *ibid.*, p.58.

[34] *ibid.*, pp.75f.; Otto Schrader in HERE II, p.33.

[35] Keith, *The Religion and Philosophy of the Veda and Upanishads*, p.231.

[36] *ibid.*, p.86; A. A. Macdonell in HERE XII, p.602.

[37] Rig-Veda I, xxv, 10f., 19f. tr. Nicol Macnicol, *Hindu Scriptures* (Everyman's Library, 944). 1938, pp.4f.

origin is Vishnu, who occupies only a subordinate place in the Rig-Veda but was destined to achieve great importance later. An indeterminate number of these gods and sometimes all of them are styled *Adityas*, sons of Aditi. This name is appropriate to their character as deities of the light of heaven and suggests that they are bright and shining, pure and holy.

In the realm of the atmosphere or the waters of the air, Indra is the most important god, and he is indeed the most prominent deity of the Rig-Veda. Strong and mighty, the wielder of the thunderbolt, he contends in battles both atmospheric and terrestrial on behalf of his people. Closely associated with him is a troop of lesser storm gods, the Maruts. The father of the Maruts is the formidable archer Rudra. Known also as the ruler of the world and its father, Rudra is deemed on this side of his nature to be beneficent, gracious and auspicious (*śiva*), the last epithet providing the name by which he is known in late Vedic times. Other aerial deities include Vayu and Vata, the wind gods, and Parjanya, the god of the thundercloud.

In the terrestrial realm, the most notable deities are Soma and Agni. Soma is the god of an intoxicating beverage made from the Soma plant, which was used as a libation to the gods and a drink for the worshipers. Agni is the personification of fire in all its forms and particularly of the altar fire used in sacrifice. Since fire was also regularly employed for the cremation of the dead, Agni was likewise the conductor of souls into the other world. There the Fathers, or spirits of the dead, dwell in the blessed abode ruled by Yama, who was the first to die. The earth herself is also worshiped in the form of the goddess Prthivi, while the rivers too, especially the Sarasvati, a small stream in the Punjab,[38] are objects of devotion.

In addition to the great gods of the celestial, aerial and terrestrial regions, we learn in the Vedas of various minor gods of nature and of certain abstract deities. Among the minor nature deities are the Gandharvas and the Apsarases. The Gandharva is a masculine creature of the heaven, a guardian of Soma, and also connected with water. The Apsaras is a water nymph, whose very name means "the goer in the water." In the Atharva-Veda the Gandharvas and Apsarases are described as dwelling in banyan and fig trees and engaging in play, song and dance to the accompaniment of the lute and cymbal.

[38] Keith, *The Religion and Philosophy of the Veda and Upanishads*, p.173.

The gods which Keith calls "abstract"[39] are ones for which a basis does not appear in some particular phenomenon of nature; rather, they personify functions or activities or faculties. Tvastr is one of these. As his name suggests, he is the great Fashioner. It was he who forged the bolt of Indra, and it was his daughter Saranyu, wife of Vivasvant, of whom were born the twins, Yama and Yami, whence came the human race. Prajapati, too, appears. The "lord of offspring," as his name means, he is a creator god. Aditi, mother of the Adityas, may also be mentioned here. Her name suggests unbinding, or freedom from bonds, and she is invoked for release from sin. A number of times spoken of as a cow, she was evidently, at least upon occasion, conceived in theriomorphic fashion.

Opposed to the gods are their enemies the demons, for whom in the later Vedas the designation *asuras* is, as we have seen, reserved. Of these the first in rank is Vritra, the "Encloser," a terrible dragon or serpent. His mother is Danu, and he bears the appellation Danava, "offspring of Danu," as do also his kinsmen, the other enemies of the gods.

While the mythology of the Vedas is far from explicit, it is possible to reconstruct the underlying stories, at least partially, by careful study of many scattered references. By such investigation, W. Norman Brown has been able to set forth an account of the creation myth of the Rig-Veda.[40] Here we find that the universe is conceived to have two parts. The first, called Sat, "the Existent," is that in which gods and men live. It includes the three divisions which have already been mentioned, the earth, the sky and the atmosphere between. The second part of the universe is Asat, "the Nonexistent."[41] It lies below the earth, separated from us by a great chasm. This is the home of the demons.

The creation myth undertakes to explain how this entire universe came into being. In the beginning, it seems, there existed the Cosmic Waters. There, too, was the great Fashioner, the god Tvastr. He made the divine pair, Dyaus or Sky, and Prthivi or Earth, and they became the parents of the gods. Among the divine beings there ensued an epic quarrel. The Danavas or descendants of Danu, led by Vritra, represented the forces of inertia and destruction; the Adityas, sprung from their mother Aditi, with Varuna as their chief, repre-

---

[39] *ibid.*, p.203.
[40] W. Norman Brown in JAOS 62 (1942), pp.85-98.
[41] W. Norman Brown in JAOS 61 (1941), pp.76-80.

sented the forces of growth and liberation. For the time being the
conservative forces were greater than those of expansion. In fact
the Cosmic Waters themselves were at this time held back, as if
within a shell, by Vritra and his cohorts, while the force of expansion,
in the person of Varuna and his associates, was impotent to accomplish a liberation. Then Indra came into being as the champion of
the gods, himself perhaps the son of Dyaus and Prthivi. By drinking
Soma he became strong and undertook battle with Vritra. Although
wounded in the fierce struggle, Indra was victorious. Forcing Heaven
and Earth apart, and himself filling the space between as the atmosphere, he released the Cosmic Waters. Coming forth, they gave
birth to the sun and themselves flowed into the atmospheric ocean.
By his mighty deed, Indra separated Sat and Asat, and this constituted creation. After that, Varuna organized all things and prescribed the laws by which they should operate. Man himself was
created to support the gods. The demons were relegated to their
place beneath the earth, whence they still emerge at night to endanger human beings.

Such was the great accomplishment of which Indra sang to his
companions:

> I slew Vritra, O Maruts, with might, having grown
> powerful through my own vigor.
> I, who hold the thunderbolt in my arms, have made these
> all-brilliant waters to flow freely for man.[42]

THE BRAHMANAS

Each of the four Vedas came in the course of time to have a body
of prose writings attached to it, the chief purpose of which was to
describe and explain the sacrificial rites with which the Vedic texts
were connected. These commentaries are known as the Brahmanas[43]
and they probably cover approximately the period of the first half
of the first millennium B.C.[44] The name is derived from the Sanskrit
brahma, which variously means magical spell, sacred rite or universal
spirit, and is obviously applicable to expositions of religious texts
and ceremonies. The priests who knew the efficacious formulas and
conducted the all-important sacrifices were called Brahmans, and
were at this time emerging into a position of supreme power and

[42] Rig-Veda I, clxv, 8. SBE XXXII, p.180.
[43] The Śatapatha-Brahmana is translated by Julius Eggeling in SBE XII, XXVI, XLI, XLIII, XLIV.
[44] CSHI p.10.

privilege in society. The cult, over which they presided, surpassed in the complexity of its ritual detail anything the world has elsewhere known.[45]

From the geographical references in the Brahmanas and other literature dealing with this period it may be seen that the center of Aryan culture had now moved eastward into the Middle Country between the Jumna and the Ganges River. Here lived such important peoples as the Kurus and the Panchalas, while farther east and destined to greater importance later were the kingdoms of Kosala, corresponding roughly to the modern district of Oudh, and Videha, in what is now northern Bihar. Among the important cities were not only Taxila in the northwest, but also Asandivat or Hastinapura on the upper Ganges, Kauśambi on the Jumna, and Kaśi which is the later Benares.[46]

Already in the Rig-Veda there is discernible a certain tendency for the various gods to merge into one another, and in the Brahmanas there are indications of an attempt to discover some deeper ground of being which underlies all the gods and all phenomena. The word Brahman appears now in the sense of divine spirit, and it is declared that "Brahman is the ultimate thing of this universe."[47]

THE UPANISHADS

Appended to and later than the Brahmanas are the Aranyakas or Forest Books, which were either composed in the forests by hermits dwelling there or were intended to be studied in the seclusion of such surroundings. In turn, attached to the Aranyakas or sometimes even incorporated in them, and thus forming a late part of the Vedic literature, are the famous Upanishads.[48]

The Sanskrit word *upanishad* probably had the original meaning of "session," and referred to a session of pupils gathered about their teacher.[49] Hence it was an appropriate name for these writings, which are usually in the form of a dialogue between an inquirer who is seeking the way of knowledge and a wise person who is already possessed of the true understanding. The Upanishads come from varying environments and advance differing, sometimes even con-

---

[45] Macdonell in HERE XII, p.601.

[46] CSHI pp.10-12.

[47] Śatapatha-Brahmana XIII, vi, 2, v.7. SBE XLIV, p.409.

[48] tr. F. Max Müller in SBE I; Robert E. Hume, *The Thirteen Principal Upanishads Translated from the Sanskrit.* 1931; Dhan Gopal Mukerji, *Devotional Passages from the Hindu Bible Adapted into English.* 1929.

[49] F. Max Müller in SBE I, p.lxxxi.

tradictory, points of view. The oldest or classical Upanishads are a dozen in number, and are believed to have been composed in the period of approximately the eighth to the sixth centuries B.C.[50] The extant manuscripts of the Upanishads, as of the Vedas as a whole, are later than A.D. 1300 in date. It is possible, however, to use the commentaries of Śankara, who lived probably in the eighth century A.D., for the determination of their text.[51]

PHILOSOPHICAL RELIGION

Whereas the Vedas had reflected primarily a worship of nature, and the Brahmanas a priestly system of sacrifices, the Upanishads represent the essential philosophical development in Indian thought.[52] This philosophy is rooted in the striving, already noted, to find a single underlying reality beneath the multiplicity of the gods, and it is now proclaimed that neither worship nor sacrifice but rather meditation is the way to knowledge of that reality. In general, the Upanishads tend toward a monistic answer to the problems of metaphysics, though dualistic and theistic ideas also get support.

"Let a man meditate on the syllable Om," begins the Chandogya-Upanishad. Om was a sacred syllable, originally denoting assent, which had to be pronounced at the beginning of the reading of a Veda or of the recitation of a Vedic hymn. Here the repetition of this syllable is intended to accomplish the concentration of the mind on a higher object of thought, of which it is the symbol. Since Om is the symbol of the Veda, and since the Veda may be taken to signify all speech and life, the syllable really stands for the spirit of life in man. Furthermore, the spirit in man may be identified with the spirit in nature, and thus one rises at last to the conception that all reality is ultimately one. Such is the pathway of meditation which is recommended in the Upanishads as alone leading to true knowledge and salvation.[53]

BRAHMAN AND ATMAN

The name of the spirit or soul of the world is Brahman. Akin at

[50] A. S. Geden in HERE XII, p.540.
[51] Müller in SBE I, p.lxxi; xv, p.xii; V. S. Ghats in HERE XI, pp.185f.
[52] Walter Ruben, *Die Philosophen der Upanishaden.* 1947.
[53] Chandogya-Upanishad I, 1-3. SBE I, pp.xxiii-xxv, 1-10; cf. J. J. Boeles in *India Antiqua, A Volume of Oriental Studies Presented by His Friends and Pupils to Jean Philippe Vogel, C.I.E., on the Occasion of the Fiftieth Anniversary of His Doctorate* (Kern Institute–Leyden). 1947, pp.40-56.

47. Painted Pottery from Mohenjo-daro (*Copyright Government of India, by permission of Arthur Probsthain, London*)

46. Paleolithic Implements from Soan Valley

49. Seal from Mohenjo-daro with Three-faced God (Copyright Government of India, by permission of Arthur Probsthain, London)

48. Portrait Statue from Mohenjo-daro (Copyright Government of India, by permission of Arthur Probsthain, London)

50. Hymn to Agni in a Manuscript
of the Rig-Veda

51. Statue of a Yaksha

52. Reliefs at Bhaja

53. Headless Statue of King Kanishka   54. Image of Vishnu as Trivikrama

55. Lad Khan Temple at Aihole

56. Lakshmana Temple
at Sirpur

57. Virupaksha Temple at Pattadakal

58. Kailasanatha Temple at Elura

59. Śiva and Parvati
on Mount Kailasa

60. Central Aisle of the Cave Temple at Elephanta

61. The Three-headed Siva

62. Kailasanatha Temple at Kanchi

63. Rajarajeśvara Temple at Tanjore

64. Hoyśaleśvara Temple at Halebid

65. Pillar in the Great Temple at Palampet

66. Kandarya Mahadeva Temple at Khajuraho

68. The Dancing Śiva

67. Lingaraja Temple at Bhuvaneśvara

69. Statue of Brahma

one time perhaps in significance to *mana*,[54] Brahman has become the essence of everything, the all-encompassing absolute. Since to attribute personality would be to imply limitation, Brahman is deemed superpersonal and neuter, and is commonly referred to as "it" or "that." Indeed it is scarcely possible to define Brahman except with negatives (*neti neti*).[55] Nevertheless, all sorts of figures of speech are employed to give an intimation of the nature of that which is fundamentally indescribable. Thus, for one example, Brahman is likened unto the fig tree "whose roots grow upward and whose branches grow downward."[56] "That," it is said, "is called Brahman. . . . All worlds are contained in it, and no one goes beyond."[57] Another passage declares: "All this is Brahman. Let a man meditate on that [visible world] as beginning, ending and breathing in it."[58] Again we read: "That from whence these beings are born, that by which, when born, they live, that into which they enter at their death, try to know that. That is Brahman."[59] "That on which the worlds are founded and their inhabitants, that is the indestructible Brahman."[60]

The name of the spirit or soul of man is Atman. The great understanding toward which the upanishadic meditations chiefly are directed is that Brahman and Atman are identical. Since Brahman is in all things, Brahman is in man and man is in Brahman. The self of the world is the same as the self of man. In the famous phrase of the Upanishads, *Tat twam asi*, "That art thou." As it is written in the Kaivalya-Upanishad, "The highest Brahman, the soul of all, the great mainstay of the universe, . . . the eternal Being, that art thou."[61]

A notable dialogue, further illustrative of this conception, is found in the sixth book of the Chandogya-Upanishad. In the dialogue a father is conversing with his son, Svetaketu, and leading him toward an understanding of man's true relation to ultimate reality. In order to show that the universal self is diffused throughout the world and yet present within the individual, the father instructs Svetaketu to

---

[54] Archer, *Faiths Men Live By*, p.200.

[55] Geden in HERE XII, p.546.

[56] This is explained as referring to a tree which sends its branches down so that they take root in the ground and form new stems, and thus one tree grows into a veritable forest.

[57] Katha-Upanishad II, vi, 1. SBE XV, p.21.

[58] Chandogya-Upanishad III, xiv, 1. SBE I, p.48.

[59] Taittiriyaka-Upanishad III, 1. SBE XV, p.64.

[60] Mundaka-Upanishad II, ii, 2. SBE XV, p.36.

[61] vi. Quoted in Albert Schweitzer, *Indian Thought and Its Development*. tr. Mrs. Charles E. B. Russell, 1936, p.35.

place some salt in a container of water and then to return in the morning.

The son did as he was commanded.

The father said to him: "Bring me the salt, which you placed in the water last night."

The son having looked for it, found it not, for, of course, it was melted.

The father said: "Taste it from the surface of the water. How is it?"

The son replied: "It is salt."

"Taste it from the middle. How is it?"

The son replied: "It is salt."

"Taste it from the bottom. How is it?"

The son replied: "It is salt."

The father said: "Throw it away and then wait on me."

He did so; but salt exists for ever.[62]

Then the father said: "Here also, in this body, forsooth, you do not perceive the True, my son; but there indeed it is.

"That which is the subtle essence, in it all that exists has its self. It is the True. It is the Self (Atman). And that art thou, Svetaketu!"[63]

It is of course within the inmost heart that this vision of the truth may best be attained, for that is where Brahman dwells. "Manifest, near, moving in the cave [of the heart] is the great Being."[64] "He is my self within the heart, smaller than a corn of rice, smaller than a corn of barley, smaller than a mustard seed, smaller than a canary seed or the kernel of a canary seed. He also is my self within the heart, greater than the earth, greater than the sky, greater than heaven, greater than all these worlds. He from whom all works, all desires, all sweet odors and tastes proceed, who embraces all this, who never speaks and who is never surprised, he my self within the heart, is that Brahman. When I shall have departed from hence, I shall obtain him. He who has this faith has no doubt."[65] As Professor Otto Strauss has said in comment on the passage just quoted, "Whoever reads these words, which are among the oldest of the kind that have come down to us, will at once feel that they disclose a vision that fills and gladdens the whole heart. We feel the original experience of the man to whom this came. . . . To have a vision of the Absolute, to *be* the Absolute—that is the central experience."[66]

[62] The translation of these two lines is disputed.
[63] Chandogya-Upanishad vi, xiii. SBE I, pp.104f.
[64] Mundaka-Upanishad II, ii, 1. SBE XV, p.36.
[65] Chandogya-Upanishad III, xiv, 3f. SBE I, p.48.
[66] Strauss in CRW p.101.

SAMSARA AND KARMA

There also emerges in the Upanishads the idea of the reincarnation of souls. According to monistic doctrine, souls are like sparks which come forth from a fire only to fall back into it again.[67] It is thus the inherent destiny of every soul, whether of man, animal or plant, to return into the universal soul whence it came forth. According to the doctrine of reincarnation, the soul is a prisoner within its body and is destined upon death to be reborn within another earthly body. This rebirth may be in a lower or in a higher form of life depending upon the evil or good done in the previous existence. If the soul is to attain the highest form of existence and to become capable of union with the universal soul, it must, as it were, earn its own redemption.[68]

The endless cycle of births and deaths through which the soul transmigrates from one body to another is known in the Sanskrit as *samsara*, while the consequences of one's deeds which determine one's future lot are called *karma*. The outworking of this inexorable system of human destiny through rebirth is not explicitly mentioned but appears to be summarized in the Brihadaranyaka-Upanishad in the sentence: "Now as a man is like this or like that, according as he acts and according as he behaves, so will he be:—a man of good acts will become good, a man of bad acts, bad."[69] "Those whose conduct has been good," it is affirmed in the Chandogya-Upanishad, "will quickly attain some good birth, the birth of a Brahman, or a Kshatriya, or a Vaisya" (these being members respectively of the priestly, warrior or kingly, and mercantile or agricultural, castes). "But those whose conduct has been evil, will quickly attain an evil birth, the birth of a dog, or a hog, or a Candala" (the last being an outcaste son of a Brahman mother and a Sudra or laboring caste father).[70] It is also possible for the soul to pass into inorganic matter,[71] or to be born again as rice, corn, an herb, a tree,[72] a worm, an insect, a fish, a bird, a lion, a boar, a serpent, or a tiger.[73] He who is impure, thoughtless and without understanding is bound inextricably within this round of births, "but he who has understanding, who is

---

[67] Mundaka-Upanishad II, i, 1. SBE XV, p.34; Brihadaranyaka-Upanishad II, i, 20. SBE XV, p.105.

[68] Schweitzer, *Indian Thought and Its Development*, pp.47-53.

[69] IV, iv, 5. SBE XV, p.176.   [70] V, x, 7. SBE I, p.82; cf. XV, p.169 n.3.

[71] Katha-Upanishad II, v, 7. SBE XV, p.19.

[72] Chandogya-Upanishad V, x, 6. SBE I, p.81.

[73] Kaushitaki-Upanishad I, 2. SBE I, p.274.

mindful and always pure, reaches indeed that place, from whence he is not born again."[74] "He who forms desires in his mind, is born again," but he who strives with strength, earnestness, and right meditation to overcome desire, is able to attain a state of passionless tranquility. "When all desires which once entered his heart are undone, then does the mortal become immortal, then he obtains Brahman. And as the slough of a snake lies on an ant hill, dead and cast away, thus lies this body; but that disembodied immortal spirit is Brahman only, is only light." Or, to change the figure of speech, "As the flowing rivers disappear in the sea, losing their name and their form, thus a wise man, freed from name and form, goes to the divine Person, who is greater than the great."[75]

[74] Katha-Upanishad I, iii, 7f. SBE XV, p.13.
[75] Mundaka-Upanishad III, ii. SBE XV, pp.40f.; Brihadaranyaka-Upanishad IV, iv. SBE XV, pp.176f.

3. THE ŚIŚUNAGA AND NANDA PERIODS, c.642-c.322 B.C.[76]

INDIAN history first becomes known to us in a more definite and detailed way in the Śiśunaga Period. At this time a number of large states existed in northern India. Among these the kingdom of Magadha was rising in importance and was destined to obtain supremacy. The territory of Magadha lay along the Ganges River in what is today southern Bihar. A dynasty was founded here by Śiśunaga which endured from c.642 to c.413 B.C. The best-known kings in this line were Bimbisara and Ajataśatru. They will come before us again in the chapters on Jainism and Buddhism for they were contemporaries of Mahavira and the Buddha. Bimbisara, known to the Jains as Śrenika, ruled around 540-490 B.C. His capital was at Rajagriha, a new city which he built near the Ganges. Ajataśatru (or Kunika) reigned c.490-c.460 B.C. His son Udaya founded a new capital at Pataliputra (near the site of modern Patna), a city which was to be for centuries the most important in India. Around 413 B.C. the line of Śiśunaga gave way to the Nanda dynasty which lasted until c.322 B.C.

In 326 B.C. Alexander the Great reached the banks of the Beas (Hyphasis) River, an upper tributary of the Sutlej, the most advanced point of his penetration of India, and had to turn back when his soldiers would go no farther.[77]

[76] For most of the dates in Indian history see CSHI.

[77] The Beas was attained in the vicinity of the modern village of Gurdaspur. For the entire expedition of Alexander the Great in central Asia see Robert Fazy in *Mitteilungen der schweizerischen Gesellschaft der Freunde ostasiatischer Kultur* (*Bulletin de la Société Suisse des amis de l'Extrême-Orient*). 4 (1942), pp.3-26.

4. THE MAURYA PERIOD, c.322-c.185 B.C.

CHANDRAGUPTA MAURYA

AT ABOUT this time a man of the Maurya family, named Chandragupta (c.322-c.298 B.C.), obtained the throne of Magadha. After the withdrawal and death of Alexander the Great, Chandragupta was able to drive the remaining Macedonian garrisons back across the Indus, and to establish his own power throughout northern India. He also concluded a treaty with Seleucus I Nicator (312-281 B.C.), who became master of Alexander's eastern provinces, whereby the Hindu Kush was established as the western frontier of his kingdom.

MEGASTHENES

An ambassador named Megasthenes was sent by Seleucus to the court of Chandragupta Maurya at Pataliputra. Megasthenes lived in India for a number of years, and wrote an account of the land. Although the original is lost, this account is cited frequently by Strabo (c.63 B.C.-after A.D. 21) in his description of India, and also by Arrian (A.D. c.96-c.180) in the "special monograph" on India which he appended to his account of the campaigns of Alexander the Great. According to Megasthenes, as quoted by both Strabo and Arrian, Pataliputra (which they called Palibothra or Palimbothra) was situated at the confluence of the Erannoboas (now the Son) and the Ganges Rivers. The city was built in the form of a large parallelogram, roughly nine miles long and two miles wide. It was surrounded by both a moat and a wooden wall. King Sandrocottus, as the Greeks called Chandragupta, evidently lived in great state, but not without fear of his life since he changed his sleeping place from time to time because of the plots against him.

Further citing Megasthenes, Strabo and Arrian report that the population of India was divided into seven castes, including philosophers, farmers, shepherds and hunters, artisans and tradesmen, soldiers, government overseers, and royal councilors. An individual's place within this system was rigidly fixed. "It is not legal for a man either to marry a wife from another caste or to change one's pursuit or work from one to another."

The philosophers were divided into two classes, Strabo reports on the authority of Megasthenes: one called Brachmanes or Brahmans, the other Garmanes or Śramanas. The Brahmans "converse more about death than anything else, for they believe . . . that death, to

[142]

those who have devoted themselves to philosophy, is birth into the
true life, that is, the happy life." They also believe "that the universe
was created and is destructible, . . . and that it is spherical in shape,
and that the god who made it and regulates it pervades the whole
of it; . . . and that the earth is situated in the center of the universe."
The Śramanas are ascetics who live in the forest or go about begging, and they are accustomed to "practice such endurance, both
in toils and in perseverance, that they stay in one posture all day
long without moving."

The Indian people in general were said by Strabo to live a simple
life, but to love beauty and personal adornment. "They wear apparel embroidered with gold, and use ornaments set with precious
stones, and wear gay-colored linen garments, and are accompanied
with sun-shades." As for their religion "the Indians worship Zeus
and the Ganges River and the local deities." "Their funerals are simple," Strabo says, "and their mounds small." In the Indus region at
least, cremation was practiced, "and wives are burned up with their
deceased husbands." There, too, they had the custom that "the dead
are thrown out to be devoured by vultures."[78]

Chandragupta Maurya was succeeded by his son Bindusara, and
then by his grandson, the famous Aśoka. Known also as Aśoka Maurya and as Aśoka-vardhana, this king succeeded to the throne around
274 or 273 B.C. and ruled until about 232 B.C.[79] In the days of his
father's reign, Aśoka had already served successfully as governor of
Taxila and of Ujjain, and upon accession to the throne his great abilities became fully manifest. His capital was at Pataliputra, the ancient center of Magadhan culture, and from here he ruled the already widely extended empire of Magadha. In addition he conquered the kingdom of Kalinga to the southeast in a sanguinary
campaign and thenceforth held sway over almost the whole of India except the extreme south. Since Aśoka was converted to Buddhism and became the great patron of that faith, more detailed
mention of his work and monuments will be given in the chapter on
Buddhism.

While Buddhism and Jainism were very important and influential
at this time, the classical Brahmanism of the Vedas and Upanishads

[78] Strabo, *Geography.* II, i, 9; xv, i, 30,36,39-49,53-55,59f.,62,69. tr. H. L. Jones,
LCL (1917-32) I, p.265; VII, pp.53,63,67-83,87-89,91,99-105,109,121; Arrian, *Anabasis
of Alexander.* v, v, 1; VIII (*Indica*), x-xii. tr. E. Iliff Robson, LCL (1929-33) II,
pp.17,335-341.
[79] CSHI pp.45,53.

still lived on. Furthermore, it is possible to show that a fusion was taking place between Aryan conceptions and other ideas deriving probably from early Dravidian backgrounds.[80] The religion which resulted from this mingling, and which has lived on in India from the first centuries B.C. to the present, is properly called Hinduism.[81]

SECTARIAN HINDUISM

In the Vedas the gods were largely the many elemental forces of nature personified, and in the Upanishads the ultimate reality was most often an impersonal Absolute with which the human soul was to realize its identity. Even in Brahmanism, however, a more theistic type of thought sometimes occurred, as for example in the Śvetaś-vatara-Upanishad. Now, in the Hinduism which more and more appealed to the popular mind, there was an increasing tendency to regard some one god as supreme among the many (not of course to the denial of the others), and to conceive the divine beings as personal and worthy of personal worship. As an adorable or worshipful being a god is a *bhagavat*, his devotee is a *bhagavata*, and the personal love and devotion which he has elicited is *bhakti*.[82]

Two great gods attained the highest importance, and around each a large sectarian movement formed. The two gods were Vishnu and Śiva, and their respective sects were those of Vaishnavism and Śaivism, each with its own numerous subdivisions.[83] Both deities had already been known in the Vedic literature but had hitherto been relatively unimportant. In the present and succeeding periods they came to play a very prominent role, while around each a multitude of other gods, many of local or aboriginal origin and all regarded as manifestations of the supreme god, was gathered. The two sects "are thus actually vast amorphous conglomerates of the most heterogeneous elements; monotheistic in essence, multifarious and grotesque polytheisms in semblance, with pantheism for a harmonising principle."[84]

THE SHRINE AT NAGARI

A Vaishnavite shrine is known to us from archeological evidence at about this time. It was devoted to the worship of the god Vasudeva, perhaps originally the divine leader of a non-Aryan clan in the

[80] CHIIA p.16. [81] Strauss in CRW p.108.
[82] Nicol Macnicol, *The Living Religions of the Indian People*. 1934, pp.39f.
[83] Sten Konow in SLR II, pp.154f.,172f. [84] MHR I, p.329.

northwest,[85] and now probably regarded as a manifestation of Vishnu.[86] The site is at Nagari, eight miles north of Chitor in the region of Rajputana. There is a village named Ghosundi about four miles northeast of Nagari, where a number of carved stones have been found which probably were brought from Nagari. One of these was an inscribed slab which had been put up within the entrance to the village well at Ghosundi, and which now has been transferred to the Victoria Museum at Udaipur. It is ascribed to the period between 350 and 250 B.C., and is thought to be the earliest extant inscription in which the Sanskrit language is used. It records the erection of a stone enclosure in connection with the worship of Vasudeva and another divinity called Samkarshana. The site of this shrine is referred to as Narayana-vata, suggesting that Vasudeva was already identified with Narayana, who is well known later as an incarnation of Vishnu.

In the course of archeological investigations at Nagari, moreover, an actual large enclosure was studied which had been built of massive blocks of laminiferous stone. Since the Ghosundi well inscription had originally formed part of a similar block, it is a convincing supposition that this is the actual enclosure to which it referred. A much later inscription, probably of the seventh century A.D., was also found on one of the stones of this wall indicating that at that time a temple of Vishnu was standing there. Thus the worship of Vasudeva-Vishnu is evidently attested at this place from the fourth century B.C. to the seventh century A.D.[87]

YAKSHAS

The Maurya Period also provides us with an actual statue probably portraying one of the popular divinities of the time. The statue, shown in Fig. 51, was found at Parkham, near Baroda, and is now in the Archaeological Museum at Muttra (Mathura). Made of sandstone, and of very large size, standing to a height of eight feet eight inches, it is the oldest known Indian stone sculpture in the round. It is believed to represent a Yaksha. The Sanskrit word *yaksha* (feminine *yakshi*) was perhaps originally a non-Aryan or at any rate a popular designation signifying practically the same as the Aryan *deva*. The Yakshas seem to have been indigenous non-Aryan deities,

---

[85] A. Eustace Haydon, *Biography of the Gods.* 1941, pp.105f.

[86] Konow in SLR II, p.149.

[87] D. R. Bhandarkar, *The Archaeological Remains and Excavations at Nagari* (MASI, 4). 1920, pp.118f.,128-133.

which were especially associated with waters, and which were looked to as the beneficent bestowers of fertility and wealth.[88] They were natural objects, therefore, of the bhakti cult. The present statue conveys an impression of mass and force, and has been called "a statement of an ideal concept in a technique that is still primitive."[89] The standing position remains typical for cult statues in early Indian art, and where these are complete they usually have the right hand raised and the left on the hip.

[88] Ananda K. Coomaraswamy, *Yakṣas* (Smithsonian Institution Publication 2926). 1928; *Yakṣas* ii (Smithsonian Institution Publication 3059). 1931.

[89] A. K. Coomaraswamy in EB xii, p.213.

5. THE ŚUNGA, ANDHRA, INDO-GREEK AND INDO-PARTHIAN PERIODS, c.185 B.C.-A.D. c.50

AFTER the splendid reign of Aśoka, the Maurya empire disintegrated rapidly. We know little more than that Aśoka's grandson, Daśaratha, ruled for a time and that the last king of the line, Brihadratha, was assassinated about 185 B.C.

The Śunga Dynasty (c.185-c.80 B.C.), whose first king was Pushya-mitra the slayer of Brihadratha, now ruled the central part of what had been Aśoka's empire. In the southeast and south the kingdoms of Kalinga and Andhra were independent, and the latter in particular maintained itself until about the middle of the third century A.D. In the northwest, the Greeks who had been settled in Bactria since the time of Alexander the Great, pressed on into the Punjab, and their most celebrated king, Menander or Milinda (c.161-c.145 B.C.), prob-ably invaded Magadha and may have reached Pataliputra. In the first century B.C. the Greeks gave way to new invaders, the Sakas and the Pahlavas. These were Scythians and Parthians, and their most famous king was the Parthian Gondophares who ruled at Taxila around A.D. 19-48.[90]

THE BESNAGAR INSCRIPTIONS

The prevalence of Vaishnavite worship in this time also is attested by two interesting inscriptions. From the type of their characters, they are probably to be dated in the second century B.C. The first is on a column at Besnagar, an important site near Bhilsa in central India. It is a votive inscription, and reads as follows: "This Garuda[91] column of Vasudeva the god of gods (*devadeva*) was erected here by Heliodorus, a Bhagavata, the son of Dion, and an inhabitant of Taxila, who came as Greek ambassador from Maharaja Antialkidas to King Kasiputra Bhagabhadra." These words are specially sig-nificant also as showing that, contrary to later practice, an alien could at this time be accepted as a devoted worshiper within the fold of Hindu society. The second inscription is on the fragment of another column which was found in a narrow street in Bhilsa, but which probably came from Besnagar, and is now in the Besnagar Museum.

[90] W. W. Tarn, *The Greeks in Bactria and India.* 1938, pp.133f.,225-269,312-350.
[91] The Sanskrit word Garuda is the name of a supernatural being who appears specially as the vehicle or bearer of Vishnu.

It also was a Garuda column, and it refers to "the excellent temple" of Vishnu.[92]

THE BHAJA RELIEFS

At the same time the nature deities of the ancient Vedic hymns lived on in the beliefs of the people and were the subjects of realistic and awe-inspiring portrayals in art. Illustration may be seen in certain reliefs which adorn the veranda of a cave at Bhaja near Poona in the Western Ghats. These sculptures date probably from the second or first century B.C. The cave evidently served as a monastery (*vihara*) and must have been Buddhist, but the sculptures under consideration were certainly from a non-Buddhist background. The reliefs are at the west end of the veranda, on either side of a doorway leading into a cell (Fig. 52). In the panel at the left we see a royal person, accompanied by two women, driving a four-horse chariot across the backs of two female demons who seem to float in the air. This is identified as Surya, the sun, driving with his two wives across the sky. On the other side of the doorway is another royal person who rides on a huge elephant and is accompanied by an attendant holding a trident standard. The elephant brandishes in his trunk an uprooted tree, and strides forward across a landscape filled with lesser figures. This is probably the storm god Indra, riding forth upon his cloud-elephant Airavata.[93]

TAXILA

The ancient city of Taxila was an important center of the Bactrian Greeks and Scytho-Parthians. At this site no less than three distinct buried cities are recognized. The most southerly is the Bhir mound which covers the older Hindu city (fifth to second centuries B.C.) where Panini taught and Aśoka served as governor. Hoards of jewelry and coins dating around 300 B.C., discovered in the Bhir mound in 1924 and 1945, provide decisive evidence of the date of these ruins.[94] To the north of the Bhir mound is that of Sirkap, which represents the city founded by the Greeks from Bactria. This was the capital of the Parthian dynasty of which Gondophares was the most illustrious member. Yet farther to the north is Sirsukh, which represents the Taxila of the later Kushan empire.

[92] Ramaprasad Chanda, *Archaeology and Vaishnava Tradition* (MASI, 5). 1920, pp.151-154.
[93] CHIIA pp.24-27.
[94] G. M. Young in *Ancient India*. 1 (Jan. 1946), pp.27-36.

The excavation of the mound of Sirkap by Sir John Marshall has laid bare a large part of Scytho-Parthian Taxila.[95] The ruins are an intricate complex of fortifications, streets, houses and shrines. Most of the shrines were Buddhist and possibly Jaina, while some distance outside the northern gate was a large temple which may have belonged to the Zoroastrian religion. Within the city the royal palace has been identified and found to consist of a series of apartments arranged around central courts. The entire complex measured over 350 by 250 feet, and was substantially built, yet not really pretentious or sumptuous. Among numerous coins unearthed in the palace were those of Gondophares and the Kushan king Kadphises I. Many of the excavated houses in the city were likewise constructed around open quadrangles, and often had two stories. The rooms of the lower story, however, did not communicate directly with the interior court or with the street, and apparently were entered only from the rooms above. Many of the houses were so extensive as to occasion the surmise that they were residences of Hindu teachers whose students were expected to live with their masters. The first century Greek philosopher Apollonius of Tyana is said to have visited Taxila, and his *Life*, written by Philostratus, gives an account of the city which is substantially in accord with the archeological findings. In particular the relative simplicity of the king's palace and the unusual character of the two-storied private houses are commented on in the Greek source.[96]

THOMAS

It is an interesting fact that until the modern discovery of his coins and inscriptions, the great king Gondophares had remained unknown to history save for the mention of his name in the apocryphal *Acts of Thomas.* This book, which was probably written at Edessa around A.D. 200, relates how the apostle Thomas journeyed to India[97] and preached the Christian message at the court of King Gundaphorus or Gondophares. The story is that Gondophares gave money to Thomas, who was taken for a carpenter, to build him a

[95] John Marshall, *A Guide to Taxila.* 2d ed. 1921, pp.67-87.
[96] Philostratus (A.D. c.170-c.245), *The Life of Apollonius of Tyana.* II, 23,25. tr. F. C. Conybeare, LCL (1912) I, pp.181,183.
[97] Parthia is named as the place of the labors of Thomas in Eusebius, *Church History.* III, i, 1; *Recognitions of Clement.* IX, 29; Socrates, *Church History.* I, 19. This may be explained, however, by the fact that in the time of Thomas north India was a part of the Scytho-Parthian empire and was ruled by a Parthian king.

palace. Thomas distributed the money to the poor and afflicted, and told the king that he was building a palace for him in heaven. Gad (or Guda), the king's brother, died and saw this palace in heaven. Being restored to life, Gad was converted to Christianity along with the king himself. After other remarkable adventures, Thomas met martyrdom in the land of another king who is referred to as Misdaeus, or the "Mazdaean."[98]

The tradition preserved in the Syrian Church of Travancore is that Thomas labored for the last twenty years of his life in south India, first on the west coast, and then on the east coast where he was martyred around A.D. 72. He is supposed to have been buried at Mylapore near Madras, where his martyr shrine, rebuilt by the Portuguese in 1547, still stands on Mount St. Thomas.[99] It is held that sometime in the century after his death, the bones of Thomas were brought back to Edessa, where a memorial church was dedicated to him.[100]

Although much of the legendary has gathered about the story of Thomas, the main facts of his work in north and south India may possibly be historical, and certainly the knowledge of, and contact with, India on the part of early Christianity is attested.[101]

[98] *Acts of Thomas.* 17-27,159-170. M. R. James, *The Apocryphal New Testament.* 1924, pp.371-376,434-438.
[99] F. C. Burkitt in EB XXII, p.143.
[100] Socrates, *Ch. Hist.* IV, 18.
[101] J. N. Farquhar in *Bulletin of the John Rylands Library, Manchester.* 10 (1926), pp.80-111; 11 (1927), pp.20-50; cf. A. Mingana, *ibid.,* 10 (1926), pp.435-514.

6. THE KUSHAN PERIOD, A.D. C.50-C.320

THE Kushans were the leading tribe among the Yueh-chi people who came out of central Asia, settled in Bactria, and in the first century A.D. pushed on into northwest India. The five principal Kushan kings were Kujala Kadphises I, Wima Kadphises II, Kanishka, Huvishka and Vasudeva. The dates of these rulers are still under debate. For Kanishka, the most important of them all, dates around A.D. 78-103, 125-150 or 144-172 have been proposed, and we may safely assume that he belongs in the second century A.D.[102]

Under Kadphises I the Kushan empire reached from the Parthian frontier to the Indus; Kadphises II extended these dominions on eastward to the Jumna and the Ganges. The latter king is well known for his gold and copper coins, on which a favorite picture is that of Siva and his bull Nandi.[103]

Kanishka, chief of the Kushans, made his Indian capital at Purushapura (Peshawar) in the northwest, in the district known as Gandhara. The city of Mathura on the Jumna River was also of much importance at this time and was famed as a religious and artistic center. Kanishka is shown in a life-sized red sandstone statue (Fig. 53) which was found at Mat in the Mathura district. The identification of the statue is guaranteed by the inscription which it carries, but the head has been lost. The king is dressed in central Asian costume, with tunic, long open coat and high heavy boots, and makes a most imposing appearance.[104]

Kanishka was converted to Buddhism, and plays a prominent part in Buddhist traditions. On his coins, however, are found representations of Hindu, Zoroastrian and Hellenistic deities as well as of the Buddha.[105]

On the coins of Huvishka both Indian and foreign deities appear, while the coinage of Vasudeva features Siva most prominently. After Vasudeva the Kushan empire disintegrated into small states where

[102] Tarn, *The Greeks in Bactria and India*, p.352. R. Ghirshman, *Bégram, recherches archéologiques et historiques sur les Kouchans.* 1946. reviewed by Richard N. Frye in *Artibus Asiae.* 11 (1948), p.242. Ghirshman, who proposes the date A.D. 144-172 for Kanishka, also gives A.D. 172-217 for Huvishka and A.D. 217-241 for Vasudeva. Sten Konow believes that Vasudeva was a predecessor and not a descendant of Kanishka. See *India Antiqua*, p.195.
[103] CSHI p.74.
[104] K. de B. Codrington, *Ancient India from the Earliest Times to the Guptas with Notes on the Architecture and Sculpture of the Medieval Period.* 1926, p.44.
[105] CSHI p.78.

various kings ruled in the third and fourth centuries, but gradually gave way to the rising Sasanian empire in the west and to the Guptas in India.

In the Kushan Period, probably by the end of the second century A.D., the two great epics of ancient India, the Ramayana and the Mahabharata,[106] seem to have been virtually completed. These present Hinduism in a popular form and, especially in the Bhagavad-Gita, state religion in terms of personal devotion.[107]

THE RAMAYANA

The Ramayana[108] means "the Career of Rama," and is the story of a noble character named Rama and of his devoted wife Sita. It is written in poetic form in more than 24,000 Sanskrit couplets. The epic is attributed to the poet Valmiki, and it may be supposed that he first brought into a homogeneous whole popular tales already current concerning Rama. This may have been done as early as the fourth century B.C., while the work had probably attained its present extent by the end of the second century A.D.[109]

The scene of the Ramayana is laid in northern India in the ancient kingdoms of Kosala and Videha. There by notable exploit, Prince Rama, eldest son of King Daśaratha of the Kosalas, won the hand of Sita, daughter of King Janaka of the Videhas. Shortly after the marriage, however, Rama was banished to the jungle for fourteen years, due to an unfortunate promise made earlier by Daśaratha to one of his wives. Sita faithfully followed her husband into exile, and they made their dwelling in the forest. But then Sita was carried off by the demon Ravana to an island in the ocean, probably Ceylon. Her whereabouts were discovered, however, by the monkey-leader Hanuman, and in alliance with the monkey-people Rama invaded Ceylon and recovered his wife. Thereafter, the fourteen years of exile having come to an end, Rama and Sita returned joyfully to Kosala, where Rama ascended the throne and reigned gloriously.

Thus in its essential outline the Ramayana is the story of an ideal man and woman who triumphed over great difficulties. In the form in which we have the epic, however, Rama is none other than the

[106] tr. Romesh C. Dutt, *The Ramayana and the Mahabharata Condensed into English Verse* (Everyman's Library, 403). 1910.

[107] Robert E. Hume, *The World's Living Religions.* 1924, p.30.

[108] tr. Ralph T. H. Griffith, *The Rámáyan of Válmíki Translated into English Verse.* 1915.

[109] A. A. Macdonell in HERE x, p.576.

incarnation (*avatara*, literally "descending") of the god Vishnu, who has consented to be born as a son of King Daśaratha in order to destroy the evil demon Ravana.

The Mahabharata means the "Great Bharata" story, and deals with a famous war between the Kurus, ruled by the House of Bharata, and a closely neighboring people. Such a conflict was doubtless a historical event, and probably took place around the beginning of the first millennium B.C.[110] The composition of the epic as we have it is generally ascribed to the period from the second century B.C. to the second century A.D., although its beginnings may go back to 400 B.C. and its amplification probably continued till A.D. 400 and even later.[111] The essential tale comprises only the kernel of the entire work, around which is accumulated a vast mass of other material, moral, religious, and philosophical. In its total extent the epic comprises about one hundred thousand Sanskrit couplets.[112]

In brief outline the central story is as follows. There are two families of cousins, both descended from a great-grandfather named Kuru. The one family is that of Dhritarashtra, who has a hundred sons, called Kauravas or Kurus. The other is that of Pandu, who dies, but leaves behind him five sons, known as Pandavas. One of these sons, named Arjuna, wins Draupadi, princess of the land of Panchala, and she becomes the wife of the five brothers. The capital of the Kurus is at Hastinapura, while the Pandavas build for themselves the city of Indraprastha, supposedly near the site of modern Delhi.

Fearful of the growing power of the Pandavas, the Kurus plan to cheat them of their kingdom in a game of dice. In this they succeed, and the five brothers with Draupadi are exiled to live for twelve years in the forest and then to pass a thirteenth year among men but in disguise. After many adventures the Pandavas return from the forest, and also successfully pass the thirteenth year in disguise. At the end of this time they should have received their kingdom again, but when this is refused they prepare for war with their cousins. The battle which then takes place is exceedingly sanguinary, but after eighteen days of fighting the Kurus are destroyed, and the Pandavas

[110] Goetz, *Epochen der indischen Kultur*, p.9.

[111] E. Washburn Hopkins, *The Great Epic of India, Its Character and Origin.* 1901, pp.386-402; and in HERE VIII, p.325.

[112] tr. Pratapa Chandra Roy and Sundari Bala Roy, *The Mahabharata of Krishna-Dwaipayana Vyasa Translated into English Prose.* 10 vols. 1893-96.

come into control of the kingdom. The eldest brother, Yudhishthira, takes the throne, and performs the famous horse-sacrifice (*asva-medha*) in token of undisputed supremacy.[113] Eventually, however, the Pandavas leave their kingdom behind, retire to the Himalayas, and thence make the ascent to heaven.

THE BHAGAVAD-GITA

Appearing as an inserted section in the sixth book of the Mahabharata is the famous Bhagavad-Gita or "Song of the Blessed One,"[114] which is "probably the most important single work ever produced in India."[115] Like the Mahabharata, the period of its composition was perhaps from the second century B.C. to the second century A.D.[116]

The scene is the plain of Kuru on which the opposing forces of the Kurus and the Pandavas are drawn up. Prince Arjuna, the famed archer among the Pandavas, gazes upon his kinsmen on the other side of the battle line, and his heart fails within him. He has no desire to begin the slaughter. Then ensues a dialogue between Arjuna and his charioteer, Krishna, whose mysterious, true nature is only gradually revealed. The conversation begins as a discussion of the immediate question of the warrior's duty, and since no task could be more difficult than to slay one's own kinsmen, the solution of this problem would cast light on all lesser duties. The essential answer of the Bhagavad-Gita is that man is bound to fulfill the duties of his calling, and that such activity, rightly conducted, is indeed a way of salvation. To be sure, it is not denied that the Brahmanic way of withdrawal from the world for mystic contemplation also leads to salvation, but the greater emphasis of the Gita is upon activity.

[113] The Aśvamedha is described in detail in the Śatapatha-Brahmana XIII, i-v. SBE XLIV, pp.274-403; and elsewhere. See P.-E. Dumont, *L'Aśvamedha, Description du sacrifice solennel du cheval dans le culte védique d'après les textes du Yajurveda blanc (Vājasaneyisaṃhitā, Śatapathabrāhmaṇa, Kātyāyanaśrautasūtra)*. Société Belge d'Études Orientales. 1927.
[114] The Bhagavad-Gita has been rendered into English by more than forty translators (see Robert E. Hume, *Treasure-House of the Living Religions*. 1932, pp.vii, 424-428), including Kashinath Trimbak Telang in SBE VIII, pp.1-131; Edwin Arnold in *The Harvard Classics*. 45 (1910), pp.799-884; Arthur W. Ryder, *The Bhagavad-Gita*. 1929; Franklin Edgerton, *The Bhagavad Gītā Translated and Interpreted*. 2 vols. (Harvard Oriental Series, 38, 39). 1944; Swami Prabhavananda and Christopher Isherwood, *Bhagavad-Gita, The Song of God*. 1944; and S. Radhakrishnan, *The Bhagavadgītā, with an Introductory Essay, Sanskrit Text, English Translation and Notes*. 1948.
[115] A. K. Coomaraswamy, *Hinduism and Buddhism*, p.4.
[116] R. Garbe in HERE II, p.538.

Renunciation and discipline of action
    Both lead to supreme weal.
But of these two, rather than renunciation of action,
    Discipline of action is superior.[117]

The proof of the necessity for activity is the simple fact that "even the maintenance of the body . . . can not succeed without action,"[118] and that if God "did not perform action," "these folk would perish."[119] The doing of one's active duty upon earth, however, must be without "attachment,"[120] that is without any trace of personal interest or desire for selfish reward. Work so done does not enchain man in bondage but on the contrary sets him free.

As the discussion in the Gita proceeds from the consideration of duty to the wider issues of religion and philosophy, the principle of loving faith and personal devotion (*bhakti*) is brought forward as the most important of all. By trust and love of God, both those who renounce the world and those who work in it, both high-caste priests and rulers, and low-caste people, women and even evil-doers, may win a sure salvation. This teaching is expressed as follows in one of the finest passages in the *Bhagavad-Gita*:

A leaf, a flower, a fruit, or water,
    Who presents to Me with devotion,
That offering of devotion I
    Accept from the devout-souled (giver).

Whatever thou doest, whatever thou eatest,
    Whatever thou offerest in oblation or givest,
Whatever austerity thou performest, son of Kunti,[121]
    That do as an offering to Me.

I am the same to all beings,
    No one is hateful or dear to Me;
But those who revere Me with devotion,
    They are in Me and I too am in them.

Even if a very evil doer
    Reveres Me with single devotion,
He must be regarded as righteous in spite of all;
    For he has the right resolution.

Quickly his soul becomes righteous,
    And he goes to eternal peace.

---

[117] v, 2. This and the following quotations are reprinted by permission of the publishers from the *Bhagavad Gita*. Edited and Translated by Franklin Edgerton (Cambridge, Mass.: Harvard University Press, 1944).
[118] III, 8.   [119] III, 24.   [120] II, 48.
[121] Kunti was the mother of Arjuna.

Son of Kunti, make sure of this:
    No devotee of Mine is lost.

For if they take refuge in Me, son of Prtha,[122]
    Even those who may be of base origin,
Women, men of the artisan caste, and serfs too,
    Even they go to the highest goal.

How much more virtuous brahmans,
    And devout royal seers, too!
A fleeting and joyless world
    This; having attained it, devote thyself to Me.

Be Me-minded, devoted to Me;
    Worshiping Me, pay homage to Me;
Just to Me shalt thou go, having thus disciplined
    Thyself, fully intent on Me.[123]

The god toward whom this devotion is directed in the Bhagavad-Gita is of course Krishna. Like Rama in the Ramayana, Krishna appears at first in the Mahabharata as a very human hero, indeed as a less admirable one than the noble Rama.[124] But in the Gita, Krishna reveals himself to Arjuna as none other than an incarnation (*avatara*) of the supreme god. In the dialogue the deity explains that he has passed through many births, even as Arjuna also has, but that unlike Arjuna he himself has memory of them all. Whenever conditions on earth become so bad as to demand it, he creates himself again, and thus is born age after age in order to destroy evil-doers and protect the good.[125]

Upon Arjuna's request the Blessed One then allows his true form to appear, and in amazement and terror Arjuna cries:

I see the gods in Thy body, O God,
    All of them, and the hosts of various kinds of beings too,
Lord Brahma sitting on the lotus-seat,
    And the seers all, and the divine serpents.

With many arms, bellies, mouths, and eyes,
    I see Thee, infinite in form on all sides;
No end nor middle nor yet beginning of Thee
    Do I see, O All-God, All-formed!

Thou art the Imperishable, the supreme Object of Knowledge;
    Thou art the ultimate resting-place of this universe;
Thou art the immortal guardian of the eternal right,
    Thou art the everlasting Spirit, I hold.

[122] Prtha was Kunti's name, earlier in life.
[123] IX, 26f.,29-34.   [124] Hermann Jacobi in HERE VII, p.196.
[125] IV, 5-8.

Touching the sky, aflame, of many colors,
  With yawning mouths and flaming enormous eyes,
Verily seeing Thee (so), my inmost soul is shaken,
  And I find no steadiness nor peace, O Vishnu![126]

The deity then resumes human form as Krishna the charioteer, and comforts Arjuna with the assurance that his devotion is still the guarantee of his salvation.

Not by the Vedas nor by austerity,
  Nor by gifts or acts of worship,
Can I be seen in such a guise,
  As thou hast seen Me.

But by unswerving devotion can
  I in such a guise, Arjuna,
Be known and seen in very truth,
  And entered into, scorcher of the foe.

Doing My work, intent on Me,
  Devoted to Me, free from attachment,
Free from enmity to all beings,
  Who is so, goes to Me, son of Pandu.[127]

[126] xi, 15f.,18,24.
[127] xi, 53-55.

7. THE GUPTA PERIOD, A.D. C.320-C.600

THE Gupta era was inaugurated by a king who bore a name already famous in Indian history. This was Chandragupta I, the first year of whose reign began on February 26, A.D. 320.[128] He ruled at Pataliputra, and held sway over the Ganges Valley as far as Prayaga (later Allahabad) at the confluence of the Ganges and the Jumna. About A.D. 335 he was succeeded by his son Samudragupta. The latter engraved an inscription on one of Aśoka's pillars, originally set up at Kauśambi and found at Prayaga, in which extensive conquests are described. These conquests were continued particularly in the west by his son Chandragupta II, who held the throne around A.D. 385-414. Under the latter the dynasty of the imperial Guptas reached the height of its splendor. The capital was now transferred to Ayodhya, and for a time the king probably also resided at Ujjain farther to the west.

FA HIEN

At about this time a Chinese Buddhist pilgrim named Fa Hien visited India and wrote an account of his travels.[129] His trip, made around A.D. 399-414, carried him across the Gobi Desert, down into the Punjab, and then through the whole Ganges Valley, from the mouth of which he sailed for home by way of Ceylon and Java. Speaking of the middle country of India, Fa Hien says: "The people are prosperous and happy. . . . The king in his administration uses no corporal punishments. . . . Throughout the country no one kills any living thing, nor drinks wine. . . ."[130]

THE WHITE HUNS

The next kings were Kumaragupta (A.D. c.414-c.455) and Skandagupta (A.D. c.455-c.470). At this time India was threatened by new invaders from central Asia, the Hunas or White Huns. They were temporarily repelled by Skandagupta, who refers to his victory over them in an inscription which also tells of his establishment of a temple and image of Vishnu at that time.[131] Afterward, however, the White Huns poured on into India and gained control of all the western

[128] CSHI p.87.
[129] Emil Abegg in *Asiatische Studien*. 1 (1947), pp.105-128.
[130] tr. H. A. Giles, *The Travels of Fa-hsien (399-414 A.D.), or Record of the Buddhistic Kingdoms*. 1923, pp.20f.; Samuel Beal, *Travels of Fah-Hian and Sung-Yun, Buddhist Pilgrims from China to India (400 A.D. and 518 A.D.)*. 1869, pp.54f.
[131] CSHI p.95.

and central dominions of the Guptas. Here the Huns continued to rule until the latter half of the sixth century. They established their capital at Sakala or Sialkot, and their greatest rulers were Toramana and his son Mihirakula. The reputation of Mihirakula was for cruelty and oppression, and he was especially remembered for his persecution of the Buddhists.

COSMAS INDICOPLEUSTES

Around A.D. 530 a visit was paid to India by Cosmas Indicopleustes ("the Indian navigator"), an Alexandrian merchant who subsequently became a monk. In his writings Cosmas makes reference to the White Huns, and to a ruler of theirs whom he calls Gollas. He describes this king, who may well be identified with Mihirakula, in the following words: "He is the lord of India, and oppressing the people forces them to pay tribute."[132]

While the imperial line of Guptas came to an end with the Hun invasion, another line of Guptas, probably a branch of the imperial family, maintained its rule in Magadha for some two centuries longer.

The Gupta rulers themselves were Hindus, and a Brahmanical revival took place within this period.[133] The era was also distinguished for its literary activity. Kalidasa, a dramatist and poet who flourished under Chandragupta II, has been called "the greatest name in Indian literature," and "the Indian Shakespeare."[134] The Panchatantra, which took its present form at about this time, has been said to be perhaps the best collection of stories in the world. The name of this work means "Five Books," and each book consists of a framing story, within which numerous other stories are inserted. Thus in book one, for example, the main outline is provided by the narrative of the broken friendship of the lion Rusty and the bull Lively, while some thirty inserted stories are told by two jackals, Victor and Cheek. The purpose of the Panchatantra is to provide a textbook on the wise conduct of life, and its message is that, granted security and freedom from anxiety, joy comes from the wise use of

[132] XI. tr. J. W. McCrindle, *The Christian Topography of Cosmas, an Egyptian Monk*. 1897, pp.370f.
[133] CSHI p.99.
[134] H. G. Rawlinson, *India, A Short Cultural History* (ed. C. G. Seligman). 1938, p.137; A. Berriedale Keith, *The Sanskrit Drama in Its Origin, Development, Theory and Practice*. 1924, pp.143-167.

one's active powers, from association with friends, and from the 'exercise of intelligence.[135]

In the realm of specifically religious literature a vast labor was performed in the collection and systematization of various teachings and lore.

THE SUTRAS

The interest in codification is especially apparent in the development of the Sutra literature. The word *sutra* means in Sanskrit "a thread," and hence is applicable to a string of rules or aphorisms. The Sutras, therefore, are systematic treatises in which a complete body of doctrine on some subject is condensed into the form of a series of concise aphoristic statements.

One large body of Sutras deals with practical matters in several different areas. The Śrauta- or Kalpa-Sutras are Books of Vedic Ritual, and give a compact description of the great sacrifices.[136] The principles involved in the Kalpa-Sutras are further discussed in the Purva Mimamsa-Sutras.[137] The Grihya-Sutras are House Books, and give the rules for the Vedic ceremonies which are to be carried out in the home.[138] The Dharma-Sutras are Law Books, and treat of both secular and religious law. Some of the older and more important Dharma-Sutras are those of Apastamba, Gautama, Vishnu, Vasishtha, and Baudhayana.[139] The Vishnu-Sutra contains this interesting and clear-cut description of the caste system: "Brahmans, Kshatriyas, Vaisyas, and Sudras are the four castes. The first three of these are [called] twice-born. . . . Their duties are: for a Brahman, to teach [the Veda]; for a Kshatriya, constant practice in arms; for a Vaisya, the tending of cattle; for a Sudra, to serve the twice-born."[140] The famous Law of Manu, which is another Dharma-Sutra still belonging to the Gupta Age, explains in its account of the creation that the four castes owe their positions to the fact of their having proceeded

[135] Franklin Edgerton, *The Panchatantra Reconstructed, An Attempt to Establish the Lost Original Sanskrit Text of the Most Famous of Indian Story-Collections on the Basis of the Principal Extant Versions, Text, Critical Apparatus, Introduction, Translation* (American Oriental Series, 2, 3). 2 vols. 1924; Arthur W. Ryder, *The Panchatantra.* 1925.

[136] F. Max Müller in SBE II, p.x, footnote.

[137] Mimamsa refers to inquiry into the connected meaning of the sacred texts, and Purva means "earlier" in distinction from the Uttara or "later" Mimamsa. George Thibaut in SBE XXXIV, pp.x-xii.

[138] Seven Grihya-Sutras are translated by Hermann Oldenberg in SBE XXIX, XXX.

[139] Translated by Georg Bühler and Julius Jolly in SBE II, VII, XIV.

[140] II, 1f.,4-8. SBE VII, p.12.

respectively from the mouth, arms, thighs and feet of the supreme god Brahman.[141] The Law of Manu also gives a detailed outline of the four stages (*ashramas*)[142] in the life of the religious man, in which he is successively a student, a married householder, a hermit in the forest, and a homeless mendicant.[143]

Another great body of Sutras is concerned not with action in practical matters, but with knowledge. The portions of the Vedic literature upon which these Sutras are based, and whose teachings they desire to systematize, are the Aranyakas and Upanishads. They are known as the Uttara Mimamsa-Sutras, or the Vedanta-Sutras, Vedanta signifying in Sanskrit the "end or final aim of the Veda." These Sutras too were probably completed before the end of the Gupta Period.[144] In form, however, they are so exceedingly condensed and abbreviated as to be almost unintelligible apart from the later commentaries of Sankara and Ramanuja which have been attached to them.[145]

THE PURANAS

The interest in compiling religious lore also gave rise in the Gupta Period to the Puranas, the oldest of which probably belong to the sixth century A.D.[146] The word *purana* means "ancient" in Sanskrit, and the Puranas are collections of Ancient Tales or Ancient Lore. They deal with many miscellaneous matters including cosmogony, theology, genealogy, and traditional history, all illustrated with numerous legends, fables and stories. Taken collectively, they have been described as "a popular encyclopaedia of ancient and mediaeval Hinduism, religious, philosophical, historical, personal, social, and political,"[147] and together with the great epics are the real Bible of the common people of India today.[148]

For a single quotation of elevated character we may give the following from the Agni Purana:

> It is the spirit of sincerity and sympathy
> That forms the backbone of virtue.

[141] I, 31. tr. George Bühler in SBE xxv, p.14. For the caste system in general see J. H. Hutton, *Caste in India, Its Nature, Function, and Origins.* 1946.
[142] Coomaraswamy, *Hinduism and Buddhism*, p.29.
[143] II, 70-246; III-V; VI, 1-32,33-97. SBE xxv, pp.43-216.
[144] HERE VIII, p.648.
[145] SBE XXXIV, XXXVIII, XLVIII.
[146] CSHI p.99; Herbert H. Gowen, *A History of Indian Literature from Vedic Times to the Present Day.* 1931, p.452.
[147] F. E. Pargiter in HERE X, p.448.
[148] J. N. Farquhar, *An Outline of the Religious Literature of India.* 1920, p.136.

> And even a small cup of water presented
> To the parched lips of a thirsty man,
> Out of a heart-felt sympathy,
> Brings immortal merit to the offerer.[149]

Many of the Vedic deities, such as Indra, Agni, Soma and Surya, appear in the Puranas, but sometimes their functions have been changed as in the case of Varuna, for example, who has now become the god of the ocean. Also, local cults are recognized, and the worship of the goddess of snakes and the veneration of the cow are mentioned. Of all the gods, however, three are the most prominent, Brahma, Vishnu and Śiva. Together they make up the Trimurti or three-fold manifestation of the supreme Brahman.[150]

Brahma is "the personalized form of the impersonal Brahman,"[151] and is the creator of the world. Sometimes praised as the highest god, he is more often considered inferior to Vishnu and Śiva, and in the further course of the centuries was to sink to a relatively insignificant place.[152]

Vishnu is the god who appeared in the Rig-Veda in only a minor role, but is now the gracious preserver of all things. He is usually said to have ten major incarnations, as follows: (1) as a fish when he saved Manu in the midst of the flood; (2) as a tortoise when he supported a mountain at the churning of the ocean, and the goddess Lakshmi and other precious things were produced; (3) as a boar when he raised the earth which had sunk to the bottom of the ocean; (4) as a man-lion when he destroyed a terrible demon; (5) as a dwarf when he outwitted another demon; (6) as Parasurama or Rama-with-the-ax when he rid the earth of all the Kshatriyas; (7) as Rama or Ramachandra, the hero of the Ramayana; (8) as Krishna, the figure in the Mahabharata; (9) as the historical Buddha; (10) as Kalki, a warrior who is yet to come at the end of the age to destroy the wicked and establish righteousness. In the Agni Purana, however, no less than twenty-four forms of Vishnu are enumerated, and in the Bhagavata Purana it is added that the incarnations of the deity are really innumerable.[153]

The Agni Purana is of special interest at this point because it also

[149] Hume, *Treasure-House of the Living Religions*, p.208. Quoted by permission of the publishers, Charles Scribner's Sons, New York.

[150] Govinda Das, *Hinduism*. 1924, p.183; J. Estlin Carpenter, *Theism in Medieval India* (Hibbert Lectures). 1926, pp.225-295.

[151] Haydon, *Biography of the Gods*, p.104.

[152] A. Hillebrandt in HERE II, p.799.

[153] Jacobi in HERE VII, pp.193f.; Pargiter in HERE X, p.452.

tells how in the sculptured representations of Vishnu each of his twenty-four forms may be differentiated.[154] The images of Vishnu usually portray him in a rather uniform way as a four-armed personage, who holds as characteristic objects a mace, a lotus, a conch and a disc. According to the Agni Purana the order in which these four objects appear in the four hands is indicative of the special aspect of the deity which is being portrayed. Thus, for example, if the lotus is in the lower right hand, the mace in the upper right, the disc in the upper left, and the conch in the lower left, the god is shown in his special form as Trivikrama, he of the three strides. The allusion is to the chief mythological feat of Vishnu, to which reference is made as early as in the Vedic hymns. There Vishnu is spoken of as "He who strode wide with his three strides across the regions of the earth";[155] and as "He within whose three wide-extended paces all living creatures have their habitation."[156] Later the Śatapatha-Brahmana explains that "by his first step he gained this same [earth], by the second this aerial expanse, and by his last [step] the sky."[157] Finally the medieval story narrates that when a demon-king was dominating the three worlds, Vishnu came to him in the form of a small dwarf and asked that he be given as much space as he could cover in three steps. When the request was granted, Vishnu strode in two paces over earth and heaven, but condescended to leave the lower world still in the demon's possession.[158] The image of Vishnu pictured in Fig. 54 is in the Indian Museum at Calcutta, and shows the god with the distinctive attributes of Trivikrama.[159]

Śiva is the god whose prototype may be recognized at Mohenjo-daro, and who is now the destroyer of the world. He has several wives, who are the mother goddesses of ancient times. These include Parvati, the lovely daughter of the Himalayas, whose son is Ganesha, the elephant-headed god of wisdom; Durga "the inaccessible," a yellow woman riding on a tiger; and Kali "the black," a terrible figure dripping with blood, encircled with snakes, and adorned with skulls.

[154] B. B. Bidyabinod, *Varieties of the Vishnu Image* (MASI, 2). 1920. For the detailed measurements and sets of proportions according to which images are to be made, as specified in the Hindu *Agamas*, see T. A. Gopinatha Rao, *Talamana or Iconometry* (MASI, 3). 1920. The Talamana was the forerunner of the later Śilpa-Śastras.
[155] Rig-Veda I, clv, 4. SBE XXXII, p.52.
[156] Rig-Veda I, cliv, 2. Macnicol, *Hindu Scriptures*, p.12.
[157] I, ix, 3, v.9. SBE XII, p.268.
[158] K. de B. Codrington in G. T. Garratt, ed., *The Legacy of India*. 1937, p.99.
[159] Bidyabinod, *Varieties of the Vishnu Image*, Pl. VII,a.

THE TANTRAS

The Gupta Period probably witnessed at least the beginnings of yet another body of writings, the Tantras, which are generally ascribed to the sixth and seventh centuries A.D. The name of these writings is derived from a word which means, in the first place, web or warp, then an uninterrupted series, and then an orderly rule or ritual. These works also bear the name of Agamas. They comprise a number of treatises, the content of which is chiefly magical or mystical. Most distinctively they have to do with the worship of the gods of the Trimurti in their female essence (Sakti), and personal devotion is directed particularly toward the wives of Śiva.[160] With these writings we reach the fourth order of Hindu literature, the four classes in the order of inspiration and authority being: (1) *śruti*, or revealed literature, including the Vedas, Brahmanas, and Upanishads; (2) *smriti*, or traditional literature, including the Epics and Sutras; (3) *purana*; (4) *tantra*.[161]

GUPTA TEMPLES

Of the most ancient Hindu temples still standing in India some probably come from the Gupta Period. One of these is shown in Fig. 55. This is the temple known as the Lad Khan at Aihole in the Deccan. It is believed to date from around the middle of the fifth century A.D. Constructed as a low, flat building, its walls are made of stone slabs set between square pilasters, and its windows also are stone slabs perforated in various patterns. The temple has a porch, on the pillars of which are figures of river goddesses. There is furthermore a cella, with a porch of its own, built on the roof of the main temple, which forms an independent shrine of the Sun.[162]

[160] D. N. Bose, *Tantras, Their Philosophy and Occult Secrets.*
[161] Gowen, *A History of Indian Literature from Vedic Times to the Present Day*, pp.459f.; Geden in HERE XII, pp.192f.
[162] CHIIA p.79, Fig. 148.

8. THE EARLY MEDIEVAL PERIOD, A.D. C.600-C.850

HARSHA VARDHANA

AFTER the collapse of the dominion of the White Huns, a number of new dynasties arose, of which the most important was the Vardhana family of Sthanviśvara or Thanesar. A member of this family became the greatest Indian ruler of the seventh century, and the dominant force at that time in the greater part of north India. This man was named Harsha, and he ruled A.D. c.606-c.647. He united the kingdoms of Thanesar and Kanauj, and then made the city of Kanauj his capital. From there he exercised sway over an empire which extended from the mouth of the Ganges to the Sutlej.

Harsha was not only a successful warrior and administrator, but also a man of literary and religious interests. In the realm of literature, three important dramas are ascribed to him.[163] In personal religion he was a Buddhist and gave active support to that faith but also paid reverence to deities such as Śiva and Surya as well as to the Buddha.[164]

HIUEN TSANG

At this time another Chinese Buddhist pilgrim came to India. This was Hiuen Tsang who arrived about A.D. 630 and stayed for some fifteen years, over half of which were spent within Harsha's dominions. Hiuen Tsang wrote a detailed account of his experiences which is known as the Si-yu-ki or Record of Western Countries, and this is supplemented by a life of the pilgrim written by his disciple Hwui Li.[165]

The achievements and conduct of Harsha were described by Hiuen Tsang as follows: "He went from east to west subduing all who were not obedient; the elephants were not unharnessed nor the soldiers unhelmeted. After six years he had subdued the Five Indies. Having thus enlarged his territory, he increased his forces; he had 60,000 war elephants and 100,000 cavalry. After thirty years his arms reposed, and he governed everywhere in peace. He then practised

---

[163] Keith, *The Sanskrit Drama in Its Origin, Development, Theory and Practice,* pp.170-181.

[164] Rawlinson, *India, A Short Cultural History,* p.112.

[165] tr. Samuel Beal, *Buddhist Records of the Western World, Translated from the Chinese of Hiuen Tsiang* (A.D. 629). 2 vols. 1906; and *The Life of Hiuen-Tsiang by the Shaman Hwui Li.* 1911. See also Emil Abegg in *Asiatische Studien.* 2 (1948), pp.56-79.

to the utmost the rules of temperance, and sought to plant the tree of religious merit to such an extent that he forgot to sleep or to eat. He forbade the slaughter of any living thing or flesh as food throughout the Five Indies on pain of death without pardon."[166]

Concerning the land and people in general, Hiuen Tsang reported: "The towns and villages have inner gates; the walls are wide and high; the streets and lanes are tortuous, and the roads winding. The thoroughfares are dirty and the stalls arranged on both sides of the road with appropriate signs. Butchers, fishers, dancers, executioners, scavengers, and so on, have their abodes without the city. In coming and going these persons are bound to keep on the left side of the road till they arrive at their homes. Their houses are surrounded by low walls, and form the suburbs. The earth being soft and muddy, the walls of the towns are mostly built of brick or tiles. The towers on the walls are constructed of wood or bamboo; the houses have balconies and belvederes, which are made of wood, with a coating of lime or mortar, and covered with tiles. . . .

"Their clothing is not cut or fashioned; they mostly affect fresh white garments; they esteem little those of mixed color or ornamented. The men wind their garments round their middle, then gather them under the armpits, and let them fall down across the body, hanging to the right. The robes of the women fall down to the ground; they completely cover their shoulders. They wear a little knot of hair on their crowns, and let the rest of their hair fall loose. . . . On their heads the people wear caps, with flower-wreaths and jeweled necklets. . . .

"With respect to the division of families, there are four classifications. The first is called the Brahman, men of pure conduct. They guard themselves in religion, live purely, and observe the most correct principles. The second is called Kshatriya, the royal caste. For ages they have been the governing class: they apply themselves to virtue and kindness. The third is called Vaisyas, the merchant class: they engage in commercial exchange, and they follow profit at home and abroad. The fourth is called Sudra, the agricultural class: they labor in ploughing and tillage. . . .

"With respect to the ordinary people, although they are naturally light-minded, yet they are upright and honorable. . . . They dread the retribution of another state of existence, and make light of the things of the present world."[167]

[166] v, 1. tr. Beal, *Buddhist Records of the Western World*, I, pp.213f.
[167] II, 5,7,11,13. tr. Beal, *ibid.*, I, pp.73-75,82f.

The capital city of Kanauj was described by Hiuen Tsang as lying near the western bank of the Ganges, and having a "dry ditch" around it, "with strong and lofty towers facing one another." On every side were flowers and woods, and "lakes and ponds, bright and pure and shining like mirrors." "The people are well off and contented," continues Hiuen Tsang. "They apply themselves much to learning, and in their travels are very much given to discussion [on religious subjects]. . . . The believers in Buddha and the heretics are about equal in number." The Hindu shrines of the place included, he said, a temple of the Sun-deva and another of Maheśvara [the god Śiva]. "The two temples are built of a blue stone of great lustre, and are ornamented with various elegant sculptures. . . . Each of these foundations has 1,000 attendants to sweep and water it; the sound of drums and of songs accompanied by music, ceases not day nor night."[168]

Concerning the important city of Benares, Hiuen Tsang wrote: "The capital borders the Ganges river. . . . Its inner gates are like a small-toothed comb; it is densely populated. The families are very rich, and in the dwellings are objects of rare value. The disposition of the people is soft and humane, and they are earnestly given to study. They are mostly unbelievers, a few reverence the law of Buddha. . . . There are a hundred or so Deva temples with about 10,000 sectaries. They honor principally Maheśvara. Some cut their hair off, others tie their hair in a knot, and go naked, without clothes; they cover their bodies with ashes, and by the practice of all sorts of austerities they seek to escape from birth and death." A copper statue of the Deva Maheśvara which Hiuen Tsang saw here was, he says, somewhat less than one hundred feet in height, and appeared grave and majestic, "as though really living."[169]

After the time of Harsha, northern India split up again into a number of small states. Meanwhile in the western Deccan the kingdom of the Chalukyas, which had arisen in the middle of the sixth century and which Harsha had been unable to conquer, maintained its existence until it was taken over by the Rashtrakutas in the middle of the eighth century. In Mysore (Maisur) the Gangas ruled from the second to the eleventh century, and in the east and south the Pallava dynasty was dominant from the fifth to the ninth century.

EARLY MEDIEVAL TEMPLES

Many fine Hindu temples belong to the Early Medieval Period,

[168] v, 1. tr. Beal, *ibid.*, ɪ, pp.206f.,223.
[169] vɪɪ, 1. tr. Beal, *ibid.*, ɪɪ, pp.44f.

of which several notable examples will be mentioned. The great
brick temple of Lakshmana at Sirpur (Fig. 56) may come from the
reign of Harsha himself, or may perhaps be as much later as the
ninth century. While the upper part of the tower is lost, the structure is still very impressive. It was richly ornamented, and the whole
was originally covered with stucco. The carving on the lintel of the
stone doorway represents the Birth of Brahma.[170]

The large temple at Pattadakal now known as the Virupaksha is
shown by the inscriptions upon it to have been built by a queen of
the Chalukya king Vikramaditya II (A.D. c.733-c.746). A photograph
of this structure, which is still in religious use, is reproduced in
Fig. 57. The temple is constructed of large blocks of stone which
are closely joined together without mortar. It was dedicated to Śiva,
and its numerous sculptures contain many representations of this
god in various forms, as well as scenes from the Ramayana and other
subjects.[171]

The Kailasanatha temple at Elura[172] is one of the most magnificent
architectural monuments in all India. It was doubtless the work of
the Rashtrakuta ruler Krishna I (A.D. c.757-c.783), among whose
achievements is said to have been the construction of a wonderful
Śiva temple in "the hill Elapura." The identification of the actual
temple at Elura with the one thus mentioned is further supported by
the name Kannara or Krishna which was still legible in the last century in an inscription on the temple. The Elura temple appears to
have been modeled after the Virupaksha at Pattadakal, but is considerably larger than the work of Vikramaditya's queen. What is
most remarkable, moreover, is that the Kailasanatha at Elura was
carved directly out of the solid rock as a complete monolithic shrine.
A rectangular pit was quarried in the sloping hillside, 50 to 100 feet
deep, 160 feet wide and 280 feet long, and the mass of rock in the
middle of this excavation was sculptured into the temple itself.

The Kailasanatha displays the main architectural features which
are characteristic of the Hindu temple. In Fig. 58 one sees in the
foreground the massive gateway which serves as the *gopura* or entrance to the whole temple complex. Behind this and connected with

[170] CHIIA pp.93f., Fig. 186.
[171] James Fergusson, *History of Indian and Eastern Architecture.* rev. ed. by James
Burgess and R. Phené Spiers. 1910, I, pp.352-355; CHIIA Fig. 188.
[172] Fergusson, *History of Indian and Eastern Architecture,* I, pp.342-348; E. B.
Havell, *The Ancient and Medieval Architecture of India: A Study of Indo-Aryan
Civilization.* 1915, pp.193-200.

it by a rock bridge is the two-storied porch or shrine of Nandi, the sacred bull of Śiva, for whom a place is always made in connection with a Śiva temple. On either side of the Nandi shrine are two square pillars (*dhwajastambhas*, literally banner staves), nearly fifty feet high, bearing the three-pronged emblem of Śiva. A further bridge leads on back to the main part of the temple. Here there is another *gopura*, and then a large square porch or *mandapam*, the terraced roof of which is supported by sixteen heavy columns. Behind this is the central shrine, which in a Hindu temple is called the *vimana* or "the vehicle of the gods." The *vimana* is usually a square or rectangular building with a pyramidal roof which may have one or several stories. Here at Elura the upper pyramid of the *vimana* rises to a height of ninety-six feet. The tower or its upper part is also known as a *śikhara*,[173] and is thought of as standing for Mount Meru, the dwelling place of gods and spirits, or in the case of a Śiva shrine like the Kailasanatha, as representing Mount Kailasa, which was the topmost peak of Meru and the retreat of Śiva.

Mount Kailasa also appears in the bold sculptures which adorn the temple at Elura. In a composition found on the south side of the temple and shown in Fig. 59, Śiva and Parvati are on Kailasa.[174] The demon king Ravana has been imprisoned within the mountain, because of his impious attempt to remove it to Ceylon, and now is attempting with all the strength of his twenty arms to break his way free. The very mountain quakes, and Parvati seizes Śiva's arm in fear, while her maid flees away. With undisturbed calm, however, Śiva holds everything in control beneath his foot.

Another impressive Śiva shrine which likewise dates from the seventh or eighth century is at Elephanta. Elephanta is a rocky island which overlooks the harbor at Bombay, and which was so named by the Portuguese because of a large stone elephant which once stood near the shore. The temple with which we are here concerned is a completely subterranean excavation, located in the island's western hill some two hundred and fifty feet above the high-water level. The main entrance is from the north, and there are also pillared porticoes on the east and west. The interior of the temple is an underground

---

[173] Strictly speaking, in the south it is only the dome of the tower which is called the *śikhara*, while in the north the name is applied to the entire tower. On the origin of the *śikhara* see E. B. Havell in *Commemorative Essays Presented to Sir Ramkrishna Gopal Bhandarkar.* 1917, pp.443-446.

[174] Codrington, *Ancient India from the Earliest Times to the Guptas with Notes on the Architecture and Sculpture of the Medieval Period*, Pl. 55.

hall, over ninety feet square, the roof of which is upheld by six rows of pillars finished with very fine ribbed cushion capitals. Fig. 60 shows the central aisle which leads straight from the northern portico to the rocky wall at the south.

Against the southern wall stands a colossal bust of the three-headed Śiva, one of the most imposing works of Indian art (Fig. 61). The entire carving, including the base, shoulders and triune head, is about twenty feet in height. According to the Vishnudhar-mottara, a manual of perhaps the seventh century on the subject of the technical details of religious art,[175] there are five faces of Śiva, each of which may be likened to one of the elements of the universe. The first is Iśana, which is compared to the invisible and omnipresent ether. This face is ordinarily not carved. The second is Tatpurusha, likened to the wind; the third, Aghora, symbolized by fire; the fourth, Vamadeva, regarded as like to water; and the fifth, Sadyojata, referred for comparison to the earth. In the Elephanta sculpture, the middle face is identified as that of Tatpurusha; the face on the spectator's left as that of Aghora, the wrathful; and the one on the right as that of Vamadeva, the blissful. The hand on the left belonging to the wrathful face has a serpent's head rising from between its fingers; the hand on the right belonging to the blissful face holds a lotus flower. All together the image represents the fully manifest Supreme Śiva.[176]

Concerning such rock and cave temples as the ones at Elura and Elephanta and others, William Rothenstein has written: "Of the individual carvers of the great rock temples we know nothing; yet the range and audacity of their achievements are astonishing. If ever there was meaning in the old idea that images lay hidden in blocks of stone, awaiting only the blows of the craftsman's mallet to be set free, then these cave carvings show the truest form of sculpture. Not from single blocks of stone or marble, but from solid hill-sides whole temples were carved. In most civilizations figures have been applied to the buildings. In India the entire fabric, with its halls and courts, its roofs and supporting shafts, its sculptured figures and enrichments, has been conceived and created from the womb of the earth itself. Building and sculpture are as the body and its organs, so

[175] III, xlviii, 1-3. tr. Stella Kramrisch, *The Vishṇudharmottara (Part III)*, *A Treatise on Indian Painting and Image-Making*. 2d ed. 1928, p.71. cf. J. V. S. Wilkinson in Richard Winstedt, ed., *Indian Art*. 1948, p.113; Stella Kramrisch in *Ancient India*. 2 (July 1946). pp.4-8, Pl. III.
[176] Stella Kramrisch in *Ancient India*. 2 (July 1946), pp.4-8.

closely united that to tear away parts would leave an open wound."[177]

This brief survey of some representative Hindu temples of the Early Medieval Period may be concluded with mention of one shrine which comes from the ancient Pallava kingdom. This is the Kailasanatha temple at Kanchi,[178] pictured in Fig. 62. It was constructed by the Pallava king Rajasimha (Narasimhavarman II), who ruled in the last quarter of the seventh century A.D. The temple is a shrine of Śiva, and is ornamented with numerous sculptures which are largely devoted to representations of Śiva and Parvati.[179]

ŚANKARA

It was in the Early Medieval Period and probably around A.D. 800 that there lived one of the greatest philosophers of Hinduism. This was Śankara, who "is regarded often as representing the standard type of Hindu thought."[180] Śankara traveled and taught throughout India from Assam to Kashmir, and from the Himalayas to Cape Comorin, and established religious centers in the four corners of the land. His purpose was the revival, explanation and inculcation of the fundamental teachings of the Upanishads. To this end he wrote numerous treatises, among which the most important are his extensive commentaries on the Upanishads and on the Vedanta-Sutras. The commentary on the Vedanta-Sutras[181] is regarded as his masterpiece both in philosophical value and in literary character. The system of the Vedanta, or "final aim of the Veda," as set forth by Śankara, is an unqualified monism. Whatever is, says Śankara, is in reality one. There is only one universal being, and that is Brahman, whose very substance is intelligence or thought. Any conceivable attribute must be denied to belong to Brahman, and the appearance

[177] Rothenstein in Codrington, *Ancient India from the Earliest Times to the Guptas with Notes on the Architecture and Sculpture of the Medieval Period*, p.5. Quoted by permission of the publishers, Ernest Benn, Ltd., London.

[178] The ancient Kanchipuram (the golden city) is the modern town of Conjeeveram.

[179] Fergusson, *History of Indian and Eastern Architecture*, I, pp.357-359; CHIIA Fig. 197.

[180] S. Radhakrishnan, *The Hindu View of Life*. 1927, p.62; cf. Paul Deussen, *Allgemeine Geschichte der Philosophie mit besonderer Berücksichtigung der Religionen*, I, 3, *Die nachvedische Philosophie der Inder*. 1908, pp.579-614; Theos Bernard, *Hindu Philosophy*. 1947, pp.7-9.

[181] tr. George Thibaut, *The Vedânta-Sûtras with the Commentary by Saṅkarâkârya.* SBE XXXIV, XXXVIII; Paul Deussen, *The System of the Vedanta According to Bâdarâyana's Brahma-Sûtras and Çaṅkaras Commentary Thereon Set Forth as a Compendium of the Dogmatics of Brahmanism from the Standpoint of Çankara.* tr. Charles Johnston, 1912.

of the world itself is due to *maya* or illusion. The enlightened soul, however, is able to look through the veil of illusion and recognize itself to be Brahman. In that recognition the self gains deliverance from the influence of *maya,* and is able in the end to assert itself in its true nature as nothing other than the absolute, eternal Brahman. Such is "the summit of Indian thought"[182] as reached in Śankara.

[182] J. N. Farquhar, *The Crown of Hinduism.* 1915, pp.243f.

9. THE LATE MEDIEVAL PERIOD, A.D. C.850-C.1200

IN THE centuries immediately preceding the Muslim invasions, India was divided into many different kingdoms of which only a few can be mentioned here. In the northern part of the land there were numerous clans of Rajputs. These "Sons of Kings" were probably descended in part from peoples who had come into India from central Asia like the White Huns and the Gurjaras[183] who followed them. The legend they cherished of their origin, however, was that when Rama-with-the-ax destroyed all the Kshatriyas and left the land masterless, the gods went to Mount Abu[184] in southern Rajputana and from the sacred fire pit there produced four "fire-born clans."[185] These four clans were the Solankis, Pawars, Chauhans, and Pariharas.

The Solankis or later Chaulukyas held sway in Gujarat, with their capital at Anhilwar (Anahilavada). Their most powerful ruler was Siddharaja (A.D. 1094-1143), who was a famous builder and a patron of the Jains. The Pawars or Paramaras ruled in Malwa from the ninth to the eleventh century. Their greatest king was Bhoja, whose capital was at Dhara, and who reigned around A.D. 1010 to 1065. In addition to his exploits on the field of battle, Bhoja was celebrated as a writer and a builder, and his name has become proverbial as the ideal Hindu monarch. The Chauhans were dominant in Ajmir, and their best-known king was Prithiviraja, of whom romantic stories are told in the popular literature of Rajputana. The Pariharas or Pratiharas ruled an extensive region around Kanauj, where their capital had been established by a king known as Bhoja I or Mihira (A.D. c.840-c.890). They were superseded at the end of the eleventh century by the Gaharwars or Gahadavalas.

Other Rajput clans included the Tomaras who founded Delhi; the Palas who ruled in Bengal, until they were succeeded by the Senas about the middle of the eleventh century; and the Chandels who held sway in Jejakabhukti, the modern Bundelkhand.[186] The Chandels probably originated from the indigenous tribe of Gonds. The most famous member of their dynasty was Dhanga who reigned from

---

[183] Their name survives in the name of the modern district of Gujarat. Likewise the name Rajputana is derived from the Rajputs.

[184] A powerful Gurjara Kingdom had come into existence at Bhinmal about fifty miles from Mount Abu, and this was the historic center of the Rajput tribes.

[185] Rawlinson, *India, A Short Cultural History*, p.200.

[186] This name is derived from the Bundelas, a clan which appeared here in the fourteenth century.

A.D. 950 to 999, and who like the other Chandel kings was a great builder.

In other parts of India there were yet other kingdoms. On the southeast coast in relatively isolated Orissa, independent rulers had maintained themselves much of the time. In the eleventh century we hear of a Somavansi dynasty, and in the twelfth century princes of the Eastern Ganga dynasty ruled there. In Mysore the dominant power was now that of the Hoyśala dynasty, whose capital was at Dorasamudra, and whose kings were originally Jains but later became Vaishnavas. Yet farther south was the area ruled by the Cholas, from whose kingdom (Cholamandalam) the Coromandel Coast derives its name. This kingdom existed as early as the time of Aśoka but rose to its highest importance under the great king Rajaraja who reigned from A.D. 985 to 1012. The Chola capital was at Tanjore.

MEDIEVAL TEMPLES

The notable development of temple architecture and sculpture which was already far advanced in the Early Medieval Period now reached its climax.[187] A vast technical literature, known as the Śilpa-Śastras, provided authoritative specifications according to which the proportions and details of statues and buildings were regulated. The medieval Śilpa-Śastras, it may be added, are still in use by Indian craftsmen.[188]

In the Śilpa-Śastras three main types of temples are differentiated. The three types are designated Nagara, Vesara and Dravida, and are found respectively in northern, central and southern India.

The southern type prevails in the Madras Presidency, and is characterized by the terraced pyramidal tower, such as we have already observed in the Kailasanatha temple at Elura. For another example we may refer to the great Rajarajeśvara temple at Tanjore (Fig. 63) which was constructed by the Chola king Rajaraja by about A.D. 1012. Old Tamil inscriptions on the base of the central shrine still enumerate the gifts of gold images, vessels and ornaments which were made to the temple by Rajaraja and also by his sister and others. As may be seen in the photograph, the most impressive feature of the temple is the enormous square pyramid of the *vimana*. The tower rises in fourteen stories to its summit dome which reaches a

[187] Stella Kramrisch, *The Hindu Temple.* 2 vols. 1946.
[188] Goetz, *Epochen der indischen Kultur*, pp.232,389f.; CHIIA p.125; EB XII, p.221.

height of one hundred and ninety feet. The temple is dedicated to the worship of Śiva.[189]

The central Indian type is found in Mysore and the Deccan. The characteristic feature of this type is that it combines elements from the southern and northern styles, and adds peculiarities of its own. The temples tend to be rather widely spread out and relatively low in elevation. They are often built on a star-shaped plan. The pyramidal towers do not have the distinctive stories of the southern temples, and they carry upward the indentations which mark the shrine below. The sculptured decoration is often very elaborate. The fullest development of this style was reached in Mysore under the Hoyśala kings, and may be illustrated by the Hoyśaleśvara temple at Halebid. The village of Halebid marks the site of Dorasamudra, the capital of the Hoyśala kings, and the temple under consideration was probably begun early in the twelfth century A.D. and finally left unfinished in A.D. 1311 due to the Muslim invasions. The Hoyśaleśvara is a double temple and contains two shrines placed side by side. It was undoubtedly intended to raise two indented pyramidal towers over these two sanctuaries, but this is a part of the work that was never completed, and the structure stands today as shown in Fig. 64. If it could have been carried out fully the architectural design would have been most impressive, and the sculptured decorations which adorn the entire building as it stands are of an almost incredible variety and beauty. A succession of friezes runs around the temple exterior, following all of its indentations. These friezes show beasts and birds, horsemen, scenes from the Ramayana, gods and heavenly beings. Among the animal friezes, that of the elephants may be specially mentioned. It is the first frieze above the temple terrace and extends in length for some seven hundred and ten feet. It contains not less than two thousand sculptured representations of elephants, many with riders and trappings, and all shown in an exceedingly lifelike and striking way. Among the gods every great figure of the Hindu pantheon appears, including Brahma, Śiva with Parvati, and Vishnu in the forms of his various avatars.[190]

For another example of exceedingly rich sculptural ornamentation in a central Indian temple of the Medieval Period, reference may be

[189] Fergusson, *History of Indian and Eastern Architecture*, I, pp.362-364; CHIIA p.122, Fig. 235; G. Jouveau-Dubreuil, *Dravidian Architecture*, ed. S. Krishnaswami Aiyangar. 1917.

[190] Fergusson, *History of Indian and Eastern Architecture*, I, pp.444-446; CHIIA p.118, Fig. 211.

made to the main temple at Palampet, a small village in the Warangal district in the Deccan.[191] This structure is built on a cruciform plan. Its exterior is adorned with long panels of carved figures, including gods, goddesses, warriors, acrobats, musicians and dancing girls. The interior likewise is filled with sculptures, which depict scenes from early myths, the Ramayana, the Puranas, and later Hindu texts. One of the four central columns of the main hall in this temple, with its very intricate ornamentation, is shown in Fig. 65.[192]

The northern type of Indian temple is represented by very numerous examples found in the Punjab, Rajputana, the Ganges Valley, the central provinces, and Orissa. The outstanding feature of this style is its lofty and aspiring vertical development. Here the entire temple is called the *śikhara*, and is distinguished by its curvilinear form. The *śikhara* is usually surmounted by an *amalaka*, a circular, corrugated coping stone carrying a flat dome in the center of which is a vaselike pinnacle.

Some of the finest northern Indian temples of the Medieval Period are at Khajuraho, which was the ancient capital of the Chandel kings, in Bundelkhand. There are some thirty important temples here, most of which are dated from their style and from inscriptions in the century between A.D. 950 and 1050. About one-third belong to the religion of Jainism, one-third to Vaishnavism and one-third to Saivism, and all are very similar architecturally. In each group there is one large temple, sometimes more than one, with smaller ones in its vicinity. The chief temple in the Saiva group, and the most imposing of all the Hindu structures, is the Kandarya Mahadeva which is pictured in Fig. 66. The pinnacle of the tower rises to an elevation of one hundred and sixteen feet above the ground, and the effect of height is greatly accentuated by the vertical lines in the structure and by the way the tower is built up of duplications of itself. Except for the tower all parts of the structure are covered with elaborate sculptures, featuring both floral themes and figures, and giving prominence to the erotic element. On and in the temple no less than eight hundred and seventy-two separate statues have been counted.[198]

Likewise of exceeding magnificence are the northern-style temples in Orissa. The greatest of these is the Lingaraja (Fig. 67) which was built at Bhuvaneśvara around A.D. 1000, and which has been

[191] Ghulam Yazdani, *The Temples at Palampet* (MASI, 6). 1922.
[192] *ibid.*, pl. XXXI,a.
[198] Fergusson, *History of Indian and Eastern Architecture*, II, pp.141-143; CHIIA p.109, Fig. 214.

called "perhaps the most majestic Indian temple now standing."[194] Here the *śikhara* is massive and solemn, yet lofty and impressive. Almost infinite labor has also been bestowed upon the carvings with which the entire structure is decorated. Other notable Orissan temples of the next century or so include the one at Puri, dedicated to Vishnu as Jagannatha or "Lord of the World," and popularly known as Juggernaut; and the one at Konarak, known as the Sun Temple or Black Pagoda, and evidently once devoted to the worship of Vishnu in the form of Surya or the sun.

As the foregoing descriptions have shown, much of Indian sculpture was an integral part of temple buildings. There were also detached works of art, however, and for illustration we show in Fig. 69 a stone statue of Brahma which came from Kuruvatti in the Bellary district, Madras, and is now in the University Museum of the University of Pennsylvania. The entire carving is about five and one-half feet in height. Brahma is portrayed with four faces, and the face at the back is bearded. The inscription at the bottom records the name of the maker of the statue. The date of the work is probably in the eleventh century.

The bronze image shown in Fig. 68 also comes from south India, and is perhaps to be dated in the twelfth century. It is a relatively early and completely intact example, over forty inches in height, of an important type of representation. The figure is known as Nataraja, the Lord of the Dance, and the subject portrayed is the cosmic dance of Śiva. Śiva is here considered not only as the destroyer but also as the sustainer, and indeed as the supreme lord of the universe. He stands within the flaming circle of the cosmos, and performs the five-fold dance of life. The details of the symbolism may be interpreted as follows. One hand holds a drum which marks the rhythm of creation; another hand is uplifted to reassure against fear and signify preservation; yet another hand carries a ball of fire which stands for destruction; the stationary leg gives the idea of repose; the uplifted one symbolizes the divine activity leading to the liberation of all beings. The seven streams of water extending from each side of the head recall the myth that Śiva once kept the heavenly Ganges imprisoned in his hair before finally releasing it in seven streams, one of which is the great river of India. Among the streams is a small figure of the river goddess Ganga.[195]

[194] CHIIA p.115, Fig. 215.
[195] F. St.G. Spendlove in *Gazette des beaux-arts.* 6th Series. 25 (1944), pp.59f.; cf. Ananda Coomaraswamy, *The Dance of Śiva.* 1924, pp.56-66; Heinrich Zimmer,

HINDUISM

RAMANUJA

The greatest Hindu philosopher of the Medieval Period was Ramanuja, who is probably to be dated around A.D. 1100. He lived in his
youth at Kanchi or Conjeeveram, and later settled at Srirangam near
Trichinopoly. He taught and wrote extensively, and like Śankara composed a commentary on the Vedanta-Sutras.[196] Ramanuja agreed with
Śankara that Brahman is the total reality, but unlike Śankara he
taught that Brahman has positive qualities of love and grace, and
that individual souls and the external world exist within the body
of God. Through personal devotion (*bhakti*) the soul gains an in-
tuitive perception of God, and upon release from earthly bondage
passes into the enjoyment of personal bliss in the eternity of Brahman.

"We know from Scripture," says Ramanuja, "that there is a Supreme Person whose nature is absolute bliss and goodness; who is
fundamentally antagonistic to all evil; who is the cause of the origi-
nation, sustentation, and dissolution of the world; who differs in
nature from all other beings, who is all-knowing, who by his mere
thought and will accomplishes all his purposes; who is an ocean of
kindness as it were for all who depend on him; who is all-merciful;
who is immeasurably raised above all possibility of any one being
equal or superior to him; whose name is the highest Brahman. And
with equal certainty we know from Scripture that this Supreme
Lord, when pleased by the faithful worship of his devotees—which
worship consists in daily repeated meditation on him, assisted by the
performance of all the practices prescribed for each caste and *ashra-
ma*—frees them from the influence of nescience which consists of
karma accumulated in the infinite progress of time and hence hard
to overcome; allows them to attain to that supreme bliss which consists in the direct intuition of his own nature: and after that does
not turn them back into the miseries of *samsara*."[197]

In the early and advanced Medieval Periods, then, Hinduism
reached a definitive stage in its development. The implications of
its fundamental philosophy were fully expounded on the monistic
and theistic sides by Śankara and Ramanuja. The expression of its

Myths and Symbols in Indian Art and Civilization. ed. by Joseph Campbell. Bollingen
Series, 6. 1946, pp.151-175.
[196] George Thibaut, *The Vedânta-Sûtras with the Commentary of Râmânuga.* SBE
XLVIII; A. Berriedale Keith in HERE X, pp.572-574.
[197] SBE XLVIII, p.770.

character in art and architecture culminated in such magnificent works as the Kailasanatha at Elura and the Kandarya Mahadeva at Khajuraho. Such achievements of thought and craftsmanship crowned thirty-five hundred years of Indian civilization.

THE MUSLIM INVASIONS

Then came the Muslim invasions, which were begun by the Arabs and continued by the Turks. The greatest threat originated at Ghazni in Afghanistan. There a Turk named Sabuktigin (A.D. 976-997), established a powerful Muslim kingdom, and his son Mahmud (A.D. c.999-1030) raided India repeatedly and in 1022 annexed the Punjab. In his most famous expedition Mahmud went all the way to Somnath on the coast of Gujarat and sacked the temple which was there dedicated to Śiva as the Lord of the Moon.

AL-BIRUNI

Two famous men of letters were active at Ghazni in Mahmud's time, Abul Kasim Mansur or Firdausi (A.D. c.940-c.1020), author of the epic history of Persia, the Shah Namah or Book of Kings; and Abu Rihan Muhammad, called al-Biruni, "the foreigner" (A.D. c.973-c.1048), who wrote an extensive work on India.[198] Al-Biruni had studied in India, and he gives much information about the country and people in this age in which the Muslim conquests were just beginning. Concerning Mahmud's aggression in India he writes with a freedom presumably only possible after the death of that king: "Mahmud utterly ruined the prosperity of the country, and performed there wonderful exploits, by which the Hindus became like atoms of dust scattered in all directions, and like a tale of old in the mouth of the people."[199]

Al-Biruni tells little or nothing of Buddhism or Jainism, but a great deal of Hinduism, with which he seems to have been most familiar in the form of Vaishnavism. His description bears the marks of a reasonably critical and impartial mind, and is reinforced by numerous quotations from Hindu writings. Concerning the faith of the educated people he writes, "The Hindus believe with regard to God that he is one, eternal, without beginning and end, acting by free-will, almighty, all-wise, living, giving life, ruling, preserving; one who in

---

[198] Edward C. Sachau, *Alberuni's India, An Account of the Religion, Philosophy, Literature, Geography, Chronology, Astronomy, Customs, Laws and Astrology of India about* A.D. *1030.* 2 vols. 1888.
[199] I, 11. Sachau, I, p.22.

his sovereignty is unique, beyond all likeness and unlikeness, and that he does not resemble anything nor does anything resemble him."[200]

A great deal of stress is laid upon transmigration or metempsychosis, which al-Biruni regards as the characteristic and distinctive doctrine of Hinduism. "As *the word of confession*, 'There is no god but God, Muhammad is his prophet,' is the shibboleth of Islam, the Trinity that of Christianity, and the institute of the Sabbath that of Judaism, so metempsychosis is the shibboleth of the Hindu religion." Continuing with a description of this belief, al-Biruni says, "The migration begins from low stages, and rises to higher and better ones. . . . The difference of these lower and higher stages depends upon the difference of the actions. . . . This migration lasts until the object aimed at has been completely attained both for the soul and matter; the *lower* aim being the disappearance of the shape of matter, except any such new formation as may appear desirable; the *higher* aim being the ceasing of the desire of the soul to learn what it did not know before, the insight of the soul into the nobility of its own being and its independent existence, its knowing that it can dispense with matter after it has become acquainted with the mean nature of matter and the instability of its shapes, with all that which matter offers to the senses, and with the truth of the tales about its delights. Then the soul turns away from matter; the connecting links are broken, the union is dissolved. Separation and dissolution take place, and the soul returns to its home. . . . The intelligent being, intelligence and its object, are united and become one."[201]

The Muslim author further reports on the caste system which he found to be very prominent. The castes, he says, are called *varna* or "colors," and are four in number: the Brahmans, Kshatriyas, Vaisyas, and Sudras, who were created respectively from the head, from the shoulders and hands, from the thighs, and from the feet of the supreme Brahman. Below the four castes are eight guilds of fullers, shoemakers, jugglers, basket and shield makers, sailors, fishermen, hunters of wild animals and birds, and weavers. Below these are classes of people like the Candalas who belong neither to a caste nor to a guild, and who are occupied with unclean work like the cleansing of the villages. From his own emancipated point of view, al-Biruni says concerning the institution of caste, "We Muslims, of course, stand entirely on the other side of the question, considering

[200] II, 13. Sachau, I, p.27.   [201] v, 24f. Sachau, I, pp.50f.

all men as equal, except in piety; and this is the greatest obstacle which prevents any approach or understanding between Hindus and Muslims."[202]

Al-Biruni also gives descriptions of various Hindu idols, of which one was of bronze and nearly the size of a man, and another of wood, covered with red leather, and with two red rubies for eyes.[203] Pilgrimages were frequent to various sites and particularly to rivers for bathing festivals. According to the author, such pilgrimages were not obligatory but were meritorious. "A man sets off to wander to some holy region, to some much venerated idol or to some of the holy rivers. He worships in them, worships the idol, makes presents to it, recites many hymns and prayers, fasts, and gives alms to the Brahmans, the priests, and others. He shaves the hair of his head and beard, and returns home."[204] Among the places of pilgrimage Benares had become one of the most sacred, as it still is today.[205]

In the time of Mahmud, the Muslim impact upon India was largely in the form of plundering raids, but a later ruler of Ghazni, Muhammad Ghori, seriously undertook the conquest of the land. He extended Muslim sway almost to Delhi, and established his slave Qutb-ud-din Aibak as governor of his Indian dominions. Aibak continued the Muslim conquests, and after the death of Muhammad Ghori in A.D. 1206 became the first Muslim sultan of Delhi and the founder of the dynasty of Slave Kings at that place.

From this time on, for centuries, Islam was the dominant religious force in India. Buddhism had already declined and now was virtually obliterated; Hinduism was greatly weakened and its material possessions much devastated. Hinduism did not perish, however, and eventually its remarkable vitality reasserted itself. A renascence took place, and in modern India the age-old belief in Śiva and Vishnu, in *samsara* and *karma*, lives on.

[202] IX, 48f. Sachau, I, pp.100f.
[203] XI, 56. Sachau, I, pp.116f.
[204] LXVI, 273. Sachau, II, p.142.
[205] E. B. Havell, *Benares, The Sacred City*. 1905.

CHAPTER IV

Jainism

JAINISM was founded by certain great ascetics, of whom the last, Mahavira, was the perhaps slightly elder contemporary of Gautama Buddha. Mahavira himself is believed to have been but the final one of a long line of twenty-four teachers which reaches back into the most remote past. These founders of the faith are known as Jinas or Conquerors, and their adherents are Jains or Jainas. The number of believers in this religion in India today is over one million.

1. THE JAINA SCRIPTURES

ACCORDING to Jaina belief, the great truths of their faith were set forth by all the Jinas of the past and were embodied in definite scriptural works in each successive age.[1] The teachings of the last founder of the religion, Mahavira, were transmitted to posterity by his followers, the Ganadharas, in the form of works known as Puvvas and Angas. These and other compositions constituted the canon, which was faithfully preserved at first but later fell into confusion. In order to restore it, a council was held at Pataliputra shortly before 300 B.C. under Sthulabhadra, a disciple of Bhadrabahu, the head of the church who was then away in another region. Despite the council's best efforts and the sending of Sthulabhadra to consult with Bhadrabahu, it was found impossible at this time to reconstitute the canon completely. Bhadrabahu could indeed recite all of the texts but he forbade the communication of the last four Puvvas to the congregation. In later years the remaining ten of the original fourteen Puvvas were also lost to knowledge, but the other sacred works were preserved and were again revised and edited in the fifth century A.D. at a council held at Valabhi under the presidency of Devarddhi. It is also indicated in Jaina traditions that the sacred texts were for the first time committed to written form at the Council of Valabhi. Since, however, perishable materials such as birch bark and palm leaves were commonly used for Indian manuscripts our oldest extant copies

[1] GJ pp.81-104.

[182]

date only from around the fourteenth century and later. The language of the oldest works is Prakrit, a later form of Sanskrit.

It must also be explained that from the time of the Council of Pataliputra on, a schism deepened within Jainism between two sects known as the Svetambaras and the Digambaras, and that while the former cherish the canon whose origin we have just described, the latter hold that not only the Puvvas but also the Angas and all the original texts have been lost and that the scriptures of the Svetambaras are therefore not genuine. They, the Digambaras, consequently adhere to a secondary and relatively modern (A.D. c.600-c.900) canon of works on history, cosmography, philosophy and ethics.

CANONICAL WORKS

Returning to the scriptures of the Svetambaras we find that they are collectively known as the Siddhanta and that they comprise the following divisions:[2] The first group contains the fourteen Puvvas (Purvas) which, as we have already explained, are no longer extant. They are frequently mentioned in other works, however, and thus we are able to give the following list of their titles and brief indication of some of their subject matter: (1) Uppaya. Origin of substances. (2) Agganiya. Basic truths. (3) Viriyappavaya. Powers of substances. (4) Atthinatthippavaya. Nature of substances from seven logical standpoints. (5) Nanappavaya. True and false perception. (6) Saccappavaya. True and false speech. (7) Ayappavaya. Characteristics of souls. (8) Kammappavaya. Nature of Karma. (9) Paccakkhanappavaya. Renunciation as the means to the eradication of Karma. (10) Vijjanuppavaya. Various sciences. (11) Avamjha. High points in the lives of 63 great men. (12) Panavaya. Medicine. (13) Kiriyavisala. Music, poetry and other arts. (14) Logavindusara. Ceremonies and salvation.

The twelve Angas make up the second division of the canon. Their titles and subject matter are as follows: (1) Ayara (Acaranga).[3] Manner of life of the ascetic. (2) Suyagada (Sutrakritanga).[4] Instructions for monks and refutation of heretical teachings. (3) Thana. Jaina concepts arranged by categories. (4) Samavaya. Continua-

[2] Walther Schubring, *Die Lehre der Jainas nach den alten Quellen dargestellt* (Grundriss der indo-arischen Philologie und Altertumskunde. Encyclopedia of Indo-Aryan Research. III, 7). 1935, pp.52-84; A. Guérinot, *Essai de bibliographie Jaina, Répertoire analytique et méthodique des travaux relatifs au Jainisme avec planches hors texte* (Annales du Musée Guimet, Bibliothèque d'Études, 22). 1906, pp.129-145.
[3] tr. Hermann Jacobi in SBE XXII.
[4] tr. Hermann Jacobi in SBE XLV.

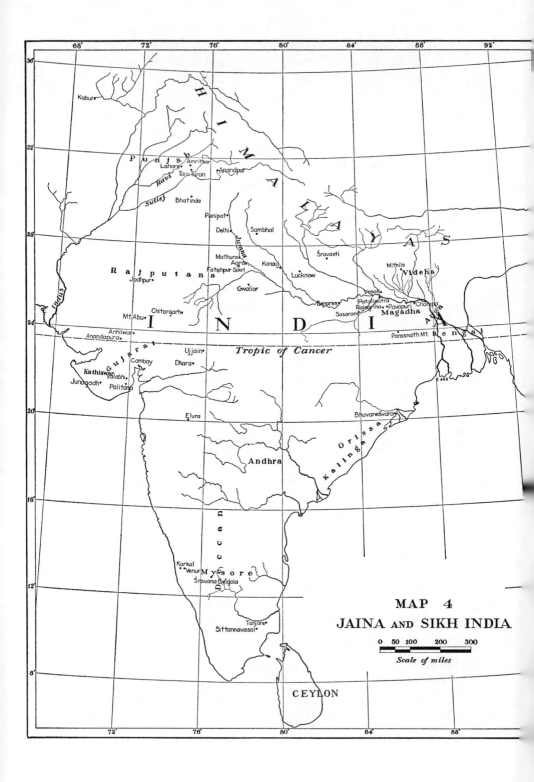

MAP 4

JAINA AND SIKH INDIA

0   50 100   200   300

Scale of miles

tion of the preceding work. (5) Viyahapannatti (Bhagavati). Jaina teachings in dialogues and legends. (6) Nayadhammakahao (Jnatadharmakatha). Narratives and parables. (7) Uvasagadasao. Legends concerning pious laymen who became adherents of Jainism. (8) Antagadadasao.[5] Narratives of ten ascetics who overcame their Karma. (9) Anuttarovavaiyadasao.[6] Legends of saints who attained to the highest heavens. (10) Panhavagaranaim. Commandments and prohibitions. (11) Vivagasuya. Legends concerning the recompense for good and evil deeds. (12) Ditthivaya. This Anga is no longer extant, but once contained five groups of texts among which were the fourteen Puvvas described in the preceding paragraph.

The third division of the canon is that of the twelve Uvangas (Upangas). (1) Uvavaiya. The preaching of Mahavira to King Kunika (Ajataśatru) at Champa. (2) Rayapasenaijja. The conversion of King Paesi by Keshi, a disciple of Pasa (Parśva). (3) Jivabhigama. The world and the beings that are in it. (4) Pannavana. Characteristics of living beings. (5) Surapannatti. Concerning the sun and moon. (6) Jambuddivapannatti. Jambuddiva, the central continent of the universe, on which India and this world are. (7) Candapannatti. Similar to Surapannatti. (8) Nirayavaliyao. War of Kunika and ten stepbrothers against King Cetaka of Vesali. (9) Kappavadimsiyao. Conversion and salvation of sons of the princes mentioned in the preceding work. (10) Pupphiyao. Pre-existences of certain deities who did reverence to Mahavira. (11) Pupphaculao. Similar to the preceding work. (12) Vanhidasao. Conversion of certain princes by Aritthanemi (Arishtanemi).

Ten Painnas (Prakirnas) constitute the fourth section of the canon: (1) Causarana. Prayers. (2) Aurapaccakkhana. Rites in preparation for death. (3) Bhattaparinna. Similar to the foregoing text. (4) Samthara. Also about matters connected with death. (5) Tandulaveyaliya. Embryology and anatomy. (6) Candavejjhaya. Concerning teachers and pupils. (7) Devindatthaya. Enumeration of god-kings. (8) Ganivijja. Astrology. (9) Mahapaccakkhana. Formulas of confession. (10) Viratthaya. Praise of Mahavira and enumeration of his names.

In the fifth group of scriptural texts we find six Cheyasuttas (Chedasutras): (1) Nisiha. Duties of monks and penalties for transgressions. (2) Mahanisiha. Moral transgressions, confession and penance.

---

[5] tr. L. D. Barnett, *The Antagaḍa-Dasāo and Aṇuttarovavāiya-Dasāo, Translated from the Prakrit* (Oriental Translation Fund, New Series, xvii). 1907.
[6] *ibid.*

(3) Vavahara. Instructions for monks and nuns. (4) Ayaradasao. Various teachings concerning the monastic life. The eighth section of this work is the Kalpasutra,[7] which contains biographies of Mahavira and the earlier Jinas. (5) Brihatkappa. Instructions for monks and nuns. (6) Pancakappa. Similar to the preceding.

The sixth section of the canon is composed of only two works: (1) Nandi. Modes of perception. (2) Anuogadara. An encyclopedia of the most varied sciences.

The seventh section comprises four Mulasuttas (Mulasutras): (1) Uttarajjhaya (Uttaradhyayana).[8] Legends, parables, dialogues and sermons. (2) Avassaya. Daily duties. (3) Dasaveyaliya. Rules for the ascetic life. (4) Pindanijjutti. The food of monks.

NONCANONICAL WORKS

In addition to the canonical works of which the chief have now been listed, the Jains also have an extensive noncanonical literature which includes theological and scientific compositions, stories, poetry and drama.[9] Several authors and works in the theological category may be mentioned here.

Umasvati (Umasvami) was the first great dogmatic writer. He lived sometime between the second and fifth centuries A.D., and wrote a work entitled Tattvarthadhigama-Sutra.[10] In this for the first time the entire system of Jaina belief was reduced to a series of condensed statements. His book is accorded the highest authority by both the Śvetambaras and the Digambaras.

Among the Śvetambaras the outstanding theological writers included Divakara (seventh century A.D.), Haribhadra (eighth century A.D.), and Hemachandra (A.D. 1088-1172). The last named was the most important of all, and his works included grammars and commentaries, an exposition of asceticism called Yogaśastra, a long epic poem entitled Trishashtiśalakapurushacaritra[11] in which the

[7] tr. Hermann Jacobi in SBE XXII; J. Stevenson, *The Kalpa Sútra and Nava Tatva: Two Works Illustrative of the Jain Religion and Philosophy, Translated from the Mágadhi with an Appendix Containing Remarks on the Language of the Original.* 1848.

[8] tr. Hermann Jacobi in SBE XLV.

[9] GJ pp.105-134.

[10] tr. J. L. Jaini, *Tattvarthadhigama Sutra (A Treatise on the Essential Principles of Jainism), by Sri Umasvami Acharya, Edited with Introduction, Translation, Notes and Commentary in English* (The Sacred Books of the Jainas, II). 1920.

[11] tr. Banarsi Das Jain, *Jaina Jātakas or Lord Rshabha's Pūrvabhavas, Being an English Translation of Book I Canto I of Hemacandra's Trishashtiśalākāpurushacaritra Originally Translated by Prof. Amūlyacharan Vidyābhushana Revised and Edited*

previous births of the Jinas and other great figures of the faith to the number of sixty-three are recounted, and a work named Pariśishtaparva in which a sort of history of the Jaina church is given.

Among the Digambaras, notable theological authors included Kundakunda, who lived sometime before A.D. 600 and possibly as early as the beginning of the Christian era, and wrote Panchastikayasara,[12] Samayasara,[13] Niyamsara[14] and other works; and Nemichandra, who flourished around A.D. 1000 and wrote Davva-Samgaha,[15] Gommatsara with two parts, Jivakanda[16] and Karmakanda,[17] and other compositions.

---

with Notes and Introduction (The Punjab Sanskrit Series, VIII). 1925; Helen M. Johnson, *Triṣaṣṭiśalākāpuruṣacaritra* (Gaekwad's Oriental Series, 51, 77). 2 vols. 1931-37.

[12] tr. A. Chakravartinayanar, *The Building of the Cosmos or Panchastikayasara (The Five Cosmic Constituents) by Svami Sri Kundakundacharya, Edited with Philosophical and Historical Introduction, Translation, Notes and an Original Commentary in English* (The Sacred Books of the Jainas, III). 1920.

[13] tr. J. L. Jaini, *Samayasara (The Soul-Essence) by Shri Kunda Kunda Acharya, The Original Text in Prakrit, with Its Sanskrit Renderings, and a Translation, Exhaustive Commentaries, and an Introduction* (The Sacred Books of the Jainas, VIII). 1930.

[14] tr. Uggar Sain, *Niyamsara (The Perfect Law) by Shri Kunda Kunda Āchārya, The Original Text in Prakrit, with Its Sanskrit Renderings, Translation, Exhaustive Commentaries, and an Introduction, in English* (The Sacred Books of the Jainas, IX). 1931.

[15] tr. Sarat Chandra Ghoshal, *Davva-Saṃgaha (Dravya-Saṃgraha) by Nemichandra Siddhānta-Chakravartī, with a Commentary by Brahma-Deva, Edited with Introduction, Translation, Notes and an Original Commentary in English* (The Sacred Books of the Jainas, I). 1917.

[16] tr. J. L. Jaini, *Gommatsara Jiva-Kanda (The Soul) by Shri Nemichandra Siddhanta Chakravarti, Edited with Introduction, Translation and Commentary* (The Sacred Books of the Jainas, V). 1927.

[17] tr. J. L. Jaini, *Gommatsara Karma-Kanda (Part I) by Shri Nemichandra Siddhanta Chakravarti, Edited with Introduction, Translation and Commentary* (The Sacred Books of the Jainas, VI). 1927.

2. THE FOUNDERS OF JAINISM

THE TIRTHANKARAS

Among the great figures of Jainism the most important are the twenty-four Tirthankaras, the title Tirthankara probably meaning one who is a guide over the ocean of Samsara.

In the introduction to the Trishashtiśalakapurushacaritra, Hemachandra addresses words of praise and prayer to the twenty-four as follows:[18]

We praise the Lord Rishabha, who was the first king, the first ascetic, the first head of a congregation.

I praise the Arhat Ajita, the sun to the lotus-bed in the form of the universe, in the clear mirror of whose omniscience the world is reflected.

May the words of the Lord of the World, Holy Sambhava, prevail at the time of his preaching—words that resemble rivers in the garden of all the souls who can attain emancipation.

May the Blessed Abhinandana, the moon for the exhilaration of the ocean of Anekanta-doctrine[19] give great joy.

May the Blessed Lord Sumati, whose toe-nails are sharpened on the whetstone of the gods' diadems,[20] grant your desires.

May the splendor of the Lord Padmaprabha's body, red as if from a burst of anger in crushing internal enemies, promote your emancipation.

Homage to the Lord of Jinas, Holy Suparśva, whose feet are honored by Mahendra (Śakra),[21] the sun to the sky in the form of the fourfold congregation.[22]

May Lord Chandraprabha's form, bright as a mass of moonbeams, as if made of embodied pure meditation, be for your prosperity.

May Suvidhi, who considers the universe as plain as a myrobalan lying in the hand by means of his wealth of omniscience, the depository of inconceivable power, be for your enlightenment.

May the Jina Sitala, a new cloud for making shoot up the bulb of the people's supreme joy, who pours forth the nectar of Syadvada, protect you.

May Śreyamsa, the sight of whom is a physician for creatures afflicted with the disease of existence, the lover of the Śri[23] of emancipation, be for your emancipation.

[18] tr. Johnson, *Triṣaṣṭiśalākāpuruṣacaritra*, I, pp.1-7; cf. Banarsi Das Jain, *Jaina Jatakas*, pp.1-5.

[19] The Anekanta doctrine is the "many-sided doctrine" or Syadvada, a distinctive feature of Jaina logic, which considers everything from seven points of view and implies that a true assertion is true only under certain conditions of time and space.

[20] The gods bow their heads so low before this great being that the jewels on their crowns come in contact with his feet.

[21] The Indra of the first heaven, the most important of the sixty-four Indras of the Jaina pantheon.

[22] The Jaina Sangha or congregation is made up of monks, nuns, laymen and laywomen.

[23] The Sanskrit *śri* means fortunate, holy or reverend, and is commonly employed when speaking of a person, king or deity with special respect. Hemachandra uses

May Vasupujya, whose acquisition of Tirthankara-nama-karma[24] has been beneficial to the whole universe, entitled to worship from gods, asuras and men, purify you.

May the words of the Lord Vimala which are like powdered clearing-nut,[25] be successful in clarifying the water of the mind of the three worlds.

May Ananta, rivaling the Svayambhuramana ocean[26] with water of the feeling of compassion, bestow on you the boundless wealth of happiness.

We worship Dharmanatha, the teacher of fourfold dharma,[27] like a kalpa-tree for attainment of creatures' desires.

May the Jina Santinatha, who has brightened the quarters of the sky by the moonlight of his nectar-like words, be a moon to you for dispelling (mental) darkness.

May the Blessed Sri Kunthunatha, lord of the wealth of the supernatural powers, supreme lord of the lords of gods, asuras and men, be for your emancipation.

May the Blessed Aranatha, the sun in the sky of the fourth division of time, grant us pleasure with the Sri of the fourth object of existence.

We praise Malli, a new cloud for the peacocks[28] in the form of lords of gods, asuras and men, Hastimalla [Indra's elephant] for the rooting up of the tree of karma.

We praise Munisuvrata's preaching, which resembles the dawn for the sleep of the world's great delusion.

May the rays of light from Nami's toe-nails which, falling on the heads of his worshipers, purify them like streams of water, protect you.

May the Blessed Arishtanemi, the moon to the ocean of the Yadu-family, a fire to the straw of karma, destroy your misfortunes.

May the Lord Parsvanatha, whose attitude of mind was the same toward Kamatha and Dharanendra[29] while each was performing actions characteristic of himself, be for your emancipation.

May there be good fortune from Holy Vira's eyes whose pupils are wide with compassion even for sinful people, moist with a trace of tears.

This and other Jaina sources provide much information about the various Tirthankaras and enable the construction of a table like the following in which are shown not only the color and emblem customarily associated with each but also his height and age and the

---

the word frequently in such a way that, as here, it might be translated "goddess," without reference, however, to Lakshmi who is known by this name in Hinduism.

24 Tirthankara-nama-karma ensures that one will at last become a Tirthankara.

25 This powder is said to remove all impurities from water in which it is dissolved.

26 The last and largest circular ocean on this earth.

27 Of dharma, usually translated "law" or "religion," Hemachandra later says: "Dharma bestows heaven and emancipation. Dharma shows the road for crossing the wilderness of samsara. Dharma nourishes like a mother, protects like a father, pleases like a friend, and is loving like a kinsman. . . . It is fourfold with the divisions of liberality, good conduct, penance, and state of mind." tr. Johnson, pp.18f.

28 With reference to the proverbial love of peacocks for clouds.

29 The demon Kamatha was the enemy of Parsvanatha, and the god Dharanendra his friend.

interval to the next Tirthankara.[30] While there is some variation among sects as to details this will provide the general picture of Jaina belief in this regard.

NAME	COLOR	EMBLEM	HEIGHT		AGE	INTERVAL TO NEXT TIRTHANKARA
1. Rishabha	Golden	Bull	500 dhanushas		84 lakhs of purvas	50 lakhs of krores of sagaras
2. Ajita	Golden	Elephant	450	"	72 lakhs of purvas	30 lakhs of krores of sagaras
3. Sambhava	Golden	Horse	400	"	60 lakhs of purvas	10 lakhs of krores of sagaras
4. Abhinandana	Golden	Ape	350	"	50 lakhs of purvas	9 lakhs of krores of sagaras
5. Sumati	Golden	Heron	300	"	40 lakhs of purvas	90,000 krores of sagaras
6. Padmaprabha	Red	Red Lotus	250	"	30 lakhs of purvas	9,000 krores of sagaras
7. Suparśva	Golden	Swastika	200	"	20 lakhs of purvas	900 krores of sagaras
8. Chandraprabha	White	Moon	150	"	10 lakhs of purvas	90 krores of sagaras
9. Suvidhi (or Pushpadanta)	White	Dolphin	100	"	2 lakhs of purvas	9 krores of sagaras
10. Śitala	Golden	Śrivatsa	90	"	1 lakh of purvas	9,999,900 sagaras
11. Śreyamsa	Golden	Rhinoceros	80	"	84 lakhs of years	54 sagaras
12. Vasupujya	Red	Buffalo	70	"	72 lakhs of years	30 sagaras
13. Vimala	Golden	Boar	60	"	60 lakhs of years	9 sagaras
14. Ananta	Golden	Falcon	50	"	30 lakhs of years	4 sagaras
15. Dharma	Golden	Thunderbolt	45	"	10 lakhs of years	3 sagaras less 3/4 palya
16. Śanti	Golden	Antelope	40	"	1 lakh of years	½ palya
17. Kunthu	Golden	Goat	35	"	95,000 years	¼ palya less 6,000 krores of years
18. Ara	Golden	Nandyavarta	30	"	84,000 years	1,000 krores less 6,584,000 years
19. Malli	Blue	Jar	25	"	55,000 years	54 lakhs of years
20. Munisuvrata (or Suvrata)	Black	Tortoise	20	"	30,000 years	9 lakhs of years
21. Nami	Golden	Blue Lotus	15	"	10,000 years	5 lakhs of years
22. Arishtanemi (or Nemi)	Black	Conch Shell	10	"	1,000 years	84,000 years
23. Parśva	Blue	Hooded Snake	9 hastas		100 years	250 years
24. Mahavira	Golden	Lion	7	"	72 years	

[30] Johnson, *Triṣaṣṭiśalākāpuruṣacaritra*, I, pp.347-349; Jagmanderlal Jaini, *Outlines of Jainism* (Jain Literature Society). 1916, table facing p.6; Hermann Jacobi in HERE VII, p.466.

The above table is self-explanatory except for the appearance of certain technical terms and statistical units. The Śrivatsa, the emblem of the tenth Tirthankara, is a curl of hair on the breast, well known as a mark of Vishnu too. The Nandyavarta, the symbol of the eighteenth Tirthankara, is a mark resembling a swastika.[31] As used by the Jains, the units of number and measure, including also a few appearing elsewhere in the present chapter, are as follows. In some cases different authorities give different values.

NUMBERS

1 lakh (Sanskrit, laksha) = 100,000[32]
1 krore (Sanskrit, koti) = 100 lakhs = 10,000,000[33]
1 kotikoti = 10,000,000 x 10,000,000 = 100,000,000,000,000[34]

MEASURES OF LENGTH AND DISTANCE

1 hasta = 18 inches[35]
1 dhanus = 4 hastas = 72 inches = 6 feet[36]
1 krośa = 8,000 hastas = 12,000 feet = 2¼ miles [37]
1 yojana = 4 krośas = 9 miles [38]
1 rajju = the distance a god can go in 6 months when he goes 100,000 yojanas in the winking of an eye[39]

MEASURES OF TIME

1 purva = $8,400,000^2$ years[40]
1 palya (or, palyopama) = the length of time required to empty a receptacle one yojana (9 miles) wide and deep, which is filled with new lamb's hairs grown within seven days, when one hair is taken out every hundred years.[41]
1 sagara (or, sagaropama), "ocean of years" = 10 krores of palyas = 100,000,000 palyas[42]

Applying these units to the table of Tirthankaras, we find, for example, that Rishabha was three thousand feet in height, and that the interval between his Nirvana and that of Ajita was 50 x 100,000 x 10,000,000 "oceans of years" (sagaras), or 50 x 100,000 x 10,000,000 x 100,000,000 palyas.

[31] GJ pp.383f.
[32] Monier Monier-Williams, *A Sanskrit-English Dictionary Etymologically and Philologically Arranged with Special Reference to Cognate Indo-European Languages.* New ed. 1899, p.891.
[33] *ibid.*, p.312.
[34] cf. Champat Rai Jain, *Ṛiṣabha Deva, the Founder of Jainism.* 1929, p.50.
[35] Monier-Williams, *A Sanskrit-English Dictionary*, p.1294.
[36] *ibid.*, p.509.   [37] *ibid.*, p.322.   [38] *ibid.*, p.858.
[39] Johnson, *Triṣaṣṭiśalākāpuruṣacaritra*, I, p.103 n.140.
[40] *ibid.*, I, p.84 n.125.   [41] *ibid.*, I, p.29 n.50.   [42] *ibid.*, I, p.71 n.97.

The most striking fact in the entire table is that, whereas enormous magnitudes of size and time are involved throughout most of the chart, there is a progressive diminution in the measurements until at the bottom of the table the figures come almost or entirely within the realm of actual earthly possibilities. Specifically, the last two Tirthankaras appear as persons of exaggerated but not utterly fantastic size, of thoroughly reasonable age-lengths of 100 and 72 years respectively, and with a relatively brief interval between them of only 250 years. The conclusion is suggested, therefore, that while the earlier Tirthankaras are purely mythological beings, Parśva and Mahavira were actual historical persons and the real founders of the religion.[43]

PARŚVA

The life of Parśva (or Parśvanatha) is narrated in the Kalpasutra, a work which contains a date nine hundred and eighty years after the death of Mahavira and is said to have been read publicly before a certain King Dhruvasena of Anandapura[44] to comfort him upon the death of his son.[45] While it is characteristic of the Jaina literature to portray all of the Tirthankaras according to one stereotyped pattern, and while the account of Parśva's life no doubt contains much that is legendary, nevertheless the kind of experience that is ascribed to him fits naturally into the background of Indian life as known from the time of the Upanishads on, and the record may not be entirely devoid of historical value.[46]

According to the Kalpasutra[47] Parśva was born in Benares as the son of King Aśvasena and Queen Vama. A commentary says that the name Parśva was bestowed upon him because before his birth Queen Vama saw a black serpent crawling about; and in the text he is given the appellation Purisadaniya, which means "the people's favorite" or "who is to be chosen among men because of his preferable Karma."

After living for thirty years as a householder, Parśva left the world behind to practice asceticism and seek salvation. He attained the en-

[43] Within Jainism itself, of course, the belief is held that even the first Tirthankara, Rishabha, was an actual man who lived "very very far back in the remoteness of hoary antiquity," who attained immortality, and who through his teachings founded the true religion. Champat Rai Jain, *Riṣabha Deva, The Founder of Jainism*, p.i.

[44] Anandapura was about a hundred and twenty miles northwest of Valabhi according to Hiuen Tsang (xi, 8f. tr. Beal, *Buddhist Records of the Western World*, ii, p.268; cf. Cunningham, *The Ancient Geography of India*, i, pp.493f.).

[45] SBE XXII, p.270.　　　[46] GJ p.19.　　　[47] SBE XXII, pp.271-275.

lightenment he sought after eighty-three days, and then spent the remainder of his life preaching his doctrine to others. At last, having abstained from food and water for an entire month, he died at the age of a hundred upon the summit of Mount Sammeta, now known in his memory as Parasnath Mountain.

The work of Parśva was very successful according to the Kalpasutra, which records that he won 164,000 men and 327,000 women as lay adherents, and 16,000 men and 38,000 women as monks and nuns. His Ganadharas or chief disciples were eight in number, Śubha (or Śubhadatta), Aryaghosha, Vasishta, Brahmacari, Saumya, Śridhara, Virabhadra and Yaśas. Of these Śubha became the leader of the church after the death of the master, and was followed in turn by Haridatta, Aryasamudra, Prabha and Keśi.[48]

MAHAVIRA

Concerning the life of Mahavira we have an extended and legend-embellished account not only in the Kalpasutra[49] but also in the Acarangasutra.[50] In these sources we learn that Mahavira was a native of Kundagrama, which was a suburb of Vesali and is probably represented by the modern village of Basukund.[51] He was going to be born of a Brahman mother, Devananda, a highly legendary portion of the narrative relates, but through the intervention of the god Śakra (Indra) an embryonic transfer was accomplished and he was born of a Kshatriya mother named Triśala. The latter was the wife of a certain Kshatriya named Siddhartha, and was herself the sister of the Licchavi king Chetaka of Vesali, whose daughter Chellana later married King Bimbisara and became the mother of King Ajataśatru. Prior to her son's birth Triśala learned, it is said, through fourteen dreams that she was to be the mother of a great saint. In these dreams she saw a white elephant, a white bull, a white lion, the goddess Śri, a garland of flowers, the white moon, the red sun, a banner, a vase, a lotus lake, a milk ocean, a celestial abode, a heap of jewels and a blazing ghee-fed fire.

At the birth of the son, it is declared, "there was a divine luster originated by many descending and ascending gods and goddesses, and in the universe, resplendent with one light, the conflux of gods occasioned great confusion and noise."[52] In Kundagrama, the parents and the townsfolk joined in extended celebrations of the auspicious event.

[48] GJ pp.22f.   [49] SBE XXII, pp.217-270.   [50] ibid., pp.189-202.
[51] Jarl Charpentier in CHI I, p.157.   [52] SBE XXII, p.251.

The personal name bestowed upon the son was Vardhamana, which is explained as follows: "In the night in which the Venerable Ascetic Mahavira was brought into the family of the Jnatris their silver increased, their gold increased, . . . the intensity of their popularity and liberality highly increased. At that time the following personal, reflectional, desirable idea occurred to parents of the Venerable Ascetic Mahavira: 'From the moment that this our boy has been begotten, our silver increased, our gold increased, . . . the intensity of our liberality and popularity highly increased. Therefore when this our boy will be born, we shall give him the fit name, attributive and conformable to his quality—Vardhamana (the Increasing One).' "[53]

It may also be noted in the foregoing passage that the family bore the name of Jnatri (Prakrit, Naya or Nata), and on this account the masculine members were designated as Jnatriputras or Nataputtas. Thus is explained the name Nataputta by which Mahavira is often called.

For thirty years Vardhamana lived the life of a householder, and then his parents died. We are told that the parents "were worshipers of Parśva and followers of the Śramanas (or Samanas; 'ascetics')," and that at the end of their lives they fasted to the death as Parśva himself had done.[54] Upon the death of his parents Vardhamana resolved to renounce the world, and first disposed of his treasures as gifts to the poor. Then "he, after fasting two and a half days without drinking water, put on a divine robe, and quite alone, nobody else being present, he tore out his hair and leaving the house entered the state of houselessness."[55]

There is reason to believe that at first Vardhamana remained in the vicinity of his home as a member of the ascetic order founded by Parśva and with which his parents seem to have been in contact.[56] Evidently finding their rules insufficiently strict, he departed from them for an utterly possessionless wandering. The Kalpasutra records: "The Venerable Ascetic Mahavira for a year and a month wore clothes; after that time he walked about naked, and accepted the alms in the hollow of his hand."[57]

For more than twelve years he sought thus for perfect salvation. A brief description of his manner of life says: "The Venerable One lived, except in the rainy season, all the eight months of summer

[53] SBE XXII, pp.248f.   [54] SBE XXII, p.194.   [55] *ibid.*, p.259.
[56] CJ p.24.   [57] SBE XXII, pp.259f.

and winter, in villages only a single night, in towns only five nights; he was indifferent alike to . . . straw and jewels, dirt and gold, pleasure and pain, attached neither to this world nor to that beyond, desiring neither life nor death, arrived at the other shore of the Samsara, and he exerted himself for the suppression of the defilement of Karma."[58] Extreme in his asceticism, he slept and ate but little, suffered attacks from animals and men without defending himself, bore pain in silence, and even if wounded never desired medical treatment.[59]

In the thirteenth year thus devoted to utterly self-forgetful meditation Vardhamana at last attained perfect understanding. "Outside of the town Jrimbhikagrama,[60] on the northern bank of the river Rijupalika, in the field of the householder Samaga, in a northeastern direction from an old temple, not far from a sal tree, in a squatting position with joined heels exposing himself to the heat of the sun, with the knees high and the head low, in deep meditation, he reached Nirvana, the complete and full, the unobstructed, unimpeded, infinite and supreme, best knowledge and intuition, called Kevala ('total'). When the Venerable One had become an Arhat and Jina, he was a Kevalin ('possessed of Kevala'), omniscient and comprehending all objects, he knew all conditions of the world, of gods, men, and demons; whence they come, where they go, whether they are born as men or animals . . . ; he saw and knew all conditions in the whole world of all living beings."[61]

Henceforth properly called Mahavira or Great Hero, the victorious ascetic lived for almost thirty years longer and preached his message widely. As before, he wandered from place to place during two-thirds of the year and only in the four months of the rainy season remained in some single city. A precise catalogue is given in the Kalpasutra of the cities in which his rainy seasons were spent throughout all forty-two years of his life as an ascetic: "Mahavira stayed the first rainy season in Asthikagrama, three rainy seasons in Champa and Prishtichampa, twelve in Vesali and Vanijagrama, fourteen in Rajagriha and the suburb of Nalanda, six in Mithila, two in Bhadrika, one in Alabhika, one in Panitabhumi, one in Sravasti, one in the town of Papa in King Hastipala's office of the writers: that was his very last rainy season."[62] Many of these places are well

---

[58] ibid., p.262.   [59] ibid., pp.79-87.
[60] Perhaps in the vicinity of Parasnath Mountain. Mrs. Sinclair Stevenson, The Heart of Jainism (The Religious Quest of India). 1915, p.38.
[61] SBE XXII, pp.201f.   [62] SBE XXII, p.264.

known, such as Champa the capital of Anga, Vesali Mahavira's own native metropolis, Rajagriha the capital of Magadha, Mithila in the kingdom of Videha, and Sravasti, celebrated in the annals of Buddhism.

Mahavira enjoyed family relationship to several of the leading rulers of his time as we have seen, and both Bimbisara (or Srenika) who ruled at Rajagriha around 540-490 B.C. and Ajatasatru (or Kunika) who succeeded his father on the same throne about 490-460 B.C. are said to have regarded his teachings with favor. The actual conversion of King Srenika by a young disciple of Mahavira is recounted in Lecture xx of the Uttaradhyayana,[63] but since that king is also claimed as a patron of Buddhism in the traditions of that religion we may suppose that he manifested a broad interest in the doctrines of various teachers rather than committing himself to any single sect.

As intimated in the quotation from the Kalpasutra given just above, death came to Mahavira in the town of Papa (or Pava). This was a place not far from Rajagriha, and is today a small village called Papapuri or Pavapuri in the region of the modern city of Bihar.[64] In the words of the Kalpasutra which follow immediately after the quotation just given: "In the fourth month of that rainy season, . . . in the town of Papa, in King Hastipala's office of the writers, the Venerable Ascetic Mahavira died, went off, quitted the world, cut asunder the ties of birth, old age, and death; became a Siddha, a Buddha, a Mukta, a maker of the end [to all misery], finally liberated, freed from all pains."

The success of Mahavira's work is indicated by the statement of the Kalpasutra that he gathered "an excellent community of 14,000 Sramanas with Indrabhuti at their head; 36,000 nuns with Chandana at their head; 159,000 lay votaries with Sankhasataka at their head; 318,000 female lay votaries with Sulasa and Revati at their head."[65] The four groups here designated, namely monks, nuns, laymen and laywomen, constitute the four orders or Tirtha of Jainism. Associated with Gautama Indrabhuti (as his full name was) in the leadership of the monks were ten other Ganadharas or chief disciples, Agnibhuti, Vayubhuti, Akampita, Arya Vyakta, Arya Sudharma, Manditaputra, Mauryaputra, Acalabhrata, Metarya and Prabhasa. All of the disciples who had wholly severed their connections with the

[63] SBE XLV, pp.100-107.
[64] Chimanlal J. Shah, *Jainism in North India 800 B.C.-A.D. 526.* 1932, p.27 n.5.
[65] SBE XXII, pp.267f.

world, that is both the monks and the nuns, were known as Nir-granthas (Niganthas) meaning "without any ties," a designation which had perhaps already been borne by Parśva's followers.[66]

THE DATES OF MAHAVIRA AND PARŚVA

The death of Mahavira, or in the language of religious faith his Nirvana, is the basic point in Jaina chronology. According to the tradition of the Śvetambaras this took place four hundred and seventy years before the beginning of the Vikrama Era (58/57 B.C.); and according to the Digambaras it was six hundred and five years before the beginning of the Śaka Era (A.D. 78).[67] By either mode of calculation the date was therefore 527 B.C. Since at death the Tirthankara had attained the age of seventy-two, his birth must have been around 599 B.C. To date the life of Mahavira around 599-527 B.C. is to make him a slightly elder contemporary of Gautama Buddha who probably lived about 567-487 B.C. This is substantiated by Buddhist sources, in which there are many references to Nataputta and the Niganthas, meaning Mahavira and the Jains; although in the Jaina canonical books there seem to be no corresponding notices of Gautama and the Buddhists. Three passages in the Buddhist canon refer specifically to the death of Nataputta the Nigantha at Pava at a time when the Buddha was still engaged in his work of teaching.[68] "Once while the lord was staying among the Sakyans at Sama-gama," it is written, "Nataputta the Nigantha had died recently at Pava."

It is true that Hemachandra states that the death of Mahavira took place one hundred fifty-five years before the accession to the throne of Chandragupta, an event which transpired in about 322 B.C. This would lead to a date around 549-477 for Mahavira and would place his death slightly later than that of the Buddha. This is supported by some scholars who criticize the Buddhist notices referred to just above as unreliable.[69]

At all events, the two great teachers, Mahavira and Gautama Bud-

---

[66] GJ pp.22,32.

[67] Schubring, *Die Lehre der Jainas nach den alten Quellen dargestellt*, p.30.

[68] Samagama Sutta. Majjhima Nikaya III, i, 104 (II, 243). tr. Chalmers, *Further Dialogues of the Buddha*, II, p.139; Pasadika Suttanta and Sangiti Suttanta. Dīgha Nikāya XXIX (III, 117); XXXIII (III, 209f.). tr. Rhys Davids, *Dialogues of the Buddha*, III, pp.111,203. For bibliographical details on the Buddhist sources see the chapter on Buddhism.

[69] Hermann Jacobi in *Sitzungsberichte der preussischen Akademie der Wissenschaften.* 1930, phil.-hist. Kl., XXVI, pp.557-561.

dha, were substantially contemporaries. In the Buddhist sources the followers of the two teachers are for the most part represented as in controversy with each other, and, as is not surprising in texts emanating from only the one group, the Buddhists are always pictured as victorious. For an example we may cite the Upali Sutta in the Majjhima Nikaya.[70] In this Sutta a prosperous householder named Upali, who is an adherent of Mahavira, enters into a conversation with Gautama Buddha, intending to refute him on a point of philosophical doctrine. Instead of succeeding, Upali finds himself not only overcome in argument but also, to his surprise, deeply impressed with both the wisdom and the magnanimity of Buddha. He forthwith announces himself to be a follower of Gautama, and closes his house to the Niganthas although at Buddha's behest he still distributes alms to them at a distance. Mahavira cannot believe the report which comes to him of the defection of his erstwhile disciple, and goes to visit Upali. The latter treats him with haughty condescension, and utters a lengthy eulogy of the Buddha. "Then and there," the Sutta concludes, "from the mouth of Nataputta the Nigantha, who could not bear to hear the lord extolled—there gushed hot blood."

While we are dealing with Buddhist notices of the Jains we may add a report on their teachings which is found in the Devadaha Sutta of the Majjhima Nikaya.[71] Gautama is supposed to be speaking: "Hereupon those Niganthas told me that Nataputta the Nigantha was all-knowing and all-seeing, with nothing beyond his ken and vision, and that he affirmed of himself that, whether walking or standing, sleeping or awake, he was always, without a break, at his spiritual best. These, they added, were his words: You have done misdeeds, Niganthas, in past existences; wear it out by severe austerities; every present restraint on body, speech and mind will undo the evil-doings of the past; hence, by expiation and purge of past misdeeds and by not doing fresh misdeeds, nothing accrues for the future; as nothing accrues for the future, misdeeds die away; as misdeeds die away, Ill dies away; as Ill dies away, feelings die away, and as painful feelings die away, all Ill will wear out and pass away. This doctrine, they added, commends itself to us and

[70] II, i, 56 (I, 371-387). tr. Chalmers, *Further Dialogues of the Buddha*, I, pp.267-278.

[71] III, i, 101 (II, 217f.). tr. Chalmers, *Further Dialogues of the Buddha*, II, p.125; cf. Culadukkhakkhandha Sutta, Majjhima Nikaya I, ii, 14 (I, 92f.). tr. Chalmers, *ibid.*, I, p.67.

has our approval, and we rejoice in it." Needless to say, in this Sutta the Buddha proceeds immediately to the refutation of the Jaina philosophy.

Having seen, then, that Mahavira and Gautama Buddha were indisputably contemporaries, and that the most probable dates for Mahavira are 599-527 B.C., we may turn to the question of the date of Parśva. There is no doubt that Parśva preceded Mahavira, since the parents of the latter were already worshipers of Parśva. Also the most reasonable explanation of the nature of Mahavira's work is that he was not the inventor of a new doctrine but the reformer of a movement already long in existence and derived from Parśva. Four vows had been enjoined on his followers by Parśva, namely: (1) not to destroy life (*ahimsa*); (2) not to speak untruth; (3) not to steal; and (4) not to own property. To these Mahavira added as a fifth the vow of chastity. This was indeed thought of as already implied in the fourth vow of Parśva, but on this point laxity had developed within the order and Mahavira deemed it necessary to make the rule explicit as a fifth regulation, additional to the four of his predecessor.[72] Furthermore, it seems that Parśva had allowed his followers to wear an under and an upper garment, but that Mahavira went to the extreme position of forbidding his monks to wear any clothing whatsoever.

There is a very interesting section (Lecture XXIII) in the Uttaradhyayana[73] in which these and other points of difference between the disciples of Parśva and those of Mahavira are set forth, and in which it is related that through an amicable discussion between Keśi, leader of the followers of Parśva, and Gautama, foremost disciple of Mahavira, the two groups were united in acceptance of the reformations of Mahavira. The following quotations will give the essence of the account:

There was a Jina, Parśva by name, an Arhat, worshiped by the people, who was thoroughly enlightened and omniscient, a prophet of the law and a Jina.

And there was a famous disciple of this light of the world, the young Sramana Keśi, who had completely mastered the sciences and right conduct.

He possessed the light of Śruta and Avadhi knowledge,[74] and was surrounded by a crowd of disciples; wandering from village to village he arrived in the town of Śravasti.

[72] A. F. R. Hoernle in HERE I, p.264.   [73] SBE XLV, pp.119-129.
[74] The second and third grades of knowledge according to the Jains.

In the district of that town there is a park, called Tinduka; there he took up his abode in a pure place to live and sleep in.

Now at that time there lived the prophet of the law, the Jina, who in the whole world is known as the venerable Vardhamana.

And there was a famous disciple of this light of the world, the venerable Gautama by name, who had completely mastered the sciences and right conduct.

He knew the twelve Angas, was enlightened, and was surrounded by a crowd of disciples; wandering from village to village he, too, arrived in Sravasti.

In the district of that town there is a park Koshtaka; there he took up his abode in a pure place to live and sleep in.

The young Sramana Kesi and the famous Gautama, both lived there. . . .

The pupils of both, who controlled themselves, who practiced austerities, who possessed virtues, and who protected their self, made the following reflection:

"Is our law the right one, or is the other law the right one? are our conduct and doctrines right, or the other?

"The law as taught by the great sage Parsva, which recognizes but four vows, or the law taught by Vardhamana, which enjoins five vows?

"The law which forbids clothes [for a monk], or that which [allows] an under and upper garment? Both pursuing the same end, what has caused their difference?"

Knowing the thoughts of their pupils, both Kesi and Gautama made up their minds to meet each other.

Gautama, knowing what is proper and what is due to the older section [of the church], went to the Tinduka park, accompanied by the crowd, his pupils.

When Kesi, the young monk, saw Gautama approach, he received him with all becoming attention. He at once offered Gautama the four pure kinds of straw and hay to sit upon.

Kesi, the young Sramana, and the famous Gautama, sitting together, shone forth with a luster like that of sun and moon.

There assembled many heretics out of curiosity, and many thousands of laymen; gods, . . . Gandharvas, Yakshas, . . . [assembled there], and there came together invisible ghosts too. . . .

[Here follows an extended conversation between Kesi and Gautama on the points at issue between the two groups, including not only the questions concerning vows and clothes but also various problems in the philosophy of religion. On each matter Gautama made such a convincing presentation that Kesi was fully persuaded, and the passage closes with these words describing the accord to which they came:]

Kesi, of enormous sanctity, bowed his head to the famous Gautama. And in the pleasant [Tinduka park] he sincerely adopted the law of the five vows, which was proclaimed by the first Tirthankara, according to the teaching of the last Tirthankara.

In that meeting of Kesi and Gautama, knowledge and virtuous conduct

70. Jaina Tablet of Homage Showing a Jaina Stupa

72. Statue of the Tirthankara Parśvanatha

71. Tablet of Homage Portraying a Jina

73. Statue of the Tirthankara
Mahavira

74. The Indra Sabha Rock Temple at Elura

75. Colossal Statue of Gommateśvara at Śravana Belgola

76. The Parśvanatha Temple at Khajuraho

77. The Temple City of Śatrunjaya

78. The Hill of Girnar and the Stairway leading to the Jaina Temples

79. The Neminatha Temple at Girnar

80. The Dome in the Temple of Vimala Shah

81. The Interior of the Temple of Tejahpala and Vastupala

82. Miniature Painting of a Tirthankara

83. A Jaina Goddess

84. The Birth of Mahavira

85. The Bath of Mahavira

86. Mahavira Gives away his Earthly Possessions

87. Queen Triśala Relates her Dreams to King Siddhartha

were for ever brought to eminence, and subjects of the greatest importance were settled.

The whole assembly was greatly pleased and fixed their thoughts on the
right way. They praised Keśi and Gautama: "May the venerable ones
show us favor!"

Parśva, then, was indubitably prior to Mahavira, and sufficient
time had elapsed since his day that a decay in the morals of the
monastic order had occurred which led to the reformation carried
out by Mahavira. This situation is in satisfactory agreement with
the more exact indication given in Jaina tradition that a period of
two hundred and fifty years had separated the two Tirthankaras.
This tradition is represented in the Kalpasutra[75] where it is stated
that from the death of Parśva to the time of the writing of the Kalpasutra 1,230 years had elapsed, and from the death of Mahavira
980 years. Reckoning two hundred and fifty years before the death
of Mahavira in 527 B.C. we reach 777 B.C. as the date of Parśva's
death, and if the latter lived for one hundred years his inclusive
dates were 877-777 B.C. Such an early date for the foundation of
Jainism is consonant with the animistic character of its basic philosophy which will appear in the succeeding section.

[75] SBE XXII, pp.270,275.

3. THE TEACHINGS OF JAINISM

THE essential ideas of Jainism, which may be supposed to go back at least as far as to Parśva,[76] include a conception of the cosmos as divided into three parts, a higher world of the gods, a middle world of men, animals and plants, and a lower world of demons; and a belief that this entire universe is filled with an infinite number of eternal, indestructible individual souls. These souls, which are called Jivas from the Sanskrit root *jiv* meaning "to live," are in themselves purely spiritual and possess unlimited wisdom, power and goodness, but their true nature is at least partially obscured by the fact that at present most of them are enveloped in matter. In other words the souls are now incarnated in the bodies of gods, men, animals, plants and demons, and are even to be found in particles of earth, cold water, fire and wind.[77] The thoughts and deeds of each embodied soul, moreover, continue to draw into itself more invisible atoms of matter which become the Karma of that soul. The eradication of this Karma and the setting free of the soul from its involvement in base matter can only be accomplished by the most rigorous regulation of all thinking and doing. To this end Parśva instituted the four vows already mentioned, which in their positive connotations call for kindness, truth, honesty and poverty. By the practice of such a way of life and by constant meditation upon its own real character, the soul may at last rise to that realm of blessedness which is lifted up like an island above the surging waves of the ocean of Samsara.

Such was the philosophical animism of early Jainism which has ever since remained characteristic of that faith. When Mahavira entered into this heritage of thought he seems not so much to have made innovations as to have systematized, and when he accepted Parśva's four vows he simply made their import unmistakable by adding the explicit fifth vow of chastity.

In its fuller development Jaina thought retained these essential foundations and built upon them an extensive system of which certain main outlines may now be indicated.[78]

WORLD STRUCTURE

As to the structure of the universe, three worlds, lower, middle and higher, are conceived as rising one above the other, all enveloped

---

[76] GJ pp.20-22.   [77] Jacobi in SBE XLV, p.xxxiii.
[78] Schubring, *Die Lehre der Jainas nach den alten Quellen dargestellt*, pp. 84-207.

in three atmospheres. Dimensions of this cosmos are given in rajjus, and it is said that the universe is fourteen rajjus high and at the base seven rajjus from north to south and seven rajjus from east to west. At the middle it tapers, however, to a width of only one rajju; above that it increases again and at half of its remaining height reaches a maximum breadth of five rajjus. The earth, which is in the middle world, is a very large circular body made up of a number of concentric rings called islands, separated from each other by ring-shaped oceans. At the center stands Mount Meru, at the foot of which is the island-continent, Jambuddiva, surrounded by the Lavanasamudra or Salt Sea. Jambuddiva itself is divided into several regions, and of these, that between the Indus and the Ganges is known as the land of Bharata. Beyond Jambuddiva and Lavanasamudra come the other continents and seas. Around Mount Meru revolve two suns, two moons and two sets of constellations.[79]

WORLD CHRONOLOGY

As to chronology, it is believed that in this world two ages follow one upon the other in constant succession. They are the "descending" age or Avasarpini, which begins with everything in the best possible condition and goes through successive periods of degeneration to the worst possible state of affairs. Then the "ascending" age or Utsarpini begins, in which conditions progressively improve again. The two ages, each with its six periods, are charted below. The quality of each period is shown by the word Sushama meaning good, or by the word Duhshama signifying bad, or by some combination of the words indicating something better or worse than the average represented by one of them alone. The duration of each period is given in units which have already been explained.

AVASARPINI
1. Sushama-sushama, "best" period, 4 kotikotis of sagaras
2. Sushama, "good" period, 3 kotikotis of sagaras
3. Sushama-duhshama, "good-bad" period, 2 kotikotis of sagaras
4. Duhshama-sushama, "bad-good" period, 1 kotikoti of sagaras less 42,000 years
5. Duhshama, "bad" period, 21,000 years
6. Duhshama-duhshama, "worst" period, 21,000 years

UTSARPINI
1. Duhshama-duhshama, "worst" period, 21,000 years

[79] Jaini, *Outlines of Jainism*, pp.119-125.

2. Duhshama, "bad" period, 21,000 years
3. Duhshama-sushama, "bad-good" period, 1 kotikoti of sagaras less 42,000 years
4. Sushama-duhshama, "good-bad" period, 2 kotikotis of sagaras
5. Sushama, "good" period, 3 kotikotis of sagaras
6. Sushama-sushama, "best" period, 4 kotikotis of sagaras[80]

The total duration of each age is ten kotikotis of sagaras. A descending and an ascending age taken together represent one complete revolution of the Kalacakra or Wheel of Time, the spokes of which are the periods of each age. The Wheel turns forever at constant speed, and thus Avasarpinis and Utsarpinis follow each other in ceaseless succession throughout eternity.

In the two periods Sushama-duhshama and Duhshama-sushama, sixty-three "great men" regularly appear, namely, 24 Tirthankaras, 12 Cakravartis (world-rulers) and 27 heroes (9 Baladevas, 9 Vasudevas and 9 Prativasudevas). It is these sixty-three who are the heroes of Hemachandra's Trishashtiśalakapurushacaritra already mentioned. One Tirthankara and one Cakravarti live in Sushama-duhshama, all the others have their existences in Duhshama-sushama, and this is so regardless of whether it is an "ascending" or "descending" age. It should also be added that various such series of "great men" appear in various portions of the world during the periods in question. Furthermore, in his life on earth each Tirthankara is accompanied by a special Yaksha and Yakshi (or Śasanadevata), and also is served by Sarasvati as a messenger goddess.

The present age of the world is Avasarpini, and it is during this age's periods of Sushama-duhshama and Duhshama-sushama that there appeared in the land of Bharata the twenty-four Tirthankaras whom we listed above and their accompanying world-rulers and heroes. Rishabha and the Cakravarti Bharata lived in Sushama-duhshama; the remaining Tirthankaras from Ajita to Mahavira, and their associates, lived in Duhshama-sushama. The Duhshama-sushama period came to an end three years and eight and one-half months after the Nirvana of Mahavira, and the world is now in the Duhshama or "bad" period of twenty-one thousand years, which will be followed by the Duhshama-duhshama or "worst" period of twenty-one thousand years. As things go thus from bad to worse, Jainism itself will disappear, but at last the time will come for the "ascending" age of Utsarpini to begin, and when the periods of

[80] Johnson, *Triṣaṣṭiśalākāpuruṣacaritra*, i, pp.93f.

Duhshama-sushama and Sushama-duhshama come, twenty-four new Tirthankaras will reestablish the true religion. The names of these future Tirthankaras will be: (1) Padmanabha; (2) Śuradeva; (3) Suparśva; (4) Svayamprabha; (5) Sarvanubhuti; (6) Devaśruti; (7) Udaya; (8) Pedhala; (9) Pottila; (10) Śatakirti; (11) Suvrata; (12) Amama; (13) Nishkashaya; (14) Nishpulaka; 15) Nirmama; (16) Citragupta; (17) Samadhi; (18) Samvara; (19) Yaśodhara; (20) Vijaya; (21) Malli; (22) Deva; (23) Anantavirya; (24) Bhadrakrit.[81]

WORLD RENUNCIATION

The teachings of the true religion lead to that mode of life through which the soul may disentangle itself from attachment to the material and ascend from the lowest reaches of the universe to the highest. This manner of life is regulated by the five vows already given and is followed in all its austerity by monks and nuns. Since, however, only a relatively small number of persons can be expected to practice extreme asceticism, lay members, both men and women, are also admitted to the Sangha or religious community. They are expected to keep the great commandments too, but only after such a fashion as is possible for those who still live in the world. Thus in the Purushartha Siddhyupaya, a treatise of high authority for all Jains, the fourth vow, not to own property, is reduced for the householder to this: "And if one is unable to wholly renounce cattle, corn, servants, buildings, wealth, etc., he also should at least limit them; because renunciation is the right principle."[82] Again the same work says: "Ratna-Traya, the Three Jewels (right belief, right knowledge, right conduct) should be followed, even partially, every moment of time without cessation by a householder desirous of everlasting liberation. . . . Even when Ratna-Traya is partially followed, whatever bondage of Karma there is, is due to its antithesis, because Ratna-Traya is assuredly the way to liberation, and can never be the cause of bondage."[83]

In yet another passage the Purushartha Siddhyupaya gives this admonition to the lay follower of the religion:

Having due regard to one's own status and capacity, a [householder] should practice the conduct of a saint, as described in the Scriptures.

[81] GJ pp.244-310.
[82] Ajit Prasada, *Purushartha-Siddhyupaya (Jaina-Pravachana-Rahasya-Kosha) by Shrimat Amrita Chandra Suri, Edited with an Introduction, Translation, and Original Commentaries in English* (The Sacred Books of the Jainas, IV). 1933, p.55, §128.
[83] *ibid.*, p.80, §209,211.

Equanimity, praising, bowing, repentance and renunciation, and giving up attachment for the body are the six [daily] duties, which should be observed.

One should carefully observe the three controls, proper control of body, proper control of speech, and proper control of mind. . . .

Forgiveness, humility, straightforwardness, truth, contentment, restraint, austerities, charity, non-attachment, and chastity are the [ten] observances to be followed. . . .

(1) Hunger, (2) thirst, (3) cold, (4) heat, (5) insect bite (6) nudity, (7) ennui, (8) women, (9) walking, (10) sitting, (11) resting, (12) abuse, (13) beating, (14) begging, (15) non-obtaining, (16) disease, (17) contact with thorny shrubs, etc., (18) dirt, (19) respect and disrespect, (20) conceit of knowledge, (21) lack of knowledge, (22) slack belief, are twenty-two sufferings. These should be ever endured without any feeling of vexation by one who desires to get rid of all cause for pain.[84]

WORLD CONQUEST

When, through the manner of life just indicated, the soul finally eradicates its karma and overcomes its worldly entanglements, it becomes a Siddha or Perfected One and is free to rise by its own nature to the highest realm of blessedness. This is a beautiful place called Ishatpragbhara, which is situated yet twelve yojanas above the highest heaven (Sarvarthasiddha)[85] of the gods. It is described as follows in Lecture xxxvi of the Uttaradhyayana:

Where do the perfected souls reside? Where do they leave their bodies, and where do they go, on reaching perfection?

Perfected souls . . . reside on the top of the world; they leave their bodies here [below], and go there, on reaching perfection.

Twelve yojanas above the Sarvartha is the place called Ishatpragbhara, which has the form of an umbrella; [there the perfected souls go].

It is forty-five hundred yojanas long, and as many broad, and it is somewhat more than three times as many in circumference.

Its thickness is eight yojanas, it is greatest in the middle, and decreases toward the margin, till it is thinner than the wing of a fly.

This place, by nature pure, consisting of white gold, resembles in form an open umbrella, as has been said by the best of Jinas.

[Above it] is a pure blessed place [called Sita], which is white like a conch-shell, the anka-stone, and Kunda-flowers; a yojana thence is the end of the world.

The perfected souls penetrate the sixth part of the uppermost krosa of the [above-mentioned] yojana.

There at the top of the world reside the blessed perfected souls, rid of all transmigration, and arrived at the excellent state of perfection. . . .

[84] *ibid.*, pp.78-80, §200-202,204,206-208.
[85] It was from the Sarvarthasiddha Vimana (or heaven) that Rishabha descended to earth (sbe xxii, p.281).

They have no [visible] form, they consist of life throughout, they are developed into knowledge and faith, and they possess paramount happiness which admits of no comparison.

They all dwell in one part of the world, and have developed into knowledge and faith, they have crossed the boundary of the Samsara, and reached the excellent state of perfection.[86]

THE NINE CATEGORIES

The extent to which the schematization and analysis of various items in the Jaina philosophy is carried is nothing less than amazing and may be indicated by a résumé of the nine categories in which the later Jaina writers organized the fundamental truths of the religion.[87]

The *first category* is Jiva or soul. All Jivas may be divided into two classes, (1) the perfected Siddhas that live in Ishatpragbhara, and (2) the unperfected jivas of samsara that live in the world. The Samsari, as the latter are called, may be divided into three groups, (1) male, (2) female and (3) neuter. According to the place where they were born, jivas may be classed in four divisions, namely those born (1) in hell, (2) in a subhuman state as in plants or animals, (3) as human beings, and (4) as spirits (*devata*), either gods or demons. A fivefold classification is possible depending upon the number of senses possessed by the jivas. (1) Ekendriya jivas possess only one sense, that of touch. Such jivas exist in stones, water, fire, wind and vegetables, which consequently are capable of pain and suffering. The length of time for which a jiva may be compelled by its karma to reside in things of this sort may extend anywhere from one moment to as much as twenty-two thousand years. According to the strictest interpretation of Jainism, the vow of Ahimsa or non-killing begins to be applicable with this very first class of jivas: therefore monks often refuse to touch a stone or fire; insist on boiling and straining water they use; make it a practice to breathe through a cloth; and avoid the eating of many vegetables—all in order to avoid injuring or destroying these jivas. (2) Beindriya jivas have two senses, touch and taste. Here are grouped animalcules, worms and creatures living in shells. The maximum term of such an existence is twelve years. For the Jaina layman the vow of non-killing is held to be in effect first with regard to this class. (3) Triindriya jivas have three senses, touch, taste and smell. Included in

---

[86] SBE XLV, pp.211-213.

[87] Stevenson, *The Heart of Jainism*, pp.94-172; Johnson, *Triṣaṣṭiśalākāpuruṣacaritra*, I, pp.437-450.

this group are ants, bugs and moths. The period of time for which a jiva may exist in such a form varies from one moment to forty-nine days. (4) Corendriya jivas possess four senses, touch, taste, smell and sight. Such creatures as wasps, scorpions, mosquitoes, gnats, flies, locusts and butterflies belong to this group. Six months is the maximum period for life in this division. (5) Pañcendriya jivas are those which enjoy five senses, namely the four hitherto enumerated plus hearing. Within this group there are four divisions: hell beings, lower animals, human beings and demigods. Remarkably enough, disease germs are classed as Pañcendriya and treated as human beings. A jiva may spend from ten thousand years to thirty-three sagaras as a hell being or demigod; from one instant to three palyas of time as a lower animal or human being (including as a disease germ).

Jivas, again, may be divided into six groups, including (1) earth, (2) water, (3) fire, (4) wind and (5) vegetable lives, with which we already have some acquaintance, and then also (6) Trasakaya. The class of Trasakaya includes all the jivas which have the power of mobility and which, when impelled by *trasa* or dread can endeavor to remove themselves from danger. A sevenfold classification of jivas divides them into (1) hell beings, which are neuter, (2) male lower animals, (3) female lower animals, (4) male human beings, (5) female human beings, (6) male demigods and (7) female demigods.

Eight classes of jivas are distinguished according to the emotions by which they are swayed or according to their complete freedom from emotion. (1) Those moved by any of the three good or three bad emotions are Saleśi and form the first class. (2) The second class comprises those dominated by Krishnaleśya, the worst of the three evil emotions, a temper so bad that it is as black as a thundercloud and rougher than a saw. (3) Jivas in the third class are ruled by Nilaleśya, an emotion blue as indigo, in which envy, gluttony and laziness are mingled. (4) Jivas of the fourth group are swayed by Kapotaleśya, a gray crookedness in thought and deed. (5) The fifth division of jivas is constituted of those who are ruled by Tejoleśya, the first of the three good emotions, red like the rising sun and sweeter than ripe mangoes. It removes evil thoughts and makes men humble and straightforward. (6) The sixth class includes the jivas whose emotion is Padmaleśya, yellow in color and named for the lotus flower. Like the lotus expanding to the sun, so their hearts are opened to all good things. (7) Śuklaleśya is the highest of the emotions and rules the jivas of the seventh class. It is white as pearls and sweeter than sugar. It brings a harmony with all nature. (8) The eighth group comprises the jivas which have risen above all emotions. Only the Siddhas are found here.

Beyond this point, further classes are made chiefly by introducing subdivisions into groupings already mentioned. Thus the classification of jivas is carried forward until a fourteenfold division is achieved; some authorities go on until they have enumerated no less than five hundred and sixty-three groupings.

The *second category* is Ajiva or non-soul. This is the realm of inanimate things, with which Jiva is entangled but toward separation from which it is struggling. Here, too, there are numerous divisions and subdivisions. The two main classes of Ajiva are Arupi, without form, and Rupi, with form. Motion, space and time are examples of divisions within Arupi. Various groupings of Pudgala, roughly translatable as "matter," are found in Rupi. Jiva and Ajiva together account for the universe; there is no need to speak of a creator.

The *third category* is Punya or merit. Here it is observed that there are nine ways of performing actions which lead to a good karma and bring peace of mind. These include (1) feeding the hungry, (2) giving drink to the thirsty, (3) offering clothes to the poor, (4) providing residence or (5) a seat or bed for a monk, (6) wishing others well or (7) exerting ourselves in their service, (8) speaking without hurting another's feelings, and (9) making reverent salutations to religious men. The reward of merit attained in these nine ways may be reaped in no less than forty-two ways, such as enjoying bodily strength or beauty.

The *fourth category* is Papa or sin. Eighteen classes of sin are recognized: (1) killing (*himsa*), (2) untruthfulness, (3) dishonesty, (4) unchastity, (5) excessive love of possessions, (6) anger, (7) conceit, (8) intrigue, (9) greed, (10) over-fondness for a person or thing, (11) envy, (12) quarrelsomeness, (13) slander, (14) telling of stories to discredit another, (15) fault-finding, (16) lack of self-control in the presence of joy or sorrow, (17) hypocrisy and (18) false faith. Among the foregoing, special emphasis is laid upon the sins of anger, conceit, intrigue and greed, these four together being called Kashaya. The results of sin are enumerated under no less than eighty-two headings. Sin affects the class of beings into which one is born in the next incarnation, it results in ugliness and deformity, it is the cause of every illness and ailment.

The *fifth category* is Aśrava which has to do with the channels for

[209]

the acquisition of karma. There are forty-two channels through which karma enters a jiva. These include the senses, the emotions and various kinds of activities, all of which are carefully listed.

The *sixth category* is Samvara, meaning methods of impeding Karma. This obviously is the converse of the preceding. Here fifty-seven ways are stated in which the inflow of karma may be arrested. These include the manner of walking so as not to injure any living thing, the guarding of the words of one's mouth, the exercise of circumspection in eating, the restraint of emotion, the endurance of hardship and illness, the performance of meditation with eyes and limbs immovable, the practice of fasting and austerity, and the cultivation of reflection aimed at a recognition of the true nature of the soul and of the manner of its release from the world.

The *seventh category* is Bandha or bondage. The enslavement of the soul to karma, it is here taught, is due to the union of the jiva with pudgala, which as has already been pointed out is roughly the equivalent of matter. The classification of such bondage is fourfold: (1) As to its nature, karma is bitter or sweet, varying with the character of the individual person. (2) As to the time required for its expiation, some karma can be eradicated in a day, some will require a thousand years. (3) In intensity, some karma is heavier than some other. (4) In thickness and thinness, karma varies with the amount of pudgala which has been attracted.

The *eighth category* is Nirjara or destruction of karma. The eradication of accumulated karma is a slow and difficult process. Exterior and interior austerities are two of the chief means. Exterior or bodily austerities include: (1) fasting for a fixed period of time or for the remainder of one's life (as Parśva and many others did); (2) partial fasting, by gradually decreasing the quantity of food consumed; (3) limited eating, involving for example a reduction in the varieties of food taken or in the number of places where one will eat; (4) abstention from certain foods in which one takes particular delight; (5) ill-treatment of the body, such as the pulling out of the hair by the roots; (6) control of the senses and restriction of exercise. Interior or spiritual austerities are also six in number: (1) confession and penance; (2) reverence to superiors; (3) service to the poor; (4) study; (5) meditation; (6) the practice of indifference to the body, to the extent of standing motionless in some sacred place until death comes.

The *ninth category* is Moksha or deliverance. As we have already seen, one who attains the state of complete deliverance is called a Siddha. He is then, by Jaina definition, "without caste, unaffected by smell, without the sense of taste, without feeling, without form, without hunger, without pain, without sorrow, without joy, without birth, without old age, without death, without body, without karma, enjoying an endless and unbroken calm."[88] Only a human being can pass directly to the state of a Siddha. If he has previously been a Tirthankara he is called a Tirtha Siddha. Interestingly enough, while a Tirthankara is an object of worship, upon becoming a Siddha he no longer receives worship since he no longer has a body. In all there are fifteen kinds of Siddhas. Factors taken into account in classification include not only previous status in life but also previous sex, influences which led to Siddhahood, and whether moksha was attained alone or in a group with others.

THE ANALYSIS OF KARMA

Prominent as karma is in the above outline, we have even yet scarcely more than hinted at the complexity of the analysis to which this central concept is subjected by the Jaina theologians. In briefest summary this analysis includes the four following points:[89]

Karma has four sources: (1) Mithyatva, false belief; (2) Avirati, attachment; (3) Kashaya, greed; (4) Yoga, adherence to worldly things. It is of two main types: (1) Nikacita, firmly bound karma which must be endured; (2) Sithila, loose karma which can be destroyed. There are one hundred and forty-eight (and some say one hundred and fifty-eight) specific kinds of karma, grouped under eight main divisions. Listing only the main divisions, we find that (1) Jñanavaraniya karma hides knowledge from us; (2) Darśanavaraniya karma keeps us from beholding the true faith; (3) Vedaniya karma determines whether we experience the feeling of pleasure or of pain; (4) Mohaniya karma causes delusion; (5) Ayu karma fixes the period of time which a jiva must spend in a given form; (6) Nama karma determines the condition of the jiva's existence as to genus of being and nature of body; (7) Gotra karma decides a man's destiny in his next existence as to whether he will be born in a high-caste or low-caste family; (8) Antaraya karma obstructs the efforts of a person toward various accomplishments.

Of the foregoing eight main kinds of karma, the first, second,

[88] Stevenson, *The Heart of Jainism*, p.169.
[89] Stevenson, *The Heart of Jainism*, pp.173-192; Johnson, *Triṣaṣṭiśalākāpuruṣacaritra*, I, pp.402-436.

fourth and eighth are the most difficult to eliminate; the others can more easily be destroyed. Three tenses are also recognized in relation to karma. (1) Satta is the name for the karma accumulated in past existences. All one hundred and forty-eight different kinds of karma are involved in satta. (2) Bandha is the karma which is being taken on even now in the present life. One hundred and twenty of the one hundred and forty-eight kinds are concerned in bandha. (3) Udaya is the karma, the fruits of which, whether good or evil, are maturing and ripening and now being experienced. One hundred and twenty-two kinds of karma are involved here.

On the ladder by which the soul climbs to emancipation from karma there are fourteen steps or Gunasthanas. (1) When a jiva is on the first step (Mithyatvagunasthana) it is in a state of delusion and does not know the truth. There are two subdivisions of this step: in the first the soul cannot tell the difference between a god and a non-god; in the second the soul knows that there is a difference but mistakes a non-deva for a deva. (2) In the second step (Saśvasadanagunasthana) the soul possesses a faint remembrance of the often forgotten distinction between truth and falsity. (3) On the third rung of the ladder (Miśragunasthana) the jiva is in the condition of knowing the truth one moment and doubting it the next. (4) In the fourth phase (Aviratisamyagdrishtigunasthana) the soul attains to faith but is not yet strong enough to take any of the vows of the Jaina life. (5) On the fifth level of progress (Deśaviratigunasthana) the soul is able to take the various vows which delimit the highest kind of life possible for the Jaina layman. (6) Step six (Pramattagunasthana) can only be ascended by the professed ascetic. Here the soul has complete self-control but is still subject to five "negligences," namely pride, enjoyment of the senses, Kashaya (i.e. anger, conceit, intrigue and greed), sleep, and idle talk. (7) At the seventh stage (Apramattagunasthana) many of the "negligences" are overcome, particularly anger, but pride, deceit and greed remain. (8) It is in the eighth stage (Niyatibadaragunasthana) that pride is conquered. (9) In the ninth (Aniyatibadaragunasthana) deceit disappears. (10) On the tenth level (Sukshmasamparayagunasthana) all pleasure in beauty and all perception of pain and fear are gone. (11) On the eleventh (Upaśantamohagunasthana) the most critical of all sins has been overcome, even greed. (12) The twelfth step (Kshinamohagunasthana) finds the soul freed from the kinds of karma which are difficult to destroy although those which are easy to destroy still

[212]

persist. (13) In the thirteenth phase (Sayogikevaligunasthana) a man may preach to others, form a Tirtha or community, and become a Tirthankara, in which state he is an object of worship. (14) The fourteenth and final step (Ayogikevaligunasthana) witnesses the destruction of all remaining karma, the separation from the body, and the attainment of moksha or release. The jiva has now become a Siddha and reached the blessed consummation of its long ascent. "Omniscience, boundless vision, illimitable righteousness, infinite strength, perfect bliss, indestructibility, existence without form, a body that is neither light nor heavy," it is declared, "such are the characteristics of the Siddha."[90]

[90] Stevenson, *The Heart of Jainism*, p.192.

4. THE LATER HISTORY OF THE RELIGION

JAINA theory conceives the present age of the world to be one of decline, and Jaina traditions describe a progressive diminution in spiritual authority on the part of the leaders of the church who came after the last Tirthankara. Mahavira's leading disciple was Indrabhuti, but he attained complete enlightenment in the very night in which his master died and, as a Kevalin, was no longer expected to be active in the administration of church affairs. Of the other Ganadharas nine had attained Nirvana even before this, and thus there was only one left to be the head of the church, namely Arya Sudharma. He served in this capacity for twelve years, at which time Indrabhuti died and he himself entered into complete enlightenment, and after that his disciple Jambusvami was the leader of the church. Jambusvami himself reached the great enlightenment one year after the death of Sudharma and then later, sixty-four years after the Nirvana of Mahavira, died. From this time on, according to Jaina belief, no man was able to achieve the great enlightenment. Since there were now no more Kevalins who possessed the authority of personally won insight into the true nature of things, understanding depended upon study of the traditions derived from the great men of the past. The next five leaders of the church were believed to possess complete knowledge of all the original texts, and hence were called Śrutakevalins. The last of these was Bhadrabahu, who is said to have died a hundred and seventy years after the Nirvana of Mahavira. After this, as we have seen, knowledge of the canonical texts tended gradually to disappear, and while the Śvetambaras think that some authentic scriptures remain the Digambaras believe that all the original texts are now lost.[91]

Despite the discouraging theory that the world has been in a "bad" period of decline since the time of Mahavira, Jainism has made many achievements of importance and has created monuments which bear witness to its significance as the faith of many believers. We will now sketch the course of the religion through several successive periods in Indian history and will mention a number of its archeological sites and remains.

[91] GJ pp.302-304.

5. THE ŚIŚUNAGA AND NANDA PERIODS, c.642-c.322 B.C.

MAHAVIRA himself lived in the Śiśunaga Period (c.642-c.413 B.C.), the first clearly defined epoch in Indian history. As we have seen, he enjoyed the favor of Kings Bimbisara and Ajataśatru. This royal patronage seems also to have been bestowed by King Udaya, son of Ajataśatru, upon the Jains of his day. Likewise the succeeding Nandas (c.413-c.322 B.C.) appear to have been friendly toward the religion. Tangible evidence for this fact is found in a badly damaged inscription of the later (second century B.C.) King Kharavela of Kalinga in which reference is made to "King Nanda" in connection with "an idol of the first Jina."[92]

[92] Charpentier in CHI I, p.164.

6. THE MAURYA PERIOD, c.322-c.185 b.c.

THE Maurya Period inaugurated by the powerful ruler Chandragupta (c.322-c.298 b.c.) is of much interest in the history of Jainism.

BHADRABAHU AND CHANDRAGUPTA

The head of the Jaina church in the time of Chandragupta's reign
was Bhadrabahu, the last of the Śrutakevalins. According to Jaina
tradition which is recorded with not a few variations in the Brihat-
kathakośa (written by Harishena in A.D. 931), the Bhadrabahucha-
rita (fifteenth century), the Munivamśabhyudaya (seventeenth century) and the Rajavalikathe (nineteenth century), Bhadrabahu
prophesied a twelve-year famine and advised or even led a migration
of a large body of Jaina monks to the south. They are supposed to
have settled in the vicinity of Śravana Belgola in Mysore, where
perhaps Bhadrabahu himself died. King Chandragupta, who was
already an adherent of the Jaina faith, left his throne at this time
and also went to Śravana Belgola where he lived for a number of
years in a cave as an ascetic, worshiping the footprints of Bhadrabahu, and finally himself died by the Jaina rite of starvation.[93]

Remarkable as this account is, it receives some substantiation from
ancient rock inscriptions at Śravana Belgola, which refer to the connection of both Bhadrabahu and Chandragupta with that place,
and speak of the king as the disciple of the great saint. The oldest
inscriptions are on a hill which is known as Chandragiri after the
king. Inscription No. 1, dating from around A.D. 600, includes this
statement: "Bhadrabahuswami, of a lineage rendered illustrious by
a succession of great men . . . , who was acquainted with the true
nature of the eightfold great omens and was a seer of the past, the
present and the future, having learned from an omen and foretold in
Ujjayani a calamity lasting for a period of twelve years, the entire
community (sangha) set out from the North to the South and
reached by degrees a country counting many hundreds of villages
and filled with happy people, wealth, gold, grain, and herds of cows,
buffaloes, goats and sheep."[94]

Another inscription (No. 67) also on the Chandragiri hill and
dated in A.D. 1129, contains the sentence: "Say, how can the greatness

[93] R. Narasimhachar, *Epigraphia Caranatica*, ii *Inscriptions at Sravana Belgola*
(Mysore Archaeological Series). rev. ed., 1923, pp.36-42; Hiralal Jain in *The Cultural
Heritage of India* (Sri Ramakrishna Centenary Memorial). i, p.221.
[94] Narasimhachar, *Epigraphia Caranatica*, ii, Translations, p.1.

be described of Bhadrabahu whose arms have grown stout by subduing the pride of the great wrestler delusion, and through the merit
of being whose disciple the renowned Chandragupta was served for
a very long time by the forest deities."[95]

Yet another text (No. 258), this one found on the Vindhyagiri hill
and dated in A.D. 1432, mentions "the lord of ascetics, Bhadrabahu,"
who "arose on the earth . . . as the full moon in the milk ocean," and
continues: "Pre-eminent for the wealth of perfect intelligence, of
brilliant perfection of conduct, breaker of the bond of karma, of a
fame increased by the growth of penance, Bhadrabahu of supernatural powers lifted up here the pure doctrine of the Siddhas beautifully
composed with faultless words. Though the last of the lords of sages,
the Śrutakevalins, on earth, Bhadrabahu became the foremost leader
of the learned by his exposition of the meaning of all the scriptures.
His disciple was Chandragupta, who was bowed to by the chief
gods on account of his perfect conduct and the fame caused by the
greatness of whose severe penance spread into other worlds."[96]

THE GREAT SCHISM

This is also the time when the Council of Pataliputra was held and
when the cleavage between the Śvetambaras and the Digambaras
began to appear. It will be recalled that even in the time of Keśi and
Gautama there was discussion on questions of monastic vows and
clothing, but that such agreement was reached that all the Jains
could be together in one community. With the great famine the
question relative to clothing became more acute. It is supposed that
the monks who went to south India were the younger and more
vigorous members of the order, who were able to maintain their
discipline in full severity and go unclad. Those who remained in
Magadha were allowed, perhaps because of age and infirmity, to
wear clothes. When the famine was over many of the emigrant monks
returned and were displeased with the laxity which had developed
among those who had remained in the north. Also they disapproved
of the Council of Pataliputra which had been held in their absence,
and questioned the validity of its revision of the canon. This estrangement developed across the succeeding years and led finally (perhaps
around A.D. 80) to actual separation between the two communities.
The spiritual descendants of the stricter southern monks became the
Digambaras (literally, sky-clad), who taught that a monk who has

[95] *ibid.*, p.25; cf. No. 64 (A.D. 1163), p.16.   [96] *ibid.*, p.116.

any property, even clothes, cannot reach Nirvana, and who disowned the canonical books as revised at Pataliputra. The others became the Śvetambaras (literally, white-clad), who maintained that the practice of dispensing with clothing had no longer been requisite since the time of the last Kevalin, Jambusvami, and who accepted the canon of Pataliputra.[97]

BINDUSARA AND AŚOKA

If Chandragupta was a complete convert to radical Jainism the same cannot be said of his two successors. His son Bindusara (c.298-c.273 B.C.) is described in the Mahavamsa[98] as supporting sixty thousand Brahmans; and his grandson Aśoka (c.273-c.232 B.C.) was deeply interested in the furtherance of Buddhism. Aśoka was tolerant, however, of all denominations and required the same attitude on the part of his officials who were in charge of religious affairs. In his seventh Pillar Edict, after telling of his own concern for the material and spiritual welfare of his subjects, he continues: "My Censors of the Law of Piety, too, are occupied with many objects of the [royal] favor, affecting both ascetics and householders, and are likewise occupied with all denominations. I have arranged, also, that they should be occupied with the affairs of the Buddhist clergy, as well as among the Brahmans and the Ajivikas, the Jains, and, in fact, various denominations. The several ordinary officials shall severally superintend their respective charges, whereas the Censors of the Law of Piety shall superintend all other denominations in addition to such special charges."[99]

As far as we know, the foregoing is the oldest actual inscriptional mention of the Jains. The passage is also of interest for its reference to the Ajivikas, another ascetic group whose founder, Gosala, was at one time closely associated with Mahavira.[100] The Ajivikas are mentioned as if they were a sect of considerable prominence at the time, and this is further borne out by the fact that both Aśoka and his grandson Daśaratha dedicated caves for the use of members of this order in the Barabar Hills near Gaya.[101]

[97] Margaret Stevenson in HERE XII, pp.123f.
[98] v, 34. tr. Geiger, pp.28f.
[99] Vincent A. Smith, *The Edicts of Asoka*, p.34.
[100] A. F. R. Hoernle in HERE I, pp.259-268.
[101] Vincent A. Smith, *Asoka, The Buddhist Emperor of India.* 3d ed. 1920, pp.134f.; Fergusson and Burgess, *The Cave Temples of India*, pp.37-43.

Daśaratha, whom we have just mentioned, seems to have ruled the eastern part of his grandfather's territories, while another grandson, Samprati, resided in Ujjain and held sway over the western regions. Samprati was converted by a famous Śvetambara monk named Suhastin, and became very zealous in the promotion of Jainism and in the building of Jaina temples. This is known on the authority of Hemachandra, who writes as follows concerning Samprati: "He showed his zeal by causing Jaina temples to be erected over the whole of Jambuddiva. During Suhastin's stay at Ujjain, and under his guidance, splendid religious festivals and processions in honor of the Arhat were celebrated, and great was the devotion manifested by the king and his subjects on this occasion. The example and advice of Samprati induced his vassals to embrace and patronize his creed, so that not only in his kingdom but also in adjacent countries the monks could practice their religion." Hemachandra also tells how Samprati had missionaries sent out, doubtless of the Śvetambara persuasion, as far as to south India: "In order to extend the sphere of their activities to uncivilized countries, Samprati sent there messengers disguised as Jaina monks. They described to the people the kind of food and other requisites which monks may accept as alms, enjoining them to give such things instead of the usual tax to the revenue collector who would visit them from time to time. Of course these revenue collectors were to be Jaina monks. Having thus prepared the way for them, he induced the superior to send monks to those countries, for they would find it in no way impossible to live there. Accordingly missionaries were sent to the Andhras and Dramilas, who found everything as the king had told. Thus the uncivilized nations were brought under the influence of Jainism."[102]

[102] Quoted by Shah, *Jainism in North India 800 B.C.-A.D. 526*, p.145.

7. BETWEEN THE MAURYA AND KUSHAN PERIODS

THE years preceding and shortly following the inception of the Christian era are relatively dark in the history of Jainism. We do know, however, that the city of Ujjain, just mentioned in connection with Samprati, continued to be an important center of the religion. A narrative known as the Kalakacaryakatha or Story of the Teacher Kalaka[103] has to do with events which took place there in the first century B.C. when a certain Gardabhilla was king.

THE STORY OF KALAKA

Although the account is legendary, and was probably not put into the form of a single written text until between the tenth and thirteenth centuries A.D., the Story of Kalaka may contain a kernel of historical truth. It relates that King Gardabhilla of Ujjain carried off the Jaina nun Sarasvati, who was the sister of the famous monk Kalaka. When Kalaka found his protests unavailing, he journeyed west of the Indus and persuaded the Śakas (Scythians) to come and attack Ujjain and overthrow Gardabhilla. The Śakas did this and established themselves in the city, where it is said that "the time passed happily for them as they devoted themselves to honoring the teaching of the Jinas, and sported like bees about the lotus-feet of the *suri* [Kalaka]."[104] Soon afterward, however, Vikramaditya, son of Gardabhilla, expelled the invaders and reestablished the native dynasty. Vikramaditya is supposed also to have adhered to the Jaina faith, and the Vikrama Era which he inaugurated in 58/57 B.C. is still in use among the Jains of north India. After one hundred and thirty-five years the Śakas regained the ascendancy and instituted their own era (A.D. 78), by which Jaina dates also are still reckoned.

THE CAVES OF ORISSA

We also know that Jainism was of importance in eastern India at this time as well as in the western regions of Ujjain. This is indicated by the existence of Jaina caves not far from Bhuvaneśvara in Orissa, the oldest of which probably date from the second century B.C. The caves are excavated in some sandstone hills known as Khandagiri, Udayagiri and Nilagiri, and served as viharas or monasteries for

---

[103] W. Norman Brown, *The Story of Kālaka, Texts, History, Legends, and Miniature Paintings of the Śvetāmbara Jain Hagiographical Work, The Kālakācāryakathā* (Smithsonian Institution, Freer Gallery of Art, Oriental Studies, 1). 1933.
[104] *ibid.*, p.60.

Jaina monks. Two of these caves in particular may be mentioned here. The Hathigumpha or Elephant Cave, as it is now known, was an extensive natural cave which was improved by the Jaina king, Kharavela of Kalinga. There is a badly damaged inscription of this king in the cave, dating around the middle of the second century B.C.,[105] which tells among other things of how he constructed rock-dwellings and gave abundant gifts to Jaina devotees. The cave now called Rani ka Naur or Queen's Palace is arranged with two stories of cells, both originally fronted by pillared verandas, and with a large courtyard cut out of the hillside. There are sculptured adornments, probably the finest of any in this entire group of caves, which include fighting scenes, the hunting of a winged deer, the carrying off of a woman, and other subjects. Although they have not been further identified, it is supposed that the portrayals are taken from Jaina legends more or less similar to the Jatakas which provided such abundant themes for Buddhist sculptures.[106]

[105] E. J. Rapson in CHI I, pp.534f.
[106] Fergusson, *History of Indian and Eastern Architecture*, II, pp.9-18; CHIIA pp.37f.

8. THE KUSHAN PERIOD, A.D. C.50-C.320

THE most famous king of the Kushan Period was Kanishka (second century A.D.), and he is well known for his patronage of Buddhism. Nevertheless Jainism also flourished in his reign and throughout this period.

MATHURA

The city of Mathura on the Jumna River was now a prominent center of Jainism as indeed it had already been for a considerable time. The ruins of a Jaina stupa as well as of two temples have been excavated in the mound called Kankali Tila at Mathura, and a second century A.D. inscription has been found which says that the stupa was "built by the gods." Evidently at that time the stupa was regarded as of immemorial antiquity. Later, in a legendary work of the fourteenth century, it is said that the stupa was built originally of gold by the goddess Kubera in honor of the seventh Jina, Suparśva, and was encased in bricks in the time of Parśva.[107]

The most important Jaina inscriptions and sculptures at Mathura, however, date probably from the first and second centuries A.D. and thus fall within the Kushan Period of which we are now speaking. The numerous inscriptions from these two centuries are of particular interest in supplying corroboration for many of the points found in the later Jaina traditions. Already, for example, the series of twenty-four successive Tirthankaras, each with his distinctive emblem, was firmly believed in, women had an influential place in the church and an order of nuns was in existence, the division between the Śvetambaras and Digambaras had come into being, and the sacred texts were being recited with verbal exactitude.[108]

The sculptures as well as the inscriptions found at and near Mathura are of much interest for the history of Jainism. A characteristic production was an Ayagapata or "tablet of homage" which was sculptured in relief and erected in a temple for purposes of adoration. Such a small sculptured tablet, dating probably from the first century A.D. and now in the Mathura Museum, is shown in Fig. 70. The inscription on the tablet begins with the words "Adoration to the

[107] Vincent A. Smith, The Jain Stûpa and Other Antiquities of Mathurâ (Archaeological Survey of India, New Imperial Series, xx). 1901, pp.10-13.
[108] G. Bühler in Wiener Zeitschrift für die Kunde des Morgenlandes. 1 (1887), pp.165-180; 2 (1888), pp.141-146; 3 (1889), pp.233-240; 4 (1890), pp.169-173,313-331; 5 (1891), pp.59-63,175-180; cj pp.42f.

Arhat Vardhamana," and indicates that it was the gift of a courtesan named Vasu, daughter of Lonaśobhika. The main representation is of a Jaina stupa, or hemispherical memorial mound, which has the same general appearance as the stupas of the Buddhists. In this case the stupa stands on a high platform surrounded by a railing, and is approached by nine steps which lead up to an ornamental gateway. On either side are Yakshis and tall columns.[109]

Another such Jaina tablet from Mathura is pictured in Fig. 71. It probably also comes from the first century A.D., and is now in the Lucknow Museum. The figure in the center is that of a seated Jina surrounded by various symbols. On the left is a pillar with a dhamma-cakka capital, and on the right a pillar with an elephant capital. The accompanying inscription reads: "Adoration to the Arhats! A tablet of homage (*ayagapata*) was set up by Sihanadika, son of the Vanika Sihaka and son of a Kośiki, for the worship of the Arhats."[110]

Larger cult images of the Jinas were also made at this time and have a general appearance similar to that of contemporary statues of the Buddha. An example is given in Fig. 72, which shows a mottled red sandstone statue found at Mathura and now in the Lucknow Museum.[111] The date is probably in the first or early second century A.D. The figure is that of the Tirthankara Parśvanatha protected by the Naga Dharanendra. The portrait type is comparable to that of the Buddha from Mathura which will be shown in Fig. 107; the sheltering of the figure beneath the hood of the snake king is a theme also familiar in Buddhist art as will be seen later (Fig. 123).[112]

[109] J. Ph. Vogel, *La sculpture de Mathura* (Ars Asiatica, xv). 1930, p.27; Smith, *The Jain Stûpa and Other Antiquities of Mathurâ*, p.61.

[110] Smith, *The Jain Stûpa and Other Antiquities of Mathurâ*, p.14.

[111] CHIIA p.57, Fig. 86.

[112] J. Ph. Vogel, *Indian Serpent-Lore or the Nāgas in Hindu Legend and Art.* 1926, p.104.

9. THE GUPTA PERIOD, A.D. C.320-C.600

MATHURA continues to provide illustration of Jaina art in the Gupta Period. From that site we show in Fig. 73 a seated image of a Tirthankara which is similar to the Buddha representation typical of the Gupta epoch (cf. Fig. 109). Thus is emphasized again the fact which is often evident, that all the Indian religions drew upon the common art of their time and place. Nevertheless, the statue is clearly Jaina rather than Buddhist. Among the points distinguishing this work from an image of the Buddha are the lack of clothing, the absence of the ushnisha and urna (p.284), and the presence of the Srivatsa symbol on the chest. Since the Srivatsa appears on various figures of Tirthankaras it may be supposed to be a general Jaina emblem at this time rather than the designation of a single Jina. The lions on the pedestal of the statue may then give us the clue to the identification of this Tirthankara as Mahavira. Between the lions are two kneeling figures and a sacred wheel.[113]

SITTANNAVASAL

In painting as well as in sculpture the Jaina art of the period may be compared with the Buddhist. Important Jaina paintings have been discovered at Sittannavasal not far from Tanjore, which are executed in the Gupta style like the Buddhist paintings at Ajanta and like some of them belong to a time around A.D. 600 or a little later. The paintings are preserved on the ceilings, capitals and upper parts of the pillars of a rock-cut Jaina temple, which was once fully decorated. The chief subject still to be seen is a large fresco adorning the entire ceiling of the veranda of the shrine. It shows a tank covered with lotus flowers, and also depicts fish, geese, buffaloes, elephants and three men. The men hold lotuses in their hands and are portrayed in a very attractive way. This is presumably some unidentified scene from Jaina history. On the capitals of the pillars are elegant painted lotuses, and on the pillars themselves are figures of *devadasis* or dancing girls of the temple.[114]

[113] Vogel, *La sculpture de Mathura*, pp.112f.; Smith, *The Jain Stûpa and Other Antiquities of Mathurâ*, p.51.
[114] G. Jouveau Dubreuil in *The Indian Antiquary, A Journal of Oriental Research*. 52 (1923), pp.45-47.

10. THE MEDIEVAL PERIOD, A.D. c.600-c.1200

DURING the Medieval Period, Jainism for the most part enjoyed the tolerance of rulers who looked upon the various religious sects with broad sympathy, and in not a few instances it was the recipient of special favor and patronage. Of this general situation several specific illustrations may be given. The great monarch Harsha (A.D. c.606-c.647) who ruled from Kanauj over most of north India, and the Pawar king Bhoja (A.D. c.1010-c.1065) who reigned at Dhara and was celebrated as an ideal Indian ruler, were both exponents of genuine tolerance. The Solanki king Siddharaja (A.D. 1094-1143) of Anhilwar, although himself a worshiper of Śiva, was pleased to have the distinguished Jaina writer, Hemachandra (A.D. 1088-1172), work at his court; and his successor, Kumarapala (A.D. 1143-1173), was actually converted by Hemachandra to Jainism. In the south the Gangas, Rashtrakutas and early Hoyśalas were Jains and supporters of the faith. The great minister Chamunda Raja or Chamunda Raya (end of the tenth century), who served under the Ganga kings Marasinha II and Rachamalla (Rajamalla) IV and whose spiritual adviser was the Jaina scholar Nemichandra, provided a notable example of active patronage of the religion. Under these favorable circumstances the religion of the Tirthankaras expanded and flowered.[115]

Tangible evidence of the splendor which Jainism attained is still to be seen in architectural monuments throughout India, several of which will now be mentioned. As in sculpture and in painting, so, too, in architecture the style of Jaina work is often not peculiar to that sect but is simply the Indian style of the time and place in which it is done. Thus we shall encounter both cave temples and structural temples which are very similar to examples of Hindu work with which we are already familiar.

ELURA

The best-known Jaina cave temple of the Medieval Period is doubtless the so-called Indra Sabha ("Court of Indra"),[116] one of

[115] GJ pp.45-60.

[116] Fergusson, *History of Indian and Eastern Architecture*, II, pp.19f.; Fergusson and Burgess, *The Cave Temples of India*, pp.496-500; James Burgess, *Report on the Elura Cave Temples and the Brahmanical and Jaina Caves in Western India, Completing the Results of the Fifth, Sixth, and Seventh Seasons' Operations of the Archaeological Survey, 1877-78, 1878-79, 1879-80; Supplementary to the Volume on "The Cave Temples of India"* (Archaeological Survey of Western India, V). 1883, pp.44-48.

several Jaina caves at Elura in Central India. There are also Buddhist and Hindu caves at Elura, and the Hindu Kailasanatha, a complete monolithic temple, has been described earlier. Like the Kailasanatha, the Indra Sabha (Fig. 74) is cut out of the solid rock.[117] The courtyard is protected by a rock screen wall which faces south. Outside of this on the east is a chapel with two pillars in front and two at the back. Entering the courtyard, there is on the right an elephant on a pedestal and on the left a monolithic column (now fallen) surmounted by a quadruple image of a Tirthankara. In the center of the court is an elaborate square porch (*mandapam*) over another quadruple image. Beyond, a sort of double veranda gives access to the lower hall of the temple which is cut on back into the rock. At the left end of the veranda are two large images of Śanti, the sixteenth Tirthankara, with an accompanying inscription: "The image of Śantibhattaraka, [made by] Sohila, a Brahmacharin [i.e. pandit of the Digambara Jains]." At the other end is a stone stairway which leads to the upper hall of the temple. Both halls are adorned with pillars, although in the lower hall these have not been completely executed and the aisles have not been finished. In the upper hall the walls of the side and back aisles are divided into compartments and filled with sculptured figures of Jinas.

Among the many sculptured figures of Jinas in the cave and its chapels, the most prominent are Parśva, Mahavira, and Gommata. The last named, Gommata or Bahubali, was a son of the first Tirthankara, Rishabha, and is specially venerated by the Digambaras. In a typical relief panel in the Indra Sabha this saint is shown, accompanied by attendants and Gandharvas, but himself standing in such complete reverie that a creeping plant has grown up and wrapped its tendrils about him. Two other large figures which have an important place in the temple are commonly identified as Indra and Indrani his wife, but are possibly intended instead to represent the Yaksha and Yakshi who are the customary companions of a Tirthankara.[118]

ŚRAVANA BELGOLA

In south India the chief center of Jainism was Śravana Belgola, the legendary connections of which place with Bhadrabahu and

---

[117] Burgess, *Report on the Elura Cave Temples and the Brahmanical and Jaina Caves in Western India*, Pl. VI.

[118] W. Kirfel, *Die Religion der Jaina's* (in Hans Haas, ed., *Bilderatlas zur Religionsgeschichte*, 12). 1928, p.xxi.

Chandragupta have already been discussed. Here in medieval and later times almost innumerable shrines were constructed. These included an ordinary type of temple known as a Basti, which contained an image of a Tirthankara; and a specially arranged kind of sanctuary called a Betta, which consisted of cloisters around an open courtyard in which stood a colossal statue of a great man of the Jaina faith.

A remarkable example of the latter type of sanctuary may be seen on the summit of the Vindhyagiri hill at Śravana Belgola. In the center of an open court surrounded by corridors adorned with Jinas and other figures stands the enormous statue pictured in Fig. 75. This huge image measuring fifty-seven feet in height and standing erect and unclothed facing north, represents Gommata (Gommateśvara). Although the figure is treated in rather conventional form there is a calm and serene expression upon the face. Anthills rise on either side and, as in the relief in the Indra Sabha, creeping plants spring from the ground and twine around the thighs and arms of the saint. Thus is symbolized the profound abstraction of the great ascetic who stands in his place of seclusion neither moving nor noticing while ants build and plants climb around him. Inscriptions (Nos. 175, 176, 179) at the side of the statue state, "Chamunda Raja caused [this image] to be made," and thus we learn that it was none other than the famous minister of Rajamalla who was responsible for the making of the monument. The date must have been about A.D. 983.[119]

Another inscription (No. 234) found at Śravana Belgola, composed by the Jaina poet Sujanottamsa (or Boppana) and dating about A.D. 1180, tells something of the character ascribed to Gommata, relates how Chamunda Raya came to have the image made, and describes its wonderful character:

I shall praise the immeasurable Gommata Jina, worshiped by the lords of men, Nagas, gods, demons and Khacharas, destroyer of Cupid by the fire of meditation and worthy to be meditated upon by ascetics. Who else is so honorable as the high-souled Bahubali, son of Puru, who, having generously handed over the kingdom of the earth to his elder brother,— who on defeat in a regular hand-to-hand fight unjustly left off speaking and when even the discus thrown by him proved a failure was seized with shame,—went forth and destroyed by his penance the enemy Karma? The

---

[119] Narasimhachar, *Epigraphia Caranatica*, II, pp.10-23; Translations, p.89; Pl. I. Two other similar colossal statues of Gommata are known, one at Karkal, 41½ feet high, erected in A.D. 1432; and one at Venur, thirty-five feet high, set up in 1604.

emperor Bharata, conqueror of all kings, son of Purudeva, caused to be made near Paudanapura, with joy of mind, an image, 525 bows high, resembling the form of the victorious-armed Bahubali-kevali. After the lapse of a long time, a world-terrifying mass of innumerable *kukkuta-sarpas*[120] having sprung up in the region near that Jina, that enemy of sin obtained, indeed, the name Kukkutesvara. Afterward that region became invisible to the common people, though seen even now by many skilled in spells and charms. There might be heard the sound of the celestial drum; why say more, there might even be seen the details of divine worship; those who have seen the brilliant charming mirror of the nails of that Jina's feet, can see the forms of their former births;—the supernatural power of that god is renowned in the world. On hearing from people of the celebrated supernatural power of that Jina, a desire arose in his mind to see him, and when he prepared himself to go, he was told by his preceptors that the region of that city was distant and inaccessible; whereupon, saying, "In that case I will cause to be made an image of that god," Gomata had this god made. Combining in himself learning, purity of faith, power, virtuous conduct, liberality and courage, the moon of the Ganga family, Rachamalla was celebrated in the world. Was it not that king's matchless power, Chamunda Raya (*alias*) Gommata, an equal of Manu, that thus caused this god to be made with great effort?

When an image is very lofty, it may not have beauty; when possessed of loftiness and real beauty, it may not have supernatural power: loftiness, real beauty and mighty supernatural power being all united in it, how worthy of worship in the world is the glorious form, comparable to itself, of Gommatesvara Jina? When it is said that Maya, the king of heaven (Indra),[121] and the lord of serpents (Adisesha)[122] are unable respectively to draw a likeness, to take a full view and to undertake the praise of it, who else are then able to draw a likeness, to take a full view and to undertake the praise of the matchless form of wondrous beauty of the southern Kukkutesvara? Birds do not fly over it even in forgetfulness; . . . who can adequately praise the glorious form of Gommatesvara Jina? . . . Why in vain do you make yourself wander in the forest of births by foolishly mistaking the various dying deities of the land for gods? Think on Gommatadeva who is of the form of the supreme soul, and you will be rid of birth, old age and other sorrows. No man shall take pleasure in killing, lying, stealing, adultery and covetousness; if he does, he will lose for ever this world and the next: lo! Gommatadeva looks as if proclaiming this standing on high.[123]

KHAJURAHO

In north India one of the important centers of Jainism was Khajuraho. As we have already seen, this was also a seat of Hinduism,

[120] The *kukkuta-sarpa* is a fowl with the head and neck of a serpent.
[121] Even though possessed of one thousand eyes.
[122] Even though possessed of two thousand tongues.
[123] Narasimhachar, *Epigraphia Caranatica*, II, Translations, pp.97-101.

and of the approximately thirty temples which stand there about one third are Vaishnavite, one third Śaivite and one third Jaina.[124] The proximity of the various temple groups to each other emphasizes their similarity, and we find that the Jaina temples are scarcely distinguishable from the Hindu except for the details of their sculptured representations.

Of all the Jaina sanctuaries the largest and finest is the Parśvanatha, which as its name indicates is dedicated to the twenty-third Tirthankara. Like most of the shrines at Khajuraho it probably belongs to the century between A.D. 950 and 1050. It is about sixty-two feet in length and half that in breadth. The outside walls are adorned with numerous bands of moldings and with three horizontal rows of sculptured statues. The appearance of the temple may be seen in Fig. 76, and may be compared with the Śaivite Kandarya Mahadeva at Khajuraho in Fig. 66.[125]

More distinctive of Jainism than the style of its individual buildings was its tendency to group its sanctuaries together into temple cities. While Buddhist stupas and viharas would of course cluster around a sacred spot as at Buddh Gaya and Hindu temples be multiplied at an important center of population such as Bhuvaneśvara, the erection of a Jaina temple was considered as a prayer in and of itself and many such structures were often built at some picturesque but relatively remote and uninhabited site. Such a temple city as would thereby arise would naturally become a place of pilgrimage (*tirtha*), but it might contain no human habitations and it might not even be permitted for men to cook or sleep within its environs.[126] Of such temple cities the greatest, where there are monuments probably dating from within the Medieval Period, are in Gujarat at Satrunjaya, Girnar and Mount Abu.

SATRUNJAYA

Śatrunjaya or the Holy Mountain is one and one-half miles from Palitana, and rises to an elevation of almost two thousand feet above sea level. It is considered specially sacred to Rishabha, the first Tirthankara. The top of the hill consists of two main ridges with a valley between, and is protected by massive battlemented walls. The temples, of which there are said to be over five hundred, are

---

124 A general view of the Jaina group is given by Lepel Griffin, *Famous Monuments of Central India.* 1886, Pl. LI.

125 Fergusson, *History of Indian and Eastern Architecture*, II, p.50, Pl. XVIII.

126 *ibid.*, II, pp.24-26.

grouped in separate enclosures generally containing one principal temple with other smaller ones. There are elaborate sculptured ornamentations, and at one time approximately sixty-five hundred separate images of Tirthankaras were counted. As for date, some of the temples are believed to be as old as the eleventh century, while the majority range from around A.D. 1500 to the present time. A general view of a portion of this sacred city of temples is given in Fig. 77.[127]

GIRNAR

The hill of Girnar (Fig. 78) is not far from Junagadh, and rises to an elevation of some 3,664 feet. The foot of the hill was chosen as a place for the recording of his Rock Edicts by Aśoka, and in Jaina faith the mountain was deemed sacred to Nemi (or Arishtanemi), the twenty-second Tirthankara. The chief group of Jaina temples, some sixteen in number, forms a sort of fort on a spectacular ledge at the top of a great cliff only six hundred feet below the summit of the peak. Of these the largest and perhaps also the oldest is the Neminatha temple (Fig. 79) erected in honor of the Tirthankara just named. Since an inscription upon it records that it was repaired in A.D. 1278, its original erection must have been considerably earlier than that and well within the Medieval Period. The temple stands in a quadrangular courtyard 195 by 130 feet, surrounded by some seventy cells each containing a seated image of a Tirthankara, and itself consists of two halls with two porches (*mandapams*), and a shrine with a large image of Nemi.[128]

MOUNT ABU

Most famous of all are the temples of the Jaina Tirtha on Mount Abu,[129] an isolated and impressive mountain which rises out of the desert of southern Rajputana and attains an elevation of some four thousand feet above sea level. In an area known as Dilvara (from *deul*, "temple," and *vara*, "place" or "precinct") stand four large temples, of which the two most important are in certain respects unrivaled anywhere in India. The older of the two was built in A.D. 1031

[127] *ibid.*, II, pp.27-30; Fischer, *Die Kunst Indiens, Chinas und Japans*, p.247.
[128] *ibid.*, II, pp.32f.; *A Handbook for Travellers in India, Burma and Ceylon* (John Murray), pp.234-238.
[129] Fergusson, *History of Indian and Eastern Architecture*, II, pp. 36-44; Diez, *Die Kunst Indiens*, p.78; Otto Fischer, *Die Kunst Indiens, Chinas und Japans* (Propyläen-Kunstgeschichte, IV). 1928, p.55; A. A. Macdonell, *India's Past, A Survey of Her Literatures, Religions, Languages and Antiquities*. 1927, pp.76f.

by a wealthy Jaina banker, Vimala Shah, and named for its founder; the other was likewise erected by bankers, two brothers named Tejahpala and Vastupala, and was completed in A.D. 1230 and dedicated to the twenty-second Tirthankara, Neminatha. Both temples are constructed entirely of white marble which must have been quarried at a distance of at least twenty or thirty miles and transported up the mountain with enormous labor.

The two temples are similar in plan, and are relatively plain on the exterior but amazingly rich in interior decoration. Each stands in a rectangular walled area, surrounded by recesses with statues of Tirthankaras and other deities. The central structure is a cell with a pyramidal roof (śikhara), lighted only from its door, and containing a statue of a Tirthankara. Connected with this is a closed hall, and in front of it in turn is an extensive open portico or assembly hall adorned with free-standing columns and with a beautiful dome upheld by eight pillars.

Some indication of the intricate decoration lavished upon these white marble sanctuaries may be given by the two following photographs. Fig. 80 shows the dome in the temple erected by Vimala Shah; Fig. 81, the interior of the temple built by Tejahpala and Vastupala.

Other interesting Jaina temples, towers and sculptures are to be found at Parasnath, Ranpur in the Jodhpur territory, Chitorgarh and Gwalior, but for the most part they are of dates later than the first great age of Jaina architecture to which our survey has been limited.[130]

ILLUSTRATED MANUSCRIPTS

Yet another characteristic and interesting development in the artistic expression of Jainism was inaugurated toward the close of the Medieval Period. This was the ornamentation of sacred manuscripts with miniature paintings. A school which produced such paintings was flourishing in Gujarat, Kathiawar and Rajputana in the early part of the twelfth century, and such work continued to be done for many centuries thereafter. Up to about A.D. 1400 the texts and illustrations were placed on palm leaf manuscripts; after that paper came into use. The work was done chiefly among the Śvetambara Jains and the texts most frequently chosen for adornment were the

[130] Fergusson, *History of Indian and Eastern Architecture*, II, pp.44-59.

Kalpasutra,[131] the Kalakacaryakatha,[132] and the Uttaradhyayanasutra.[133] The earliest known examples of such miniatures are two paintings found in a palm leaf manuscript preserved in the Santinatha Temple (Nagin Das) of the Svetambara Jains at the ancient port city of Cambay in Gujarat. Here the text is that of the Jnatasutra and next three Angas, together with the commentary of Abhayadeva, a Svetambara scholar of the eleventh century A.D. The manuscript itself bears a date equivalent to A.D. 1127.[134]

These two miniatures are shown in Figs. 82 and 83. In Fig. 82 the personage in the center is a Jina, probably Mahavira, or possibly Rishabha. He is seated upon a pedestal like that used for images in temples; behind his head is a halo, and above an ornament of leaves. On either side is a fly-whisk (*chauri*) bearer, presumably a god. In Fig. 83 the chief figure is probably the goddess Sarasvati, often associated with Mahavira, although another interpretation would make her Cakresvari, the Yakshi of Rishabha, the first Tirthankara. The goddess is portrayed with four arms, and carries in her upper hands lotuses and in her lower hands a rosary and a manuscript. In front of her is a peacock, and on either side a worshiper, these perhaps being the two laymen who were the donors of the entire manuscript.

The finest miniatures of the Jaina school were produced in the fourteenth and fifteenth centuries.[135] While thus exceeding the chronological limits otherwise adhered to in this chapter, these paintings are of such importance and interest that several examples may be given. Two varieties of style are distinguished, the first of which may be observed in Figs. 84 and 85. Here the composition and background remain relatively simple, as in the earlier miniatures already shown. Both of the present paintings are from a palm leaf manuscript of the Kalpasutra and Kalakacaryakatha which bears a date equivalent to A.D. 1370. The one illustration (Fig. 84) depicts the birth of Mahavira; the other (Fig. 85), his bath at birth. The second style is marked by richness of background and profusion of detail, executed

[131] W. Norman Brown, *A Descriptive and Illustrated Catalogue of the Miniature Paintings of the Jaina Kalpasūtra as Executed in the Early Western Indian Style* (Smithsonian Institution, Freer Gallery of Art, Oriental Studies, 2). 1934.

[132] W. Norman Brown, *The Story of Kālaka, Texts, History, Legends, and Miniature Paintings of the Śvetāmbara Jain Hagiographical Work, The Kālakācāryakathā* (Smithsonian Institution, Freer Gallery of Art, Oriental Studies, 1). 1933.

[133] W. Norman Brown, *Manuscript Illustrations of the Uttarādhyayana Sūtra Reproduced and Described* (American Oriental Series, 21). 1941.

[134] Brown, *The Story of Kālaka*, pp.18,116; Figs.1,2.

[135] W. Norman Brown in *Journal of the Indian Society of Oriental Art*. June-Dec. 1937, pp.2-12; Figs.2,3,7,9.

usually with very fine lines. It may be studied in Figs. 86 and 87. Fig. 86 is a painting from a palm leaf manuscript of the Kalpasutra, not dated but belonging probably to the last half of the fourteenth century. Mahavira is shown giving away his possessions as he abandoned his worldly life. Fig. 87 is from a paper manuscript of the Kalpasutra, probably of the first half of the fifteenth century. The subject depicted is the recital by Queen Triśala to King Siddhartha of her fourteen wonderful dreams.

CHAPTER V

Buddhism

BUDDHISM originated in India and spread from there to many other lands. Its world membership is estimated at over 155,-000,000, but in the land of its birth it has today probably not more than half a million members.[1]

1. INDIA IN THE ŚIŚUNAGA PERIOD, c.642-c.413 B.C.

THE founder of Buddhism lived in the sixth and early fifth centuries B.C. during what is known in Indian history as the Śiśunaga Period. This period and some of its kings have already become known to us in the chapters on Hinduism and Jainism, but because more detailed references are required in the present chapter a recapitulation and amplification of earlier notices of the historical situation is appropriate.

Numerous kingdoms and clans existed in northern India at the time. Of the kingdoms the four most important were those of Magadha, Kosala, Vamsa and Avanti.[2] Magadha, already described, lay along and south of the Ganges River, and was ruled by the dynasty from which this historical period takes its name. The most famous Śiśunaga kings were Bimbisara (Śrenika), c.540-490 B.C., and his son Ajataśatru (Kunika), c.490-c.460 B.C., both of whom ruled at Rajagriha. Ajataśatru's son Udaya established a new capital at Pataliputra. The Kosalas dwelt to the northwest, with their capitals at Savatthi (Śravasti) and Saketa. Their rulers included King Pasenadi and his son Vidudabha. The kingdom of the Vamsas lay to the southwest along the banks of the Jumna River. Their most important king was named Udena, and his capital was at Kauśambi on the south bank of the Jumna. The Avantis were yet farther to the southwest, with their capital at Ujjeni. Their king was Pajjota, who was called "the Fierce." Of these kingdoms that of Kosala was then the most

---

[1] A Handbook for Travellers in India, Burma and Ceylon (John Murray, 15th ed. 1938), p.lxviii.
[2] T. W. Rhys Davids, Buddhist India. 1903, pp.1-41; and in CHI I, pp.172-191.

important, but that of Magadha was the most progressive and was growing in power and size, and was ultimately to absorb the other kingdoms including Kosala.

Among the most important clans and tribes which existed at the same time were the following, each group being mentioned together with its capital or chief city: the Sakyas (Sakiyas) of Kapilavastu (Kapilavatthu), the Bulis of Allakappa, the Koliyas of Ramagama, the Mallas of Pava, the Mallas of Kusinara, the Moriyas of Pipphali-vana, the Licchavis of Vesali, and the Angas of Champa. Insofar as they are exactly or approximately known, the geographical locations of these groups and their towns are shown on Map 4. Most of the groups were organized as republics, and carried out their administrative and judicial business in public assemblies meeting in so-called Mote Halls. Some of them enjoyed complete or partial independence, while others such as the Sakyas, Bulis, Koliyas and Moriyas were vassals under the more powerful states like Kosala.[3]

[3] Bimala C. Law, *India as Described in Early Texts of Buddhism and Jainism.* 1941, p.134.

2. THE BUDDHIST SCRIPTURES

THE literature of the Buddhist religion is very extensive and represents a process of compilation which was carried on over many years. Gautama Buddha himself was a native of Kosala and spent much of his ministry in Magadha; presumably, therefore, he taught in the contemporary dialect or dialects of those lands. Buddhaghosa, a celebrated Buddhist scholar and writer who flourished early in the fifth century A.D., makes explicit reference to "the language of the Magadhas spoken by the All-enlightened."[4] The earliest written texts of Buddhism are composed in the Pali language, an Indic dialect descended from the Vedic Aryan. It may be that this is the same as the Magadhi language to which Buddhaghosa refers; on the other hand it may be that in the meantime the teachings had been rewritten in a new dialect.[5] In the Kullavagga (v, xxxiii, 1. SBE xx, pp. 150f.) an incident is recorded where the monks desired to versify the teachings, doubtless as an aid to memory, but this request was refused. It was first in Ceylon under King Vattagamani Abhaya (c.29-c.17 B.C.) that the monks of that country caused the teachings and their commentaries to be written in books. This fact is recorded in the fourth and sixth century Ceylonese chronicles, the Dipavamsa and the Mahavamsa, in almost identical words. Speaking of the reign of King Vattagamani, the Dipavamsa says: "Before this time, the wise Bhikkus had orally handed down the text of the three Pitakas and also the Atthakatha. At this time, the Bhikkus who perceived the decay of created beings, assembled and in order that the religion might endure for a long time, they recorded [the above-mentioned texts] in written books."[6] This was done in the Pali language.

PALI WRITINGS

The Pali canonical literature is known as the Tipitaka (Sanskrit, Tripitaka) or "Three Baskets."[7] The word *pitaka* refers to a basket

---

[4] Quoted by Edward J. Thomas, *The Life of Buddha as Legend and History* (The History of Civilization). 1927, p.254.

[5] Ralph L. Turner in EB xvii, pp.145f.

[6] xx, 20f. tr. Hermann Oldenberg, *The Dipavamsa: An Ancient Buddhist Record.* 1879, p.211; cf. Mahavamsa xxxiii, 100f. tr. Wilhelm Geiger, *The Mahāvamsa or the Great Chronicle of Ceylon Translated into English* (Pali Text Society). 1912, p.237.

[7] Bimala C. Law, *A History of Pāli Literature.* 1933, i. Selected passages from these scriptures are translated by Henry C. Warren, *Buddhism in Translations, Passages Selected from the Buddhist Sacred Books and Translated from the Original Pali into English* (Harvard Oriental Series, iii, 8th issue). 1922; and by Edward J. Thomas, *Early Buddhist Scriptures.* 1935.

containing manuscripts, and as the name of the entire collection suggests, the Pali scriptures comprise three major groups.

THE VINAYAPITAKA

The first is the Vinayapitaka or "Discipline Basket," which contains the rules and regulations for the Buddhist orders of monks and nuns. The Vinayapitaka consists of four books as follows: (1) Suttavibhanga. This means expositions of the Suttas, the word Sutta having the same meaning as the Sanskrit Sutra (p.160). The rules here explained are those contained in the Patimokkha, shortly to be mentioned. The Suttavibhanga is itself divided into two sections, Parajika and Pacittiya. Parajikas are offences for which the punishment is expulsion from the order; Pacittiyas are those for which some expiation is specified. (2) Khandhakas. Here again there are two sections, the larger being the Mahavagga, and the smaller the Kullavagga. The Mahavagga[8] records certain historical incidents in the life of the Buddha, and then lays down numerous regulations and gives various medical prescriptions as well. The Kullavagga[9] also contains anecdotes from the life of the Buddha and the history of the order, and sets forth numerous rules concerning legal and other matters. (3) Parivarapatha. This is a digest or learned review of the other parts of the Vinayapitaka. At the end it is said to have been composed by "the highly wise, learned, and skillful Dipa, after he had inquired here and there into the methods followed by former teachers." (4) Patimokkha. This is a long tabulation of offences requiring confession and expiation, composed for use in penitential assemblies of the members of the Buddhist orders.

THE SUTTAPITAKA

The second Pitaka is the Suttapitaka or "Discourse Basket," which contains sermons, sayings and dialogues of the Buddha and his disciples. According to their length or subject matter, these discourses are grouped into five Nikayas (or Agamas) as follows:[10] (1) Digha Nikaya.[11] This is a collection of thirty-four long Suttas or discourses,

[8] tr. T. W. Rhys Davids and Hermann Oldenberg, SBE XIII, XVII.
[9] *ibid.*, XVII, XX.
[10] Selected discourses from the Suttapitaka are translated by T. W. Rhys Davids in SBE XI as follows: Tevijja Sutta, Mahaparinibbana Suttanta and Mahasudassana Suttanta, from the Digha Nikaya; Sabbasava Sutta, Akankheyya Sutta and Cetokhila Sutta, from the Majjhima Nikaya; and Dhammacakkappavattana Sutta, from the Samyutta Nikaya.
[11] tr. T. W. and C. A. F. Rhys Davids, *Dialogues of the Buddha, Translated from the Pali of the Digha-Nikāya* (Sacred Books of the Buddhists, II, III, IV). 3 vols. 1899-1921.

each dealing fully with certain matters of Buddhist doctrine. (2) Majjhima Nikaya.[12] Here there are about one hundred and fifty medium-length Suttas, which, taken as a whole, treat almost all the points of the Buddhist religion. (3) Samyutta Nikaya.[13] This is a collection of "Grouped Suttas," and comprises fifty-six Samyuttas or groups of teachings, dealing mostly with psychological, ethical and philosophical problems. (4) Anguttara Nikaya.[14] In this Nikaya the materials are grouped numerically and in ascending order, running from the "Book of the Ones" to the "Book of the Elevens." The topics considered include such varied subjects as "energetic effort," "punishments," "fools," "fears," "the worthy man," "earthquakes," and "perfect purity." (5) Khuddaka Nikaya. Here there are some sixteen independent books, written for the most part in verse, and containing all the most important works of Buddhist poetry. They are listed as follows: (i) Khuddakapatha,[15] a selection of four short texts or Pathas, which include the Buddhist creed and ten commandments, and of five Suttas; (ii) Dhammapada,[16] a compilation of the Buddha's teachings in four hundred and twenty-three verses divided into twenty-six Vaggas or chapters; (iii) Udana,[17] an arrangement of Buddhist stories and utterances in eight Vaggas; (iv) Itivuttaka,[18] an anthology of the Buddha's ethical teachings; (v) Sutta Nipata,[19] one of the oldest books of the Pali canon, composed in five Vaggas,

[12] tr. Lord Chalmers, *Further Dialogues of the Buddha, Translated from the Pali of the Majjhima Nikāya* (Sacred Books of the Buddhists, v, vi). 2 vols. 1926-27; Bhikkhu Sīlācāra, *The Majjhima Nikāya, The First Fifty Discourses from the Collection of the Medium-Length Discourses of Gotama the Buddha, Freely Rendered and Abridged from the Pali* (Veröffentlichungen der deutschen Pali-Gesellschaft, 6). 2 vols. 1912-13.

[13] tr. Mrs. Rhys Davids and F. L. Woodward, *The Book of the Kindred Sayings (Sanyutta-Nikāya), or Grouped Suttas* (Pali Text Society). 5 vols. 1917-30.

[14] tr. F. L. Woodward and E. M. Hare, *The Book of the Gradual Sayings (Anguttara-Nikāya), or More-Numbered Suttas* (Pali Text Society). 5 vols. 1932-36.

[15] tr. Mrs. Rhys Davids, *The Minor Anthologies of the Pali Canon, Part I, Dhammapada: Verses on Dhamma, and Khuddaka-Pāṭha: The Text of the Minor Sayings* (Sacred Books of the Buddhists, vii). 1931.

[16] *ibid.*; also tr. by F. Max Müller in sbe x; and by Irving Babbitt, *The Dhammapada, Translated from the Pali with an Essay on Buddha and the Occident.* 1936.

[17] tr. F. L. Woodward, *The Minor Anthologies of the Pali Canon, Part II. Udāna: Verses of Uplift, and Itivuttaka: As It Was Said* (Sacred Books of the Buddhists, viii). 1935.

[18] *ibid.*; also tr. Justin H. Moore, *Sayings of Buddha, The Iti-vuttaka, A Pali Work of the Buddhist Canon, for the First Time Translated with an Introduction and Notes* (Columbia University Indo-Iranian Series, v). 1908.

[19] tr. V. Fausböll in sbe x; Lord Chalmers, *Buddha's Teachings, Being the Sutta-Nipāta or Discourse-Collection Edited in the Original Pali Text with an English Version Facing It* (Harvard Oriental Series, xxxvii). 1932; E. M. Hare, *Woven Cadences of Early Buddhists* (Sacred Books of the Buddhists, xv). 1944.

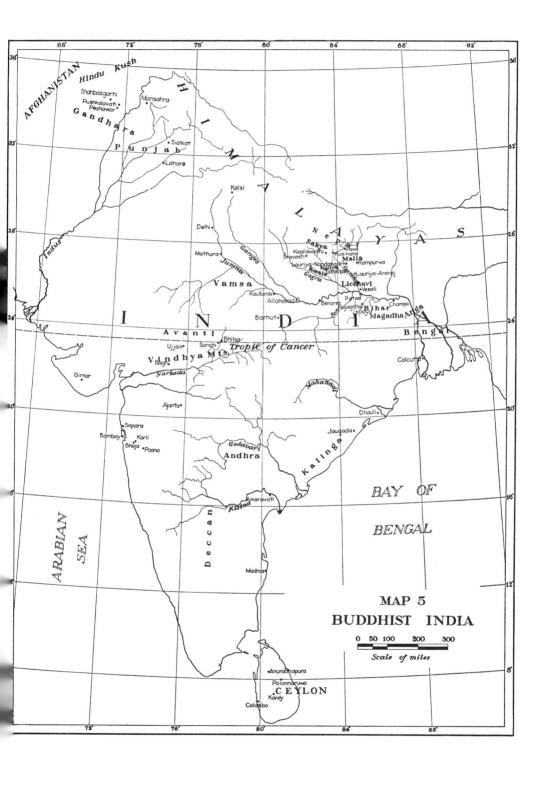

MAP 5
BUDDHIST INDIA

0 50 100   200   300

Scale of miles

and presenting the Buddhist faith from an ethical point of view; (vi)
Vimanavatthu,[20] a description in poetry of the abodes of blessedness
and punishment which lie beyond this earth; (vii) Petavatthu,[21] a
series of stories about the spirits of the deceased; (viii) Theragatha,[22]
poems attributed to two hundred and sixty-four Theras or elders of
the Buddhist order; (ix) Therigatha,[23] poems attributed to seventy-
three nuns; (x) Jataka,[24] a work containing five hundred and forty-
seven birth stories, in which events in previous existences of the Buddha are narrated; (xi) Mahaniddesa and (xii) Cullaniddesa, commentaries on portions of the Sutta Nipata; (xiii) Patisambhidamagga,
an analysis of various religious concepts; (xiv) Buddhavamsa, a history of the twenty-four Buddhas who preceded the historical Gautama Buddha; (xv) Cariyapitaka, thirty-five stories in verse, parallel
to the Jataka tales in prose; (xvi) Apadana, tales in verse of the great
deeds of five hundred and fifty monks and forty nuns.

THE ABHIDHAMMAPITAKA

The third Pitaka is the Abhidhammapitaka or "Basket of Higher
Expositions," which gives a scholastic treatment of the doctrines of
the Suttapitaka. The material is largely in the form of catechetical
questions and answers, and is arranged in seven works as follows:
(1) Dhammasangani.[25] This is a textbook on psychological ethics.
(2) Vibhanga. Here there are eighteen chapters further analyzing
the matters dealt with in the Dhammasangani. (3) Kathavatthu.[26]
This is a book of debates, discussions and refutations relating to con-

[20] tr. Jean Kennedy and Henry S. Gehman, *The Minor Anthologies of the Pali
Canon, Part IV, Vimāna Vatthu: Stories of the Mansions, and Peta Vatthu: Stories
of the Departed* (Sacred Books of the Buddhists, xii). 1942.

[21] *ibid.*, cf. Bimala C. Law, *The Buddhist Conception of Spirits*. 2d ed. 1936.

[22] tr. Mrs. Rhys Davids, *Psalms of the Early Buddhists*, ii, *Psalms of the Brethren*
(Pali Text Society). 1913.

[23] tr. Mrs. Rhys Davids, *Psalms of the Early Buddhists*, i, *Psalms of the Sisters*
(Pali Text Society). 1909.

[24] E. B. Cowell, ed., *The Jātaka, or Stories of the Buddha's Former Births, Trans-
lated from the Pali by Various Hands*. 6 vols. 1895-1907. The introduction to the
Jataka known as the Nidanakatha is tr. by T. W. and Mrs. Rhys Davids, *Buddhist
Birth-Stories (Jataka Tales), The Commentarial Introduction Entitled Nidāna-Kathā,
The Story of the Lineage* (Broadway Translations). rev. ed.

[25] tr. Caroline A. F. Rhys Davids, *A Buddhist Manual of Psychological Ethics of the
Fourth Century B.C., Being a Translation Now Made for the First Time, from the
Original Pali, of the First Book in the Abhidhamma Piṭaka Entitled Dhamma-Sangaṇi
(Compendium of States or Phenomena)* (Oriental Translation Fund, New Series,
xii). 1900.

[26] tr. Shwe Zan Aung and Mrs. Rhys Davids, *Points of Controversy or Subjects of
Discourse, Being a Translation of the Katha-Vatthu from the Abhidhamma-Piṭaka*
(Pali Text Society). 1915.

troversial points of doctrine. (4) Puggalapannatti.[27] This work classifies the various types of individuals according to the qualities they possess and the perfections they have achieved. (5) Dhatukatha. Here a discussion is given, supplementary to the Dhammasangani, of the mental characteristics generally associated with persons of religious faith. (6) Yamaka. In this book an arrangement of pairs of questions provides the outline for an analysis of psychological matters. (7) Patthana. Here there is an analysis of the relations of things in twenty-four groups.

NONCANONICAL BOOKS IN PALI

In addition to the Pali canonical books just described there is an extensive noncanonical Buddhist literature in the same language.[28] Among the works which were probably written in the period from c.20 B.C. to the end of the fourth century A.D., the most important include: (1) Nettipakarana and (2) Petakopadesa, methodical expositions of Buddhist texts; (3) Milinda Panha or the Questions of Milinda,[29] a Pali translation of a book which may have been written originally in north India in Sanskrit, and which recounts the conversations on Buddhist subjects of King Milinda or Menander (first century B.C.) with Thera Nagasena; and (4) Dipavamsa,[30] the oldest known Pali chronicle of Ceylon, which closes with an account of the reign of King Mahasena in the middle of the fourth century A.D. In or around the fifth century A.D. were written the extensive commentaries of Buddhadatta, Dhammapala, and Buddhaghosa. (1) Buddhadatta lived in south India, and was the author of various volumes of prose and metrical comments, several of which are known as Buddhadatta's Manuals. (2) Dhammapala resided in Kanchipuram, and wrote commentaries on the Vimanavatthu, Petavatthu, Theragatha, and Cariyapitaka. (3) Buddhaghosa[31] is said to have been born at Gaya in Magadha near the famous Bo tree. Later he went to the island of Ceylon when Mahanama was king there (first part of the fifth century A.D.), and dwelt at Anuradhapura to study

[27] tr. Bimala C. Law, *Designation of Human Types (Puggala-Paññatti)* (Pali Text Society). 1922.

[28] Law, *A History of Pāli Literature*, II.

[29] tr. T. W. Rhys Davids, SBE XXXV, XXXVI; cf. Mrs. Rhys Davids, *The Milinda-Questions, An Inquiry into Its Place in the History of Buddhism with a Theory as to Its Author*. 1930.

[30] tr. Hermann Oldenberg, *The Dipavaṃsa: An Ancient Buddhist Historical Record.* 1879.

[31] Bimala C. Law, *The Life and Work of Buddhaghosa* (Calcutta Oriental Series, 9,E,3). 1923; T. W. Rhys Davids in HERE II, pp. 885-887.

and write. His name means the Voice of the Buddha, and was conferred on him because of his eloquence. Among his exceedingly voluminous writings, greatest fame attaches perhaps to the Visuddhimagga,[32] which is a summary and veritable encyclopedia of the Buddhism of his time. His commentaries covered all the major parts of the Tipitaka, and include such works as the Atthasalini,[33] which is an explanation of the Dhammasangani, and the Kathavatthu-atthakatha,[34] which is an exposition of the Kathavatthu. Doubtless the most important work of the sixth century was the Mahavamsa or Great Chronicle of Ceylon,[35] a history written by a poet named Mahanama, and based upon the earlier Dipavamsa. At different times and by different authors a series of additions was made to the Mahavamsa. These are known collectively as the Culavamsa.[36] Of yet later works we may mention only the Dathavamsa[37] or history of the tooth-relic of the Buddha, an account which was probably translated into Pali in A.D. 1200 but written originally much earlier; and the Abhidhammattha-Sangaha,[38] which was written by a teacher named Anuruddha sometime between the eighth and twelfth centuries A.D. and which has served as a basic primer of Buddhist psychology and philosophy in Ceylon and Burma ever since.

SANSKRIT WRITINGS[39]

The Pali literature we have described belongs to the sect of Buddhism to which its own adherents gave the name Theravada or Song of the Elders, referring to the immediate disciples of the Buddha. The canon of the Theravadins was roughly paralleled by another canon which belonged to the Sarvastivada school of Buddhism.

[32] tr. Pe Maung Tin, *The Path of Purity, Being a Translation of Buddhaghosa's Visuddhimagga* (Pali Text Society). 3 vols. 1923-31.

[33] tr. Maung Tin, *The Expositor (Atthasālinī), Buddhaghosa's Commentary on the Dhammasangani, The First Book of the Abhidhamma Piṭaka* (Pali Text Society). 2 vols. 1920-21.

[34] tr. Bimala C. Law, *The Debates Commentary (Kathāvatthuppakaraṇa-Aṭṭhakathā), Translated into English for the First Time* (Pali Text Society). 1940.

[35] tr. Wilhelm Geiger, *The Mahāvaṃsa, or The Great Chronicle of Ceylon Translated into English* (Pali Text Society). 1912.

[36] tr. Wilhelm Geiger, *Cūlavamsa, Being the More Recent Part of the Mahāvaṃsa* (Pali Text Society). 2 vols. 1929-30.

[37] tr. Bimala C. Law, *The Daṭhavamsa (A History of the Tooth-Relic of the Buddha), Edited and Translated* (The Punjab Sanskrit Series, 7). 1925.

[38] tr. Shwe Zan Aung, *Compendium of Philosophy, Being a Translation Now Made for the First Time from the Original Pali of the Abhidhammattha-Sangaha* (Pali Text Society). 1910.

[39] Maurice Winternitz, *A History of Indian Literature*, II, *Buddhist Literature and Jaina Literature*. tr. S. Ketkar and H. Kohn. 1933, pp. 226-401.

Whereas Ceylon provided a center of the Theravada, the Sarvasti-vadins were found in Gandhara and Kashmir and spread from there into central Asia, Tibet and China. The name of this school means "the all-is doctrine," referring to the teaching that everything exists permanently. The writings accepted as authoritative in this sect were composed in Sanskrit. Unlike the well-preserved Pali canon, this collection is known only from fragments of manuscripts, quotations in other Buddhist Sanskrit works, and translations into Tibetan and Chinese. From these remnants it is possible to ascertain that the wording and arrangement of texts in the Sanskrit canon was very similar in many points to the Pali canon but that there were also not a few differences. From this it is surmised that both canons derive from a common source, perhaps a lost Magadhi canon, from which the Pali writings branched off in one part of India and, later, the Sanskrit in another region.

The Sanskrit texts of the Sarvastivadins, like the Pali literature of the Theravadins, belong to that major division of Buddhism called Hinayana, but most of the remaining Sanskrit works have either been influenced by or belong outright to the Mahayana form of the faith.

The following works may be described as representing an area of transition between the Hinayana and the Mahayana: (1) Maha-vastu or the Great Story. This claims to be a Hinayana work but definitely exhibits features which resemble the Mahayana. It comes from the school of the Lokottaravadins who taught that the Buddhas are "exalted above the world" (*lokottara*). In the maze and mass of legends which it contains is a miracle-embellished biography of Gautama Buddha. The nucleus of the book may date from the second century A.D.

(2) Lalita-vistara.[40] The name of this work means "detailed account of the sports [of the future Buddha]," and it gives a narrative of the Buddha's life from his decision to be born down to the uttering of his first sermon. In part the account of the Buddha's life is in close agreement with the oldest Pali records such as those in the Mahavagga of the Vinayapitaka; again, however, there is a conspicuous exaggeration of the miraculous element and the Buddha appears as an exalted supernatural being. It is therefore surmised that we have here a recast of an older Hinayana text, perhaps a biography of

[40] tr. P. E. Foucaux, *Le Lalita Vistara, Développement des Jeux, contenant l'histoire du Bouddha Çakya-Mouni depuis sa naissance jusqu'a sa prédication, traduit du sanscrit en français* (Annales du Musée Guimet, 6, 19). 1884-92.

the Buddha once current in the Sarvastivada school, which has been revised in the spirit of the Mahayana. The date of the completed work may be in the third century A.D. In its final form the book is one of the most sacred Mahayana texts.

(3) Buddha-charita.[41] This is a poetic Life of Buddha, written by Aśvaghosha. A contemporary of King Kanishka (second century A.D.), Aśvaghosha was one of the most prominent poets of Sanskrit literature and a pioneer of the Mahayana school. In the Buddha-charita old legends have been clothed in a new poetical garment and brought into an artistic arrangement which constitutes a truly magnificent epic. While many of the doctrines are still those of the Hinayana there is also not a little of the Mahayana. In about A.D. 420 this work was translated from the Sanskrit into Chinese by Dharma-raksha under the title Fo-sho-hing-tsan-ching.[42]

(4) Sutralamkara.[43] This work is ascribed to Aśvaghosha by Chinese authorities, but was probably written rather by his younger contemporary Kumaralata. Preserved only in a Chinese translation of the fifth century, it consists of a collection of Buddhist legends with moral teachings.

(5) Avadana literature. The Sanskrit word *avadana* (Pali, *apadana*) means a "noteworthy deed" or a "moral or religious feat." In the sense in which it is used here it refers to a recital by the Buddha of a story of the present and a story of the past, together with a moral. Various Avadana books contain collections of such stories. Among these are the Avadana-Śataka or the Hundred Avadanas, the Karma-Śataka or the Hundred Karma Stories, and the Divyavadana or the Heavenly Avadanas.

Whereas the foregoing works have affinities with both the Hinayana and the Mahayana, those next to be mentioned belong entirely to the Mahayana. There is no Mahayana canon as such, since the Mahayana is not itself a unified movement. There are, however, a great many so-called Mahayana-Sutras and among these nine Dharmas or Vaipulya-Sutras, meaning "discourses of great extent," take rank as of supreme importance. They are the following:

(1) Lalita-vistara, already mentioned above in connection with its early Hinayana materials but in its finished form accounted a

---

[41] tr. E. B. Cowell in SBE XLIX. cf. Ananda Coomaraswamy, *Buddha and the Gospel of Buddhism.* 1916, pp. 303-309.

[42] tr. Samuel Beal in SBE XIX.

[43] tr. Édouard Huber, *Sûtrâlaṃkâra, traduit en français sur la version chinoise de Kumârajîva.* 1908.

Mahayana text. (2) Saddharma-pundarika or the Lotus of the True Law.[44] This book probably dates from about A.D. 200, and is regarded as the most important and characteristic single work of Mahayana Buddhism. In it the Buddha is represented as an infinitely exalted being, a god above all gods. (3) Ashtasahasrika-Prajña-Paramita. A Prajña-Paramita is a "wisdom-perfection" or metaphysical treatise dealing with the "perfections" of a Bodhisattva, especially the highest perfection of "wisdom," which consists in the knowledge of Śunyata, "emptiness," i.e. the non-reality of all phenomena. This doctrine is usually elaborated in a series of dialogues between the Buddha and various of his disciples. In the Ashtasahasrika, probably the earliest of the books of this kind, there are thirty-two chapters of such dialogues.

(4) Gandavyuha. This work deals with the wanderings of a youth named Sudhana in search of enlightenment. His journeys throughout India are undertaken on the advice of the Bodhisattva Manjuśri, and finally he obtains the object of his quest through the Bodhisattva Samantabhadra. At the end of the book is a beautiful prayer concerning the life of piety which has been much used in worship in all Mahayana Buddhist countries since the fourth century A.D. (5) Dasabhumiśvara. Here the Bodhisattva Vajragarbha expatiates on the ten steps (*dasabhumi*) by which Buddhahood may be attained. The work was translated into Chinese in A.D. 297. (6) Lankavatara, or more fully, Saddharma-Lankavatara-Sutra, the Revelation of the Good Religion in Lanka (Ceylon).[45] This work discusses the tenets of a number of different philosophical schools of Mahayana Buddhism. Its own principal teaching is a modification of the Śunyavada or doctrine of emptiness, known as the Vijñanavada or doctrine of consciousness. Here the reality of the external world is still denied but the subjective reality of the phenomena of consciousness is recognized.

(7) Samadhiraja. Here it is shown how a Bodhisattva can attain to the highest knowledge by various meditations of which the supreme is the "king of meditations" to which the title of the work refers. (8) Suvarna-Prabhasa or Splendor of Gold. The contents of this work are partly philosophical and partly ethical. A fine passage

[44] tr. H. Kern in SBE XXI.

[45] tr. Daisetz T. Suzuki, *The Lankavatara Sutra, A Mahayana Text, Translated for the First Time from the Original Sanskrit.* 1932; cf. Suzuki, *Studies in the Lankavatara Sutra, One of the Most Important Texts of Mahayana Buddhism, in Which Almost All Its Principal Tenets Are Presented, Including the Teaching of Zen.* 1930.

in praise of love toward all beings is included. Tantric ritual is also emphasized and various female deities mentioned. A great deal of space is occcupied with telling how much merit can be obtained by the reading of the book itself. Chinese translations were made in the fifth and later centuries. (9) Tathagataguhyaka. As foreshadowed in the Suvarna-Prabhasa, the influence of Tantrism increasingly penetrated some sections of Mahayana Buddhism, and in the work here mentioned we have an actual Buddhist Tantra. The book was accepted as very authoritative as early as the seventh century.

Among other Mahayana-Sutras, not included in the nine Vaipulya-Sutras, may be mentioned: (1) Karanda-vyuha, or more fully, Avalokiteśvara-Gunakaranda-vyuha, the Detailed Description of the Basket of the Qualities of Avalokiteśvara. This is a glorification of the Bodhisattva Avalokiteśvara, the "Lord who looks down (i.e. with infinite pity on all beings)." As the typical Bodhisattva, Avalokiteśvara refuses to become a Buddha until all beings are redeemed, and in the performance of his task of redemption visits hell, converts cannibal witches and preaches to insects and worms. (2) Sukhavati-vyuha, or Detailed Description of the Blessed Land.[46] The Blessed Land, Sukhavati, is the western paradise presided over by Amitabha, the Buddha of Boundless Light. This being is also the Buddha of Boundless Life in his form of Amitayus, and of Boundless Compassion in his Bodhisattva form of Avalokiteśvara. In the present work it is taught that those who think on Amitabha are reborn after death in his pleasant Buddha-land.

In listing the above works we have already met two individual authors of great renown, (1) Aśvaghosha, who lived in the time of King Kanishka (second century A.D.) and wrote the Buddha-charita, and (2) Kumaralata, his younger contemporary, who composed the Sutralamkara. Other important authors of Sanskrit Buddhist works include the following. (3) Nagarjuna. Likewise a contemporary of Aśvaghosha, Nagarjuna was reputed to be a great scientist and sorcerer as well as philosopher. He systematized the Śunyavada doctrine of unreality found in the Prajña-Paramitas, himself writing a large commentary called Maha-Prajña-Paramita-Śastra[47] and an important work named Madhyamika-Śastra. The Madhyamika school with its doctrine of the Void as its theory of the nature of ultimate

[46] tr. F. Max Müller in SBE XLIX.

[47] tr. Étienne Lamotte, *Le traité de la grande vertu de sagesse de Nāgārjuna (Mahāprajñāpāramitāśāstra)*. Université de Louvain, Institut Orientaliste, Bibliothèque du Muséon, 18. I, 1944.

reality became one of the two most important sects of Mahayana Buddhism. (4) Aryadeva. This man was a pupil and successor of Nagarjuna, and in his writings, of which the most famous is the Catuh-Śataka, defended the doctrines of the Madhyamika school.

(5) Asanga and (6) Vasubandhu. These were two of a family of three brothers born in Purushapura in the fourth or fifth century A.D., all of whom became Sarvastivada monks. Asanga and Vasubandhu were converted to Mahayana Buddhism, however, and through their writings are recognized as the founders of the Yogachara school which ranks along with the Madhyamika as one of the two most important of the Mahayana. Their distinctive doctrine is essentially an elaboration of the Vijñanavada as found in the Lankavatara, involving a defense of the reality of pure consciousness. The Yogachara-Bhumi-Śastra contains the revelations made to Asanga by Maitreya, probably a historical teacher confused in later legend with the future Buddha of the same name. The Abhidharmakośa, the Vijñaptimatrata Trimśika and Vimśatika[48] are the most celebrated works of Vasubandhu. It may be said that Asanga and Vasubandhu occupy a place of as much importance in Mahayana Buddhism as Śankara in Hinduism and Thomas Aquinas in Roman Catholicism.

As has been noted frequently in the foregoing listings, the Sanskrit Buddhist works were often translated into other languages such as Chinese, and in many cases it is only the translations which are now extant. Also original Buddhist writings were often composed in lands such as Nepal, Tibet and Japan, as well as China, and were included in the Mahayana canons which came to prevail in these places. All together these scriptures are exceedingly voluminous, and the Chinese canon, to which the Tibetan and Japanese approximately correspond, contains more than sixteen hundred different works in over five thousand volumes.[49]

[48] tr. Clarence H. Hamilton, *Wei Shih Er Shih Lun or The Treatise in Twenty Stanzas on Representation-Only by Vasubandhu, Translated from the Chinese Version of Hsüan Tsang, Tripiṭaka Master of the T'ang Dynasty* (American Oriental Series, 13). 1938.
[49] August K. Reischauer in JGRMW p.110.

3. THE LIFE AND TEACHINGS OF GAUTAMA BUDDHA[50]

THE following statement appears in the Mahavamsa: "Be it known, that two hundred and eighteen years had passed from the nibbana of the Master unto Aśoka's consecration."[51] The Pali word *nibbana* is the equivalent of the Sanskrit *nirvana,* and refers here to the death of the Buddha, an event which is described in terms of entering Nirvana in the Mahaparinibbana Suttanta.[52] In the same Suttanta it is indicated that the Buddha was eighty years of age at the time of his death.[53] The great emperor Aśoka began to rule around 273 B.C., and his actual coronation followed four years later, or about 269 B.C. Reckoning, then, two hundred and eighteen years before this date, we arrive at 487 B.C. as the year of the Buddha's decease, and counting eighty years before this we come to 567 B.C. as the year of his birth. These dates for the life of the Buddha must be at least approximately correct, since in the Buddhist scriptures Kings Bimbisara (c.540-c.490 B.C.) and Ajataśatru (c.490-c.460 B.C.) figure as his contemporaries, and the latter is represented as on the throne at the time of the Buddha's death.[54]

Three outstanding points in the life of Gautama Buddha are indicated in the Kathavatthu[55] in these words: "Now the Exalted One

[50] The personal name of the founder of Buddhism is given as Siddhattha, Siddhartha, or Sarvarthasiddha, these variant forms all having some such meaning as "he whose aim is accomplished." Siddhartha's clan name was Gotama or Gautama, and non-Buddhists are commonly represented as referring to him by this name, or by the title Mahasamana signifying "the great ascetic." He was also frequently called Sakyamuni or "the sage of the Sakyas." After his enlightenment he received the title of Buddha or "the enlightened," and prior to that time he was a Bodhisatta or Bodhisattva, that is "a being destined for enlightenment." In his own discourse he often spoke of himself as Tathagata, a title which etymologically means "he who has come thus." His disciples referred to him as Bhagava or Bhagavat, this term meaning "lord" and being in common use among the Hindu sects to designate their founders or special deities. Thomas, *The Life of Buddha as Legend and History,* p.1 n.1, p.44.

[51] v, 21. tr. Geiger, p. 27.

[52] vi, 8f. Digha Nikaya II, xvi, 156. tr. Rhys Davids, *Dialogues of the Buddha,* II, pp. 173-175. There is a distinction in Buddhism between Nirvana attained at enlightenment and Nirvana at death, the latter being when the *skandhas* or parts which make up a human being finally fall apart. The two terms *nirvana* and *parinirvana* are often held to refer to these two types of Nirvana respectively, but according to E. J. Thomas (in *India Antiqua,* pp. 294f.) this is incorrect. Rather the distinction involved in these two words is purely grammatical: Nirvana expresses the state, Parinirvana the attaining of the state.

[53] II, 25. Digha Nikaya II, xvi, 100. tr. Rhys Davids, *ibid.,* p.107.

[54] Janavasabha Suttanta 4. Digha Nikaya II, xviii, 202; Mahaparinibbana Suttanta vi, 24. Digha Nikaya II, xvi, 164. tr. Rhys Davids, *Dialogues of the Buddha,* II, pp.238, 187.

[55] I, iii, 8. tr. Aung and Rhys Davids, p.72.

88. Ceylon Manuscript on Silver Plates, with Text
of the Dhammacakkappavattana

89. Column of Aśoka at
Lauriya Nandangarh

90. Capital of the Aśoka Column at
Sarnath (*Copyright reserved by the
Archaeological Survey of India*)

92. Jataka Scenes on the Railing of the Stupa of Barhut

91. Yaksha and Yakshi
on a Sculptured Pillar
of the Stupa at Barhut

93. Sculptured Medallions from the Stupa of Barhut

94. Pasenadi-Post of the Southern Gate at the Stupa of Barhut

95. Stone Railing at Buddh Gaya

97. Pillars of the Eastern Gate at Sanchi

96. Northern Gate of the Great Stupa at Sanchi

98. Architraves
of the Eastern
Gate at Sanchi

99. Façade of
the Chaitya
Hall at Karli

100. Interior of the Chaitya Hall at Karli

101. Reliquary of
King Kanishka

102. Standing Statue of Buddha
from Gandhara

103. Head of Buddha from the Gandharan School

105. Votive Relief from Gandhara

104. Gautama as an Emaciated Ascetic

106. Statue of a Bodhisattva from Gandhara

107. The Buddha as Sculptured at Mathura

109. The Buddha as Sculptured at Sarnath (*Copyright reserved by the Archaeological Survey of India*)

108. Sculptured Slab from Amaravati

110. Veranda of
Cave I
at Ajanta

111. Fresco of the
Great Bodhisattva
at Ajanta (*By the
kind permission of
the Archaeological
Department, the Ni-
zam's Government,
Hyderabad [Dec-
can], India*)

112. Head of the Great Bodhisattva (*By the kind permission of the Archaeological Department, the Nizam's Government, Hyderabad [Deccan], India*)

113. Mingalazedi
Pagoda at Pagan

114. Seated Buddha
from Anuradhapura

117. Stone Head of Buddha of the Sukhothai Type

116. Bronze Head of Buddha of the
Sukhothai Type

115. Model Stupa of the Sukhothai

was born in Lumbini, became supremely enlightened at the foot of the Bodhi Tree, and set turning the Norm Wheel at Benares."

Giving our attention first to the birth and birthplace of the Buddha, we find that the place Lumbini is also mentioned in the Nalaka Sutta,[56] where the gods inform the sage Asita: "The Bodhisatta, the excellent pearl, the incomparable, is born for the good and for a blessing in the world of men, in the town of the Sakyas, in the country of Lumbini." The identification of the site of Lumbini has been made possible by the discovery of a pillar which King Aśoka erected to commemorate his visit there, and which still stands in its original place. It is near the village of Padaria in the Tarai district of Nepal, and it has the following inscription: "By His Sacred and Gracious Majesty the King when he had been consecrated twenty years, having come in person and reverence having been done—inasmuch as 'Here was born Buddha, the sage of the Sakyas'—a stone bearing a horse was caused to be made and a stone pillar was erected. Inasmuch as 'Here the Holy One was born,' the village of Lummini was released from religious taxes and required to pay [only] one-eighth as land revenue."[57] There can be no doubt that the village of Lummini, as it was called by Aśoka, is the same as the place Lumbini, which the Buddhist scriptures name as the birthplace of Gautama.

In the quotations just given it was stated that the Buddha was a member of the Sakyas, a clan which, as we have noted, was a part of the kingdom of Kosala. Similarly in a conversation with King Bimbisara of Magadha, recorded in the Pabbajja Sutta of the Sutta Nipata, the Buddha said: "Flanking Himalaya, in Kosala, yonder extends a land both rich and brave. By lineage 'the Kinsmen of the Sun' are we, and Sakiyans by family.—Such was the stock I left behind me, sire, having no appetite for pleasure's toys."[58] Since the Sakyas claimed descent from an ancient Brahman *rishi* named Gotama, they were also known as Gotamas or Gautamas. It was because of these relationships, then, that the Buddha bore the name Gautama and was often called Sakyamuni, the Sage of the Sakyas. The chief Sakya city was Kapilavastu, a place which must have been a few miles west of Lumbini, but whose exact location is debatable.[59]

---

[56] Sutta Nipata III, xi, 5 (683). tr. Fausböll, SBE X, ii, p.125.
[57] Vincent A. Smith, *Asoka, The Buddhist Emperor of India.* 3d ed. 1920, pp.221f.
[58] Sutta Nipata III, i, 18f. (422f.). tr. Chalmers, *Buddha's Teachings*, p.101.
[59] Bimala C. Law, *Geography of Early Buddhism.* 1932, pp.28-30.

According to the Mahapadana Suttanta[60] and the Buddhavamsa,[61] the father of Gautama Buddha was named Suddhodana (Sanskrit, Śuddhodana), and the mother Maya. The account of Gautama's birth may be found in the Acchariyabbhutadhamma Sutta,[62] in the form of a recital by the disciple Ananda to the Buddha, and also in the Nidanakatha,[63] which forms an introduction to the Jataka. In the latter source it is narrated that Queen Maya was journeying from Kapilavastu to Devadaha, and tarried in the Lumbini grove where "at that time, from the roots to the topmost branches, it was one mass of fruits and flowers; and amidst the blossoms and branches swarms of various-colored bees, and flocks of birds of different kinds roamed warbling sweetly." There in that beautiful place the Bodhisatta was born. Abundant marvels transpired at the birth, and in the Acchari-yabbhutadhamma Sutta, Ananda relates: "As soon as he is born, the Bodhisatta firmly plants both feet flat on the ground, takes seven strides to the north, with a white canopy carried above his head, and surveys each quarter of the world, exclaiming in peerless tones: In all the world I am chief, best and foremost; this is my last birth; I shall never be born again. As soon as the Bodhisatta issues from his mother's womb, throughout the entire world with its gods and Maras and Brahmas there appears, to all recluses and brahmins and to all gods and men, a measureless and vast effulgence—surpassing the gods' own celestial splendor and penetrating even those vast and murky interspaces between worlds where gloomy darkness reigns and no light may enter of sun and moon for all their power and might —so that by this effulgence the denizens of those interspaces can behold one another and recognize that other creatures dwell with them there; and withal the ten thousand worlds tremble and shake and quake; and this too, sir, I hold to be—like all the foregoing—wonderful and a marvel in the Lord."

Of the luxurious life he lived prior to his renunciation, the Buddha is represented in the Anguttara Nikaya[64] as giving the following account: "Monks, I was delicately nurtured, exceeding delicately nurtured, delicately nurtured beyond measure. For instance, in my father's house lotus-pools were made thus: one of blue-lotuses, one of

[60] Digha Nikaya II, xiv, 3-12 (2-7). tr. Rhys Davids, *Dialogues of the Buddha*, II, pp.5-7.

[61] Law, *A History of Pāli Literature*, I, p.290.

[62] Majjhima Nikaya III, cxxiii, 118-124. tr. Chalmers, *Further Dialogues of the Buddha*, II, pp.222-226.

[63] tr. Rhys Davids, *Buddhist Birth-Stories*, pp.153f.

[64] III, iv, 38 (I, 145). tr. Woodward, *The Book of the Gradual Sayings*, I, p.128.

red, another of white lotuses, just for my benefit. No sandal-wood powder did I use that was not from Kasi [Benares]: of Kasi cloth was my turban made: of Kasi cloth was my jacket, my tunic and my cloak. By night and day a white canopy was held over me, lest cold or heat, dust or chaff or dew, should touch me. Moreover, monks, I had three palaces: one for winter, one for summer, and one for the rainy season. In the four months of the rains I was waited on by minstrels, women all of them. I came not down from my palace in those months. Again, whereas in other men's homes broken rice together with sour gruel is given as food to slave-servants, in my father's home they were given rice, meat and milk-rice for their food."

Doubts arose in the mind of Gautama, however, concerning the ultimate value of worldly enjoyments, and in the section of the Anguttara Nikaya from which we have just quoted he goes on to say: "To me, monks, thus blest with much prosperity, thus nurtured with exceeding delicacy, this thought occurred: Surely one of the uneducated manyfolk, though himself subject to old age and decay, not having passed beyond old age and decay, when he sees another broken down with age, is troubled, ashamed, disgusted, forgetful that he himself is such an one. Now I too am subject to old age and decay, not having passed beyond old age and decay. Were I to see another broken down with old age, I might be troubled, ashamed and disgusted. That would not be seemly in me. Thus, monks, as I considered the matter, all pride in my youth deserted me. Again, monks, I thought: One of the uneducated manyfolk . . . when he sees another person diseased, is . . . disgusted, forgetful that he himself is such an one. Now I too am subject to disease. Were I to see another diseased, I might be troubled. . . . That would not be seemly in me. Thus, monks, as I considered the matter, all pride in my health deserted me. Again, monks, I thought: One of the uneducated manyfolk . . . when he sees another person subject to death . . . is . . . ashamed, forgetful that he himself is such an one. Now I too am subject to death. . . . Were I to see another subject to death, I might be troubled. . . . That would not be seemly in me. Thus, monks, as I considered the matter, all pride in my life deserted me."

Due to the rise of such thoughts in his mind, and, according to the Nidanakatha,[65] to the actual sight of an old man, an ill man, and a dead man, and also of a mendicant friar who had renounced the world, Gautama decided upon his own great renunciation. Various

[65] tr. Rhys Davids, *Buddhist Birth-Stories*, pp.166f.

accounts of this event are found in the Buddhist scriptures. In some passages Gautama is described as having been "quite young" at the time, and again his age is more precisely indicated as having been twenty-nine years. In the Ariyapariyesana Sutta[66] the Buddha recalls: "There came a time when I, being quite young, with a wealth of coal-black hair untouched by grey and in all the beauty of my early prime—despite the wishes of my parents, who wept and lamented—cut off my hair and beard, donned the yellow robes and went forth from home to homelessness on Pilgrimage." And in a conversation with a certain Subhadda which took place shortly before his own death, and which is recorded in the Mahaparinibbana Suttanta,[67] the Buddha says:

> But twenty-nine was I when I renounced
> The world, Subhadda, seeking after Good.
> For fifty years and one year more, Subhadda,
> Since I went out, a pilgrim have I been
> Through the wide realm of System and of Law—
> Outside of that no victory can be won!

A more detailed account, telling how Gautama gazed for the last time upon his sleeping wife and son, and then rode away in the night to the accompaniment of various miracles, appears in the Nidana-katha.[68]

In the course of his search for truth, Gautama first sought the guidance of two religious teachers,[69] and then for some six years practiced austerities together with five disciples. "I lived to torment and to torture my body," he afterward reported, according to the Mahasihanada Sutta.[70] "I took up my abode in the awesome depths of the forest, depths so awesome that it was reputed that none but the passion-less could venture in without his hair standing on end. When the cold season brought chill wintry nights, then it was that, in the dark half of the months when snow was falling, I dwelt by night in the open air and in the dank thicket by day. But when there came the last broiling month of summer before the rains, I made

[66] Majjhima Nikaya I, iii, 26 (163). tr. Chalmers, *Further Dialogues of the Buddha*, I, p.115. The same passage occurs also in the Mahasaccaka, Bodhirajakumara and Sangarava Suttas, Majjhima Nikaya I, iv, 36 (240); II, iv, 85 (93); v, 100 (212). tr. Chalmers, ibid., I, p.173; II, pp.48,122.

[67] v, 27. Digha Nikaya II, xvi, 151. tr. Rhys Davids, *Dialogues of the Buddha*, II, p.167.

[68] tr. Rhys Davids, *Buddhist Birth-Stories*, pp.172f.

[69] Ariyapariyesana Sutta. Majjhima Nikaya I, iii, 26 (163-165). tr. Chalmers, *Further Dialogues of the Buddha*, I, pp.115-117.

[70] Majjhima Nikaya I, ii, 12 (78f.). tr. Chalmers, *ibid.*, I, pp.54f.

my dwelling under the baking sun by day and in the stifling thicket by night. Then there flashed on me these verses, never till then uttered by any:—

> Now scorched, now frore, in forest dread, alone,
> naked and fireless, set upon his quest,
> the hermit battles purity to win."

Finally concluding that such extreme austerities were no more profitable than his earlier extreme indulgence in luxurious living, Gautama then turned to a "middle way" of thought and action, and attained the great enlightenment. "Still in search of the right, and in quest of the excellent road to peace beyond compare," he later narrated, according to the Ariyapariyesana Sutta,[71] "I came, in the course of an alms-pilgrimage through Magadha, to the Camp township at Uruvela and there took up my abode. Said I to myself on surveying the place:—Truly a delightful spot, with its goodly groves and clear flowing river with ghats and amenities, hard by a village for sustenance. What more for his striving can a young man need whose heart is set on striving? So there I sat me down, needing nothing further for my striving. Subject in myself to rebirth—decay —disease—death—sorrow—and impurity, and seeing peril in what is subject thereto, I sought after the consummate peace of Nirvana, which knows neither rebirth nor decay, neither disease nor death, neither sorrow nor impurity;—this I pursued, and this I won; and there arose within me the conviction, the insight, that now my Deliverance was assured, that this was my last birth, nor should I ever be reborn again."

The unnamed river in the foregoing account is identified in the Mahavagga[72] as the Neranjara. This is probably the same as the modern Nilajan, and the ancient district of Uruvela must have extended along this river and have included the modern Buddh Gaya which is just to the west, and six miles south of the city of Gaya.[73] In the same passage in the Mahavagga the Buddha is said, following his great experience, to have "sat cross-legged at the foot of the Bodhi tree uninterruptedly during seven days, enjoying the bliss of emancipation"; and in the miracle-embellished account of the enlightenment in the Nidanakatha[74] he is likewise said to have been seated at the time at the foot of the Bo tree. The Bodhi tree means

[71] Majjhima Nikaya I, iii, 26 (167). tr. Chalmers, *ibid.*, I, pp.117f.
[72] Mahavagga I, i, 1. tr. Rhys Davids and Oldenberg, SBE XIII, p.74.
[73] Benimadhab Barua, *Gayā and Buddha-Gayā*. I (1931), pp.101f.
[74] tr. Rhys Davids, *Buddhist Birth-Stories*, pp.189f.

the Tree of Enlightenment. In the Mahapadana Suttanta[75] it is stated that the tree was an Assattha, this being a pipal tree or sacred fig (*Ficus religiosa*).

Although he was naturally reluctant to go forth and preach what he had won so hardly and what "men sunk in sin and lusts would find it hard . . . to grasp," the Buddha now made his way to Benares, and in the Deer Park of Isipatana found the five disciples who had been with him in his austerities but who had deserted him when he had abandoned that extreme way. While three of them went abroad for alms he taught the other two, or while two went out he instructed the other three, and thus led them all at last to the same insight and conviction which he himself had attained.[76]

In the Dhammacakkappavattana Sutta we have the sermon which the Buddha is supposed to have delivered to the five disciples at that time. The title of this Sutta includes the important Buddhist term Dhamma (Sanskrit, Dharma) meaning doctrine, norm, law, or righteousness,[77] and may be translated as The Foundation of the Kingdom of the Norm (or of Righteousness). In the sermon the five disciples are addressed as Bhikkus, this being the regular designation (feminine, Bhikkunis) for members of the Buddhist monastic order. An outline is given of four noble truths and an eightfold path, which provides a clear-cut and convenient summary of Buddhist teachings. So important is the passage that it appears more than once in the canon.[78] Here we give an extended quotation from the translation by T. W. Rhys Davids, which was made from a beautiful Ceylon manuscript on silver plates, now in the British Museum and shown in Fig. 88.[79]

There are two extremes, O Bhikkus, which the man who has given up the world ought not to follow: the habitual practice, on the one hand, of those things whose attraction depends upon the passions, and especially of sensuality—a low and pagan way, unworthy, unprofitable, and fit only for the worldly-minded; and the habitual practice, on the other hand, of asceticism, which is painful, unworthy, and unprofitable.

There is a middle path, O Bhikkus, avoiding these two extremes, dis-

[75] Digha Nikaya II, xiv, 3-12 (2-7). tr. Rhys Davids, *Dialogues of the Buddha*, II, p.6.
[76] Ariyapariyesana Sutta. Majjhima Nikaya I, iii, 26 (168-173). tr. Chalmers, *Further Dialogues of the Buddha*, I, pp. 118-123.
[77] I. B. Horner in *Artibus Asiae*. 11 (1948), p.115.
[78] Mahavagga I, vi, 17-47. tr. Rhys Davids and Oldenberg, SBE XIII, pp.94-102; Samyutta Nikaya V, xii (lvi), 2 (420ff.). tr. Woodward, *The Book of the Kindred Sayings*, V, pp.356-365.
[79] SBE XI, pp.137-155.

covered by the Tathagata—a path which opens the eyes, and bestows understanding, which leads to peace of mind, to the higher wisdom, to full enlightenment, to Nirvana!

What is that middle path, O Bhikkus, avoiding these two extremes, discovered by the Tathagata—that path which opens the eyes, and bestows understanding, which leads to peace of mind, to the higher wisdom, to full enlightenment, to Nirvana? Verily, it is this noble eightfold path; that is to say:

> Right views;
> Right aspirations;
> Right speech;
> Right conduct;
> Right livelihood;
> Right effort;
> Right mindfulness; and
> Right contemplation.

This, O Bhikkus, is that middle path, avoiding these two extremes, discovered by the Tathagata—that path which opens the eyes, and bestows understanding, which leads to peace of mind, to the higher wisdom, to full enlightenment, to Nirvana!

Now this, O Bhikkus, is the noble truth concerning suffering. Birth is attended with pain, decay is painful, disease is painful, death is painful. Union with the unpleasant is painful, painful is separation from the pleasant; and any craving that is unsatisfied, that too is painful. In brief, the five aggregates which spring from attachment are painful. . . .

Now this, O Bhikkus, is the noble truth concerning the origin of suffering. Verily, it is that thirst, causing the renewal of existence, accompanied by sensual delight, seeking satisfaction now here, now there—that is to say, the craving for the gratification of the passions, or the craving for life, or the craving for success. . . .

Now this, O Bhikkus, is the noble truth concerning the destruction of suffering. Verily, it is the destruction, in which no passion remains, of this very thirst; the laying aside of, the getting rid of, the being free from, the harboring no longer of this thirst. . . .

Now this, O Bhikkus, is the noble truth concerning the way which leads to the destruction of sorrow. Verily, it is this noble eightfold path; that is to say:

> Right views;
> Right aspirations;
> Right speech;
> Right conduct;
> Right livelihood;
> Right effort;
> Right mindfulness; and
> Right contemplation.

Such was the essence of the sermon in which "the royal chariot wheel of the truth" was "set rolling onwards by the Blessed One."

Here then was the Buddha's answer to the religious problem of his time. Brahmanism was ancient and deeply entrenched, yet its priestly sacrifices and rituals and its many gods evidently appeared to him irrelevant to real salvation. Its proponents were often mired in a life of worldly pleasure. According to the Anguttara Nikaya, the Buddha once said to a certain Brahman, "One who is ablaze with lust, overwhelmed with lust, infatuated thereby, plans to his own hindrance, to that of others, to the hindrance both of self and others, and experiences mental suffering and dejection."[80] The heretical orders which had arisen, like those of the Jains and the Ajivikas, and had resorted to an austere asceticism, were likewise to him a failure. In a characterization given by the Buddha of a typical ascetic, as found in the Anguttara Nikaya, we can scarcely mistake the features of a Jaina recluse or one much like unto him. "A certain one goes naked. . . . He is a beggar from one house only, an eater of one mouthful. . . . He is a plucker out of hair and beard. . . . He remains standing and refuses a seat. . . . In divers ways he lives given to these practices which torment the body."[81] Neither the householder with his sacrificial ceremonies nor the ascetic with his mortification of the body could attain the goal. The one was a "hardened sensualist," the other a "self-tormentor."[82]

To these two opposite types of practice the Buddha opposed his own "midway practice." It was a way which avoided both extremes and was characterized by intellectual, ethical and psychological discipline. To elucidate the condensed statement found in the foregoing sermon it may be said that the intellectual discipline consists in adoption of a true view of the nature of things and in resolve to renounce the world. The ethical discipline involves refraining from speaking falsely or maliciously, refraining from killing and stealing, and refraining from earning livelihood in an improper manner. The psychological discipline calls for exertion to cleanse the mind of evil thoughts, for constant awareness of all that is going on in the body and mind, and for sustained practice of meditation. This is the middle path.[83]

[80] III, vi, 53. tr. Woodward, *The Book of the Gradual Sayings*, I, p.140.
[81] III, xvi, 151. tr. Woodward, *ibid.*, I, pp.272-274.
[82] *ibid.*
[83] Nalinaksha Dutt, *Early Monastic Buddhism* I (Calcutta Oriental Series, 30). 1941, pp.198-202.

Afterward, the Buddha converted a noble youth of Benares named Yasa, and his father and mother and former wife, and fifty-four friends as well. These followers were then sent out to preach, with the charge, "Go ye now . . . and wander, for the gain of the many, for the welfare of the many, out of compassion for the world, for the good, for the gain, and for the welfare of gods and men." They brought back many persons from different regions and different countries who desired to join the Sangha or Buddhist monastic order, and the Buddha gave instructions for their ordination as follows: "Let him [who desires to receive the ordination] first have his hair and beard cut off; let him put on yellow robes, adjust his upper robe so as to cover one shoulder, salute the feet of the Bhikkus [with his head], and sit down squatting; then let him raise his joined hands and . . . say [three times]: 'I take my refuge in the Buddha, I take my refuge in the Dhamma, I take my refuge in the Sangha.' "[84]

Later the Buddha went to Rajagriha (Rajagaha), the capital of Magadha, and met King Bimbisara. The king is reported to have said that five wishes which he had made earlier were then fulfilled, namely that he might become king, that the Buddha might visit his kingdom, that the king might pay his respects to him, that the Buddha might preach, and that the king might understand the doctrine. At Rajagriha the Buddha also converted two young Brahmans, named Sariputta (Sanskrit, Śariputra) and Moggallana (Sanskrit, Maudgalyayana) who became his foremost disciples.[85]

Such were some of the chief events in the life of the Buddha during the year of his enlightenment. Before his death at the age of eighty, forty-five years of ministry ensued, the events of which are known to us in only a rather disconnected way. During the rainy season of each year it was his custom to reside in one place, and then during the dry season he would journey about the land. A principal place of his residence was at Śravasti or Savatthi, the capital of Kosala, a place some seventy miles northwest of modern Gorakhpur and now represented by the ruined city called Saheth-Maheth on the south bank of the Rapti River.[86] Here King Pasenadi became his royal patron, as Bimbisara had been in Magadha, and the whole

[84] Mahavagga I, vii-xii. tr. Rhys Davids and Oldenberg, sвE xiii, pp.102-115.
[85] Mahavagga I, xxii-xxiv. tr. Rhys Davids and Oldenberg, sвE xiii, pp.136-151. For the chief place of Sariputta and Moggallana among the disciples cf. Digha Nikaya II, xiv, 3-12 (2-7). tr. Rhys Davids, *Dialogues of the Buddha*, II, p.6.
[86] Law, *Geography of Early Buddhism*, p.5 n.2; and in masi 50 (1935), p.1.

of the Kosala Samyutta of the Samyutta Nikaya[87] is devoted to incidents concerning this king and his conversations with the Buddha.
The Buddha also revisited Kapilavastu, and there is said to have
won the members of his own family, and also such important disciples as Ananda and Devadatta. Ananda became the permanent
attendant of the Buddha and has been called the "beloved disciple,"
while Devadatta has been likened to the Judas of Christian history,
since he later became the leader of a schismatic group and even
plotted with Ajataśatru for the slaying of both the Buddha and Bimbisara.[88] As a result of this plot, Bimbisara was finally killed by Ajataśatru, but the Buddha was only lightly wounded by Devadatta,
and lived on to die at last a natural death.

The circumstances connected with the passing away of the Buddha are recounted at length in the Mahaparinibbana Suttanta or
the Book of the Great Decease.[89] Gautama was staying at the time
in a sal tree grove at Kusinara in the land of the Mallas, and remained right there even though Ananda urged that he should not die
in "a small wattle-and-daub town, a town in the midst of the jungle,
a branch township," but should proceed to one of the great cities
such as Champa, Rajagriha, Savatthi, Saketa, Kosambi, or Benares.
Kusinara is described as located "on the further side of the river
Hiranyavati," this probably being the river now called the Little
Gandak. The site of the ancient city may possibly be represented by
the present-day village of Kasia.[90]

As the Buddha's death drew near the monks were distressed to
think that they would no longer be able to journey to some place
where they could see and meet their master, but he told them that
there were four spots which the believer could always visit with
feelings of reverence, namely the place where the Tathagata was
born, where he attained enlightenment, where he began to turn the
Wheel of the Norm, and where he died or achieved complete Nirvana. Again as they were troubled by the thought that the word
of their teacher would be heard no more, he said to them, "The
truths, and the rules of the order, which I have set forth and laid
down for you all, let them, after I am gone, be the teacher to you."

[87] i, iii, 1-3 (68-102). tr. Rhys Davids, *The Book of the Kindred Sayings*, i,
pp.93-127.
[88] Thomas, *The Life of Buddha as Legend and History*, pp.97-102,122f.,131-138.
[89] Digha Nikaya ii, xvi, 72-167. tr. Rhys Davids, *Dialogues of the Buddha*, ii,
pp.78-191.
[90] Law, *Geography of Early Buddhism*, p.14.

Finally, as his last word, he said this: "Behold now, brethren, I exhort you, saying:—Decay is inherent in all component things! Work out your salvation with diligence!"

A funeral pyre was prepared by the Mallas of Kusinara to the east of their city, and the body of the great teacher was cremated there. Claims for a share in the relics were made by Ajataśatru of Magadha, by the Licchavis, by the Sakyas, by the Bulis, by the Koliyas, by a certain Brahman named Vethadipaka, by the Mallas of Pava and by the Mallas of Kusinara, and each of these erected a sacred cairn over the portion of the remains received. These cairns were put up in Rajagriha, Vesali, Kapilavastu, Allakappa, Ramagama, Vethadipa, Pava, and Kusinara. Another Brahman named Dona received the vessel in which the remains had been collected, and made a cairn over it; while the Moriyas of Pipphalivana received and similarly commemorated the embers of the fire. "Thus were there eight cairns for the remains," states the Mahaparinibbana Suttanta in conclusion, "and one for the vessel, and one for the embers. This was how it used to be."

4. BUDDHISM IN THE MAURYA PERIOD, c.322-c.185 B.C.

IT IS clear that Buddhism had its origin in northeastern India, and that by the time of the death of Gautama Buddha it had won there a considerable following. The rapid and wide expansion of the faith began in the Maurya Period (c.322-c.185 B.C.) and in particular in the reign of King Aśoka (c.273-c.232 B.C.). It has already been related (pp.142f.) that the Maurya dynasty was founded by Chandragupta Maurya (c.322-c.298 B.C.) in Magadha, and that this king was followed upon the throne by his son Bindusara (c.298-c.273 B.C.) and then by his grandson Aśoka Maurya. From his capital at Pataliputra (modern Patna) Chandragupta held sway over territories which extended from the Narbada River to the Himalaya Mountains and the Hindu Kush. This empire was preserved by Bindusara and then further extended by Aśoka.

AŚOKA

While Aśoka[91] acceded to the throne about 273 B.C., his solemn consecration or coronation seems not to have followed until four years later or around 269 B.C., and it is from this point that he dates his regnal years in his inscriptions. In the inscriptions he regularly refers to himself by official hereditary titles, which in fullest form are Devanampiya Piyadasi Raja, meaning something like His Sacred and Gracious Majesty the King.

In his ninth regnal year (261 B.C.) Aśoka undertook and accomplished the conquest of the kingdom of Kalinga in southeast India, thus extending the Maurya rule over almost the entire land with the exception of the extreme south. Two special edicts by the king, still preserved at Dhauli and Jaugada, stated the principles according to which the newly conquered provinces should be governed. It was immediately after the conquest of Kalinga that Aśoka became a Buddhist, and a revulsion against the horrors of war was intimately connected with his acceptance of the faith. The king's own statement concerning this is to be found in his Rock Edict XIII, which reads in part as follows:

The Kalingas were conquered by His Sacred and Gracious Majesty the King when he had been consecrated eight years. One hundred and fifty

[91] Vincent A. Smith, *Asoka, The Buddhist Emperor of India.* 3d ed. 1920; D. R. Bhandarkar, *Asoka.* 1925. For the emperor's inscriptions see E. Hultzsch, *Inscriptions of Asoka* (Corpus Inscriptionum Indicarum, I). New ed. 1925; Vincent A. Smith, *The Edicts of Asoka, Edited in English with an Introduction and Commentary.*

[260]

thousand persons were thence carried away captive, one hundred thousand were there slain, and many times that number perished.

Directly after the annexation of the Kalingas, began His Sacred Majesty's zealous protection of the Law of Piety, his love of that Law, and his giving instruction in that Law (dharma). Thus arose His Sacred Majesty's remorse for having conquered the Kalingas, because the conquest of a country previously unconquered involves the slaughter, death, and carrying away captive of the people. That is a matter of profound sorrow and regret to His Sacred Majesty. . . .

Thus of all the people who were then slain, done to death, or carried away captive in the Kalingas, if the hundredth or the thousandth part were to suffer the same fate, it would now be matter of regret to His Sacred Majesty. Moreover, should any one do him wrong that, too, must be borne with by His Sacred Majesty, if it can possibly be borne with. Even upon the forest folk in his dominions His Sacred Majesty looks kindly and he seeks their conversion. . . . For His Sacred Majesty desires that all animate beings should have security, self-control, peace of mind, and joyousness.

And this is the chiefest conquest in the opinion of His Sacred Majesty —the conquest by the Law of Piety—this it is that is won by His Sacred Majesty both in his own dominions and in all the neighboring realms as far as six hundred leagues. . . .

And, again, the conquest thereby won everywhere is everywhere a conquest full of delight. Delight is found in the conquests made by the Law. That delight, however, is only a small matter. His Sacred Majesty regards as bearing much fruit only that which concerns the other world.

And for this purpose has this pious edict been written in order that my sons and grandsons, who may be, should not regard it as their duty to conquer a new conquest. If, perchance, they become engaged in a conquest by arms, they should take pleasure in patience and gentleness, and regard as [the only true] conquest the conquest won by piety. That avails for both this world and the next. Let all joy be in effort, because that avails for both this world and the next.[92]

For some two and one half years the king was a lay disciple in the Buddhist faith, without however exerting himself strenuously, as he puts it in his Minor Rock Edict I.[93] Then in his eleventh regnal year (259 B.C.) he actually joined the Buddhist order as a monk, and began to perform vigorous religious works. He gave up his former "tours of pleasure" or hunting trips, and substituted "tours of piety" in which he visited holy persons and places and carried to the people instruction in the Buddhist law (Rock Edict VIII).[94] He also organized preaching missions and sent out envoys to proclaim the faith. According to the names of places and kings mentioned in Rock

[92] Smith, *The Edicts of Asoka*, pp.18-21.　　　　　[93] *ibid.*, p.3.
[94] *ibid.*, pp.13f.

[261]

Edicts II and XIII these missionaries went not only throughout all
of India but also to Ceylon, Syria and Egypt.[95] Through such works
the great king "transformed the creed of a local Indian sect into a
world-religion."[96]

The teachings which he was thus strenuously promoting were
summarized by Aśoka in his Minor Rock Edict II in these words:
"Father and mother must be hearkened to; similarly, respect for living creatures must be firmly established; truth must be spoken. These
are the virtues of the Law of Piety which must be practiced. Similarly, the teacher must be reverenced by the pupil, and towards relations fitting courtesy should be shown. This is the ancient nature
[of piety]—this leads to length of days, and according to this men
must act."[97] As an even more concise and aphoristic statement the
king composed the precept, "Let small and great exert themselves"
(Minor Rock Edict I).[98] While he thus most frequently stated the
meaning of the Buddhist faith in his own words, in one edict Aśoka
declared that "whatsoever . . . has been said by the Venerable Buddha all of that has been well said," and then went on to recommend
seven passages in the scriptures which he thought of special value
for study and meditation (Bhabra Edict).[99] Aśoka was also tolerant
of other varieties of Indian religion. He said, "all denominations are
reverenced by me with various forms of reverence" (Pillar Edict
VI);[100] and he carved out caves in the Barabar Hills near Gaya for
the Ajivika ascetics who were more like the Jains than like the Buddhists.

It was in his thirteenth regnal year (257 B.C.) that Aśoka first began to issue religious inscriptions such as these from which we have
been quoting. In his Pillar Edict VI where he tells of the inauguration of this practice, he calls them "pious edicts," and says that they
were written in order to help mankind attain welfare and happiness.[101] The first inscription composed was probably that now known
as Minor Rock Edict I, and in it the king states his resolution that
"this purpose must be written on the rocks, both afar off and here,
and wherever there is a stone pillar it must be written on the stone
pillar."[102] As this passage suggests, the king's inscriptions were set
up in two chief forms, as Rock Edicts and as Pillar Edicts. There

95 *ibid.*, pp.7,20.
96 Smith, *Asoka, The Buddhist Emperor of India*, p.46.
97 Smith, *The Edicts of Asoka*, p.5.
98 *ibid.*, p.3. 99 *ibid.*, pp.5f. 100 *ibid.*, p.32.
101 *ibid.*, pp.31f. 102 *ibid.*, p.3.

were fourteen chief Rock Edicts, all published by 256 B.C., and seven chief Pillar Edicts, published in 243-242 B.C., in addition to other minor inscriptions. More or less complete copies of the Rock Edicts have been found at Shahbazgarhi, Mansahra, Kalsi, Sopara, Girnar, Dhauli, and Jaugada; and Pillar Edicts have been discovered at Delhi, Allahabad where the pillar probably came from Kauśambi, Lauriya-Araraj, Lauriya-Nandangarh, and Rampurwa. The inscriptions are composed in one or another of the Aryan vernacular dialects known collectively as Prakrit, most of them being in the dialect of Magadha. The characters are those of the ancient Brahmi alphabet, from which most of the later Indian alphabets are descended; save that the inscriptions on the northwestern frontier are in the Kharoshthi script which was of Aramaic origin.

In his twenty-first regnal year (249 B.C.) Aśoka made a "pious tour" on which he visited traditional sites in the life of the Buddha. It was at this time that he erected a commemorative pillar at Lumbini where Gautama was said to have been born. Another pillar found some miles away indicates that on the same trip the king visited a stupa of Buddha Konakamana which he says he had enlarged for the second time six years before.[103] The mention of Buddha Konakamana shows that already at this time belief existed in previous Buddhas who had lived before Gautama Buddha. According to literary tradition Aśoka was guided on this journey by the saint Upagupta, and went to see not only the Lumbini garden where the Buddha was born, but also Kapilavastu the scene of his youth, the Bodhi tree at Buddh Gaya where he attained enlightenment, Isipatana near Benares where he turned the wheel of the law, Kusinara where he died, Śravasti where he lived long in the Jetavana monastery, and the stupas of Vakkula and of Ananda. At the various places the king erected monuments and gave gifts. The benefaction at the stupa of Ananda, Gautama's faithful disciple, is said to have amounted to six million pieces of gold, but that at the stupa of Vakkula was only a single copper coin since this saint had had few obstacles to overcome and had done little good to his fellows.[104] Thus, even if the great king did not erect all the eighty-four thousand stupas which legend says he did,[105] he made notable contributions to the monumental and architectural development of Buddhism as well as to its missionary expansion.

103 Smith, *Asoka, The Buddhist Emperor of India*, p.224.
104 *ibid.*, pp.40,252-254.   105 *ibid.*, p.106.

Aśoka's capital city of Pataliputra is buried beneath modern Patna, his palaces and monasteries are destroyed, and his stupas have generally been rebuilt in later structures; but, as already indicated, many of his widely scattered Rock Edicts and Pillar Edicts remain as original monuments of his time, while we also have other uninscribed pillars which he likewise put up. The pillars provide our finest known examples of Maurya art.[106]

One of the uninscribed pillars stands at Bakhra, near the village of Besarh, which probably represents the ancient Vesali. The lower part of this column has been buried in the ground, and its base is even below the present water level down to which excavation has been carried. The height of the shaft above water level is thirty-two feet, and it is a monolith of polished sandstone, tapering from a diameter of about fifty inches to thirty-nine inches. It is surmounted by a bell-shaped capital with an oblong abacus or platform on which is a life-sized and realistic statue of a lion. The total weight of the monument must be about fifty tons.[107]

One of the inscribed pillars is to be seen at Lauriya-Nandangarh (Fig. 89). It is designed like the column at Bakhra, but is thinner and lighter. The shaft is a single block of polished sandstone nearly thirty-three feet high, and tapering from a diameter of about thirty-five inches at the base to twenty-six inches at the top. There is a bell-shaped capital with a circular abacus ornamented with geese and surmounted by a statue of a lion.[108]

The most magnificent capital was discovered near portions of its broken shaft at Sarnath, which is the ancient Deer Park of Isipatana by Benares. A photograph of it is shown in Fig. 90. On the abacus a bull, horse, lion and elephant, and wheels, are carved in relief. Above are the large figures of four lions, and they in turn once supported a stone wheel of which now only fragments remain. Such was the splendid sculpture with which Aśoka commemorated the place where the Buddha first turned the wheel of the law.

[106] J. Ph. Vogel, *Buddhist Art in India, Ceylon and Java.* tr. A. J. Barnouw. 1936, pp.10f.

[107] Alexander Cunningham, *Reports of the Archaeological Survey of India.* 1 (1871), pp.59-61.

[108] *ibid.*, pp.72f.; BEIS I, Pl. 4.

5. ARCHITECTURE AND SCULPTURE IN THE ŚUNGA (c.185-c.80 b.c.) AND EARLY ANDHRA (c.70-c.25 b.c.) PERIODS

EARLY in the second century b.c. the Maurya rule gave way to the Śunga dynasty (c.185-c.80 b.c.), while in the southeast and south Kalinga and Andhra became independent and in the northwest the Bactrian Greeks ruled in the Punjab (cf. p.147). Pushyamitra, the first king of the Śunga dynasty, may possibly have persecuted the Buddhists,[109] but the faith continued to live, and certain impressive monuments were produced which remain until today as evidences of its character.

The Stupa[110] (Sanskrit *stupa*, Pali *thupa* or *thupo*, Singhalese *dagaba* or *dagoba*, English *tope*) was the most widely used kind of architectural monument in the Buddhist religion. Possibly in its remote origins a type of grave for a king or hero, the stupa now served either to mark some specially sacred spot or to enshrine some relic or other object of the faith. Thus the cairns traditionally said to have been erected over the relics of the Buddha were no doubt stupas, while the great king Aśoka was credited, as we have seen, with the erection of no less than eighty-four thousand such structures.

In its oldest preserved form in India the stupa was a massive, hemispherical mound, surrounded by a railing with from one to four gateways (*toranas*) at the cardinal points. Within this railing a processional pathway (*pradakshina patha*) encircled the stupa, while steps led up to a second such pathway, likewise protected by its own fence, on the terrace at the immediate base of the stupa. On the summit of the mound was an ornamental structure surmounted by one or more umbrellas. The exterior of the mound was generally covered with stucco and ornamented with paintings or reliefs. It was an act of devotion in the Buddhist faith to visit a stupa and walk around it three or more times, always keeping the mound on the right hand.

BARHUT

The remains of a stupa of the Śunga Period have been found at

---

[109] H. Kern, *Manual of Indian Buddhism* (Encyclopedia of Indo-Aryan Research, III, 8). 1896, p.118.

[110] Ernst Diez, *Die Kunst Indiens* (Handbuch der Kunstwissenschaft). p.13.

Barhut[111] near the town of Satna southwest of Allahabad. Most of the structure was destroyed by plunderers, but portions of the railing and gateways have survived and are now preserved in the Indian Museum at Calcutta. Inscriptions on two of the gateways state that they were erected "in the sovereignty (or within the dominion) of the Śungas."[112] The inscription on the eastern gateway also names a certain Dhanabhuti as the builder, and he may have been a feudal king subject to the overlordship of the Śunga monarchs.[113] The gates and railing may therefore be dated around 150 B.C.

The railing was very massive, the pillars being some seven feet high and the coping stones about the same in length, while the gateways loomed high above. The whole was elaborately sculptured with floral decorations, with figures of animals and deities, and with scenes from Buddhist history and legend. In many cases inscriptions identify the persons or events portrayed.

One of the sculptured pillars is shown in Fig. 91.[114] The large standing figures are a Yaksha and a Yakshi. The Yaksha, who stands upon a cast-down demon, is Kuvera, recognized in later Buddhism as one of the four guardians of the world. The Yakshi, who in characteristic gesture is holding the branch of a tree, is identified as Chanda.[115]

The coping which crowned the entire circle of pillars had a total length of three hundred and thirty feet and was sculptured on both the inner and outer sides. Lotus and creeper designs adorn the outer side, while on the inner side the creepers frame panels in which are portrayed scenes from the former existences of the Buddha as narrated in the Jataka. Two sections of these beams are pictured in Fig. 92.[116] On the upper beam the scene at the right has not yet been interpreted, but that at the left represents Story No. 400 in the Jataka.[117] This tale concerns a time when the Bodhisatta (Sanskrit Bodhisattva), as the Buddha is called in his previous lives, was existing as the spirit of a tree standing on the banks of a river. At this

---

[111] Benimadhab Barua, *Barhut* (Indian Research Institute Publications, Fine Arts Series, 1-2). 2 vols. 1934.

[112] Benimadhab Barua and Kumar Gangananda Sinha, *Barhut Inscriptions.* 1926, pp.1-3.

[113] E. J. Rapson in CHI I, p.523.   [114] BEIS I, Pl. 19, left.

[115] Vincent A. Smith, *A History of Fine Art in India and Ceylon.* 2d ed. rev. by K. de B. Codrington. 1930, p.71; cf. Aśvaghosha, Buddha-charita, IV, 35. SBE XLIX, p.40.

[116] BEIS I, Pl. 26.

[117] Dabbhapuppha Jataka. ed. Cowell, III, pp.205-207.

time a jackal went out to get a fish for his jackal-wife. Two otters had just caught a fish together, and were arguing over its division. The jackal, asked to serve as arbiter, gave the head of the fish to one and the tail to the other, and made off with the middle portion as his own fee. The otters lamented the folly of their quarreling in this verse:

> But for our strife, it would have long sufficed us without fail:
> But now the jackal takes the fish, and leaves us head and tail.

And the jackal brought the portion of fish to his wife with these words:

> By strife it is their weakness comes, by strife their means decay:
> By strife the otters lost their prize: Mayavi, eat the prey.

Also on the lower beam shown in Fig. 92 the scene at the right remains uninterpreted, although accompanied by the inscription, "Vedhuka milks 'Katha,' on the mountain, Nadodha"; while the representation at the left is based upon Story No. 488 in the Jataka.[118] In this narrative the Bodhisatta was born as the son of a rich man but gave away his inherited treasure and went with his six brothers and one sister to a hermitage in the Himalayas. Each brother in turn gathered fruit and lotus stalks and divided these into portions to supply the needs of all. In order to test the Bodhisatta, Sakka, king of the gods, made his share disappear for three days. The Bodhisatta summoned his brothers and sister to seek an explanation, and an elephant and a monkey who lived near by also came. All, including the animals, solemnly protested their innocence, and then Sakka appeared and returned the Bodhisatta's food with this confession:

> Myself to test these sages stole away
> That food, which by the lakeside I did lay.
> Sages they are indeed and pure and good.
> O man of holy life, behold thy food!

Of the numerous sculptured medallions on the Barhut railing, four are shown in Fig. 93.[119] At the upper left is the Dream of Maya, the future mother of Gautama, who according to the Nidanakatha[120] saw the Buddha descend in the shape of a white elephant. At the upper right is the Legend of the Jetavana Garden. As related in the Kullavagga[121] a very rich industrialist named Anathapindika in-

---

[118] Bhisa Jataka. ed. Cowell, IV, pp.192-197.
[119] BEIS I, Pls. 30, upper right; 31, upper right, lower left; 32, upper left.
[120] tr. Rhys Davids, *Buddhist Birth-Stories*, p.150.
[121] SBE XX, pp.187-189.

vited the Buddha to Śravasti, and undertook to find a dwelling place for him. The garden of Prince Jeta seemed desirable, but the owner said that it was not for sale even for a sum so great that the pieces of money would cover the entire ground if laid side by side. "I take, Sir, the garden at the price," replied Anathapindika. When the court of justice ruled that an actual bargain had thus been made, Anathapindika brought cartloads of gold coins and covered the Jetavana with pieces laid side by side. Then he proceeded to erect an extensive monastery for the use of the Buddha. On our medallion Anathapindika appears twice, once superintending the laying out of the square pieces of gold, and once pouring water from a jug to consecrate the ground. The water is supposed to flow over the hands of the Buddha, and the latter is symbolized by the hedged-in tree.

At the lower left in Fig. 93 is an unidentified scene, evidently of comic character. Under the supervision of a group of monkeys, a man's tooth is being extracted by an elephant pulling an enormous forceps. Relative to this and other comical scenes on the stupa at Barhut, Vincent A. Smith remarks: "The rollicking humour and liberty of fancy unchecked by rigid canons, while alien to the transcendental philosophy and ascetic ideals of the Brahmans, are thoroughly in accordance with the spirit of Buddhism, which, as a practical religion, does not stress the spiritual to the extinction of human and animal happiness."[122] Finally at the lower right in our illustration is a lotus medallion enclosing a royal head.

On the posts of the gateways at Barhut there were extremely detailed sculptures, some of which are of special historical interest. On the corner jamb of the western gate one of the scenes represents the coming of King Ajataśatru to Gautama in remorse after the slaying of his father King Bimbisara; and on a post of the southern gate is a portrayal of a visit of King Pasenadi (also called Prasenajit) of Kosala to the Buddha in the Jetavana cloister. While Pasenadi was never actually converted we know that he was very favorable to the new movement, and often called upon the Buddha for consultation or conversation. An entire book of the Samyutta Nikaya is devoted to the record of such talks.[123] The reliefs on the southern gate post just mentioned are shown in Fig. 94. The three columns represent respectively the two sides and the edge of the pillar.

[122] *A History of Fine Art in India and Ceylon*, p.31. Quoted by permission of the publishers, the Clarendon Press, Oxford.
[123] Kosala. Samyutta I, 68-102 (III). tr. Rhys Davids and Woodward, *The Book of the Kindred Sayings*, I, pp.93-127.

At the top of the left column is the Visit of Pasenadi, the Buddha being represented in the portrayal by the Dhammacakka (Dharmacakra) or Wheel of the Law. In the middle is the story of the Naga King Erapata who sought to have a mysterious inscription read as a clue to finding the Buddha; and at the bottom is, according to the accompanying legend, the fig tree Bahuhastika upon the Mountain Nadodha Bahuhastika, "where many elephants dwelt." At the top of the center column is the Bodhi Tree at Buddh Gaya where the Enlightenment of the Buddha took place. The tree is shown with a throne at its base and an enclosing structure around it. This structure probably was a temple erected by Aśoka at the sacred site. In the middle of the same column the Sudhavasa gods in the eastern quarter of heaven are represented, as is indicated by the accompanying inscription; and at the bottom is the Dance of the Apsarases, these being the celestial nymphs in the heaven of Indra.[124] In the upper scene on the third column is the Adoration of a Stupa, and in the middle and bottom are pairs of donors or worshipers.[125]

It may be noted that at this period in Buddhist art the Bodhisattva was portrayed in human form, but Gautama Buddha himself was represented only by symbols such as the tree and the wheel.

BUDDH GAYA

The sculptures at Barhut and also, as we shall see, those at Sanchi show a temple built around the Bodhi tree at Buddh Gaya, and it is very possible that such a temple was erected by King Aśoka. The temple which now stands at this place is of modern date, but around it are the remains of a large rectangular stone fence which enclosed the area at an early time. This railing is adorned with sculptures[126] the style of which is somewhat more advanced than that at Barhut and suggests a date in the first half of the first century B.C. Inscriptions on two of the pillars state that they were presented by the Queens of King Indramitra and King Brahmamitra respectively, but it is not known whether these kings were connected with the Śunga dynasty or not.[127]

[124] The Apsarases may have originated as personifications of mist and clouds. Chintamoni Kar, *Classical Indian Sculpture 300 B.C. to A.D. 500.* 1950, p.5.

[125] BEIS I, pp.23f., Pl. 23.

[126] Ananda K. Coomaraswamy, *La sculpture de Bodhgayā* (Ars Asiatica, XVIII). 1935.

[127] J. H. Marshall in CHI I, pp.626f.; Benimadhab Barua, *Gayā and Buddha-Gayā.* II (Indian Research Institute Publications, Fine Art Series, 4. 1934), p.119.

A portion of this railing is shown in Fig. 95.[128] It carries on one pillar an inscription of Kurangi, wife of Indramitra. On the coping is a continuous band of flowers, on the crossbars are lotus medallions, and on the upright pillars are standing figures or medallions with busts, animals and various scenes.

SANCHI

We turn next to the vicinity of Bhilsa, which lies far to the southwest of Barhut. The modern town is near the ancient site of Vidisa, which was the capital of Eastern Malwa and was taken by the Andhras after the end of the Śunga dynasty.[129] A large community of Buddhists must have existed here since there are numerous ruins of stupas and monasteries in the region. We are concerned with the Great Stupa on the hill of Sanchi,[130] near the small village of the same name, about five and one-half miles southwest of Bhilsa.

The Great Stupa was probably built originally as a much smaller brick structure by King Aśoka, and the lion-crowned capital of a column erected by the same king was found not far away. Perhaps a century later by the addition of a stone casing the stupa was enlarged to its present size with a diameter of over one hundred and twenty feet and a height of about fifty-four feet. Also a plain but massive stone railing was built around the base. Then probably in the Early Andhra Period (c.70-c.25 B.C.) the four magnificent ornamental gateways were constructed.

Stylistic and architectural considerations suggest that the Southern Gate was the first erected, and that it was followed in succession by the Northern, Eastern and Western Gates. All were built according to the same general design, the main features of which may be seen in Fig. 96 where the Northern Gateway, best preserved of the four, is pictured.[131] Two massive square pillars are surmounted by capitals which in turn support a superstructure of three slightly arched horizontal beams placed one above the other. The capitals are carved with elephant, lion or dwarf figures, while Yakshis act as supports to the projecting ends of the lowest horizontal beam. Between and above the beams are other figures and dominating all at the top was the Wheel of the Law flanked by guardian Yakshas and trisul emblems. The surfaces of the pillars and beams both in the front and back are covered with the most intricate sculptures in bas-relief.

[128] BEIS I, Pl. 35.
[130] John Marshall, A Guide to Sanchi. 1918.

[129] Rapson in CHI I, p.533.
[131] BEIS I, Pl. 48.

The nature of the Sanchi reliefs may be further illustrated by reference to the Eastern Gateway, the scenes on which have been the object of a special study by A. Foucher.[132] The front sides of the two square pillars of this gateway are shown in Fig. 97.[133] On the right column there are six panels each with pillars representing the front of a palace in which a god is seated with his attendants. These are the first six heavens or Devalokas of the Buddhist paradise, being dwelling places respectively for (1) the Four Great Kings who guard the four cardinal points; (2) the Thirty-three Gods ruled by Indra; (3) those over whom Yama reigns; (4) the Tushita or Satisfied Gods among whom the Bodhisattva lived before he descended again the last time to earth; (5) the gods who ordain for their own creations; and (6) the gods who ordain for the creations of others, and whose king is Mara, ruler also over the five lower heavens. Above these six panels there is yet another where two more gods and their attendants appear upon a balcony. This must be the lowest portion of the Brahmaloka or heaven of Brahma, one plane higher than the highest Devaloka, and just visible to human eyes.

On the left column we see in the lowest panel King Bimbisara coming forth from Rajagriha to visit the Buddha who is symbolized by an empty throne. An account of this visit is given in the Mahavagga (I, xxii, 2f. SBE XIII, pp.136f.).

According to the Mahavagga, Bimbisara's visit to the Buddha took place just after the conversion of Kassapa. In order to accomplish this conversion the Buddha performed various miracles, and one of these is appropriately enough depicted in the next higher panel on our column. This miracle is narrated in the Mahavagga (I, xx, 16. SBE XIII, pp.130f.) as quoted below. It may be explained that the designation Gatila given Kassapa means a Brahmanical ascetic, and that the title "great Samana" with which he addresses the Buddha signifies Great Ascetic. The miracle story is as follows:

At that time a great rain fell out of season; and a great inundation arose. The place where the Blessed One lived was covered with water. Then the Blessed One thought: "What if I were to cause the water to recede round about, and if I were to walk up and down in the midst of the water on a dust-covered spot." And the Blessed One caused the water to recede round about, and he walked up and down in the midst of the water on a dust-covered spot.

---

[132] *La porte orientale du Stûpa de Sânchi (Moulage du Musée Guimet)*. Annales du Musée Guimet, Bibliothèque de Vulgarisation. 34 (1910), pp.153-230.
[133] BEIS I, Pl. 59.

And the Gatila Uruvela Kassapa, who was afraid that the water might have carried away the great Samana, went with a boat together with many Gatilas to the place where the Blessed One lived. Then the Gatila Uruvela Kassapa saw the Blessed One, who had caused the water to recede round about, walking up and down in the midst of the water on a dust-covered spot. Seeing him, he said to the Blessed One: "Are you there, great Samana?"

"Here I am, Kassapa," replied the Blessed One, and he rose in the air and stationed himself in the boat.

In the panel under discussion on the Sanchi column the flooded river is shown washing the branches of the trees where monkeys have taken refuge, while waterfowl are all about. Paddling in a canoe on the flood, Kassapa and two companions come to the rescue. Gautama is walking unharmed, however, in the midst of the water, as is indicated by showing his promenade. At the bottom of the picture Kassapa does homage to the Buddha, now represented by his seat or throne at the lower right-hand corner.

In the third panel from the bottom on the same left pillar of the Eastern Gate we have, as at Barhut, the Bodhi tree at Buddh Gaya symbolizing the Enlightenment of the Buddha. A throne is at the foot of the tree, and its branches grow out through the upper windows of the Aśokan temple by which it is enclosed. Above, in the two rows of the uppermost panel, are groups of deities looking on from their celestial realms.

The front panels of the three horizontal beams or architraves of the Eastern Gateway are shown in Fig. 98.[134] In the center of the first beam we recognize again the Bodhi tree and temple at Buddh Gaya. At the right a king and queen dismount from an elephant and then do homage to the tree. At the left a procession advances to the sound of music, and its foremost members carry pitchers for the watering of the tree. This evidently represents the visit of Aśoka and his queen to the Bodhi tree. According to legend, Queen Tishyarakshita was jealous because of the king's attentions to the tree, and cast a spell on it. The tree began to wither, but when Aśoka declared that he would not live longer than it did, the queen put a stop to her witchcraft. Then the king and queen came together to water and restore the sacred tree, as here depicted. It may also be noted that on the projecting ends of the beam with this scene there are pairs of peacocks, the peacock (Sanskrit *mayura*) being the symbol of the Maurya dynasty.

[134] Lepel Griffin, *Famous Monuments of Central India.* 1886, Pl. xiii.

On the middle horizontal beam the departure of Gautama from Kapilavastu in his great renunciation is portrayed. At the left is the city with its wall and moat, and coming forth from the gate is the horse Kanthaka, its hoofs supported by Yakshas lest any sound give the alarm.[135] An embroidered rug serves as a saddle, and the attendant Chandaka (or Channa) holds up a parasol, but the figure of Gautama himself is not shown. To the right the same group is shown three more times to suggest the progress of the fleeing prince. Then at the extreme right Kanthaka and Chandaka take leave of their master, whose presence is symbolized by gigantic wheel-marked footprints[136] surmounted by the parasol. Finally at the bottom at the right, horse and groom are shown going back to Kapilavastu, Chandaka carrying the jewels which Gautama has discarded. In the center of the composition is a jambo tree which suggests the young Bodhisattva's first meditation, said to have taken place beneath such a tree, the shadow of which did not move while he sat under it.

On the highest horizontal beam of the Eastern Gate the seven last Buddhas are symbolized, the first and last by thrones beneath Bodhi trees, the others by stupas.

KARLI

As we have already seen, the stupa was the central object of interest in Buddhist architecture. Around important stupas other buildings naturally came to be erected, including chapels and monasteries. The customary designation for the chapel is chaitya hall.[137] The word *chaitya* is derived from a root meaning to heap up, and is properly applicable to the stupa itself, but is also used for structures connected with the stupa and for other objects of reverence. The chaitya hall as we are speaking of it was a chapel enclosing a stupa. Its characteristic plan was similar to that of an early Christian basilica. A long hall was divided by two rows of columns into a nave and two narrow side aisles, and at the end was an apse in which the stupa stood.

The early chaitya halls were built wholly or partly of wood, and have mostly perished although their remains are occasionally found

---

[135] Nidanakatha. tr. Rhys Davids, *Buddhist Birth-Stories*, p.174.

[136] One of the thirty-two marks of a great man destined to be either a universal monarch or a supreme Buddha is that "on the soles of his feet, wheels appear with a thousand spokes, with tire and hub, in every way complete." Digha Nikaya II, xiv, 32 (17); III, xxx, 1, 2 (143). tr. Rhys Davids, *Dialogues of the Buddha*, II, p.14; III, pp.137f.; Lalita-vistara VII. tr. Foucaux, *Le Lalita Vistara*, I (6), p.96.

[137] Diez, *Die Kunst Indiens*, p.26.

as for example at Sanchi. The wooden buildings were, however, copied in the form of chapels hewn in the solid rock, and of such chaitya caves many are still in existence. The largest, finest and best preserved is at Karli, between Bombay and Poona, and dates probably from the first century B.C.

The exterior of the Karli chaitya cave is shown in Fig. 99. At the left we see a heavy sixteen-sided column surmounted by carved lions. A corresponding column doubtless stood originally at the right, where now a small modern temple is. Immediately beyond the lion column are the remains of the outer screen. It was composed of two octagonal pillars supporting a mass of rock, once adorned with wooden carvings, above which was a row of four short columns. The porch behind this screen was fifteen feet deep, over fifty feet high and equally wide. Three doorways gave entrance to the hall, the central one opening into the nave and the other two into the side aisles. Above is a great horseshoe-shaped window, containing a wooden framework. This window allowed light to fall into the nave and upon the stupa inside, but left the side aisles in comparative obscurity.

The interior is pictured in Fig. 100. On either side fifteen octagonal columns, with vaselike bases and with lotus capitals carrying animal and human figures, separate the nave from the side aisles. In the apse seven plain octagonal columns form a semicircle behind the stupa. The stupa is hewn out of the solid rock, like the rest of the hall, but is crowned with an umbrella of wood. The vaulted roof is ornamented with ribs of wood, and terminates in a semidome at the apsidal end of the hall. The hall is over one hundred and twenty-four feet long and forty-five feet wide, and the apex of the roof is forty-five feet high. The entire effect of this place of devotion is both solemn and grand.[138]

Like the chaitya halls the monasteries, too, were often hewn from the solid rock. They are technically called viharas or sangharamas.[139] A *vihara* may be the "abiding place" of even a single monk, and when a series of such cells is ranged together it forms a *sangharama* or "community garden." It is also customary, however, to call the entire cloister a vihara. When such a vihara was built in the open air it comprised a group of cells surrounding an open court, and

[138] James Fergusson and James Burgess, *The Cave Temples of India*. 1880, pp.232-240; BEIS II, Figs. 66, 69.
[139] Diez, *Die Kunst Indiens*, p.37.

when it was hewn in the solid rock there was generally a veranda in front and one or more rows of cells behind. For an example of such a monastery we may recall the vihara at Bhaja, not far from Karli, which has already been mentioned (p.148) in connection with its non-Buddhist sculptures showing Surya and Indra.

6. NORTHWEST INDIA UNDER THE BACTRIAN GREEKS (SECOND CENTURY B.C.) AND THE KUSHANS (A.D. c.50-c.320)

TURNING now to northwest India, we know that in the second century B.C. the Greco-Bactrian king Menander was ruling there (p.147). According to Strabo[140] this monarch extended his power even farther east than Alexander the Great had done. There is no doubt that Menander is the same as Milinda, the king who figures in the Milinda Panha or Questions of Milinda, a Buddhist historical romance which must have originated not too long after Menander's death.[141] According to this work, Milinda ruled in a city called Sagala, which is doubtless to be identified with the modern Sialkot.[142] The city is described as fortified "with many and various strong towers and ramparts, with superb gates and entrance archways; and with the royal citadel in its midst, white walled and deeply moated," and it is said that it was "so full . . . of money, and of gold and silver ware, of copper and stone ware, that it is a very mine of dazzling treasures."[143] The king himself was "learned, eloquent, wise, and able," and conversant with many arts and sciences including philosophy, arithmetic, music, medicine, astronomy, magic, war and poetry. "As a disputant he was hard to equal, harder still to overcome; the acknowledged superior of all the founders of the various schools of thought. And as in wisdom so in strength of body, swiftness, and valor there was found none equal to Milinda in all India. He was rich too, mighty in wealth and prosperity, and the number of his armed hosts knew no end."[144]

It was the custom of the king, according to the Milinda Panha, to engage in conversations with the most learned men he could find, but when none could match him in disputation he thought to himself, "All India is an empty thing, it is verily like chaff! There is no one, either recluse or Brahman, capable of discussing things with me and dispelling my doubts."[145] Then the venerable Nagasena, a Thera or Elder of the Buddhist order, came to Sagala. So remarkable was his scholarship in the Buddhist religion that at the age of twenty he had recited from memory the seven books of the Abhidhamma in

---

[140] Geography. XI, xi, 1.
[141] Tarn, The Greeks in Bactria and India, p.414.
[142] Law, India as Described in Early Texts of Buddhism and Jainism, pp.69,88.
[143] I, 2. SBE XXXV, pp.2f.   [144] I, 9. SBE XXXV, pp.6f.
[145] I, 14. SBE XXXV, p.10.

full in seven months.[146] King Milinda visited Nagasena at the hermitage where he was staying, and even at his first sight of the large assembly gathered around the famous teacher the king experienced the emotion of fear and "felt like an elephant hemmed in by rhinoceroses, . . . like a jackal surrounded by boa-constrictors, . . . like a snake in the hands of a snake charmer, or . . . like a man who has lost his way in a dense forest haunted by wild beasts."[147] There followed then a long series of conversations, in which Milinda propounded all manner of religious and philosophical questions and Nagasena answered so successfully as to constrain the king again and again to say something like, "Very good, Nagasena! That is so, and I accept it as you say."[148]

For a single short example we may quote the following:

The king said: "Nagasena, is there any one who after death is not re-individualized?"

"Some are so, and some not."

"Who are they?"

"A sinful being is reindividualized, a sinless one is not."

"Will you be reindividualized?"

"If when I die, I die with craving for existence in my heart, yes; but if not, no."

"Very good, Nagasena!"[149]

Conversations such as this and others much longer and more complex make up the body of the Milinda Panha, the whole of which is introduced with this poem:

> King Milinda, at Sagala the famous town of yore,
> To Nagasena, the world famous sage, repaired.
> (So the deep Ganges to the deeper ocean flows.)
> To him, the eloquent, the bearer of the torch
> Of Truth, dispeller of the darkness of men's minds,
> Subtle and knotty questions did he put, many,
> Turning on many points. Then were solutions given
> Profound in meaning, gaining access to the heart,
> Sweet to the ear, and passing wonderful and strange.
> For Nagasena's talk plunged to the hidden depths
> Of Vinaya and of Abhidhamma
> Unraveling all the meshes of the Suttas' net,
> Glittering the while with metaphors and reasoning high.
> Come then! Apply your minds, and let your hearts rejoice,
> And hearken to these subtle questionings, all grounds
> Of doubt well fitted to resolve.[150]

[146] I, 27. SBE XXXV, p.22. [147] I, 43. SBE XXXV, p.38.
[148] e.g., IV, 28. SBE XXXV, p.225. [149] II, i, 6. SBE XXXV, p.50.
[150] I, 1. SBE XXXV, pp.1f.

The Milinda Panha concludes with the conversion of the king to the Buddhist faith.[151] According to Plutarch (A.D. c.46-c.120), Menander died on a campaign, and the different cities disputed about the honor of his burial until at last they agreed to divide the relics among them and severally erect monuments over them.[152] This story is of course very similar to that of the disposition of the relics of the Buddha.

KANISHKA

Continuing now to the Kushan Period (A.D. c.50-c.320), we have to speak particularly of King Kanishka who ruled in the second century A.D. at Purushapura (modern Peshawar) in the district of Gandhara. Reference has been made earlier to his extant statue and also to his coins on which the Buddha as well as Hindu and western deities appear. Here we may also show the relic casket (Fig. 101) which was found in the ruins of his great stupa near Peshawar.[153] It has a height of over seven inches, and is made of gilt copper alloy. On the lid is a figure of the Buddha seated on a lotus and with a nimbus around his head. On either side of him is a standing figure, and these are usually identified as Brahma and Indra. On the side of the lid is a frieze of geese, while on the main cylinder we see a seated Buddha, other deities, and a figure of Kanishka. Despite the syncretistic impression given by his coins and this memorial, the king was a convert to Buddhism and is claimed in Buddhist traditions as a great protector of the faith.

According to these traditions as preserved by the seventh century Chinese Buddhist pilgrim Hiuen Tsang,[154] Kanishka was in the habit of consulting the Buddhist scriptures frequently, and of having a Buddhist priest enter the palace daily to preach the law. There were, however, various schools of belief, and their different views were so contradictory that the king was filled with doubt and uncertainty. An honored Buddhist patriarch named Parśva explained to him, "Since Tathagata left the world many years and months have elapsed. The different schools hold to the treatises of their several masters. Each keeps to his own views, and so the whole body is torn by divisions."

The king thereupon resolved, as Hiuen Tsang reports: "I will

---

[151] VII, vii, 20. SBE XXXVI, pp.373f.

[152] Reipublicae Gerendae Praecepta, 28. *Plutarchi Chaeronensis varia scripta quae moralia vulgo vocantur.* 1820, v, p.105.

[153] BEIS II, Pl. 148.

[154] Beal, *Buddhist Records of the Western World*, I, pp.151-156.

dare to forget my own low degree, and hand down in succession the teaching of the law unimpaired. I will therefore arrange the teaching of the three Pitakas of Buddha according to the various schools." To this end he summoned from far and near a holy assembly. After the elimination of those less fit for such deliberations, this body consisted of five hundred sages and saints, and met under the presidency of the venerable Vasumitra. As a place of gathering for the assembly the king founded a monastery.

The labors of these scholars resulted in three commentaries on the three Pitakas, which totaled no less than 300,000 verses. "There was no work of antiquity to be compared with their productions; from the deepest to the smallest question, they examined all, explaining all minute expressions, so that their work has become universally known and is the resource of all students who have followed them." For a permanent record King Kanishka had the discourses inscribed on copper sheets and enclosed in a stone receptacle, and over this he erected a stupa.

The council summoned by Kanishka is thus supposed to have ended the period of old quarrels between the sects, but actually at about this time the major cleavage in all Buddhist history comes into view. This is the division between Hinayanism and Mahayanism.

HINAYANA AND MAHAYANA

Hinayana means Little Vehicle, and refers to the earlier form of Buddhism in which the goal is for the individual to become a saint or Arhat and enter into the oblivion of Nirvana. The Theravadins, Sarvastivadins, Lokottaravadins and other early sects all agreed in teaching that man should strive for such individual liberation. Since only a few could reach this objective, however, the doctrine appeared to others to be an inadequate vessel, insufficient to provide for the salvation of the many. Thus it was that the adherents of the later Mahayana disparagingly called the earlier kind of Buddhism the Hinayana, the Little Vehicle.

The Mahayana or the Great Vehicle, its followers believed, was capable of bringing all humanity to salvation. According to this teaching the ideal is not the "saint for himself" but rather the Bodhisattva, "one whose essence is enlightenment." Such a being is destined for Nirvana and thus is a "future Buddha." For the present, however, he voluntarily refrains from entering the final state in order to act as a helper of humanity and a savior to others who are seeking salvation. It is in line with this doctrine that Gautama Buddha himself is designated as a Bodhisattva in his previous existences. By worshiping the Bodhisattvas, by practicing generosity and self-denial and by showing pity and kindness to all beings, even the ordinary man can make progress toward salvation.

The Hinayana thinkers themselves had believed in a number of Buddhas but the theologians of the Mahayana carried the multiplication of divine beings much farther. Thousands of Buddhas, myriads of Bodhisattvas, and numerous deities adopted from Hinduism as associates of the Buddhas and Bodhisattvas came to fill the Mahayana pantheon. In the Hinayana, as represented by the Pali canon, the Buddha was described as a superhuman being, but it was through his enlightenment that he attained this status. According to the Lokottaravadins the Buddhas were supernatural personages who came down to earth for a time. Being actually far "exalted above the world," any acts of everyday life which they performed were purely external adaptations. A Buddha would eat food, for example, but not because of any necessity, for hunger never touched him; he might use medicine, but in reality he suffered no illness. Finally in the Mahayana doctrine the Buddhas are completely divine beings, and their appearance on earth and entry into Nirvana are entirely illusory. A Buddha has three bodies (*trikaya*), it was taught. The *dharma-kaya* or dharma-body is the essential or ultimate form; the *sambhoga-kaya* or body of enjoyment is the superhuman body in which the Buddhas enjoy their glory and wisdom; and the *nirmana-kaya* or transformation body is the assumed form in which they appear to do their work on earth.[155]

While such a sect as that of the Lokottaravadins was clearly a forerunner of the Mahayana, the two most important individuals in its rise were doubtless Aśvaghosha and Nagarjuna, to whose literary productions reference has already been made. Both are connected in Buddhist traditions with the time of Kanishka. Aśvaghosha, poetic author of the Buddha-charita and other works, and a pioneer of the Mahayana, is said to have lived and worked at the court of Kanishka; and Nagarjuna, first great philosophical systematizer of Mahayana doctrines, is supposed to have been born at the very time of the council convoked by the same king. Of later Mahayana thinkers, the greatest were Asanga and Vasubandhu, whose works have also been referred to above.

[155] Edward J. Thomas, *The History of Buddhist Thought.* 1933, pp.242f.

Since Hinayanism prevails for the most part in such lands as Ceylon, Burma and Thailand, it is sometimes called Southern Buddhism; and since Mahayanism developed in north India and spread to countries like China and Japan it is sometimes called Northern Buddhism.[156]

[156] L. de la Vallée Poussin in HERE VIII, pp.330-336; Winternitz, *A History of Indian Literature*, II, pp.228-231,240; Helmuth von Glasenapp, *Der Buddhismus in Indien und im Fernen Osten, Schicksale und Lebensformen einer Erlösungsreligion.* 1936, pp.79f.; Ryukan Kimura, *A Historical Study of the Terms Hīnayāna and Mahāyāna and the Origin of Mahāyāna Buddhism.* 1927, pp.70f.; E. Lamotte, *La somme du Grand Vehicule.* 1939.

7. BUDDHIST ART IN THE KUSHAN (A.D. c.50-c.320) AND LATER ANDHRA (FIRST TO THIRD CENTURIES A.D.) PERIODS

THE time of the reign of the Kushan kings in northwest India was approximately the same as that of the Later Andhras in the Deccan, namely the first, second and third centuries of the Christian era. We have now to speak of the achievements of Buddhist art in this period, and we shall find that the relevant materials are scattered all the way from the domain of the Kushans to the territory of the Andhras.

GANDHARA

The most important single fact is that whereas in the art of earlier periods the Buddha was represented only by symbols now he is portrayed in numerous statues and his figure is given a central and dominant place in many reliefs. An intimation of this development has already come before us in the reliquary of Kanishka, where we saw that the Buddha, seated on a lotus, was in the central position among the three figures on the lid. Our most numerous early Buddha figures come from Gandhara where Kanishka and the other Kushans ruled, and it seems probable that the school of art which produced them enjoyed the patronage of these kings. It is not usually possible to assign specific dates to individual sculptures but the first three centuries of the Christian era were certainly the time when the Gandharan school was flourishing. Since the Gandhara Buddha figures are the oldest extensive group of such figures we have, it is quite generally supposed that this type of representation actually originated here. At all events the same Buddha type is afterward found throughout India and all Asia wherever the Buddhist faith spread.

Gandhara was the region where Hellenism in its eastward course and Buddhism in its westward movement met. For this reason it is not surprising to find an unmistakable Hellenistic atmosphere about the art although its subject matter is thoroughly Buddhist, and it is generally recognized that a mingling has taken place here of Hellenistic art forms and Indian religious beliefs. In consequence the Gandharan school is often called Greco-Buddhist.[157]

[157] A. Foucher, L'art gréco-bouddhique du Gandhâra (Publications de l'école française d'extrême-orient). 3 vols. 1905-23; The Beginnings of Buddhist Art and Other Essays in Indian and Central-Asian Archaeology (tr. by L. A. and F. W. Thomas). 1917, pp.111-137; William Cohn, Buddha in der Kunst des Ostens. 1925, pp.xxv-xxvii; Tarn, The Greeks in Bactria and India, pp.403-405; Smith, A History of Fine

At the same time there was a definite theological or philosophical reason for the transformation which is observed in Buddhist art at this time. In early Buddhism, which generally speaking was of the Hinayana type, the conception of Nirvana was expressed largely in terms of negations. Since through his Parinirvana the Buddha had entered a state completely transcending all that man experiences in this world, no positive concept could express the truth about him. Early Buddhist artists therefore represented the Buddha only by symbols connected with his earthly life, such as his footprints, the wheel of the law indicating the role he played as a great teacher, the empty throne, or the seat on which he sat when a teacher but which is now empty because the revered instructor has passed on into the great beyond. In later Buddhism, however, particularly in the Mahayana type in which the Bodhisattva becomes so prominent, it was equally natural that the Buddhist artists should represent not only the Bodhisattva but even the eternal Buddhas as ideal human figures. Though worthy to enter the Nirvana state, the Bodhisattva remains in the realm of human beings to save others, and therefore he can be represented as an ideal human figure in much the same way in which Greek art portrayed Greek deities, that is as ideal humans. Also in Mahayana Buddhism even the eternal Buddhas, though in their deepest nature completely transcending all that is human, are often thought of as manifesting themselves to man in terms of ideal human figures since the finite mind cannot grasp the nature of the Buddha as absolute being and he must be expressed in terms which the finite mind can grasp. Thus the artist of later Buddhism need have no hesitation in picturing the eternal Buddha as the perfect human. If the artist is also a philosopher he will realize that the chisel or brush can never adequately represent the nature of the divine, but he can at least indicate the direction in which the divine lies, namely through and beyond the ideal human. Even Hinayana Buddhism eventually began to represent the Buddha through pictures and statues of ideal humans instead of the older symbols, but at least at first this was with the Buddha in mind as he was before he experienced Parinirvana. They therefore drew rather heavily on the birth stories of the Pali canon which picture the Buddha in his many incarnations as a sort of Bodhisattva who comes again and again into this world to save others. Then further, the later Buddhist

---

Art in India and Ceylon from the Earliest Times to the Present Day, pp.97-131; Diez, *Die Kunst Indiens*, pp.114-116; CHIIA pp.50-55.

artists, even in Hinayana Buddhism, under the influence of the Buddhism of the masses which made the Buddha himself into one of the popular gods, had little hesitation in representing the Buddha even after he had passed into the great beyond in terms of the ideal human.

In the time with which we are presently concerned, the most prominent objects of art are statues of the Buddha, either standing or seated, reliefs in which he is the chief figure, and figures of Bodhisattvas. The Hellenistic influence is particularly noticeable in the general plasticity of form, in the treatment of the garments and their folds, and in the pose of the standing Buddha who looks much like a Greek philosopher or teacher. Most of the details of the iconography, however, are Indian. Among the distinctive marks of the Buddha figure as they appear on different statues are the following: (1) The *ushnisha,* or prominence on the top of the head. This occurs as early as the first century B.C. on a statue of Indra,[158] and in the Buddhist scriptures is named as one of the thirty-two marks of a great man (see the references cited above, note 136). (2) The *urna,* a mole or tuft of hair between the eyebrows. This is also one of Buddhism's thirty-two marks of a great man. (3) The hair cut short, lying close to the head and curling to the right. This accords with the description in the Nidanakatha of how Gautama cut his hair at the time of his great renunciation.[159] (4) The elongated ear lobes. These presumably reflect the wearing of heavy earrings in Gautama's princely days, but no earrings are shown because, as the Nidanakatha states,[160] he gave all such ornaments to Channa as he left the world behind. (5) The *mudras,* or symbolic positions of the hands and fingers. According to Buddhist traditions these positions are: *abhaya* or assurance, where the right hand is raised in a gesture signifying "do not fear"; *bhumisparśa* or earth-touching, where the right hand rests upon the right knee with the palm downward and the tips of the fingers touching the ground; *dharmacakra* or teaching, where both hands are raised against the chest and the thumb and forefinger are held together; *dhyana* (*samadhi*) or meditative, where the hands lie upon the lap with palms open, one upon the other; *varada* or gift-bestowing, where the right hand is stretched forward.[161] (6) The manner of sitting, which is in general like a yogi

158 CHIIA p.32 n.9.   159 tr. Rhys Davids, *Buddhist Birth-Stories,* p.177.
160 *ibid.*
161 Benoytosh Bhattacharyya, *The Indian Buddhist Iconography Mainly Based on the Sādhanamālā and Other Cognate Tantric Texts of Rituals.* 1924, p.2.

and harks back all the way to Mohenjo-daro (p.127). Specific modes are distinguished, as for example on a lion throne (*in simhasana*), or on a lotus seat (*in padmasana*). The lotus (*padma*) is of course a motif of great antiquity in Indian art and is often used as the seat or pedestal of a divine being in Hinduism as well as Buddhism.[162] As for the nimbus which appears around the head of the Buddha in the Gandharan sculptures, we do not know if it was of Indian, Iranian or western origin.[163]

A standing statue of the Buddha which was found at Pushkalavati or Peukelaotis, one of the ancient capitals of Gandhara about seventeen miles northeast of Peshawar,[164] is shown in Fig. 102.[165] Although the statue is somewhat damaged it may be presumed that the right hand was lifted in the gesture which signified "fear not" (*abhaya mudra*). On the base is portrayed the adoration of the alms bowl of the Buddha. A fine head of the Buddha, also of the Gandharan school, is pictured in Fig. 103. A seated statue from Gandhara is reproduced in Fig. 104.[166] Here Gautama is shown in the condition of terrible emaciation to which he came through the practice of severe austerities in the early period of his search for truth.[167] The hands are in the position of meditation (*dhyana mudra*). On the base of the statue, disciples are shown in attitudes of worship. Such a dreadful representation as this of the Buddha is very rare, however, and the prevailing characterization emphasizes his attainment of supreme peace.

A Gandharan votive relief is pictured in Fig. 105.[168] Here the Buddha is seated upon a lotus which rises out of a body of water on which lotus blossoms are floating and in which fish are swimming. He is garbed in a close-fitting robe which leaves the right shoulder bare, and he exhibits the teaching position of the hands (*dharmacakra mudra*). Above his head a crown is held, while all around are more than thirty seated and standing figures including Buddhas, Bodhisattvas and Devas. The man and woman standing

[162] A. A. Macdonell and L. A. Waddell in HERE VIII, pp.142-144.

[163] CHIIA pp.41,57.

[164] Alexander Cunningham, *The Ancient Geography of India.* I, *The Buddhist Period, Including the Campaigns of Alexander and the Travels of Hwen-Thsang.* 1871, pp.49f.

[165] Cohn, *Buddha in der Kunst des Ostens*, p.5.

[166] Otto Fischer, *Die Kunst Indiens, Chinas und Japans* (Propyläen-Kunstgeschichte, IV). 1928, p.168.

[167] Mahasihanada Sutta. Majjhima Nikaya I, ii, 12 (80). tr. Chalmers, *Further Dialogues of the Buddha*, I, p.56.

[168] Diez, *Die Kunst Indiens*, Fig. 136.

on either side of the lotus are probably the donors of the relief. Finally a standing statue of a Bodhisattva from Gandhara is shown in Fig. 106.

MATHURA

An important school of sculptors also arose at the ancient city of Mathura (modern Muttra) in the central part of northern India. For the most part the work of these artists is readily recognizable from the distinctive red and black sandstone which they usually employed. The carving shown in Fig. 107 is of black sandstone and bears an inscription in characters of probably the second century A.D. The inscription contains a dedication "for the welfare and happiness of all beings," and calls the figure portrayed a Bodhisattva. Because the foliage above is that of a pipal tree, this must be Gautama before he attained the great enlightenment. He is seated on a lion throne (*simhasana*), and holds up his right hand in the gesture of reassurance (*abhaya mudra*). The symbol of the wheel is visible in the palm of his hand, and also appears on the soles of his feet. The *ushnisha* is in a spiral form, and the nimbus is adorned with scallops. On either side are attendants, and in the air above are two deities.[169]

AMARAVATI

Amaravati is a town of the present day near the site of an ancient center of Buddhism in southeast India. A large stupa stood in the vicinity until comparatively recent times, but has now been destroyed. Portions of its sculptures, probably dating from around A.D. 150-250, are preserved in the Museum at Madras and in the British Museum at London. The stupa was surrounded by a magnificent railing some six hundred feet in circumference and fourteen feet high. The surfaces of this structure had an area of about 16,800 square feet and were completely covered with sculptured reliefs. The stupa itself was over one hundred and sixty-two feet in diameter, and its lower part was covered with casings which were also richly carved. One of the slabs from this casing is shown in Fig. 108. The principal object depicted is a beautifully ornamented stupa together with its gateway and railing. No doubt this may be taken as a good representation of how a decorated stupa, like the one at Amaravati itself, originally looked. Intricate and elaborate sculptures fill the

[169] Smith, *A History of Fine Art in India and Ceylon from the Earliest Times to the Present Day*, pp.143f.; cHIIA p.234.

rest of the slab, and the frieze at the top alone contains nearly fifty figures. In the central panel, seen through the gateway, and on the panels at the right and left the Buddha is represented only symbolically by his throne, but at the top in the scene of the Temptation by the Daughters of Mara, the Evil One,[170] he is shown in bodily likeness, seated in fashion as a yogi.

[170] Samyutta Nikaya I, iv, 3, 5 (124-127). tr. Woodward, *The Book of the Kindred Sayings*, pp.156-159; Nidanakatha. tr. Rhys Davids, *Buddhist Birth-Stories*, pp.202-204; Lalita Vistara XXI. tr. Foucaux, *Le Lalita Vistara*, I, pp.274f.

8. THE GUPTA PERIOD, A.D. c.320-c.600

THE Gupta Period, with its famous kings Chandragupta I (A.D. c.320-c.335) and Chandragupta II (A.D. c.385-c.414), was a splendid time in the history of Indian culture. A revival of Hinduism took place (p.159), and Buddhism also was strong.

FA HIEN

According to Fa Hien, the Chinese Buddhist pilgrim who visited India in the time of Chandragupta II, there was enmity between the Brahmans and the Buddhists, and at Śravasti, for example, the former attempted to destroy certain Buddhist structures but were miraculously hindered: "The heretic Brahmans, growing jealous, wished to destroy them; whereupon the heavens thundered and flashed lightning with splitting crash, so that they were not able to succeed."[171] In general, however, the Chinese visitor found Buddhism prospering. In the record of his travels we read concerning the Punjab: "The Faith is very flourishing under both the Greater and Lesser Vehicles"; and concerning the region of Mathura: "The Faith is here becoming very popular."[172] Telling of the numerous Buddhist monasteries in Middle India, Fa Hien says: "From the date of Buddha's disappearance from the world, the kings, elders, and gentry of the countries round about, built shrines for making offerings to the priests, and gave them land, houses, gardens, with men and bullocks for cultivation. Binding title-deeds were written out, and subsequent kings have handed these down one to another without daring to disregard them, in unbroken succession to this day. Rooms, with beds and mattresses, food, and clothes, are provided for resident and traveling priests, without fail; and this is the same in all places. The priests occupy themselves with benevolent ministrations, and with chanting liturgies; or they sit in meditation."[173]

As a pious pilgrim Fa Hien journeyed to many sacred sites of Buddhism and he tells of the numerous shrines and pagodas which he saw, and of the various relics of the Buddha, such as his tooth or his alms bowl, which were preserved in different places. The region of Kapilavastu was described as frequented by dangerous white elephants and lions, and as "just like a wilderness, except for priests and some tens of families"; but a large number of pagodas still ex-

---

[171] tr. Giles, *The Travels of Fa-hsien*, p.30.
[172] *ibid.*, pp.19f.   [173] *ibid.*, pp.21f.

isted to mark the spots where particular events in Gautama's life transpired.[174] The royal garden called Lumbini was said to be located fifty *li*[175] to the east of the city. Fa Hien also found the city of Gaya "a complete waste within its walls"; but in the vicinity were pagodas and monasteries marking such places as where Gautama suffered self-mortification for six years and where he finally attained to Buddhaship. In the same region Fa Hien visited the cave where, prior to his enlightenment, Gautama was supposed to have sat and reflected, "If I am to become a Buddha, there should be some divine manifestation in token thereof." Fa Hien reports: "At once the silhouette of a Buddha appeared upon the rock; it was over three feet in height and is plainly visible at the present day."[176]

An important objective of Fa Hien was to secure copies of the Buddhist scriptures to take back with him to China, "but in the various countries of Northern India these were handed down orally from one patriarch to another, there being no written volume which he could copy." For this reason he extended his journey to central India, and there in a monastery of the Greater Vehicle he was successful in obtaining a copy. Also in Ceylon, where he went later, he was able to secure other manuscripts, and with these he returned at last to China.[177]

SARNATH

In the Gupta Period Buddhist sculpture attained its high point. Among its most typical expressions are both seated and standing statues of the Buddha, who is usually shown garbed in a smooth, close-fitting robe. For a single example of outstanding importance we may turn to Sarnath where the Seated Buddha pictured in Fig. 109 was found. This world-famous carving, now in the Sarnath Museum of Archaeology, Benares, is of white sandstone, and is over five feet high. The Buddha is portrayed sitting upon a richly ornamented throne, and with a particularly beautiful nimbus behind his head. As is appropriate to Sarnath where his first sermon was preached, the hands of the Buddha are in the teaching position (*dharmacakra mudra*). Above hover two Devas, while on the lower part of the throne is the wheel of the law, and the five disciples to whom Gautama first proclaimed his message. The woman with the child at the left may be the donor of the image. The entire composi-

---

[174] *ibid.*, pp.36-38.
[175] One *li* was approximately one-third of a mile.
[176] tr. Giles, pp.53-56.   [177] *ibid.*, pp.64,76.

tion expresses almost perfectly the attainment of cosmic peace and illumination on the part of the Enlightened One.

The art of painting was practiced in India from ancient times, and the kings of Magadha and Kosala are said to have had houses adorned with painted figures and patterns.[178] In the Gupta age this art was developed to a very high degree, and our finest known examples of Buddhist paintings come from about this time. We will speak here of the paintings preserved in the Buddhist caves at Bagh and Ajanta.

The Bagh caves are cut in a sandstone cliff in a valley on the southern slopes of the Vindhya Mountains. There are nine caves all together, but several have already collapsed. They were elaborately decorated both with sculpture and with painting. Good statues of the Buddha and his attendants are found in Cave II, and the best remaining paintings are on the outer surface of the front wall of Caves IV and V. There was originally a continuous veranda, two hundred and twenty feet in length and with some twenty heavy pillars, in front of these two caves, but it is now destroyed. The paintings formed a great mural, the chief subject of which seems to have been some kind of city pageant or festival. A splendid procession is shown with finely depicted horses and elephants, and there are groups of dancers and musicians, and other persons. While these subjects seem secular, we shall see at Ajanta how comparable themes were suffused with religious feeling. According to a recently discovered inscription on a copper plate, the caves at Bagh date around the beginning of the sixth century A.D.[179]

At Ajanta there are no fewer than twenty-nine caves, cut in the cliffs of a beautiful and secluded valley, which once served as monasteries and temples of the Buddhist faith.[180] The walls, ceilings and

[178] Rhys Davids, *Buddhist India*, p.96.

[179] John Marshall, M. B. Garde, P. Vogel, E. B. Havell and J. H. Cousins, *The Bagh Caves in Gwalior State, Published by the India Society in Co-operation with the Department of Archaeology, Gwalior, for His Late Highness Maharaja Sir Madhav Rao Scindia Alijah Bahadur*. 1927; GCE, II, pp.160f.; AJA 50 (1946), p.411.

[180] It is possible but not certain that Hiuen Tsang was describing Ajanta when he wrote concerning the region of Maharashtra: "On the eastern frontier of the country is a great mountain with towering crags and a continuous stretch of piled-up rocks and scarped precipice. In this there is a sangharama constructed in a dark valley. Its lofty halls and deep side-aisles stretch through the face of the rocks. Story above story they

pillars of nearly all of these were once decorated with paintings, and portions of the frescoes still remain in thirteen of the caves. In date the various paintings range all the way from before the Christian era to the seventh century A.D. The most excellent level of work was probably attained in the second half of the fifth and the beginning of the sixth centuries A.D.[181]

The chief subjects of the frescoes are events in the historical life of the Buddha, including his birth, departure from Kapilavastu, enlightenment, miracles and death; and from his previous existences as related in the Jataka tales in which he was, for example, a prince, a deer, a moose and an elephant. In addition there are portraits of Buddhas, Bodhisattvas and various deities; scenes of court life and daily life; and decorative figures of mythological creatures and of animals, trees and flowers. Indeed, since in his various successive existences the Buddha is supposed to have passed through all the experiences of earth, the pictures in their entirety give us a veritable pageant of ancient Indian life in all its phases. The prevailing impression is not secular, however, but religious, and the great Bodhisattva who moves through the scenes seems to look upon the manifold life of the world with tenderness and compassion. As William Rothenstein says: "On the hundred walls and pillars of these rock-carved temples a vast drama moves before our eyes, a drama played by princes and sages and heroes, by men and women of every condition, against a marvelously varied scene, among forests and gardens, in courts and cities, on wide plains and in deep jungles, while above the messengers of heaven move swiftly across the sky. From all these emanates a great joy in the surpassing radiance of the face of the world, in the physical nobility of men and women, in the strength and grace of animals and the loveliness and purity of birds and flowers; and woven into this fabric of material beauty we see the ordered pattern of the spiritual realities of the universe."[182] And René Grousset sums up the "multifarious impressions" of Ajanta

---

are backed by the crag and face the valley." XI, 3. tr. Beal, *Buddhist Records of the Western World*, II, p.257; Thomas Watters, *On Yuan Chwang's Travels in India 629-645 A.D.* (Oriental Translation Fund, New Series, XIV, XV). 1904-05, II, p.240.

[181] Jeanne Auboyer in *Art and Letters, India and Pakistan.* New Series XXII, 1. First Issue for 1948. pp.20-28.

[182] In *Ajanta Frescoes, Being Reproductions in Colour and Monochrome of Frescoes in Some of the Caves at Ajanta after Copies Taken in the Years 1909-1911 by Lady Herringham and Her Assistants, with Introductory Essays by Various Members of the India Society.* 1915, p.23. Quoted by permission of the India Society and the Oxford University Press, London.

"in a single formula," by saying that "the predominant feature of Ajaṇṭā is an intimate and harmonious fusion of the old Indian naturalism of Sāñchī, with its youthful freshness, and the infinite gentleness of Buddhist mysticism. And it is this which makes Ajaṇṭā a complete expression of every side of the Indian soul."[183]

For specific illustration we will select Cave Number I.[184] It is situated at the southeast end of the valley and architecturally is considered one of the finest viharas in India. The porch which once stood in front has fallen and carried away part of the rock above, but the veranda still stands as shown in Fig. 110.[185] The dimensions of the veranda are sixty-four feet in length, over nine feet in width and thirteen feet in height. The columns and horizontal bands above are intricately sculptured. A large ornamental door leads into the great hall which is nearly sixty-four feet square and has a roof supported by a colonnade of twenty richly carved pillars. At the back of the hall an antechamber leads into a shrine, about twenty feet square, in which is a colossal statue of the Buddha. In the interior of the rock are also fourteen cells.

All the walls and ceiling of the cave were once adorned with paintings, and of these considerable portions still remain. While these decorations were probably executed between A.D. 600 and 650 at the height of the Chalukya dynasty, and thus belong strictly speaking to the beginning of the Medieval Period, it is proper to describe them as done in the Gupta style. The fresco on the back wall of the cave to the left of the antechamber is shown in Fig. 111.[186] The doorway which appears in the picture is that of the first cell to the left of the entrance to the antechamber. The principal figure in the painting is the Great Bodhisattva. A detail of the painting, showing the Bodhisattva's head, is reproduced in Fig. 112. He is depicted on a scale larger than life-size, is garbed in a dhoti of striped silk, and wears on his head a high jeweled crown. In his right hand he holds a blue lotus, and because of this symbol may probably be identified

[183] GCE II, p.159. Quoted by permission of the publisher, Alfred A. Knopf, Inc., New York and London.
[184] Fergusson and Burgess, *The Cave Temples of India*, pp.320-332; Victor Goloubew, *Documents pour servir à l'étude d'Ajanta, Les peintures de la première grotte* (*Ars Asiatica*, x). 1927; *Ajanta, The Colour and Monochrome Reproductions of the Ajanta Frescoes Based on Photography, with an Explanatory Text by G. Yazdani.* Part I, Text and Plates, 1930; GCE II, p.150.
[185] Goloubew, *Documents pour servir à l'étude d'Ajanta, Les peintures de la première grotte*, Pl. VIII.
[186] *Ajanta, The Colour and Monochrome Reproductions of the Ajanta Frescoes Based on Photography, with an Explanatory Text by G. Yazdani*, Part I, Pl. XXIV.

as the Bodhisattva Padmapani, "the lotus-handed," or Avalokiteśvara.[187] Elsewhere in the picture are a dark-skinned princess, a mace-
bearer, human couples, heavenly musicians, flying figures, peacocks
and monkeys.

[187] CHIIA p.99.

9. THE MEDIEVAL PERIOD, A.D. c.600-c.1200

As SHOWN by the artistic monuments just described, Buddhism reached a high point in its influence in the Gupta Period. After that it began to decline. Weakened by its own divisions, and facing increased competition from a Hinduism strengthened by such notable teachers as Śankara and Ramanuja, Buddhism gradually lost ground. Finally upon the onslaught of Islam, it disappeared almost completely from the land of its origin.

HIUEN TSANG

It was just at the beginning of this long period of decline that the Chinese Buddhist pilgrim Hiuen Tsang visited India (A.D. c.630-c.645).[188] His writings will provide us with the last glimpse, for which there is space in this chapter, of Buddhism in its own homeland.

Hiuen Tsang mentions numerous Buddhist monasteries, and writes as follows concerning their manner of building: "The sangharamas are constructed with extraordinary skill. A three-storied tower is erected at each of the four angles. The beams and the projecting heads are carved with great skill in different shapes. The doors, windows, and the low walls are painted profusely; the monks' cells are ornamental on the inside and plain on the outside. In the very middle of the building is the hall, high and wide. There are various storeyed chambers and turrets of different height and shape, without any fixed rule. The doors open toward the east; the royal throne also faces the east."[189]

Of the various divisions of Buddhism the Chinese observer says: "The different schools are constantly at variance, and their contending utterances rise like the angry waves of the sea. The different sects have their separate masters, and in various directions aim at one end. There are eighteen schools, each claiming pre-eminence. The partisans of the Great and Little Vehicle are content to dwell apart. There are some who give themselves up to quiet contemplation, and devote themselves, whether walking or standing still or sitting down,

[188] For Hiuen Tsang's visit to Harsha, and his public disputation on behalf of the Great Vehicle, see Beal, *The Life of Hiuen-Tsiang by the Shaman Hwui Li*, pp.171-181. Fa Hien and Hiuen Tsang were admired and emulated by yet a third Buddhist pilgrim from China, I-Tsing, who visited India toward the end of the seventh century and wrote an extensive account of Buddhist customs. See J. Takakusu, *A Record of the Buddhist Religion as Practised in India and the Malay Archipelago* (A.D. 671-695), *by I-Tsing*. 1896.
[189] II, 5. tr. Beal, *Buddhist Records of the Western World*, I, p.74.

to the acquirement of wisdom and insight; others, on the contrary, differ from these in raising noisy contentions about their faith. According to their fraternity, they are governed by distinctive rules and regulations, which we need not name."[190]

Many cities which figure in Buddhist history were visited by Hiuen Tsang in his travels, and of these we will select Benares and Kusinara for mention. Having quoted already from Fa Hien's description of Kapilavastu and Gaya, this will give us from the pens of the two pilgrims eyewitness accounts of the four most sacred regions of Buddhism, namely where the Buddha was born, attained enlightenment, began to preach, and passed away. In Benares itself Hiuen Tsang learned that the Buddhists were far outnumbered by their rivals, but at the famous Deer Park near by he found a great monastery in which fifteen hundred priests were studying the Little Vehicle. In its enclosure was a vihara about two hundred feet high. On its sides were a large number of niches in each of which was a golden figure of Buddha, and in the middle was a life-size copper statue representing the Buddha as turning the wheel of the law. "To the southwest of the vihara," Hiuen Tsang continues, "is a stone stupa built by Aśoka-raja. Although the foundations have given way, there are still 100 feet or more of the wall remaining. In front of the building is a stone pillar about 70 feet high. The stone is altogether as bright as jade. It is glistening, and sparkles like light; and all those who pray fervently before it see from time to time, according to their petitions, figures with good or bad signs. It was here that Tathagata, having arrived at enlightenment, began to turn the wheel of the law."[191]

Concerning Kusinara, Hiuen Tsang writes: "The capital of this country is in ruins, and its towns and villages waste and desolate. The brick foundation walls of the old capital are about ten li in circuit. There are few inhabitants, and the avenues of the town are deserted and waste. At the northeast angle of the city gate is a stupa which was built by Aśoka-raja. . . . To the northwest of the city three or four li, crossing the Ajitavati [Hiranyavati] river, on the western bank, not far, we come to a grove of sal trees. . . . In this wood are four trees of an unusual height, which indicate the place where Tathagata died. There is here a great brick vihara, in which is a figure of the Nirvana of Tathagata. He is lying with his head to the north as if asleep. By the side of this vihara is a stupa built by Aśoka-raja;

[190] ii, 10. tr. Beal, *ibid.*, i, p.80.   [191] vii, 1. tr. Beal, *ibid.*, ii, p.46.

although in a ruinous state, yet it is some 200 feet in height. Before it is a stone pillar to record the Nirvana of Tathagata; although there is an inscription on it, yet there is no date as to year or month."[192]

[192] vi, 4. tr. Beal, *ibid.*, ii, pp.31-33.

118. Angkor Wat

119. Air View of the Bayon

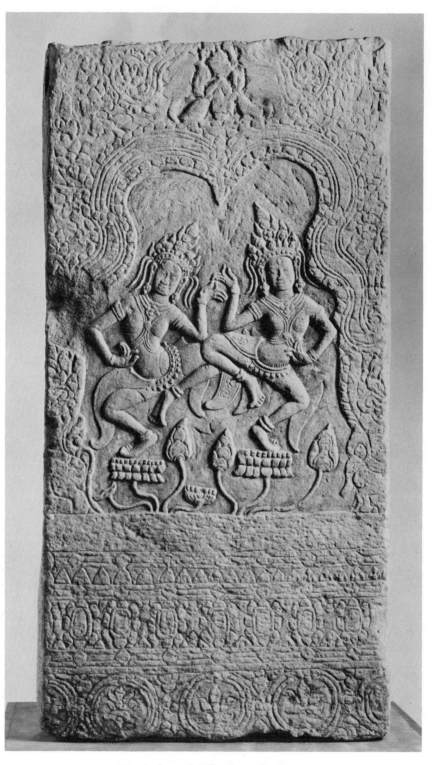

120. Sculptured Pillar from the Bayon

121. Tower of the Bayon

123. Buddha Sheltered by the Serpent

122. Cambodian Buddha Head

125. Great Terrace of Borobudur

126. Bas-Relief at Borobudur

124. Air View of Borobudur

127. Cave Painting at Qizil near Kucha

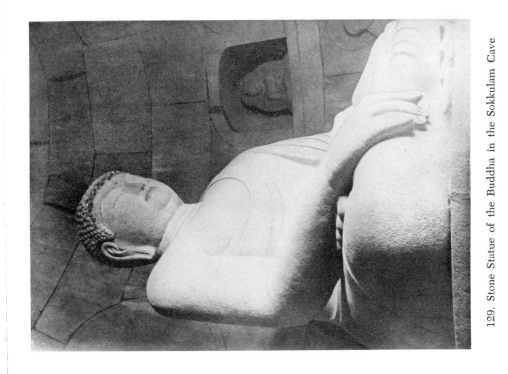

129. Stone Statue of the Buddha in the Sokkulam Cave

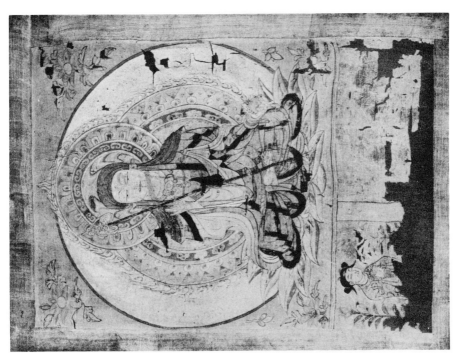

128. Painting from Tunhwang of the Bodhisattva Kshitigarbha

130. The Sukhavati Paradise of Amitabha as Painted at Wan Fo Hsia

131. Golden Hall, Middle
Gate and Pagoda at Horyuji

132. Buddhist Trinity in
the Golden Hall at Horyuji

133. Wall Painting of the Paradise of Shaka, in the Golden Hall at Horyuji

134. Tibetan Painting of Gautama Buddha

135. Tibetan Mandala

10. BUDDHISM IN OTHER LANDS

LONG before the period of its decline and virtual disappearance in India, and largely due as we will remember to the initial impetus of the missionary zeal of Aśoka. Buddhism had gone out from the land of its birth and become a vital faith in many other countries. Within the limits of the present chapter it will be possible only very briefly to indicate the chief of these other lands into which Buddhism went and to mention a few of the earliest or most significant archeological sites and monuments of this faith, in them.

SOUTHERN LANDS

The countries first to be mentioned are all in southeast Asia and adjacent regions. In some of them, as for a notable example in Cambodia, it was at one time the Mahayana form of Buddhism which was in the ascendancy, but in most of them it is now the Hinayana school which prevails.

CEYLON

According to the Mahavamsa[193] and the record of Hiuen Tsang,[194] the chief work in the conversion of Ceylon (which was called Lanka or Simhala) to the Buddhist faith was done by Mahinda (or Mahendra), son (or younger brother) of King Aśoka. The king of Ceylon at that time was named Tissa, and he became the great protector of the new religion on the island. At his capital city of Anuradhapura, Tissa erected various sacred structures, including the Mahavihara or Great Monastery where a portion of the Bodhi tree brought from Gaya was planted.[195] In the same city at the beginning of the first century B.C. the great king Dutthagamani built the large Ruanweli dagoba which is described in detail in the Mahavamsa;[196] and toward the end of the same century King Vattagamani Abhaya constructed the Abhayagiri vihara.[197] The ruins or rebuilt remains of these and other ancient structures are still to be found at Anuradhapura; and on the platform of the Ruanweli dagoba there stood until modern times several colossal statues dating probably from around A.D. 200. In the forest not far away was the statue of the Buddha pictured in

---

[193] XIII-XIV. tr. Geiger, pp.88-96.
[194] XI, 1. tr. Beal, *Buddhist Records of the Western World*, II, pp.246f.
[195] Mahavamsa XV-XIX. tr. Geiger, pp.97-135.
[196] XXVIII-XXXI. tr. Geiger, pp.187-219.
[197] Mahavamsa XXXIII, 81. tr. Geiger, p.235.

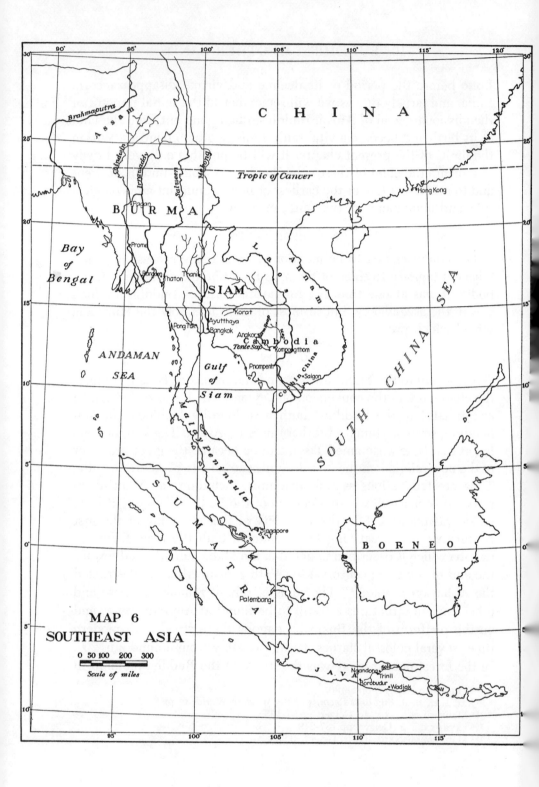

CHINA

Brahmaputra

Assam

Tropic of Cancer

Hong Kong

BURMA

Pagan

Prome

Bay
of
Bengal

Prandon
Thaton

Thani

Laos

SIAM

Korat

Ayutthaya

Pong Tuk
Bangkok

Angkor

Cambodia

TonleSap

Kompongthom

ANDAMAN

SEA

Gulf
of
Siam

Pnompenh

Cochin-china

Saigon

SOUTH CHINA SEA

Malay Peninsula

SUMATRA

Singapore

BORNEO

Palembang

MAP 6
SOUTHEAST ASIA

0 50 100   200   300

Scale of miles

JAVA

Ngandong

Solo

Trinil

Borobudur

Wadjak

Bali

Fig. 114. This figure is larger than life-size, and probably belongs to the third century A.D. It is now in the Museum at Colombo.

In the ninth century A.D. the kings transferred their residence to Polonnaruwa, where medieval dagobas, temples and viharas still stand; and in the sixteenth century the capital was moved to Kandy, where the most famous sanctuary is the Dalada Maligawa or Temple of the Tooth. This temple dates in its present form from the eighteenth century, and is the repository of a supposed tooth-relic of the Buddha. According to the Dathavamsa,[198] when the relics of the Buddha were distributed after his cremation this tooth was given to Brahmadatta, king of Kalinga, and then later in time of war it was sent by King Guhasiva to Ceylon where it was given to King Kittisi-rimegha. This was in the latter part of the fourth century A.D., and when Fa Hien visited Ceylon in the early fifth century he found that the tooth was kept in a specially built shrine and brought forth at regular intervals to be carried in a procession and made the object of homage in extended ceremonies.[199] After being kept first at Anuradhapura and then at Polonnaruwa, it is said to be the same tooth that is now at Kandy. At any rate the Temple of the Tooth at Kandy is of importance as having probably been built on much the same plan as the ancient temples of Anuradhapura.[200]

BURMA

Burma was in the circle of influence of India from the beginning of the Christian era on, and probably by the fifth century A.D. the cities of Prome on the Irrawaddy River and Thaton on the southern coast were centers of Hindu and Buddhist culture. The oldest epigraphic records in Burma were found at the village of Hmawza, six miles north of modern Prome. They belong probably to the sixth century A.D., and contain extracts from Pali Buddhist texts.[201] Thaton was a royal capital, but in the eleventh century A.D. was conquered by Anawrahta of Pagan, the king who first achieved the unification of all Burma. The latter king returned to Pagan with valuable Buddhist relics and scriptures, and devoted himself to spreading the religion of Buddhism throughout his realm. Pagan remained a great center of Buddhism from that time on until it was destroyed by a

---

[198] Law, The Dathavamsa, pp.15f.,36f.,42-51.
[199] Giles, The Travels of Fa-hsien, pp.69-71.
[200] A. M. Hocart, The Temple of the Tooth in Kandy (Memoirs of the Archaeological Survey of Ceylon, IV). 1931.
[201] Nihar-ranjan Ray, Sanskrit Buddhism in Burma. 1936, pp.3f.

Chinese army in A.D. 1287. The ruins of the ancient city and its environs extend over an area about twenty miles in length and five miles in breadth along the Irrawaddy River, and in this district the remains of more than five thousand pagodas and monasteries can be traced.[202] Some of the pagodas were cylindrical or hemispherical like the stupas with which we are already familiar; others like the thirteenth century Mingalazedi (Fig. 113)[203] anticipated the modern type which is best known from the famous Shwe Dagon Pagoda in Rangoon. Among the decorations of these structures were stone reliefs, wall paintings, and bronze figures.

THAILAND

The introduction of Buddhism into Thailand at some time in the early centuries of the Christian era is attested by a small bronze statue of the Buddha found, along with the ruins of an ancient temple, at Pong Tük, and by a similar figure discovered at Korat, both of which are judged from their style to have come from Amaravati in India. During the second half of the first millennium the land was inhabited by people of the Mon race, who practiced the Buddhist religion according to the Hinayana school and carved statues of the Buddha which are very similar in appearance to those of the Gupta Period in India. Then for a time the Khmer people dominated Siam, but were gradually displaced by the Thai. The latter were a Mongoloid race who are believed to have come from south China. By the last part of the thirteenth century A.D. a united state was in existence under the rule of a certain Ram Kamheng who takes rank as the first great Thai king of Siam.

The capital city of Ram Kamheng was at Sukhothai, near modern Thani. Among the ancient ruins of Sukhothai are the temples of Maha-Tat and Sri Chum. The former is said to have comprised originally no less than a hundred and eighty-nine different structures, of which the chief were a stupa with its annexes and a huge vihara. The ruined stupa and the lower portions of the columns which supported the roof of the vihara are still to be seen, as is also an enormous standing statue of the Buddha. The temple of Sri Chum is later in date than that of Maha-Tat, and probably belongs to the reign of Dharmaraja I, grandson of Ram Kamheng, in the middle of the fourteenth century. It was built of brick and stucco, and had a rectangular

[202] *A Handbook for Travellers in India, Burma and Ceylon* (John Murray), p.703; Th. H. Thomann, *Pagan, Ein Jahrtausend buddhistischer Tempelkunst.* 1923.
[203] CHIIA Fig. 313.

sanctuary in which there is still a gigantic image of the seated Buddha.

Near the temple of Maha-Tat an obelisk was discovered with an inscription of Ram Kamheng written in the earliest form of Thai script. In it the king told how he and all his people without any distinction of rank or sex followed the observances of the Buddhist religion devoutly; how in the midst of Sukhothai there were temples and statues of the Buddha, some of the latter being as much as thirty feet in height; and how he built a monastery for a renowned teacher of Buddhism who came from the Malay Peninsula. Another inscription found at Sukhothai belongs probably to the reign of Dharmaraja I, and tells among other things of the coming of another famous Buddhist teacher, a venerable monk who had studied in Ceylon.

The style of architecture and sculpture which was developed at Sukhothai spread throughout the land, and the Sukhothai school is recognized as representing the ideal of Siamese art. The general type of stupa or pagoda which was built may be indicated by the twelve-inch-high bronze model with ivory pinnacle shown in Fig. 115.[204] Representations of the Buddha characteristic of the Sukhothai school may be seen in a bronze head (Fig. 116) in the National Museum at Bangkok and a stone head (Fig. 117) at Gump's in San Francisco. Notable aspects of this type of portrayal include the elongated head, the sharply defined, aristocratic features, the half-closed eyes, gentle smile and calm, meditative expression.[205]

CAMBODIA

Present-day Cambodia is but the remnant of a once much larger kingdom. In the first centuries of the Christian era this kingdom, which included Cochin China, Laos and southern Siam in addition to Cambodia, was known as Funan. In Funan the cults of both Śiva and Buddha were practiced, and the art was definitely Indianesque. In about A.D. 540 the power of Funan was destroyed and their kingdom passed into the hands of the Khmer people. The latter were of Sino-Tibetan origin, and in their legends claimed descent from an Apsaras (or celestial nymph) named Mera, or from a Nagini (the feminine of Naga, a half-human, half-serpentine being) called Soma.

[204] Reginald Le May, *A Concise History of Buddhist Art in Siam.* 1938. Fig. 151.
[205] George Coedès, *Les collections archéologiques du Musée National de Bangkok* (Ars Asiatica, XII). 1928, p.32; Le May, *A Concise History of Buddhist Art in Siam*, pp.15-20,21f.,120-134; cf. Kenneth E. Wells, *Thai Buddhism, Its Rites and Activities.* 1939.

As far as religion is concerned, both Hinduism and Mahayana Buddhism flourished in the kingdom of the Khmers, and the Hinayana school must also have been known since eventually it prevailed over the Mahayana. In about A.D. 802 Angkor became the Khmer capital, and from that date to the end of the thirteenth century is the classic period of Cambodian art, an art which was devoted to the service of both Hinduism and Buddhism.[206]

Angkor is the Cambodian form of the Sanskrit word *nagara*, meaning "capital," and Angkor Thom, as the full name now runs, signifies "the great capital." The ancient name of the city was Yasodharapura. Angkor Wat, as the temple about a mile south of the city is called, means "the temple of the capital."

The site of Angkor is on the right bank of the Siem Reap River which flows into the Tonle Sap or Great Lake. If we approach from the south we come first to Angkor Wat.[207] It is the best-preserved example of Khmer architecture, and shows impressively the type of temple construction developed by this people. The entire structure is surrounded by a large moat, across which on the west side a paved bridge protected by Naga parapets leads to the main monumental entrance. Within, a paved causeway likewise guarded by a Naga balustrade leads on to the temple proper. Here a double gallery, richly sculptured with scenes of Hindu mythology, encloses the inner terraces. These rise one above the other to the innermost court where five great towers loom up, the highest reaching a total elevation of over two hundred and ten feet above the level of the ground. A view of the temple from the inner causeway is shown in Fig. 118.[208]

Proceeding to Angkor Thom, we find that the ancient city had large reservoirs or artificial lakes on either side, and that it was itself surrounded by a moat three hundred feet wide and by walls which enclosed a practically perfect square some two miles long on each side. Within the city was also a sort of inner city, itself protected by moats now dry. The royal palace which probably once stood in this area has been destroyed, but other monuments are still to be seen, including the pyramidal temple called Phimeanakas, and the royal terrace with its procession of elephants, almost natural size, sculptured in relief.

[206] Von Glasenapp, *Der Buddhismus in Indien und im Fernen Osten*, pp.122f.; CHIIA pp.180-186.

[207] *Le Temple d'Angkor Vat* (Mémoires archéologiques publiés par l'École Française d'Extrême-Orient, II). 7 vols. 1929-32.

[208] *ibid.*, Part 1, vol. I, Pl. 56.

At the very center of the entire city square rose the enormous Bayon temple, shown in Fig. 119 in an air view. It was built on much the same general plan as Angkor Wat, with encircling galleries and successive stories. Contributing a great deal to the impressiveness of the temple are its approximately fifty towers and one hundred and seventy-two great sculptured human faces. The faces are thought to represent the Bodhisattva Lokeśvara or Avalokiteśvara, and if this is correct the Bayon probably originated as a Buddhist temple. Other decorations include a great variety of relief scenes which depict trees, flowers, animals, fishes, festivals, processions, naval combats, events in daily life, ordinary men and women, princes and princesses, gods and goddesses. A sculptured pillar from the Bayon, with two dancing figures on lotuses, is pictured in Fig. 120. In Fig. 121 one of the mighty towers is shown, with its colossal faces looking out, eyes half closed and an enigmatical, elusive smile upon the lips. This is the "smile of Angkor," doubtless intended as a mysterious and mystic reflection of the inward blessedness of enlightenment.[209]

A similar facial expression appears upon many of the Buddha statues characteristic of classic Khmer art. This may be seen, for example, in the case of the Buddha head pictured in Fig. 122. Particularly interesting and typical of Cambodian art also is the type of statue shown in Fig. 123. Here the Buddha is seated upon a coiled serpent which raises its seven heads protectingly behind the Buddha's head. The literary reference which illuminates the conception may be found in various sources including the Lalita-vistara.[210] There it is narrated that in the fifth week after his enlightenment the Buddha was staying in the house of the king of the Nagas, Mucilinda. At this time there was very bad weather, and the serpent king protected the Buddha from the cold winds by enveloping him with seven coils and sheltering him with his heads.[211]

[209] George Groslier, *Angkor* (Famous Art Cities). 1933, pp.45-52; *The Madrolle Guides: Indochina.* 1939, pp.27-43; GCE II, pp.318-320.
[210] XXIV. tr. Foucaux, *Le Lalita Vistara,* I, p.316.
[211] Adhémard Leclère, *Le Buddhisme au Cambodge.* 1899, pp.448,453; George Coedès, *Bronzes Khmèrs, Étude basée sur des documents recueillis par M. P. Lefèvre-Pontalis dans les collections publiques et privées de Bangkok et sur les pièces conservées au Palais Royal de Phnom Penh au Musée du Cambodge et au Musée de l'École Française d'Extrême-Orient* (Ars Asiatica, V). 1923, pp.32-41; *Arts et archéologie Khmers, Revue des recherches sur les arts, les monuments et l'ethnographie du Cambodge, depuis les origines jusqu'à nos jours.* 1 (1921-23), Pls. XVII, XVIII; Vogel, *Indian Serpent-Lore or the Nāgas in Hindu Legend and Art,* pp.102f.; Pierre Dupont in *Artibus Asiae.* 13 (1950), pp.39-62.

JAVA

Both Hinduism and Buddhism must have been introduced into Java in the early centuries of the Christian era. As far as Buddhism is concerned it was the creed of the Hinayana which gained the most adherents at first, but in the eighth century A.D. the Mahayana school gained the ascendancy. Finally in the fifteenth century the faith of Islam spread over the entire island.

From about A.D. 750 to 850 Middle Java was ruled by the Sailendra dynasty whose center was at Palembang in Sumatra. It was at this time that Mahayanism flourished and it is from this time that the chief Buddhist monuments of Java come. Of these the greatest is Borobudur.

Borobudur[212] is the common native name of a mighty structure which stands on an eminence in the plain of Kedu commanding a striking panorama of green fields and lofty conical volcanoes. A rounded hill was terraced to support the construction and was veritably clothed in a mantle of stone. The six lower terraces are square, while the upper three are circular. Each of the lower terraces provides a gallery the walls of which are richly adorned with reliefs which illustrate the life of Buddha according to the Lalita-vistara and scenes from other Buddhist literature; while on the upper platforms no fewer than seventy-two small perforated stupas are arranged in three concentric circles around a larger central stupa. All together the monument constitutes a sort of mystic diagram in stone. As the pilgrim walks around the terraces the teachings of Buddhism are spread before his eyes in the long succession of sculptured reliefs. As he climbs toward the summit he comes up to levels where figured representations are left behind and there are only the "pure forms" of the stupas. Thus is symbolized the progress of the follower of Buddhist teachings who rises out of the world of appearances into perfect enlightenment.

An air view of this remarkable monument is shown in Fig. 124; and a portion of its broad base terrace and elaborately ornamented wall is pictured in Fig. 125. Also, from the series of reliefs on the first gallery which gives scenes from the life of Gautama Buddha according to the Lalita-vistara, we show in Fig. 126 the Attainment of the

[212] N. J. Krom and T. Van Erp, *Beschrijving van Barabudur* (Archaeologisch Onderzoek in Nederlandsch-Indie, III). 5 vols. 1920-31; N. J. Krom, *Barabudur, Archaeological Description.* 2 vols. 1927; J. Ph. Vogel, *The Relation between the Art of India and Java.* 1925, pp.23-33.

Highest Wisdom.[213] Since the immediately preceding reliefs have depicted the final attacks upon Gautama by Mara and his daughters, there can be no doubt that this scene represents the actual achievement of the Great Enlightenment by the Buddha. The relevant passage in the Lalita-vistara reads in part as follows: "In the late watch of the night when the day began to break, the Bodhisattva with such lofty comprehension, according to an insight that absorbed in unity of thought and time all that could be known, thought, achieved, seen and contemplated, attained the highest and most perfect Wisdom, and acquired the threefold knowledge. Thereupon the gods spake: 'Strew flowers, O friends, Bhagavat hath attained the Wisdom.' Then the sons of the gods strewed divine flowers over the Tathagata till a knee-deep layer of the blossoms was formed."[214] In the relief showing this scene the Buddha is seated upon a throne while the Bodhi tree bends over him to form a round niche and on either side stands a flowering plant. The gods sit to the right and left, some holding bowls of flowers, and others hover above, also with flowers and vases to honor the Enlightened One with a rain of blossoms.

NORTHERN LANDS

In its remarkable missionary expansion Buddhism went also into the lands of northern Asia, and in these regions it is the Mahayana which now chiefly prevails.

SINKIANG

Of the routes of intercourse between India and the north none is more interesting than that marked out by the pilgrim feet of Fa Hien who, in about A.D. 399 journeyed overland from China to seek Buddhist documents in the land of that faith's origin. Departing from Ch'ang-an, Fa Hien and his party went by way of Changyeh to Tunhwang at the end of the Great Wall, and then set out across a fearsome desert which is described in his record as follows: "In this desert there are a great many evil spirits and also hot winds; those who encounter them perish to a man. There are neither birds above nor beasts below. Gazing on all sides as far as the eye can reach in order

[213] Krom and Van Erp, *Beschrijving van Barabudur*, Atlas III, Pls. 11, 64; Atlas I, Pl. XLVIII, No. 96.
[214] XXII. tr. Foucaux, *Le Lalita Vistara*, I, pp.293f.; N. J. Krom, *The Life of Buddha on the Stūpa of Barabuḍur According to the Lalitavistara-Text*. 1926, p.107.

to mark the track, no guidance is to be obtained save from the rotting bones of dead men, which point the way."[215]

Fa Hien was here journeying across a portion of the Gobi desert, and heading toward and across what today is called Sinkiang. Two chains of oases mark and make possible the caravan routes which lead on to the west and southwest. The route skirting the central waste on the north touches Turfan, Qara Shahr, Kucha and Kashgar; while the other route on the south goes through Lop Nor, Niya, Khotan and Yarkand. Of these places the following are mentioned in the record of Fa Hien: the region of Lop Nor, Qara Shahr, Turfan, Khotan and Kashgar. Beyond Sinkiang the pilgrims crossed mountains where there was snow in both winter and summer alike, and where according to their record there were "also venomous dragons, which, if provoked, spit forth poisonous winds, rain, snow, sand, and stones." "Of those who encounter these dangers," says Fa Hien, "not one in ten thousand escapes." Finally they followed "a difficult, precipitous, and dangerous road, the side of the mountain being like a stone wall ten thousand feet in height. On nearing the edge, the eye becomes confused; and wishing to advance, the foot finds no resting-place."[216] Below, however, they saw the Indus River, and descending at last from the terrible hills found themselves in the land which was their goal.

At this point in our study we are dealing with the northward spread of Buddhism, and we note with interest that Fa Hien reports the existence of the faith in the form of either the Little or the Great Vehicle at most of the places he visited in Sinkiang. There is also archeological evidence from the same region in the form of Buddhist sculptures and paintings, and in sufficient abundance that it is possible to distinguish the contributions of varied schools of art such as the Gandharan, the Gupta and the Sasanian.[217]

For a single concrete example of this Buddhist art of central Asia we will turn to the region of Kucha. In this vicinity there is a series of caves with Buddhist paintings dating from around the fourth to the eighth centuries A.D. The painting reproduced in Fig. 127 is from a cave at Qizil near Kucha, and dates probably from the seventh century A.D. There are several copies of this scene at Kucha, and on the edge of one the name of Ajataśatru was scratched as a tiny in-

[215] tr. Giles, *The Travels of Fa-hsien*, p.2.
[216] *ibid.*, pp.8f.
[217] GCE III, pp.147-176; J. Hackin in *Studies in Chinese Art and Some Indian Influences*, pp.1-14.

scription. This was doubtless to assist the memory of some monk who guided pilgrims to see the pictures, and it also gives the clue to the identification of the following curious and little-known legend as that represented in the scene. According to Tibetan tradition, at the time when Gautama Buddha died and the accompanying earthquake took place, the important disciple Kassapa (Kaśyapa) the Great was staying at Rajagriha. He feared that the shock of the Buddha's death might be too much for King Ajataśatru unless the news were broken to him with certain precautions. Kassapa therefore told a nobleman of Magadha named Varshakara of the danger and instructed him how to proceed. Varshakara was to prepare a picture which depicted the chief events of the life of Gautama including his Parinirvana in death at Kusinara. Also he was to make ready seven large jars full of fresh ghee, and one of pulverized sandalwood. Then, said Kassapa to Varshakara, "when the king comes to the gate of the park, you must ask him if he would not like to see the picture; and when he looks at the scenes you will explain them to him beginning with the first. When he hears that the Enlightened One is dead, he will fall to the earth. You must then place him in one of the jars filled with fresh ghee, and when the butter begins to melt you must put him in the jar of powdered sandalwood, and he will recover."

In our painting we see in the lower right hand corner a large circle enclosing a sea and mountain. The mountain is breaking apart and falling down, while the sun and moon roll to the ground. This represents the earthquake which was concomitant with the death of the Buddha. In the upper left-hand corner two royally attired persons are seated upon thrones, accompanied by attendants, and in earnest conversation with a young man who sits on a near-by stool. This must be King Ajataśatru and his queen talking with Varshakara. At the right is a second and subsequent scene. We note a number of large jars in the foremost of which is the figure of the king, still wearing his crown, but wrapped now in bandages and lifting his arms in fear. Before him stands Varshakara, holding up a large cloth roll covered with pictures. On this, four scenes may be distinguished. At the lower left is the Nativity, with Queen Maya and a body of light descending at her side. At the upper left is the attack of the hosts of Mara upon Gautama just before his Enlightenment. At the lower right is the preaching of the Buddha in the Deer Park at Benares; at the upper right is his death. In many of the graceful figures we recognize the Gupta style of painting which we first met at far-away Ajanta.[218]

CHINA

Buddhism was known in China at least as early as A.D. 61 when according to legend the later Han emperor Ming Ti was supposed to have been led by a dream to send to India for Buddhist statues, writings, and teachers. Probably it was there even earlier. The routes by which the Buddhist faith came to China must have been various, and doubtless included the way of the sea from south India to Tonkin and south China, and the mountain passes from Burma to Yunnan and southwest China, as well as the caravan routes across the wastes of Sinkiang to west China of which we have just been speaking. Despite the formidable mountains and deserts which might have barred less devoted pilgrims and missionaries, this last way was the most important in the whole history of the introduction of Buddhism to China.[219] We will continue on it, therefore, in our own presentation, and enter China at the western frontier city of Tunhwang whence long ago Fa Hien departed.

Tunhwang was not only on the great east-west trade route across Asia but also at the intersection point with it of the high road between Mongolia in the north and Tibet in the south. This location exposed the city to not infrequent attacks, and it was probably some such incursion which led to the hiding away of the treasure of which we are about to speak. This is a quantity of Buddhist paintings on silk, all crumpled up as if thrust away hurriedly, which were recovered from a recess in one of the Ch'ien Fo Tung or Caves of the Thousand Buddhas at Tunhwang.[220] While the caves themselves are of much interest for their frescoes and sculptures,[221] special attention may be given to the paintings just mentioned, along with which

[218] Albert Grünwedel, *Alt-Kutscha, archäc゙ ̣gische und religionsgeschichtliche Forschungen an Tempera-Gemälden aus buddhistischen Höhlen der ersten acht Jahrhunderte nach Christi Geburt* (Veröffentlichung der preussischen Turfan-Expeditionen mit Unterstützung der Bässler-Instituts). 1920, Pls. XLII-XLIII; II, pp.101-107; A. von Le Coq, *Bilderatlas zur Kunst und Kulturgeschichte Mittel-Asiens.* 1925, p.82, Fig. 157.

[219] O. Franke in SLR I, pp.229f.

[220] Aurel Stein, *Serindia, Detailed Report of Explorations in Central Asia and Westernmost China.* 1921, II, pp.791-894; and *The Thousand Buddhas, Ancient Buddhist Paintings from the Cave-Temples of Tun-huang on the Western Frontier of China.* 1921.

[221] Paul Pelliot, *Les Grottes de Touen-Houang, peintures et sculptures bouddhiques des époques des Wei, des T'ang et des Song* (Mission Pelliot en Asie Centrale). 6 vols. 1914-24.

some paintings on linen and on paper, and also a few specimens of embroidered pictures, were likewise found. For the importance of such pictures we may recall the illustrated cloth which we have just seen Varshakara holding up before King Ajataśatru in the wall painting at Kucha.

The Tunhwang paintings were probably hidden away soon after the close of the tenth century A.D., and the period of their execution is believed to have been the T'ang Period, seventh to tenth centuries A.D., when Chinese art reached great heights. In the style of the paintings Indian, Tibetan and Chinese traditions are recognizable, and in their subjects special prominence is given to various ones of the Bodhisattvas who are such important objects of devotion in Mahayana Buddhism.

Of all the Bodhisattvas the most beloved is Avalokiteśvara, the incarnation of Pity and the spiritual son of Amitabha, ruler of the blessed Western Paradise. Avalokiteśvara is known to the Chinese as Kwan-yin (and to the Japanese as Kwannon) and may appear in either male or female form.[222] In later art the female representation is almost universal, but at Tunhwang the male is still predominant. Next in popularity to Avalokiteśvara is Kshitigarbha, known in China as Ti-tsang (and in Japan as Jizo), and recognized as breaker of the powers of hell and illuminator of its darkness, and as patron of travelers. Other Bodhisattvas are Manjuśri, embodiment of the spirit of wisdom; Samantabhadra, representative of the power of the Church; Bhaishajyaraja, lord of medicine; and Maitreya, the Buddha who is yet to come. All of these are portrayed on the Tunhwang paintings, as well as Gautama Buddha himself, the Guardians of the Four Quarters of the World, and the blessed inhabitants of the Happy Land of Amitabha.

We select for illustration in Fig. 128 an attractive picture of the Bodhisattva Kshitigarbha as the Patron of Travelers.[223] The painting is on pale green silk, and the other chief colors are brownish red, yellow and black. The Bodhisattva is seated upon an open lotus and holds a pilgrim's staff in the right hand and a ball of crystal in the left. The head and shoulders are draped in a traveler's shawl. Below

---

[222] For the various forms of Avalokiteśvara, see Alice Getty, *The Gods of Northern Buddhism, Their History, Iconography and Progressive Evolution through the Northern Buddhist Countries.* 2d ed. 1928, pp.55-107. For Kwan-yin as the goddess of mercy and the most popular deity of China see Lewis Hodous, *Folkways in China* (Probsthain's Oriental Series, xviii). 1929, pp.68-74.

[223] Stein, *The Thousand Buddhas, Ancient Buddhist Paintings from the Cave-Temples of Tun-huang on the Western Frontier of China*, Pl. xl.

in the left corner is the figure of the donor of the painting. The whole atmosphere of the work is that of serene beatitude.

For one other illustration of Buddhist art in China we may continue to Wan Fo Hsia, three days' march east of Tunhwang, where a ninth century cave is adorned with wall paintings. One of these is pictured in Fig. 130. The scene is the Sukhavati or Western Paradise of Amitabha. Amitabha is seated in the center upon a throne which is on a platform built on piles over the Sukhavati Lake, and on either side is a Bodhisattva seated upon a lotus. The one on Amitabha's left is Avalokiteśvara, who holds a flask with lotus flowers; the one on his right is Mahasthamaprapta, who is his other customary attendant. Around each of the side figures are five smaller Bodhisattvas, while two kneeling figures present offerings at the throne of Amitabha. On the smaller pier in front of the throne platform an Apsaras is dancing to the accompaniment of seated musicians, while on either side at the front are terraces with seated Buddhas. Behind and above these various deities are the Palaces of Delight, with their verandas overlooking the lake.[224]

Tunhwang and Wan Fo Hsia of course bring us only barely within the frontiers of China and give us only early glimpses of Buddhism in that land. They do provide us, however, with the type of material which it is the primary purpose of this book to notice. Beyond that, to follow the expansion of Buddhism throughout China's vast reaches and to note the wealth of monuments which mark its later history there, would far exceed the necessary limits of the present chapter and is a task which cannot be undertaken here. This does not mean that the tremendous role played by Buddhism in the life of the Chinese people is to be minimized.[225]

KOREA

The geographical location of Korea made it the natural recipient of Buddhism from China and in turn the mediator of that faith to Japan. According to Korean legend the kingdom of Tjoson (Japanese, Chosen) was first founded prior to 2000 B.C. Throughout much

[224] Langdon Warner, *Buddhist Wall-Paintings, A Study of a Ninth-Century Grotto at Wan Fo Hsia* (Harvard-Radcliffe Fine Arts Series). 1938, Pl. XXIII. For the Sukhavati abode, cf. Franke in SLR I, pp.237f.

[225] MHR I, pp.79-92; Franke in SLR I, pp.229-247; GCE III, pp.176-278; Ernest J. Eitel, *Hand-book of Chinese Buddhism, Being a Sanskrit-Chinese Dictionary with Vocabularies of Buddhist Terms in Pali, Singhalese, Siamese, Burmese, Tibetan, Mongolian and Japanese.* 2d ed. 1888; D. Tokiwa and T. Sekino, *Buddhist Monuments in China.*

of the first millennium A.D. three kingdoms existed in the land. These were: Silla (Japanese, Shiragi), which was located in the southeast, had its capital at Kyongju (Keishu), and lasted from 57 B.C. to A.D. 935; Pekche (Kudara), which was in the southwest, and endured from 37 B.C. to A.D. 663; and Kokuryo (also called Kokurai, Kokuli or Kuma), which was in the north, had its capital at Pyongyang (Heijo), and existed from 17 B.C. to A.D. 668. From A.D. 918 to 1392 the whole land was ruled by the Koryo dynasty, with the capital at Songto (Kaesong or Kaijo). From Koryo (Japanese, Korai), meaning Land of Beautiful Mountains, comes the name "Korea." In 1392 the I (Yi) dynasty arose which ruled until modern times. Under this dynasty the capital was at Seoul (Kyongsong, Keijo), and the country was once more known as Tjoson, the Land of Morning Cool.

It was in the fourth century A.D., according to Korean traditions, that Buddhism was first introduced into the land.[226] In A.D. 369 a priest named Sundo is said to have come to the northern kingdom of Kokuryo from a small Chinese kingdom on the upper border of Korea bringing Buddhist idols and sacred texts. In A.D. 384 when the people of Pekche learned of the new faith which was being practiced in Kokuryo they asked the Emperor of China to send them a famous priest named Marananda, and he and other priests who soon followed from China spread the faith in the southwestern kingdom. Finally around A.D. 424 a priest from Pyongyang named Mukocha came to Silla and preached Buddhism to the southeastern kingdom.

The story is that Mukocha first hired himself out as a plowman to a farmer who concealed him upon occasion in a cave. Later in Kyongju the priest was able to accomplish the cure of the illness of the king's daughter by burning incense and offering prayer before a Buddhist image. Soon after that the king acceded to a request from Mukocha to bring artists from China to carve figures in the rock walls of his cave in order to make it into a chapel. In these labors the artists are said to have spent forty years.

For a single impressive monument of Buddhism in Korea we may speak of the Sokkulam or Temple of the Rock Cave not far southeast of Kyongju.[227] Some would identify this cave with that of Mukocha,

[226] Frederick Starr, *Korean Buddhism*. 1918, pp.4-11; Charles A. Clark, *Religions of Old Korea*. 1932, pp.27f.
[227] P. Andreas Eckardt, *Geschichte der koreanischen Kunst*. 1929, pp.48-51,106, 114-117.

but in certain ancient chronicles there is mention of the building of the Sokpulsa or Temple of the Rock-Buddha near Kyongju in the tenth year of King Kyongtokwang, and if this is to be identified with the Sokkulam it would date this work in A.D. 752.

The Sokkulam is constructed according to a remarkably symmetrical plan and is adorned with masterly reliefs and statues. The approach to the cave is flanked by life-sized granite figures of guardians of the Buddhist law, while the open entrance, over eleven feet wide, is protected by two carved doorkeepers. Next there is an antechamber with reliefs on both sides portraying the four kings of heaven, and beyond this there is a portal with massive columns and an arched beam through which access is gained to the innermost shrine or rotunda. Here the walls are lined with more granite relief slabs showing four Bodhisattvas and ten Arhats or Lohans, as the enlightened saints were known in Chinese, and, at the back of the rotunda, an eleven-headed Kwannon. On either side above the reliefs of the Bodhisattvas and Lohans are niches with small seated figures of Buddhas and Bodhisattvas. In the center of the rotunda on a high pedestal is a colossal and majestic statue of the Buddha as shown in Fig. 129.[228]

JAPAN

In the preceding section we have learned of the kingdom of Pekche in southwest Korea into which Buddhism was introduced from China in the latter part of the fourth century A.D. It was a king of Pekche who was instrumental in transmitting the faith to Japan. Under attacks from Kokuryo and Silla, Pekche turned to Japan for assistance and frequently received help from that source. In recognition of this aid and in hope of its continuation in the future, King Sungwang of Pekche sent emissaries to the court of Emperor Kimmei of Japan in the year A.D. 552. As the most valuable gifts he could present, the king of Pekche sent to his ally an image of the Buddha and certain Buddhist books.

For many years it was a question whether the new faith thus made known to Japan would be accepted or rejected. It was favored by the influential Soga family, but opposed by the conservative families of Mononobe and Nakatomi. After protracted controversy the opposition was at last overcome in an actual battle in A.D. 588 and Buddhism was free to spread unhindered. In the same year another mis-

[228] *ibid.*, Fig. 178.

sion from Pekche brought monks and also expert builders, including temple architects, tilers, a caster of pagoda spires and a painter, to Japan. It was no doubt with their assistance that the first large Buddhist monasteries were erected, the Shitennoji in Osaka, and the Hokoji in Asuka. Of this introduction of Buddhist architecture into Japan in the last quarter of the sixth century A.D. it has been said that it "was at the same time a first introduction to monumental architecture in general. More than this, it was the beginning of Japanese architectural history."[229]

The earliest monastery of which the buildings remain substantially intact today is the Horyuji near Nara. The first completion of Horyuji is dated by an inscription in A.D. 607, and the majority of important structures still standing date either from that time or from a rebuilding sometime within the following century. As revealed at Horyuji the nucleus of a monastery of this period was a group of buildings enclosed in a four-sided walled colonnade (Horo). Entrance was through a middle gate (Chumon) on one side of the rectangle, and within were two chief structures, a pagoda or To, and a Buddha hall or Kondo, the last name literally meaning a "golden" hall. Other buildings in the entire complex must have included an assembly hall, dining hall and sleeping quarters. A photograph of the nucleus of original buildings at Horyuji taken from the inner courtyard is shown in Fig. 131. The Golden Hall is at the left, the Pagoda at the right, and the Middle Gate in the center at the back.[230]

From the sculptures which crowd the Golden Hall we show in Fig. 132 a group in bronze, once covered with gold, which was probably executed in the first quarter of the seventh century A.D. by the famous sculptor Kuratsukuri no Obito Tori. Sakyamuni is seated in the center, with his robes descending in wide-spreading folds. On either side stands an attendant Bodhisattva, while behind the heads are enormous nimbuses with a decoration of flames.[231]

The Golden Hall is also splendidly decorated with wall paintings which probably date from the beginning of the eighth century,[232] Their style reveals a tradition derived from Ajanta (particularly

---

[229] Alexander C. Soper, *The Evolution of Buddhist Architecture in Japan* (Princeton Monographs in Art and Archaeology, xxii). 1942, p.5.

[230] *ibid.*, pp.23f.,297, Fig. 5.

[231] Cohn, *Buddha in der Kunst des Ostens*, p.101; Karl With, *Buddhistische Plastik in Japan bis in den Beginn des 8. Jahrhunderts n. Chr.* 2 vols. 1919, pp.33-42.

[232] Naitō Tōichirō, *The Wall-Paintings of Hōryūji.* tr. and ed. by William R. B. Acker and Benjamin Rowland, Jr. (American Council of Learned Societies Studies in Chinese and Related Civilizations, 5). 1943, pp.289f.

Cave I), by way of Kucha and Tunhwang, and after Ajanta these paintings are regarded as the greatest masterpieces of the Buddhist world.[233] The pictures at Horyuji include four paradise scenes on four large wall sections and eight Bodhisattvas on eight small wall sections. The four paradises are the realms in which four great Buddhas reside and into which they receive faithful believers.[234] In each of the four scenes the respective Buddha is seated in the center surrounded by Bodhisattvas, saints and disciples, while celestial beings, clouds and flowers also adorn the picture. The painting reproduced in Fig. 133 is from the large east wall section and represents the Paradise of Shaka (Sakyamuni).[235] The Bodhisattvas who stand on either side of the Buddha are portrayed in the Indian style, as may be seen for example by comparing the head of the Bodhisattva at Sakyamuni's right with the head of the Bodhisattva Padmapani in Cave I at Ajanta and noting that the treatment of such a detail as the eyebrows is absolutely identical. While in his compassion the Bodhisattva at Ajanta bends near to humanity, the Bodhisattvas of Horyuji retain a transcendental detachment even though they too are the incarnation of refuge and salvation.

As in China, so too in Japan the necessary concentration of our attention upon only a very few of the earliest monuments must not be taken to minimize the importance of the long history and wide spread of the Buddhist faith in the land. In Japan no less than a dozen sects of Buddhism arose, or thirty if subsects be counted. Of these six attained the greatest importance: Tendai, Shingon, Zen, Jodo, Shin, and Nichiren. To study them, however, and to catalogue later objects of Buddhist art in Japan would lead far beyond the limits necessarily imposed upon the present chapter.[236] That which has been recorded here provides at all events at least a glimpse of the introduction of the faith into the land in which it still plays an important part in the lives of the inhabitants.

TIBET

Finally a word will be said concerning Tibet, where the prevailing

[233] GCE IV, p.56.

[234] M. Anesaki, *Buddhist Art in Its Relation to Buddhist Ideals with Special Reference to Buddhism in Japan*. 1915, p.15.

[235] Naitō, *The Wall-Paintings of Hōryūji*, pp.127f., Pl. 5.

[236] MHR I, pp.115-141; K. Florenz in SLR I, pp.348-422; GCE IV, pp.15ff.; Daisetz Teitaro Suzuki, *Zen Buddhism and Its Influence on Japanese Culture* (The Ataka Buddhist Library, 9). 1938; Anesaki, *Buddhist Art in Its Relation to Buddhist Ideals with Special Reference to Buddhism in Japan*.

religion of Lamaism represents an amalgamation of elements from the aboriginal demonistic animism called Bon with the later intro- duced Buddhism.[237] The Buddhist faith was brought to Tibet during the reign and through the leadership of King Srong-btsan-sgam-po who reigned from about A.D. 630 to 650. This important king who made Lhasa the capital of his realm, married both a Nepalese and a Chinese princess and thus symbolized the relationship of his country with its neighbors on both sides, a relationship which was clearly influential in the development of Tibetan Buddhist art.

In the eighth century a celebrated Indian monk named Padma- sambhava was brought to Tibet from Magadha. He taught Buddhism in a strongly Tantric form which was full of sorcery and magic, and was similar to Śaivite Hinduism in the worship of the Śaktis or femi- nine principles of the gods. Such teachings were widely acceptable in a land long accustomed to demonolatry, and were never entirely eliminated despite the later reforms of such monks as Atiśa (eleventh century) and Tsong-kha-pa (A.D. 1357-1419) through whom the an- cient "Red" sects were partially suppressed and the "Yellow" church established as the dominant ecclesiastical organization.

The spiritual successors of Tsong-kha-pa were the Dalai Lamas who were able to establish a kind of papacy which had its center at Lhasa and which ruled both church and state. All the more ex- alted members of the hierarchy were called lamas or "superior per- sons," and were regarded as earthly manifestations of higher powers, while the Dalai Lama was considered the incarnation of no less a being than Avalokiteśvara.

Tibetan art finds its chief expressions in the architecture of palaces, temples, monasteries, and stupas which are known as Chortens; in sculpture, much of which is in bronze; and in painting, which is largely directed toward the production of votive banners for the temples. While most of the painted banners which are known date only from the eighteenth century or later, the painters have usually worked under the strictest requirements for the exact reproduction of earlier designs and hence the scenes themselves may be regarded

[237] J. E. Ellam, *The Religion of Tibet, A Study of Lamaism* (The Wisdom of the East Series). 1927; W. Y. Evans-Wentz, *The Tibetan Book of the Dead or the After- Death Experiences on the Bardo Plane, According to Lama Kazi Dawa-Samdup's English Rendering.* 1927; and *Tibetan Yoga and Secret Doctrines or Seven Books of Wisdom of the Great Path, According to the Late Lāma Kazi Dawa-Samdup's English Rendering, Arranged and Edited with Introductions and Annotations to Serve as a Commentary.* 1935; Li An-che in *Journal of the Royal Asiatic Society of Great Britain and Ireland.* 1948, pp.142-163; and in Ferm, ed., *Forgotten Religions,* pp.253-269.

as of much greater antiquity. The subjects include events in the life of Gautama Buddha or portraits of the latter with other scenes grouped around him; representations of other Buddhas, tutelary deities (Yi-dams), Bodhisattvas, female deities among whom the most important is the Śakti of Avalokiteśvara named Tara, and Guardians of the Religion (Dharmapalas) who are demons of terrifying aspect; pictures of local saints and heroes such as Padmasambhava; and scenes of Tantric character employing a symbolism based on terror and mystic sensuality.[238]

In the painting shown in Fig. 134 the central place is occupied by Gautama Buddha. Standing below his ornate throne are his two most eminent disciples, Sariputta and Moggalana. At the top are three tutelary deities, Sang-dui, the Master of Secrets; Yamantaka, the Conqueror of Yama, the Lord of Death; and Samvara, or Best Happiness. Beneath the throne the personage riding on the lion is Kubera, who is the Lord of Riches and one of the Defenders of the Faith. At the bottom the two elephant-headed figures are two forms of Ganeśa. The remaining scenes illustrate events in the life of Gautama. Reading up from the bottom at the left, across, and down the right side, they depict: (1) Buddha in the Tushita heaven, waiting to descend to earth in the shape of a white elephant; (2) the dream of Maya; (3) the birth of Gautama; (4) his marriage and life in the pleasure palace; (5) his leaving home; (6) the cutting of his hair; (7) his life as an ascetic; (8) his preaching to the Nagas; (9) the temptation by Mara; (10) the enlightenment; (11) the first preaching; and (12) the entrance into Nirvana.

The painting reproduced in Fig. 135 is a *mandala* or ritual diagram which is used in making invocations to the deities. Here the central figure is Amitayus, the Buddha of Infinite Life, surrounded by eight facsimiles of himself. Around the outer rim of the large circle are the Eight Emblems and the Seven Jewels of Buddhism. The Eight, along the upper edge of the circle, are the umbrella, conch, covered vase, canopy, two fish, lotus, endless knot, and wheel of the law; the Seven, below, are the jewel, wheel, wife, elephant, horse, minister, and military leader. Across the top of the painting are Sitatapatra, Manjuśri, Amitabha, Sadakshari, and Ushnishavijaya; and across the bottom are Jambhala, Sitajambhala, Hayagriva, Kalajambhala, and Vasudhara.[239]

[238] GCE IV, pp.264-300; W. J. G. Van Meurs, *Tibetaansche Tempelschilderingen.* Eng. tr. May Hollander. 1924; George Roerich, *Tibetan Paintings.* 1925.
[239] Antoinette K. Gordon, *The Iconography of Tibetan Lamaism.* 1939, pp.27f.

CHAPTER VI

Confucianism

CHINA is a vast land stretching back from its four thousand miles of Pacific coast line to the remote plateaus and deserts of Tibet, Sinkiang and Mongolia.[1] Between the ocean and the outlying regions, three great river valleys mark out the three major areas of China proper. These are the basins of the Hwang, Yangtze, and Si, in north, central, and south China respectively. The Hwang Ho originates among the western mountains and flows approximately twenty-five hundred miles to empty into the Yellow Sea. The name of the stream literally means Yellow River and is derived from the valuable loess or yellow earth with which its waters are so heavily laden.[2] Sometimes swift and again shallow and meandering, and in its lower reaches often altering its course, the Hwang has been of little value for commerce but has often devastated the land with terrible floods. The Yangtze Kiang rises in the high country between Tibet and Sinkiang, and has a course estimated at over three thousand miles in length before it pours into the sea not far from Shanghai. Known also as Ch'ang Kiang (Long River) or Ta Kiang (Great River), this river is navigable for sixteen hundred miles above its mouth, and provides China's chief natural artery of commerce. The Si Kiang starts on the plateau of Yunnan and flows east and south for some twelve hundred and fifty miles to enter the South China Sea not far from Hong Kong. It, too, is of major commercial importance.[3]

There are eighteen provinces[4] in the region of the three river valleys just described, and although they occupy only about two-fifths of the entire area of the country they contain the bulk of its population or over four hundred million persons. When the estimated number of inhabitants in the outlying provinces and sections is also added in, the grand total is nearer five hundred million.[5]

[1] Albert Herrmann, *Historical and Commercial Atlas of China* (Harvard-Yenching Institute Monograph Series, 1). 1935.
[2] Henri Maspero, *The Origins of the Chinese Civilization* (from the Smithsonian Report for 1927, pp.433-452). Publication 2946. 1928, p.443.
[3] H. G. W. Woodhead, *The China Year Book 1929-30*, pp.12-26.
[4] Anhwei, Chekiang, Fukien, Honan, Hopeh, Hunan, Hupeh, Kansu, Kiangsi, Kiangsu, Kwangsi, Kwangtung, Kweichow, Shansi, Shantung, Shensi, Szechwan, Yunnan.
[5] *China Handbook 1937-1943.* 1943, p.2.

1. THE BEGINNINGS OF CULTURE IN CHINA

THE life of man in the region of China began in the Paleolithic Age as we know from the discovery of skeletal remains of *Sinanthropus pekinensis* near Chou K'ou Tien (p.25), and it is thought possible that the modern Chinese are directly descended from these remote ancestors.[6]

THE NEOLITHIC AGE

In the Neolithic Age the remains of human life and culture are more abundant.[7] Like the Paleolithic site at Chou K'ou Tien, the Neolithic sites now known are for the most part in the great basin of the Hwang Ho.[8] They reveal a culture which in general was similar to that of other Neolithic peoples elsewhere in the world. That is to say, the men of this age practiced agriculture as well as hunting and fishing, they made weapons and tools of polished stone, and they manufactured much pottery.

The first discovery of a settlement of this period was made by J. G. Andersson in 1921 near Yang Shao Ts'un in western Honan.[9] The oldest pottery at this place was a coarse, gray ware, with simple designs which had been pressed into the wet clay. Typical shapes included pots with pointed bottoms, and two kinds of "tripod" pots. The first of the tripod vessels is technically known as a *li*. This has three hollow, bulging legs, and it is surmised that it originated from leaning three pots with pointed bottoms together over the fire, and then later merging these in one vessel. The second tripod, known as a *ting*, is simply a bowl supported on three relatively thin, solid legs. It may also have originated in two stages from placing a clay vessel on three stones, and then replacing the stones with attached clay legs. While vessels more or less like the *ting* may also be found in other lands, the *li* seems to be a peculiarly characteristic invention of the Chinese area. Vessels are still made in both of these shapes in China today. Examples of the two typical forms from the Yang Shao

[6] J. Gunnar Andersson, *Children of the Yellow Earth, Studies in Prehistoric China.* 1934, pp.94-126; Franz Weidenreich in *Bulletin of the Geological Society of China.* 14 (1935), pp.438,458.

[7] CBC pp.43-51; CSECC pp.170-218.

[8] The present mouth of the Hwang Ho is very recent, and anciently this river flowed into the Po Hai (Gulf of Chihli) after passing between the sites of modern Tientsin and Peiping.

[9] J. G. Andersson in *Bulletin of the Museum of Far Eastern Antiquities* (*Östasiatiska Samlingarna*), Stockholm. 19 (1947), pp.1-124.

culture are shown in Fig. 136 with the *li* on the left and the *ting* on the right.[10]

A later pottery likewise found at Yang Shao Ts'un and related sites is of much finer quality than the coarse ware just mentioned, and is also much advanced in its decoration. This is a painted pottery with attractive designs in various colors. Several of the sherds unearthed at Yang Shao Ts'un illustrate its character in Fig. 137.[11] Similar pottery has also been found abundantly at sites out in the province of Kansu, and mortuary urns from that region are pictured in Fig. 138.[12] This geographical distribution of the finds suggests that the Yang Shao painted pottery may have been an introduction into China from somewhere in the west. The time when the Yang Shao culture flourished has not yet been determined with any accuracy. Dates suggested for it range all the way from early in the third millennium to early in the second millennium B.C.[13]

Yet a third type of Neolithic pottery represents still further technical advance. It is a very fine ware, made on a wheel, and finished with a glossy black surface. This was found first at Ch'eng Tzu Yai in Lung Shan Hsien, where excavations were conducted in 1930 and 1931 by the National Research Institute of History and Philology. Along with the black pottery were found other wares in white, pink, red and brown. This Lung Shan culture appears to have been simply an outgrowth of the Yang Shao culture, and the direct line of development is indicated by the continued and frequent occurrence of the *li* and *ting* types of vessels. The people of Ch'eng Tzu Yai, it may be added, lived in a large rectangular city, surrounded by walls of pounded earth more than thirty feet wide at the base and still standing in places to a height of ten feet.

THE HSIA DYNASTY

From many similarities, not the least of which are the common use of the "tripod" vessels and of the technique of building with pounded earth, the Neolithic cultures just dealt with and the Shang civilization shortly to be described may be regarded as standing in a continuous line of evolution. The question has not been solved, however,

[10] Andersson, *Children of the Yellow Earth*, pp.218-223, Pl. 21.

[11] T. J. Arne in *Palaeontologia Sinica* (Geological Survey of China). Ser. D, I, 2 (1925), Pl. III.

[12] Nils Palmgren in *Palaeontologia Sinica*. Ser. D, III, 1 (1934), Pl. XXXVI.

[13] Oswald Menghin, *Weltgeschichte der Steinzeit*. 1931, p.81; cf. Ssu Yung Liang, *New Stone Age Pottery from the Prehistoric Site at Hsi-yin Tsun, Shansi, China* (Memoirs of the American Anthropological Association, 37). 1930, p.75.

as to where the Hsia dynasty belongs in this development. This is a dynasty spoken of in Chinese literary traditions as preceding the Shang dynasty. It has not yet been possible to substantiate the existence of such a dynasty by archeological discoveries, and so it may be surmised that the Hsia kings were little more than the headmen of some of the Neolithic villages and towns. Perhaps they were able to form some sort of a state, but it does not appear that they constituted a dynasty in the usual sense of the word. The traditions suggest that if such a state existed its location was in the region of the lower Hwang Ho valley.[14]

The literary sources also profess to provide us with dates for the Hsia dynasty. The traditional chronology of ancient China, it may be explained, is based upon a table found in the second part of the twenty-first chapter of the Ch'ien Han Shu, or History of the Former Han Dynasty, written by Pan Ku who died in A.D. 92.[15] Another chronology is given in the Chu Shu Chi Nien, or Annals of the Bamboo Books, a work which was found in a tomb in A.D. 280 or 281 and is believed to have been compiled in the state of Wei in the early part of the third century B.C.[16] Yet a third chronological system is based upon a critical reconstruction of the text of the Bamboo Books just mentioned, made by Wang Kuo-wei.[17] All of the authorities are in general agreement concerning the dating of events from 841 B.C. on, but the farther one goes back of that date the more there is divergence. Thus the Hsia dynasty is dated 2205-1765 B.C. in the traditional chronology; 1989-1558 B.C. in the system of the Bamboo Books in their current text; and 1994-1523 B.C. in the scheme based upon a reconstitution of the supposed ancient text of the Bamboo Books.

[14] CSECC pp.97-131.

[15] For the traditional chronology see Mathias Tchang, *Synchronismes chinois, Chronologie complète et concordance avec l'ère chrétienne de toutes les dates concernant l'histoire de l'Extrême-Orient (Chine, Japon, Corée, Annam, Mongolie, etc.) (2357 av. J.-C.–1904 apr. J.-C.)* (Variétés sinologiques, 24). 1905.

[16] On the chronology in the Bamboo Books see C. W. Bishop in JAOS 52 (1932), pp.232-247.

[17] For these dates reduced to terms of the Christian era, see CSECC, p.xvii.

2. THE SHANG PERIOD

Out of the prehistoric cultures glimpsed by archeology as thus far indicated, emerged the first historic Chinese civilization, that of the Shang Period. In the traditional chronology the Shang dynasty is dated 1765-1122 B.C.; in the chronology of the current text of the Bamboo Books it is placed at 1558-1050 B.C.; and in the chronology of the revised text of the Bamboo Books it is 1523-1027 B.C.

According to later literary tradition, the founder of the Shang dynasty was a hero called T'ang. In the T'ang Shih, probably written in the Chou Period, he is pictured as a vassal of the last Hsia king, who rose up in rebellion against the latter because of the wickedness of his reign. "It is not I, the little child," T'ang is reported to have said, "who dare to undertake a rebellious enterprise; but for the many crimes of the sovereign of Hsia, Heaven has given the charge to destroy him. . . . The sovereign of Hsia is guilty, and, as I fear God, I dare not but punish him."[18]

In the time of a later Shang king named P'an Keng it is possible to correlate the traditional history with actual archeological discovery. P'an Keng ruled from 1401 to 1374 B.C. according to the traditional chronology (or 1315-1288 B.C. according to the Bamboo Books), and is said to have moved his people to a new capital city. The move is narrated in a literary work called the P'an Keng, in which we read of this king, "P'an Keng wished to remove [the capital] to Yin."[19] This document probably dates from the Chou Period, in which time the ancient Shang capital evidently was known as Yin. Another later writing, the Hsiang Yü Pen Chi of the Shih Chi, indicates the location of the city by stating that certain events transpired "on the site of the ruins of Yin, south of the Huan River."[20]

ANYANG

The geographical position just indicated agrees with that of an ancient city excavated since 1928 at Anyang in northern Honan. The excavations have been done by the National Research Institute of History and Philology in collaboration with the Freer Gallery of Art, and there can be little doubt that the result is the rediscovery of the one-time capital of P'an Keng. From inscriptions on oracle bones

[18] Shu King IV, i. SBE III, p.85.
[19] Shu King IV, vii, 1. SBE III, p.104.
[20] Shih Chi VII, 10b. Quoted in CSECC p.64.

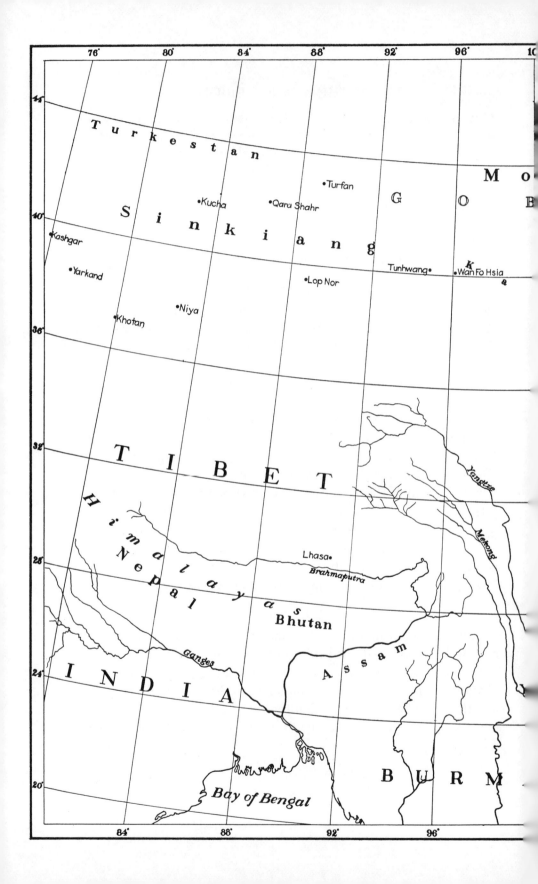

MAP 7
CHINA

0 50 100 200 300

Scale of miles

found there and shortly to be described in more detail, we learn that the ancient name of the place was "the great city Shang."[21]

The city was on a level plain, and utilized a bend in the river for natural protection. Probably there were also earthen walls, but the remains of these have not yet been found. The houses and buildings of the city were constructed with foundations of pounded earth and superstructures of wood. The roofs seem to have been gabled, and to have been supported on three rows of pillars. The base of each pillar was usually set upon a large rock, sunk into the earthen foundation platform. The wooden portions of these buildings have of course vanished almost entirely, but the foundation terraces and pillar bases remain to show their outlines clearly. The structural principles, it may be added, are essentially the same as those of modern Chinese houses, save that now the middle row of supports for the roof no longer comes down to the floor as pillars but rests upon horizontal beams supported by the side pillars. Interestingly enough, one of the characters in the inscriptions on the oracle bones is 　　 and this is probably a pictograph of one of the large buildings, perhaps a temple, seen from the end.[22]

While the people of the Great City Shang still practiced hunting, they also possessed domesticated animals including cattle and horses, and their principal source of livelihood was agriculture. In the realm of ceramics, the Shang people made a white pottery which seems to have been directly descended from the white pottery of the Lung Shan culture. While the Lung Shan ware was left a plain white, however, the Shang pottery was adorned with an elaborate ornamentation. The fundamental pattern in this decoration is technically known as the angular volute or meander. Sometimes this is worked out in purely geometrical designs, but again it takes on a theriomorphous character, that is, it represents animals or at least suggests them in a highly stylized way. An illustration may be seen in Fig. 139 where a white pottery amphora, now in the Freer Gallery, Washington, D.C., is shown. The decoration around the body of the jar is geometrical but in the frieze about the neck the motif of an eye with bands going off from it on either side is introduced.

RITUAL BRONZES

In the excavations at Anyang many objects of bronze were brought to light, and other bronzes of comparable character and date are

[21] CSECC p.65.　　　　　　　　　　[22] CBC pp.62,67.

known from many other sources. Thus it is shown that the people of the Shang Period had already made the very important transition from the Stone Age to the Bronze Age. As far as we know, the Lung Shan culture was the direct predecessor of the Shang civilization, and in the strata representing that culture at Ch'eng Tzu Yai and elsewhere, no metal whatsoever was found. In the Shang Period, immediately following, bronze was well known, and bronze casting was practiced with a technique equal to the best that can be done today. This suggests the hypothesis that the art of bronze working had been introduced into China from the outside and at a relatively advanced stage of development. Even if the Shang people derived this art from others, however, there is no question that they themselves raised it to very great heights. Indeed it is generally recognized that Shang bronzes are of a distinctive excellence which is unsurpassed and has seldom even been attained anywhere else in the world.[23]

The bronze objects of the Shang Period include weapons, tools, ornaments, helmets and chariot-fittings, but most important are the many vessels known as ritual bronzes.[24] These vessels were cast in a variety of shapes. Among them we recognize at once the bowl supported on three legs, which was familiar as a clay vessel in Yang Shao times and has now been translated into bronze. It appears in the form of a *li*, a *ting*, and also a *li-ting* where the two types of tripods have been combined. Similar to the *ting* is the *chia*, also a three-legged bowl but with a pair of short, capped columns on the rim to facilitate its removal from the fire. The *ting* now also may have handles on the rim, and both the *ting* and the *chia* are sometimes found with four legs rather than three. Another three-legged vessel is the *chüeh*, the bowl of which looks like an inverted helmet, and which has a handle and a spout as well as the capped columns on the rim. The *hsien* is a steamer made out of a *li* with a large pot on top of the tripod. The *p'ou* is a round container with sloping shoulders and a body which gives the appearance of sagging. The *lei* is a large *p'ou*, and the *kuei* looks like the same vessel with a very wide mouth. The *ku* is a tall vase shaped like a trumpet; and the *tsun* is a large vase of more ordinary form and much stouter than the *ku*. The *yu* is a potlike container with a cover, and often with a handle.

In the decoration of the Shang bronzes the first main style was

---

[23] CSECC pp.220-234; CBC pp.108-125.
[24] Phyllis Ackerman, *Ritual Bronzes of Ancient China.* 1945; Charles F. Kelley and Ch'en Meng-Chia, *Chinese Bronzes from the Buckingham Collection.* 1946.

adornment with incised representations, the grooves of which were probably filled originally with red or black pigment. The prevailing motifs were much the same as those already noted on the Shang white pottery. For an illustration we show in Fig. 140 an early Shang *ting*, which may be compared with the pottery amphora in Fig. 139. The body of the bowl carries a complex meander pattern, and under the rim is the same arrangement of lines on either side of an eye as was found on the amphora. In some cases there are naturalistic representations of animals, for example of frogs or fish, on the bronzes, but more often it is the highly conventionalized figures which prevail. These may include combinations of various animals, real and imaginary; often the conceptions are so very abstract that if it were not for the eyes they might be taken for purely geometric patterns.

A very characteristic representation shows a monster with one head and two bodies, or, otherwise expressed, with a severed body the two halves of which are laid out symmetrically on either side. To this figure it has become customary to give the name *t'ao-t'ieh* meaning "ogre mask." Such a *t'ao-t'ieh* may be seen on the body of the fine *tsun* pictured in Fig. 141. On the same vessel there are dragons on the foot, other animals and raised heads on the shoulder, serpents on the neck, and standing triangles on the outside of the mouth. Small notched flanges delimit the main areas of decoration.

The second main style of decoration employed the same theriomorphic motifs but rendered them in bold relief. A fine example may be seen in the *yu* pictured in Fig. 142. As usual, the *t'ao-t'ieh* occupies the most prominent position. Specially notable are the curved horns of the monster, with pointed tips turned upward. The flanges on the vessel are very pronounced and serve to emphasize its structure.

To what use were these vessels put? It is possible that some of them were employed for ordinary household purposes, but as their customary designation, "ritual bronzes," implies, it is believed that for the most part they were intended for religious purposes. Already at this time, as so persistently thereafter, the Chinese people seem to have worshiped the spirits of the elements and of their ancestors. To do proper reverence to these spirits was deemed of great importance, and customary practices included the making of offerings of food and drink. The ritual bronzes, according to the most probable interpretation of their character, were the necessary vessels for use in these ceremonies. Thus, for example, a jug like the *yu* may have held the sacrificial wine; a bowl like the *ting* may have contained an offering of food or liquid; a cup like the *chüeh* may have been used to pour out a libation; and a beaker such as the *ku* may have been employed to drink from in symbolical communion with the deities.

That such an interpretation is not entirely hypothetical is shown by the inscriptions which are frequently found on the bronzes. These may say, for example, "For Father Ting"; or again they may express the wish that sons and grandsons may value and employ the vessels for ten thousand years. This is clear proof that such objects were used in the ancestor cult. While most of the bronzes now known came from tombs, it is surmised that many of them were kept in ancestral temples before they were placed in the graves.[25]

What then was the significance of the decoration on the bronzes? It must have had an ornamental purpose, of course, as we recognize in the very fact of calling it decoration. But the persistent appearance of the many fantastic creatures including the *t'ao-t'ieh* suggests some deeper meaning as well. The character of the figures is scarcely such as to justify their identification with the elemental and ancestral spirits to whom the cult worship was chiefly addressed. Indeed, as far as we otherwise know, there was no tendency at this time to portray the deities in either animal or human form. Rather, the nature of the forms makes us think that they are intended for demons, and in that case the primary purpose of placing them on the sacred vessels must have been to ward off evil and safeguard the consecrated contents. When we also recall the geometrical but elusive manner of the portrayal, in which the component parts of the creatures are so placed that an animal form seems to materialize before our eyes and then almost dissolve again into purely angular patterns, we may go further and say with MM. Charles Vignier and René Grousset that the decorations convey a "haunting suggestion" of "that omnipresent mystery which was always ready to resolve itself into terror." Thus "the Chinese race was already uncompromisingly practical, though intensely impregnated with a sense of mystery."[26]

ORACLE BONES

The Shang Period not only marks the transition from the epoch of stone to that of bronze, but also from the era of illiteracy to that

[25] Ludwig Bachhofer, *A Short History of Chinese Art.* 1946, pp.28f.

[26] GCE III, pp.31-33. Quoted by permission of the publisher, Alfred A. Knopf, Inc., New York and London. See also Carl Hentze, *Objets rituels, croyances et dieux de la Chine antique et de l'Amérique.* 1936, pp.101f.

of writing. Our knowledge of this last fact is based upon the famous oracle bones which have come to light in the vicinity of Anyang.[27] These are pieces of oxbone, and also of tortoise shell, which were employed for purposes of divination, and on some of which inscriptions are found. Many of them are from the reign of Wu Ting, who ruled at Anyang from 1324 to 1266 b.c. according to the traditional chronology; others may go back to the time of P'an Keng. A group of the inscribed bones is shown in Fig. 143, although the specimen in the upper left-hand corner is an example of a forged inscription in imitation of the ancient ones. These inscriptions provide us with the earliest known examples of Chinese writing, and it is interesting to learn that all of the important principles in the formation of modern Chinese characters were already employed, at least to some extent, at that time. More than two thousand different characters appear upon the oracle bones as now known.

The use to which the bones were put is of significance for our study. As already intimated, they were employed as a means of obtaining the counsel of the deities and the ancestral spirits in answer to questions. The essential part of the method consisted in the application of heat to the bone or shell, thus producing a T-shaped crack, the specific character of which was interpreted as giving either an affirmative or a negative answer.

Occasionally, say about one time in ten to judge from the examples at hand, the question to which an answer was sought was actually written out on the bone. The question was often as simple as, "Will it rain tonight?" and on one bone where this interrogation was recorded there was also a later notation, "It really didn't rain." Other queries concerned sacrifices, trips, wars, hunting, farming, illness and all kinds of miscellaneous subjects.

From the inscriptions additional information has been derived concerning the deities worshiped at this time. Most important, of course, were the spirits of ancestors, sometimes going back for many generations. Then there were the elemental spirits such as of the earth, of the wind, of a river, of east, west and south, of below and above [of earth and heaven?]. Yet other deities were named the Dragon Woman, the Eastern Mother, the Western Mother, and Ti or Shang Ti. The last named, Ti or Shang Ti, is of obscure character at this time, though connected in the inscriptions with such things as war,

[27] cbc pp.21-26,158-173, 185-196,205-210, Pl. i; csecc pp.33-42; F. H. Chalfant and R. S. Britton, *Seven Collections of Inscribed Oracle Bone.* 1938; *The Hopkins Collection of Inscribed Oracle Bone.* 1939.

136. Pottery of the Yang Shao Culture: A Li and a Ting

137. Sherds of Painted Pottery from Yang Shao Ts'un

139. White Pottery Amphora of the Shang Period

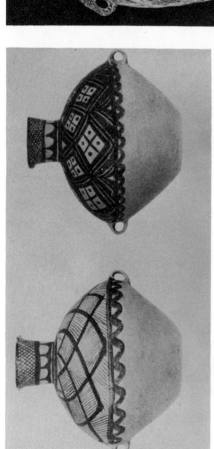
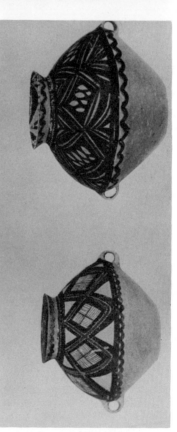

138. Painted Mortuary Urns of the Yang Shao Period, from Kansu

140. An Early Bronze Ting
of the Shang Period

141. A Bronze Tsun of the Shang Period

142. A Bronze Yu of the Shang Period

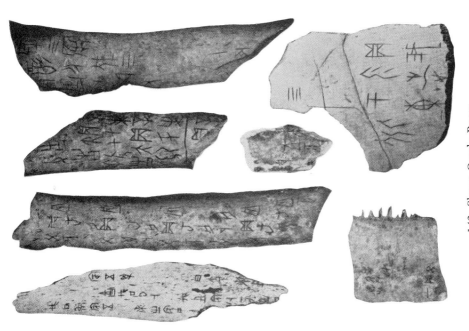

144. A Shang Ceremonial Bronze Ax

143. Shang Oracle Bones

145. A Bronze Kuei of the Western Chou Period

146. A Bronze Pilgrim's Bottle in the Huai Style

148. Bronze Winged Dragon of Late Chou Period

147. Bronze Statuette
of a Kneeling Servant

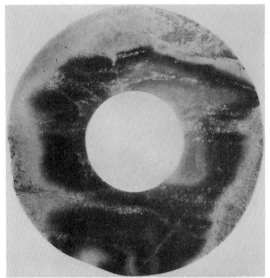

149. Jade Pi of
the Chou Period

151. Human Figure in
Jade, Chou Period

150. Jade Ts'ung
of the Chou Period

152. The Tomb of Confucius at Chufou

153. The Tumulus of Shih Huang Ti near Si-an

154. The Great Wall of China

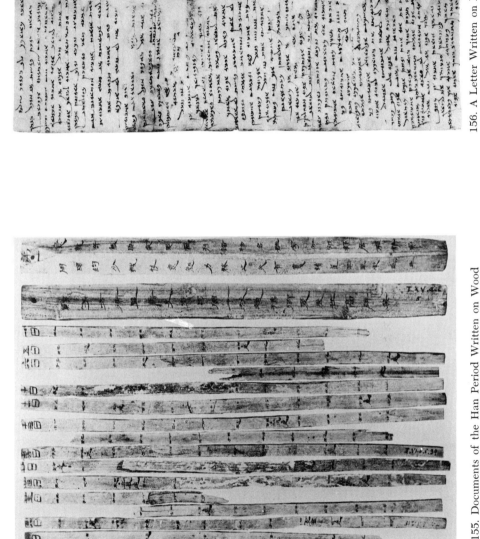

155. Documents of the Han Period Written on Wood

156. A Letter Written on Paper, from the Han Period

157. Painted Pottery Vessel of the Han Period

158. Stone Horse in Front of the Tomb of Ho Ch'ü-ping

160. Wu Liang Tz'u Relief with Scenes from History and Mythology

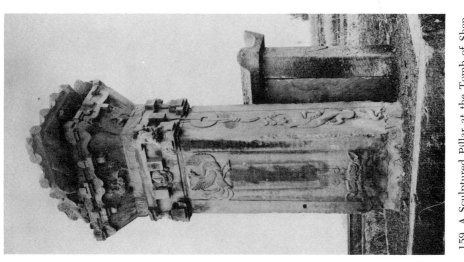

159. A Sculptured Pillar at the Tomb of Shen

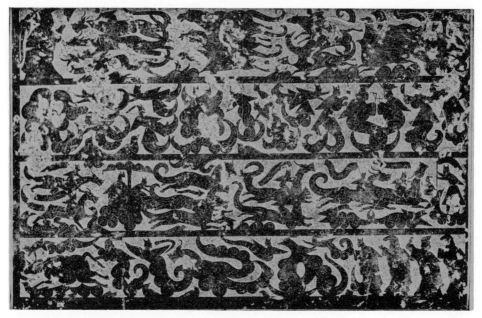

161. Wu Liang Tz'u
Relief Showing the
Kingdom of the Air

162. Colossal Monster
of the Period of the
Six Dynasties

163. Tomb Figures of the Six Dynasties Period

164. The Cross on the
Nestorian Monument

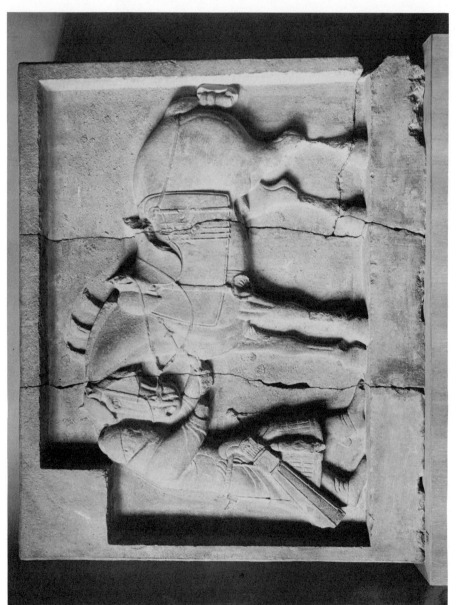

165. War Horse of the Emperor T'ai Tsung

166. Scene in the T'ang Copy of the Roll of Ku K'ai-chi

167. Tomb Figures of the T'ang Period

168. Sung Painting of Scholars Collating Classic Texts

rain, and fortune or misfortune in general. Later this god was to attain great importance.

The oracle bone inscriptions seem also to mention human sacrifice, and the discovery of mass burials of decapitated persons at Anyang is taken to substantiate the existence of this practice. The pictograph on the oracle bones which is interpreted as sometimes signifying human sacrifice (and again, attack as in war), is clearly that of a man who is laying the blade of a dagger-ax across the neck of another. This pictograph may be seen on the oracle bone in the upper right-hand corner of Fig. 143. It also appears at the top of the left side of the Shang bronze ax in Fig. 144. On the same instrument at the right is the picture of a *hsien* or steamer, which is used in the bone inscriptions with the meaning "to sacrifice." It is supposed therefore that this ax was a ceremonial weapon used for such sacrifices.

The inscriptions furthermore testify to the existence in their time of written books. They employ a pictograph meaning "book," and showing several vertical lines joined by a loop. The vertical lines represent strips of wood or bamboo, and the loop is the cord with which these were tied together. Books made in exactly this fashion, with each wooden strip containing a column of characters running from top to bottom, and the whole resembling a miniature picket fence, are known from the Han Period, but all those of the ancient Shang Period have doubtless long since perished.

3. THE CHOU PERIOD

THE Shang Period came to an end and the Chou Period was inaugurated in 1122 B.C. according to the traditional chronology; or 1050 B.C. according to the figures given in the Bamboo Books; or 1027 B.C. according to the revised scheme growing out of the critical reconstruction of the text of the Bamboo Books. It is possible but not certain that the Shang capital had remained at Anyang (Yin) until the end. The genuine text of the Bamboo Books states: "From the time when P'an Keng moved to Yin down to the fall of Chou [the last Shang king] . . . the capital was not again moved."[28] Supporting this statement in part is the fact of the existence of inscribed oracle bones doubtless found at Anyang and dating from the reign of Ti I (traditionally dated in 1191-1155 B.C.), the next to the last Shang king; whether any bone inscriptions are to be ascribed to the reign of the last Shang ruler is uncertain.[29]

The last ruler of the Shang people was Ti Hsin, ordinarily called Chou. He was notorious, at least in the later literary traditions which took form under his conquerors, for misrule, cruelty and immoderation in every way. He was supposed to have been the first to use ivory chop sticks, and one of his ministers named Kitsu is reported to have remarked: "Today it was ivory chop sticks, tomorrow it will be jade cups. The eating of bears' paws will follow. Such extravagance and covetousness will bring the empire to ruin."[30]

WESTERN CHOU

This corrupt representative of the great Shang dynasty was overthrown by a confederation of western barbarians under the leadership of the Chous.[31] The tribe or tribes known by the name of Chou lived in the valley of the Wei River over three hundred and fifty miles west and south of Anyang. Their capital city was at Feng, and shortly after the conquest of Shang was moved to Hao. They seem to have been descended from the same Neolithic ancestors as the Shangs, but to have had a more primitive civilization until their contact with the latter. Then they learned rapidly and soon adopted many elements of Shang writing, art, architecture, religion and divination. Through their own extensive conquests they spread the Shang culture widely.

[28] Quoted in CSECC p.12 n.24.   [29] CSECC pp.133f.
[30] John Ross, *The Origin of the Chinese People.* 1916, p.21.
[31] CBC pp.219-245.

The conquest of Shang is supposed to have been planned by the Chou king Wen, whose name means "the Acomplished." The plan was carried out successfully by his son, King Wu, "the Martial." A very considerable part of north China seems to have submitted to the new conqueror. In order to maintain a form of control over this large area, many of the lands were apportioned to various chiefs and rulers, and the result was the establishment of a feudal system of government.

After the death of King Wu, traditionally dated in 1116 B.C., his young son King Ch'eng succeeded to the throne, but actual authority was exercised for a number of years by the Duke of Chou, brother of the Martial King. Some of the Shang people had hitherto been allowed to remain under the vassal rule of a son of Ti Hsin, and they rebelled at this time. The revolt was suppressed by the Duke of Chou, and K'ang Shu, another brother of the Martial King, was made ruler of a newly created State of Wei in the area of Anyang. His capital was at Ch'ao Ke, about thirty miles south of the Great City Shang.

When King Ch'eng became old enough to rule for himself, the Duke of Chou retired from direction of the government. Although the Chou capital remained in the Wei valley, a new city and sort of secondary capital was built at this time farther east at Loyang.

Of the early centers of the Chous, Feng and Hao can be at least approximately located in the Wei basin, and present-day villages near the two sites still have Feng and Hao as part of their names; the site of the city at Loyang was just to the northwest of modern Loyang, while a second Chou city ten miles east of Loyang is still marked by its walls standing in places fifteen feet high. As for Ch'ao Ke, just a few miles north of this site at Hsün Hsien more than eighty tombs of Chou date have been excavated by the Honan Archaeological Research Association in cooperation with the National Research Institute. These were subterranean burial places, filled up with pounded earth, and left level with the surrounding ground. They contained not only ritual bronzes but also chariots, armor, weapons and other objects. It is believed that they were the tombs of the rulers of the State of Wei. Furthermore the tombs of Kings Wen, Wu, Ch'eng and K'ang and of the Duke of Chou still exist on the plateau of Pi about four miles north of the present city of Hsien Yang. Each is surmounted by a lofty tumulus or artificial mound of earth, relatively well preserved after all the centuries.[32]

[32] CBC pp.246-253.

The establishment of the Chou dynasty has now been related in sufficient detail for our purposes. From the inauguration of the dynasty down to 771 B.C. the royal capital remained in the west, and this time is therefore known as the Western Chou (or Early Chou) Period. It is neither necessary nor indeed possible to recount the political history of this period in full. The essential point is that in this time the Chou rulers were able to maintain their supreme sovereignty in fact. The general trend of events, however, was toward the destruction of a centralized authority. On the one hand, weaker kings succeeded the vigorous founders of the dynasty; on the other hand, the various vassal states grew in power and their princes became more and more independent in attitude. There were also threats and attacks from barbarian peoples on the frontiers of the land.

For two examples of the increasing misfortunes of the Chou rulers we may recall that King Chao did not come back from a military expedition to the Yangtze River in 1002 B.C.; and that King Li, who took the throne in 878 B.C., suppressed his people severely but was driven from the throne and spent the last fourteen years of his life as a refugee.

The last of the Western Chou monarchs was King Yu. According to the stories about him, he reigned both foolishly and feebly. In 771 B.C. he was killed in a barbarian attack, and the days when the House of Chou could claim to really rule the land were at an end. The vassal princes established Yu's heir on the throne as King P'ing, but he and his successors were little more than petty chiefs and often quite powerless in the hands of their erstwhile subordinates. Since the capital was now moved to Loyang, this was known as the Eastern Chou dynasty.

EASTERN CHOU

The Eastern Chou dynasty endured from 771 to 256 B.C., and it was not until 221 B.C. that the next great dynasty, the Ch'in was inaugurated. It is customary to divide the Eastern Chou Period into two parts. Recalling that the time of the Western Chou dynasty was the Early Chou Period, these may be named the Middle and the Late Chou Periods; or, using the names of books of the time as Chinese scholars do, they may be designated the Period of "Spring and Autumn Annals" (Ch'un Ch'iu) and the Period of "Warring States" (Chan Kuo).[33] In either case the dividing point between the

[33] Friedrich Hirth, *The Ancient History of China to the End of the Chóu Dynasty.* 1908, pp.179,262.

two parts of the Eastern Chou Period falls not far from the time of the death of Confucius, 478 B.C.

China was now divided into a large number of states. In the seventh century B.C. five of these were most important: Ch'i in the northeast in what are now the provinces of Shantung and Hopei; Chin in the north in present day Shansi; Ch'in in the west in modern Shensi; Sung in the center in the vicinity of Honan; and Ch'u in the south in the region of Hupeh. In the sixth century much power was attained by the State of Wu in what is now Kiangsu; in the fifth century, Yüeh in modern Chekiang became very strong. Chou itself was only one of the smaller and less important states; and so too was Lu, the state which had been founded by the Duke of Chou in southern Shantung, where later Confucius was born.

In the "Warring States" Period seven chief states contended for mastery. These were Ch'i, Ch'in and Ch'u, with which we are already familiar; Han, Wei (or Liang), and Chao, which were fragments of the former Chin; and Yen, a state with its capital where Peiping now is. The struggle for power among these groups narrowed gradually to a contest between Ch'u in the south and Ch'in in the west, Chou meanwhile being entirely eliminated with the death of its last king in 256 B.C. Ch'u finally was overcome too, and in 221 B.C. all of China was unified in the empire of the Ch'in.

ART IN THE CHOU PERIOD

As in the Shang Period, so too throughout the entire Chou Period the making of ritual bronzes continued to be the most important task toward which artistic effort was directed. The brilliance of the achievements, however, was now somewhat diminished. There was a sharp reduction in the number of types of vessels produced as well as in the variety of their decorative motifs. Around 1000 B.C. the *t'ao-t'ieh* virtually disappeared, and of the many animals both real and imaginary which were on the Shang bronzes, only the dragon and the bird were frequently used. The *kuei* shown in Fig. 145 will provide an example of the relatively severe but yet attractive style of the Western Chou Period. This vessel has an inscription which dates it in the third year of a ruler who was probably King Hsüan (827-781 B.C.), the immediate predecessor of King Yu.

In the Eastern Chou Period several artistic styles were developed. Of these we will select for illustration only one, namely the Huai Style, which is so designated from the Huai River in the vicinity of which the first vessels so decorated were discovered. The nature of the style at its best may be seen in the pilgrim's bottle in Fig. 146. The body of the bottle is flat, and divided by bands into recessed, rectangular areas, in which the characteristic Huai pattern appears. The particular interest of this style for us lies in the fact that it prevailed during the last seventy-five years of the Period of "Spring and Autumn Annals," which is almost exactly the time of the life of Confucius.

At about the time just mentioned, another development comes into view, namely the sculptured representation of man in isolated figures. An example probably contemporary with the period of the Huai Style (end of the sixth or beginning of the fifth century B.C.) is shown in Fig. 147. This is a bronze statuette nearly ten inches high. The small tube in front of the knees and that in the hands were probably intended to hold something like a torch, and the figure is generally identified as a "kneeling servant" or a "torchbearer."

From the late Chou Period, probably, we have also the large bronze dragon pictured in Fig. 148. This is a winged figure covered with fine spiral ornaments, and so sculptured as to portray a remarkable degree of menace and of watchfulness.[34]

In the Chou Period not only bronze but also jade seems to have been in quite common use for objects of art. Among the jade objects which probably come from this period are ceremonial disks and tubes; knives, daggers, chisels and ax-heads; representations of insects, animals and animal heads; ornaments; and human statuettes. For the most part it is supposed that these were employed in various ceremonies, sacrifices and funeral rites. The ceremonial disks called *pi*, like the one pictured in Fig. 149, are interpreted as emblems of the sun or of heaven; the hollow tubes (*ts'ung*) cylindrical on the inside but square on the outside, like the one in Fig. 150, are thought to have symbolized the earth or the four cardinal points. An extremely interesting human figure in jade, also ascribed to the Chou Period by Berthold Laufer, is shown in Fig. 151. Simple slits indicate the eyes and mouth, and incised lines mark the pointed, triangular beard. The body is enveloped in a long robe which completely hides both hands and feet. Perhaps this is the conventionalized figure of a sage.[35]

[34] Bachhofer, *A Short History of Chinese Art*, Fig. 50.
[35] Berthold Laufer, *Archaic Chinese Jades Collected in China by A. W. Bahr, Now in Field Museum of Natural History, Chicago*. 1927, pp.9f.,16,29,48, Pl. IV, 2, XVI, XXXIII; Una Pope-Hennessy, *Early Chinese Jades*. 1923, pp.29-42,133f.; see also

LITERATURE IN THE CHOU PERIOD

Although it was a time of feudalism and warfare, the Chou Period was, as we have just seen, also a time of important artistic achievement. Yet more significant was the development of literature in this epoch. So intense was the activity in this regard, that the era is commonly known as the Classical Age of Chinese history. Even in early Chou times, it is estimated, the number of documents written must have amounted to tens or hundreds of thousands. So numerous were the literary works prior to Confucius, that he and his disciples are supposed to have devoted much of their time to collecting, editing and interpreting these books.

As time went on there came to be so many compilations and commentaries that it is now difficult to disentangle the component parts and ascertain which truly belong to a given period. The inscriptions on the oracle bones and ritual bronzes provide important materials for comparison, however, and by the use of these and other standards it is possible to check on the authenticity and antiquity of the documents. In brief it may be said that by such tests no books now survive from the Shang Period although several purport to be of such date; that not a few ascribed to Chou times are actually yet later; but that many important writings still extant are authentic representatives of the Chou Period.[36]

The works regarded as most important were ultimately assembled in the so-called "Confucian canon." These comprised the Wu Ching or Five Classics, which were probably brought together in the time of the Han dynasty (202 B.C.-A.D. 220); and the Ssu Shu or Four Books, which were first collectively designated by this name in the Sung period (A.D. 960-1279).[37] It has been commonly held that Confucius was the compiler of the first four of the Classics and the author of the fifth; while the Four Books are attributed to the work of his disciples and descendants.[38] Modern criticism of these opinions will be reflected below, where the chronological notations will at all events indicate that most of these books originated in the Chou Period. Certain related works will also be mentioned in addition to the nine canonical books.

Berthold Laufer, *Jade, A Study in Chinese Archaeology and Religion* (Field Museum of Natural History Publication 154, Anthropological Series, x). 1912; Paul Pelliot, *Jades archaïques de Chine appartenant à M. C. T. Loo.* 1925.

[36] CBC pp.254-275.
[37] Lewis Hodous in JGRMW p.2.
[38] MHR I, p.5.

THE FIVE CLASSICS

(1) I Ching (Yi King),[39] or Book of Changes.[40] Speaking of course of the original text and not of the appended commentaries, this is regarded as the first complete work in Chinese literature, among extant productions, to have reached its present form. One tradition ascribes the work to the Accomplished King, and it is probable that it does belong to the very beginning of the Chou Period. The I Ching is a book of divination. It is based upon sixty-four diagrams which represent various possible combinations of six lines either whole or broken. Evidently the diviner manipulated sticks to form one of these diagrams, and then consulted the text to ascertain its explanation.

Here, for one example, is the tenth diagram in the book, called the Li Hexagram, and the accompanying text:

```
 —————————————
 —————————————
 —————    —————
 —————————————
 —————————————
 —————————————
```

This suggests the idea of one treading on the tail of a tiger, which does not bite him. There will be progress and success.

1. The first line, undivided, shows its subject treading his accustomed path. If he go forward, there will be no error.
2. The second line, undivided, shows its subject treading the path that is level and easy;—a quiet and solitary man, to whom, if he be firm and correct, there will be good fortune.
3. The third line, divided, shows a one-eyed man who thinks he can see; a lame man who thinks he can walk well; one who treads on the tail of a tiger and is bitten. All this indicates ill-fortune. We have a mere bravo acting the part of a great ruler.
4. The fourth line, undivided, shows its subject treading on the tail of a tiger. He becomes full of apprehensive caution, and in the end there will be good fortune.
5. The fifth line, undivided, shows the resolute tread of its subject. Though he be firm and correct, there will be peril.
6. The sixth line, undivided, tells us to look at the whole course that is trodden, and examine the presage which that gives. If it be complete and without failure, there will be great good fortune.[41]

(2) Shu Ching, or Document Classic; also called Shang Shu, or Preserved Books; and commonly known in English as the Book of

---

[39] The word *ching* (or *king*, as it is also spelled in English) is usually translated "classic." It means originally the warp of a web, and hence signifies what is a rule, and is applicable to a canonical book.
[40] tr. James Legge in SBE XVI.
[41] SBE XVI, pp.78-80; Herbert A. Giles, A *History of Chinese Literature*. 1901, p.22.

History.[42] This is a compilation of many different documents. Of these the T'ang Shih, Pan Keng, Kao Tsung Yung Jih, Hsi Po K'an Li, and Wei Tzu have been attributed to the Shang Period, but careful comparison with the indisputably genuine language and ideas in the inscriptions of the Shang oracle bones indicates that they are actually fabrications of later date.[43] Of the entire book perhaps one fourth can be assigned to a time before 600 B.C., while the other parts are yet later, in some cases as late as the third century A.D. The older parts include speeches, proclamations and communications by various rulers and military leaders, as well as documents concerning the building of the city at Loyang.

(3) Shih Ching, or Book of Poetry.[44] This was an anthology of three hundred and eleven poems of which three hundred and five still exist. They are traditionally supposed to have been selected by Confucius from three thousand pieces, but it is now questioned if the great sage actually made the collection. Many of the poems probably date from around 800 to 600 B.C., and were used by Confucius and his followers as texts for moral instruction. One section, known as the Shang Sung, has been attributed to a time as early as the Shang Period, but this is probably not correct.[45] For the most part the poems of the Shih Ching are lyric rather than epic in character, and a variety of subjects is dealt with including courtship, marriage, war, agriculture, hunting, feasting and sacrifice. Many of the poems were doubtless once set to music, but this has been lost.

For one example, we quote here a portion of a sacrificial song as translated by Arthur Waley:

> In due order, treading cautiously,
> We purify your oxen and sheep.
> We carry out the rice-offering, the harvest offering,
> Now baking, now boiling,
> Now setting out and arranging,
> Praying and sacrificing at the gate.
> Very hallowed was this service of offering;
> Very mighty the forefathers.
> The Spirits and Protectors have accepted;
> The pious descendant shall have happiness,

---

[42] tr. James Legge in SBE III, pp.1-272; and in *The Chinese Classics, with a Translation, Critical and Exegetical Notes, Prolegomena, and Copious Indexes.* III (1865).

[43] CSECC pp.55-89.

[44] tr. James Legge in SBE III, pp.273-446; and in *The Chinese Classics.* IV (1871); Arthur Waley, *The Book of Songs, Translated from the Chinese.* 1937.

[45] CSECC pp.49-54.

They will reward him with great blessings,
With span of years unending.

We mind the furnaces, treading softly;
Attend to the food-stands so tall,
For roast meat, for broiled meat.
Our lord's lady hard at work
Sees to the dishes, so many,
Needed for guests, for strangers.
Healths and pledges go the round,
Every custom and rite is observed,
Every smile, every word is in place.
The Spirits and Protectors will surely come
And requite us with great blessings,
Countless years of life as our reward.[46]

(4) Li Chi, or Ceremonial Records.[47] Here we have a large collection of treatises on the rules of propriety. Instructions are given for ceremonial procedure in connection with such things as weddings, funerals, mourning, sacrifices, banquets, appearances at court, war, education, and capping, which was the rite signalizing the passage of a youth from immaturity into manhood. The keynote of the book is struck in its opening sentence, "Always and in everything let there be reverence." In its present form, the work may have been completed in the second century A.D.[48] Another book of similar character was the Chou Li, or Ceremonies of Chou, which may date from the first century A.D. or earlier.[49] Older still was yet a third manual of ceremonial procedure, called the I Li, or Book of Etiquette and Ceremony.[50] This book may have appeared in the second century B.C., and it probably contains materials from and reflects practices of the Chou Period.

(5) Ch'un Ch'iu, or Spring and Autumn Annals.[51] This work is supposed to have been written by Confucius, although the attribution is questioned by some modern scholars. At any rate it is a chronicle of events in the Sage's native state of Lu, extending from 721 to 478 B.C. It notices such events as beginnings of seasons, eclipses, deaths of prominent persons, state covenants and wars.

[46] Waley, *The Book of Songs*, pp.209f. Quoted by permission of the publishers, Houghton Mifflin Company, Boston and New York.

[47] tr. James Legge in SBE XXVII, XXVIII.

[48] Legge in SBE XXVII, p.2.

[49] K. S. Latourette, *The Chinese, Their History and Culture.* 2d ed. 1934, I, p.67.

[50] tr. John Steele, *The I-li, or Book of Etiquette and Ceremonial* (Probsthain's Oriental Series). 2 vols. 1917.

[51] tr. James Legge in *The Chinese Classics.* v (1872).

Many other historical chronicles were of course written at various times, and we have already mentioned (p.320) in connection with the chronological framework of Chinese history the Ch'ien Han Shu, or History of the Former Han Dynasty,[52] and the Chu Shu Chi Nien, or Annals of the Bamboo Books. Here we may also note two other treatises. The first is the Tso Chuan,[53] which is traditionally regarded as a commentary on the Ch'un Ch'iu but is probably of independent origin. It contains chronicles covering the time from 722 to 468 B.C. The second is the Chan Kuo Ts'e, or Documents of the Warring States. It is a collection of historical episodes dealing with the last troubled years of the Chou Period.[54]

Mention of one other classic may also be inserted here, although it is not one of the five accorded highest place. This is the Hsiao Ching, or Classic of Filial Piety.[55] It is a relatively brief book, and its essential character is indicated by its title. It is traditionally connected with the name of Tseng Shen, a pupil of Confucius, but that he was actually the author is now regarded as improbable.[56]

THE FOUR BOOKS

(1) Lun Yü, or Analects.[57] This is a collection of the sayings of Confucius and a record of conversations in which he engaged. A variety of themes are discussed, among which the most prominent are ethics and government. For the most part the teachings contained may be regarded as deriving authentically from Confucius, although in their formulation they may have undergone a long process of smoothing and polishing. The compilation of the work is thought to have been done by a second generation of Confucian scholars, that is by pupils of the first followers of the great sage. Since Book VIII refers to the last illness of Tseng-tzu who died in 437 B.C., and since Mencius (372-289 B.C.) quotes several passages in language virtually identical with the present text, it may be reasonably

---

[52] tr. Homer H. Dubs, *The History of the Former Han Dynasty by Pan Ku, A Critical Translation with Annotations.* 2 vols. 1938-44.
[53] tr. Legge in *The Chinese Classics,* v.
[54] Latourette, *The Chinese, Their History and Culture,* I, p.68.
[55] tr. James Legge in SBE III, pp.447-488.
[56] Richard Wilhelm, *Confucius and Confucianism.* tr. George H. Danton and Annina P. Danton. 1931, p.139.
[57] tr. James Legge, *The Chinese Classics.* I (2d ed. 1893), pp.137-354; Lionel Giles, *The Sayings of Confucius, A New Translation of the Greater Part of the Confucian Analects* (Wisdom of the East). 1907; Leonard A. Lyall, *The Sayings of Confucius.* 2d ed. 1925; Arthur Waley, *The Analects of Confucius, Translated and Annotated.* 1938.

surmised that the work was written around 400 B.C. A manuscript found in the house of Confucius in 150 B.C., and probably hidden there around 213-211 B.C. when Shih Huang Ti was trying to destroy the classical writings, is the chief authority for the text in its present form.[58]

It may be added in this connection that another work entitled Chia Yü, or the School Conversations, existed at the time of the burning of the books by Shih Huang Ti, and was also rediscovered later. The present-day book of the same title, however, was probably not written or published until the beginning of the third century A.D. It contains numerous anecdotes and conversations, but represents a later stratum of tradition than the Lun Yü.[59]

(2) Ta Hsüeh, or the Great Learning.[60] This work is ordinarily supposed to have been written by Tseng-tzu, who was mentioned just above. There is some evidence in its style and philosophy, however, for a later date, say about the middle of the fourth century B.C., in which case it would have to be attributed to an unknown Confucianist.[61] The book calls for the cultivation of the individual self through the extension of knowledge, and then for the consequent ordering in harmony of family, state, and all society.

(3) Chung Yung, or the Doctrine of the Mean (also rendered, the Mean-in-action).[62] Tradition uniformly ascribes this book to Tzu Ssu (also called K'ung Chi), the grandson of Confucius. Such an authorship seems probable for the body of the work, but it is possible that certain sections are from a later unknown writer of the second half of the third century B.C.[63] The theme is the harmonious development of human nature through right action and the practice of the principle of reciprocity. While the Ta Hsüeh and Chung Yung were thus singled out for special emphasis they are both actually sections of the Li Chi.

(4) Meng Tzu Shu, or the Book of Mencius.[64] This work is made

[58] Lyall, The Sayings of Confucius, p.xii.
[59] Wilhelm, Confucius and Confucianism, pp.134-136.
[60] tr. Legge, The Chinese Classics, I, pp.355-381; E. R. Hughes, The Great Learning and the Mean-in-Action. 1943.
[61] Hughes, op.cit., p.103.
[62] tr. Legge, The Chinese Classics, I, pp.382-434; Ku Hung Ming, The Conduct of Life, or the Universal Order of Confucius, A Translation of One of the Four Confucian Books, Hitherto Known as the Doctrine of the Mean (Wisdom of the East). 1906; Hughes, The Great Learning and the Mean-in-Action; Leonard A. Lyall and King Chien-kün, The Chung-Yung, or The Centre, The Common. 1927.
[63] Hughes, The Great Learning and the Mean-in-Action, pp.99f.
[64] tr. James Legge, The Chinese Classics. II (2d ed. 1895); Leonard A. Lyall,

up of seven sections, and contains in a fairly authentic form the teachings of the philosopher Mencius, who lived around 372-289 B.C. He set forth the doctrines of Confucius in his own way and gave them a somewhat more popular tone. As might be expected, the main topics of discussion are ethics and politics.

RELIGION IN THE CHOU PERIOD

Before proceeding to tell about Confucius and his philosophy in particular, we will say a word concerning the kind of religion in general which prevailed at this time. In its main aspects, religion in the Chou Period[65] was a development of the beliefs and practices with which we already have some familiarity from Shang times. As before, the basic belief was in elemental and ancestral spirits. Now, however, one of the spirits has attained preeminent position and is generally recognized as the chief deity. This is Shang Ti, who will be remembered as mentioned on the Shang oracle bones in connection with such things as war and rain. Not only does Shang Ti now figure as the highest spirit, but an identification has also evidently taken place between Shang Ti and another deity called T'ien or Heaven. It may be supposed that the latter was a chief god among the Chou people, and that when they found Shang Ti occupying a somewhat similar place among the Shangs they merged the two.[66] At any rate both names are now used for the same deity, and T'ien occurs even more frequently than Shang Ti. Furthermore the Chou kings customarily used T'ien Tzu, "the Son of Heaven," as their title.

The spirits of the dead were of course still as important as ever. They were generally thought of as living in the heavens, but the idea also occurs that they dwell beneath the earth at a place named the Yellow Springs. The maintenance of sacrifices to the deceased was deemed of the greatest significance, and the inscriptions on the ritual bronzes express again and again some such wish as, "May my sons and grandsons for ever treasure and use this vessel."

The twin centers of religion were the ancestral temple and the "altar of the land."[67] Each family was united around its own ancestral temple, and the whole land looked toward the ancestral temple of

---

Mencius. 1932; Lionel Giles, *The Book of Mencius (Abridged), Translated from the Chinese* (Wisdom of the East). 1942.

[65] CBC pp.332-345.

[66] Ch'en Meng-chia in H. F. MacNair, ed., *China* (The United Nations Series). 1946, pp.63f.

[67] Marcel Granet, *Chinese Civilization*. tr. K. E. Innes and M. R. Brailsford. 1930, pp.239-241.

the king as a focal point. Wooden tablets bearing the names of the ancestors were placed in the temples, and the spirits were believed to answer the summons to come there upon ceremonial occasions. The "altar of the land" was a mound of earth which first had symbolized the soil as a deity, and now stood in each community as a focus of its religious activity. Various officials and servants maintained the temples, and wizards and witches were available to assist in communication with the spirits.

It was supposed that both benefit and harm came from the spirits, and that they sometimes manifested themselves as ghosts to accomplish their purposes. Prayers were naturally offered both for protection from danger and for positive blessings. Longevity, numerous descendants, the necessities of daily life, and qualities of calmness and wisdom, were things for which supplication was made. The prayers were commonly written out, recited in connection with a sacrifice, and then burned, all in order to bring them to the attention of the deities. Oracles were still sought by the divinatory methods used by the Shangs as well as by the procedure for which the I Ching provided a handbook.

4. EARLY CONFUCIANISM

THE history of China has now been sketched briefly to the end of the Chou Period, and the general framework of contemporary political events, artistic achievements and religious beliefs has been outlined. This was the setting within which the work of China's two great teachers, Confucius and Lao Tzu, was done. We are concerned with Confucius and Confucianism in this chapter, and will deal with Lao Tzu and Taoism in the next. As a modern religion, Confucianism is estimated to have 250,000,000 adherents.

THE LIFE AND WORK OF CONFUCIUS

The earliest chronologically arranged account of the life of Confucius[68] is found in Chapter XLVII of the Shih Chi, or Historical Records, of Ssu-ma Ch'ien.[69] Ssu-ma Ch'ien was a court official who lived about 140-80 B.C.,[70] and his book, based largely upon earlier documents and works, covers the history of China and the lives of many of its important personages from the beginning down to his own day. While not all the details of Ssu-ma Ch'ien's biographies are considered reliable by Sinologists, the record about to be quoted provides the basis of all the later lives of the great sage.[71] The section concerning Confucius begins as follows: "Confucius was born in the State of Lu, in the District of Ch'ang P'ing, in the city Chou [or Tsou]. His ancestor was from the State of Sung and was called K'ung Fang-shu. Fang-shu begat Po-hsia. Po-hsia begat Shu-Liang Ho. Late in life, Ho was united in matrimony with the daughter of the man, Yen, and begat Confucius. His mother prayed to the hill, Ni, and conceived Confucius. It was in the twenty-second year of Duke Hsiang of Lu that Confucius was born [551 B.C.].[72] At his birth, he

---

[68] Confucius is the Latinized form of the Chinese K'ung-fu-tzu, meaning Master K'ung, or K'ung the philosopher. As appears in the quotation given above, K'ung was the family name; Tzu is the usual designation for Master, or Philosopher.

[69] The Shih Chi is translated in part by Édouard Chavannes, Les mémoires historiques de Se-Ma Ts'ien, traduits et annotés. 5 vols. 1895-1905. Chapter XLVII, with which we are here concerned, is found in vol. v, pp.283-435, of the work by Chavannes; and is translated into English in Wilhelm, Confucius and Confucianism, pp.3-70, from which source the present quotations are taken.

[70] Richard Wilhelm, A Short History of Chinese Civilization. tr. Joan Joshua. 1929, pp.25f.

[71] cf. Derk Bodde, Statesman, Patriot, and General in Ancient China, Three Shih Chi Biographies of the Ch'in Dynasty (255-206 B.C.), Translated and Discussed (American Oriental Series, 17). 1940, pp.68f.

[72] According to other sources the date was 552 B.C. Richard Wilhelm, Kung-tse, Leben und Werk. 1925, p.188 n.1; cf. James Legge, The Life and Teachings of Con-

[343]

had on his head a bulging of the skull, whence he is said to have received the name Hill (Ch'iu). His style of appellation was Chung Ni, his family name K'ung. When he was born, his father, Shu-Liang Ho, died."

The child, even in early years, manifested special religious interest. "Confucius was always wont to set up sacrificial vessels in his childish play," Ssu-ma Ch'ien relates, "and to imitate ceremonial gestures." Being of a poor family, he entered into employment as soon as he was old enough. His work was done with punctilious care, and matters in his charge prospered. "Confucius was poor and of low estate, and when he grew older he served as a petty official of the family Chi, and while he was in office his accounts and the measures were always correct. Thereupon, he was made Chief Shepherd; then the beasts grew in numbers and multiplied." He is said to have married at the age of nineteen.

By the time he was in his thirties, Confucius was a scholar of such repute as to attract the attention of the Minister of Lu, Meng Hsi-tze. As the latter was dying, he advised his son, I-tze, and his nephew, Nan-Chung Ching-shu, to take Confucius as their teacher in decorum.[73] It was in company with Nan-Chung Ching-shu that Confucius made a memorable journey to the imperial capital of Loyang in Honan. The purpose of the trip was to study the ancient ceremonial rites of the land. The Prince of Lu provided the two young travelers with a chariot, two horses, and a servant. "Thus they went together to Chou [the residence of the Emperor at Loyang]," the Shih Chi narrates, "and inquired about the rites."

The Shih Chi also indicates that Confucius made the acquaintance of Lao Tzu while on this journey, but this portion of the account is almost certainly apocryphal. When Confucius took leave of Lao Tsu, the latter, in parting, is stated to have addressed him as follows: "I have heard that rich and noble persons make parting gifts; but good people give words in farewell. I am neither rich nor noble, but I am held a good man, so I should like to give you these words upon your way: Shrewd and clever people are near to death, for they love to pass judgment on others. Those who know a great deal and do things

---

fucius. 6th ed. 1887, p.58; Herrlee G. Creel, *Confucius, The Man and the Myth.* 1949, pp.254-296f.

[73] Ssu-ma Ch'ien dates this event in the seventeenth year of Confucius' life, but this is a mistake based upon faulty use of a source. The true date, verified by calculation of the time of an eclipse of the sun which is mentioned in another source, was almost certainly 518 B.C. Wilhelm, *Confucius and Confucianism,* pp.76f.

on a large scale endanger their persons, for they disclose the mistakes of mankind. He who is the son of another has nothing for himself; he who is the official of another has nothing for himself."

The fame of Confucius was enhanced by this journey, and after his return to Lu he gradually attracted more pupils to himself. Duke Ching of Ch'i also became interested in him, and for a time Confucius took service in that state. When the Duke questioned him regarding government, Confucius gave this succinct advice: "Let the prince be prince, the servant servant, the father father, the son son." On another occasion he pronounced this aphorism on the same subject: "Governing consists in being sparing with the resources." Despite the evident wisdom in these counsels, opponents of Confucius spoke against him to the Duke. They said: "Scholars are smooth and sophisticated; they cannot be taken as a norm; they are arrogant and conceited; they cannot be used to guide the lower classes. . . . Confucius splendidly forms the rules of behavior, increases the ceremonies of reception and departure, and the customs in walking and in bowing, so that many generations would not be enough to exhaust his teachings. Years would not suffice to plumb his rules of decorum. If you wish to use him to change the manners of Ch'i, this is not the correct way to lead the common people." So at last Duke Ching dismissed him, and Confucius went back to Lu.

In his own state, conditions were now far from favorable. "From the highest dignitaries down, every one was grasping of power, and all had departed from the true way." "Therefore," states Ssu-ma Ch'ien, "Confucius accepted no office. He lived in retirement, and arranged the odes, the records, the rites and music. And his pupils grew ever greater in number, while from all sides, from far distant regions, disciples flocked to him."

It was not until he was fifty years old, and Duke Ting was on the throne of Lu, that Confucius' great opportunity for public service came. The Duke appointed him ruler of the middle district known as Chung Tu, and within a year "his neighbors on all sides took him as a model." From the management of this district he was soon advanced to the position of Minister of Public Works, and then to that of Minister of Justice. In his last year of public service he received the post of Acting Chancellor. So successful was his administration of affairs that it is written in the Shih Chi, "After Confucius had conducted the government of the state for three months, the sellers of lambs and of suckling pigs no longer falsified their prices, and men and women walked on different sides of the road. Lost objects were not picked up on the streets. Strangers who came from all sides did not need to turn to the officials when they entered the city, for all were received as if they were returning to their own homes."

Such success made the people of the neighboring state of Ch'i fear that Lu would become dominant over all, and they contrived the scheme of presenting Duke Ting with eighty beautiful dancing girls and a hundred and twenty magnificent horses in order to divert his mind from politics to pleasure. The plan worked as they desired, and when Confucius saw that his prince was neglecting the government and the all-important ceremonial sacrifices, he himself regretfully took his departure. He was now fifty-six years old, having been in public service in the State of Lu for six years (501-495 B.C.).

Fourteen years of wandering and hardship ensued. While many details of this period are given in the Shih Chi, we may content ourselves with quoting the summary statement in the same source. "Finally he left Lu, was abandoned in Ch'i, was driven out of Sung and Wei, suffered want between Ch'en and Ts'ai.[74] Thereupon he returned to Lu. Confucius was nine feet six inches tall. All the people called him a giant and marveled at him. Lu again treated him well; so he returned to Lu."

"But finally it turned out that they could not make use of Confucius in Lu. And neither did Confucius strive for official position." For the rest of his days he devoted himself to his literary work and teaching. Although his methods of instruction were severe, he gathered about him some three thousand pupils whom he instructed in the odes, records, rites and music. "He gave no help to him who was not zealous. If he presented one corner of a subject as an example, and the pupil could not transfer what he had learned to the other three corners, Confucius did not repeat."

Of his habitual demeanor the following description is given in the Shih Chi: "In everyday life, Confucius was altogether modest, as though he were not able to speak. In the ancestral temple and at court, he was eloquent, yet his speeches were always cautious. At court, he conversed with the upper dignitaries in exact and definite terms; with the lower dignitaries he was free and open. Whenever he entered in at the Duke's door, he walked as though bowed over, with quick steps; he approached as if on wings. Whenever the

[74] Ch'en and Ts'ai were small states just south of Sung. Herrmann, *Historical and Commercial Atlas of China*, pp.14f.

Prince commanded his presence at a reception of guests, his appearance was serious. Whenever a command of the Prince summoned him, he left his house without waiting for the horses to be put to his chariot."

Such was the relative obscurity in which he passed his last years that he once drew a deep sigh and said, "Alas, no one knows me!" Upon being questioned about this, he continued, however: "I do not murmur against Heaven. I do not grumble against man. I pursue my studies here on earth, and am in touch with Heaven above. It is Heaven that knows me!"

The same melancholy was with him in his last illness. It is reported that he sighed and sang:

> The Sacred Mountain[75] caves in,
> The roof beam breaks,
> The Sage will vanish.

Then he wept and said to Tze Kung, one of his disciples: "For a long time the world has been unregulated; no one understood how to follow me. The people of Hsia placed the coffin upon the east steps, the people of Chou placed it on the west steps, the people of Yin placed it between the two pillars. Last night I dreamed that I was sitting before the sacrificial offerings between the two pillars. Does that mean that I am a man of Yin?" Seven days later Confucius passed away, having attained an age of seventy-three years (478 B.C.).[76]

"Confucius was buried north of the city, on the bank of the River Szu," Ssu-ma Ch'ien states as he brings to a close his chapter on the life of the great teacher. "All the disciples mourned him for three years. When the three years of the mourning of the heart were over, then they separated and went their ways, and once more each one wept bitter tears wrung from his heart. Some there were who remained even longer. Tze Kung alone built himself a hut by the grave mound. He remained, in all, six years before he departed. There were over a hundred families of the disciples of Confucius and of the people of Lu who went thither and built houses by the grave. So they called the place the Hamlet of Confucius. In Lu, the custom was handed down from generation to generation to offer sacrifices at the grave of Confucius at fixed times of the year. And the scholars

---

[75] T'ai Shan in Shantung.
[76] Other calculations make this date 479 B.C. See Legge, *The Life and Teachings of Confucius*, p.87; Wilhelm, *Kung-tse, Leben und Werk*, p.63.

also practiced the rites of a communal banquet and held a great archery contest at the grave of Confucius. The burial place of Confucius is one hundred acres in extent. The Hall in which the pupils of Confucius dwelt was later turned into a temple in which the clothes, hats, lute, chariots, and books of Confucius were preserved. All of this was kept for over two hundred years, until the Han period. When the first emperor of the Han Dynasty came through Lu, he offered a great sacrifice to Confucius. When princes, dignitaries, and ministers come, they always first visit the temple, before they go about their business. . . .

"The Chief Historian says: 'In the Book of Odes it is written:

> The high mountain, he looked toward it;
> The distant road, he walked along it.'

"Even if a person does not reach his goal, yet his heart ever seeks to attain it. I read the writings of Confucius, and I pictured to myself what sort of man he had been. I went to Lu, and in the temple of Chung Ni I contemplated his chariot, his garments, and his ceremonial implements. At a fixed time, scholars performed the rites of his house. So I remained there, full of reverence, and could not tear myself away. There were on earth many princes and sages who, in their lifetime, were famous, but whose names were no longer known after their death. Confucius was a simple man of the people. But after more than ten generations, his doctrine is still handed down, and men of learning honor him as Master. From the Son of Heaven, and from kings and princes on, all who practice the six free arts in the Middle Kingdom take their decisions and their measure from the Master. That can be designated the highest possible sanctity."

While the native place of Confucius was at Tsou (or Chou), he lived afterward at Chufou (also spelled Ch'ü-fou, Kufow) and it was in the vicinity of the latter place that he was buried.[77] There the tomb of the great sage is still to be seen, as shown in Fig. 152. The burial mound itself is covered with plants and shaded by trees. In front of it stands an inscribed stone tablet which forms the back for a stone table of sacrifice, with its candelabra and incense vessels. The inscription reads simply, "Ancient, Most Holy Teacher."[78]

THE TEACHINGS OF CONFUCIUS

Within the framework of our study it will suffice to deal briefly

[77] Chavannes, *Les mémoires historiques de Se-ma Ts'ien*, v, p.283 n.2.
[78] Franz X. Biallas, *Konfuzius und sein Kult, Ein Beitrag zur Kulturgeschichte Chinas und ein Führer zur Heimatsstadt des Konfuzius*. 1928, p.83.

with the teachings of Confucius. Indeed some idea of the nature of his interests and outlook has already been given in telling of his life and work. As far as religion in the sense of reference to the supernatural is concerned, it may be said that he simply took for granted the general framework of ideas which prevailed in his time. He was not primarily a religious leader but he did believe in the spirits and had a sense of personal relationship to Heaven. An expression of this sense of relationship has already come before us in his remark that although no man knew him, Heaven knew him. He believed in the importance of sacrifices and stood for a dignified fulfillment of one's proper duties to the supernatural.

One of his sayings in particular has been taken to show that Confucius was fundamentally agnostic in religion. This is found in the Lun Yü (vi, 20) where, according to a quite literal and frequently encountered translation,[79] he advised men to "keep aloof" from the spirits. The meaning is rather, however, that men should "maintain the proper distance"[80] in relations with the spirits, that is not fawn upon them for the sake of personal advantage but always act toward them in the manner prescribed by custom and courtesy.[81] As translated by Ku Hung-ming, the entire statement means: "To know the essential duties of man living in a society of men, and to hold in fear and awe the Spiritual Powers of the Universe, while keeping aloof from irreverent familiarity with them, that may be considered as understanding."[82]

"The essential duties of man living in a society of men," was of course the subject of deepest interest to Confucius. His major attention was devoted to the problem of the organization of society in accordance with ethical principles.[83] As far as these principles were concerned, he believed that they came down out of an immemorial past and that he himself was not their originator but only their transmitter. The following quotations from several of the oldest sources

[79] e.g. Lyall, *The Sayings of Confucius*, p.25.
[80] cf. tr. in CBC p.338.
[81] Herrlee G. Creel in *T'oung Pao ou Archives concernant l'histoire, les langues, la géographie, l'ethnographie et les arts de l'Asie orientale*. 29 (1932), pp.55-99.
[82] *Discourses and Sayings of Confucius*, quoted by Creel, *ibid.*, p.90 n.1.
[83] For detailed studies of the political and economic teachings of Confucius see, for example, Leonard Shihlien Hsü, *The Political Philosophy of Confucianism, An Interpretation of the Social and Political Ideas of Confucius, His Forerunners, and His Early Disciples* (The Broadway Oriental Library). 1932; Chen Huan-Chang, *The Economic Principles of Confucius and His School* (Studies in History, Economics and Public Law, edited by the Faculty of Political Science of Columbia University, xliv, xlv, 112, 113). 2 vols. 1911.

will reveal the basic attitude of Confucius and state some of the fundamental thoughts advanced by him and his early followers.

From the Lun Yü, or Analects, we give these sayings of Confucius:

The Master said, I have "transmitted what was taught to me without making up anything of my own." I have been faithful to and loved the Ancients. . . . I have never grown tired of learning nor wearied of teaching others what I have learnt.

The Duke of She asked Tzu-lu about Master K'ung. Tzu-lu did not reply. The Master said, Why did you not say "This is the character of the man: so intent upon enlightening the eager that he forgets his hunger, and so happy in doing so, that he forgets the bitterness of his lot and does not realize that old age is at hand. That is what he is."

The Master said, I for my part am not one of those who have innate knowledge. I am simply one who loves the past and who is diligent in investigating it.

The Master said, At fifteen I set my heart upon learning. At thirty, I had planted my feet firm upon the ground. At forty, I no longer suffered from perplexities. At fifty, I knew what were the biddings of Heaven. At sixty, I heard them with docile ear. At seventy, I could follow the dictates of my own heart; for what I desired no longer overstepped the boundaries of right.

The Master said, It is Goodness that gives to a neighborhood its beauty. One who is free to choose, yet does not prefer to dwell among the Good— how can he be accorded the name of wise?

The Master said, Without Goodness a man

> Cannot for long endure adversity,
> Cannot for long enjoy prosperity.

The Good Man rests content with Goodness; he that is merely wise pursues Goodness in the belief that it pays to do so.

Of the adage "Only a Good Man knows how to like people, knows how to dislike them," the Master said, He whose heart is in the smallest degree set upon Goodness will dislike no one.

The Master said, In the morning, hear the Way; in the evening, die content.

The Master said, In the presence of a good man, think all the time how you may learn to equal him. In the presence of a bad man, turn your gaze within!

The Master said, He who will not worry about what is far off will soon find something worse than worry close at hand.

The Master said, The gentleman who takes the right as his material to work upon and ritual as the guide in putting what is right into practice, who is modest in setting out his projects and faithful in carrying them to their conclusion, he indeed is a true gentleman.

The Master said, A gentleman is distressed by his own lack of capacity; he is never distressed at the failure of others to recognize his merits.

The Master said, A gentleman has reason to be distressed if he ends his days without making a reputation for himself.

The Master said, The demands that a gentleman makes are upon himself; those that a small man makes are upon others.

The Master said, A gentleman is proud, but not quarrelsome, allies himself with individuals, but not with parties.

The Master said, A gentleman does not

> Accept men because of what they say,
> Nor reject sayings, because the speaker is what he is.

Tzu-kung asked saying, Is there any single saying that one can act upon all day and every day? The Master said, Perhaps the saying about consideration: "Never do to others what you would not like them to do to you."[84]

From the Ta Hsüeh, or Great Learning, we quote a famous passage on how to order all society aright through the cultivation of the self. The first paragraph was supposed to be by Confucius and the second, with its amplified and logically articulated statement of the same idea, by the later author of the book.

The Way of learning to be great consists in shining with the illustrious power of moral personality, in making a new people, in abiding in the highest goodness. To know one's abiding place leads to fixity of purpose, fixity of purpose to calmness of mind, calmness of mind to serenity of life, serenity of life to careful consideration of means, careful consideration of means to the achievement of the end.

Things have their roots and branches, human affairs their endings as well as beginnings. So to know what comes first and what comes afterward leads one near to the Way. The men of old who wished to shine with the illustrious power of personality throughout the Great Society, first had to govern their own states efficiently. Wishing to do this, they first had to make an ordered harmony in their own families. Wishing to do this, they first had to cultivate their individual selves. Wishing to do this, they first had to put their minds right. Wishing to do this, they first had to make their purposes genuine. Wishing to do this, they first had to extend their knowledge to the utmost. Such extension of knowledge consists in appreciating the nature of things. For with the appreciation of the nature of things knowledge reaches its height. With the completion of knowledge purposes become genuine. With purposes genuine the mind becomes right. With the mind right the individual self comes into flower. With the self in flower the family becomes an ordered harmony. With the families ordered harmonies the State is efficiently governed. With states efficiently governed the Great Society is at peace. Thus from the Son of

---

[84] vii, 1f.,18f.; ii, 4; iv, 1-4,8,17; xv, 11,17-23; tr. Waley, *The Analects of Confucius*, pp.123,127,88,102f.,105,197f. Quoted by permission of the publishers, George Allen and Unwin Ltd., London.

Heaven down to the common people there is unity in this: that for everybody the bringing of the individual self to flower is to be taken as the root.[85]

From the Chung Yung, or Doctrine of the Mean, we give three sections. The first is plainly set forth as a quotation from Confucius, the second seems to mingle the thoughts of Confucius and Tzu Ssu, and the third is probably a summary or interpretation by a later editor.

The Master said: "The Way is not far removed from men. If a man pursues a way which removes him from men, he cannot be in the Way. . . . The treatment which you do not like for yourself you must not hand out to others."

The true ruler must not fail to cultivate his self; and, having it in mind to do this, he must not fail to serve his parents; and having it in mind to do this, he must not fail to have knowledge of men; and, having it in mind to have this knowledge, he must not fail to have knowledge of Heaven.

There are five things which concern everybody in the Great Society, as also do the three means by which these five things are accomplished. To explain, the relationship between sovereign and subject, between father and son, between husband and wife, between elder and younger brother, and the equal intercourse of friend and friend, these five relationships concern everybody in the Great Society. Knowledge, human-heartedness, and fortitude, these three are the means; for these qualities are the spiritual power in society as a whole. The means by which this power is made effective is unity.

That which Heaven entrusts to man is to be called his nature. The following out of this nature is to be called the Way. The cultivation of the Way is to be called instruction in systematic truth. The Way, it may not be abandoned for a moment. If it might be abandoned, it would not be the Way. Because this is so, the man of principle holds himself restrained and keyed up in relation to the unseen world. Since there is nothing more manifest than what is hidden, nothing more visible than what is minute, therefore the man of principle is on guard when he is alone with himself.

To have no emotions of pleasure and anger and sorrow and joy surging up, this is to be described as being in a state of equilibrium. To have these emotions surging up but all in tune, this is to be described as a state of harmony. This state of equilibrium is the supreme foundation, this state of harmony the highway, of the Great Society. Once equilibrium and harmony are achieved, heaven and earth maintain their proper positions, and all living things are nourished.[86]

[85] Taken from *The Great Learning and the Mean-in-Action*, tr. by E. R. Hughes, published by E. P. Dutton and Co., Inc., New York. Copyrighted by E. R. Hughes, 1943. By permission of the publishers.
[86] *ibid.*, pp.111,119f.,105f.

"WARRING STATES" AND COMPETING PHILOSOPHIES

The period following the death of Confucius was that of the "Warring States," in which the various political units of China struggled for supremacy. It was also a time in which numerous other philosophies arose to compete with that of Confucius for followers. As a matter of fact, for a hundred years or more Confucianism seemed to grow weaker rather than stronger. Of this course of events Ssu-ma Ch'ien says in the Shih Chi: "After the death of Confucius, his seventy disciples scattered and traveled among the feudal lords. The important ones became teachers and ministers [of the feudal lords]. The lesser ones became friends and teachers of the officials or went into retirement and were no longer seen. . . . During this period there was fighting everywhere throughout the empire between the Warring States, and Confucianism declined. Only in the states of Ch'i and Lu did learning still continue."[87]

So many divergences of thought came into existence that within little more than a century after the death of Confucius reference was made to "the doctrines of the Hundred Schools."[88] We of course cannot discuss all of these. We will, however, tell of Taoism and its leaders such as Lao Tzu, Yang Chu, and Chuang Tzu, in the next chapter; and at this point we will give a brief description of one other philosophy as a single example out of the many schools. It is the remarkable system of thought originated by Mo Tzu and known as Mohism.

Mo Tzu, or Master Mo,[89] was also known by the personal name of Ti. Concerning him there is this brief statement in the Shih Chi: "Mo Ti seems probably to have been a great officer in the state of Sung. He was skillful in maintaining military defenses, and taught economy of use. Some say that he was contemporary with Confucius, others that he was after him."[90] According to recent research the latter alternative suggested by Ssu-ma Ch'ien as to the date of Mo Tzu is the more probable, and his life fell within the century after the death of Confucius (somewhere between 478 and 381 B.C.).

The central interest of Mo Tzu was the welfare of man. He once said, "The purpose of the magnanimous lies in procuring benefits for the world and eliminating its calamities";[91] or, more concisely trans-

[87] tr. in FHCP p.106.   [88] FHCP pp.132-169.
[89] FHCP pp.76-105; Yi-pao Mei, *Motse, The Neglected Rival of Confucius* (Probsthain's Oriental Series). 1934.
[90] tr. in FHCP p.76.
[91] tr. Yi-pao Mei, *The Ethical and Political Works of Motse, Translated from the Original Chinese Text* (Probsthain's Oriental Series). 1929, p.87.

lated, "Promote general welfare and remove evil"; and this utterance has been called the motto of his entire movement.[92]

In order to accomplish this end Mo Tzu advocated frugality, universal love, and the condemnation of offensive war. Extravagance was to be avoided, he thought, both in government and in personal life, and only those expenditures made which really brought benefit to the people. Concerning the realm of government he said, "To cut out useless expenditures is the way of the sage-kings and a great blessing to the world."[93] In personal affairs he suggested avoiding lavish funerals and shortening the period of mourning.

Universal love, likewise, was seen as necessary by Mo Tzu if universal well-being were to be achieved. The great evils of the world, he held, were caused by the absence of such love. He said: "Mutual attacks among states, mutual usurpation among houses, mutual injuries among individuals; the lack of grace and loyalty between ruler and ruled, the lack of affection and filial piety between father and son, the lack of harmony between elder and younger brothers—these are the major calamities in the world." Whence do such calamities arise? "They arise out of want of mutual love." What, then, is the way of universal love and mutual aid? "It is to regard the state of others as one's own, the houses of others as one's own, the persons of others as one's self."[94]

The condemnation of offensive war grew naturally out of the foregoing analysis. War brings no benefit to Heaven, nor to the spirits, nor to men. "Now to capture a state and to destroy an army, to disturb and torture the people, and to set at naught the aspirations of the sages by confusion—is this intended to bless Heaven? But the people of Heaven are gathered together to besiege the towns belonging to Heaven. This is to murder men of Heaven and dispossess the spirits of their altars and to ruin the state and to kill the sacrificial animals. It is then not a blessing to Heaven on high. Is it intended to bless the spirits? But men of Heaven are murdered, spirits are deprived of their sacrifices, the earlier kings are neglected, the multitude are tortured and the people are scattered. It is then not a blessing to the spirits in the middle. Is it intended to bless the people? But the blessing of the people by killing them off must be very meager. And when we calculate the expense, which is the root of the calamities to living, we find the property of innumerable people is

[92] Chan Wing-tsit in MPEW p.38.
[93] tr. Yi-pao Mei, *The Ethical and Political Works of Motse*, p.119.
[94] *ibid.*, pp.81f.

exhausted. It is then not a blessing to the people below either." Therefore the conclusion is inescapable: "Now if the rulers and the gentlemen of the world sincerely desire to procure benefits and avert calamities for the world—if they desire to do righteousness and be superior men, if they desire to strike the way of the sage-kings on the one hand and bless the people on the other—if so, the doctrine of condemnation of offensive war should not be left unheeded."[95]

In all of this the strongly practical and utilitarian emphasis of Mo Tzu is evident. Hate harms the people; love benefits everybody, not least of all the one who practices it. "Whoever loves others is loved by others." "How can there be anything that is good but not useful?" asks this pragmatic thinker.[96]

Religion itself was approached by Mo Tzu from this same kind of interest in its usefulness. "If all the people in the world believed that the spirits are able to reward virtue and punish vice," he asked, "how could the world be in chaos?"[97] Because of its practical effectiveness as the sanction of right order in the world, religion was strongly championed by Mo Tzu. Also in his religious thinking he set forth a more personal conception of Shang Ti than had been known before.[98] Here is the famous passage in which he set forth his quaint reasons for his sublime belief that "Heaven loves the people":

How do we know Heaven loves the people? Because it teaches them all. How do we know it teaches them all? Because it claims them all. How do we know it claims them all? Because it accepts sacrifices from them all. How do we know it accepts sacrifices from all? Because within the four seas all grain-eating [i.e., civilized] people feed oxen and sheep with grass, and dogs and pigs with grains, and prepare clean cakes and wine to do sacrifice to Supreme God [Shang Ti] and the spirits. Claiming all the people, why will Heaven not love them? Moreover, as I have said, for the murder of one innocent individual there will be one calamity. Who is it that murders the innocent? It is man. Who is it that sends down the calamity? It is Heaven. If Heaven should be thought of as not loving the people, why should it send down calamities for the murder of man by man? So, I know Heaven loves the people.[99]

MENCIUS

In the Period of the "Warring States," then, there was not only contention among political groups but also rivalry among philosophi-

[95] ibid., pp.108f.,116.   [96] ibid., pp.83,89.
[97] ibid., p.160.   [98] Hodous in JGRMW p.10.
[99] tr. Yi-pao Mei, The Ethical and Political Works of Motse, p.139.

cal schools. The ultimate victorious emergence of Confucianism as the most widely accepted philosophy in China was due largely to the work of Mencius and Hsün Tzu. Continuing the statement from which we quoted above (p.353), Ssu-ma Ch'ien speaks of these two teachers as follows: "During the reigns of Kings Wei [357-320 B.C.] and Hsüan [319-301 B.C.] of Ch'i there were such persons as Meng Tzu [Mencius] and Hsün Ch'ing [Hsün Tzu], who followed the teachings of the Master [Confucius] and developed them, becoming famous in their generation for their learning."

The biographical statement of the same historian concerning Mencius is this: "Meng K'o was a native of Tsou. He received his education from the disciples of Tzu Ssu [the grandson of Confucius]. When his learning had become comprehensive, he traveled to serve King Hsüan of Ch'i, but the latter was unable to employ him. He then went to the state of Liang, but King Hui of Liang [370-319 B.C.] was insincere in his words and considered [Mencius] as pedantic and far from reality. . . . The empire was then engaged in forming vertical [north-to-south] and horizontal [east-to-west] alliances [among the states], and held fighting as something worthy. Whereas Meng K'o was [intent on] transmitting the virtues of . . . the Three Dynasties, so that those whom he visited were not willing to listen to him. So he retired and together with his disciple, Wan Chang, and others, put the Shih and Shu into order, transmitted the doctrines of Confucius, and composed the Mencius in seven books."[100]

As the passage just quoted indicates, the birthplace of Mencius was in Tsou, a tiny state on the border of Lu in the present Shantung, and like Lu a center of Confucianism. The dates of his life were probably 372-289 B.C. As also stated in the foregoing quotation, the writings of Mencius took the form of seven books customarily known by his own name.[101]

In this work Mencius describes the confusion of argument in his time, and tells how he has made it his task to defend Confucianism and to oppose Yang Chu and Mo Ti, the leaders of Taoism and of Mohism respectively. "Sage-kings cease to arise, and the feudal lords give rein to their lusts. Unemployed scholars indulge in unreasonable discussions.[102] The words of Yang Chu and Mo Ti fill all below heaven. The words of all below heaven come home to Mo, if they do not come home to Yang. Yang's school is for self. It has no lord.

[100] tr. in FHCP p.107.
[101] For the translations of his work see above, p.340 n.64.
[102] tr. in FHCP p.132.

Mo's school loves all alike. It has no father. Without father and without lord we are birds or beasts. . . . If the ways of Yang and Mo are not stopped, if the way of Confucius is not seen, crooked words will bewitch the people, and choke love and right. When love and right are choked, beasts are led to eat men, and men will eat each other. I am afraid, therefore. I defend the way of bygone holy men, withstand Yang and Mo, stop the rise of crooked speakers, and banish wanton words. Working in man's heart they hurt his business; working in his business they hurt his conduct. When a holy man rises again he will not change my words."[103]

From the above we learn that the objection of Mencius to Yang's school was that it was centered in selfishness; his criticism of the school of Mo was that it taught love for all alike. As for himself, Mencius advocated the principle of benevolence, but believed that there were necessary levels of love. He distinguished liking for animals, love for mankind, and devotion to kinsfolk as successively higher levels of attachment. He said, "A gentleman likes living things, but he does not love them. He loves the people, but not as he loves his kinsmen. He is a kinsman to his kin, and loves the people. He loves the people and likes living things."[104]

Furthermore, Mencius took issue with the utilitarianism of Mo. He himself believed that human nature was essentially good, and therefore taught the practice of virtue as a necessary expression of that nature, quite apart from the material benefits which might also result. To illustrate Mencius' belief in the fundamental goodness of human nature we may recall the famous saying in which he argued that man tends to seek good just as water tends to run downhill. The statement was made in opposition to a contrary statement by a little-known philosopher named Kao Tzu. "Kao Tzu said, Our nature is like a whirlpool: if a breach is made to the east, the water flows east; if a breach is made to the west, it flows west. As water does not discern between east and west, so man's nature does not discern between good and evil. Mencius said, Truly water does not discern between east and west, but does it not discern between up and down? Man's nature is good, as water flows down. No man but is good, no water but flows down. Hit water and make it leap, you can send it above your forehead; force it, and you can bring it up a

---

[103] tr. Lyall, *Mencius*, pp.96f. This quotation and those following are by permission of the publishers, Longmans, Green and Company, London and New York.
[104] *ibid.*, p.222.

hill. But is that the nature of water? It is done by force; and when man is brought to do evil, the same is done to his nature."[105]

For an expression of his advocacy of doing good regardless of expectation of profiting thereby, we may turn to a conversation which Mencius had with King Hui of Liang. The king asked what gain the counsel of Mencius might be expected to bring, and Mencius replied: "Why must you speak of gain, King? There is love too and right, and they are everything. When the king says, What gain can I get for my land? the great men say, What gain can I get for my house? the knights and common men say, What gain can I get for myself? then high and low fight one another for gain, and the kingdom is shaken. . . . When gain is put before right, only robbery can fill the maw. Love never forsakes kinsmen, right never puts his lord last. You too, King, should speak of love and right and of nothing else; why must you speak of gain?"[106]

Two more brief quotations must suffice to complete our sampling of the teachings of this penetrating thinker:

Mencius said, The great man is he that does not lose the child heart.

Mencius said, Man's heart is love, man's road is right. To leave the road unfollowed, [to] let the heart stray and not know where to seek it, is sad indeed!

If a man's dog or hen strays, he knows where to seek it; but when his heart strays he knows not where to seek it! The scholar's way is no more than seeking our stray heart.[107]

HSÜN TZU

Mencius may be called the developer and Hsün Tzu the systematizer of Confucianism. The latter, known also as Hsün Ch'ing, lived probably around 320-235 B.C.,[108] in other words near the close of the Period of the "Warring States." The Shih Chi says of him: "Hsün Ch'ing was a native of Chao. When he was fifty, he first came to spread his teachings abroad in Ch'i. . . . T'ien P'ien and the other scholars associated with him were already all dead in the time of King Hsiang of Ch'i [283-265 B.C.], and Hsün Ch'ing was the most eminent [surviving] learned scholar. Ch'i was still repairing the gaps in the ranks of the 'great officers,' and Hsün Ch'ing was three times

[105] *ibid.*, pp.168f.
[106] *ibid.*, pp.1f.; cf. pp.188f.; Liang Chi-chao, *History of Chinese Political Thought During the early Tsin Period.* 1930, pp.54f.
[107] tr. Lyall, *Mencius*, pp.122,178.
[108] Homer H. Dubs, *Hsüntze, The Moulder of Ancient Confucianism* (Probsthain's Oriental Series). 1927, pp.22-25.

officer for the sacrificial wine offering. Among the people of Ch'i were some who slandered Hsün Ch'ing, and he thereupon went to Ch'u, where Prince Ch'un-shen made him magistrate of Lan-ling.[109] When Prince Ch'un Shen died [238 B.C.], Hsün Ch'ing lost his Lan-ling position. Li Ssu, who later became Prime Minister of Ch'in, was his disciple. Hsün Ch'ing hated the governments of his corrupt generation, its dying states and evil princes, who did not follow the Way (Tao), but gave their attention to magic and prayers and believed in omens and luck. It was a generation of low scholars who had no learning. [Thinkers] such as Chuang Chou [Chuang Tzu], on the other hand, were specious and threw the customs into disorder. Therefore he expounded the prosperity and decay that come from putting into practice the Confucian and Mohist doctrines and virtues. By the time of his death he had written and arranged in order several tens of thousands of words. He was buried in Lan-ling."[110]

In the "several tens of thousands of words" which Hsün Tzu has left behind,[111] we can see that he undertook to give a well-rounded and consistent expression to the fundamental Confucian philosophy. In doing so he paid high tribute to Confucius, but sharply criticized Mencius. His most striking difference from the latter was that whereas Mencius believed human nature was fundamentally good, Hsün Tzu regarded it as basically bad. On this point Hsün Tzu formulated his opinion very concisely: "The nature of man is evil; his goodness is only acquired training."[112]

If this is correct, then virtue cannot be just the development of innate impulses as Mencius would lead one to suppose. Rather, Hsün Tzu argues, for the proper training of human nature in goodness, standards of action are needed which can only come from an external authority. These norms are to be found in the rules of propriety which were enunciated by the sage-kings of the past and should be enforced by the wise ruler of the present. "Anciently the sage-kings knew that man's nature was evil, that it was partial, bent on evil, and corrupt, rebellious, disorderly, without good government, hence they established the authority of the prince to govern man; they set forth clearly the rules of proper conduct and justice to reform him; they established laws and government to rule him; they

---

[109] A place in southern Shantung.
[110] tr. in FHCP p.279.
[111] Homer H. Dubs, *The Works of Hsüntze, Translated from the Chinese, with Notes* (Probsthain's Oriental Series). 1925.
[112] *ibid.*, p.301.

made punishments severe to warn him; and so they caused the whole country to come to a state of good government and prosperity, and to accord with goodness. This is the government of the sage-kings, the reforming influence of the rules of proper conduct and justice."[113]

With this strong emphasis upon authority it may be said that the most splendid age of Chinese thought came to its downfall.[114] The spirit of intellectual emancipation which had fostered a variety of inquiries into the nature of reality, gave way to the authoritarianism which always thereafter remained characteristic of Confucianism.

Hsün Tzu may also be seen as completing the development of Confucianism into a thoroughly naturalistic humanism. In the thought of Confucius, Heaven seems to have been a ruling and personal providence, and the spirits were actual beings toward whom a gentleman should maintain a bearing full of respect. With Hsün Tzu, Heaven was depersonalized and conceived as naturalistic law, while the very existence of the spirits was denied. Man was therefore cast upon his own resources and challenged to do his utmost to achieve advance through his own unaided efforts. The following words will give some of Hsün Tzu's own statements on the matter, and will conclude our consideration of this philosopher: "Heaven has a constant regularity of action. . . . The fixed stars make their round; the sun and moon alternately shine; the four seasons come in succession; the Yin and Yang[115] go through their great mutations. . . . The results of all these changes are known, but we do not know the invisible source—this is what is meant by the work of Heaven. . . . Prosperity and calamity do not come from Heaven. . . . Therefore the superior man is anxious about what is within his power, and does not seek for what comes from Heaven—this causes daily progress. . . . If a person neglects what men can do and seeks for what Heaven does, he fails to understand the nature of things."[116]

With the systematization of its doctrines and the explicit statement of its implicit authoritarianism and naturalism by Hsün Tzu, early Confucianism may be said to have attained its henceforth most characteristic form. We will now follow more briefly the developments in later periods.

[113] *ibid.*, p.308.
[114] Hu Shih, *The Development of the Logical Method in Ancient China.* 1928, p.168.
[115] The negative and positive cosmic principles which were so important in medieval Chinese philosophy. See Alfred Forke, *The World-Conception of the Chinese, Their Astronomical, Cosmological and Physico-Philosophical Speculations* (Probsthain's Oriental Series). 1925, pp.163-223.
[116] tr. Dubs *The Works of Hsüntze*, pp.173,175,177,179,183.

5. THE CH'IN PERIOD, 221-207 B.C.

SHIH HUANG TI

THE story of the Ch'in dynasty is virtually that of a single man, Shih Huang Ti.[117] This remarkable leader was a prince of Ch'in, the state from the name of which our word China is probably derived. He succeeded in overcoming all of the other Chinese states and bringing them together into a single unified empire with himself as the absolute ruler. Shih Huang Ti was king of Ch'in from 246 to 221 B.C., and emperor of all China from 221 to 210. His imperial capital was at Kwan-chung, modern Si-an (or Si-an-fu), in the same plain of the River Wei where the Western Chou capitals had been and where later the capitals of the Former Han, Sui and T'ang dynasties would be. The title assumed by the new master of China in 221 B.C. may be translated First Emperor, Shih meaning "first," and Huang and Ti being royal titles out of the legendary past. It was intended that following rulers should be called Erh Huang Ti, San Huang Ti, etc., meaning Second Emperor, Third Emperor, etc. In view of the fact that the Chinese empire thus founded lasted in substantially the same form, although under different dynasties, for over two thousand years—from 221 B.C. to A.D. 1911—the work of Shih Huang Ti may properly be described as "the most enduring political achievement ever wrought by man."[118] "With him," it has also been said, "the ancient history of China closes and a new era begins."[119]

Since many of the scholars, who were devoted to the past, preferred the ancient feudal ways to the new autocracy, and since freedom of philosophic discussion was conducive to criticism of the government, Shih Huang Ti undertook drastic repressive measures against these apparently subversive forces. He caused many of the literati to be killed, and ordered the collection and burning of the ancient literature (213 B.C.).[120] In this act, as in his entire career, he was encouraged and guided by his chief minister, Li Ssu, who had learned as a pupil of Hsün Tzu to believe in the absolute power of the prince.[121]

[117] Granet, *Chinese Civilization*, pp.96,392f.; Tsui Chi, *A Short History of Chinese Civilization*. 1943, pp.71-79.
[118] E. W. Bishop in JAOS Supplement 4 (1939), p.60.
[119] J. J. L. Duyvendak, *The Book of Lord Shang, A Classic of the Chinese School of Law* (Probsthain's Oriental Series). 1928, p.1.
[120] Leo Wieger, *China throughout the Ages.* tr. E. C. Werner. 1928, p.305.
[121] Derk Bodde, *China's First Unifier, A Study of the Ch'in Dynasty as seen in the Life of Li Ssŭ* (280?-208 B.C.) (Sinica Leidensia, III). 1938, pp.10f.

Against external enemies, particularly the Hsiung Nu (probably the same as the Huns of European history) in the northwest, Shih Huang Ti built the Great Wall of China. The feudal kingdoms in the north had already erected various lines of defense against the barbarians, and Shih Huang Ti was able to utilize these scattered ramparts in the completion of his more extensive barrier. As established in 214 B.C. his wall ran from Shan-hai-kuan on the Gulf of Liao-tung to Lin-t'ao in southern Kansu. As it stands today the Great Wall is the result not only of the work of Shih Huang Ti but also of enlargements, restorations and even alterations of its course made during many centuries since his time. This present wall is a parapet of earth and stone faced with brick, some twenty or thirty feet high, with square watch towers at intervals, and stretching across northern China for fourteen hundred miles.[122] The photograph reproduced in Fig. 154 shows the Great Wall in the vicinity of the Nan-k'ou Pass.

Shih Huang Ti died in 210 B.C. and the great earthen mound or tumulus where he was buried (Fig. 153) may still be seen some distance east of Si-an.[123] The following account of his burial is found in the Shih Chi of Ssu-ma Ch'ien:

In the ninth moon the First Emperor was buried in Mount Li, which in the early days of his reign he had caused to be tunneled and prepared with that view. Then, when he had consolidated the empire, he employed his soldiery, to the number of 700,000, to bore down to the Three Springs [that is, until water was reached], and there a foundation of bronze was laid and the sarcophagus placed thereon. Rare objects and costly jewels were collected from the palaces and from the various officials, and were carried thither and stored in vast quantities. Artificers were ordered to construct mechanical crossbows, which, if any one were to enter, would immediately discharge their arrows. With the aid of quicksilver, rivers were made, the Yangtze, the Hwang Ho, and the great ocean, the metal being poured from one into the other by machinery. On the roof were delineated the constellations of the sky, on the floor the geographical divisions of the earth. Candles were made from the fat of the man-fish [walrus], calculated to last for a very long time.

The Second Emperor said, "It is not fitting that the concubines of my late father who are without children should leave him now"; and accordingly he ordered them to accompany the dead monarch to the next world, those who thus perished being many in number.

[122] Stein, *Serindia*, II, pp.722f.; Oswald Sirén in EB V, p.556; Owen Lattimore, *Inner Asian Frontiers of China* (American Geographical Society Research Series, 21). 1940, pp.25,440.

[123] Victor Segalen, Gilbert de Voisins and Jean Lartigue, *Mission archéologique en Chine (1914 et 1917)*, Atlas, I, *La sculpture et les monuments funéraires (Provinces du Chàn-si et du Sseu-tch'ouan)*. 1923, Pl. I; I, *L'art funéraire à l'époque des Han.* 1935, pp.18-20.

When the interment was completed, some one suggested that the workmen who had made the machinery and concealed the treasure knew the great value of the latter, and that the secret would leak out. Therefore, so soon as the ceremony was over, and the path giving access to the sarcophagus had been blocked up at its innermost end, the outside gate at the entrance to this path was let fall, and the mausoleum was effectually closed, so that not one of the workmen escaped. Trees and grass were then planted around, that the spot might look like the rest of the mountain.[124]

[124] tr. Giles, *A History of Chinese Literature*, pp.107f.

6. THE HAN PERIOD, 202 B.C.-A.D. 220

IT WAS not long after the death of Shih Huang Ti that a period of anarchy ensued out of which was established the Han dynasty. The founder of the new house was Liu Pang (also called Kao Tsu) and the name of the dynasty was that of his own native state, Han. The period may be divided into two parts, Former Han (202 B.C.-A.D. 9) and Later Han (A.D. 25-220), the dividing point between the two being the time early in the first century A.D. when a usurper named Wang Mang held the throne. Since the Later Han capital was at Loyang this period is also called Eastern Han. The greatest Han emperor was doubtless Wu Ti who reigned during the Former Han Period from 140 to 87 B.C.; the emperor of most interest to us in the Later Han Period was Ming Ti (A.D. 58-76).

As the Han empire reached its apex under Wu Ti it was not far from the size of the realm which Rome was contemporaneously mastering in the west, and next to that domain it was the greatest power on earth. Largely through the western explorations of Chang Ch'ien,[125] minister of Wu Ti, the east and west were brought into contact, and the silks of China began to go by way of the caravan routes of Sinkiang to Rome.

In order to protect this highway of trade as it stretched out into central Asia, Wu Ti extended China's "Great Wall" to the northwest and pushed a line of fortifications into the forbidding desert beyond Tunhwang. As explored in this remote region by Aurel Stein, the remains of the wall show that it was built with bundles of sticks placed crosswise in layers alternating with layers of stamped clay and gravel. This type of construction was planned to withstand the destructive effects of the wind-driven sand of the desert. Behind the wall and not far from it was a long chain of square brick watch-towers, with adjacent quarters for the military detachments posted there.[126]

As far as religion is concerned, Taoism was favored by Liu Pang and his immediate successors as it had been by Shih Huang Ti; Buddhism attracted the attention of the court by the time of Ming Ti; but Confucianism was, under Wu Ti, elevated to the religion of state, a position it retained until A.D. 1912.

There is a story, indeed, that already in the last year of his reign Liu Pang himself visited the tomb of Confucius at Chufou and

[125] GCBD p.12.   [126] Stein, *Serindia*, II, pp.578-790.

offered sacrifice, but the historicity of this account has been questioned, and if the event did take place it was probably at most a political gesture.[127] Wu Ti, however, gave Confucianism his strong patronage. The reasons leading to the official adoption of Confucian doctrines included the following, according to the analysis of the situation by John K. Shryock: Experience had shown that some of the principles followed by Shih Huang Ti, although apparently successful in time of war, were inadequate as a basis for a lasting government, since the Ch'in dynasty had collapsed so soon after the death of its founder. The burning of the Confucian books by Shih Huang Ti and Li Ssu had actually had an opposite effect from that intended; interest in this literature had increased and Confucian sentiment had grown stronger, while the differences between the scholars and the emperor had grown less. Wu Ti himself was credulous by nature and when certain ominous portents were experienced at the close of his predecessor's reign readily concluded that a radical change was called for. He loved ceremony and ritual too, and naturally turned to the Confucians as authorities in such things.[128]

In line with the renewed and increased interest in Confucianism, a great deal of effort was given at this time to recovering the writings of the past, so many of which had suffered in the earlier "burning of the books." Much historical work likewise was done. Of the ancient texts the following were now included in the list of canonical books: the I Ching, Shu Ching, Shih Ching, Li Chi, Chou Li, I Li, Ch'un Ch'iu, Hsiao Ching, Lün Yü, Meng Tzu Shu, and Erh Ya, the last often being called the oldest Chinese dictionary. In the compilation of historical records a leading part was played by Ssu-ma Ch'ien who was active under the reign of Wu Ti, and from whose work we have already quoted frequently. He is often referred to as the father of Chinese history. Another work of importance for its graphic description of the social order of the time is the Yen T'ieh Lun, a treatise on economic and political problems, written by Huan K'uan in the first century B.C.[129]

WRITINGS ON WOOD AND ON PAPER

Hundreds of written documents dating from the first century B.C.

[127] John K. Shryock, *The Origin and Development of the State Cult of Confucius.* 1932, p.97.

[128] *ibid.*, pp.34-38.

[129] tr. Esson M. Gale, *Discourses on Salt and Iron, A Debate on State Control of Commerce and Industry in Ancient China, Chapters I-XIX, Translated from the Chinese of Huan K'uan with Introduction and Notes* (Sinica Leidensia, II). 1931.

to the middle of the second century A.D. have been recovered by Aurel Stein from the ruins of the "Great Wall" in the region of Tunhwang, and from these we can learn what books of the Han Period were like, and verify the surmise already made on other grounds (p.329) as to the appearance of ancient Chinese books.[130] A collection of portions of such books is shown in Fig. 155. These are slips of wood approximately nine inches (or one foot in the reckoning of the Han Period) in length, containing writing in vertical columns. It will be convenient first to look at the fifteen pieces of practically uniform width which fill the whole central part of the plate, all of which belong to a single "book." Upon close inspection each piece is seen to have three small notches, uniformly spaced, in its left edge. Furthermore there is no text on the reverse side of these slips. It is almost certain, therefore, that the slips were tied with strings so that they could be folded together, blank back to blank back, for carrying and storage, and opened out, like the bellows of an accordion, for perusal. Such was the customary wooden "book" of that time and of earlier times.

The fifteen pieces just dealt with, it may be explained further, were found by Aurel Stein at the station on the "Great Wall" which he labels T. VI. b. i. Upon decipherment it was learned that the "book" to which they belonged was an elaborate calendar for the year 63 B.C., probably used by the officer in command at this post for the correct dating of his official correspondence.

The two panels at the extreme left of our same illustration are the two sides, both inscribed, of a single slip of wood. In this case we have an administrative record, in which is noted the issue in the year 60 B.C. of a linen tunic to a soldier by the captain of a certain company, together with the price of the garment.

The two panels at the extreme right likewise represent two views of the same object, in this case a prismatic, triangular-shaped piece of wood, with writing on its three faces. This was found at the station of the Wall which Stein labels T. XV. a. i. In this document we have the complete opening paragraph of a lexicographical text, named the Chi Chiu Chang, which was composed originally in the period 48-33 B.C. The slip itself was found in company with another piece dated in the year A.D. 67, and may doubtless be assigned to a com-

[130] Stein, *Serindia*, II, pp.644-651,672,698-766; Édouard Chavannes, *Les documents chinois découverts par Aurel Stein dans les sables du Turkestan oriental, publiés et traduits.* 1913, pp.6f.,10-14,20; Pl. I.

parable date. While there might be some question as to whether the calendar and the administrative record should be described as "books," here there is no doubt but that we are dealing with a portion of a book properly so called. This then is one of the oldest known manuscripts of a Chinese book.

The Han Period and the desert ruins of the "Great Wall" give us tangible examples not only of China's ancient wooden books, but also of that important invention, paper, which the same country also contributed to the literary work of the world. According to the Hou Han Shu or Later Han Annals, written by Fan Yeh (d. A.D. 445), the invention of paper was made by Ts'ai Lun in A.D. 105. "In ancient times," writes Fan Yeh, "writing was generally on bamboo or on pieces of silk, which were then called *chih*.[131] But silk being expensive and bamboo heavy, these two materials were not convenient. Then Ts'ai Lun thought of using tree bark, hemp, rags and fish nets. In the first year of the Yüan-hsing Period [A.D. 105] he made a report to the Emperor on the process of paper making, and received high praise for his ability. From this time paper has been in use everywhere and is called the 'paper of Marquis Ts'ai.' "[132]

That paper was actually in use in China not long after the time when tradition affirms it to have first been invented, is shown by Aurel Stein's discovery of documents written on this material as well as on wood in the ruins of the western "Great Wall." Some eight letters, written on paper and carefully folded, were recovered, at the station known as T. XII. a. The paper was found upon microscopic analysis to have been made from rags which had been reduced to a pulp by a rough process of stamping. The script in which the letters were composed is identified as Early Sogdian.[133] Since the definitely dated documents found in the various stations of the "Great Wall" do not go later than A.D. 137 (or possibly A.D. 153), these letters are doubtless also not later than the middle of the second century. A photograph of one of the letters (now labeled T. XII. a. ii. 2) is reproduced in Fig. 156. The size of the sheet is about nine by sixteen inches, and it was enclosed in an envelope also bearing writing, probably an address, on the outside.[134]

[131] This character is now the ordinary word for paper.
[132] Quoted in T. F. Carter, *The Invention of Printing in China and Its Spread Westward.* rev. ed 1931, p.3.
[133] The Sogdians were an East Iranian people.
[134] Stein, *Serindia*, IV, Pl. CLIV, left.

HAN ART

As in preceding ages, so too in the Han Period there was artistic expression in objects of clay, bronze and jade. Without dealing with these in detail it may be said that in form and decoration they reveal an elegant simplicity of line and sense of movement expressive of released force.[135] For a single example we show in Fig. 157 a painted pottery vessel of the period, adorned with ferocious winged dragons.

The desire to provide the finest possible burials for the deceased is responsible for giving us some further very interesting glimpses of the times. The customary arrangement of an important tomb included not only the large tumulus or earthen mound above the burial place proper, but also a chapel or chapels immediately in front of the grave for the making of sacrifices to the dead, and a ceremonial approach lined with pillars or animal statues.

Such a tomb was that of Ho Ch'ü-ping (or Ho K'iu-ping) at Hsü-ping-hsien near modern Si-an. Ho Ch'ü-ping was a brilliant general who warred successfully against the Hsiung Nu, and died at the age of twenty-four in 117 B.C.[136] His tomb was erected at the command of the emperor. As shown in Fig. 158, one of the figures of the guardian animals of the tomb is still standing in place. This is a relatively primitive and more than life-size granite statue of a horse. Prostrate on his back and trampled beneath the feet of the horse is the figure of a man. This man represents the Hsiung Nu against whom Ho Ch'ü-ping had warred, and the entire sculpture doubtless has some of the same magical connotation as the similar portrayals in the Sasanid rock reliefs.[137]

One of two gateway pillars of another tomb, that of Shen (second century A.D.) at Ch'ü-hsien in remote Szechwan, is pictured in Fig. 159. It is adorned with elegant relief carvings: on the front face a "red bird," the symbol of the south; above that a *t'ao-t'ieh*; yet above that a funeral cavalcade; and on the inner face a sinuous "white tiger" and above, a barbarian archer.[138]

There were also relief sculptures in the chapels and chambers of the graves. A fine group of these was found in the burial chambers of the Wu family at Chia-hsiang-hsien in Shantung, often referred to from the name of one of the sons as the Wu Liang Tz'u, or sanctuary

---

[135] GCE III, pp.48-68.　　　　[136] GCBD pp.260f.

[137] Segalen, de Voisins and Lartigue, *Mission archéologique en Chine* (1914), I, pp.33-43; Atlas, I, Pl. III.

[138] *ibid.*, I, pp.55-67; Atlas, I, Pl. XVI,left.

of Wu Liang.[139] Inscriptions here belong to the years from 147 to 167 A.D. To make the reliefs at Wu Liang Tz'u the artists hollowed out the stone around the design and let the figures appear with perfectly flat surfaces. The result has been called "paintings with the chisel," and it is very possible that the reliefs in the tombs were in fact copies of contemporary paintings which adorned the homes of the living.

The Wu Liang Tz'u reliefs contain scenes from history and mythology, and in them a variety of fantastic creatures appears. The relief reproduced in Fig. 160 shows, in the first panel, a charioteer protecting his wounded master by holding above him the top from the chariot; in the second panel, the attempt of Ching K'o to assassinate the Prince of Ch'in who later became Shih Huang Ti;[140] and in the third panel, the two mythical founders of civilization, Fou-hsi (on the right) and his sister Niu-kua, represented with bodies terminating in intertwined serpents' tails.

Another relief portrays the mythological kingdom of the waters. Here we see a deity proceeding in a car drawn by fishes, while around him are frogs, tortoises, fish armed with weapons, men riding on fish, and gnomes with bodies ending in fish tails. Yet another relief (Fig. 161) represents the kingdom of the air, and in this it is evident that the very clouds of heaven have become living things, endowed with the attributes of animals and gods. In the first panel of this relief there are winged quadrupeds with heads of birds and tails of serpents, some ridden by winged gnomes; in the second panel Fou-hsi and Niu-kua appear again; in the third panel winged horse-dragons are pulling cars or ridden by winged gnomes; and in the bottom panel there are swirling, spiraling clouds with heads of birds and tails of serpents.

[139] Otto Fischer, *Die chinesische Malerei der Han-Dynastie.* 1931, pp.33-36.
[140] Bodde, *Statesman, Patriot, and General in Ancient China, Three* Shih Chi *Biographies of the Ch'in Dynasty* (255-206 B.C.), *Translated and Discussed*, pp.34f.,51f.

7. THE SIX DYNASTIES, A.D. 220-581

THE period from A.D. 220 to 581 is known as that of the Six Dynasties. In this time China broke up again into a multiplicity of kingdoms and also suffered invasion by the northern barbarians. The most characteristic artistic monuments of the period, aside from those of Buddhism, are doubtless the large stone sculptures of lions and monsters which guarded the approaches to the tombs. The fearsome and fantastic character of these beasts is another expression of the "art of terror" which was almost as old as China.[141] For a single example we show in Fig. 162 the head of one of the winged lions which guard the tomb of Duke Hsiao Ching (d. A.D. 528) near Nanking. With his upraised head, cavernous mouth and lolling tongue, this monster is indeed a fear-inspiring apparition.[142]

In the tombs, funeral statuettes were often placed. These figures were probably intended to guarantee to the deceased the companion-ship and the services of the persons or creatures represented.[143] From the Six Dynasties Period comes the group of tomb figures shown in Fig. 163. There are three girls playing musical instruments, three with harvesting implements.

In these troubled times the refuge offered by the monasteries and the philosophy of Buddhism proved increasingly attractive, and that faith attained an integral and influential place in the life of China. The relative lack of learning and prevalence of ignorance also con-duced to the spread of the superstitions which had more and more become a part of Taoism. Confucianism was at a low ebb, yet not without influence. Liu Shao, who lived at the beginning of this period, claimed the inspiration of Confucius in the composition of his own Jen wu chih (A.D. 240-250). Remarking that "if Chung Ni had not examined his disciples, he could not have improved them," the author proceeds to a detailed and systematic "study of human abilities," and sets forth an applied psychology of character which

[141] GCE III, pp.119-122.
[142] Segalen, de Voisins and Lartigue, *Mission archéologique en Chine*, Atlas, II, *Monuments funéraires* (*Région de Nankin*), *Monuments bouddhiques* (*Province du Sseu-tch'ouan*). 1924. Pl. LXXVII; Osvald Sirén, *A History of Early Chinese Art: Sculpture.* 1930, pp.21f.
[143] C. Hentze, *Chinese Tomb Figures, A Study in the Beliefs and Folklore of Ancient China.* 1928, p.17.

is still of importance and value.[144] A growing degree of veneration was also directed toward the person of Confucius. In A.D. 442 a temple was erected to the sage at Chufou, where his tomb was, and in A.D. 505 a temple was built at the capital.[145]

[144] J. K. Shryock, *The Study of Human Abilities, The* Jen wu chih *of Liu Shao, with an Introductory Study* (American Oriental Series, 2). 1937.
[145] Hodous in JGRMW p.11.

8. THE SUI (A.D. 581-618) AND T'ANG (A.D. 618-906) DYNASTIES

AFTER the four centuries of chaos and convulsion just alluded to, a new and brilliant period ensued. The unity of the land was restored by the Duke of Sui who founded the short-lived Sui dynasty (A.D. 581-618), and this in turn was followed by the T'ang dynasty which reigned in splendor for three centuries (A.D. 618-906).[146]

T'AI TSUNG

Of the T'ang rulers, T'ai Tsung (A.D. 627-649) was without doubt the greatest. He extended the Chinese empire to boundaries even more extensive than those of Han times, and he ruled wisely at home. The empire was divided in his time into ten *tao* or provinces, and these were divided into *chou* or prefectures, and *hsien* or sub-prefectures. In A.D. 639 there were 358 *chou* in all.

The family of T'ai Tsung claimed to be descended from Lao Tzu, and the emperor therefore had a natural leaning toward Taoism. Nevertheless he did much to strengthen Confucianism. In A.D. 630 he commanded the erection of a temple to Confucius in each of the *chou* and *hsien* in the empire, and he also ordered sacrifices to be made in them by scholars and officials of the government. Not only Confucius but also noteworthy disciples and Confucian scholars were objects of veneration in these temples where at this time, perhaps as a result of Buddhist influence, they were customarily represented by actual statues. These images were made of wood but in A.D. 960 clay figures were ordered to be substituted. Thus for all practical purposes Confucius was treated as a god and his cult was scarcely distinguishable from that addressed to any other deity. In 1530, however, the appearance of idolatry was eliminated by the removal of the clay images, and wooden tablets, bearing the names of the respective worthies, were set up in the temples.[147]

For the most part T'ai Tsung and the other early T'ang rulers were not only friendly toward all three of the faiths already deep-rooted in Chinese life, namely Confucianism, Taoism and Buddhism, but were also tolerant toward other foreign religions which were becoming known in the land at this time. These included Judaism, Zoroas-

[146] Woodbridge Bingham, *The Founding of the T'ang Dynasty, The Fall of Sui and Rise of T'ang, A Preliminary Survey* (American Council of Learned Societies Studies in Chinese and Related Civilizations, 4). 1941.

[147] Shryock, *The Origin and Development of the State Cult of Confucius*, pp.134-139,237-264; T. Watters, *A Guide to the Tablets in a Temple of Confucius*. 1879.

trianism, Islam, Manicheism and Nestorian Christianity. The introduction of the last-named faith took place in A.D. 635 under the reign of T'ai Tsung, as is attested by the famous and interesting Nestorian stone inscription.

THE NESTORIAN MONUMENT

The monument just mentioned is an inscribed stone tablet which was discovered beneath ground some thirty or forty miles from Si-an in A.D. 1625 and afterward set up in Ch'ang-an near Si-an.[148] The upper part of the entire stone is carved with entwined dragons on either side of a plaque which carries the title of the monument. The top of this plaque is triangular in shape, and adorned with the cross as shown in Fig. 164. The lower part of the stone, over three feet wide and six feet high, is covered on the front and sides with the inscription and lists of names.

The title reads, "A monument of the diffusion through the Middle Kingdom of the Brilliant Teaching of Ta-ch'in." Ta-ch'in was the Chinese name for the Near East, and is used here in reference to the place whence the Christian teaching had come. The inscription continues with a very lengthy text from which we quote the following excerpts:

Behold! The unchanging in perfect repose, before the first and without beginning; the inaccessible in spiritual purity, after the last and wonderfully living; he who holds the mysterious source of life and creates, who in his original majesty imparts his mysterious nature to all the sages; is this not the mysterious Person of our Three in One, the true Lord without beginning, A-lo-he. . . .[149] He made and perfected all things; he fashioned and established the first man. He gave him special goodness and just temperament, he commanded him to have dominion over the ocean of creatures. . . . It came to pass that So-tan [Satan], propagating falsehood, borrowed the adornment of the pure spirit. He insinuated [the idea of] equal greatness [with God] into the original good. . . .

In consequence of this three hundred and sixty-five sects followed side by side crossing one another's tracks, vying one with another in weaving the web of religion. . . . For all their activity they attained nothing, being consumed by their own feverish zeal. They deepened darkness on the road of perdition, and wandered long from the [way of] return to happiness.

Upon this the divided Person of our Three in One, the brilliant and reverend Mi-shih-he [Messiah], veiling and hiding his true majesty, came to earth in the likeness of man. An angel proclaimed the good news; a

---

[148] P. Y. Saeki, *The Nestorian Monument in China.* 1916; A. C. Moule, *Christians in China Before the Year 1550.* 1930, pp.27-52, Fig. 2.

[149] The name is probably the Chinese transcription of the Syriac word for God.

virgin gave birth to the sage in Ta-ch'in. A bright star told of good fortune; Persians saw its glory and came to offer gifts. He brought to completion the letter of the ancient law of the twenty-four sages, regulating the state on the great principle; he founded the new teaching unexpressed in words of the most holy Spirit of the Three in One, modeling the practice of virtue on right faith. . . . He disclosed life and abolished death. He hung up a brilliant sun to take by storm the halls of darkness; the wiles of the devil were then all destroyed. He rowed the boat of mercy to go up to the palaces of light; those who have souls were then completely saved. His mighty works thus finished, he ascended at midday to the spiritual sphere.

Of scriptures there were left twenty-seven books which explain the great reformation to unlock the barriers of the understanding. The water and the Spirit of religious baptism wash away vain glory and cleanse one pure and white. . . .

The true and eternal way is wonderful and hard to name; its merits and use are manifest and splendid, forcing us to call it the brilliant teaching. Yet the way without a prophet will not flourish; a prophet without the way will not be great. When way and prophet match and tally all under the sky is civilized and enlightened.

When T'ai Tsung, the polished Emperor, was beginning his prosperous reign in glory and splendor, with light and wisdom ruling the people, there was in the land of Ta-ch'in one of high virtue called A-lo-pen, who, auguring by the blue clouds, carried the true scriptures; watching the harmony of the winds, hastened to meet difficulties and dangers. In the ninth Cheng-kuan year [A.D. 635] he came to Ch'ang-an. The Emperor sent the Minister of State, Duke Fang Hsüan-ling, to take an escort to the west suburb to meet the guest and bring him to the palace. When the books had been translated in the library and the doctrine examined in his private apartments, [the Emperor] thoroughly understood their propriety and truth and specially ordered their preaching and transmission. . . .[150]

Near the close of the inscription the date is given when the monument was erected. It is equivalent to February 4, A.D. 781.

ART

As far as art inspired by religion is concerned, the T'ang Period is the great Buddhist age of Chinese history.[151] Since the Buddhist works do not concern us here, we can speak briefly of other artistic expressions of the time. The keynote of T'ang art may be said to be realism, and the subjects chosen often reflected the military aspect of the day. From the tomb of T'ai Tsung at Li Ch'üan-hsien in Shensi, a burial place begun by the emperor himself in A.D. 636, we have six reliefs showing his own war horses. One of these is reproduced in

[150] tr. Moule, *Christians in China Before the Year 1550*, pp.34-39.
[151] GCE III, pp.147f.,176-218.

Fig. 165. The animal has been wounded in battle, but is standing patiently while the commander K'iou Sing-kung extracts the arrow which has penetrated his chest.

Funeral statuettes, such as we have already noticed in the Period of the Six Dynasties, are particularly numerous in the T'ang Period. From this time come the figures of a lady carrying a drum and a lady carrying a ball shown in Fig. 167.

National schools of painting now flourished, and the names of a number of famous painters are preserved in literary sources. Perhaps the most interesting work is an illustrated scroll, now in the British Museum, by an unknown artist. Although his identity is not known, it is believed certain that he based his paintings upon a lost original which had been produced by a notable artist of the time of the Six Dynasties named Ku K'ai-chi (A.D. 321-379). The roll is entitled "The Admonitions of the Instructress to Court Ladies," and consists of pictures which illustrate short didactic sayings written beside them. The text was composed by a certain Chang Hua (A.D. 232-300). In general, it may be said that the admonitions are intended to promote proper conduct in the midst of a refined society. The painting reproduced in Fig. 166 is from this source. It portrays a family group and has the purpose of emphasizing counsel on harmonious life.[152]

Other artistic productions of the time included bronze mirrors, cups of crystal, silver and gold, beautiful polychrome glazed pottery, and objects of porcelain.[153] Before the end of the period, also, block printing was invented.[154]

[152] Laurence Binyon, *L'art asiatique au British Museum* (*Sculpture et peinture*) (*Ars Asiatica*, VI). 1925, p.39, Pl. XIV,2,upper; GCE III, pp.262f.,275-278; Bachhofer, *A Short History of Chinese Art*, pp.93f.

[153] R. L. Hobson, *Chinese Art, One Hundred Plates in Colour Reproducing Pottery and Porcelain of All Periods, Jades, Lacquer, Paintings, Bronzes, Furniture, etc., etc., Introduced by an Outline Sketch of Chinese Art.* 1927, pp.9f.

[154] Carter, *The Invention of Printing in China and Its Spread Westward*, pp.28f.

9. THE FIVE DYNASTIES (A.D. 907-960), THE SUNG (A.D. 960-1279) AND YÜAN (A.D. 1279-1368) DYNASTIES

THE "refined" society of the T'ang dynasty was supported upon a substratum of peasant poverty, and collapse came ere long. There followed an extended period of disintegration and eventual conquest by invaders. In the half century from A.D. 907 to 960, "Five Dynasties" succeeded one another swiftly at Loyang, while yet other houses were practically sovereign in outlying provinces. Then a new national dynasty called Sung was established which endured for some three centuries, though it was under a succession of threats from the north to which it finally succumbed. One of the most notable statesmen of the times was Wang An Shih (A.D. 1021-1086), who foresaw the coming disasters and as Prime Minister endeavored to forestall them by radical economic and political reforms.[155] These failed, however, and in A.D. 1125 the northern Sung capital, K'aifeng in Honan, was abandoned to the invaders, a Tartar people known as the Juchen. After that the Sung emperors continued to rule in the south with their capital at Hangchow. In the north the Juchen (or Kin) kingdom centered in the city later named Peking (Peiping). Finally came the Mongols. They attacked northern China within the lifetime of their leader Jenghiz Khan (d. 1227) and soon afterward (1234) succeeded in conquering the Kin kingdom; in 1279, with Kublai Khan (d. 1294), grandson of Jenghiz Khan, at their head, they overwhelmed the Sung empire. The Yüan dynasty which Kublai Khan founded ruled China from then on until 1368.

Troubled as these times were politically, culturally and religiously they were far from lacking in brilliance and importance. Indeed, even when the Mongols came, the conquerors adopted the civilization of the conquered and regarded themselves as its patrons.

Ancestor worship continued of course to be a very strong factor in the lives of the people, and the proper burial of the dead occupied much attention. Two graves of the Sung dynasty came to light in 1941 during excavation in the refugee campus of Fukien Christian University at Shaowu. Stone tablets still stood in front of the graves, with inscriptions revealing that this was the last resting place of a scholar named Li Yung Shih and his wife. The date was probably in the second half of the twelfth century. On each side of each tablet

---

[155] H. R. Williamson, *Wang An Shih, A Chinese Statesman and Educationalist of the Sung Dynasty* (Probsthain's Oriental Series). 2 vols. 1935-37.

was an earthen jar. These contained some grains of rice and both paper and genuine money. Fifty-eight pieces of money for the man and sixty-two for his wife indicated their respective ages at the time of death. The grave itself was an underground chamber built of bricks with slabs of stone for roofing. The wood of the coffin was in a state of decay but pieces were recovered bearing a brilliant red varnish made of tung oil and pigment. Inside the coffin were three lacquer bowls and saucers, black and dark brown in color. Both varnish and lacquer were of high quality.[156]

Of outstanding distinction was the painting of the Sung Period. Portraiture and especially landscape painting were emphasized. At this point we will show only a single example, the picture reproduced in Fig. 168. This painting dates probably from the eleventh century, and the subject is of interest for our study since it portrays a group of scholars of Ch'i at work upon the collation of the classical texts. The Sung landscapes will be discussed in our next chapter.

THE CONFUCIAN RENAISSANCE

After the previous ascendency of Buddhism during the T'ang Period, Confucianism experienced a strong revival in the periods here dealt with. The Confucian renaissance was ushered in by the printing of the nine classical books and their commentaries in a text carefully edited by the scholars. This was done under the administration of Feng Tao (A.D. 881-954), a remarkable minister who served under no less than ten sovereigns of four houses of the Five Dynasties. The work was proposed in a memorial issued in A.D. 932 and reading in part as follows: "During the Han Dynasty, Confucian scholars were honored and the Classics were cut in stone. . . . In T'ang times also stone inscriptions containing the text of the Classics were made in the imperial school. Our dynasty has too many other things to do and cannot undertake such a task as to have stone inscriptions erected. We have seen, however, men from Wu and Shu who sold books that were printed from blocks of wood. There were many different texts, but there were among them no orthodox Classics. If the Classics could be revised and thus cut in wood and published, it would be a very great boon to the study of literature. We, therefore, make a memorial to the throne to this effect."[157] The labors of

[156] Tiao-hsin Wang in *Artibus Asiae*. 11 (1948), pp.111-114.
[157] This passage is from the Ts'e Fu Yüan Kuei written about A.D. 1005 by Wang Hsin-jo, and translated in Carter, *The Invention of Printing in China and Its Spread Westward*, p.50.

editing and printing thereupon inaugurated lasted for twenty-one years and were completed in A.D. 953 when a hundred and thirty volumes of the classics and their commentaries were presented to the emperor.

The renewed interest thus manifested in Confucian antiquity in the Period of the Five Dynasties was an even more conspicuous feature of the Sung Period. A vigorous Neo-Confucian school (as it is now called) arose in this time which maintained that the solution of social and political problems was to be found by a return to the teachings of classical antiquity. Among the leaders of this movement were Ssu-ma Kuang (A.D. 1019-1086), opponent of the "innovator" Wang An-shih,[158] and author of the Tzu Chih T'ung Chien, a famous history of China from the fifth century B.C. to the tenth century A.D.;[159] and Chu Hsi (A.D. 1130-1200), who revised the history of Ssu-ma Kuang and wrote extensive commentaries on the Confucian classics.[160]

As Chu Hsi was doubtless the greatest of the Neo-Confucianists, we may give the following brief statement of his philosophy. The universe, he believed, came into being because of one supreme principle called Li or Ultimate Reason. From this principle the two forces of Ying, the Negative, and Yang, the Positive, developed. The ceaseless interaction of these two forces produces all matter and life, and the endless process of creation which is thus going on may be called Chi or Activating Energy. While Li is the metaphysical element in creation, Chi is the physical. The same two elements are present in an individual, Li being responsible for his innate goodness, and Chi being represented by his powers of action, emotion and thought. The secret of life, then, is to place one's abilities and desires under the guidance of Ultimate Reason so that the inner self may be developed in harmony with the purpose of creation. "From the Li within us," Chu Hsi wrote, "can be traced the origin of our saintly inclination to be good. And from the human faculties within us are developed all of our earthly wants. Thus, the saints entertain human desires such as hunger and thirst in the same manner that villains

---

[158] H. R. Williamson, *Wang An Shih, A Chinese Statesman and Educationalist of the Sung Dynasty* (Probsthain's Oriental Series). 2 vols. 1935-37.

[159] GCBD pp.669-671.

[160] Derk Bodde has translated the section on Chu Hsi from the second volume of the *History of Chinese Philosophy* by Fung Yu-lan in the *Harvard Journal of Asiatic Studies.* 7 (1942-43), pp.1-51. See also J. Percy Bruce, *Chu Hsi and His Masters, An Introduction to Chu Hsi and the Sung School of Chinese Philosophy* (Probsthain's Oriental Series). 1923.

can be expected to show such saintly inclination as sympathy. The teaching of our Sage is to have Li, our saintly inclination within us, to be our master, and to subject our earthly wants to its direction." Again he said: "Heaven and Earth [i.e., the supernatural] has for its purpose the creation of matter. All matter, including human beings, have in them the same purpose as that of Heaven and Earth. ... This purpose, to summarize, is Love. Love is behind all creation. Were we able to recognize its meaning and keep it, we would be in possession of the source of goodness and the foundation of living."[161]

The Sung Period may be regarded as the climactic point for the survey undertaken in this chapter. It was the period which saw the "definitive establishment of the Chinese canon of art,"[162] and the rise of the Neo-Confucian school of philosophy which has continued its work until modern times.[163] The Yüan Period has already been mentioned, and it will suffice in addition to state that the two dynasties which followed were the Ming (A.D. 1368-1644), under which Peking became the national capital and the Altar of Heaven at that place the center of national worship; and the Ch'ing (A.D. 1644-1912), when the Manchus maintained a rule that was ended only by the Revolution of 1911-1912.

[161] tr. Gung-Hsing Wang, *The Chinese Mind.* 1946, pp.136f.
[162] GCE III, p.279.
[163] Chan Wing-tsit in MPEW pp.54-68. For Wang Yang-ming (A.D. 1472-1529), doubtless the most eminent Neo-Confucianist after Chu Hsi, see F. G. Henke, *The Philosophy of Wang Yang-ming, Translated from the Chinese.* 1916.

CHAPTER VII

Taoism

IN THE Six Dynasties Period (A.D. 220-581) the phrase arose which is frequently translated "the three religions" but which might better be "the three doctrines," since the Chinese word involved means basically "to teach." The three schools of thought thus singled out as of chief importance among the many which had flourished in China were Confucianism, Taoism, and Buddhism. Confucianism has been dealt with in the preceding chapter, Buddhism's entry into the land was described briefly in the chapter on that faith, and now we turn to Taoism. The number of adherents of Taoism at the present time is sometimes given as 40,000,000, but actually it is very difficult to say who is or is not a Taoist, and any such figure must be taken as only a very broad approximation and as a testimony to the fact that Taoism has been widely influential in Chinese life.

1. THE LEADERS AND THE WRITINGS OF EARLY TAOISM

LAO TZU

THE rise of Taoism is traditionally associated with the name of Lao Tzu. The Shih Chi of Ssu-ma Ch'ien (145-86 B.C.) gives an account concerning this philosopher which contains the following statements:[1]

"Lao Tzu was a native of Ch'ü-jen hamlet, in Li-hsiang, in the district of K'u, in the state of Ch'u. His given name was Erh, his style was Tan, and his family name was Li. He was a clerk in the Chamber for Preserving and Storing [Records] of the Chou [kings].

"Confucius visited the Chou [capital] in order to question Lao Tzu about the rules of propriety. [When Confucius, speaking of propriety, praised reverence for the sages of antiquity], Lao Tzu said: 'The men of whom you speak, Sir, have, if you please, together with their bones moldered. Their words alone are still extant. If a

[1] tr. in FHCP p.171; Homer H. Dubs in JAOS 61 (1941), p.217; SBE XXXIX, pp.34f.; cf. Arthur Waley, *The Way and Its Power, A Study of the Tao Tê Ching and Its Place in Chinese Thought.* 1934, pp.106-108.

noble man finds his time he rises, but if he does not find his time he drifts like a roving plant and wanders about. I observe that the wise merchant hides his treasures deeply as if he were poor. The noble man of perfect virtue assumes an attitude as though he were stupid. Let go, Sir, your proud airs, your many wishes, your affectation and exaggerated plans. All this is of no use to you, Sir. That is what I have to communicate to you, and that is all.' Confucius left. He addressed his disciples, saying: 'I know how birds can fly, fish swim, and animals run. But the runner may be snared, the swimmer hooked, and the flyer shot by the arrow. But there is the dragon: I cannot tell how he mounts on the wind through the clouds, and rises to heaven. Today I have seen Lao Tzu, and can only compare him to the dragon.'

"Lao Tzu practiced the Way (Tao) and the Power (Te). His doctrine aimed at self-effacement and namelessness. Lao Tzu resided in Chou most of his life. When he foresaw the decay of Chou, he departed and came to the frontier. The custom-house officer Yin Hsi said: 'Sir, since it pleases you to retire, I request you for my sake to write a book.' Thereupon Lao Tzu wrote a book of two parts consisting of five thousand and odd words, in which he discussed the concepts of the Way and the Power. Then he departed. No one knows where he died.

"Some say that Lao Tzu was also a man of Ch'u. He wrote fifteen sections of writings, speaking for the use of Taoists. He was a contemporary of Confucius.

"It seems that Lao Tzu lived to be more than one hundred and sixty years old, and some say more than two hundred years, because he cultivated the Way and nourished his old age. One hundred twenty-nine years after the death of Confucius, the histories record that the historian Tan of the House of Chou had an interview with Duke Hsien of Ch'in [384-362 B.C.]. . . . Some say that this Tan was the same as Lao Tzu, and others say he was not. No one in the world knows if it is correct or not.

"Lao Tzu was a superior man who lived a retired life [or, a recluse gentleman]. His son was named Tsung. Tsung became a general of the state of Wei, and was enfeoffed [as a noble, with his fief] at Tuan-kan. Tsung's son was Chu and Chu's son was Kung. Kung's great-great-grandson was Chia, who held office under Hsiao Wen-ti [179-157] of the Han dynasty. Chia's son, Chieh, became grand tutor to An, prince of Chiao-hsi, and so moved his home to Ch'i."

The circumstantial details given in the first and last paragraphs from Ssu-ma Ch'ien above, would seem to guarantee the actual historicity of Lao Tzu. Accepting Ssu-ma Ch'ien's statements as they stand, we learn that Lao Tzu's combined family and personal name was Li Erh or Li Tan. The appellation by which he is more commonly known, Lao Tzu, means "Old Master," or "Old Philosopher," and may have been given him later as a title; on the other hand it is possible that Lao was actually an inherited family name.[2] Evidently due to similarity in names, Lao Tzu was sometimes confused with Lao Lai Tzu, a Taoist teacher who was a contemporary of Confucius; and with Tan, a historian who lived in the fourth century.

The tiny village that was the birthplace of Lao Tzu was in the district of K'u, which was probably at or near modern Lu-yi in eastern Honan.[3] Later Lao Tzu went to the Chou capital, Loyang, where he was an official in the imperial library.[4]

In mentioning the book which Lao Tzu composed before disappearing beyond the frontier, Ssu-ma Ch'ien was no doubt giving the current belief as to the origin of the Taoist scriptures known as the Lao-tzu, or popularly the Tao Te Ching (Tao Teh King).

The date of Lao Tzu remains uncertain. Traditionally he is placed in the sixth century B.C., and the account given by Ssu-ma Ch'ien of a visit by Confucius to Lao Tzu of course agrees with this dating. The story may be only apocryphal, however, and intended to increase the prestige of Taoism in its controversies with Confucianism. Abandoning the traditional date, some scholars have put Lao Tzu around 300 B.C.[5] or 240 B.C.[6] The latter date, for example, rests upon the argument that the grammar and style of the Tao Te Ching are such as prevailed at the end of the "Warring States" Period. On the other hand the type of reasoning used to establish these late dates has itself been subjected to criticism, and it may be felt that the evidence is not yet sufficient to require this large shift in the dating of Lao Tzu and the Tao Te Ching.[7]

THE TAO TE CHING

Although we are uncertain whether the Tao Te Ching dates from

[2] Richard Wilhelm, *Lao-Tse und der Taoismus.* 1925, p.15.
[3] Dubs in JAOS 61 (1941), p.217.
[4] Wilhelm, *Lao-Tse und der Taoismus,* p.16.
[5] Dubs in JAOS 61 (1941), pp.215-221.
[6] FHCP p.170; Waley, *The Way and Its Power,* pp.86,127f.
[7] Hu Shih in *Harvard Journal of Asiatic Studies.* 2 (1937), pp.373-397; Erwin Rousselle in *Sinica.* 16 (1941), p.120; Herrymon Maurer, *The Old Fellow.* 1943, pp.290f.

the sixth century or the third B.C., and for that matter whether it was composed by Lao Tzu himself or by a later writer or writers, it is still our most important literary source for early Taoism, and probably may be safely regarded as embodying to a greater or lesser degree the teachings of Lao Tzu. The Tao Te Ching[8] means the Classic of the Tao and the Te. It is written in about five thousand Chinese characters, and is usually divided into two parts, I, "Concerning Tao" (chapters 1-37), and II, "Concerning Te" (chapters 38-81). A photograph of a T'ang manuscript of the work, found at Tunhwang and now in the British Museum, is shown in Fig. 169.

It is clear that the two words Tao and Te are of crucial importance for the teaching contained in this work. The word *tao* in the Chinese language has the primary meaning of "road" or "way." Then it may also be used metaphorically to signify the "Way of man," that is, human conduct and morality; and metaphysically to mean the "Way of the universe," that is, the course of nature and the immanent principle of the cosmos.[9] It is chiefly with these philosophical connotations of an ultimate way of nature and of an ethical way for man, that the word Tao is used in the Tao Te Ching. Hence we may render it as "Way."

The word *te* may be translated as "power" or "virtue." It is essentially the efficacy or the principle which is inherent in an individual thing.[10] In the teaching of Lao Tzu, the Te is the outcome of the Tao. Rendering this term as "Power," we may translate the title of the Tao Te Ching as the Classic of the Way and the Power.

One other expression should be explained before we proceed to give quotations from the Tao Te Ching. This is *wu wei*, which means "not to do anything for," and which is generally translated as "inaction." Lao Tzu uses the phrase, however, for an unassertive, effortless behavior which actually accomplishes much more than blus-

---

[8] tr. Stanislas Julien, *Le Livre de la Voie et de la Vertu, composé dans le VIe siècle avant l'ère chrétienne par le philosophe Lao-Tseu, traduit en français, et publié avec le texte chinois et un commentaire perpétuel.* 1842; James Legge in SBE XXXIX, pp.45-124; Lionel Giles, *The Sayings of Lao Tzu, Translated from the Chinese, with an Introduction* (Wisdom of the East). 1905; Arthur Waley, *The Way and Its Power, A Study of the Tao Tê Ching and Its Place in Chinese Thought.* 1934; cf. also Bhikshu Wai-Tao and Dwight Goddard, *Laotzu's Tao and Wu-Wei, A New Translation.* 2d ed. 1935; Witter Bynner, *The Way of Life According to Laotzu, An American Version.* 1944.

[9] FHCP p.177; J. J. M. DeGroot, *Religion in China, Universism: A Key to the Study of Taoism and Confucianism.* 1912, pp.6f.

[10] FHCP p.179.

tering, violent effort. Hence *wu wei* really signifies something like simplicity, spontaneity, or naturalness.[11]

Now we may quote a number of passages from the Tao Te Ching in which the characteristic doctrines of early Taoism will appear. Concerning the nature and manner of working of the Tao it is stated:

> The Way that can be told of is not an Unvarying Way;
> The names that can be named are not unvarying names.
> It was from the Nameless that Heaven and Earth sprang;
> The named is but the mother that rears the ten thousand creatures,
> each after its kind.[12]
> There was something formless yet complete,
> That existed before heaven and earth;
> Without sound, without substance,
> Dependent on nothing, unchanging,
> All pervading, unfailing.
> One may think of it as the mother of all things under heaven.
> Its true name we do not know;
> "Way" is the by-name that we give it. . . .
> The ways of men are conditioned by those of earth. The ways of
> earth, by those of heaven. The ways of heaven by those of Tao, and
> the ways of Tao by the Self-so [the "what-is-so-of-itself"].[13]
> Great Tao is like a boat that drifts;
> It can go this way; it can go that.
> The ten thousand creatures owe their existence to it and it does not
> disown them;
> Yet having produced them, it does not take possession of them.
> Tao, though it covers the ten thousand things like a garment,
> Makes no claim to be master over them,
> And asks for nothing from them.
> Therefore it may be called the Lowly.
> The ten thousand creatures obey it,
> Though they know not that they have a master;
> Therefore it is called the Great.[14]
> Tao never does;
> Yet through it all things are done.
> If the barons and kings would but possess themselves of it,

[11] Chan Wing-tsit in MPEW pp.35f.; J. J. L. Duyvendak in *Asiatische Studien, Zeitschrift der Schweizerischen Gesellschaft für Asienkunde.* 1 (1947), pp.81-102.

[12] This quotation and those following are from the translation by Waley, *The Way and Its Power*, and are made by permission of the publishers, George Allen and Unwin Ltd., London, and Houghton Mifflin Company, Boston. The reference here is chapter I of the Tao Te Ching, and p.141 of the book by Waley. In each case the chapter of the Tao Te Ching is cited by a Roman numeral, while the page number gives the reference to Waley's translation.

[13] XXV; p.174.   [14] XXXIV; p.185.

The ten thousand creatures would at once be transformed.[15]
When there is not Tao in the empire
War horses will be reared. . . .[16]

Concerning the way of life which is patterned after the silent, ceaseless working of the Tao, we read:

The highest good is like that of water. The goodness of water is that it benefits the ten thousand creatures; yet itself does not scramble, but is content with the places that all men disdain. It is this that makes water so near to the Way.[17]

Nothing under heaven is softer or more yielding than water; but when it attacks things hard and resistant there is not one of them that can prevail. . . . That the yielding conquers the resistant and the soft conquers the hard is a fact known by all men, yet utilized by none.[18]

How did the great rivers and seas get their kingship over the hundred
lesser streams?
Through the merit of being lower than they; that was how they got
their kingship.
Therefore the Sage
In order to be above the people
Must speak as though he were lower than the people.
In order to guide them
He must put himself behind them.
Only thus can the Sage be on top and the people not be crushed by
his weight.
Only thus can he guide, and the people not be led into harm.
Indeed in this way everything under heaven will be glad to be pushed by him and will not find his guidance irksome. This he does by not striving; and because he does not strive, none can contend with him.[19]

Here are my three treasures. Guard and keep them! The first is pity; the second, frugality; the third: refusal to be "foremost of all things under heaven."

For only he that pities is truly able to be brave;
Only he that is frugal is truly able to be profuse.
Only he that refuses to be foremost of all things
Is truly able to become chief of all Ministers.[20]
Without leaving his door
He knows everything under heaven.
Without looking out of his window
He knows all the ways of heaven.
For the further one travels
The less one knows.
Therefore the Sage arrives without going,

---

[15] xxxvii; p.188. [16] xlvi; p.199. [17] viii; p.151.
[18] lxxviii; p.238. [19] lxvi; p.224. [20] lxvii; p.225.

> Sees all without looking,
> Does nothing, yet achieves everything.[21]

The same quiet, plain, secluded way of life is proposed as ideal for the entire state. The author describes what a wise ruler would do with even a tiny state:

Given a small country with few inhabitants, he could bring it about that though there should be among the people contrivances requiring ten times, a hundred times less labour, they would not use them. He could bring it about that the people would be ready to lay down their lives and lay them down again in defense of their homes, rather than emigrate. There might still be boats and carriages, but no one would go in them; there might still be weapons of war but no one would drill with them. He could bring it about that "the people should have no use for any form of writing save knotted ropes, should be contented with their food, pleased with their clothing, satisfied with their homes, should take pleasure in their rustic tasks. The next place might be so near at hand that one could hear the cocks crowing in it, the dogs barking; but the people would grow old and die without ever having been there."[22]

> The more prohibitions there are, the more ritual avoidances,
> The poorer the people will be.
> The more "sharp weapons" there are,
> The more benighted will the whole land grow.
> The more cunning craftsmen there are,
> The more pernicious contrivances will be invented.
> The more laws are promulgated,
> The more thieves and bandits there will be.
> Therefore a sage has said:
> So long as I "do nothing" the people will of themselves be transformed.
> So long as I love quietude, the people will of themselves go straight.
> So long as I act only by inactivity the people will of themselves become prosperous.[23]

War is naturally abhorrent to the adherent of Tao.

> He who by Tao purposes to help a ruler of men
> Will oppose all conquest by force of arms;
> For such things are wont to rebound.
> Where armies are, thorns and brambles grow.
> The raising of a great host
> Is followed by a year of dearth.[24]

Fine weapons are none the less ill-omened things. . . . The slaying of multitudes is a matter for grief and tears; he that has conquered in battle is received with rites of mourning.[25]

[21] XLVII; p.200.   [22] LXXX; pp.241f.
[23] LVII; p.211.   [24] XXX; p.180.
[25] XXXI; p.181. cf. E. H. v. Tscharner in *Asiatische Studien*. 1 (1947), pp.6-9.

Even while the national and international implications of Taoist teachings are thus set forth, the primary appeal of the Tao Te Ching remains a call to the individual. He must follow the Way, treating all kinds of people alike, and ultimately this will bring all into harmony with the Tao.

> Of the good men I approve,
> But of the bad I also approve,
> And thus he gets goodness.
> The truthful man I believe, but the liar I also believe,
> And thus he gets truthfulness.[26]

A profound paradox attaches to the teaching of the Great Way, and it is at once extremely simple and extremely difficult to apprehend. Therefore Lao Tzu (if it is really he speaking) declares:

> My words are very easy to understand and very easy to put into practice. Yet no one under heaven understands them; no one puts them into practice. . . .
> Few then understand me; but it is upon this very fact that my value depends. It is indeed in this sense that "the Sage wears hair-cloth on top, but carries jade underneath his dress."[27]

YANG CHU

Another early leader of Taoism was Yang Chu, who probably lived around 440-366 B.C.[28] If Lao Tzu lived in the sixth century B.C., Yang Chu was one of his successors; if Lao Tzu is to be dated around 300 B.C., Yang Chu was his predecessor and possibly the first leader of the Taoist movement.

Concerning Yang Chu our information is relatively scanty. As we have already seen (pp.356f.), Mencius opposed him vehemently, and it may therefore be that the statements concerning Yang Chu from this source are not entirely free of polemical bias. We have already quoted Mencius in the declaration that "Yang's school is for self." In another passage the same authority stated: "The principle of Yang Tzu is, 'Each one for himself.' Though he might have benefited the whole world by plucking out a single hair, he would not have done it."[29]

Another statement which casts additional light upon the teaching of Yang Chu occurs in the Huai-nan-tzu, a miscellaneous compilation of the second century B.C. concerning various schools of thought.

---

[26] XLIX; p.202.   [27] LXX; p.230.
[28] Chan Wing-tsit in MPEW p.34.
[29] tr. in FHCP p.133; cf. Lyall, *Mencius*, p.213.

There the positions of Confucius, Mo Tzu, Yang Chu, and Mencius are referred to in succession as follows: "The orchestra, drum and dance for the performance of music; obeisances and bowing for the cultivation of good manners; generous expenditures in funerals and protracted mourning for the obsequies of the dead: these were what Confucius established and were condemned by Mo Tzu. Universal love, exaltation of the worthy, assistance to the spirits and anti-fatalism: these were what Mo Tzu established, and were condemned by Yang Tzu. Completeness of living, preservation of what is genuine, and not allowing outside things to entangle one's person: these were what Yang Tzu established, and were condemned by Mencius."[30]

The teachings of Yang Chu as well as Mo Ti were also discussed from much the same point of view as that of Mencius by Wang An Shih (A.D. 1021-1086), the Sung Period statesman and author. His essay on the subject declares: "The doctrines of Yang and Mo may be said to attain to the teachings of Confucius in one point, but to fall short of them in a hundred others. Anyway, the doctrines of Confucius embrace the teachings of Yang and Mo, and are applicable to all times and circumstances.

"The teachings of Mo Ti are summarized in the sentence, that 'if by rubbing his body smooth he could benefit his fellows he would do so.' The teachings of Yang Chu are likewise summarized in the sentence, 'He would not pluck so much as a hair out of his head for the benefit of his fellows. . . .'

"The main tenet of Yang Chu's teachings is 'self-interest.' But 'self-interest' is but the first principle of the Confucian doctrine. The summum bonum of Mo Ti's teachings is 'altruism.' But 'altruism' in the Confucian system is only of secondary importance. . . .

"The conclusion of the whole matter is that Yang Chu's teaching is relatively nearer to the doctrine of Confucius, and that of Mo Ti relatively remote from orthodoxy. They are both different from Confucianism, but distinctions should be made between them in regard to the reason why they offend the Confucianists."[31]

The positive conclusion to be extracted from these statements is that Yang Chu must have taught simplicity of life even as Lao Tzu, and that he specially regarded personal integrity as of greater worth than material things and worldly profits.

[30] tr. in FHCP p.134. For the Huai-nan-tzu see *ibid.*, p.395; Wieger, *China throughout the Ages*, p.469.
[31] tr. Williamson, *Wang An Shih*, II, pp.381-383.

CHUANG TZU

Chuang Tzu (or Chuang Chou) was the third of the three thinkers who formulated the characteristic doctrines of early Taoism. He probably lived around 369-286 B.C., and the following account of his life is found in the Shih Chi:

"Chuang Tzu was a native of Meng.[32] His personal name was Chou. He held a small post at Ch'i-yüan, in Meng. He was a contemporary of Kings Hui of Liang [370-319 B.C.] and Hsüan of Ch'i [319-301 B.C.]. His erudition was most varied, but his chief doctrines were based upon the sayings of Lao Tzu. His writings, which run to over 100,000 words, are for the most part allegorical. His literary and dialectic skill was such that the best scholars of the age were unable to refute his destructive criticism of the Confucian and Mohist schools.[33] His teachings were like an overwhelming flood which spreads unchecked according to its own will, so that from rulers and ministers downward, none could apply them to any practical use.

"King Wei of Ch'u [339-329 B.C.], hearing good of Chuang Tzu, sent messengers to him, bearing costly gifts, and inviting him to become Prime Minister. At this Chuang Chou smiled and said to the messengers: 'A thousand taels of gold is valuable indeed, and to be Prime Minister is an honorable position. But have you never seen the sacrificial ox used for the suburban sacrifice? When after being fattened up for several years, it is decked with embroidered trappings and led to the altar, would it not willingly then change place with some uncared-for pigling? Begone! Defile me not! I would rather disport myself to my own enjoyment in the mire than be slave to the ruler of a state. I will never take office. Thus I shall remain free to follow my own inclinations.' "[34]

From this biographical sketch it is clear that Chuang Tzu belonged to the same tradition as Lao Tzu and Yang Chu. It is explicitly stated that he based his main teachings upon the utterances of Lao Tzu, and a description is given of his attitude toward wealth and position which reminds one at once of the determination of Yang Chu to avoid any entanglements with "outside things."

The Shih Chi also states that Chuang Tzu wrote extensively, and a body of writings has come down connected with his name and

[32] Meng was a place in the state of Sung, now in modern Honan.
[33] cf. the mention of Chuang Tzu in another passage from the Shih Chi, quoted above, p.359.
[34] tr. in FHCP p.221.

called the Chuang-tzu.[35] We may turn to these texts now for further information on the doctrines of this philosopher and his school. At once we perceive that the basic concept of the Tao is the same with Chuang Tzu as it was with Lao Tzu. "Tao has reality and evidence, but no action and form. It may be transmitted, but cannot be received. It may be attained, but cannot be seen. It exists by and through itself. It exists prior to heaven and earth, and indeed for all eternity. It causes the gods to be divine, and the world to be produced. It is above the zenith, but it is not high. It is beneath the nadir, but it is not low. It is prior to heaven and earth, but it is not ancient. It is older than the most ancient, but it is not old."[36]

It is when we ask how the Tao can be apprehended that we come to the most distinctive emphases of Chuang Tzu. At this point we find that he is the exponent of a mysticism centered in nature. The mystical way by which oneness with the Tao may be attained is described in the Chuang-tzu as "the fast of the mind," and as "sitting in forgetfulness." These terms are introduced in a series of apocryphal conversations between Confucius and his disciple, Yen Hui. The first method is outlined by Confucius in the following words: "Maintain the unity of your will. Do not listen with ears, but with the mind. Do not listen with the mind, but with the spirit. The function of the ear ends with hearing; that of the mind, with symbols or ideas. But the spirit is an emptiness ready to receive all things. Tao abides in the emptiness; the emptiness is the Fast of the Mind." The second description of the experience is reported by Yen Hui like this: "I have abandoned my body and discarded my knowledge, and so have become one with the Infinite. This is what I mean by Sitting in Forgetfulness."[37]

On the road toward the union with Tao, the contemplation of the silent vastnesses of nature is of extreme importance. "How does the sage sit by the sun and moon, and hold the universe in his arm? He blends everything into a harmonious whole. . . . He blends together

[35] tr. James Legge in SBE XXXIX, pp.125-392; XL, pp.1-232; Herbert A. Giles, *Chuang Tzŭ, Mystic, Moralist, and Social Reformer, Translated from the Chinese.* 2d ed. 1926. (Selections from the first edition of the same translation appear in Lionel Giles, *Musings of a Chinese Mystic, Selections from the Philosophy of Chuang Tzŭ.* Wisdom of the East. 1906); Fung Yu-lan, *Chuang Tzŭ, A New Selected Translation with an Exposition of the Philosophy of Kuo Hsiang.* 1931. Most of our quotations are from the translation by Fung Yu-lan, permission to use which has been granted by The Commercial Press, Ltd., Shanghai. For the quotations from Giles, acknowledgment is made to Kelly and Walsh, Ltd., Shanghai.

[36] tr. Fung Yu-lan, *Chuang Tzŭ*, p.117.

[37] *ibid.*, pp.79f.,128 (cf. FHCP p.241; SBE XXXIX, pp.209,257).

ten thousand years, and stops at the one, the whole, and the simple."³⁸ "The universe is very beautiful, yet it says nothing. The four seasons abide by a fixed law, yet they are not heard. All creation is based upon absolute principles, yet nothing speaks. And the true sage, taking his stand upon the beauty of the universe, pierces the principles of created things. Hence the saying that the perfect man does nothing, the true sage performs nothing, beyond gazing at the universe."³⁹

How tremendous is this great universe, and how tiny is man in comparison with it! "The Four Seas—are they not to the universe but like puddles in a marsh? The Middle Kingdom—is it not to the surrounding ocean like a tare-seed in a granary? Of all the myriad created things, man is but one. And of all those who inhabit the land, live on the fruit of the earth, and move about in cart and boat, an individual man is but one. Is not he, as compared with all creation, but as the tip of a hair upon a horse's skin?"⁴⁰

To realize his true place in the infinite system of nature brings the sage a sense of calmness and of trust with regard to death as well as life. "Wherever a parent tells a son to go, east, west, south, or north, he simply follows the command. Nature, the Yin and Yang, is no other than a man's parent. If she bid me die quickly, and I demur, then I am obstinate and rebellious; she does no wrong. The universe carries me in my body, toils me through my life, gives me repose with old age, and rests me in death. What makes my life a good makes my death a good also."⁴¹

Indeed, in the great process of the universe death is nothing more than a transition from one form of existence to another. If, therefore, we find that this life is a goodly thing we may assume that the next will be, too. "To have attained to the human form is a source of joy. But, in the infinite evolution, there are thousands of other forms that are equally good. What an incomparable bliss it is to undergo these countless transitions!"⁴² Perhaps the next life will so far surpass the present one, that to attain it may be compared to coming home after being long lost, or to awakening after being in the unreal world of dreams. "How do I know that the love of life is not a delusion? How do I know that he who is afraid of death is not like a man who was lost from his home when young and therefore does not want to return?

³⁸ *ibid.*, p.61.   ³⁹ tr. Giles, *Chuang Tzŭ*, pp.279f.
⁴⁰ *ibid.*, p.202.   ⁴¹ tr. Fung Yu-lan, *Chuang Tzŭ*, p.122.
⁴² *ibid.*, pp.116f.

... Those who dream ... do not know that they are dreaming. ...
Only when they are awake, they begin to know that they dreamed.
By and by comes the Great Awakening, and then we shall find out
that life itself is a great dream."[43]

When Chuang Tzu himself was about to die, it is said that his
disciples wished to prepare a splendid funeral for him, but he turned
again to the thought of the majesty of nature, and replied: "With
Heaven and Earth for my coffin and shell; with the sun, moon, and
stars, as my burial regalia; and with all creation to escort me to the
grave—are not my funeral paraphernalia ready to hand?"[44]

This exaltation of nature is perhaps the greatest contribution of
Chuang Tzu, and at the same time it reveals the fundamental divergence of Taoism from Confucianism. Confucianism's main interest
and center was in man; but such humanism loses its importance
when man's small place in the universe is realized as it is in Taoism.
Then it becomes appropriate for him to center his attention not
upon himself, but upon that vaster natural order by which he is
sustained and in which at last he may perceive the great Tao.

[43] *ibid.*, pp.61f. (cf. FHCP p.236).   [44] tr. Giles, *Chuang Tzŭ*, p.434.

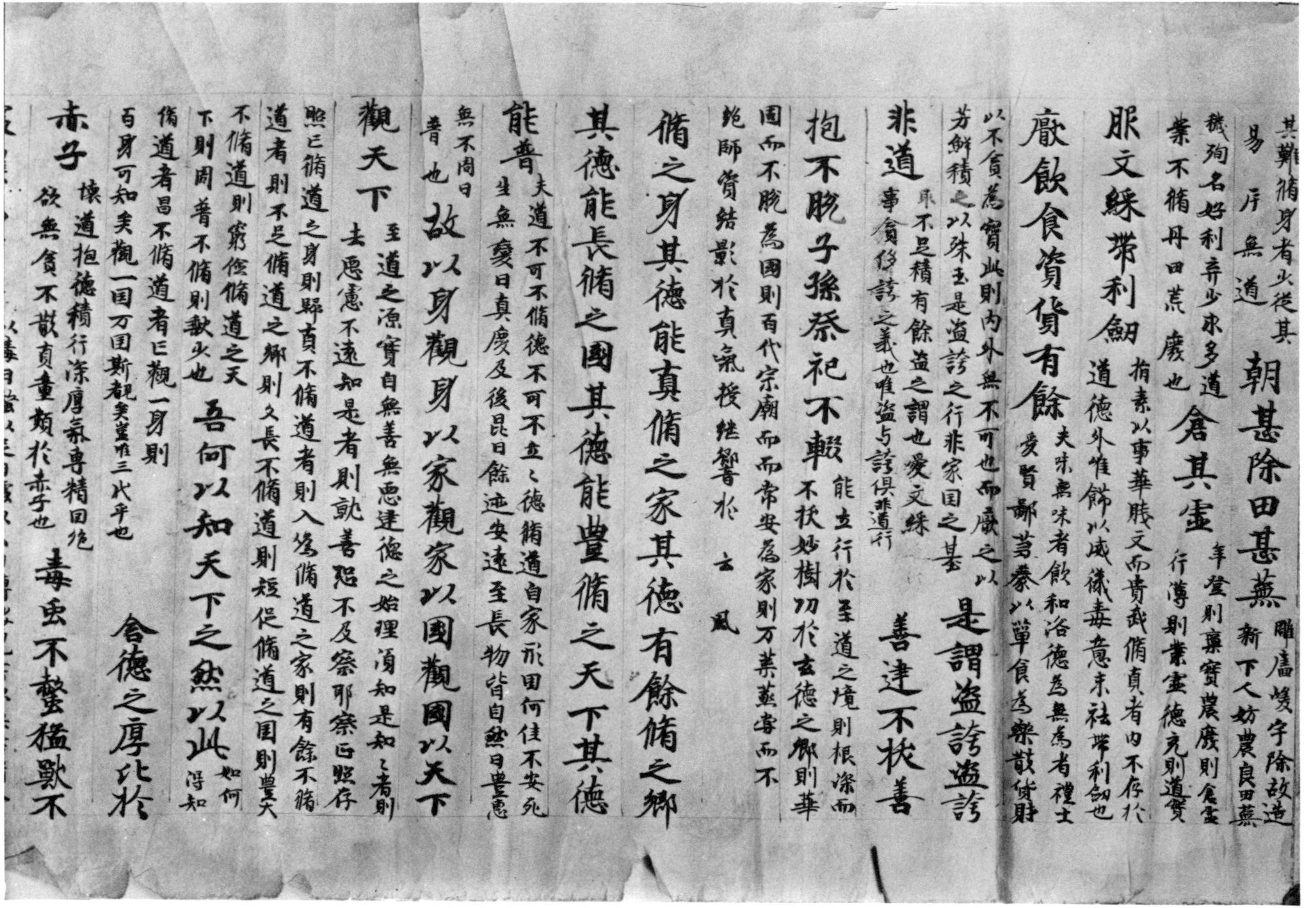

169. Manuscript of the Tao Te Ching

170. Mirror with Taoist Deities

171. Genii of the Five Holy Mountains

172. The Court of Hades

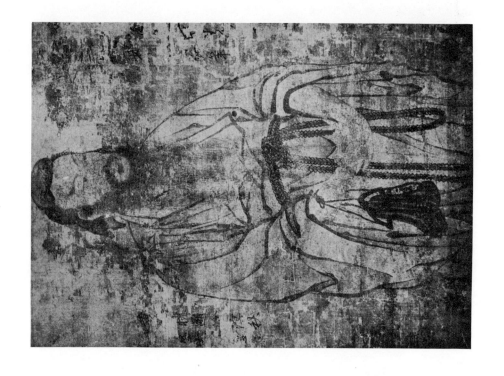

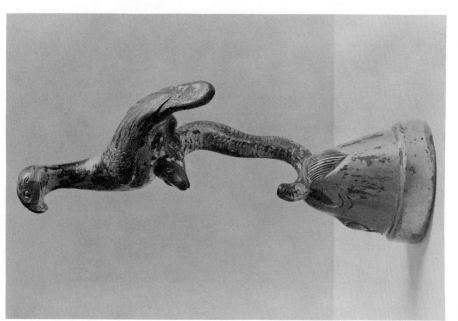

173. Bronze Statuette with Symbols of the Three Governors

176. Bare Willows and Distant Mountains

175. A Temple among the Snowy Hills

177. Summer

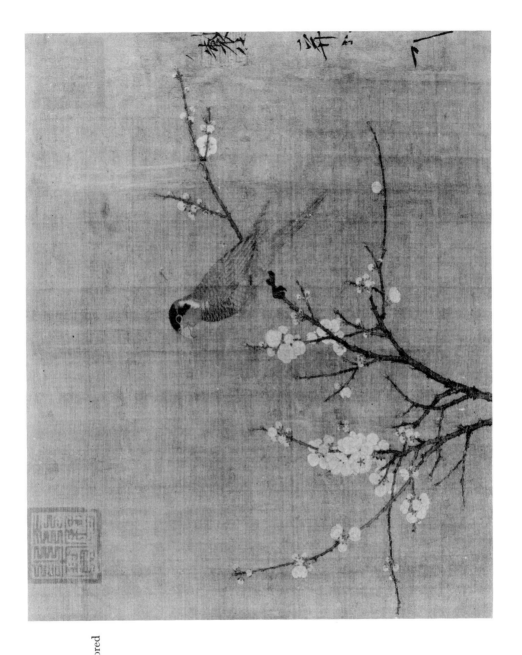

178. The Five-Colored
Parakeet

179. Two Sages and an Attendant under a Plum Tree

180. Mountain Landscape with Blossoming Trees

181. Mountain Brook

182. Temple Overlooking the Sea

183. Taoist Magicians Preparing the Elixir of Life

184. Chung K'uei, the Exorciser of Demons

185. A Taoist Immortal Ascending to Heaven

186. A Taoist Immortal Seated on the Ground

2. POPULAR TAOISM IN THE CH'IN (221-207 B.C.) AND HAN (202 B.C.-A.D. 220) PERIODS

In TERMS of historical periods, the story told thus far of Taoism has fallen within the limits of the epoch called Eastern Chou (771-256 B.C.). We will speak now of Taoism in the Ch'in (221-207 B.C.) and Han (202 B.C.-A.D. 220) Periods. At this time the religion came into imperial favor. Shih Huang Ti, who burned many of the books of Confucian antiquity because they supported resistance to his innovations, adopted the Taoist faith because its doctrine of "inaction" seemed likely to make the people submissive to his domination; and the first Han kings likewise gave their support to this religion. At the same time, Taoism had already to a large extent degenerated from its original lofty philosophical speculations into a mass of popular superstitions.

This state of affairs is described concisely in a fourteenth century work on religion, written by Wu Wei and entitled Ts'ing Yen Ts'ung Lu: "From the time of the Former Han Dynasty on, when Wen Ti[45] was emperor and Ts'ao Ts'an minister, this [system of the] Tao was utilized for purposes of government, and thereby the people were kept quiet and united. Thus it was actually possible to support the administration and the empire by the help of this Tao [system]. Then, however, this system of knowledge was transformed into an art of dealing with genii and magical practices, and beyond that into a doctrine of rice-magic and wine-offering. These things developed to the extent of constituting a heresy. The art of dealing with genii and magical practices was divided into two parts, one part having to do with the preparation of the elixir of immortality and the other with the proper use of food. These two comprise today the teaching of Perfect Truth. The doctrine of rice-magic and wine-offering likewise was divided into two parts, talismans and secret signs. These two comprise today the teaching of Right Unity."[46]

ALCHEMY AND THE "ISLES OF THE IMMORTALS"

As Wu Wei indicates, this decadent or popular Taoism was much concerned with the concocting of an "elixir of immortality" and with the "proper use of food." We have already seen that the union with the Tao which Chuang Tzu taught, brought with it an assurance

---

[45] Wen Ti, also known as Liu Heng, was the fourth ruler of the Han dynasty, and occupied the throne from 180 to 157 B.C. GCBD pp.500,873.

[46] tr. O. Franke in SLR I, p.223.

of life after death. It was now believed that this immortality could be obtained by the use of certain foods and medicines in which the vital forces of the universe particularly resided. A great deal of effort was therefore directed toward the determination of regimens and the preparation of mixtures which would prolong life and eventually produce immortality, and it is to these alchemical and dietary procedures that Wu Wei refers.

In this connection we may also note the widespread belief of the time in the existence of the "Isles of the Immortals," where, if only they could be reached, the food of immortality would be readily available. These wonderful islands were described as follows by Ssu-ma Ch'ien: "It is reported that in the midst of the Eastern Sea, there are three supernatural islands. Their names are P'eng Lai, Fang Chang, and Ying Chou. . . . They are not far removed from human beings, but unfortunately, at the very time when one is on the point of arriving at the islands, one's boat is blown back by the wind and one finds one's self at a distance. In ancient times—to tell the truth —there were people who succeeded in reaching the islands. It is there that the immortals may be found, and the drug which prevents death. There, all beings—even birds and quadrupeds—are white. The palaces are made of gold and silver. People have not succeeded in reaching the islands a second time. They see the islands from a distance, like a cloud, but when they approach, the islands are submerged in the water, and when they come quite near, the wind suddenly forces their boat into the open sea. In short, no one has been able to land."[47]

Shih Huang Ti, whose adherence to Taoism we have already noted, was particularly interested in the effort of this religion to obtain the means of immortality. Since the "drug which prevents death" was to be found on the Isles of the Immortals, the emperor was persuaded to send a naval expedition to search for these islands. According to the history of Ssu-ma Ch'ien, this was at the request of the celebrated magician Hsü She. "Hsü She and his companions tendered the following request: 'We make supplication that we be permitted—after we have purified ourselves—to depart with a company of youths and maidens, to seek these islands. . . .' The emperor was well pleased. He gave to Hsü She seeds of the five grains and dispatched him upon his voyage with three thousand young men and women, and laborers for all kinds of work. Hsü She sailed away,

[47] This translation of Ssu-ma Ch'ien and those immediately following are from Obed S. Johnson, A Study of Chinese Alchemy. 1928, pp.66-68.

and discovered a locality noted for its peace and fertility. There he tarried, was made king, and did not return."

Despite the failure of this expedition, Shih Huang Ti still sought ways of obtaining the wonderful drug. "When the emperor had reunited the empire," states Ssu-ma Ch'ien, "he set his face toward the seashore. At that time, magicians in numbers too numerous to be estimated gave expression to their views concerning the immortal islands. The emperor feared that were he himself to make trial of the sea, he might not succeed. . . . The following year, he returned to make his pilgrimages along the seashore. Three years later he betook himself to Chieh Shih and made a series of inquiries among the magicians who navigate the sea. . . . Five years later he journeyed southward and made ascent of the lofty Huai Chi Mountain. It was his custom to promenade up and down the seashore, in the hope that he might in some manner obtain the wonder-working drug of the three sacred islands in the midst of the sea—but he never obtained it. He returned to Sha Ch'iu—and there he died."

THE LIEH-TZU

Further light is cast upon the Taoism of the time by the Lieh-tzu.[48] This is a book which bears the name of a legendary Taoist, Lieh Tzu (or Lich Yü-k'ou), who was supposed to have lived in the fourth century B.C. While it may contain some older materials, the book as we have it probably comes from the Han Period.[49]

Lieh Tzu was thought to have been a man who made remarkable achievements in the Taoist faith. Chuang Tzu used him as an illustration of one who had attained a pure experience of the Tao and thereby come to enjoy absolute freedom. "He could ride upon the wind," said Chuang Tzu of Lieh Tzu, "and travel whithersoever he wished staying away as long as fifteen days."[50] In the Lieh-tzu he is represented as giving this account of his achievement in the ninth year of his Taoist studies: "Internal and external were blended into unity. After that, there was no distinction between eye and ear, ear and nose, nose and mouth: all were the same. My mind was frozen, my body in dissolution, my flesh and bones all melted together. I

---

[48] tr. Lionel Giles, *Taoist Teachings from the Book of Lieh Tzu, Translated from the Chinese, with Introduction and Notes* (Wisdom of the East). 1912.

[49] Wieger, *China throughout the Ages*, p.478; GCBD p.482.

[50] tr. Giles, *Chuang Tzŭ*, p.5. Although the Taoists called this "absolute" freedom, Lieh Tzu still had to have the wind in order to get around. Chuang Tzu noted this: "Yet although Lieh Tzu was able to dispense with walking, he was still dependent upon something"; and made the point that all happiness is dependent upon something.

was wholly unconscious of what my body was resting on, or what was under my feet. I was borne this way and that on the wind, like dry chaff or leaves falling from a tree. In fact, I knew not whether the wind was riding on me or I on the wind."[51]

Other stories in the Lieh-tzu, which show the kind of interest then prevailing, tell of a man who emerged out of a solid rock cliff and hovered in the air amidst flames and smoke; of a magician who carried a king of Chou high into the sky to see his aerial palace; and of another wonder-worker who successfully constructed an automaton which could walk and sing.[52]

As for the Isles of the Immortals, the Lieh-tzu is able to give this report on conditions there: "The vegetation is miraculous, the flowers are sweet-scented, and if the fruits of these islands are eaten, they will preserve the eater from old age and death." Of the inhabitants of the Isles it is said: "They do not eat the five grains, but inhale air and drink dew."[53]

CHANG TAO LING

A famous Taoist of the Later Han Period was Chang Tao Ling. Gaining prestige by his proficiency in magical practices, he acquired a sufficient following to inaugurate the Yellow Turban Rebellion of A.D. 184. Deriving its name from the headdress worn by the rebels, this uprising so weakened the Han rule that anarchy ensued and the dynasty eventually fell.[54]

The traditional history of his life places his birth in A.D. 34 in Chekiang, and makes him a descendant of Chang Liang, minister of Liu Pang, the founder of the Han dynasty. Dwelling first in Kiangsi and later in Szechwan, Chang Tao Ling is said to have devoted his life to the study of alchemy and magic and to the search for the elixir of immortality. It is reported that a compound known as "Blue Dragon and White Tiger" was at last developed, and that upon tasting it Chang Tao Ling, then already sixty years of age, regained his youth. He supported himself by the practice of medicine, his fee for each case being five bushels of rice, for which reason he was later called "Rice-thief." He lived to an advanced age and then ascended to heaven after having bequeathed to his son, Chang Heng, his magical formulas and equipment. "Take these precious gifts," he

[51] tr. Giles, *Taoist Teachings from the Book of Lieh Tzu*, p.42.
[52] *ibid.*, pp.50,58-61,90-92.
[53] tr. in Johnson, *A Study of Chinese Alchemy*, pp.53,55.
[54] Teng Ssu-yü in MacNair, ed., *China*, pp.78f.

said, "kill demons, chase off hobgoblins, protect the kingdom, bring peace to the people and let my dignity pass from father to son without ever leaving the family."[55]

The words just quoted reflect the historical fact that the descendants of Chang Tao Ling assumed a spiritual headship of Taoism which was ultimately accorded imperial recognition. In A.D. 748 the T'ang emperor, Hsüan Tsung (712-756), confirmed the hereditary privileges of the family, and bestowed posthumously upon Chang Tao Ling and all his successors the title of Master of Heaven, or Celestial Teacher. A Taoist society still exists, with a head living at the Dragon-Tiger Mountain in Kiangsi, who claims descent from Chang Tao Ling.

[55] Henry Doré, *Researches into Chinese Superstitions.* IX, tr. D. J. Finn. 1931, pp.69-86.

3. TAOISM IN THE SIX DYNASTIES PERIOD (A.D. 220-581)

WITH the fall of the Han dynasty there was a general revolt against the customs of the past and in particular a reaction against Confucianism. Under these circumstances Taoism experienced a revival.[56] Among leaders of the early Six Dynasties Period (A.D. 220-581) who criticized Confucianism and emphasized Taoist doctrines were Wang Pi and Ho Yen. The former is dated A.D. 226-249, and the latter must have lived about the same time. Both men wrote commentaries on the Tao Te Ching, but when Ho Yen read that written by Wang Pi he admired it so much that he destroyed his own. The two teachers founded a school which was known as the T'an Hsüan Chia or "the school which discusses profundity." They regarded the doctrine of *wu wei* or "inaction" as the fundamental principle of the universe.

Another school which appeared a little later in the same century was that of the Seven Sages of the Bamboo Grove. This was a group of young noblemen who held meetings in a grove of bamboo, and comported themselves in ways at variance with the established standards of correct and ceremonious conduct. Among their number were Chi K'ang (A.D. 223-262), who practiced alchemy and took exercises in breathing in order to attain immortality; and Hsiang Hsiu, who prepared a commentary on Chuang Tzu.

The Period of the Six Dynasties was not only marked by the revolt against custom, particularly Confucian custom, but was also characterized by a general neglect of learning. This, too, was conducive to the spread of Taoism or at least of the superstitions which had increasingly tended to attach themselves to this ancient philosophy.

FENG SHUI

The pseudo-science known as Feng Shui, literally meaning Wind and Water, was not unknown hitherto in China but was now, at the hands of a third century Taoist, given its definitive development particularly as applied to graves. In the system of Feng Shui, ever afterward so pervasive a part of Chinese life, wind and water are regarded as the visible signs of Yin and Yang, the negative and positive principles of the universe. It is believed that these forces act in different ways in different localities, depending upon such factors as the forms of the hills, the directions of the streams, the nature

---

[56] Shryock, *The Study of Human Abilities*, pp.14-16.

of man-made objects, and the relationships to the heavenly bodies. On such presuppositions it is obviously important that houses, temples and graves be so placed as to take advantage of favorable configurations of cosmic influence, and it is toward the ascertaining of such propitious locations that the calculations of Feng Shui are directed.[57]

The working out of this system with regard to ascertaining proper places of burial was the achievement of Kuo P'o. Born in Wen-hsi in Shansi, Kuo P'o lived from A.D. 276 to 324. He was a scholar of attainment and became famous as an exponent of the doctrines of Taoism. The biography of Kuo P'o, contained in the history of the Tsin dynasty, under which he lived, narrates that in his youth he received from another teacher "a Book on the Contents of the Blue Bag, in nine chapters," and that from this "he thoroughly understood the arts relating to the five elements, astrology and divination, knowing how to expel calamities, how to avert disasters, and how to bring complete succour in hopeless cases."

As an example of his skill in the proper location of a grave, we read in the same source: "Having lost his mother, he resigned his office, and with a tortoise shell sought out a burial place for her in Ki-yang. The spot being not farther from the borders of the water than some hundred paces, there was much gossip abroad about its being too near; but P'o declared that the water would soon become dry ground. Afterwards sand was flooded up over an area of several tens of miles from the grave, and entirely converted into orchards and fields."[58]

Kuo P'o was an author of repute, and the Book on Burial, a standard Feng Shui treatise, is attributed to him, though perhaps incorrectly. At any rate his successors in the so-called geomantic art have continued to look upon him as the patriarch of their profession and indeed as its patron divinity.

KO HUNG

With its elixirs of everlasting life, Isles of Immortality, and geomantic procedures about burials, Taoism was far removed from the system of speculative thought it had been in its origin. Indeed it was being transformed from a mystic philosophy into a popular re-

[57] J. J. M. DeGroot, *The Religious System of China, Its Ancient Forms, Evolution, History and Present Aspect, Manners, Customs and Social Institutions Connected Therewith*. III (1897), pp.935-1056.
[58] tr. *ibid.*, pp.1001f.

ligion. With this transformation, Ko Hung, a Taoist of the fourth century, had much to do.[59]

Known also as Pao P'u Tzu, Ko Hung was born in Kiangsu. As a youth he was very poor, but earned money by cutting firewood to buy paper and ink for his studies, in which he was very zealous. In A.D. 326 he was appointed to an official post and was able to journey to Cochin China to secure cinnabar for alchemical researches in which he was engaged.

A written work of his known as the Pao-p'u-tzu contains a discussion, in the first part, of the transmutation of metals, the preparation of elixirs of immortality, and the ascetic rules by which life may be prolonged; in the second part, it goes on into matters of government and politics. Here is a sample of the prescriptions contained in this source: "Take three pounds of genuine cinnabar, and one pound of white honey. Mix them. Dry the mixture in the sun. Then roast it over a fire until it can be shaped into pills. Take ten pills the size of a hemp seed every morning. Inside of a year, white hair will turn black, decayed teeth will grow again, and the body will become sleek and glistening. If an old man takes this medicine for a long period of time, he will develop into a young man. The one who takes it constantly will enjoy eternal life, and will not die."[60]

THE TAOIST PANTHEON

Another work by Ko Hung was called Biographies of the Gods. As the title indicates, the Taoism promulgated by this authority gave full recognition to divine beings. Having begun as a naturalistic philosophy, from the fourth century A.D. on, Taoism developed a multiplicity of gods. Some of these were nature and astral deities, as is understandable when we recall how much attention was given to dealing with the spiritual forces supposedly at work in earth and heaven. Others were adopted from Buddhism, or invented in imitation of the numerous divine beings recognized in that faith. Yet others were genii, immortals, and deified personages. Lao Tzu himself was elevated to the rank of a deity in A.D. 666.[61]

To bring order out of confusion, a hierarchical grouping was eventually established. At the head of the pantheon was the triad of the Three Pure Ones, evidently formed in imitation of Buddhist ideas, dwelling in the three heavens. The highest of the three was Yuan

[59] Shryock, *The Study of Human Abilities*, p.19; GCBD p.372.
[60] tr. in Johnson, *A Study of Chinese Alchemy*, p.63.
[61] Franke in SLR I, p.228.

Shih T'ien Tsun (or Yuan Shih T'ien Wang), the "Original Beginning, Honored of Heaven," who appeared as the First Principle of
the universe in the cosmogony set forth by Ko Hung.[62] Later this
deity had his place taken by, or was himself merged in the character
of the god Yu Huang Shang Ti. The name of this divinity means
the Jade Emperor, or, since jade is the symbol of purity, the August
Pure One. The highest heaven in which he resides is called Yuh
Ts'ing or "Pearly Azure," and his throne is there placed upon the
Jade Mountain.

The god of second rank was Tao Chün or "Honorable Tao," also
known as Ling Pao T'ien Tsun or "Mystic Jewel, Honored of
Heaven." His heaven was Shang Ts'ing or "Upper Azure," and he
was in control of the relationships of Yin and Yang. The third deity
was Lao Tzu, who dwelt in the heaven of T'ai Ts'ing or "Supreme
Azure," and expounded the doctrine emanating from Honorable
Tao.[63]

In the three heavens presided over by these three great deities
were arranged many other divine beings. These included the Saints
in the highest heaven, the Perfect or Elevated in the second heaven,
and the Immortals or Genii in the lowest heaven.

There was also a hierarchy of deities in Hades. Here the chief
ruler was T'ai Shan. T'ai Shan was originally the sacred mountain of
that name in the province of Shantung, the most famous of all such
places in China. Considered as a god, T'ai Shan ruled over the des-
tinies of men not only on earth but also after death. His court is
held in the seventh division of Hades, where terrible penalties are
meted out to evildoers.

Almost innumerable other gods had a place in the fully developed
pantheon. These included, for example, deities of city, kitchen, fire,
pestilence, medicine, north star, happiness, office, and age. Three
Mandarins, or Three Governors as they were called, were also much
worshiped. Of these the first ruled heaven, the second earth, and
the third the seas, lakes, rivers and canals.

The Genii or Immortals, mentioned above as being represented in
the third heaven, and alluded to by Wu Wei (p.393) as having a
prominent place in the Taoist religion, deserve special mention. As
Taoist beliefs were eventually elaborated, there are no less than
five classes of these supernatural beings: (1) Demon Immortals, dis-

[62] *ibid.*, p.221.
[63] cf. E. T. C. Werner, *A Dictionary of Chinese Mythology.* 1932, pp.399f.

embodied spirits without a resting place; (2) Human Immortals, men who have attained freedom from the troubles of the spirit and the infirmities of the flesh; (3) Earthly Immortals, human beings who have achieved immortality in this world; (4) Deified Immortals, spirits which have gone to live on the three islands of the blessed; and (5) Celestial Immortals, glorified beings who enjoy everlasting life in heaven.

At least in the Yüan Period (A.D. 1279-1368), there was a group of Eight Immortals about whose names many legends had gathered and to whom much veneration was paid. They were: (1) Chung-li Ch'üan, pictured with a fan as his symbol, believed to have lived in the Han dynasty, to have transmuted metals and obtained the formula for immortality, and thus to have become the first and greatest of the Eight Immortals; (2) Lü Yen (or Lü Tung-pin), an eighth century A.D. scholar and recluse, represented with a sword; (3) Chang Kuo, a magician of the seventh or eighth century A.D., who rode on a donkey which he was supposed to be able to fold up like a piece of paper when not in use; (4) Lan Ts'ai Ho, generally pictured as a woman, with a flute as a symbol; (5) Han Hsiang, a nephew of the celebrated scholar Han Yü (ninth century A.D.), portrayed with a basket of peaches, supposedly a fruit of immortality; (6) Ts'ao Kuo-chiu, said to have lived in the ninth or tenth century A.D., and usually pictured with castanets as his emblem; (7) Ho Hsien Ku, the daughter of a shopkeeper, seventh century A.D., shown in pictures with a lotus flower; (8) Li T'ieh-kuai, represented as a beggar with an iron staff.[64]

The bronze mirror shown in Fig. 170 is attributed to the period of which we have been speaking, perhaps as early as the third century A.D. As may be seen, the back is elaborately ornamented with figures in relief, and these are believed to represent Taoist deities.[65]

[64] Peter C. Ling in *Journal of the North-China Branch of the Royal Asiatic Society.* 49 (1918), pp.53-75; see GCBD under the respective names.

[65] For Chinese mirrors, cf. Schuyler Cammann in *Archaeology.* 2 (1949), pp.114-120.

4. TAOISM IN THE T'ANG PERIOD (A.D. 618-906)

IT HAS already been noted in the chapter on Confucianism that the great T'ang ruler, T'ai Tsung (A.D. 627-649), claimed descent from Lao Tzu himself, and therefore manifested a natural inclination toward Taoism. His later successor, the sixth emperor of the T'ang Dynasty, Hsüan Tsung[66] (A.D. 712-756), was also very favorably disposed toward the faith.

HSÜAN TSUNG

According to texts dealing with his reign, Hsüan Tsung experienced dreams which moved him to favorable actions with regard to the Taoist religion. In the most remarkable of these dreams the Emperor saw a statue of Lao Tzu which was duly found and set up as an object of reverence. The place of the discovery was at Chou-chih, west of Ch'ang-an, where one tradition placed the tomb of Lao Tzu. Not far away was supposed to be the house of the customs officer to whom Lao Tzu had given the Tao Te Ching, before he rode away on his ox over Western Pass, never to return. As Duyvendak has pointed out, Hsüan Tsung's experience looks like an imitation of that of Ming Ti, the Later Han emperor, whose dream of a statue of the Buddha, afterward discovered in India, played an important part in the introduction of Buddhism into China.[67]

WU TAO TZU

Superstitious and dissolute as he was, Hsüan Tsung was a patron of literature and art and surrounded himself with poets and artists. Among these was Wu Tao Tzu, whom he raised from an insignificant post in Shantung to the court position of Imperial Artist-in-chief. Becoming one of the most famous personages in Far Eastern art, Wu Tao Tzu was named the Prince of Painters of all generations. Possessed of an original and powerful style, he drew human and animal forms as well as pictures of buildings and foliage with great skill. Particularly noteworthy in his compositions were heroic and demoniac figures, and the spirits, gods and demons of Taoism provided him with almost inexhaustible materials.[68]

No original works of Wu Tao Tzu are known to be in existence

---

[66] Also known as Li Lung-chi or Ming Huang.
[67] J. J. L. Duyvendak in *India Antiqua*, pp.102-108.
[68] GCBD pp.889f.; V.-F. Weber, "Ko-ji Hô-ten," *Dictionnaire à l'usage des amateurs et collectionneurs d'objets d'art japonais et chinois*. 1923, II, p.451.

now, but there are recognized copies both in the form of engravings on stone and drawings on paper, while his influence has been traced widely.[69] An album of fifty drawings is extant, most of the pictures in which probably are actually copies of his works.[70] The first twenty-six pictures depict genii, planetary spirits and other heavenly beings of the Taoist pantheon. The next fourteen drawings have to do with the Taoist Hades, where the king of the underworld sits upon his throne, attended by various demons, and passes judgment upon the people who are brought before him. The last ten pictures in the album, although of a style not unrelated to the first, appear to be clearly from a different artist.

In Fig. 171 we show from this collection the drawing of the genii of the five holy mountains (Wu Yo) of China: the holy mountain of the east, T'ai Shan in Shantung; of the south, Heng Shan in Hunan; of the center, Sung Shan in Honan; of the west, Hua Shan in Shensi; and of the north, Heng Shan in Shansi.[71] In Fig. 172 we reproduce one of the scenes from the underworld. The ruler of Hades sits upon his throne, stern of countenance, while a man kneels before him, guarded by an ax-bearing demon. Another demon at one side reads the man's record from a scroll. Elsewhere in the picture are other figures, including two women at the lower left with chains about their necks, also watched by demons.[72]

Another interesting object of art, probably of T'ang date, is the bronze statuette pictured in Fig. 173. The base is the upturned head of a fish; in the mouth of the fish is a snake; and on the neck of the snake sits a bird, perhaps a pheasant. These figures are believed to symbolize the Taoist Three Governors of water, earth and heaven respectively.[73]

THE T'AI I CHIN HUA TSUNG CHIH

The influence of Buddhism was very evident in the Taoist thought of the T'ang Period. A striking example of the amalgamation which resulted may be seen in the book called the T'ai I Chin Hua Tsung Chih or The Secret of the Golden Flower.[74] This work is supposed

[69] Zoltán de Takács in *Artibus Asiae.* 7 (1937), pp.161-170; 11 (1948), pp.70-73.
[70] F. R. Martin, *Zeichnungen nach Wu Tao-tze aus der Götter- und Sagenwelt Chinas.* 1913.
[71] Werner, *A Dictionary of Chinese Mythology,* pp.578-580.
[72] Martin, *Zeichnungen nach Wu Tao-tze aus der Götter- und Sagenwelt Chinas,* Pls. 5,32.
[73] Alfred Salmony in *Gazette des beaux-arts.* 6th Series. 25 (1944), pp.315-317.
[74] tr. Richard Wilhelm, *The Secret of the Golden Flower, A Chinese Book of Life, Translated and Explained.* tr. Cary F. Baynes. 1931.

to embody the teachings of Lü Yen, or Lü Tung-pin as he is also named, a Taoist recluse and teacher born about A.D. 755 and accounted one of the Eight Immortals. A portrait of Lü Tung-pin, painted according to the later added inscription by Teng Tschang-yeu in the latter part of the ninth century, is shown in Fig. 174.[75]

The special form of faith which Lü Tung-pin promulgated was known as Chin Tan Chiao or the Golden Elixir of Life. While this name suggests the same kind of magical practices with which we have already become familiar, the movement of Lü Tung-pin was in fact somewhat of a reformation in which the old language of alchemy was employed to symbolize psychological processes. It was in the elaboration of its psychology that the T'ai I Chin Hua Tsung Chih drew extensively upon the resources of Buddhist thought. Buddhist writings are quoted from time to time, and a specifically Buddhist type of meditation is recommended.

This way of meditation is called "fixating contemplation" (Chih Kuan), and is described in the book as follows: "Fixating contemplation is a Buddhist method which by no means has been handed down as a secret. One looks with both eyes at the end of the nose, sits upright and in a comfortable position, and holds the heart to the center in the midst of conditions [on the fixed pole in the flight of phenomena]. In Taoism it is called the yellow middle, in Buddhism the center in the midst of conditions. The two are the same. It does not necessarily mean the middle of the head. It is only a matter of fixing one's thinking on the point which lies exactly between the two eyes. Then all is well. The Light is something extremely mobile. When one fixes the thought on the mid-point between the two eyes, the Light streams in of its own accord."[76]

As shown in the concluding part of the preceding quotation, the purpose of the practice of contemplation is to cause the mystic Light of the universe to flow into the being of the devotee. When this is done a spirit-body is formed which is capable, upon the death of the individual, of attaining immortality and becoming part of the great Tao. In the not always wholly lucid words of the book:

The Golden Flower is the Light. . . . When the Light circulates, the powers of the whole body arrange themselves before its throne, just as when a holy king has taken possession of the capital and has laid down the fundamental rules of order, all the states approach with tribute; or,

[75] Ernst Diez, *Einführung in die Kunst des Ostens.* 1922, pp.143f., Fig. 38.
[76] tr. Wilhelm, *The Secret of the Golden Flower,* pp.38f.

just as when the master is quiet and calm, men-servants and maids obey his orders of their own accord, and each does his work.

Therefore you only have to make the Light circulate: that is the deepest and most wonderful secret. The Light is easy to move, but difficult to fix. If it is allowed to go long enough in a circle, then it crystallizes itself: that is the natural spirit-body. This crystallized spirit is formed beyond the nine Heavens. It is the condition of which it is said in the Book of the Seal of the Heart: Silently in the morning thou fliest upward.

In carrying out this fundamental truth you need to seek for no other methods, but must only concentrate your thoughts on it. The book Leng Yen[77] says: By collecting the thoughts one can fly and will be born in Heaven. Heaven is not the wide blue sky, but the place where the body is made in the house of the creative. If one keeps this up for a long time, there develops quite naturally in addition to the body, yet another spirit-body.

The Golden Flower is the Elixir of Life. All changes of spiritual consciousness depend upon the Heart. Here is a secret charm, which, although it works very accurately, is yet so fluent that it needs extreme intelligence and clarity, and complete absorption and calm. People without this highest degree of intelligence and understanding do not find the way to apply the charm; people without this utmost capacity for concentration and calm cannot keep fast hold of it.[78]

PERSECUTION AS PROPOSED AND AS PRACTICED

While the position of Taoism in the T'ang Period was, on the whole, favorable, it was the increasing effort of Confucianism to stamp the mark of heresy upon it as well as upon Buddhism, both of which religions were held to be foreign to the classical traditions of China. An example of the attack which was made may be found in the essay, "On the True Faith of a Confucianist," written by the celebrated poet and statesman, Han Wen Kung, who lived from A.D. 768 to 824. This leader wrote: "The followers of Lao Tzu say, 'Confucius was a disciple of our Master.' The followers of Buddha say, 'Confucius was a disciple of *our* Master.' And the followers of Confucius, by dint of hearing this so often, have at length fallen so low as themselves to indulge in such random talk, saying, 'Our Master also respected Lao Tzu and Buddha.' Not only have they uttered this with their tongues, but they have written it down in books; and now, if a man would cultivate morality, from whom should he seek instruction? Great is the straining of mankind after the supernatural! Great is their neglect of fundamentals in this yearn-

[77] The Buddhist Lankavatara Sutra.
[78] tr. Wilhelm, *The Secret of the Golden Flower*, pp.23-25.

ing for the supernatural alone. . . . Let us . . . insist that the followers of Lao Tzu and Buddha behave like ordinary mortals. Let us burn their books. Let us turn their temples into dwelling houses."[79]

The Taoists were still too strong, however, to be the victims of any wholesale confiscation and expropriation of their property as urged by Han Wen Kung. Indeed by the middle of the ninth century they had experienced such a new access of power that they themselves were able to instigate terrible persecutions of the faiths which they regarded as foreign. It was the Emperor Wu Tsung (A.D. 841-846), an ardent Taoist, who in A.D. 845 conducted the most severe religious persecution which had ever been witnessed in China. The chief object of his wrath was Buddhism, which had now grown very strong, and along with it Christianity and Zoroastrianism were included.

The edict[80] launching the persecution of A.D. 845 was entitled, "The proclamation ordering the destruction of the Buddhist monasteries." It began with the observation that there was no such thing as Buddhism in ancient China, and that it was only after the Han dynasty that "the Image-Teaching gradually began to flourish. And once established, in that degenerate age, this strange custom prevailed far and wide, and now the people are soaked to the bone with it." Continuing to specific charges against Buddhism, the edict declared: "Wasting human labor in building; plundering the people's purse by golden decorations; ignoring parents and the sovereign in contributions; neglecting both husband and wife by their vigil-keeping; no teaching is more harmful than this Buddhism." Then confiscation was announced of 4,600 monasteries as well as of 40,000 temples and lesser establishments, while 260,500 monks and nuns were ordered to "return to secular life so that they may be able to pay the taxes."

Following this condemnation of Buddhism, the proclamation contained this paragraph: "Examining into the teachings from the foreign lands in the Empire, We have discovered that there are over 3,000 monks from Ta-ch'in and Mu-hu-fu; and these monks also shall return to lay life. They shall not mingle and interfere with the manners and customs of the Middle Kingdom." As we know from the Nestorian Monument, those from Ta-ch'in were the Christians;[81]

[79] tr. in Herbert A. Giles, *Confucianism and Its Rivals* (The Hibbert Lectures, 2d Series). 1915, pp.218f.

[80] tr. Saeki, *The Nestorian Monument in China*, pp.86-89; cf. Moule, *Christians in China before the Year 1550*, pp.70f.

those from Mu-hu-fu are identified as Zoroastrians. Economically motivated as this persecution obviously was, it also witnesses to the intolerance of the Taoism of the time, when occupying a position of unlimited power.

[81] Perhaps it was at this very time that the Nestorian Stone was buried for safety.

5. TAOISM IN THE SUNG (A.D. 960-1279) AND YÜAN (A.D. 1279-1368) PERIODS

THE T'AI SHANG KAN YING P'IEN

As WE come to the Sung Period we find an increased emphasis upon ethics in Taoism. Despite the Taoist attack upon Buddhism recorded in the preceding section, the influence of that faith upon Taoism is clearly evident in the ethical teachings which are now to be noted. We find precise calculations of present and future retributions and rewards; these can be explained as an attempt to make tangible and practical for the ordinary man the doctrine of *karma*. We observe a new stress upon love of all creatures; this must reflect the similar doctrine of the Mahayana.

These teachings may be studied in the T'ai Shang Kan Ying P'ien or Book of the Exalted One on Rewards and Punishments.[82] While the Exalted One in whose name the text is set forth is supposed to be Lao Tzu, in actuality the book was probably first published in the time of the Sung dynasty. The work is relatively brief, being written in somewhat more than twelve hundred Chinese characters, and as a popular tract on Taoist morals has been circulated very widely.

The introduction to the book states the general theory of rewards and punishments, which is that various spiritual beings keep an accurate record of the good deeds and the crimes of men and then lengthen or shorten their lives accordingly. "The Exalted One says: Curses and blessings do not come through gates, but man himself invites their arrival. The reward of good and evil is like the shadow accompanying a body, and so it is apparent that heaven and earth are possessed of crime-recording spirits. According to the lightness or gravity of his transgressions, the sinner's term of life is reduced. Not only is his term of life reduced, but poverty also strikes him. Often he meets with calamity and misery. His neighbors hate him. Punishments and curses pursue him. Good luck shuns him. Evil stars threaten him; and when his term of life comes to an end, he perishes. ... Of all the offences which men commit, the greater ones cause a

---

[82] tr. James Legge in SBE XL, pp.233-246; Teitaro Suzuki and Paul Carus, *T'ai-Shang Kan-Ying P'ien, Treatise of the Exalted One on Response and Retribution, Translated from the Chinese, Containing Introduction, Chinese Text, Verbatim Translation, Translation, Explanatory Notes and Moral Tales.* 1906; James Webster, *The Kan Ying Pien, Book of Rewards and Punishments, The Chinese Text, with Introduction, Translation and Notes.* 1918. The quotations here are from the translation by Suzuki and Carus.

loss of twelve years, the smaller ones of a hundred days. These their offences, great as well as small, constitute some hundred affairs, and those who are anxious for life everlasting, should above all avoid them."

After this comes the following series of miscellaneous moral injunctions: "The right way leads forward; the wrong way backward. Do not proceed on an evil path. Do not sin in secret. Accumulate virtue, increase merit. With a compassionate heart turn toward all creatures. Be faithful, filial, friendly, and brotherly. First rectify thyself and then convert others. Take pity on orphans, assist widows; respect the old, be kind to children. Even the multifarious insects, herbs, and trees should not be injured. Be grieved at the misfortune of others and rejoice at their good luck. Assist those in need, and rescue those in danger. Regard your neighbor's gain as your own gain, and regard your neighbor's loss as your own loss. Do not call attention to the faults of others, nor boast of your own excellence. Stay evil and promote goodness. Renounce much, accept little. Show endurance in humiliation and bear no grudge. Receive favors as if surprised. Extend your help without seeking reward. Give to others and do not regret or begrudge your liberality."

Having set forth these exhortations, the blessings are stated which may be expected by the person who obeys them. "Those who are thus, are good: people honor them; Heaven's Reason (Tao) gives them grace; blessings and abundance follow them; all ill luck keeps away; angel spirits guard them. Whatever they undertake will surely succeed, and even to spiritual saintliness they may aspire. Those who wish to attain heavenly saintliness should perform one thousand three hundred good deeds, and those who wish to attain to earthly saintliness should perform three hundred good deeds."

Then the book goes on to describe evildoers at much length. A few of the things which such people do are these: "Right and wrong they confound. . . . Though they know their mistakes they do not correct them; though they know the good they do not do it. . . . Improperly they have grown rich, and withal they remain vulgar. . . . They crush that which is excellent in others. . . . They break into others' houses to take their property and valuables. . . . They shorten the foot, they narrow the measure, they lighten the scales, they reduce the peck. . . . With the members of their own family they are angry and quarrelsome. . . . They spit at falling stars and point at the many-colored rainbow."

The punishments for such doers of wrong are then discussed and it is stated that if at death any guilt remains unpunished the penalties will be transferred to the children and grandchildren of the culprit.

Finally the following exhortation concludes the book: "Therefore, blessed is the man who speaketh what is good, who thinketh what is good, who practiceth what is good. If but each single day he would persevere in these three ways of goodness, within three years Heaven will surely shower on him blessings. Unfortunate is the man who speaketh what is evil, who thinketh what is evil, who practiceth what is evil. If but each single day he would persevere in these three ways of evil-doing, within three years Heaven will surely shower on him curses. Why shall we not be diligent and comply with this?"

CHEN TSUNG

In preceding sections we have noticed some of the occasions on which Taoism attained its greatest outward successes and was most prominent politically. We have seen how its doctrine of "inaction" lent itself to the purposes of Shih Huang Ti; how its superstitions flourished in the disturbed time of the Six Dynasties; and how it was favored by the T'ang emperors and espoused by Wu Tsung, the persecutor of the foreign faiths in the land. Yet another apex of external success was reached under the third emperor of the Sung dynasty, Chen Tsung.

Known also as Chao Heng, Chen Tsung reigned A.D. 968-1022. The founder of his line had strongly supported Confucianism, but Chen Tsung became an adherent of Taoism. Being mild and superstitious by nature, he fell an easy prey to charlatans. Written revelations were brought to him, which he received as of divine origin and had placed in special temples. In A.D. 1008 the high official Wang Ch'in-jo presented the Emperor with a twenty-foot-long letter written on silk which was supposed to convey divine congratulations upon the prosperity of the land and the justice of the government. At the reading of this supernatural document other officials declared that they saw a purple cloud, which had the shape now of a dragon and again of a phoenix, hanging low over the palace buildings. So flagrant was the hoax that a scholar asked, quoting Confucius, "I have heard that God does not even speak; how then should he write a letter?"[83]

---

[83] tr. Giles, *Confucianism and Its Rivals*, p.221.

Later the same Wang Ch'in-jo served as master of ceremonies for a pilgrimage which the Emperor was induced to make to the sacred mountain T'ai Shan. Returning from this journey, Chen Tsung visited the birthplace of Confucius and conferred upon the sage the title of "King." Some years afterward he went to a temple which he had erected in honor of Lao Tzu and bestowed upon him the yet higher title of "Emperor." Again Chen Tsung called together a large assembly of Taoist and Buddhist priests to discuss an appearance of the planet Venus in the daytime, and to conduct prayers to ward off any evil consequences which might otherwise follow from this portent.

So complete was the obsession of the Emperor with Taoist superstitions and so thorough was his subjection to the will of the Taoist magicians, that the ultimate result was a strong reaction against this religion which played upon imperial credulity to further its own purposes. The new movement took the form of an attack on all heterodox teaching and a revival of Confucianism. The greatest leader was Chu Hsi (A.D. 1130-1200), whom we have already met (p.378) as the philosopher through whom Neo-Confucian doctrines were put in the form which was to be regarded as orthodox until the twentieth century. Here we may give certain additional information on his attitude toward Taoism.

CHU HSI ON TAOISM

As a youth Chu Hsi studied Taoism as well as Buddhism,[84] but in his maturity condemned them both, withal opposing Buddhism even more uncompromisingly than Taoism. The argument which he presented against Taoism and its Buddhistic leanings was this: "Taoism was at first confined to purity of life and to inaction. These were associated with long life and immortality, which by and by became the sole objects of the cult. Nowadays, they have thought it advisable to adopt a system of magical incantations, and chiefly occupy themselves with exorcism and prayers for blessings. Thus, two radical changes have been made. The Taoists have the writings of Lao Tzu and Chuang Tzu. They neglected these, and the Buddhists stole them for their own purposes; whereupon the Taoists went off and imitated the Sutras of Buddhism. This is just as if the scions of some wealthy house should be robbed of all their valuables, and then go off and gather up the old pots and pans belonging to the thieves.

[84] Bruce, *Chu Hsi and His Masters*, pp.62f.

Buddhist books are full of what Buddha said, and Taoist books are similarly full of what Tao said. Now Buddha was a man, but how does Tao manage to talk? This belief, however, has prevailed for eight or nine centuries past. Taoism began with Lao Tzu. Its Trinity of the Three Pure Ones is copied from the Trinity of the Three Persons as taught by Buddhism. By their Trinity the Buddhists mean (1) the spiritual body [of Buddha], (2) his joyful body [showing Buddha rewarded for his virtues], and (3) his fleshly body, under which Buddha appears on earth as a man. The modern schools of Buddhism have divided their Trinity under three images which are placed side by side, thus completely missing the true signification [which is Trinity in Unity]; and the adherents of Taoism, wishing to imitate the Buddhists in this particular, worship Lao Tzu under [another version of] the Three Pure Ones, namely, (1) as the original revered God, (2) the supreme ruler Tao, and (3) the supreme ruler Lao Tzu. Almighty God (T'ien) is ranked below these three, which is nothing short of an outrageous usurpation. Moreover, the first two do not represent the spiritual and joyful bodies of Lao Tzu, and the two images set up cannot form a Unity with him; while the introduction of the third is an aggravated copy of the mistake made by the Buddhists. Chuang Tzu has told us in plain language of the death of Lao Tzu, who must now be a spirit; how then can he usurp the place of Almighty God? The doctrines of Buddha and Lao Tzu should be altogether abolished; but if this is not possible, then only the teachings of Lao Tzu should be tolerated, all shrines in honor of him, or of his disciples and various magicians, to be placed under the control of the directors of Public Worship."[85]

As a result of the anti-Taoist and pro-Confucian movement just described, Taoism was more and more pushed into the background, at least as far as official standing was concerned. Individual Sung emperors like Hui Tsung (p.416) might still take an interest in the faith, and under Jenghiz Khan and Kublai Khan the religion might enjoy an important period of imperial favor; but, after the end of the Yüan dynasty, Confucianism was definitely the dominant force in relation to the government.[86]

Deprived of its ability to sway the affairs of state, Taoism continued to flourish among the common people as a system of magic, geomancy, divination, exorcism and idolatry. Some thinkers, however, were challenged to return to the more nearly pure idealism of

[85] *ibid.*, pp.237-239.   [86] Franke in SLR I, p.228.

Lao Tzu and the nature mysticism of Chuang Tzu, and thus the nobler forms of Taoism have never utterly perished. Indeed, in its majestic conception of the Tao, in its affirmation of the value of life, in its ethical principles of simplicity and overcoming evil with good, and in its deep love of nature, Taoism made enduring contributions.[87]

THE APPRECIATION OF NATURE

The appreciation of nature just referred to had far-reaching effects. As will be remembered, it was Chuang Tzu more than any other philosopher who centered attention upon the great natural world, and who described the true sage as "taking his stand upon the beauty of the universe," and doing nothing "beyond gazing at the universe." The influence of this attitude was felt powerfully among the poets of the T'ang Period, and through them it passed on to the painters of the Sung Period. Of course it was not only Taoists who wrote poems and painted pictures about nature, but it cannot be doubted that among those who did, Taoists were prominent, and that in the entire movement in this direction the Taoist tradition was very influential.

It has been observed that the Chinese artist "was usually both a Confucian scholar in his training and a Taoist recluse in his longings";[88] and Chuang Tzu has been called "the main fountain of inspiration and imagination to Chinese artists, particularly landscape painters," even unto the present day.[89]

POETS

If we try to trace this line of influence, we find that among the numerous poets whose work brought honor to the T'ang Period were the Taoists, T'ao Han and Chang Ch'ien.[90] T'ao Han held a government position during the years between A.D. 713 and 742, but later devoted himself exclusively to the care of his aged mother. Chang Ch'ien likewise entered upon an official career in A.D. 727, but afterward retired to the mountains and lived as a hermit. Both men were ardent followers of the cult of Tao, and both were very sensitive to the beauties of the natural world in which they found intimations of profound truth.

[87] Y. C, Yang, *China's Religious Heritage.* 1943, pp.161-166,171-174.
[88] George Rowley, *Principles of Chinese Painting, with Illustrations from the Du Bois Schanck Morris Collection* (Princeton Monographs in Art and Archaeology, XXIV). 1947, p.13.
[89] Chan Wing-tsit in MPEW p.45; cf. F. S. C. Northrop, *The Meeting of East and West, An Inquiry Concerning World Understanding.* 1946, pp.330-334.
[90] GCBD pp.52,718; Wieger, *China throughout the Ages,* pp.280-402.

Here, for example, is a poetic description by T'ao Han of a visit to a convent in the mountains: "The pines and cypresses conceal the mountain gorge, but I have discovered a narrow path on the west. The sky clears, a peak shows itself, and, as though born out of space, a convent rises up before my eyes. The building seems to stand upon a terrace of clouds, it raises its tall pavilion into the air amid the steep rocks. Night falls, the monkeys and the birds are silent. The sound of bells and the chant of the bonzes[91] rise above the chill clouds. I gaze upon the blue peaks and the moon, which mirrors itself in the waters of the lake; I listen to the sound of the springs and the wind as it lashes the leaves at the torrent's edge. My soul has soared beyond what is visible, at once wanderer and captive, in a wondrous ravishment. And so the dawn surprises me; soon the face of all things will change. Already the darkness is melting away towards the east on the slope of the giant rocks; already the surface of the waters is lit up with a sparkling gleam, the herald of the dawn, and little by little the paling rays of the moon are losing their brightness."[92]

And here is a poem about a night among the mountains by Chang Ch'ien: "Seated upon a slope of the mountain, I followed with my eyes a frail bark, the symbol of our destiny, as it floated lightly upon the deep waters. It sailed away and was lost to sight, it melted into the vast sky, while the sun was quenching its fires on the opposite horizon. Suddenly all that was passing before my eyes was plunged into the half-light of an uncertain dimness. The sun's last rays now lit up only the tree-tops and the summits of the rocks. The surface of the waters became darker and darker. Soon none but a few red clouds marked where the sun had disappeared. The islands in the lake stood out black upon the tranquil waters, on which still lay a lingering light reflected from the sky, but already the darkness lay heavy upon the woods and hills, and the horizon was now no more than a vague line before my powerless eyes. Night falls, the air is keen, there is a stir in it afar off, the north wind harshly raises its whistling note, the water-birds seek a shelter on the sandy shore, where they will wait for dawn, cowering among the reeds."[93]

PAINTERS

Then as we come to the great painters who were the glory of the

---

[91] A term applied to both Buddhist and Taoist monks.

[92] tr. in GCE III, p.292. This quotation and the one following are made by permission of the publisher, Alfred A. Knopf, Inc., New York and London.

[93] *ibid.*, III, pp.295f.

Sung Period (p.377), we find that their favorite subjects were land-scapes, in which powerful and poignant expression was given to the vastness and the consoling power of nature. Not a few of the paint-ings are virtually translations into this realm of art of such visions of the poets as we have been citing. Several of these Sung landscapes may now be shown, arranged in the chronological order of the artists to whom they are attributed.

The painting in Fig. 175 is a winter scene, showing a temple among the snowy hills. It is ascribed to Fan K'uan, an artist who flourished around A.D. 990-1030.

In Fig. 177 we see a painting called "Summer," which is usually attributed to Hui Tsung (A.D. 1082-1135).[94] Hui Tsung (also known as Chao Chi) was none other than the eighth emperor of the Sung dynasty, and an artist as well. He came to the throne in A.D. 1100 when the currents of Neo-Confucianism were already gathering strength, but was himself devoted to Taoism, and spent large sums of money for assemblies of Taoist recluses.[95] The painting we are con-sidering here is an almost perfect expression of the spirit of Taoism, for it shows a man seated against a tree upon a mountain ledge, and gazing out to the sky where a few clouds are drifting and two cranes are flying up into the vastness. Almost irresistibly we are re-minded of the saying of Chuang Tzu: "The wise man looks into space, and does not regard the small as too little, nor the great as too much."[96]

As the quotation just made reminds us, it was in harmony with the attitude of Taoism to be aware of the details of the natural scene as well as of its vast and stupendous aspects. This may be illustrated by another and exquisite painting by the Emperor Hui Tsung (Fig. 178). It is called "The Five-Colored Parakeet."

Because of the similarity of its composition to that of "Summer" by Hui Tsung, we will not reproduce but only mention "The Scholar Gazing at the Moon," by Ma Yüan. As in the aforementioned picture, here too there is a rock in the foreground and a cliff and tree at one side, while in the distance the moon floats in the haze. This artist, Ma Yüan, was active around A.D. 1190-1224, and is regarded as one of the greatest painters not only of China but of the entire world.[97] From his other works we show "Two Sages and an Attendant under

[94] Bachhofer, A Short History of Chinese Art, Fig. 103.
[95] GCBD pp.56f.   [96] tr. Giles, Chuang Tzŭ, pp.202f.
[97] Bachhofer, A Short History of Chinese Art, p.114.

a Plum Tree" (Fig. 179), "Bare Willows and Distant Mountains" (Fig. 176), and "Mountain Landscape with Blossoming Trees" (Fig. 180). In the case of the last picture, the execution may be of later date, but the composition doubtless originated with Ma Yüan.[98] The several persons who are wandering or resting amidst the grandeur of the mountains should be noticed.

The son of Ma Yüan, named Ma Lin (flourished A.D. 1215-1225), was also a noted painter. In Fig. 182 we show a painting attributed to him which we may call "Temple Overlooking the Sea." It is almost an illustration of the poem by T'ao Han (p.415) telling about the convent which seemed to be "born out of space," to "stand upon a terrace of clouds," and to raise "its tall pavilion into the air amid the steep rocks."

Even greater than Ma Yüan, perhaps, was his contemporary Hsia Kuei, who worked around A.D. 1195-1224. One of his masterpieces may appropriately climax our presentation of the Sung landscapes. This is the painting known as "Mountain Brook" (Fig. 181). It bears the name of Ma Yüan, but this is doubtless a later addition, while the half-effaced signature of Hsia Kuei most probably indicates the actual author of the subject. Of it Ludwig Bachhofer has written: "The motive could not be simpler: a wall of rocks, polished by the little rivulet for millions of years, a few trees upon the high ledge, and a slight haze over the brook. But here is the grandeur of nature, before which all the sorrows and ambitions of man become utterly insignificant."[99]

Before concluding this chapter we will show several other paintings, of date more or less comparable with the preceding, which illustrate some specific aspects of Taoism that have become familiar to us in the course of our study. Fig. 183 reproduces a painting in which the natural scene is only the background for a group of Taoist magicians who are engaged in the preparation of the elixir of life.[100]

In Fig. 184 we see, seated at the foot of a tall tree, Chung K'uei, an imaginary character of the Taoist faith, believed to possess the power of exorcising evil demons. As here, he is regularly depicted as an old man in ragged clothes. The legend concerning him may date from the T'ang dynasty, and this painting is ascribed to an

[98] Osvald Sirén, *Chinese and Japanese Sculptures and Paintings in the National Museum, Stockholm.* 1931, p.42, Pl. 45.

[99] Bachhofer, *A Short History of Chinese Art*, p.116. Quoted by permission of the publishers, Pantheon Books Inc., New York.

[100] Wilhelm, *A Short History of Chinese Civilization*, Pl. 30.

otherwise unidentified artist of the Yüan dynasty named Ku Lo.[101]

The painting reproduced in Fig. 185 is probably also from the Yüan Period. It shows a Taoist Immortal who is ascending to heaven. Three women attendants and two men accompany him, while higher up in the clouds other heavenly beings await him. Two storks fly in the extreme upper right hand corner.[102]

The personage in Fig. 186 is a Taoist Immortal, seated on the ground. He is wearing a mantle which leaves his right shoulder bare. The right hand holds a small box, and there is a jar on the ground beside him. The date of the painting may be in the early fourteenth century, or perhaps as late as the beginning of the Ming Period.[103]

[101] Sirén, *Chinese and Japanese Sculptures and Paintings in the National Museum, Stockholm,* pp.39f., Pl. 42; GCBD p.207.
[102] Sirén, *Chinese and Japanese Sculptures and Paintings in the National Museum, Stockholm,* p.39, Pl. 41.
[103] *ibid.,* p.42, Pl. 44.

CHAPTER VIII

Shinto

THE Japanese islands form an arc off the coast of northeast Asia. Four main islands, named Hokkaido, Honshu, Shikoku and Kyushu, together with many smaller ones, constitute Japan proper, while to the north and the south respectively extend the Kurile and the Ryukyu groups. The area of the central archipelago is approximately 150,000 square miles, or slightly less than that of the State of California.

Some seventy-five per cent of the country is mountainous, and only about fifteen per cent of the total area of the land is under cultivation. The highest peak is the symmetrical volcanic cone of Mount Fuji, which reaches an elevation of 12,461 feet. If the Kurile and Ryukyu Islands are included, there are more than five hundred volcanoes within the land. Not far off the eastern coast of Japan the ocean bed descends to depths of twenty and thirty thousand feet below sea level, thus making a difference in elevation between the high peaks and the ocean depths of seven or eight miles. The geological stresses set up by this enormous differential are believed responsible for the frequent earthquakes which are felt throughout the area. There is snow and relatively cold weather in Japan in the winter, and rain and heat in the summer.

The largest approximately level region is the Kwanto Plain around modern Tokyo, most of which has been built up as an alluvial fan by the numerous rivers which flow down out of the mountains. Central Honshu, whence these rivers descend, is the most mountainous region in all Japan. Northern Honshu is also rugged, and has a more severe climate, as does also the northernmost island of Hokkaido. Western Honshu is hilly rather than mountainous, and facing on the island-dotted Inland Sea is perhaps the most beautiful part of the entire picturesque land. Shikoku is the smallest of the main islands and the least important; Kyushu, by virtue of its location, has long served as a connecting link with China and the South Seas.[1]

---

[1] For the geography of Japan see Glenn T. Trewartha, *Japan, A Physical, Cultural and Regional Geography.* 1945; George B. Cressey, *Asia's Lands and Peoples, A Geography of One-Third the Earth and Two-Thirds Its People.* 1944, pp.170-252.

1. PREHISTORIC JAPAN

THE ANCESTRAL AINUS

As FAR as is now known there was no Paleolithic culture in Japan, and the earliest inhabitants belonged to the Neolithic Age. This epoch probably began in Japan in the third millennium B.C. and lasted until near the end of the pre-Christian era.[2] The most ancient people of this period lived primarily by hunting and fishing, and are known to us chiefly from the thousands of shell mounds, or kitchen middens, which they left around the coasts of the islands.[3] Mixed in with the discarded shells in these refuse heaps are animal bones, stone implements and weapons, and broken pottery. The stone objects include picks, axes, scrapers, knives, and heads for arrows and spears. The pottery fragments are from all sorts of vessels such as jars, pots, bowls, cups and bottles. The manufacture of the pottery was by hand, and it was relatively coarse in material but ornate in decoration. Much of it was of the "rope-pattern" type, so-called because it was built up by coiling strips of clay or was ornamented with the coil as a conventional design.

It is thought that the people represented by this Neolithic culture were not indigenous to the islands but had come from elsewhere in several successive waves of immigration. Their racial origin is not certainly known, but it is surmised that they were of Caucasoid affinity. There seems little doubt that the Ainus, an aboriginal people now living on the northern island of Hokkaido, are their modern descendants; hence the ancient Neolithic people may conveniently be called the ancestral Ainus.[4]

The religion of the present-day Ainus probably has much in common with that of their prehistoric ancestors, and a few words concerning it may cast light upon the kind of beliefs which prevailed in the Neolithic Age. This religion is characterized by animism and nature worship. Almost every object in the universe, whether ani-

[2] Menghin, *Weltgeschichte der Steinzeit*, pp.81,297-302.
[3] Neil G. Munro, *Prehistoric Japan*. 1908, pp.44f. This book is still, despite its date, the only comprehensive study of the period. See Hugh Borton, Serge Elisséeff, and Edwin O. Reischauer, *A Selected List of Books and Articles on Japan in English, French and German*. 1940, p.18.
[4] H. Matsumoto in *American Anthropologist, New Series, Organ of the American Anthropological Association, The Anthropological Society of Washington, and the American Ethnological Society of New York*. 23 (1921), pp.50-76; Carl W. Bishop in *Annual Report of the Board of Regents of the Smithsonian Institution, Showing the Operations, Expenditures, and Condition of the Institution for the Year Ending June 30, 1925* (Publication 2836). 1926, pp.550f.; SJSCH pp.1-5.

mate or inanimate, organic or inorganic, is supposed to be the seat of personal, intelligent life. In the skies the highest deity is the sun, while on earth the chief deity is of related character, namely, fire. The spirit of fire, which is worshiped on every pagan hearth, is regarded as a goddess and is commonly called Fuji, meaning "ancestress." Since the same Ainu word is the name of Japan's highest mountain, it may be supposed that this famous volcano was an object of worship to the prehistoric Ainus. Other nature deities include spirits of stars, clouds, seas and vegetation. Over against the beneficent spirits are many demons of air and land, the exorcism of which is a part of their religious practice.[5]

THE YAMATO CONQUEST

In the last centuries B.C. and the first centuries A.D. other people made their way into the islands and began to push the Ainus before them. These invaders probably came for the most part from the Asiatic mainland by way of Korea, and are believed to have been of Mongoloid stock with perhaps an admixture of a proto-Malay element from the tropical South.[6] It is at this time that Japan begins to figure in Chinese writings. The earliest reference is in an ancient treatise on geography called the Shan-hai-ching, where it is stated that the northern and southern Wo are tributary to the Chinese state of Yen. Since Yen ceased to exist as an independent state about 226 B.C., this statement must have to do with a time in the third or even fourth century B.C. Again we are told of the Ta Wo Wang or Great King of the Wo who ruled in the region of Ye-ma-t'ai south of Korea. This place must have been on the island of Kyushu, and the name Ye-ma-t'ai is evidently the same as Yamato, by which the Japanese people have ever afterward designated themselves.[7]

Since Yamato is also the name later applied to a province in central Honshu, we may assume that from an original stronghold on Kyushu the Yamato people pushed gradually forward onto the larger island. The region of Yamato is near Lake Biwa, and the establishment of this as their center shows that the Yamato people had made large gains against the Ainus. Another independent kingdom, closely related to the kingdom of Silla in Korea, also came into existence in western Honshu.

[5] J. Batchelor in HERE I, pp.239-252; Carl Etter, *Ainu Folklore, Traditions and Culture of the Vanishing Aborigines of Japan.* 1949, pp.51f.

[6] Katsuro Hara, *An Introduction to the History of Japan.* 1920, pp.39-49.

[7] Bishop in *Annual Report of the . . . Smithsonian Institution . . . 1925*, pp.554f.

136° 138° 140° 142° 144°

HOKKAIDO

N

O F

H

A

N

O

S

N

O

Nikko•

P

•Tokyo
+Fuji •Kamagawa
       •Yokohama
Adzuchi •Kamakura

Kyoto•
Yamato
Osaka• Nara•
  Asuka•
    Ise•

A

MAP 8

JAPAN

0   50   100   150

Scale of miles

42°
40°
38°
36°
34°
32°

136° 138° 140° 142°

The invaders of whom we have been telling had a culture much more advanced than that of the Ainus. Whereas the latter were still a people of the Stone Age, the Yamato enjoyed all the advantages of the use of iron. Since relatively few bronze remains have been found in Japan, it is supposed that with the arrival of the newcomers the land witnessed a transition from the Neolithic Age to the Iron Age with scarcely any intervening Bronze Age at all. Among the numerous objects of iron now found, are not only axes, chisels, swords and daggers, but also bits and stirrups which give us the important additional information that the horse was introduced and ridden. As a matter of fact it was doubtless the practice of fighting on horseback as well as with weapons of iron which gave the conquerors their superiority over the Ainus. The possession of domesticated animals also made possible the practice of true agriculture in distinction from such hoe culture as may have prevailed previously.

One other mark of this time was the practice of burying important deceased persons in dolmens. These tombs were megalithic structures built out of huge rough boulders, covered with mounds of earth and surrounded by moats. Iron objects of the kind already mentioned were found in these burial places, and also wheelmade pottery and interesting terra cotta figures technically called *haniwa*. The last are generally in the form of cylinders surmounted by a bust of a man or woman. Sometimes it is a soldier in armor who is represented, and occasionally it is a horse or even a house. These figures were probably set up around the edges of the tomb terraces, and may have been substitutes for living beings who were buried with the deceased in earlier times. A group of such *haniwa* is shown in Fig. 187.[8]

While exact dates are not available for the times of which we have been speaking, it may be safely affirmed that the culture just described was flourishing in Japan in the second century A.D. It is also known that the dolmen type of burial prevailed until in the seventh or eighth century, and that by that time the Ainus had been pushed northward to a line approximately corresponding to the thirty-seventh parallel of latitude. Not until the tenth century was the subjugation of the Ainus completed on Honshu, and by then there was a considerable admixture of Ainu blood in the Japanese race. Meanwhile, in the fifth and sixth centuries respectively, the art of writing

[8] Otto Kümmel, *Die Kunst Chinas, Japans und Koreas* (Handbuch der Kunstwissenschaft). 1929, p.103; Mary A. Nourse, *Kodo, The Way of the Emperor, A Short History of the Japanese.* 1940, pp.30f., Fig. facing p.31,upper.

and the faith of Buddhism were introduced into Japan from Korea and China.[9]

ANCIENT TIMES ACCORDING TO THE OLDEST WRITTEN RECORDS

Thus far our account has been based primarily upon archeological studies, and while lacking in many details concerning which we would like to be informed, has the relative dependability of a grounding upon tangible remains of the past. Japanese myths, legends and chronicles also reach back into these same ancient times, and supply a great many details which are extremely vivid but unfortunately do not always have the same kind of dependability.

The two earliest written sources we have are the Kojiki or "Record of Ancient Things" and the Nihongi (also called Nihon-shoki) or "Chronicles of Japan," which were compiled respectively in A.D. 712 and 720. A facsimile of the first page of the Preface to the Kojiki is reproduced in Fig. 188.

THE KOJIKI[10]

In the preface of the Kojiki it is related that the Emperor Temmu (A.D. 673-686) was concerned over the inaccuracies to be found in the official records then existing, and that he therefore issued the following decree: "I hear that the chronicles of the emperors and likewise the original words in the possession of the various families deviate from exact truth, and are mostly amplified by empty falsehoods. If at the present time these imperfections be not amended, ere many years shall have elapsed, the purport of this, the great basis of the country, the grand foundation of the monarchy, will be destroyed. So now I desire to have the chronicles of the emperors selected and recorded, and the old words examined and ascertained, falsehoods being erased and the truth determined, in order to transmit [the latter] to after ages."[11]

At that time, it is further narrated, there was a retainer named Hiyeda no Are who had such a remarkable memory that he could repeat anything he ever read and remember anything he ever heard. This man was therefore commanded to memorize the genealogies of the emperors and the "words of former ages." Meanwhile, how-

[9] Bishop in *Annual Report of the . . . Smithsonian Institution . . . 1925*, pp.559, 561f.,566f.

[10] tr. Basil H. Chamberlain, *"Ko-ji-ki,"* or *"Records of Ancient Matters"* (Transactions of the Asiatic Society of Japan, Supplement to Vol. x). 1882; 2d ed. with annotations by W. G. Aston, 1932. The references here are to the original edition.

[11] tr. Chamberlain, p.9.

ever, Emperor Temmu died and no further progress was made on the matter until under the Empress Gemmyo (A.D. 708-721). Then a court official named Yasumaro was commissioned to put into written form the materials which had been preserved in the memory of Are for the past twenty-five years. Coming to this event in his preface, Yasumaro says, referring to the Empress: "She, on the eighteenth day of the ninth moon of the fourth year of Wa do,[12] commanded me Yasumaro to select and record the old words learnt by heart by Hiyeda no Are according to the Imperial Decree, and dutifully to lift them up to her."[13]

As completed, the work written by Yasumaro covered events from the mythological beginnings of heaven and earth to the end of the reign of the Empress Suiko (A.D. 593-628), and was laid before Empress Gemmyo in three volumes only a little more than five months after it was first commissioned. This is stated by the writer in the conclusion of his preface: "All together the things recorded commence with the separation of Heaven and Earth, and conclude with the august reign at Woharida.[14] So from the Deity Master-of-the-August-Center-of-Heaven down to His Augustness Prince-Wave-Limit-Brave-Cormorant-Thatch-Meeting-Incompletely makes the First Volume; from the Heavenly Sovereign Kamu-yamato-ihare-biko down to the august reign of Homuda makes the Second Volume; from the Emperor Oho-Sazaki down to the great palace of Woharida makes the Third Volume. All together I have written Three Volumes, which I reverently and respectfully present. I Yasumaro, with true trembling and true fear, bow my head, bow my head.

"Reverently presented by the Court Noble Futo no Yasumaro, an Officer of the Upper Division of the First Class of the Fifth Rank and of the Fifth Order of Merit, on the twenty-eighth day of the first moon of the fifth year of Wa do."[15]

As Yasumaro indicated in his preface, the Kojiki opens with the beginning of heaven and earth. At this time numerous deities began to come into existence, of whom the first one was mentioned in the preface, namely the Deity Master-of-the-August-Center-of-Heaven

---

[12] Wa do is the name of a Japanese "year-period" which extended from A.D. 708 to 714, and the date indicated corresponds to November 3, 711. For a list of these "year-periods," see Ernest W. Clement in *Transactions of the Asiatic Society of Japan*. 30 (1902), pp.57-60; and, for detailed tables, Supplement of Vol. 37 (1910) of the same *Transactions* (for Wa do, pp.54f.).

[13] tr. Chamberlain, p.11.

[14] Woharida was the residence of Empress Suiko.

[15] tr. Chamberlain, pp.12f. The last date is equivalent to March 10, 712.

(Ame-no-mi-naka-nushi-no-kami). Here is the situation as described in the first two sentences of the Kojiki: "The names of the deities that were born [literally, that became] in the Plain of High Heaven when the Heaven and Earth began were the Deity Master-of-the-August-Center-of-Heaven, next the High-August-Producing-Wondrous-Deity, next the Divine-Producing-Wondrous-Deity. These three deities were all deities born alone, and hid their persons."[16]

These words evidently mean that three gods came into being out of nothing at the same time that the heaven and the earth came into existence. The "Plain of High Heaven" was presumably the sky or some mythical place in it, and so it may be supposed that these were sky gods. The statement that they "hid their persons" would seem to indicate that they made themselves invisible to human sight.[17] The fact that the Deity Master-of-the-August-Center-of-Heaven is not mentioned again after this first appearance, while the High-August-Producing-Wondrous-Deity and the Divine-Producing-Wondrous-Deity are active in the events which follow, has been interpreted as showing that the first god was comparatively lofty and transcendent.[18]

The next two deities "were born . . . from a thing that sprouted up like unto a reed-shoot when the earth, young and like unto floating oil, drifted about medusa-like," and were named Pleasant-Reed-Shoot-Prince-Elder-Deity and Heavenly-Eternally-Standing-Deity. After these, a dozen more gods and goddesses came into being, with translated names such as Deity Mud-Earth-Lord, Deity Oh-Awful-Lady, Deity the Male-Who-Invites, and Deity the Female-Who-Invites. The last two are often referred to by their Japanese names, Izanagi-no-kami and Izanami-no-kami, or simply Izanagi and Izanami.

After this the Kojiki proceeds to relate how through Izanagi and Izanami the Japanese islands came into being. "Hereupon all the Heavenly Deities commanded the two Deities His Augustness[19] the Male-Who-Invites and Her Augustness the Female-Who-Invites, ordering them to 'make, consolidate, and give birth to this drifting land.' Granting to them a heavenly jeweled spear, they [thus] deigned

[16] I, 1. tr. Chamberlain, p.15.
[17] I. Dooman in *Transactions of the Asiatic Society of Japan.* 25 (1897), pp.67f.
[18] Genchi Kato in *Transactions of the Asiatic Society of Japan.* 36 (1908), pp.137-162; and in *Annales du Musée Guimet, Bibliothèque de vulgarisation.* 50 (1931), pp.68-72.
[19] The Japanese title is Mikoto.

to charge them. So the two deities, standing upon the Floating Bridge of Heaven, pushed down the jeweled spear and stirred with it, whereupon, when they had stirred the brine till it went curdle-curdle,[20] and drew [the spear] up, the brine that dripped down from the end of the spear was piled up and became an island. This is the island of Onogoro [i.e. Self-Curdling]."[21]

Izanagi and Izanami then descended upon the island just created and there became the parents of the other Japanese islands and also of a host of additional deities. Not a few of these deities were produced upon an occasion when Izanagi was performing a ceremonial purification. As he divested himself of his garments a new god came into being with each item of apparel removed, and the same thing happened at each new stage in the washing of himself. Of these deities we are particularly concerned with the one who is said to have been born as Izanagi "washed his left august eye." This was the goddess Ama-terasu-o-mi-kami or the Heaven-Shining-Great-August-Deity.

Reading on a little ways farther we find that Izanagi bestowed upon Amaterasu the rule of the Plain of High Heaven, that is of the sky, and signalized this event by giving her the string of jewels which had been about his own neck. These jewels, incidentally, were turned into more deities a little later. Thus, according to mythology, did Amaterasu attain the position of sun goddess in which she has always been so prominent for Japanese religion.

Some time after this, the brother of Amaterasu, named His Brave-Swift-Impetuous-Male-Augustness (Take-haya-susa-no-wo-no-miko-to), did a number of things which caused grave offence and fright to the sun goddess. For example he caused damage to be done to the rice-fields, and he also flayed backward a "heavenly piebald horse" and flung it through the roof of the hall where Amaterasu was weaving garments for the gods. The sun goddess thereupon retired into the Rock-Cave of Heaven and made fast the door. "Then the whole Plain of High Heaven was obscured and all the Central Land of Reed-Plains darkened."

The darkness caused by the withdrawal of the sun goddess was a matter of much concern to the "eight hundred myriad" deities, and they assembled at the Tranquil River of Heaven to devise a plan for coping with the situation. Under the inspiration of the Thought-

[20] This is an onomatopoeic expression in the Japanese.
[21] I, 3. tr. Chamberlain, pp.18f.

Combining-Deity, they proceeded as follows. They gathered "long-singing birds of eternal night" and set them singing. They made a long string of brilliant jewels and a large and beautiful mirror. They obtained a Sakaki tree[22] from the Heavenly Mount Kagu,[23] and hung the jewels on its upper branches, the mirror on its middle branches, and gifts of cloth on its lower branches. After that they recited a grand liturgy together, and Her Augustness Heavenly-Alarming-Female performed a dance in front of the door of the Rock-Cave of Heaven.

"Then," continues the Kojiki, "the Plain of High Heaven shook, and the eight hundred myriad deities laughed together. Hereupon the Heaven-Shining-Great-August-Deity was amazed, and, slightly opening the door of the Heavenly Rock-Dwelling, spoke thus from the inside: 'Methought that owing to my retirement the Plain of Heaven would be dark, and likewise the Central Land of Reed-Plains would all be dark: how then is it that the Heavenly-Alarming-Female makes merry, and that likewise the eight hundred myriad deities all laugh?' Then the Heavenly-Alarming-Female spoke, saying: 'We rejoice and are glad because there is a deity more illustrious than Thine Augustness.' While she was thus speaking, His Augustness Heavenly-Beckoning-Ancestor-Lord and his Augustness Grand-Jewel pushed forward the mirror and respectfully showed it to the Heaven-Shining-Great-August-Deity, whereupon the Heaven-Shining-Great-August-Deity, more and more astonished, gradually came forth from the door and gazed upon it, whereupon the Heavenly-Hand-Strength-Male-Deity, who was standing hidden, took her august hand and drew her out, and then His Augustness Grand-Jewel drew the bottom-tied rope along at her august back, and spoke, saying: 'Thou must not go back further in than this!' So when the Heaven-Shining-Great-August-Deity had come forth, both the Plain of High Heaven and the Central-Land-of-Reed-Plains of course again became light."[24]

The sequel to the foregoing events was the expulsion from heaven of His Brave-Swift-Impetuous-Male-Augustness for having caused all the trouble. This deity thereupon descended to the Land of Izumo where he found that certain earthly deities were terrorized by an eight-forked serpent. His Brave-Swift-Impetuous-Male-Augustness

[22] Identified as the *cleyera japonica*, and still a sacred tree in the Shinto religion.
[23] Kagu was a mountain in Yamato, and is here thought of as having a counterpart in heaven.
[24] I, 16. tr. Chamberlain, pp.58f.

slew this serpent and in its middle tail found a sword which is the Herb-Quelling Great Sword (Kusa-nagi-no-tachi). Although he informed Amaterasu of his exploit and perhaps presented her with the sword, His Brave-Swift-Impetuous-Male-Augustness seems not to have been readmitted to heaven, since afterward we find him building a palace for himself in the Land of Izumo.

Numerous earthly deities seem to have been dwelling on the Japanese islands, and things in general there were in a great state of tumult. Amaterasu resolved to send her son, His Augustness Truly-Conqueror-I-Conquer-Conquering-Swift-Heavenly-Great-Great-Ears (Masa-ka-a-katsu-kachi-hayabi-ame-no-oshi-ho-mimi-no-mikoto),[25] to be the ruler there, but when he went and looked down from the Floating Bridge of Heaven he saw so much violence that he turned back. A long process of pacifying the land then ensued, and by the time it was completed His Augustness Heavenly-Great-Great-Ears (as we may call him for short) was himself the father of a son named His Augustness Heaven-Plenty-Earth-Plenty-Heaven's-Sun-Height-Prince-Rice-ear-Ruddy-Plenty (Ame-nigishi-kuni-nigishi-ama-tsu-hi-daka-hiko-ho-no-ni-nigi-no-mikoto). The father now proposed that the son be sent, and so Prince-Rice-ear-Ruddy-Plenty was commissioned with these words: "This Luxuriant Reed-Plain-Land-of-Fresh-Rice-ears is the land over which thou shalt rule."[26]

Prince-Rice-ear-Ruddy-Plenty was given as marks of his authority the jewels and mirror which had been on the tree in front of Amaterasu's heavenly rock-cave, and the sword which had come from the tail of the eight-forked serpent. The mirror in particular was to symbolize the spirit of the sun goddess, Amaterasu. "Regard this mirror," he was told, "exactly as if it were our august spirit, and reverence it as if reverencing us." Also certain of the heavenly deities were appointed to accompany him. When all was ready, Prince-Rice-ear-Ruddy-Plenty made his great descent and came down upon a mountain peak on the island of Tsukushi, which is modern Kyushu.

There he married Princess Blossoming-Brilliantly-Like-the-Flow-

[25] The word *mimi* or "ears" is a part of many ancient Japanese names. Large ears were considered lucky in Japan as well as in China and Korea. Chamberlain, *op.cit.*, p.48 n.18.

[26] I, 33. tr. Chamberlain, p.107. In the Nihongi, of which we will tell in the next section, the commission reads more fully: "Then she [Amaterasu] commanded her August Grandchild, saying:—'This Reed-plain-1500-autumns-fair-rice-ear Land is the region which my descendants shall be lords of. Do thou, my August Grandchild, proceed thither and govern it. Go! and may prosperity attend thy dynasty and may it, like Heaven and Earth, endure for ever'" (II, 16. tr. Aston, I, p.77).

[430]

ers-of-the-Trees, daughter of the Deity Great-Mountain-Possessor, and became the father of three sons known as Fire-Shine, Fire-Climax and Fire-Subside. His Augustness Fire-Shine was a skillful fisherman, and His Augustness Fire-Subside, also known as His Augustness Heaven's-Sun-Height-Prince-Great-Rice-ears-Lord-Ears (Ama-tsu-hi-daka-hiko-ho-ho-de-mi-no-mikoto), was a mighty hunter. One day they exchanged occupations, but His Augustness Fire-Subside lost his elder brother's fishhook and had to go on a long journey to the realm of the Deity Ocean-Possessor to recover it. There he married this monarch's daughter, Luxuriant-Jewel-Princess, and obtained certain wonderful jewels by virtue of which, upon his return home, he became master over his elder brother.

His Augustness Fire-Subside and Her Augustness Luxuriant-Jewel-Princess had a son named His Augustness Heaven's-Sun-Height-Prince-Wave-limit-Brave-Cormorant-Thatch-Meeting-Incompletely (Ama-tsu-hi-daka-hiko-nagisa-take-u-gaya-fuki-ahezu-no-mikoto). He in turn married his mother's younger sister, Her Augustness Jewel-Good-Princess (Tamayori-hime-no-mikoto), and had four sons. They were named His Augustness Five-Reaches, His Augustness Boiled-Rice, His Augustness August-Food-Master, and His Augustness Young-August-Food-Master, or His Augustness Divine-Yamato-Ihare-Prince.

Volume I of the Kojiki closes with the crossing over of His Augustness August-Food-Master to the Eternal Land, and the departure of His Augustness Boiled-Rice for the Sea-Plain which was the land of his deceased mother. This left two brothers out of the four, namely the youngest one, His Augustness Divine-Yamato-Ihare-Prince or Kamu-yamato-ihare-biko-no-mikoto, and the oldest one, His Augustness Five-Reaches or Itsu-se-no-mikoto, and Volume II of the work opens with the account of a conference which these two held as to their future plans. At the time they were still living in a palace at the mountain where Prince-Rice-ear-Ruddy-Plenty had first descended upon Kyushu, and the question they raised was: "By dwelling in what place shall we [most] quietly carry on the government of the Empire?" Their conclusion was: "It were probably best to go east."

The progress to the east was a matter of military campaigns extending from Kyushu on to Honshu and lasting over many years. Defeats as well as successes are recorded, and in one battle Itsu-se was wounded and later died. Kamu-yamato-ihare-biko was ultimately successful, however, and we read that "having thus subdued and pacified the savage deities, and extirpated the unsubmissive people, [he] dwelt at the palace of Kashibara near Unebi, and ruled the Empire."[27] The place indicated was probably in Yamato in central Honshu.

Although the work of Kamu-yamato-ihare-biko is filled with much that is fabulous and fantastic, it is probable that here at last we have a reflection of actual happenings even if in a highly legendary form. The military campaigns pushing eastward from Kyushu and resulting in the establishment of rule in central Honshu sound very much like what we may suppose to have been the actual progress of the Yamato people earlier discussed, and Kamu-yamato-ihare-biko may have been an actual leader of theirs. All the later Japanese histories consider him to have been the first emperor of Japan. In the eighth century A.D. it became customary to bestow a "canonical name" upon each emperor after his death, and at that time such "canonical names" were also selected for the sovereigns who had reigned previously. Kamu-yamato-ihare-biko, the first of these, received the name Jimmu. To this is ordinarily added Tenno, meaning sovereign, and thus it is that we are most familiar with the legendary original potentate of Japan as Jimmu Tenno.

THE NIHONGI

We now leave the Kojiki and turn to the Nihongi,[28] the second oldest Japanese chronicle. Unlike the Kojiki, the Nihongi has no preface to tell about its authorship. A series of commentaries was soon written on it, however, and several of these, known as Shiki or "private notes," are preserved in the thirteenth century Shaku-nihongi. Of these the Konin Shiki, ascribed to the "year period" A.D. 810-823, informs us that the Nihongi was compiled by Prince Toneri and Yasumaro Futo no Ason and laid before the Empress Gemmyo in A.D. 720. The Yasumaro here mentioned was the same as the one who took down the Kojiki from the lips of Are, but the Kojiki is not mentioned in the Nihongi nor does much use seem to have been made of it.[29]

The Nihongi is composed of thirty books, and there was also orig-

---

[27] II, 50. tr. Chamberlain, p.145.
[28] tr. W. G. Aston, *Nihongi, Chronicles of Japan from the Earliest Times to A.D. 697, Translated from the Original Chinese and Japanese* (Transactions and Proceedings of the Japan Society, London, Supplement I). 2 vols. 1896.
[29] *ibid.*, pp.xiii,xix.

inally a book of genealogies of the emperors which is no longer extant. In size the Nihongi is perhaps twice as large as the Kojiki, and it carries the history somewhat further, closing with the year A.D. 697. As far as the early mythology is concerned, the Kojiki is fuller, but the Nihongi presents some interesting variants. In the later history, the Nihongi is more detailed and therefore perhaps more useful.

The Nihongi also provides a complete chronology with dates as far back as the beginning of the reign of Jimmu Tenno, which is placed in 660 B.C. Unfortunately these dates do not prove dependable until about the beginning of the sixth century A.D. As a matter of fact it was not until about A.D. 603 that a calendar was adopted for the first time in Japan,[30] and it is now supposed that the chronologists of the seventh century arrived at the beginning date of 660 B.C. quite arbitrarily. The theory is that they used the Chinese idea of a cycle of 1,260 years from one event of world-shaking importance to another, and counting back from A.D. 601 when, under Empress Suiko, the Prince-Regent Shotoku Taishi was working on important governmental reforms, came to 660 B.C. as the date of Jimmu's coronation. Modern studies have introduced a large revision, and it is now thought that Jimmu's rule may have started around 40 B.C. We append below a list of all the emperors of Japan with their traditional accession dates, and show also in parentheses the critically revised dates for the first twenty-seven sovereigns after which the usual dates seem to be accurate within one year.[31]

(1) Jimmu, 660 B.C. (c.40 B.C.)	(14) Chuai, 192 (c.356);
(2) Suizei, 581 B.C. (c.10 B.C.)	Jingo Kogo, Regent, 201
(3) Annei, 548 B.C. (A.D. c.20)	(c.363)
(4) Itoku, 510 B.C. (A.D. c.50)	(15) Ojin, 270 (c.380)
(5) Kosho, 475 B.C. (A.D. c.80)	(16) Nintoku, 313 (c.395)
(6) Koan, 392 B.C. (A.D. c.110)	(17) Richu, 400 (c.428)
(7) Korei, 290 B.C. (A.D. c.140)	(18) Hanzei or Hansho, 406 (c.433)
(8) Kogen, 214 B.C. (A.D. c.170)	(19) Ingyo, 412 (c.438)
(9) Kaika, 157 B.C. (A.D. c.200)	(20) Anko, 454 (c.455)
(10) Sujin, 97 B.C. (A.D. c.230)	(21) Yuryaku, 457 (c.457)
(11) Suinin, 29 B.C. (A.D. c.259)	(22) Seinei, 480 (c.490)
(12) Keiko, A.D. 71 (A.D. c.291)	(23) Kenso, 485 (c.495)
(13) Seimu, 131 (c.323)	(24) Ninken, 488 (c.498)

[30] N. Sakuma in *Transactions of the Asiatic Society of Japan*. 30 (1902), p.72.

[31] Herbert H. Gowen, *An Outline History of Japan*. 1927, pp.xvii-xviii; REJH I, pp.13f.,77-84; Émile Gaspardone in *Journal asiatique, Recueil trimestriel de mémoires et de notices relatifs aux études orientales, publié par la Société Asiatique*. 230 (1938), pp.240f.

(25) Buretsu, 499 (c.504)
(26) Keitai, 507 (c.510)
(27) Ankan, 534 (c.527)
(28) Senka, 536
(29) Kimmei, 540
(30) Bidatsu, 572
(31) Yomei, 586
(32) Sushun, 588
(33) Suiko, Empress, 593
(34) Jomei, 629
(35) Kokyoku, Empress, 642
(36) Kotoku, 645
(37) Saimei, 655
(38) Tenchi, 661
(39) Kobun, 672
(40) Temmu, 673
(41) Jito, Empress, 687
(42) Mommu, 697
(43) Gemmyo, Empress, 708
(44) Gensho, Empress, 715
(45) Shomu, 724
(46) Koken, Empress, 749
(47) Junnin, 759
(48) Shotoku, 765
(49) Konin, 770
(50) Kammu, 782
(51) Heijo, 806
(52) Saga, 810
(53) Junna, 824
(54) Nimmyo, 834
(55) Montoku, 851
(56) Seiwa, 859
(57) Yozei, 877
(58) Koko, 885
(59) Uda, 888
(60) Daigo, 898
(61) Suzaku, 931
(62) Murakami, 947
(63) Reizei, 968
(64) Enyu, 970
(65) Kazan, 985
(66) Ichijo, 987
(67) Sanjo, 1012
(68) Go-Ichijo, 1017
(69) Go-Suzaku, 1037
(70) Go-Reizei, 1046
(71) Go-Sanjo 1069

(72) Shirakawa, 1073
(73) Horikawa, 1087
(74) Toba, 1108
(75) Sutoku, 1124
(76) Konoe, 1142
(77) Go-Shirakawa, 1156
(78) Nijo, 1159
(79) Rokujo, 1166
(80) Takakura, 1169
(81) Antoku, 1181
(82) Go-Toba, 1186
(83) Tsuchi-mikado, 1199
(84) Juntoku, 1211
(85) Chukyo, 1222
(86) Go-Horikawa, 1231
(87) Yojo, 1232
(88) Go-Saga, 1242
(89) Go-Fukakusa, 1246
(90) Kameyama, 1259
(91) Go-Uda, 1274
(92) Fushimi, 1288
(93) Go-Fushimi, 1298
(94) Go-Nijyo, 1301
(95) Hanazono, 1308
(96) Go-Daigo, 1318
(97) Go-Murakami, 1339
(98) Go-Kameyama, 1373
(99) Go-Komatsu, 1382
(100) Shoko, 1414
(101) Go-Hanazono, 1429
(102) Go-Tsuchi-mikado, 1465
(103) Go-Kashiwabara, 1521
(104) Go-Nara, 1536
(105) Ogimachi, 1560
(106) Go-Yojo, 1586
(107) Go-Mizuo, 1611
(108) Myosho, Empress, 1630
(109) Go-Komyo, 1643
(110) Go-Nishio, 1656
(111) Reigen, 1663
(112) Higashiyama, 1687
(113) Naka-mikado, 1710
(114) Sakuramachi, 1720
(115) Momozono, 1747
(116) Go-Sakuramachi, Empress, 1763
(117) Go-Momozono, 1771

(118) Kokaku, 1780

(119) Jinko, 1817

(120) Komei, 1847

(121) Meiji, 1868

(122) Taisho, 1912

(123) Hirohito, 1925.

In general it may be said of the Nihongi, that while it deals with the early Emperors in a very legendary manner, the narrative becomes more realistic as it proceeds, and from around the beginning of the sixth century A.D. on, appears to be a trustworthy record.

2. THE ASUKA PERIOD, A.D. 552-645

IN WHAT has been said thus far it has become evident that real history, in distinction from the earlier mythological and legendary periods, only begins in Japan in about the sixth century A.D. This was also, it will be remembered (p.312) the time when Buddhism was introduced under Kimmei Tenno. This sovereign reigned from A.D. 540 to 571, and it was in the thirteenth year of his reign, A.D. 552, that Buddhism came. This year may be taken as the opening date of the first historical period in Japan, a time that extended from A.D. 552 to 645.

In order to obtain a name for this and succeeding periods, it is not possible to refer to successive dynasties since there was only one house of rulers throughout all Japanese history, and therefore another system must be utilized. That which is most customary is to designate the periods by the names of the places from which the supreme authority was exercised at the time. In this earliest period of which we are now speaking, however, the capital was moved with the accession of each new ruler, and hence we simply take the most prominent single place and use its name to mark the whole time. This was Asuka. Actually the various early capitals were all quite close together in the region of Yamato, and also the later and more famous capitals like Nara and Kyoto were located in the same district.[32]

It is in the reign of Kimmei's second successor, Yomei Tenno (A.D. 586-587), that we first encounter the actual term Shinto. Concerning this ruler we read in the Nihongi, "The Emperor believed in the Law of Buddha and reverenced the Way of the Gods (Shinto)."[33] The phrase, "the Way of the Gods," is a literal translation of "Shinto," *shin* (Chinese, *shen*) meaning "gods," and *to* (Chinese, *tao*), "way." Since *to* already means "way" or "doctrine," it is not necessary to add "ism" to form the proper name of this religion. The equivalent in pure Japanese of the basically Chinese name Shinto, is Kami no Michi.

The fact that the name Shinto appears now for the first time does not mean that the religion arose only at this time. Actually this was the ancient, long-known religion of Japan, and not a few of its basic

[32] For detailed maps of the region and the capitals, see REJH II, pp.27-36; for tables of the periods, SJSCH p.xviii; Soper, *The Evolution of Buddhist Architecture in Japan*, pp.xv-xvi.
[33] XXI, 1. tr. Aston, II, p.106.

ideas, particularly in the realm of nature worship, prevailed already among the ancestral Ainus. What happened here in the sixth century was simply that with the introduction of Buddhism it became necessary for the first time to have a term by which to distinguish the ancient faith of the land from the newly imported religion. The foreign teaching was Butsudo, "the Way of the Buddha"; the indigenous cult was Shinto, "the Way of the Gods."[34]

SHINTO SHRINES

The place of worship characteristic of Shinto is the shrine (*jinja*). At the outset, objects of nature such as rocks and trees were doubtless worshiped directly; after that, it is thought, sacred areas were marked out for worship with rows of evergreen branches. When the mirror and the jewels and the sword, of which we have heard in the myths, became divine symbols, a house was necessary in which to keep them. This was constructed in the same fashion as an ordinary dwelling, being little more than a wooden hut with a thatched roof. Large size was not even necessary, because there was no congregational worship, and the individual visitor simply stood outside to make obeisance or present some supplication.[35]

After the introduction of Buddhism, Shinto architecture was strongly influenced by the Chinese habits incorporated in Buddhist temple design: complex symmetrical plans, southward orientation, surrounding walls and colonnades and gate buildings, painting, gilding, sculptural decoration, curving roof lines. Nevertheless, the typical Shinto shrine remained always relatively simple and presented a comparatively austere appearance.

In the literary traditions, shrines are mentioned from time to time. In noting several of these references, we may begin with the account in the Nihongi relating to the reign of Sujin Tenno (97-30 B.C. by the traditional chronology; A.D. c.230-c.258 by the revised). It seems that at this time there was a great plague. Hitherto both the goddess Amaterasu and the god Yamato-no-o-kuni-dama (The Spirit of the Great Land of Yamato) had been worshiped in the palace of the emperor, but the latter now felt a sense of fear at having these two powerful beings so close to him. Accordingly separate shrines were established for them elsewhere. That of Amaterasu, in which we are specially interested, was placed at the village of Kasanuhi some distance northeast of Asuka, and the emperor's own daughter Toyo-

[34] MHR I, p.93.   [35] SJSCH pp.57f.

suki-iri-hime-no-mikoto was installed there as high priestess. The mirror which was the symbol of the sun goddess, and the legendary sword, Kusa-nagi, were both put in the new shrine.

The Nihongi makes reference to this event in these words: "Before this the two gods Ama-terasu-o-mi-kami and Yamato-no-o-kuni-dama were worshiped together within the Emperor's Great Hall. He dreaded, however, the power of these gods, and did not feel secure in their dwelling together. Therefore he entrusted Ama-terasu-o-mi-kami to Toyo-suki-iri-hime-no-mikoto to be worshiped at the village of Kasanuhi in Yamato, where he established the sacred enclosure of Shiki. Moreover, he entrusted Yamato-o-kuni-dama-no-kami to Nunaki-iri-hime-no-mikoto to be worshiped. But Nunaki-iri-hime-no-mikoto was bald and lean, and therefore unfit to perform the rites of worship."[36]

In the reign of the next emperor, Suinin Tenno (29 B.C.-A.D. 70; or A.D. c.259-c.290), the shrine of Amaterasu was established at Ise, where it remained permanently thereafter. The daughter of Suinin Tenno, named Yamato-hime-no-mikoto, was priestess of the shrine, and it was to her that the command of the sun goddess came for the transferal. As the Nihongi records: "Now Ama-terasu-o-mi-kami instructed Yamato-hime-no-mikoto, saying:—'The province of Ise, of the divine wind, is the land whither repair the waves from the eternal world, the successive waves. It is a secluded and pleasant land. In this land I wish to dwell.' In compliance, therefore, with the instruction of the Great Goddess, a shrine was erected to her in the province of Ise."[37]

Yamato-hime-no-mikoto was still serving as high priestess of the shrine at Ise when her brother, Keiko Tenno, was on the throne (A.D. 71-130; or c.291-c.322). At this time we get an interesting glimpse of the custom of repairing to the shrine before proceeding on an important mission. Yamato-dake-no-mikoto, son of Keiko Tenno, was ordered to subdue the Eastern Barbarians, and as he set out upon his journey he went first to notify the sun goddess. "He turned aside from his way," records the Nihongi, "to worship at the shrine of Ise. Here he took leave of Yamato-hime-no-mikoto, saying:—'By order of the Emperor, I am now proceeding on an expedition against the East to put to death the rebels, therefore I am taking leave of thee.' " Since the expedition was of great importance, the high priestess gave him the famous sword, of which we have already heard, to

[36] v, 3f. tr. Aston, I, pp.151f.　　　[37] vi, 16. tr. Aston, I, p.176.

use. "Hereupon Yamato-hime-no-mikoto took the sword Kusa-nagi and gave it to Yamato-dake-no-mikoto, saying:—'Be cautious, and yet not remiss.' "[38]

While the foregoing quotations have dealt chiefly with the central sanctuary of Amaterasu at Ise, there were many other shrines throughout the land. The earliest statistical record is from the eighth century, and from this we learn that in A.D. 737 there were more than three thousand shrines which were officially recognized, and that about one-fourth of these were supported at government expense.[39]

Being made of wood, the shrines were not of great durability and had to be rebuilt frequently. In comparatively recent times it has been the custom to rebuild the Ise shrine every twenty years. In such reconstructions, however, care was expended to make the new shrine a replica of its predecessor, and thus the essential forms of antiquity were long preserved.

THE IZUMO SHRINE

The most primitive type of sanctuary still existing is represented by the Great Shrine of Izumo, known in Japanese as the Izumo-no-oyashiro. It is second only to the Shrine at Ise in national popularity, and like that sanctuary also has connections with the earliest mythology.

It will be remembered that after Take-haya-susa-no-wo-no-mikoto was expelled from heaven for offending Amaterasu, he made his way to the land of Izumo. There he had numerous descendants, among whom the most important was a son of perhaps the sixth generation,[40] named Oho-kuni-nushi-no-kami or Deity Master-of-the-Great-Land.[41] When the heavenly deities were pacifying the Japanese islands in preparation for the inauguration of the rule of the grandson of Amaterasu, Oho-kuni-nushi-no-kami abdicated his throne and surrendered his territory to the emissary of the sun goddess.[42] Remembered particularly for this act, Oho-kuni-nushi-no-kami was the chief deity worshiped at Izumo-no-oyashiro.

When the Great Shrine was first erected we cannot tell, but it must have been at an early time. It certainly was in existence in the third century, for we know that in the reign of Sujin Tenno

[38] VII, 23. tr. Aston, I, p.205. [39] SJSCH p.58.
[40] See the genealogical table in REJH II, p.39.
[41] Kojiki. I, 20. tr. Chamberlain, p.67.
[42] Kojiki. I, 32. tr. Chamberlain, pp.99-105.

(A.D. c.230-258 by the revised chronology) a certain Izumo Furone (d. A.D. c.255) was in charge of the sacred treasures of the shrine.[43]

The Great Shrine[44] is shown in Fig. 189. It is surrounded by a small veranda, and approached by a steep stairway. The building is entered from the end, through a doorway to the right of the central vertical pillar. Inside, there is a single pillar in the center, and a partition separating the rear of the room from the front. The style of construction is called Oyashiro-zukuri.

On top of the building near either end of the roof ridge is seen a pair of crossed timbers (*chigi*). These are regarded as sacred symbols, and probably survive from an earlier method of building in which the roof was supported by beams reaching from the ground and crossing at the top. The short round pieces of wood (*katsuogi*) laid horizontally across the roof ridge are likewise inseparable attachments of a Shinto shrine, and probably are remnants of the timbers which were employed in earlier times to hold down the straw-thatched roof.

THE ISE SHRINE

We return now to the shrine of Amaterasu at Ise, a number of references to the history of which have already been given. There are two sacred areas at Ise, that of the Outer Shrine occupying two hundred acres, and that of the Inner Shrine, three and one-half miles away, extending over one hundred and seventy-five acres. The grounds of the Inner Shrine are approached by a bridge over the Isuzu River, back of which rises a heavily wooded mountain, Mount Kamiji. The Inner Shrine itself is located within a rectangular fenced space known as Omiyanoin. The measurement around this area is 1,386 feet. There are four entrances, one in each direction of the compass, the southern being the principal. Ascending broad, gently sloping steps (Fig. 191), the visitor to the shrine passes under a plain torii, a post and lintel construction commonly found at all Shinto shrines,[45] and enters through a gateway. Within, there are yet other fences and gates. In an innermost precinct, flanked by other structures, stands the Seiden or main building. It is shown from a distance, seen through the trees, in Fig. 190. Architecturally, the chief difference from the Izumo Shrine consists in the fact that here the

---

[43] REJH I, p.117.
[44] W. L. Schwartz in *Transactions of the Asiatic Society of Japan.* 41 (1913), pp.491-681; Aisaburo Akiyama, *Shintô and Its Architecture.* 1936, pp.59,62f.
[45] Akiyama, *Shintô and Its Architecture,* pp.82-86.

187. Haniwa of the Dolmen Period

188. A Facsimile Page of the Kojiki

189. The Great
Shrine of Izumo

190. The Great
Ise Shrine, Seen
through the Trees

191. Entrance
to the Great
Ise Shrine

192. The Kasuga Shrine in an Ancient Picture Scroll

193. Praying in Seclusion at the Kasuga Shrine

194. The Kasuga Shrine

195. The Kitano Shrine

197. Shinto Goddess

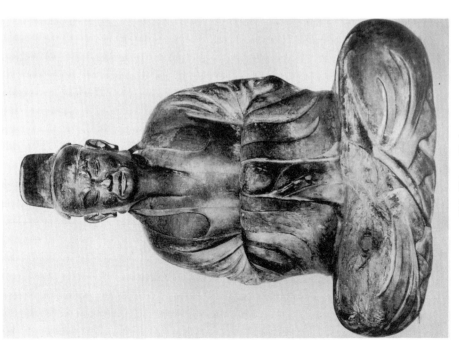

196. Shinto God

199. Nakatsu-hime

198. Hachiman

200. The Shrine of Hachiman

202. Sugawara Michizane

201. Tamayori-hime

203. Winter Landscape, by Sesshu

204. The Yomei Gate of the Toshogu Shrine, Nikko

205. Moon upon the Snow, by Kano Tanyu

206. Mount Fuji, by Okyo

207. Mount Fuji seen through High Waves, by Hokusai

main building has been turned around and the entrance placed at the center of the long side. This change made the Ise design fit into general Far Eastern practice; perhaps it was due to Chinese influence filtering in through Korea along with new ideas in building palaces. Except for this difference the general appearance of the shrine is much the same as that of the structure at Izumo. The *chigi* and the *katsuogi* of course appear upon the roof. In technical terminology the advanced architectural style exemplified here at Ise is known as the Shimmei-zukuri.[46]

In summary, then, the Asuka Period, when Buddhist art unfolded in monumental architecture and rich sculpture, only serves to throw into sharp relief the essential simplicity of Shinto. The centers of the faith then, as before and since, were relatively crude wooden structures in the richest of which there were no more impressive treasures than the symbolic mirror, jewels and sword.

[46] *ibid.*, pp.66f.; Seichi Taki, *Japanese Fine Art*. tr. Kazutomo Takahashi. 1931, pp.45f.; Tokugoro Nakamura, *Kotaijingu Shi* (The History of the Grand Imperial Shrine). 1921, pp.407-417.

3. THE NARA PERIOD, A.D. 645-794

THE next division in Japanese history may be called the Nara Period. The capital of the country was not actually established at Nara until A.D. 710, but even so the years from 645 to 710 are often looked upon as preparatory and called "Early Nara" or "Proto-Nara"; hence for our purposes it will be simplest to apply the one name to the entire period.

The most important event in the political situation was doubtless the Great Reform of A.D. 645. Some forty-five years before, the Prince-Regent Shotoku Taishi had done much to improve the government of Japan, but the growing power of the Soga family, which he had favored and which had grown more and more grasping of power after his death, seemed an ever increasing menace. It will be remembered (p.312) that this was the family which had welcomed Buddhism upon its first arrival; and as for Shotoku Taishi, so strong was his support of that faith that he has been called the Constantine of Japanese Buddhism. Of the two families which had stood against the acceptance of Buddhism, the Mononobe clan had lost prestige because of defeat in the struggle, but the Nakatomi family was still a force to be reckoned with. It was from the latter clan that the leader of the Great Reform arose.

This leader was Kamatari. Although his family had long been devoted to Shinto, Kamatari took up an intensive study of the Chinese classics and from these sources derived his ideal of government. The details do not concern us here, suffice it to say that the net result of his work was the transformation of Japan from a tribal confederation into a centralized bureaucracy patterned after the government of China. In the process the dominance of the Soga clan was destroyed, and the Nakatomi family, henceforth known as Fujiwara, achieved the position of great power which it occupied for the next four or five centuries.

In the edict embodying these reforms and published in the first month of A.D. 646, one provision called for the imperial capital to be "regulated."[47] Up to this time the capital had been moved with the accession of each new ruler, a thing that was not too difficult to do since the palaces were probably like the Shinto shrines hitherto described, simple structures of wood thatched with straw or reeds. Now with the increased complexity of government, larger and more dur-

[47] REJH I, p.147.

able buildings were needed, and such transferals would be less easy. Furthermore, knowledge was now had of the magnificent T'ang capital at Ch'ang-an, and along with the imitation of things Chinese in general, came the desire to have a similar fine center of rule. Such were some of the factors which led in A.D. 710 to the building of Nara, Japan's capital for the next seventy-five years.

Nara was located on a level plain nearly surrounded by mountains. The city was rectangular in plan, like its Chinese model. As compared with preceding capitals, it was large and elaborate. Perhaps the most beautiful buildings were the many temples and shrines. Of these, the most numerous and of course the most ornate were the Buddhist. On the mountain eastward above the city, however, there was a relatively large and important Shinto shrine, the Kasuga-no-jinja, which deserves special mention.

THE KASUGA SHRINE

As already indicated, the Fujiwara clan had long been devoted to the Shinto faith. Indeed, the family traced its descent from no less a personage than Ame-no-koyane-no-mikoto (His Augustness Heavenly-Beckoning-Ancestor-Lord), who had played a prominent part in the mythological episode of enticing Amaterasu forth from the Rock-Cave of Heaven. The wife of Ame-no-koyane-no-mikoto, and Takemikazuchi-no-kami and Futsunushi-no-kami who had led in the pacification of the Japanese islands prior to the descent of the grandson of Amaterasu, were the other deities worshiped by the Fujiwara, and it was to these four deities that the Kasuga Shrine was dedicated.[48]

A fourteenth century picture scroll called the Kasuga Gongenrei Kenki[49] contains pictures of worship at the Kasuga Shrine. From this source we show two scenes, identified according to legends in the scroll. In the first (Fig. 192) a priest is ordering the stopping of the drum music; in the second (Fig. 193) people are praying in seclusion at the shrine.

In the sixteenth century, the Jesuit missionary, Luis Alameida, visited Nara (1565) and wrote an extended description of the Kasuga Shrine. According to this source, the shrine was set in the midst of a dense forest and approached by an avenue lined with cedars and

[48] REJH II, p.161.
[49] *Nihon Emakimono Shusei.* 1929, IV, Fig. 10; III, Fig. 64; cf. Kenji Toda, *Japanese Scroll Painting.* 1935, pp.108-110.

pines. The missionary expressed the opinion that he had never seen such fine trees in all his life. The avenue had also a double row of stone pillars in which were set lanterns made of black wood. These were lighted throughout every night, for when such a lantern was set up it was required that the donor provide a sufficient yearly endowment for this purpose. At the end of the avenue stood a house in which dwelt the lady bonzes, whose chief duty was to give tea to drink to the numerous pilgrims who came to the shrine. From this house a covered alley led up to the temple itself. Beyond the alley no one was allowed to go except certain men who were dedicated to the service of the idol, the Jesuit said. He also told of seeing some of these priests, who were robed in silk gowns and wore tall caps. They collected the alms which the people threw onto the veranda of the temple.[50]

Approaching the Kasuga Shrine today, one passes along an avenue lined with cryptomeria trees and stone lanterns. There are four main buildings, similar to each other in appearance and dedicated to the four deities previously mentioned, as well as numerous other structures which were added later. The architectural style is essentially similar to that with which we have already become familiar. One important development, however, is the employment of curved lines. Furthermore, the buildings are painted red like contemporary Buddhist temples and Chinese architecture generally; this is a significant change from the natural wood surface seen earlier.[51] A photograph of the shrine is reproduced in Fig. 194.

RYOBU SHINTO

The strong influence of Buddhism in the Nara Period led in some instances to outright amalgamation between that faith and Shinto. An interesting evidence of this trend appeared in the year 715 when for the first time a Buddhist temple annex was established at a Shinto shrine.[52] Again, in A.D. 750, the Shinto war god, Hachiman-no-kami,[53] was brought from his shrine at Usa on Kyushu to the Todai-ji Tem-

---

[50] George Schurhammer, *Shin-tō, The Way of the Gods in Japan, According to the Printed and Unprinted Reports of the Japanese Jesuit Missionaries in the 16th and 17th Centuries.* 1923, pp.61-63.

[51] Akiyama, *Shintô and Its Architecture*, pp.68f.; Garrett C. Pier, *Temple Treasures of Japan.* 1914, pp.92-95; *Handbook of the Old Shrines and Temples and Their Treasures in Japan* (Bureau of Religions). 1920, pp.87f.

[52] REJH I, p.174.

[53] According to some legends, this god was the deified Emperor Ojin, son of the warrior queen, Jingo Kogo, conqueror of Korea. W. G. Aston, *Shinto (The Way of the Gods).* 1905, pp.178f.

ple in Nara to pay his respects to the Great Statue of the Buddha (Daibutsu); and there he remained in a specially built shrine as the guarding spirit of the temple.[54]

The process of intermixture between Shinto and Buddhism was also advanced by an event which took place in A.D. 735. In that year a terrible epidemic of smallpox which had started in Kyushu reached the capital. Under the impact of this calamity it was deemed necessary to placate the divine forces, under whatever name known. The common people turned to the old gods for help; the Emperor Shomu resolved to erect a new and colossal statue of the Buddha (the Daibutsu at Nara). At this juncture the Buddhist patriarch Gyogi was sent to the Shrine at Ise to seek the blessing of the sun goddess for the emperor's project. The oracle was favorable, and the succeeding night the emperor himself experienced a dream in which Amaterasu declared herself identical with Vairocana, a great Buddha of the Mahayana. From here on it was easy to identify every native Japanese deity with some Buddha or Bodhisattva, and thus a theological basis was provided for a thoroughgoing syncretism. The mixture of Shinto and Buddhism which thus arose in the eighth and ninth centuries, and prevailed for a thousand years, is called Ryobu Shinto, the Twofold Way of the Gods.[55]

THE NORITO

Important as Ryobu Shinto became, "pure" Shinto also lived on. An interesting glimpse of its primitive character is obtainable in the *norito* or ancient Shinto rituals.[56] In the performance of a Shinto rite, for example the presentation of an offering to a god, it was customary to read a sort of liturgy in which the grounds of the worship were stated and the offerings enumerated. This liturgy is called a *norito*. It may be composed for a single special occasion, or the same formulation may be used repeatedly.

An example of the *norito* is a ritual called Praying for Harvest which comes probably from the reign of Konin (A.D. 770-782) and thus from the period of which we are here speaking.

The reader of the liturgy is supposed to be giving the words of none other than the emperor, to whom the introductory formula, "He says," refers. Beginning with a salutation to the assembled priests and to the gods, the text continues:

[54] REJH I, p.193.   [55] MHR I, pp.94,118f.
[56] tr. Ernest Satow in *Transactions of the Asiatic Society of Japan.* 7 (1879), pp.97-132,393-434; 9 (1881), pp.183-211; Karl Florenz, *ibid.*, 27 (1900), pp.1-112.

He says: "I declare in the presence of the sovereign gods of the harvest. If the sovereign gods will bestow in many-bundled ears and in luxuriant ears the late-ripening harvest which they will bestow, . . . then I will fulfill their praises by setting-up the first fruits in a thousand ears and many hundred ears. . . ."

He says: "Parting the words,[57] I declare in the presence of the Heaven-Shining-Great-Deity who sits in Ise. Because the sovereign great deity bestows on him the countries of the four quarters over which her glance extends, as far as the limit where heaven stands up like a wall, as far as the bounds where the blue clouds lie flat, as far as the bounds where the white clouds lie fallen; the blue-sea-plain as far as the limit whither come the prows of the ships without letting their poles or paddles be dry, the ships which continuously crowd on the great-sea-plain; the road which men go by land, as far as the limit whither come the horses' hoofs, with the baggage-cords tied tightly, treading the uneven rocks and tree-roots and standing up continuously in a long path without a break; making the narrow countries wide and the hilly countries plane, and as it were drawing together the distant countries by throwing many tens of ropes over them, [because she does all this,] he will pile up the first-fruits like a range of hills in the great presence of the sovereign great deity, and will tranquilly take to himself the remainder."[58]

[57] i.e., taking up a fresh theme.
[58] tr. Satow, *op.cit.*, 7 (1879), pp.113-116.

4. THE HEIAN PERIOD, A.D. 794-1185

IN A.D. 794 the capital of Japan was established at Heian-kyo ("the capital of peace and tranquility"), later called simply Kyoto, meaning "the capital." If Nara had been a relatively permanent center in contrast with the frequent changes of the seat of government before that time, the new capital endured amazingly longer still. Kyoto was the capital for over a thousand years, or until the reformation of 1868 ushered in the modern period. Counting from the establishment of the city, the first four centuries, approximately, constitute the so-called Heian Period.

Like Nara, Heian-kyo was patterned after Ch'ang-an. It occupied a rectangle three and one-third miles from north to south and three miles from east to west. An enclosure in the north central part contained the Greater Imperial Palace and the chief government buildings. Not far away were other offices and institutions, and near the southern gate was the large and important university. All the buildings, of course, were of wood.[59]

SHRINES AT HEIAN-KYO

Several shrines already existed at the site before Heian-kyo was built, and gained added prestige with the coming of the capital. Two of these were the Kamo-no-mioya-no-jinja or Shimo-kamo-no-jinja, and the Kamo-no-wakiikatsuchi-no-jinja or Kami-kamo-no-jinja, which are also known collectively as the Kamo-no-jinja. The deities worshiped there are the Kamo-no-kami, and include Takemikazuchi-no-kami who was also mentioned in connection with the Kasuga-no-jinja. The architectural style is called "Nagare," meaning a stream, or flowing. This has reference particularly to the smooth-flowing lines of the roof, the front of which is carried far out over the front porch.[60]

Another shrine existent before the building of the capital was the Yasaka-no-jinja or Gion-no-yashiro, dedicated to Take-haya-susa-no-wo-no-mikoto, built in the "Gion" style with a gabled roof, and serving as the center for a great annual Shinto festival (Gion-no-go-ryo-e).[61]

Other Shinto shrines and also many Buddhist temples were erected

[59] SJSCH pp.191-194.
[60] REJH II, pp.157f.; Akiyama, *Shintô and Its Architecture*, p.70f.; *Handbook of the Old Shrines and Temples and Their Treasures in Japan*, pp.56-58.
[61] Akiyama, *Shintô and Its Architecture*, p.75; *Handbook of the Old Shrines and Temples and Their Treasures in Japan*, pp.52f.

after the founding of the capital. These spread over the plain on which the city stood, and also were placed on the surrounding hills. Indeed, so numerous were the sanctuaries becoming throughout the country, and so extensive were the lands which were becoming the tax-free properties of the temples, that Kammu (A.D. 782-806), the first emperor to rule at Heian-kyo, was constrained to issue an edict in which he said, "If this continues, in a few years there will be no land which is not temple property." He therefore forbade the selling or donating of land to religious institutions, and established limitations to the building of temples and the admission of persons to the priesthood.[62]

One of the later shrines at Heian-kyo was the Kitano-no-jinja, where Sugawara Michizane was worshiped. Sugawara Michizane was a scholar and statesman who taught at the university and then held the very highest governmental posts under the Emperors Uda (A.D. 888-898) and Daigo (898-930). His advancement was in opposition to the Fujiwara family, and when the final test of strength came, they prevailed. Michizane was sent away to a minor position in distant Kyushu, and thus virtually banished. There in exile he died in A.D. 903.

Prior to his departure from home, Michizane wrote this poem to a plum tree in his garden:

> When the east wind blows,
> Emit thy perfume
> Oh thou plum blossom;
> Forget not the spring,
> Because thy master is away.

According to legend, a branch of this tree broke off of its own accord and went with him into banishment. Other marvels transpired before his death, it is said, and after that event his ghost began to take vengeance on his enemies and to disturb the nation. Finally in A.D. 947 a six-year-old boy transmitted the following oracle from Michizane: "All the thunder-gods and demons to the number of 168,000 have become my servants. If any one does evil I have him trampled to death by them. Pestilence, eruptive diseases, and other calamities have been placed in my hands by the Supreme Lord of Heaven, and no kami, however powerful, can control me. But I will give help to those who piously express their sorrow." In order to placate this

[62] SJSCH p.192.

dangerous spirit, therefore, the Kitano Shrine was forthwith erected to him in Heian-kyo. His spirit was called Temmangu, and was supposed to preside over affairs of learning and literature. As it stands, the architecture of the Kitano Shrine is late in plan and ornament. It combines Shinto and Buddhist influences, and exemplifies the Yatsu-mune ("eight-roofed") style, which features a complicated and elegant system of roofs. A photograph of the Kitano Shrine is reproduced in Fig. 195.[63]

SHINTO AND BUDDHISM

A famous Buddhist priest named Kobo Daishi, who lived in the early Heian Period, did much to further the process of assimilation which was going on between Shinto and Buddhism. Returning from residence in China in A.D. 806, Kobo Daishi founded the Shingon sect of Buddhism. Following the formula already introduced by Gyogi, Kobo taught that the various aboriginal deities of Japan were in reality Buddhas and Bodhisattvas which had anciently visited the land in the guise of Kami to bring blessing to the people. In Buddhism the deeper nature of these beings was made known, and thus that faith appeared as only an unfolding of the hidden meaning of Shinto itself. The common man could be a Shintoist and a Buddhist at the same time, without contradiction.[64]

Due to Buddhist influence, the Shinto religion which had originally been content with such symbols as the mirror, jewels and sword, now had images of the deities similar to those so long used by the Indian faith. For illustration we may turn to the Matsuno-o-no-jinja, a Shinto shrine of national prominence not far west of Kyoto. There we find the striking and powerful wooden statues of a Shinto god and a Shinto goddess pictured in Figs. 196 and 197. They were carved probably in the ninth century A.D. Only the garb distinguishes them from cult statues of the Buddhists.[65]

Again, in the Yakushi-ji Temple at Nara there are the two wooden statues shown in Figs. 198 and 199. They also belong to the ninth century. The first portrays the war god Hachiman in a fully Buddhist guise; the second shows his wife, Nakatsu-hime. Not only are these images actually in a Buddhist temple they are supposed to have

[63] Aston, *Shinto*, pp.179-183; Noritake Tsuda, *Handbook of Japanese Art.* 1935, pp.391-394; Akiyama, *Shintô and Its Architecture*, p.79.
[64] MHR I, pp.119f.
[65] *Japanese Temples and Their Treasures*, 1910, II, Pls. 283,284; Kümmel, *Die Kunst Chinas, Japans und Koreas*, p.128.

been carved by a Buddhist priest named Eisho who lived during the era A.D. 889-898.[66] Thus the role of Buddhism in the development of such representations of Shinto deities is clearly demonstrated.

[66] *Japanese Temples and Their Treasures,* 1910, II, Pls. 298,299; Pier, *Temple Treasures of Japan,* p.47.

5. THE KAMAKURA PERIOD, A.D. 1185-1392

IN THE later part of the Heian Period, extravagance and luxury became more common, the power of the Fujiwara weakened, and general disorder spread. Two great families, the Taira and the Minamoto, then struggled for dominance, and the Minamoto emerged victorious. No more than the Fujiwara, would the Minamoto have thought of abolishing the divinely-descended imperial house of Japan. The emperors simply continued to reign in name, while the feudal lords exercised authority in fact.

The leader of the Minamoto was Yoritomo, and this remarkable leader now devoted himself to building up a powerful military society. He himself was the shogun or military governor; under him were his lords, each with his retainers or samurai. The residence of Yoritomo and the center of the shogunate were established at Kamakura, two hundred and fifty miles east of Kyoto. This explains the name applied to the period now under discussion.

The code of moral principles which prevailed in the military system of the time is known as Bushido, the Way of the Warrior. This was developed out of elements from all three of the major teachings then known in Japan. The political and ethical precepts of Confucianism, calling for a careful ordering of all the relationships of society and favorable toward aristocracy and conservatism, provided the chief basis for the code. Buddhism gave a sense of calm submission to the inevitable; and Shinto contributed a strong emphasis on patriotism and loyalty.[67]

Two Shinto deities whom we have already met were of particular prominence at the time. They were Sugawara Michizane or Temmangu, who served as god of literature and of civil affairs in general; and Hachiman, who was god of war. Hachiman had been closely connected with the Minamoto family from the beginning, and as a deity of battles was understandably important in a military society. In A.D. 1191 Yoritomo erected a great shrine to Hachiman in Kamakura. This sanctuary is approached by an avenue lined with pines and spanned by three torii. In the court is the Wakamiya Shrine,[68] dedicated to a son of the war god, and beyond it is the Shirahata Shrine, consecrated to Yoritomo himself. The Hachiman Shrine

[67] Inazo Nitobé, *Bushido, The Soul of Japan.* rev. ed. 1905, pp.11-22.
[68] Wakamiya means a branch shrine. It is usually one for the son of the deity, or for a second relic of the deity, who is worshiped in the main shrine. REJH II, p.242.

proper is accessible by a flight of steps, and is surrounded by an open colonnade. In its style of architecture both Shinto and Buddhist influences are blended.[69] A photograph of this shrine is reproduced in Fig. 200.

The ability of the god of war was soon put to the test. In A.D. 1274 and again in 1281, Kublai Khan attempted to invade Japan. On both occasions great storms broke and drove back the ships of the enemy with heavy losses. The worshipers who had thronged to the shrines of Hachiman and the other deities to plead for help believed that their prayers had been answered, and the myth of a divinely guarded and impregnable nation was much furthered.[70]

Despite the military aspect of the times, the arts were promoted and indeed manifested a new vitality in the Kamakura Period. Both sculpture and painting flourished. Here we show two examples of such work in this period. The statue in Fig. 201 is a representation of the Shinto goddess, Tamayori-hime-no-mikoto, legendary mother of Jimmu Tenno. She is portrayed in the garb of a court lady of the time. The figure is made of wood, painted, and is dated A.D. 1251. It is in the Shinto shrine, Yoshino-take-mikumari-jinja near Nara.[71] The portrait in Fig. 202 is of the scholar-statesman-deity, Sugawara Michizane. Although not signed, the work is attributed to Tosa Tsunetaka, around A.D. 1240. It is in the collection of Ulrich Odin.[72]

[69] Wilhelm Gundert, *Japanische Religionsgeschichte, Die Religionen der Japaner und Koreaner in geschichtlichem Abriss dargestellt.* 1935, pp.52,110f.; Pier, *Temple Treasures of Japan*, pp.117-119.

[70] Mary A. Nourse, *Kodo, The Way of the Emperor.* 1940, pp.107-113.

[71] *Japanese Temples and Their Treasures*, III, Pl. 425; Fischer, *Die Kunst Indiens, Chinas und Japans*, pp.117,615.

[72] *Peintures chinoises et japonaises de la collection Ulrich Odin, avec une introduction et des notices de M. Ulrich Odin et un avant-propos de M. Sylvain Lévi* (Ars Asiatica, XIV). 1929, p.29, Pl. XII.

6. THE MUROMACHI PERIOD, A.D. 1392-1568

EVEN though Japan was wonderfully delivered from the invasions of Kublai Khan, the wars of that time brought an aftermath of economic troubles and general disorder. In the struggles which followed, Kamakura was destroyed by fire (A.D. 1333), Kyoto became once more the seat of government, and the Ashikaga family gradually secured the chief power in the land. By 1392 the Ashikaga shogunate was fully established, and this date is taken as the beginning of a fresh period in Japanese history. The name of the period, Muromachi, is that of the Ashikaga residence at Kyoto.[73]

The new shogunate was not as powerful or centralized as that at Kamakura, and the entire period was one of almost continual civil war. Kyoto itself was burned in 1467, but afterward rebuilt with lavish expenditure by the shoguns. Despite much warfare, the arts flourished and the period was by no means lacking in brilliance.

Shinto was much overshadowed by Buddhism, yet due to its compromises with that faith, lived on. The ancestral deities of the land were never forgotten, and the custom of pilgrimage to the Shrine of the Sun Goddess at Ise grew in popularity. Religious dances which had doubtless long been performed in front of the Shinto shrines, developed into the form of lyric drama known as No. A Shinto priest named Kwanami (A.D. 1333-1384) and his son Seami (1363-1444) perfected the No, and in their dramatic work enjoyed the patronage of the third Ashikaga shogun, Yoshimitsu (1368-1393).[74]

The finest artistic work was doubtless that done in painting, and here the chief subject matter was now sought in nature. It is generally recognized that the master painters of the time were much influenced by Zen Buddhism, which was introduced into Japan from China in A.D. 1191.[75] This form of Buddhism had become to some extent amalgamated with the temper of Taoist quietism in China, and agreed with that religion in a love of nature and a desire to attain through contemplation a tranquil sense of identity with the universe. Hence we can understand how Zen Buddhism helped to inspire in Japan paintings strongly reminiscent of the slightly earlier Sung paintings in China (pp.415f.). At the same time we should not forget that an appreciation of the beauty of nature was native to the Japanese people, and had been fostered in the Shinto religion from the

[73] SJSCH pp.325f.　　　　[74] ibid., pp.384-488.
[75] K. Florenz in SLR I, pp.373-381; Anesaki, History of Japanese Religion, pp.206-214.

earliest times. Hence the paintings of the period are not irrelevant to our present concern with Shinto.

Perhaps the greatest painter of the time was Sesshu, himself a Buddhist priest. He lived from 1420 to 1506, and spent a period of two years in study in China. He painted in ink, and produced landscapes scarcely excelled in all East Asia. For a single example, we show in Fig. 203 his Winter Landscape, which is in the Manjuin Temple in Kyoto.[76]

[76] Jon Carter Covell, *Under the Seal of Sesshū*. 1941.

7. THE MOMOYAMA (A.D. 1568-1615) AND YEDO (A.D. 1615-1867) PERIODS

AFTER centuries of civil war, three dictators began to forge the unity of modern Japan. The first was Oda Nobunaga (A.D. 1534-1582), a descendant of the illustrious family of Taira (p.451). Forming a powerful feudal army, he set out upon campaigns which brought half of Japan into his control. Among the obstacles to a unified country were the very powerful Buddhist temples and monasteries, and many of these were reduced by his troops. On the other hand, the Spanish Jesuit missionary Francis Xavier, who arrived in Japan in 1549, was looked upon with favor. The headquarters of Nobunaga were at the powerful castle of Adzuchi which he built on the shore of Lake Biwa.

The second man of conquest was Toyotomi Hideyoshi, who had been a general in the army of Nobunaga. Upon the assassination of the latter, Hideyoshi took power and continued the program already begun. So successful was he that by 1590 all Japan had submitted to his mastery. His ambition was not yet satisfied, however, and he planned an Asiatic empire which should also include Korea, China, India and Persia. Wars intended to accomplish this purpose were begun in Korea, but ended in disaster, and Japan's attempt at foreign conquest was abandoned, at least for three hundred years. Like his predecessor, Hideyoshi at first was favorable to Christianity, but becoming suspicious of the imperialistic intentions of the Spaniards, he issued an edict of persecution in 1597. A colossal, moated, granite castle at Osaka was the stronghold of Hideyoshi; and at a suburb of Kyoto called Momoyama he built an ornate palace for his residence. The latter place gives its name to the period (A.D. 1568-1615) of which we are now speaking.

The third of the dictators was Tokugawa Ieyasu. He worked in unity with Hideyoshi, and ruled in the Kwanto Plain where he had a fortress at Yedo (or Edo, now Tokyo). Upon the death of Hideyoshi (1598), Ieyasu had to struggle with rivals but eventually (1615) succeeded in claiming the mastery of all Japan.

Through the work of Ieyasu, the Tokugawa family was established in a supremacy which it maintained for over two hundred years. The emperors were in virtual seclusion at Kyoto, restricted to the performance of little but ceremonial functions. The shogunate wielded the real power, and its seat, Yedo, was practically the capital of the country. Hence, to use the same kind of terminology hitherto employed, this epoch of Tokugawa dominance may be called the Yedo Period (A.D. 1615-1867).

Ieyasu died in A.D. 1616, having expressed the wish to be buried at Nikko. This is an extremely picturesque place in the hills ninety miles north of Tokyo. Its antiquity as a religious center goes far back of the time of Ieyasu. When the first Shinto shrine was erected there we do not know, but the first Buddhist temple is said to have been built in A.D. 767. This was done by Shodo Shonin (735-817), a pioneer of Buddhism among the mountains and a man possibly also influenced by Taoism.[77]

The wish of Ieyasu was carried out by his son and successor, Hidetada. A mausoleum was erected at Nikko, and the remains of Ieyasu buried there with much ceremony in the year 1617. This mausoleum was rebuilt in its present form by the third Tokugawa shogun, the grandson of Ieyasu, Iyemitsu, the work being completed in 1626. Iyemitsu himself was slain upon a visit to this tomb in 1651, and his sepulcher is also at Nikko.

The mausoleum of Ieyasu comprises an extensive complex of buildings which are known collectively as the Toshogu Shrine. A gigantic granite torii spans the approach avenue, which leads on past various structures. These include the Honji-do Temple, dedicated to Yakushi, a god of healing who was worshiped by Ieyasu as his tutelary Buddha. At last one stands before the Yomei-mon. This is probably the finest architecture of the entire shrine, and is a notable example of the "divine gate" (*shim-mon*) which was now a characteristic feature in many Shinto shrines.[78] As the photograph in Fig. 204 shows, the Yomei Gate is built in two stories and is everywhere covered with intricate carvings. What is not shown in a black and white picture is the resplendent polychrome decoration of the whole, which stands out brilliantly against the surrounding forest. On the ceiling of the first story there are monochrome dragons and various heavenly beings in color, which were executed by Tanyu (A.D. 1602-1674), one of the famous Kano family of artists.[79]

Beyond the Yomei-mon is the smaller Kara-mon, and beyond that are the Hall for Prayers (Hai-den), the Stone-floored Chamber (Ishi-

[77] Anesaki, *History of Japanese Religion*, p.92 n.4.
[78] Akiyama, *Shintô and Its Architecture*, p.109.
[79] *Handbook of the Old Shrines and Temples and Their Treasures in Japan*, p.20.

no-ma), and the Main Shrine (Hon-den). The Main Shrine, decorated in exquisite detail, is built in the Gongen style, which is similar to the Yatsu-mune style and like it combines Shinto and Buddhist motifs.[80]

The tomb of Ieyasu is a little distance away on a high mound. The path which leads to it passes beneath another gate made famous by a carved cat springing out of a peony plant, the work of the notable sculptor, Hidari Jingoro (A.D. 1594-1634). The tomb is in the form of a bronze stupa standing upon a platform of steps, with a tall bronze candlestick of stork design in front of it.[81]

The Shrine of Iyemitsu, known as the Daiyu-in, is in a separate quarter west of the Toshogu. It was begun in 1651 and completed in 1653. This shrine is on the whole comparable to that of Ieyasu, but on a somewhat less grand scale. Whereas the Shinto element was strong in the Toshogu, the Buddhistic influence is stronger here.[82]

In addition to the two Tokugawa shrines, there are numerous other buildings at Nikko. These include the Shinto shrine, Futa-ara-jinja, and the Buddhist temple, Rinnoji, the existence of which at the same sacred site further emphasizes the thorough interrelatedness of the two faiths at this time.

THE WARONGO

An important literary expression of Ryobu Shinto appeared at about this time. This is the Warongo or Japanese Analects,[83] published in ten volumes in 1669. While the names of various compilers are given in the text, ranging in date from the Kamakura Period to the early Tokugawa shogunate, it has been shown that the entire work was probably in actuality the product of one author, Sawada Gennai, otherwise known as Sasaki Ujisato, who lived in the middle of the seventeenth century.

The Warongo consists in the main of a collection of oracles of various Shinto deities together with sayings of certain princes, priests and others. Strongly Japanese as the work is, the Shinto it expresses is a syncretistic religion in which both Buddhist and Confucian elements are prominent. Thus in the Oracle of the Sea God, Watatsumi Daimyojin, it is said:

[80] Akiyama, *Shintô and Its Architecture*, p.78.
[81] Pier, *Temple Treasures of Japan*, pp.298f.
[82] *Handbook of the Old Shrines and Temples and Their Treasures in Japan*, pp.22f.
[83] tr. Genchi Kato in *Transactions of the Asiatic Society of Japan*. 45 (1917), pp.1-138.

Not only in Japan doth one and the same Japanese God of Heaven manifest himself in different forms but also in many other lands.

In India he was born as the Buddha Gautama, the Supremely Enlightened One. . . . In China the three sages, K'ung-fu-tzu, Lao-tzu, and Yen Hui, were neither more nor less than our own kami.

You may ask: Why does one and the same God assume such varied forms? It is simply because, being one and the same God, he desires to preach the selfsame truth, and therefore he takes forms differing only in appearance from each other, so that he may best adapt his teaching to the understanding of every man.[84]

Similarly in a saying ascribed to Fujiwara Kanetomo (A.D. 1435-1511) it is concluded: "Thus viewed, the introduction of Confucianism and Buddhism in olden days is not to be understood as something utterly new and foreign imported then for the first time into Japan, but as the revival of the ancient Shinto teachings disguised in the form of Buddhism and Confucianism which, having penetrated into foreign lands [India and China] from their original home in Japan, had returned hither in a quickened form."[85]

PAINTING

In the earlier discussion of the Nikko shrines were introduced the names of two of the foremost artists of those days, Hidari Jingoro the sculptor, and Kano Tanyu the painter. An additional word about painting will enlarge our conception of the artistic work then being done. It was the Kano family, to which Tanyu belonged, which provided the continuity of tradition from the Muromachi Period into the Momoyama and Yedo Periods. The founder of their school of painting was Kano Masanobu, who had lived about 1453 to 1490 and been a personal friend of the great Sesshu. To illustrate the work which this school produced in the later times we can do nothing better than show one of the paintings of Kano Tanyu (1602-1674) himself. This is a picture in the collection of Ulrich Odin, and is known as Moon Upon the Snow (Fig. 205).[86]

Another great painter was Maruyama Okyo (1753-1795), whose landscapes breathe a sense of reverie and mystery. For one example of his work we present a painting dated in 1772, showing Mount Fuji among the clouds (Fig. 206).[87] Yet a final name may be men-

[84] *ibid.*, p.75. [85] *ibid.*, p.77.
[86] *Peintures chinoises et japonaises de la collection Ulrich Odin*, p.42, Pl. xxxvi.
[87] *ibid.*, pp.48f., Pl. xlviii.

tioned here, that of Katsushika Hokusai (1760-1849),[88] who devoted to the same sacred mountain of Japan a series of thirty-six paintings. In them he has grouped around the peak almost every aspect of the Japanese life and land. One of the series is reproduced in Fig. 207. Here Fuji is seen across the sea from near Kamagawa, dramatically framed by a breaking wave, and with boats tossing on the waters. The waves are animated by a mysterious power, an almost divine life, the force of which is infinitely greater than man.[89]

Perhaps it is not without significance that here in the last of the periods covered in our survey, we have come upon a fresh interest in that sacred mountain to which also the most primitive people of Japan had directed their worship, and upon a sense of a divine power permeating the natural world which was also shared in their own way by those same early ancestors.

MOTOORI

At all events in this same Yedo Period there was a distinct revival of interest in the ancestral faith and philosophy of the land. After all the years of ready acceptance of the doctrines of Buddhism and Confucianism, there was now a distinct movement calling for the repudiation of Chinese teachings and for a return to the inspiration of the ancient Japanese literature, and for a reestablishment of "pure" Shinto.

The leader of this movement who is of most significance for us was Motoori (A.D. 1730-1801). He was born in the province of Ise, home of the shrine of the sun goddess, and as a man he devoted himself to intensive studies of the ancient writings of the land. His greatest work was a thoroughgoing commentary on the Kojiki, known as the Kojiki-den.[90]

One fateful result of such studies was a renewed sense of the divine dignity of the imperial dynasty of Japan, and there was a growth of feeling against the shogunate through which the emperors had been pushed so much into the background.

The ultimate outcome, to which of course many other factors also contributed, was the revolution of 1868 in which the shogunate was abolished and the emperor "restored" as actual ruler of Japan. In the period following World War II, "state" Shinto was officially abol-

---

[88] W. Boller in *Mitteilungen der schweizerischen Gesellschaft der Freunde ostasiatischer Kultur.* 7 (1945), pp.39-59.

[89] GCE IV, p.246.

[90] Anesaki, *History of Japanese Religion*, p.308; Aston, *Shinto*, p.373.

ished and the Emperor Hirohito issued a formal denial of his own divinity as monarch. "Sectarian" Shinto survived, and in 1945 the number of its adherents was estimated at over twenty million.

CHAPTER IX

Islam

THE religion of Islam originated in Arabia, and now has more than 250,000,000 believers throughout the world, mostly in the Eastern Hemisphere. In the land where it began, of the nine million inhabitants at least ninety-nine per cent are numbered among the faithful.[1]

Arabia is the world's largest peninsula. Projecting 1,500 miles southeastward from the mainland of Asia, it has an area of 1,000,000 square miles, as much as that of the United States east of the Mississippi. On each of its three seacoast sides there are lowlands backed by mountain ranges. The mountains paralleling the western coast are the highest, Jebel al-Maqla in the north being over 9,500 feet in elevation, and Jebel Hadhur in the south over 12,000 feet. Near the eastern coast, Jebel Sham is 9,900 feet high. Between the western ramparts and the eastern, the land may be described in general as a vast plateau, sloping gently eastward.

In the entire land there is not a single permanent river, but a network of wadis carries off the occasional rainfall. Deserts and steppes comprise the greater part of the country, but there are also many oases where springs exist or the subterranean waters are not too far beneath the surface of the ground. At the oases and also around the edges of the peninsula where the rainfall is slightly more, permanent habitations are possible. Actually the bulk of the population is found in the settlements, and the Bedouins who follow a truly nomadic life number perhaps only around one million.

Of the various regions which may be distinguished in the country, that in the west where the important cities of Mecca and Medina are, is called the Hejaz. The central tableland is the Nejd, to the north, east and south of which are the Nefud, Dahana and Rab' al-Khali deserts. In the southwest are the highlands of Yemen, in the southeast those of Oman, and in between the Aden Protectorate and the region of Hadhramaut. In the extreme northeast is Kuwait. Yemen, Oman and Kuwait have long been independent countries, and

---

[1] Samuel M. Zwemer, *A Factual Survey of the Moslem World with Maps and Statistical Tables.* 1946, pp.10-15.

Aden belongs to Great Britain, but otherwise the bulk of the peninsula is included in the Kingdom of Saudi Arabia, named after the royal house of Saud. The capital of Saudi Arabia is at Riyadh.

The Greek and Roman writers of classical antiquity divided the land into three main parts, and spoke of Arabia Deserta, the "desert" region of the north; Arabia Felix, the "happy" area with more water in the south; and Arabia Petraea, the "rocky" portion in the northwest including Sinai[2] and much of what is now Transjordan.

Due to its isolation and forbidding character, Arabia has remained less well known to the outside world than most of the lands with which we have dealt. Indeed it has been said that prior to World War I there was nowhere else on earth except in the polar areas so large an unexplored and unmapped region as here.[3] Archeological exploration is likewise not far advanced, nevertheless considerable information is already available concerning the period before Muhammad as well as after.

The earliest evidences of the existence of man on the Arabian peninsula are flints of the Paleolithic Age, such as have been found for example in Wadi Hadhramaut, where prehistoric hunters gathered to manufacture their primitive implements and weapons.[4]

In historical times, Arabia, projecting as it does between Asia and Africa, was an object of interest to the neighboring peoples including the Egyptians, Assyrians, Hebrews, Greeks and Romans. The records of these peoples contain many references which relate to Arabian history, the general nature of which it will be helpful to indicate at this point.

The Egyptians prized both the minerals of Sinai and the frankincense of South Arabia. Probably as early as in the First Dynasty, King Semerkhet carried on mining operations in the Wadi Maghara and, as later Pharaohs also did, left there a memorial in the form of an inscription and a relief showing himself smiting a Bedouin.[5] In the Fifth Dynasty King Sahure, like many a later ruler including the famous Queen Hatshepsut, sent a sea expedition to Punt to get incense and ointment and recorded the same in his inscriptions.[6] The

[2] For Sinai as a part of Arabia, cf. Galatians 4:25.

[3] Cressey, *Asia's Lands and Peoples*, p.397.

[4] G. Caton Thompson, *The Tombs and Moon Temple of Hureidha* (*Hadhramaut*) (Reports of the Research Committee of the Society of Antiquaries of London, xiii). 1944, pp.3f.

[5] James H. Breasted, *A History of Egypt from the Earliest Times to the Persian Conquest*. 1905, p.48 and Fig. 28; are i, §168f.

[6] *ibid.*, pp.127,274-278; are i, §161; ii, §246-295.

name Punt probably referred to what is now Somaliland, and may have also included portions of Arabia across the Straits of Bab el-Mandeb, whence similar products were to be obtained.[7]

The Assyrians came into military conflict with the people of the peninsula to the south of them, and the "Monolith Inscription" of Shalmaneser III (858-824 B.C.) provides the first explicit reference to the "Arabians." This is the inscription which in a list of conquered enemy forces contains the name of Ahab, the Israelite. A little farther on in the same list we encounter "Gindibu', the Arabian," and find that he is described, appropriately enough for a desert leader, as commanding a force of one thousand camels.[8] Tiglath-pileser III (744-727 B.C.) mentions "Samsi, queen of Arabia," as well as Saba and the Sabeans.[9] Sargon II (721-705 B.C.) writes: "From Pir'u (Pharaoh), king of Egypt, Samsi, queen of Arabia, It'amra, the Sabean, the kings of the seacoast and the desert, I received gold, products of the mountain, precious stones, ivory, seed of the maple, all kinds of herbs, horses, and camels, as their tribute."[10] Sennacherib (704-681 B.C.) mentions "Karibi-ilu, king of Saba'."[11]

The relationship of the Hebrews and the Arabians was relatively close by reason of geography and also of language, Hebrew and Arabic being cognate Semitic tongues. Commercial cooperation evidently existed in the time of King Solomon. The famed Queen of Sheba probably came from the Arabian kingdom of Saba and doubtless visited Solomon for business purposes as well as because of interest in his notable wisdom (I Kings 10:1-10). Likewise the navy of ships which Solomon built in Ezion-geber for trade with Ophir (I Kings 9:26-28) went probably to South Arabia. According to I Kings 10:14f., the trade with Arabia was a not unimportant part of the sources of Solomon's wealth: "The weight of gold that came to Solomon in one year was six hundred and sixty-six talents of gold, besides what came from the traffic of the merchants and from all the kings of the Arabs and from the governors of the land."[12] Intermittent warfare is also recorded. "The Arabians that are beside the Ethiopians" invaded Judah in the time of King Jehoram (II Chronicles 21:16); and Uzziah fought against "the Arabians that dwelt in Gurbaal, and the Meunim" (II Chronicles 26:7).[13] "Geshem the Arabi-

---

[7] HHA p.34.   [8] ARAB I, §611.   [9] ARAB I, §778.
[10] ARAB II, §18, cf. 55.   [11] ARAB II, §440.
[12] From The Bible, An American Translation. cf. II Chronicles 9:13f.
[13] Hezekiah also fought against the Meunim (I Chronicles 4:41).

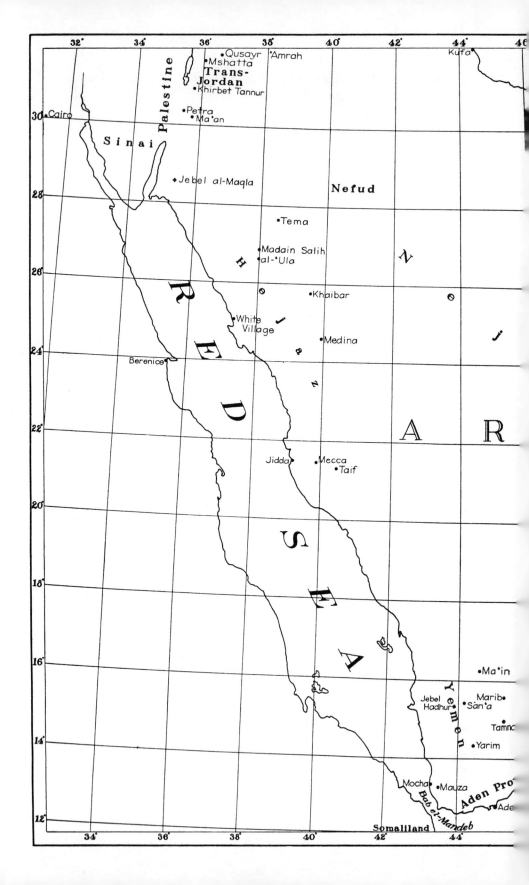

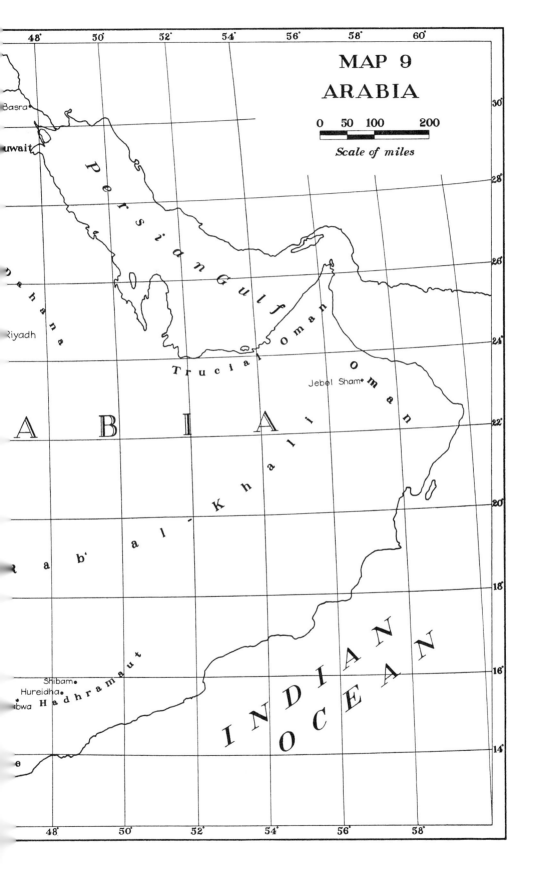

MAP 9

ARABIA

0 50 100 200

Scale of miles

48° 50° 52° 54° 56° 58° 60°

30°

28°

26°

24°

22°

20°

18°

16°

14°

Basra

uwait

P e r s i a n   G u l f

hana

Riyadh

T r u c i a l   O m a n

Jebel Sham

O m a n

A   B   I   A

r   a   b'   a   l   ' K   h   a   l   i

Shibam

Hureidha

bwa H a d h r a m a u t

e

I N D I A N

O C E A N

an" was an opponent of Nehemiah (Nehemiah 2:19); and Sheba or the Sabeans raided Job (Job 1:15).

Commercial, military and scientific interests motivated the concern of the Greeks and Romans with Arabia, and there are numerous references to this land in their geographical and historical writings. The names which appear in these sources include the *Sabaei* (Sabeans), *Minaei* (Mineans), *Homeritae* (Himyarites), *Scenitae* (tent-dwellers or Bedouins), *Nabataei* (Nabateans), *Catabanei* (Qatabanians), *Chatramotitae* (people of Hadhramaut), *Omanitae* (inhabitants of Oman), and *Sachalitae* (people of the southern coast line).[14]

The earliest classical authorities to speak of Arabia are the Greek botanist, Theophrastus (c.372-c.287 B.C.), and the Alexandrian mathematician, astronomer and geographer, Eratosthenes (c.276-c.195 B.C.). Theophrastus writes in his *Enquiry into Plants*: "Now frankincense, myrrh, cassia and also cinnamon are found in the Arabian peninsula about Saba, Hadramyta, Kitibaina and Mamali."[15] Eratosthenes provides the following information, as quoted by Strabo in his *Geography*.[16]

But I return to Eratosthenes, who next sets forth his opinions concerning Arabia. He says concerning the northerly, or desert, part of Arabia, which lies between Arabia Felix and Coele-Syria and Judaea, extending as far as the recess of the Arabian Gulf, that from the City of Heroes, which forms a recess of the Arabian Gulf near the Nile, the distance in the direction of the Petra of the Nabataeans to Babylon is five thousand six hundred stadia, the whole of the journey being in the direction of the summer sunrise and through the adjacent countries of the Arabian tribes, I mean the Nabataeans and the Chaulotaeans and the Agraeans. Above these lies Arabia Felix, which extends for a distance of twelve thousand stadia towards the south, to the Atlantic Sea. The first people who occupy Arabia Felix, after the Syrians and Judaeans, are farmers. After these the soil is sandy and barren, producing a few palm-trees and a thorny tree and the tamarisk, and affording water by digging, as is the case in Gedrosia; and it is occupied by tent-dwellers and camel-herds. The extreme parts towards the south, lying opposite to Aethiopia, are watered by summer rains and are sowed twice, like India; and the rivers there are used up in supplying plains and lakes. The country is in general fertile, and abounds in particular with places for making honey; and, with the exception of horses and mules and hogs, it has an abundance of domesticated animals; and, with the exception of geese and chickens, has all kinds of birds. The extreme part of the country above-mentioned is occupied by the four largest tribes; by the Minaeans, on the side towards the Red Sea, whose largest city is Carna or Carnana; next to these, by the Sabaeans, whose metropolis

[14] HHA p.44 n.1.   [15] IX, iv, 2. tr. Arthur Hort, LCL (1916), II, pp.233-235.
[16] XVI, iv, 2.

is Mariaba; third, by Cattabanians, whose territory extends down to the straits and the passage across the Arabian Gulf, and whose royal seat is called Tamna; and, farthest toward the east, the Chatramotitae, whose city is Sabata.

An interesting source of the Roman period which deals with Arabia is *The Periplus of the Erythraean Sea*.[17] The author is unknown but must have been a Greek resident in Egypt and a Roman subject. He was a merchant and made a voyage around Arabia for commercial reasons. The present work, written perhaps about A.D. 60, is a report on that trip and on the various ports, markets and products which the author had observed. *Periplus* means "a sailing round" or "the account of a coasting voyage," and the term Erythraean Sea was at that time applied to the Indian Ocean together with the Arabian Gulf (or Red Sea of modern times) and the Persian Gulf.

Starting from Berenice, Egypt, he crossed the Gulf to White Village, from which as he says "there is a road to Petra, which is subject to Malichas, King of the Nabataeans." "Directly below this place," the author continues, "is the adjoining country of Arabia, in its length bordering a great distance on the Erythraean Sea. Different tribes inhabit the country, differing in their speech, some partially, and some altogether. The land next the sea is similarly dotted here and there with caves of the Fish-Eaters, but the country inland is peopled by rascally men speaking two languages, who live in villages and nomadic camps, by whom those sailing off the middle course are plundered, and those surviving shipwrecks are taken for slaves. And so they too are continually taken prisoners by the chiefs and kings of Arabia; and they are called Carnaites. Navigation is dangerous along this whole coast of Arabia, which is without harbors, with bad anchorages, foul, inaccessible because of breakers and rocks, and terrible in every way. Therefore we hold our course down the middle of the gulf and pass on as fast as possible by the country of Arabia until we come to the Burnt Island; directly below which there are regions of peaceful people, nomadic, pasturers of cattle, sheep and camels.

"Beyond these places, in a bay at the foot of the left side of this gulf, there is a place by the shore called Muza,[18] a market-town es-

[17] tr. Wilfred H. Schoff, *The Periplus of the Erythraean Sea, Travel and Trade in the Indian Ocean by a Merchant of the First Century, Translated from the Greek and Annotated.* 1912.

[18] The name seems to include both the modern seaport of Mocha and the inland market-town of Mauza.

tablished by law, distant altogether from Berenice for those sailing southward, about twelve thousand stadia. And the whole place is crowded with Arab shipowners and seafaring men, and is busy with the affairs of commerce; for they carry on a trade with the far-side coast and with Barygaza,[19] sending their own ships there.

"Three days inland from this port there is a city called Saua. . . . And after nine days more there is Saphar,[20] the metropolis, in which lives Charibael, lawful king of two tribes, the Homerites and those living next to them, called the Sabaites; through continual embassies and gifts, he is a friend of the Emperors."

Proceeding on his adventurous voyage, the author of the *Periplus* entered "a narrow strait," the course through which was "beset with rushing currents and with strong winds blowing down from the adjacent ridge of mountains." This was the strait now known as Bab el-Mandeb or Gate of Tears.

Having negotiated this passage he arrived at Eudaemon Arabia, or the modern Aden. "After Eudaemon Arabia," he goes on, "there is a continuous length of coast, and a bay extending two thousand stadia or more, along which there are Nomads and Fish-Eaters living in villages; just beyond the cape projecting from this bay there is another market-town by the shore, Cana, of the Kingdom of Eleazus, the Frankincense Country. . . . Inland from this place lies the metropolis Sabbatha,[21] in which the King lives. All the frankincense produced in the country is brought by camels to that place to be stored, and to Cana on rafts held up by inflated skins after the manner of the country, and in boats. And this place has a trade also with the far-side ports, with Barygaza and Scythia and Ommana and the neighboring coast of Persia." Farther than this we will not follow the nameless merchant who has provided such vivid glimpses of first century Arabia.

In the second century A.D. the Greco-Egyptian geographer Ptolemy listed a large number of known places in Arabia. His map of that land is shown in Fig. 208.[22]

[19] The city on the west coast of India now known as Broach.

[20] Saphar is called Zafar by the Arabian geographers and is identified with ruins near modern Yarim.

[21] Probably to be identified with ruins sixty miles west of modern Shibam.

[22] *Geography.* v, 16, 18; vi, 7. Edward L. Stevenson, *Geography of Claudius Ptolemy, Translated into English and Edited, Based upon Greek and Latin Manuscripts and Important Late Fifteenth and Early Sixteenth Century Printed Editions, Including Reproductions of the Maps from the Ebner Manuscript, ca. 1460.* 1932, pp.128f.,130f., 137-140. Sexta Asiae tabula.

1. THE SABEO-HIMYARITE PERIOD, c.1000 B.C.-A.D. c.525[23]

Now we will turn to systematic consideration of a number of the early Arabian kingdoms which have been mentioned in the foregoing accounts. All those to be dealt with have become known to modern archeology through their own monuments and inscriptions as well as through the references of outside peoples such as we have been citing. For the most part the centers of these kingdoms were in South Arabia, an area which has been penetrated by comparatively few scientific explorers. Among those who were pioneers, special prominence attaches to the names of the Dane, Carsten Niebuhr (1763); the Frenchmen, Louis Arnaud (1843) and Joseph Halévy (1869); and the Austrian, E. Glaser (1882-1889).[24] Despite the difficulties, the work of these men and others has resulted in making known many sites and monuments, and in particular in collecting a large body of inscriptions.[25] These are written in an alphabet which is related to the Hebrew and, like it, probably derived from the proto-Sinaitic alphabetic symbols.[26]

References to and descriptions of various ancient monuments are also to be found in the writings of later Arabic authors. In this regard, the most important name is that of al-Hamdani (d. A.D. 945), a native of San'a and a student of astronomy, geography and history. He wrote a geography of Arabia entitled Sifatu Jazirat al-'Arab, and a large treatise on the history and antiquities of Yemen called al-Iklil, The Crown.[27] Book VIII of the latter work deals with the citadels and castles of South Arabia,[28] and will be cited in the following discussion. Where it has been checked by modern explorers it has proved remarkably dependable.

[23] For most of the dates and periods in Arabian history see HHA.

[24] David G. Hogarth, *The Penetration of Arabia, A Record of the Development of Western Knowledge Concerning the Arabian Peninsula* (The Story of Exploration). 1904, pp.39-62,128-131,200-203,203f.

[25] *Corpus Inscriptionum Semiticarum ab Academia Inscriptionum et Litterarum Humaniorum conditum atque digestum.* Pars Quarta, *Inscriptiones Himyariticas et Sabaeas continens.* 1889- .

[26] Martin Sprengling, *The Alphabet, Its Rise and Development from the Sinai Inscriptions.* OIC 12 (1931), pp.54f.

[27] Reynold A. Nicholson, *A Literary History of the Arabs.* 2d ed. 1930, pp.11f.

[28] tr. David H. Müller, *Die Burgen und Schlösser Südarabiens nach dem Iklîl des Hamdânî.* 2 parts. Sitzungsberichte der kaiserlichen Akademie der Wissenschaften, Wien, phil.-hist. Cl. 94 (1879), pp.335-423; 97 (1881), pp.955-1050; Nabih Amin Faris, *The Antiquities of South Arabia, Being a Translation from the Arabic with Linguistic, Geographic, and Historic Notes of the Eighth Book of Al-Hamdânî's al-Iklîl, Reconstructed from al-Karmali's Edition and a MS in the Garrett Collection, Princeton University Library.* 1938.

The first kingdoms we will take up are the four which are mentioned by both Theophrastus and Eratosthenes. Theophrastus, it will be remembered, alludes to the lands of Saba, Hadramyta, Kitibaina and Mamali; and Eratosthenes speaks of the Minaeans, Sabaeans, Cattabanians and Chatramotitae. Since Mamali in the text of Theophrastus is probably an error for Minea,[29] the two lists are in agreement. Theophrastus gives the names of the countries; Eratosthenes the names of the peoples inhabiting them. The order of reference in the latter source is evidently geographical, coming down the coast of the Red Sea to the Bab el-Mandeb and then turning eastward to Hadhramaut. We will follow the order in Theophrastus, beginning with Saba, probably the oldest of these kingdoms.

THE SABEANS, c.1000-c.115 B.C.

Since Saba[30] and the Sabeans are mentioned by the Assyrian kings as far back as Tiglath-pileser III, we know that the Sabean kingdom was in existence at least as anciently as the eighth century B.C. If, as the virtual identity of names suggests and as there seems no sufficient reason to doubt, the Biblical Queen of Sheba was from the land of Saba, then that kingdom was also old enough to be contemporaneous with Solomon (c.965-c.926 B.C.). The rule of a queen need not be astonishing, since an Arabian queen is explicitly named by Sargon only two hundred and fifty years later.[31] In the legends of Islam the Queen of Sheba is a prominent figure. She appears in the Qur'an (xxvii, 20-45), and is generally known in the Muslim world by the name of Bilqis.[32]

The oldest known capital of the Sabeans was at Sirwah, a day's journey west of Marib.[33] The ruins at this site include a castle, an elliptical temple, and numerous monolithic pillars. In the center of the temple stands a large block of stone, seventy feet long, thirty-five inches high and eighteen inches thick, covered on both sides with a

---

[29] De Lacy O'Leary, *Arabia Before Muhammad* (Trubner's Oriental Series). 1927, p.107 n.2.

[30] Tkač in Wilhelm Kroll and Kurt Witte, eds., *Paulys Real-Encyclopädie der klassischen Altertumswissenschaft, Neue Bearbeitung begonnen von Georg Wissowa.* Zweite Reihe, i, ii, cols. 1298-1515; and (J. Tkatsch) in EI iv, pp.3-19.

[31] D. S. Margoliouth, *The Relations between Arabs and Israelites Prior to the Rise of Islam* (The British Academy, Schweich Lectures, 1921). 1924, pp.49f.

[32] B. Carra de Vaux in EI i, p.720. Josephus, on the other hand, states that the royal visitor to Solomon was a "queen of Egypt and Ethiopia"; and Ethiopian tradition holds that their first king, named Menelik, was the son of Solomon and Makkeda, the latter being identified with the Queen of Sheba (*Antiquities*. viii, vi, 5. tr. H. St. J. Thackeray and Ralph Marcus, LCL v [1934], pp.660f. and note e).

[33] HHA p.54.

lengthy Sabean inscription. Many of the pillars also contain inscriptions. The temple was built by a Mukarrib or priest-king named Yada'il Dharih, and was dedicated to Almaqah.[34]

Almaqah (or Ilmuqah) was the moon god, corresponding to Sin in Mesopotamia, and was the chief deity of the Sabeans. Throughout South Arabia this divinity was conceived of as masculine, and was known to the Mineans by the name of Wadd, to the Qatabanians as 'Amm, and to the Hadhramautians as Sin. His consort was the sun, Shams, the same as Shamash in Mesopotamia. Their son, who completed the triad of most important deities, was 'Athtar. He was the planet Venus, and corresponded to the Babylonian Ishtar and Phoenician Astarte. Many other heavenly bodies were considered divine, and were believed to spring from the moon god and sun god.[35]

The later and more famous capital of Saba was Marib.[36] The town is situated 3,900 feet above sea level. The ancient city wall of Marib encloses a parallelogram roughly one thousand yards square. The wall is some three feet thick, and the positions of eight gates are still recognizable in it. According to inscriptions the wall was originally built by a son of the Mukarrib Sumuhu-'alaya Yanaf. Of him it is said that he "built a wall around Marib by command of and with the help of 'Athtar."

Al-Hamdani states that there were three citadels within the city, Salhin, al-Hajar and al-Qashib. Salhin was the royal residence, and al-Hamdani says that it was the citadel of Bilqis. The pillars of the throne were still standing when he wrote, and were so solidly imbedded in the stone, he said, that even many men would not be able to topple them over.[37]

Some distance east of the city are the ruins to which the modern designation of Haram Bilqis attaches. Actually these are the remains of an elliptical temple like the one at Sirwah, and like it, consecrated to the moon god, Almaqah. An inscription of Ilsarah, son of Sumuhu-'alaya, king of Saba, found here, dedicates walls and towers which he had built to Almaqah because this deity had answered his prayer and bestowed benefits upon him. Another dedication to Almaqah was written by Tabi'karib, a priest and a general under three Sabean kings. Yet another stated: "Karib'il Watar Yuhan'im, king of Saba

[34] Adolf Grohmann in EI IV, pp.450f.
[35] Ditlef Nielsen in *Handbuch der altarabischen Altertumskunde*. I (1927), pp.177-250.
[36] Adolf Grohmann in EI III, pp.280-294.
[37] Faris, *The Antiquities of South Arabia*, p.36.

and Raidan, son of Dhamar'alayi Bayyin, and Halak'amar, son of Karib'il, restored the wall for Almaqah for the good of the citadel Salhin and the city Marib."[38]

Southwest of the city at a distance of an hour or two was the Marib dam, the most famous structure of all. It was located at the place where the Wadi Dana opens out between the Balaq hills. Although the Wadi is often waterless in the summertime, in the rainy season a stream pours through it of such size and force as often to be uncrossable for some months. In order to protect Marib from floods and to control the waters for irrigation, the Sabeans undertook the construction of an elaborate system of barriers and sluices. The main dam was of earth, over two thousand feet long, and faced on the side which met the water with small stones strongly held together with mortar. On either side were large sluices, in connection with which stone towers and other buildings were erected. From here canals ran out to distribute the waters to the whole Marib plain, enabling it to flourish as a veritable garden-land.

Various inscriptions have been found at the dam. Two of these, on what are probably some of the oldest constructions on the right side nearest the city, name Sumuhu-'alaya Yanuf and his son Yithi'amar Bayyin as builders of the sluice-works on that side. These kings probably belong to the earlier part of the Sabean Period.[39] Eventually the great dam weakened, and inscriptions of the fifth and sixth centuries A.D. tell of breaches and of attempts at repair. The last of these records is dated in A.D. 542, and the final disastrous break in the dam must have occurred sometime after that date and before the rise of Islam. This allowed a terrible flood to devastate the valley, which afterward returned to desert.[40]

In the Qur'an this catastrophe is interpreted as a punishment upon the people of Saba for their sins: "For Sheba . . . there was a sign in their dwelling-place—two gardens, on the right and on the left: 'Eat of the provision of your Lord, and show gratitude to him; a good soil and a forgiving Lord.' But they turned away, so We sent upon them the flood of the dam and gave them instead of their two gardens, two which produced bitter fruit, and tamarisks and lotetrees a few."[41]

[38] *Corpus Inscriptionum Semiticarum*, Pars Quarta, II, pp.20-28 (Nos. 373-375).

[39] Müller, *Die Burgen und Schlösser Südarabiens nach dem Iklîl des Hamdânî*, II, pp.965-967.

[40] Grohmann in EI III, pp.290f.

[41] XXXIV, 14f. tr. Richard Bell, *The Qur'ān, Translated with a Critical Re-arrangement of the Surahs*. 2 vols. 1937-39, II, p.423.

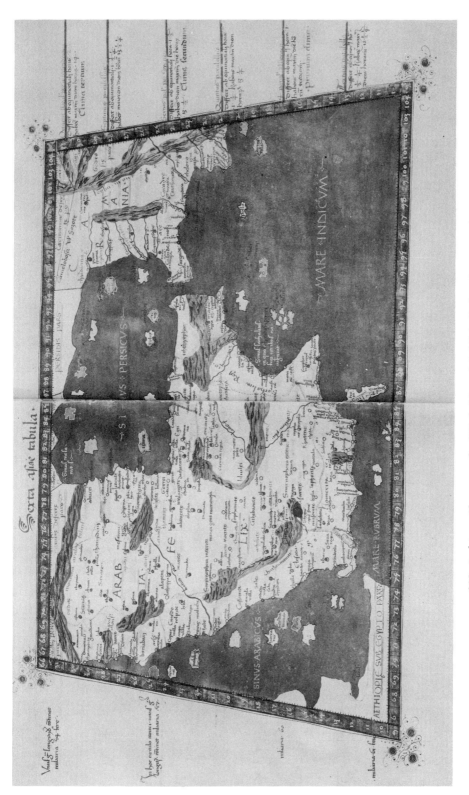

208. Arabia as Shown on the "Sixth Map of Asia" in Ptolemy's *Geography*

209. Baetyl in the Moon Temple
at Hureidha

210. Image in the Moon Temple
at Hureidha

211. Minean Inscription from al-'Ula

212. Mask of Kaddat

213. Head of a Woman

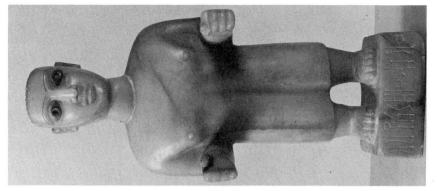

214. Statuette of 'Ammyada

215. Stela of 'Igli

217. Amulet of Ilza'adi and Hillqahi

216. Fragment of a Funeral Stela

219. Tomb at Madain Salih

218. The Khazneh at Petra

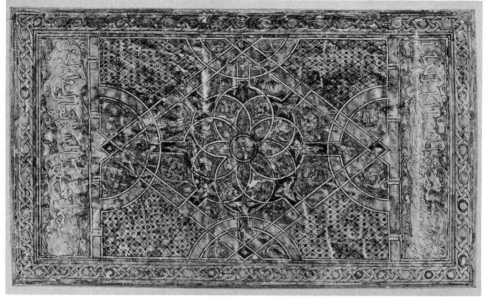

221. Colophon Page
in a Persian Qur'an

220. A Page in the Samarkand Kufic Qur'an

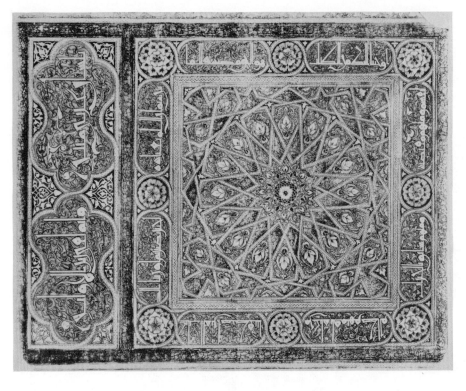

223. Qur'an of Sultan Sha'ban

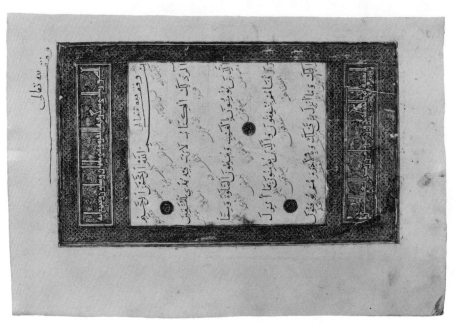

222. Page with Beginning of Surah 2 in a Persian Qur'an

224. Mecca and the Sacred Mosque

225. The Ka'bah at Mecca

226. The Mosque of the Prophet at Medina

227. Inside the Dome
of the Rock

228.   The Great Mosque at Damascus (*From Creswell, "Early Muslim
Architecture," Clarendon Press*)

229. Qusayr 'Amrah from the Air (*From Creswell, "Early Muslim Architecture," Clarendon Press*)

230. Carved Tower of Mshatta (*From Creswell, "Early Muslim Architecture," Clarendon Press*)

231. The Ruins of the Great Mosque at Samarra (*From Creswell, "Early Muslim Architecture," Clarendon Press*)

232. The Great Mosque of Qayrawan (*From Creswell, "Early Muslim Architecture," Clarendon Press*)

233. Inside the Great Mosque of Qayrawan (*From Creswell, "Early Muslim Architecture," Clarendon Press*)

234. The Pulpit in the Great Mosque of Qayrawan (*From Creswell, "Early Muslim Architecture," Clarendon Press*)

235. The Mosque of ibn-Tulun (*From Creswell, "Early Muslim Architecture," Clarendon Press*)

236. In the Sanctuary of the Mosque of ibn-Tulun (*From Creswell, "Early Muslim Architecture," Clarendon Press*)

237. The Mosque of al-Azhar

When al-Hamdani visited Marib the break in the dam had long since taken place, but the aqueducts through which the waters were led to the fields still stood "as though the builders had completed their construction only yesterday." So impressive were the ruins that al-Hamdani was not uninclined to accept the attribution of the original construction of the dam to Luqman ibn-'Ad, a mythical person to whom many institutions of antiquity were ascribed.[42]

Marib is now being excavated by the American Foundation for the Study of Man, under the presidency and leadership of Wendell Phillips.

THE HADHRAMAUTIANS

The Chatramotitae, as Eratosthenes named them, were the people of the land which Theophrastus called Hadramyta and which we know as Hadhramaut.[43] According to Eratosthenes the capital city of Hadhramaut was Sabata, which is identified with the modern town of Shabwa.[44] Pliny (A.D. 23-79) spoke of the city under the name of Sabota and said that it was situated on a lofty mountain, was surrounded by walls and contained sixty temples.[45]

Another ancient town of Hadhramaut was at modern Hureidha, some distance east of Shabwa. Excavations were conducted here in 1937-1938 by Gertrude Caton Thompson.[46] Hureidha is on the Wadi 'Amd. In this Wadi the remains of an extensive ancient irrigation system were traced. As in the case of the larger and more famous system at Marib, there were dams, sluices and channels to control and impound the waters and to lead them to the fields.

In the ruins of the ancient town the most important discovery was that of a temple to the moon god, the first such structure to be excavated in Arabia. As revealed by the digging, this temple stood on a slight eminence in the cultivated valley. It was built upon an oblong platform of paved stone, the corners of which were oriented to the four cardinal points. The main façade faced to the southwest. Three building periods were distinguished, in the course of which the temple was enlarged to its final dimensions. Five stone pillar-

---

[42] Faris, *The Antiquities of South Arabia*, pp.34f.

[43] Probably to be identified with Hazarmaveth in Genesis 10:26.

[44] HHA p.55; Adolf Grohmann in EI IV, pp.244f.

[45] *Natural History.* VI, xxxii, 155; XII, xxx, 52. tr. H. Rackham, LCL (1938-) II, p.455; IV, p.37.

[46] G. Caton Thompson, *The Tombs and Moon Temple of Hureidha (Hadhramaut)* (Reports of the Research Committee of the Society of Antiquaries of London, XIII). 1944.

bases still stood near the center of the platform. These may have supported wooden pillars upon which the sanctuary roof was carried.

Lying beside one of these pillars was a stone offering table. It was made from a rectangular slab of limestone, and there was a depression in the upper surface evidently intended to receive libations. A projection on one side was roughly shaped into a bull's head, and an inscription (No. 7)[47] gave the name of the one who had dedicated the table.

In one of the shrines later added to the temple there was a large stone altar, and around the base of this were various votive objects. In addition to pottery vessels these included two remarkable pieces of limestone. The first had been roughly hammer-dressed into a conical shape with a flattened base; the second was a rectangular brick with one end crudely shaped into a human head. The place where they were found shows that both stones must have had some sort of religious character. We may call the first a baetyl or sacred stone, and may suppose that it was an aniconic representation of a god. The second stone is clearly a semi-anthropomorphic image, and may be held to represent the worshiper or to be a cult image. In the two, then, we have two stages on the way to the fully sculptured images of which we will present examples in speaking of the Himyarite Period. Crude as they are, the stones are therefore of much significance, and we reproduce them in Figs. 209 and 210.[48]

Some fifty inscriptions were found at Hureidha, written in the Hadhramautic dialect. Twenty-two of these preserve dedications to the moon god, Sin, and there are also explicit references to the temple and the town. Inscription No. 4 refers to the "town of Madabum," thus giving us the ancient name of Hureidha; No. 10 mentions the "anterior façade [of the temple] of Madabum"; and No. 54 names the god of the city, "Sin of Madabum."[49]

Two cave tombs were also excavated and a considerable body of pottery recovered as well as two stone seals and a number of beads. The beads resemble eastern Mediterranean beads of the seventh to fifth centuries B.C.;[50] the seals reveal Achaemenian (sixth to fourth centuries B.C.) influence.[51] A tentative date, therefore, for the Hureidha tombs and temple is in the fifth and fourth centuries B.C.,

[47] ibid., pp.160f. ("Epigraphy" by G. Ryckmans).
[48] ibid., Pls. xv,left; xiv,left.
[49] ibid., pp.158-160,162f.,173 (Ryckmans).
[50] ibid., pp.96-101 (H. C. Beck).
[51] ibid., pp.101-103 (Henri Frankfort).

with later phases of the temple building belonging perhaps to the third century.[52]

THE QATABANIANS

The statement of Eratosthenes concerning the Qatabanians leads us to locate this people along the strait, Bab el-Mandeb. Their capital, according to the same authority, was Tamna. For some time a number of inscriptions in the Qatabanian dialect have been known. These give the names of some of the Qatabanian kings, and tell of campaigns in which they fought with and also against the Sabeans. On the basis of these materials it has been judged that the Qatabanian kingdom came into existence around 500 B.C. and endured until around the beginning of the Christian Era.[53] The site of ancient Tamna, or Timna,[54] has very recently been identified, forty miles south of Marib. Explorations and excavations were conducted there in 1950 and 1951 by the American Foundation for the Study of Man, under the leadership of Wendell Phillips, with William F. Albright as chief archeologist. Thick beds of ashes have been revealed, marking the final conflagration in which the capital city was destroyed. This event, doubtless coinciding with the end of Qataban as an independent kingdom, is now placed about 50 B.C. in round numbers.[55]

THE MINEANS

From the statement of Eratosthenes we gather that the territory of the Mineans was to the north of that of the Sabeans, and we learn that their largest city was Carna. Carna is identified with the modern Ma'in, northeast of San'a. Outposts of Minean power were at Ma'an near Petra, and at Daydan (Old Testament Dedan) which is represented by modern al-'Ula.[56]

Many inscriptions in the Minean dialect have been found in both South and North Arabia. The Minean inscriptions which were found

[52] *ibid.*, pp.93,153.
[53] J. Tkatsch in EI II, pp.809-814; and (Tkač) in *Paulys Real-Encyclopädie der klassischen Altertumswissenschaft.* Zweite Reihe, I, ii, cols. 1457-1459; Nikolaus Rhodokanakis, *Der Grundsatz der Öffentlichkeit in den südarabischen Urkunden.* 1915, pp.33-49; *Katabanische Texte zur Bodenwirtschaft.* 1919 (Sitzungsberichte der [kais.] Akademie der Wissenschaften in Wien, phil.-hist. Kl., 177, 2 and 194, 2); W. F. Albright in BASOR 119 (Oct. 1950), pp.5-15; cf. A. Jamme in BASOR 120 (Dec. 1950), pp.26f.
[54] Although Timna is the form now more widely used, Eratosthenes has Ταμνα, which points to Tamna as more accurately representing the ancient vocalization.
[55] W. F. Albright in BASOR 119 (Oct. 1950), pp.5-15.
[56] HHA pp.52,54. Daydan was the capital of the Lihyanites, whom the Mineans probably succeeded at that place.

at al-'Ula by the French explorers Pères Jaussen and Savignac contain the names of three kings of Ma'in, Ilyafa' Yashur, Abikarib Yathi' and Waqah'il Nabat, and refer frequently to the "gods of Ma'in."[57] One of these inscriptions, naming Abikarib Yathi' and mentioning some of the gods of Ma'in, is reproduced in Fig. 211.

It has been thought by some that the Minean kingdom originated even before the Sabean and went back to 1200 B.C. or earlier. Various objections have been raised to this view, however, and it now appears probable that the Minean kingdom was later than the Sabean.[58] Possible dates for its duration are from c.500 B.C. to A.D. c.50.[59] If, however, the Meunim of the Old Testament are to be identified with the Mineans, then this people must have been in existence as early as the eighth century B.C. since both Uzziah (785-747) and Hezekiah (725-697) are said to have fought against them.[60]

THE HIMYARITES, C.115 B.C.-A.D. C.525

Toward the end of the second century B.C. the dominant power in South Arabia passed from the Sabeans to the Himyarites.[61] These were a people related to the Sabeans in race and language, and the heirs of their culture. The center of the Himyarites was at Raidan, and about 115 B.C. the title "King of Saba and Raidan" appears in the inscriptions.[62] Raidan was later known as Saphar (Sephar in Genesis 10:30) or Zafar, under which name it appears, as we have seen, in *The Periplus of the Erythraean Sea*. The same source gives us our first mention by name of the Homerites or Himyarites, and states that their king (who also ruled over the Sabeans) was Charibael. This ruler is probably the same as the Karib'il Watar Yuhan'im, king of Saba and Raidan, whom we have already met in a late inscription at the Haram Bilqis at Marib. Pliny[63] also mentions the Homeritae in connection with the Roman expedition which Aelius Gallus led to disaster in Arabia in 25 B.C. Gallus, says Pliny, reported that the Homeritae constituted the most numerous tribe in the land. Strabo[64] describes the same expedition and states that at the time Marsiaba (Marib) belonged to the tribe of the Rhammanitae who

[57] Jaussen and Savignac, *Mission archéologique en Arabie* (Publications de la Société des Fouilles Archéologiques). II, *El-'Ela, d'Hégra a Teima, Harrah de Tebouk* (1914), pp.256-263,270-273,301-304 (Nos. 11,12,17,31); Atlas, Pl. LXXIV, No. 17.

[58] Tkatsch in EI IV, pp.12-15.

[59] F. V. Winnett in BASOR 73 (Feb. 1939), pp.3-9.

[60] II Chronicles 26:7; I Chronicles 4:41.

[61] J. H. Mordtmann in EI II, pp.310-312.   [62] HHA p.55.

[63] *Natural History*, VI, xxxii, 161.   [64] *Geography*. XVI, iv, 22-24.

were subject to Ilasarus. Ilasarus is probably the Ilsarah Yahdub, king of Saba and Raidan, who is also known in the inscriptions.

The ruins of the Himyarite capital of Zafar[65] crown the summit of a circular hill near the modern village of Yarim. Al-Hamdani tells of the place at some length and quotes the expressions of various Arabic poets concerning it. He says that the city had nine gates and that from the main gate to the inner city was a mile in distance. The guardhouse at this gate was connected by a golden chain with the place where the king held audience so that the approach of visitors could be signaled. One of the castles at Zafar, reports al-Hamdani, was adorned with silver and white stones on the outside, and paneled with aloe wood, mosaic, onyx and different kinds of precious stones on the inside. So splendid was this castle that legend attributed its erection to the jinn or demons.[66]

Another notable Himyarite castle was the Ghumdan in San'a, which al-Hamdani calls the oldest, most remarkable and most famous of all those with which he deals. According to one view, it was built by none other than Shem, the son of Noah. In the time of al-Hamdani the castle was reduced to a gigantic ruin, opposite the great mosque of San'a, but this authority collected much information on its earlier appearance. It was built in terraces, he says, to a height of twenty stories. Each façade was built of stone of a different color, one front red, one white, one green and one black. The uppermost story was roofed with marble so transparent that, looking up, one could distinguish between a crow and a stork. At the four corners stood lions of copper which roared whenever the wind blew.[67]

The Himyarite Period is divided into two parts, the first from around 115 B.C. to around A.D. 300, the second from that date to about A.D. 525. Early in the first part colonists from South Arabia settled in the "land of Cush" and laid the foundations of the kingdom of Aksum (first century A.D.) which developed into the later Abyssinia. During the second part there were one or two relatively brief times of Abyssinian invasion and rule in Arabia, but mostly the native Himyarite kings maintained their position until the final date indicated.[68]

Both Judaism and Christianity were in South Arabia in the latter part of the Himyarite Period. According to Philostorgius in his

---

[65] J. Tkatsch in EI IV, pp.1185-1187.
[66] Faris, *The Antiquities of South Arabia,* pp.20-29.
[67] *ibid.,* pp.8-20.   [68] HHA pp.56f.,60.

Church History (written sometime between A.D. 425 and 433), Christianity was taken to the Himyarites by the Indian Theophilus under the Emperor Constantius (A.D. 337-361). The evangelist succeeded in building churches in several towns, including the metropolis of Tapharon (probably Zafar), Aden, and a place at the mouth of the Persian Gulf. At the same time there were already numerous Jews in the land.[69]

Along with the two monotheistic faiths which had come in from the outside, the indigenous polytheism of Arabia continued to flourish, and worship was still directed to Almaqah, 'Athtar and other deities. Philostorgius says of the Himyarites in the same passage just cited: "They sacrifice to the sun and moon and spirits of the land."

The extant remains by which the popular beliefs are known include many funerary objects. As other peoples throughout the world have done, the ancient Arabians buried with the dead a variety of things which were valuable to them and desired for the life beyond. Among these, for example, are jars and saucers, cosmetic boxes and necklaces of semiprecious stones. Small altars and incense burners attest some kind of religious rites. Most interesting of all are the statuettes and bas-reliefs. These usually provide a representation of the deceased and are presumably animistic in conception, being intended to be a "support" for the soul after the burial of the inanimate body.[70]

The items which will be shown here have all been recovered in various ways from burial places in southwest Arabia. The inscriptions, which are in various South Arabian dialects, provide some clues for dating. For the most part it may be said that the objects belong to the time between 150 B.C. and A.D. 200, that is at the end of the Sabean and in the earlier part of the Himyarite Periods.

Fig. 212 pictures a limestone mask in which the human countenance is represented in a geometrical form. The inscription at the base is in archaic characters, and gives a name which has been read

[69] III, 4. ed. Joseph Bidez, *Philostorgius Kirchengeschichte mit dem Leben des Lucian von Antiochien und den Fragmenten eines arianischen Historiographen, herausgegeben im Auftrage der Kirchenväter-Commission der königl. preussischen Akademie der Wissenschaften* (Die griechischen christlichen Schriftsteller der ersten drei Jahrhunderte). 1913, pp.32-34. For the struggles between the Jews and the Christians and the persecution of the Christians by the Jewish king Masruq (dhu-Nuwas in the Muslim tradition), see Axel Moberg, *The Book of the Himyarites, Fragments of a Hitherto Unknown Syriac Work, Edited, with Introduction and Translation* (Skrifter Utgivna Av Kungl. Humanistiska Vetenskapssamfundet I Lund, 7). 1924.

[70] Léon Legrain in AJA 38 (1934), pp.329-337.

as Kaddat or Kadabat.[71] Fig. 213 shows an even more strongly geometrical woman's head executed in alabaster. In Fig. 214 we see a complete statuette in the round, also carved in alabaster. The modeling is done with care, but the lower part of the body is quite out of proportion, due no doubt to considering the head as the most important part. The inscription on the base gives the name of 'Ammyada of Shukaymim.[72]

Of the relief carvings three examples will be shown. The first (Fig. 215) is an alabaster stela with two panels of reliefs. In the upper panel the deceased man is shown at the right, garbed in a long robe and seated upon a low stool. He holds a bowl in one hand, and in front of him is a table with another bowl and a large vase. A servant with cup or bowl stands by the table, while at the left is a woman with a two-stringed musical instrument. This would appear to represent the master at a feast. In the lower panel the same deceased one is shown, evidently returning from an expedition. He rides upon a horse and, with brandished spear, drives a camel before him. At the top an inscription invokes the protection of the god 'Athtar for the monument: "Funeral image and stela of 'Igli, son of Sa'dlati Qurain. And may 'Athtar of the East smite him who effaces it!"[73]

The second relief (Fig. 216) is now but a fragment. At the top is part of an inscription calling the object a tombstone and giving several names; below this is a scene showing a peasant guiding a plow drawn by two oxen; and at the bottom are the heads of three persons.[74]

The third stela (Fig. 217) is identified by the inscription at the top as an "amulet" belonging to Ilza'adi and his brother Hillqahi. The carving shows a front view of the heads of two bulls. Their horns form almost perfect crescents or new moons, and on this ground the heads may probably be interpreted as symbols of Almaqah, the moon god.[75]

THE NABATEANS

In the time with which we have thus far been dealing there were

---

[71] G. Ryckmans in *Le Muséon, Revue d'études orientales*. 48 (1935), p.175.

[72] *ibid.*, pp.170f.

[73] *Corpus Inscriptionum Semiticarum*, Pars Quarta, II, pp.143f. (No. 445); J. H. Mordtmann in *Zeitschrift der deutschen morgenländischen Gesellschaft*. 32 (1878), pp.200-203; 35 (1881), pp.432-438,440.

[74] *Corpus Inscriptionum Semiticarum*, Pars Quarta, III, pp.127f. (No. 706).

[75] *ibid.*, pp.118f. (No. 695); Ditlef Nielsen, *Die altarabische Mondreligion und die mosaische Ueberlieferung*, 1904, pp.110-112.

also various kingdoms in North Arabia, but for the most part they were of less prominence than those in the South. For this reason the important southern kingdoms of the Sabeans and Himyarites have been allowed to give their names to the entire period. Of the northern kingdoms, it will suffice to mention here the earliest and greatest, that of the Nabateans, before passing on to the next main chronological period.

The Nabateans appear first in the inscriptions of Ashurbanipal in the seventh century B.C.,[76] and were mentioned by Eratosthenes, in the passage already quoted, among other North Arabian tribes. They succeeded the Moabites and Edomites in Transjordan, and made their capital at the famous city of Petra which they wrested from the Edomites. Their kingdom flourished from the fourth century B.C. to the second century A.D., reaching its greatest height in the first century A.D.

Petra, the Sela (or Selah) of the Old Testament (Isaiah 16:1; 42: 11; II Kings, 14:7; cf. Jeremiah 49:16; Obadiah 3; II Chronicles 25: 12), was a spectacular city, carved largely out of the solid and colorful rock in a high mountain valley east of the Wadi el-Arabah. Rockhewn temples like the Khazneh (Fig. 218), houses, tombs, cisterns, aqueducts, and altars remain to attest the splendor which this place enjoyed when caravans brought in and out of it the riches of all the East.[77]

Of the many Nabatean deities the best known was dhu-al-Shara (the lord of Shara) or Dushara. He was worshiped at Petra in the form of an unhewn, rectangular black stone. In an inscription[78] at Petra, dating probably from the first century A.D., a tomb is entrusted to the care of this god in the following words:

This sepulcher, and the large vault within it, and the small vault inside, within which are burying-places fashioned into niches, and the wall in front of them . . . and the rest of all the entire property which is in these places, is the consecrated and inviolable possession of Dushara, the god of our lord, and his sacred throne, and all the gods, [as specified] in deeds relating to consecrated things according to their contents. And it is the order of Dushara and his throne and all the gods that, according to what

[76] ARAB II, §821.

[77] M. Rostovtzeff, *Caravan Cities.* tr. D. and T. Talbot Rice. 1932, pp.37-53; M. A. Murray, *Petra, The Rock City of Edom.* 1939.

[78] Although they spoke Arabic the Nabateans wrote in script derived from the Aramaic, and this developed into the script of North Arabic, particularly the round script called *naskhi* in distinction from the angular writing practiced in the city of Kufa and hence called Kufic (HHA p.70).

is in the said deeds relating to consecrated things, it shall be done and not altered. Nor shall anything of all that is in them be withdrawn; nor shall any man be buried in this sepulcher save him who has in writing a contract to bury, [specified] in the said deeds relating to consecrated things—for ever.[79]

Elsewhere in southern Transjordan the sites of more than five hundred Nabatean towns, fortresses, watch-towers and temples have now been surveyed. For a strikingly located temple we may refer to Khirbet Tannur on the summit of high, isolated Jebel Tannur not far from the Dead Sea. Here, as the sculptured remains show, the Nabateans worshiped Syrian deities like Hadad and his consort Atargatis.[80] Farther south in Arabia another Nabatean center was at Madain Salih or al-Hegr, where the rock-hewn monuments are almost as impressive as at Petra. One of the tombs at this place, dated in the year 1 B.C., is pictured in Fig. 219.[81]

The decisive blow to the Nabatean kingdom was the capture of Petra by the Romans in A.D. 106, after which time the rival city of Palmyra successfully attracted the trade which had previously enriched the merchants of Nabatea. The people of Palmyra, it may be added, were also of Arabian descent, and built in the Syrian desert a caravan city of amazing splendor. Their religion was a distinctive blend of Arabian, Parthian, Babylonian, Syrian and Greek elements, and their gods included a trinity made up of Bel (with Malak-bel as his messenger), Yarhibol and Aglibol, and the other deities Belshamin the rival of Bel, Shamash, Ishtar, Nanaia, Nergal, Hadad, Atargatis, Eshmun, Sama, Allat, Chai al Qaum, Arsu, Azizu and Satrapes.[82]

---

[79] *Corpus Inscriptionum Semiticarum*, Pars Secunda, *Inscriptiones Aramaicas continens*. I (1889), pp.307-311 (No. 350); G. A. Cooke, *A Text-Book of North-Semitic Inscriptions, Moabite, Hebrew, Phoenician, Aramaic, Nabataean, Palmyrene, Jewish.* 1903, pp.241-244 (No. 94).

[80] Nelson Glueck, *The Other Side of the Jordan.* 1940, pp.158-200.

[81] Jaussen and Savignac, *Mission archéologique en Arabie*, I, *De Jérusalem au Hedjaz, Médain-Saleh* (1909), pp.301-441; II, pp.78-108; Atlas, Pl. XL.

[82] Rostovtzeff, *Caravan Cities*, pp.91-152; Hoyningen-Huene and David M. Robinson, *Baalbek, Palmyra.* 1946, pp.59-127.

2. THE JAHILIYAH PERIOD, A.D. c.525-622

FROM the Muslim point of view the entire time prior to the rise of Islam was *jahiliyah*. This word appears several times in the Qur'an and is variously translated "Time of Ignorance" or "Paganism."[83] Finding such a designation not altogether appropriate to the relatively advanced civilizations hitherto discussed, the modern historian is inclined to limit the word to the century just before the establishment of Islam.[84]

The chief feature of Arabian life at this time was the return to nomadism.[85] In the south the breaking of the Marib dam symbolized the downfall of the urban civilization there; in the north the Nabatean state had already disintegrated and its powerful cities lost their greatness. Elsewhere in the north, in Hejaz and Nejd, nomadic life had always been most characteristic of the people.

Only three cities of importance were to be found in Hejaz. These were Taif, Mecca and Medina. Taif[86] enjoyed a picturesque and fertile location in the mountains and Medina[87] (then known as Yathrib) was in a well-watered plain, but Mecca[88] stood in a barren, rocky valley. Despite the sterility and extreme heat of the place, Mecca enjoyed the possession of a famous well called Zamzam and an ancient sanctuary known as the Ka'bah, and was also where important commercial routes intersected.

The Bedouins of the desert, who comprised the majority of North Arabia's population, were basically animistic in their religion. Springs and wells, stones and trees were the dwelling-places of spirits, and wild animals and fearsome places of the wilderness were inhabited by jinn or demons. Higher gods also were worshiped, and among these the most important, for our account, were Allah, Allat, al-'Uzza and Manat.[89]

While Allah is best known as the principal god of Mecca, he was also worshiped in other places throughout Arabia as is shown by the occurrence of the name in Sabean, Minean and particularly Lihya-

[83] III, 148; v, 55; xxxiii, 33; xlviii, 26. tr. Bell, I, pp.60,101; II, pp.414,523.
[84] HHA p.87.
[85] Giorgio Levi della Vida in FAH pp.43f.,55.
[86] H. Lammens in EI IV, pp.621f.   [87] Fr. Buhl in EI III, pp.83-92.
[88] H. Lammens in EI III, pp.437-442.
[89] J. Wellhausen, *Reste arabischen Heidentums gesammelt und erläutert.* 2d ed. 1897; Theodor Nöldeke in HERE I, pp.659-673; cf. Samuel M. Zwemer, *The Influence of Animism on Islam, An Account of Popular Superstitions.* 1920.

nite inscriptions.[90] The Qur'an (xxix, 61) refers to the belief of the pagans in Allah as the creator of the heavens and the earth; and Muhammad's own father bore the name of 'Abd Allah or 'Abdullah, meaning the slave or worshiper of this god. In Mecca, Allah was worshiped in the Ka'bah and possibly represented by the famous Black Stone in that place.

Allat, according to recent study of the complicated inscriptional evidence,[91] is believed to have been introduced into Arabia from Syria, and to have been the moon goddess of North Arabia. If this is the correct interpretation of her character, she corresponded to the moon deity of South Arabia, Almaqah, Wadd, 'Amm or Sin as he was called, the difference being only the oppositeness of gender. Mount Sinai (the name being an Arabic feminine form of Sin) would then have been one of the centers of the worship of this northern moon goddess.

Similarly, al-'Uzza is supposed to have come from Sinai, and to have been the goddess of the planet Venus. As the moon and the evening star are associated in the heavens, so too were Allat and al-'Uzza together in religious belief, and so too are the crescent and star conjoined on the flags of Arab countries today.

As for Manat, her original home seems to have been in Hejaz. The etymology of the name is judged to be connected with the root mana, meaning "to determine" or "to mete out," and it is thus suggested that she was a goddess of fortune or fate. The same root is at the basis of the name of the god Meni or Destiny mentioned in Isaiah 65:11.

Prior to the rise of Islam, these three goddesses were associated with Allah as his daughters,[92] and all were worshiped at Mecca and other places in the vicinity. Articles about all three of them were written by the scholar Ibn al-Kalbi (d. A.D. c.820) in his Kitab al-Asnam or Book of Idols, extensive portions of which are preserved in the *Geographical Dictionary* of Yaqut (d. A.D. 1229).[93] According to Ibn al-Kalbi the sanctuary of Allat was in Taif where the goddess was represented by a rectangular block of stone, over which a build-

[90] HHA p.100.

[91] F. V. Winnett in *The Moslem World*. 30 (1940), pp.113-130.

[92] In the tablets found at ancient Ugarit (Ras Shamra), three daughters are ascribed to Baal, which strengthens the theory of North Syrian influence in the formation of the Meccan pantheon. Cyrus H. Gordon, *The Loves and Wars of Baal and Anat and Other Poems from Ugarit*. 1943, p.23.

[93] The extracts in Yaqut are collected and translated by Wellhausen, *Reste arabischen Heidentums*, pp.10-64. See now N. A. Faris, *The Book of Idols*. 1952.

ing was erected.[94] Al-'Uzza "stood," says the same authority, in the valley of Nakhla to the right of the road from Mecca to Iraq. This manner of speech leads us to suppose that al-'Uzza also was worshiped in the form of a stone pillar, and Ibn al-Kalbi speaks expressly of the house which was built over her. Manat was the oldest of the three deities, according to the same authority, and was a large stone in the valley of Qudaid between Mecca and Medina. The Aus and Khazraj tribes of Medina were the most prominent worshipers of Manat, while the Quraish of Mecca paid much reverence to Allat and al-'Uzza, most of all to the latter. The Quraish were the tribe to which Muhammad belonged, and Ibn al-Kalbi states that before the prophet began to preach his own message he himself once offered a white sheep to al-'Uzza. Such was the "paganism" in which Muhammad was reared and which he later came to believe it was his mission to dispel.

The milieu of the prophet was not one, however, of polytheistic paganism untouched by any other influences. As in South Arabia, so too in North the monotheistic faiths of Judaism and Christianity had long since become known. When the first Jewish communities were established in North Arabia we do not know, but a plausible hypothesis supposes that the enhanced commercial opportunities consequent upon the residence at Tema (Taima) of the Babylonian king Nabonidus (Nabunaid) attracted colonists as early as the latter half of the sixth century B.C. From there they followed on down the main caravan route to establish other colonies in Khaibar, Medina and Mecca.[95] The influence of Christianity was brought to bear upon Arabia both from Syria in the northwest and from Mesopotamia in the northeast. In the sixth century A.D. the Arabic kingdoms of the Ghassanids in Syria and the Lakhmids in Mesopotamia were allied respectively with the Byzantine and the Persian empires and were strong centers respectively of Monophysite and of Nestorian Christianity. From these regions and in this time if not also earlier, Christian ideas spread on into the farther reaches of Arabia.[96]

[94] The idol-stone of Allat which Charles M. Doughty was shown at Taif in the last century was an "unshapely crag" of gray granite nearly twenty feet in length (*Travels in Arabia Deserta*. 1921, ii, p.516).

[95] Charles C. Torrey, *The Jewish Foundation of Islam* (The Hilda Stich Stroock Lectures [Established 1927] at the Jewish Institute of Religion). 1933, pp.10-15; cf. Ilse Lichtenstädter in *Proceedings of the American Academy for Jewish Research*. 10 (1940), pp.185-194.

[96] Richard Bell, *The Origin of Islam in Its Christian Environment* (The Gunning Lectures, Edinburgh University, 1925). 1926, pp.18-28.

A careful study of the relevant data particularly in the Qur'an shows that Muhammad had a very considerable store of knowledge of Judaism and Christianity, and that it was of the sort which he would have been most likely to obtain through oral channels and personal observation over a long period of time. He was specially impressed, it seems, with the fact that both the Jews and the Christians were People of a Book, and it was his desire likewise to provide his own people with a Book which would be to them what the Torah was to the Jews and the Bible to the Christians.[97]

[97] Julian Obermann in FAH pp.58-119; cf. Heinrich Speyer in EI IV, pp.1146-1148; W. F. Albright in JAOS 60 (1940), p.301; W. St. Clair-Tisdall, *The Sources of Islam, A Persian Treatise*. tr. William Muir. 1901.

3. THE AUTHORITATIVE WRITINGS OF ISLAM

THE QUR'AN

THE book which Muhammad gave to his people was the Qur'an (Koran).[98] The name of this book is the noun from the verb *qara'a* which is used in the work itself with the meaning "to read," "to discourse," or "to recite"; hence it must signify something like "lecture," "discourse," or "what is uttered."[99] More than fifty other names are applied to the Qur'an, of which one of the most frequent is Kitab, simply meaning "book" or "scripture." The individual chapters of the book, of which there are one hundred and fourteen, are called Surahs, a word the derivation of which has not been satisfactorily explained.[100] Smaller sections are known as *aya* (plural *ayat*), probably meaning "token," or "token of belief."

The contents of the Qur'an are extremely miscellaneous in character, as might indeed be expected from its own statement that it is "a clear setting forth of everything" (XII, 111). Not only the variety of subject matter but also the abruptness of transitions and the great number of repetitions conduce to the impression of confusion given by the materials of the Qur'an.

Critical study of these materials attempts to bring them into some sort of chronological order. According to present investigation,[101] three periods may be distinguished. In the first, Muhammad was still

[98] tr. George Sale, *The Koran, Commonly Called the Alcoran of Mohammed, Translated into English Immediately from the Original Arabic; with Explanatory Notes, Taken from the Most Approved Commentators. To Which is Prefixed a Preliminary Discourse.* 1734. 6th ed. 1876; E. M. Wherry, *A Comprehensive Commentary on the Qurán: Comprising Sale's Translation and Preliminary Discourse, with Additional Notes and Emendations, Together with a Complete Index to the Text, Preliminary Discourse, and Notes* (Trübner's Oriental Series). 4 vols. 1896; J. M. Rodwell, *El Kor'ân; or, the Korân: Translated from the Arabic, The Suras Arranged in Chronological Order; with Notes and Index.* 1861. 2d ed. 1876; E. H. Palmer in SBE VI, IX. 1880; Maulvi Muhammad Ali, *The Holy Qur-án, Containing the Arabic Text with English Translation and Commentary.* 2d ed. 1920; Richard Bell, *The Qur'ān, Translated, with a Critical Re-arrangement of the Surahs.* 2 vols. 1937-39; cf. Allama Sir Abdullah al-Mamun al-Suhrawardy, *The Sayings of Muhammad* (Wisdom of the East). 1941. For other translations and the literature related to the Qur'an see Gustav Pfannmüller, *Handbuch der Islam-Literatur.* 1923, pp.206-229. The translation employed in this chapter is that by Bell.

[99] D. S. Margoliouth in HERE X, pp.538f.; F. Buhl in EI II, pp.1063f.; and in A. J. Wensinck and J. H. Kramers, eds., *Handwörterbuch des Islam.* 1941, pp.347f.

[100] F. Buhl in EI IV, pp.560f.

[101] Bell, *The Qur'ān, Translated, with a Critical Re-arrangement of the Surahs,* I, pp.v-vii; II, pp.689f.; John E. Merrill in *The Moslem World.* 37 (1947), pp.134-148; cf. Theodor Nöldeke, *Geschichte des Qorāns.* 2d ed. by Friedrich Schwally. 1909-19, I, pp.58-234.

in Mecca, and his preaching was a summons to the worship of Allah alone, based specially upon "signs" which Allah had set forth in nature. A sample passage from this period runs as follows (XIII, 2): "Allah it is who hath raised up the heavens without pillars that ye can see; then sat firm upon the throne managing the affair; and hath subjected the sun and the moon to service, each running its course to a fixed term; he maketh the signs distinct, mayhap of the meeting with your Lord ye will be convinced."

The second period covers the latter part of Muhammad's time in Mecca and the first year or two of his residence in Medina. In this period Muhammad recited many stories with which he had become familiar in the traditions of the Jews and the Christians, and evidently felt that he was preaching to his own people the same revelation which had already come to the peoples of the Law and the Gospel. Passages originating in this period may be found in Surah XXVI, for example, where stories of Moses, Abraham, Noah and others are related.

The third period is that of the prophet's later time in Medina. He had now become opposed to Judaism and Christianity and had determined upon the establishment of a religious community independent of both. For that community he consciously undertook to prepare a Book which would have the same place as was occupied by the Old Testament and the New Testament among the Jews and the Christians.

The transition to this period and to the type of material characteristic of it may be seen in Surah II, which is believed to have been composed for the most part during Muhammad's second and third years at Medina. Some portions of the Surah contain appeals to the Jews, but in verses 105-107 the prophet speaks against Jews, Christians, and pagan Arabs alike:

They say: "No one but those who are Jews or Christians will enter the Garden"; that is what they take on trust; say (thou): "Produce your proof, if ye speak the truth."
Nay, whoever surrenders himself to Allah, being a well-doer, has his reward with his Lord, fear rests not upon him nor does he grieve.
The Jews say: "The Christians have no ground to stand on," and the Christians say: "The Jews have no ground to stand on"; (this) though they both recite the Book. So also those who have no knowledge[102] say much the same. Allah will judge between them on the Day of Resurrection in regard to that in which they have been differing.

[102] These are the pagan Arabs who have no knowledge of revealed religion.

While the Jews and the Christians both want him to accept their teachings, he feels that he will be under the divine displeasure unless he adheres to the revelation of which he has been made the recipient, and to that alone. These are the words which come to him (v.114): "Neither the Jews nor the Christians will be satisfied with thee until thou followest their creed; say: 'The guidance of Allah is the guidance': if thou followest their desires after the knowledge which has come to thee, there will be for thee from Allah neither protector nor helper."

After all, the religion which he is proclaiming is older, he believes, than either the Law of Moses or the Gospel of Jesus. It is, indeed, nothing other than the original religion of Abraham (v.129): "They say: 'Be ye Jews or Christians and ye will be guided'; Say (thou): 'Nay, the creed of Abraham, who was a Hanif, but was not one of the idolaters.' " The word Hanif, applied here to Abraham, occurs frequently in the Koran as the name of those who have the true religion.[103] In other verses (125f.) Muhammad calls Abraham a Muslim even more explicitly: "Who is averse to the creed of Abraham but him who is essentially stupid? We surely have chosen him in this world, and in the Hereafter he is among the upright. When his Lord said to him: 'Surrender thyself,'[104] he said: 'I have surrendered myself to the Lord of the worlds.' Abraham charged his sons therewith, and Jacob also: 'O my sons, Allah hath chosen the religion for you, so die not without becoming submissive.' "[105]

As an outward sign of the new independence of his movement, Muhammad changed the Qibla[106] or direction of prayer for his followers. Hitherto they had practiced the Jewish custom of praying in the direction of Jerusalem. In preparation, possibly, for the change, Muhammad declared (v.109): "To Allah belong the East and the West; whichever way ye turn, the face of Allah is there; verily Allah is unrestricted, knowing." Then he brought the following message, abrogating for his adherents the observance of the Jewish Qibla and instituting the custom of praying toward the Ka'bah in Mecca (vv. 136-139): "The stupids among the people will say: 'What has turned them from the qibla which they have been observing?'; say (thou): 'To Allah belongs the East and the West; he guideth whom he willeth to a straight path.' Thus have We made you a community in the middle, that ye may be witnesses in regard to the people, and

---

[103] Fr. Buhl in EI II, pp.258-260.
[105] That is, "becoming Muslims."
[104] That is, "become Muslim."
[106] C. Schoy in EI II, pp.985-989.

the messenger be in regard to you a witness. We appointed the qibla which thou hast been observing only that We might know those who would follow the messenger from those who would turn on their heels, though it was a big thing except to those whom Allah guided. But Allah was not one to let your faith go lost; verily Allah is with the people gentle and compassionate. We see thee turning thy face about in the heaven. So We shall put thee in possession of a qibla that will satisfy thee; turn thy face in the direction of the Sacred Mosque, and wherever ye are, turn your faces in its direction. Those to whom the Book has been given know that it is the truth from their Lord, and Allah is not neglectful of what they do."

Such are some of the main points in Surah II, a chapter which Muhammad very probably intended to serve as the first in the new and definitive Book which he was to give to his people. In line with this, we find in the first sentence of the Surah (v.1) the statement: "That is the Book, in which there is no doubt, guidance for those who act piously."

Are we to suppose that Muhammad was personally responsible for the recording of his revelations and pronouncements? It is not impossible that he was, either by dictation to others or by actually doing the writing himself. Dr. Bell, whose hypothesis as to the chronological periods in which the various Surahs originated has here been followed, is of the opinion that Muhammad wrote personally. He pictures the prophet as setting down his messages on small pieces of writing material as occasion permitted, and from time to time revising, correcting, and making additions between the lines, on the margins and on the backs of the sheets. Thus it is possible to explain the abundant confusion in the materials.[107]

Whether or not the theory just mentioned is correct, there can be little doubt that written collections of the prophet's sayings were in existence shortly after his death. The orthodox belief is that the scattered portions of the Qur'an were brought together in the year after the prophet's death by his secretary, Zayd ibn-Thabit, and again revised by the same person under the Caliph 'Uthman (A.D. 644-656). Modern critical study of the text of the Koran leads to the conclusion, rather, that there were various codices with varying readings in different Muslim centers until 'Uthman designated as authoritative the text used at Medina and ordered the others destroyed.[108]

[107] Bell, *The Qur'ān, Translated, with a Critical Re-arrangement of the Surahs*, I, p.vi.
[108] Arthur Jeffery, ed., *Materials for the History of the Text of the Qur'ān*, The Old

The arrangement of the Surahs in the completed Qur'an was in accordance with their length, running from the longest (Surah II) to the shortest (Surah CXIV). The following short prayer was placed as a preface to the entire collection (Surah I):

> In the Name of Allah, the Merciful, the Compassionate.
> Praise belongs to Allah, the Lord of the worlds,
> The Merciful, the Compassionate.
> Wielder of the Day of Judgment.
> Thee do we serve, and on Thee do we call for help;
> Guide us (in) the straight path,
> The path of those upon whom thou hast bestowed good,
> Not (that) of those upon whom anger falls, or those who go astray.

The making of copies of the Qur'an was always an important expression of Islamic faith, and as time went on much attention was devoted to executing these in the most beautiful manner possible. The art of calligraphy, practiced largely on such works, was most highly regarded throughout the Muslim world. Thus a fourteenth century author, Muhammad ibn-Mahmud al-Amuli, in an encyclopedic work on Muslim arts and sciences entitled *Nafa'is al-Funun*, says: "The art of writing is an honorable one and a soul-nourishing accomplishment; as a manual attainment it is always elegant, and enjoys general approval; it is respected in every land. . . . The Prophet (peace be upon him!) said: 'Beauty of handwriting is incumbent upon you, for it is one of the keys of man's daily bread.' "[109]

As we have already noted,[110] there were two kinds of North Arabic script, a round form called *naskhi* and an angular variety known as Kufic. The latter name is derived from Kufa, a city which was founded by the Muslims in A.D. 638 near the site of Babylon, and which became a very important center of Qur'anic studies.[111] The Kufic script was evidently regarded as possessing a sort of hieratic character, and for the first four centuries or so almost all the copies of the Qur'an seem to have been written in it.[112] Later the round

---

Codices, The Kitāb al-Maṣāḥif of Ibn Abī Dāwūd Together with a Collection of the Variant Readings from the Codices of Ibn Ma'sūd, Ubai, 'Alī, Ibn 'Abbas, Anas, Abū Mūsā and Other Early Qur'ānic Authorities Which Present a Type of Text Anterior to That of the Canonical Text of 'Uthmān. 1937, pp.7f.

[109] tr. Thomas W. Arnold, *Painting in Islam, A Study of the Place of Pictorial Art in Muslim Culture.* 1928, p.2.

[110] cf. above p.480 n.78; and see B. Moritz in EI I, pp.381f.,387f.

[111] K. V. Zetterstéen in EI II, pp.1105-1107.

[112] See Section I in B. Moritz, ed., *Arabic Palaeography, A Collection of Arabic Texts from the First Century of the Hidjra till the Year 1000* (Publications of the Khedivial Library, Cairo, No. 16). 1905.

script was used too, of course with certain variations in the different countries into which the Muslims went.

One of the oldest known copies of the sacred book of Islam is the famous Samarkand Kufic Qur'an. This is a parchment codex which was long in the Mosque of Khodzah-Akhrar in Samarkand, was sent to the St. Petersburg Public Library in 1869, and was returned in the early days of the Soviet Government to Samarkand. Although it is said not to have been heard of since its return, the manuscript was photographed in Russia by Dr. S. Pissareff in 1905. It is believed to have been written not later than the beginning of the second century of the Muslim era, perhaps in Iraq.[113] A photograph of a page of this manuscript is reproduced in Fig. 220.[114]

A handsome and relatively early example of a Qur'an in the Naskhi writing is the manuscript numbered N.E.-P. 27 in the University Museum of the University of Pennsylvania. This is a Persian Qur'an of the Seljuq Period, richly illuminated and definitely dated. The date appears in a colophon at the end, where we are also given the name of the master calligrapher and illuminator who did the work, as well as the place of its execution. This colophon reads: "Mahmud ibn al-Husayn, the scribe from Kirman[115] wrote it and illuminated it in the city of Hamadhan,[116] may Allah who is exalted guard it, in the last days of Jumada I of the year 559 [April, 1164]. Praise to Allah, the Lord of the Worlds, and blessing on Muhammad and his family and his relatives." The first (fol. 212-b) of the two pages containing the colophon is shown in Fig. 221. The text, with the name of the scribe and the city, appears in the narrow rectangles at the top and bottom of the page; the center is filled with a diamond-shaped figure featuring a rosette of intersecting circles together with half-circles and arabesques. The page (fol. 2-a) containing the beginning of Surah II of the Qur'an is reproduced in Fig. 222. The border of the page is composed of interlacing designs of geometrical character. As is the case throughout the work, between the lines of the text an Arabic commentary is written, on the slant, in a smaller Naskhi script.[117]

[113] Isaac Mendelsohn in *The Moslem World*. 30 (1940), pp.375-378; citing A. Shebunin in *Zapiski Vostochnago Otdieleniia Imperatorskago Russkago Arkheologicheskago Obshchestva*. 6 (1891), pp.69-133.

[114] S. Pissareff, *Curan coufique de Samarcand écrit d'après la tradition de la propre main du troisième calife Osman qui se trouve dans la bibliothèque impériale publique de St. Pétersbourg*. 1905.

[115] The same as Kerman.

[116] A rare but still standard spelling of Hamadan.

[117] Richard Ettinghausen in *Bulletin of the American Institute for Persian Art and Archaeology*. 4 (1935-36), pp.92-102.

For another example of the exquisite and detailed work lavished upon copies of the Qur'an, we show in Fig. 223 a page from a Qur'an of the Mamluk Sultan, Sha'ban (A.D. 1363-1376). It is dated in A.H. 770 = A.D. 1369.[118]

THE HADITH

Next to the Qur'an in authority for the Muslim world stands the great body of tradition known as Hadith.[119] This word means "news" and can relate to a communication or narrative of any kind. Here it is used for the whole mass of inherited information about the doings and sayings of Muhammad and his companions. At first this information was handed down orally, and then later was committed to writing in various collections.

The first of the written collections was made, according to Muslim belief, about one hundred years after the time of Muhammad, and other compilations were certainly prepared in the next two centuries or so. Any given tradition to be complete should contain two parts: first, the *isnad* or "support" which is a list of the persons who have handed down the information from one to another; second, the *matn* or text itself. In the earlier compilations the materials were arranged according to their transmitters, and such a collection was called a *musnad* or body of "supported" traditions. In the later arrangements the traditions were put together according to their content, and a collection so ordered was known as *musannaf* or "arranged."

Of the first type of collection the most important example was doubtless the Musnad of Ahmed ibn-Hanbal[120] who lived in Baghdad in the second century of the Muslim era (A.D. 780-855). As edited by his son 'Abd Allah, this voluminous work contained nearly thirty thousand traditions grouped under the names of seven hundred companions of the prophet.

Of the second type, some six collections, all of which arose during the third Muslim century, attained the highest recognition. These were made by the following authorities: (1) al-Bukhari (d. A.D. 870); (2) Muslim (d. A.D. 875); (3) Abu Dawud (d. A.D. 888); (4) al-Tirmidhi (d. A.D. 892); (5) al-Nasa'i (d. A.D. 915); (6) ibn-Madja

[118] B. Moritz, ed., *Arabic Palaeography, A Collection of Arabic Texts from the First Century of the Hidjra till the Year 1000* (Publications of the Khedivial Library, Cairo, No. 16). 1905, Pl. 57.

[119] Th. W. Juynboll in EI II, pp.189-194; Alfred Guillaume, *The Traditions of Islam, An Introduction to the Study of the Hadith Literature.* 1924; cf. A. J. Wensinck, *A Handbook of Early Muhammadan Tradition.* 1927.

[120] Goldziher in EI I, pp.188-190.

(d. A.D. 886). Together these works are known as "the six books" (al-Kutub al-Sitta), while the first two are singled out for designation as *sahih* or "sound," meaning that their tradition is utterly faultless. The first, by al-Bukhari, is the most highly regarded. Its remarkable author is said to have been acquainted with six hundred thousand traditions, to have himself memorized more than two hundred thousand, and to have put more than seven thousand in his book. His labors were performed with the utmost piety. His inspiration came, he said, from a dream in which he was driving flies away from Muhammad. An interpreter explained the flies as falsehoods which had gathered around the tradition of the prophet, and it was these which he made it his task to dispel. He never put a tradition in his collection without first making an ablution and offering a prayer.

So vast was the total literature of the Hadith that it became desirable also to make synopses and anthologies. Of these we may mention, for a single example, the Mishkatu-l-Masabih or The Niche of the Lamps by Waliu-l-Din Abu 'Abd Allah, who flourished in the fourteenth century A.D.

4. THE LIFE AND TEACHINGS OF MUHAMMAD

THE three most important sources for the life of Muhammad are the Qur'an, the Hadith, and the Arabic biographies of the prophet.[121] The nature of the first two has been dealt with in the preceding section; here we may also cite an important example of the last. This is the large biographical work of ibn-Sa'd, who died in Baghdad in A.D. 845. It is entitled Kitab al-Tabaqat or Book of the Classes, and narrates the lives of Muhammad and of his companions and successors down to the author's own time.[122]

HIS CAREER

The first definitely fixed date in the life of Muhammad is that of his migration from Mecca to Medina which took place in A.D. 622. The year of this event, known as the Hijra (Hegira), was taken as the first year of the Muslim era (A.H.).[123] Since tradition regularly places the call of Muhammad thirteen years before the Hijra, and makes the prophet forty years of age at the time of his call, we may suppose that he was born around A.D. 570. The date of his death was ten years after the removal to Medina, or A.D. 632.[124]

Many legends cluster around the birth of Muhammad, and the Qur'an itself contains a passage (LXI, 6) in which Jesus is stated to have predicted his coming: "Jesus, son of Mary, said: 'O Children of Israel, I am Allah's messenger to you, confirming the Torah which was before me, and announcing the good tidings of a messenger who will come after me, bearing the name Ahmed.'" The possible basis for this is John 16:7 where in Greek the word for Comforter($\pi\alpha\rho\acute{\alpha}\kappa\lambda\eta\tau\sigma\varsigma$) is very similar to the word for "renowned" ($\pi\epsilon\rho\iota$-

---

[121] Pfannmüller, Handbuch der Islam-Literatur, pp.128-132.

[122] E. Mittwoch in EI II, pp.413f.

[123] The Hijra occurred on September 25 but the era was reckoned from the beginning of the year which was on July 16, A.D. 622. B. Carra de Vaux in EI II, pp.302f.; Leone Caetani, Chronographia islamica ossia riassunto della storia di tutti i popoli musulmani dall'anno 1 all'anno 922 della Higrah (622-1517 dell'Era Volgare), corredato della bibliografia di tutte le principali fonti stampate e manoscritte. 1912-, I, p.3. Since the Muslim year has only 354 days, it shifts all the while in relation to the Christian year. Thus the New Year of A.H. 1367 began on November 15, 1947.

[124] For the life of Muhammad see Tor Andrae, Mohammed, The Man and His Faith. tr. Theophil Menzel. 1936; D. S. Margoliouth, Mohammed and the Rise of Islam (Heroes of the Nations). 3d ed. 1905; William Muir, The Life of Mohammad from Original Sources. rev. ed. by T. H. Weir. 1912; M. M. Ali, Mohammad, the Prophet. 1924; G. I. Kheirallah, Islam and the Arabian Prophet. 1938; A. Sprenger, Das Leben und die Lehre des Mohammad nach bisher grösstentheils unbenutzten Quellen. 3 vols. 1861-65.

κλυτός), the latter being the meaning of the names Ahmed and Muhammad.

It is fact that Muhammad was a member of the Quraish tribe in Mecca. His father was 'Abdullah and his mother Aminah. The father died before the son was born, and the mother when he was only six. He was raised then in the home of his grandfather, 'Abd al-Muttalib, who was in charge of giving water from the well Zamzam to pilgrims to Mecca. This well, incidentally, was believed to have sprung up at the command of Allah to provide water for Ishmael, son of Hagar and ancestor of the Arabs. After the grandfather's death two years later, Muhammad was kept by his uncle, Abu Talib. Although he never became a Muslim, Abu Talib always defended his nephew strongly. At the age of twenty-five Muhammad married Khadijah, a wealthy widow of forty years of age. She likewise was always a great source of strength to him. As he later thought upon Allah's kindness to him in all these regards, as well as in showing him the true religion, Muhammad wrote (Surah XCIII):

> By the morning brightness,
> By the night when it is still,
> Thy Lord hath not taken leave of thee, nor despised thee.
> The last is for thee better than the first;
> Assuredly in the end thy Lord will give thee to thy satisfaction.
> Did he not find thee an orphan and give (thee) shelter?
> Did he not find thee erring, and guide (thee)?
> Did he not find thee poor, and enrich (thee)?
>   So as for the orphan, be not (thou) overbearing;
>   And as for the beggar, scold not;
>   And as for the goodness of thy Lord, discourse (of it).

The vision which came to Muhammad in the fortieth year of his life and which marked his call to be a prophet is described as follows in the Qur'an (LIII, 1-12): "By the star when it falls, your comrade has not gone astray, nor has he erred; nor does he speak of (his own) inclination. It is nothing but a suggestion suggested, taught (him) by One strong in power, forceful; he stood straight, upon the high horizon, then he drew near, and let himself down, till he was two bow-lengths off or nearer, and suggested to his servant what he suggested. The heart did not falsify what it saw. Do ye debate with it as to what it sees?" The "One strong in power" who thus appeared to him may have been thought of by Muhammad as Allah himself, since this deity is described by the similar epithet of "Possessor of Strength" in LI, 58. On the other hand he may have

[495]

been regarded as an angel, since in another account (LXXXI, 19f.) of the same vision the divine visitant is called "a noble messenger, powerful, beside him of the throne established."

For thirteen years Muhammad is said to have preached in Mecca. His proclamation of the message of Allah seems not always to have involved a complete repudiation of the old "paganism." According to a tradition which is hardly likely to have been invented, Muhammad at one time taught that the three goddesses worshiped at Mecca as daughters of Allah were in fact angels to whom requests for intercession with the one god might properly be addressed. "Have ye considered Allat, and al-'Uzza, and the third, Manat, the other (goddess)?" Muhammad said, "These are the swans exalted; whose intercession is to be hoped for."[125] Later this compromise with polytheism was repudiated, the uttering of the teaching attributed to the inspiration of Satan, and the offending words removed from the Qur'an.[126]

When Muhammad boldly attacked the ancient Meccan faith and called for worship of Allah alone, he aroused the strong opposition of the Quraish. They called him an "insolent liar" (Surah LIV, 25f.) and subjected him to some persecution. Certain followers were won, however, among whom were the prophet's own wife Khadijah, his cousin 'Ali, son of Abu Talib, his more distant relative Abu Bakr, and 'Umar, destined to play an important part in the political establishment of Islam. Muhammad was also encouraged by the reception of further revelations, and by the experience called the "night-journey." As reported in Muslim tradition, the latter was a miraculous trip in which the prophet was taken by night from the Ka'bah at Mecca to the Temple at Jerusalem and from there up into the Seventh Heaven. The celestial part of the journey was variously supposed to have begun at the Wailing Wall or the Sacred Rock in Jerusalem, and transportation was provided by Buraq, a winged horse with a woman's head and a peacock's tail. The Qur'an makes the following reference to this event (XVII, 1): "Glory be to him who journeyed by night with his servant from the Sacred Mosque to the Furthest Mosque around which We have bestowed blessing, that We might show him some of our signs; verily he is the one who hears and sees."

In A.D. 620 the two persons who had done most to strengthen and

[125] Surah LIII, 19f. Bell, *The Qur'ān, Translated, with a Critical Re-arrangement of the Surahs,* II, p.540 n.8.
[126] cf. Surah XXII, 51. SBE IX, p.62 n.1.

protect the prophet, Khadijah and Abu Talib, died. In danger of his life in Mecca and perceiving opportunity in Medina, Muhammad made the fateful "flight" to that city in A.D. 622. Whereas the single tribe of the Quraish, now his avowed enemies, dominated Mecca, in Medina the Aus and Khazraj tribes were in strife with one another and the time seemed ripe for the arrival of a strong leader.

Taking full advantage of his opportunities, and drawing upon his continuing revelations for authorization, the prophet now embarked upon a remarkable political and military career. He speedily gained the loyalty of the people of Medina save for the three tribes of Jews resident there, and all of these, when it became evident that they could not be converted, he either drove out or slaughtered. The caravans of his old enemies, the Quraish, were raided even in the month of truce, and several pitched battles were fought with the same foes. Remarkable as it may seem, eight years after he had fled from Mecca in danger of his life, Muhammad returned to the same city as conqueror, and ere he died two years later he was actually the master of most of Arabia. Of these campaigns it is not necessary to tell more here. A detailed account may be read in the Kitab al-Maghazi or Book of the Wars by al-Waqidi, an Arab historian who lived in Medina in the second century of the Muslim era (d. A.D. 822).[127]

The home of Muhammad in Medina was a natural center for his followers. The story is that when the prophet first rode into Medina on his camel, he took the place where the beast stopped as the site for his residence. This dwelling place was built of sun-dried mud bricks, and had a large open courtyard. After the death of Khadijah, Muhammad had married two more wives, the widow Sawdah and the child 'A'ishah, and apartments were constructed for them against the outer wall of the courtyard at the south end of the east side. As the prophet took yet other wives additional places were built for them until finally there were nine huts in all. Each house was known as a *hujrah*, and had a curtained door opening into the court.

The simplicity of these structures is evident from references to them in the writings of Ibn Sa'd. This historian quotes the reports of men who saw the place within the first century of the Muslim era, as follows: "'Abd Allah ibn-Yazid relates that he saw the houses in which the wives of the Prophet dwelt, at the time when 'Umar ibn-

---

[127] tr. J. Wellhausen, *Muhammed in Medina, Das ist Vakidi's Kitab alMaghazi in verkürtzter deutscher Wiedergabe.* 1882.

'Abd al-'Aziz, governor of Medina [A.H. c.100], demolished them. They were built of unburnt bricks, and had separate apartments with partitions of palm-branches, daubed with mud; he counted nine houses, each having separate rooms, in the space extending from the house of 'A'ishah to the house of Asma' daughter of al-Husain. . . . A citizen . . . was present . . . when the dispatch of the Caliph 'Abd al-Malik (A.H. 86-88) was read aloud, commanding that these houses should be taken down and the site brought within the area of the Mosque, and he never witnessed sorer weeping than there was amongst the people that day. One exclaimed: 'I wish, by the Lord! that they would leave these houses alone just as they are; then would those that spring up hereafter in Medina, and strangers from the ends of the earth, come and see what kind of building sufficed for the Prophet's own abode, and the sight thereof would deter men from extravagance and pride.' "[128]

Although it was a private residence, the courtyard of Muhammad's home was used as a place for prayers and for the conversations of the prophet with those who came to see him. There were three doors, the principal one, through which visitors came, on the south, and one on the west and one on the east, the last being regularly used by Muhammad himself. The direction of prayer was at first toward the north, that is toward Jerusalem, and the north wall was left unbroken. When the Qibla was changed, the south door was walled up and the main entrance placed in the north wall. It is said that the companions who joined Muhammad in prayers complained of the heat of the sun in the open courtyard, and so a portico was built with palm trunks as columns supporting a roof of palm branches covered with mud. From the flat roof Muhammad later had the stentorian-voiced Abyssinian, Bilal, utter the summons to prayer. The use of the formal call to prayer (adhan) was decided upon by the prophet a year or two after coming to Medina as a mark of distinction from the Christians who summoned their faithful to church with a wooden gong, and from the Jews who employed horns. The discourses of Muhammad were delivered at first as he leaned casually against a palm trunk in the place of prayer. As his prominence increased and more people came to listen, he had a sort of pulpit constructed of tamarisk wood. This was known as a minbar, and consisted of three steps on the top one of which the prophet would sit to speak.

[128] tr. Muir, The Life of Mohammad from Original Sources, pp.534f.

The home of Muhammad was also his place of death and burial. The prophet died in the arms of his beloved wife 'A'ishah, and when the question of the burial place was raised, Abu Bakr recalled that Muhammad had once said that a prophet is buried where he passes away. He was laid to rest, therefore, in the apartment of 'A'ishah, where in their turn both Abu Bakr and 'Umar also at last were placed. 'A'ishah herself, however, by her own wish was interred in the cemetery of Baqi outside the eastern city wall of Medina.[129]

HIS RELIGION

The religion instituted by Muhammad is outlined in terms of five duties to be performed and five doctrines to be believed. Since Muhammad was not a systematic theologian, we may take it that this schematization was the work of later theologians. Nevertheless the elements of the outline are already present in the Qur'an.

The five practical duties are known as the "pillars of Islam."[130] These are the following: (1) Recital of the Profession of Faith. The profession of faith (*shahada*) comprises two conjoined affirmations: "I witness that there is no god but Allah and I witness that Muhammad is the apostle of Allah." This is virtually a combination of Surah xxvii, 26: "Allah, there is no god but he";[131] and vii, 157: "I am the messenger of Allah to you all."

(2) Recital of Prayers (*salat*). Traditionally, there are five times of prayer every day: dawn, midday, afternoon, sunset, and nightfall. The Qur'an simply says (Surah ii, 239): "Remember the prayers, the middle prayer included, and stand (in worship) to Allah reverently." The call to prayer (*adhan*), uttered from the minaret (*ma'-dhana*) of a mosque by the muezzin (*mu'adhdhin*), consists of repetition of the phrases: "Allah is most great (*Allahu akbar*). I witness that there is no god but Allah. I witness that Muhammad is the apostle of Allah. Come to prayer! Come to salvation! Allah is most great. There is no god but Allah." At the morning call the words, "Prayer is better than sleep," are added, usually between the fifth and sixth of the foregoing formulas.[132] Before prayers, ablutions must be performed in accordance with Surah v, 8: "When ye stand up for the prayer, wash your faces and your hands up to the elbows, and

---

[129] Nabia Abbott, *Aishah, The Beloved of Mohammed.* 1942, pp.69,86,100,215,218.

[130] A. J. Wensinck, *The Muslim Creed, Its Genesis and Historical Development.* 1932, p.19 n.5; H. Lammens, *Islām, Beliefs and Institutions.* tr. E. Denison Ross. 1929, pp.56-62.

[131] cf. Surah xxviii, 88.

[132] Th. W. Juynboll in ei i, p.133.

wipe your heads and your feet up to the ankles." The verse following provides that sand may be used for this if water is not available. Certain postures and prostrations are also prescribed in tradition to accompany the prayers. A complete set of prostrations together with the recital of the first Surah and at least two more verses of the Qur'an is called a *rak'a*.

(3) Almsgiving (*zakat*). This is inculcated in the Qur'an in passages like the following: "They will ask thee (for) what they should contribute; say: 'The good ye have contributed is for parents, relatives, orphans, the poor, and the follower of the way; whatever good ye do Allah knoweth" (Surah II, 211); "What ye give for usury that it may increase amongst the wealth of the people will gain no increase with Allah, but what ye give as Zakat desiring the favor of Allah—these are the ones who gain the double" (Surah XXX, 38).

(4) Fasting (*sawm*). "O ye who have believed, fasting is prescribed for you as it was for those before you; mayhap ye will show piety," declares the Qur'an (II, 179). As the passage immediately following specifies, the required fast is that of "the month of Ramadan, in which the Qur'an was sent down as guidance for the people." The fast must be kept during every day of this month, but eating and drinking are permitted throughout the night "until so much of the dawn appears that a white thread may be distinguished from a black." Other fasts are voluntary.[133]

(5) Pilgrimage to Mecca (*hajj*). "Pilgrimage to the house is due to Allah from the people, whoever is able to make his way thither," states the Qur'an (III, 91), and more details concerning the observance are specified by tradition.[134] The practice of pilgrimage was in fact very important: necessitating long journeys and meetings with pilgrims from other nations, many of whom had at least a smattering knowledge of Arabic, it furthered the diffusion of ideas and helps to explain the rather uniform appearance of Muslim art in spite of tremendous distances, differences in ethnic stock and national heritage.

The five basic doctrines are listed in a negative statement in Surah IV, 135: "Whoever disbelieves in Allah and his angels and his books and his messengers and the last day, has strayed into error far." Teachings of Muhammad on each of these five points are scattered throughout the Qur'an.

[133] C. C. Berg in EI IV, pp.192-199.
[134] A. J. Wensinck in EI II, pp.196-201.

(1) Allah. A concise definition of the nature of Allah appears in Surah cxii, a verse which Muhammad himself is traditionally reported to have declared equal in value to two-thirds of the Qur'an:[135]

> Say: "He is Allah, One,
> Allah, the Eternal;
> He brought not forth, nor hath he been brought forth;
> Co-equal with him there hath never been any one."

Slightly longer is the "verse of the throne" (Surah ii, 256), often inscribed in mosques:[136] "Allah—there is no god but he, the Living, the Eternal; slumber affects him not nor sleep; to him belongs whatever is in the heavens and whatever is in the earth; who is there that will intercede before him except by his permission? He knoweth what is before them and what is behind them, and they comprehend not anything of his knowledge but what he willeth; his throne extendeth over the heavens and the earth, to guard them wearieth him not; he is the Exalted, the Mighty."

All together, it is reckoned that ninety-nine appellations are applied to Allah in the Qur'an, and the repetition of these names is regarded as a matter of merit in accordance with the injunction of Surah vii, 179: "To Allah belong the most beautiful names; so call upon him by them."[137]

Many-sided as this multiplicity of names would indicate the character of Allah to be, his chief attribute is undoubtedly his unlimited power. In line with this, predestination is a dominant doctrine in the Qur'an.[138] Surah lxxiv, 34 states: "Thus Allah doth send astray whom he willeth and guideth whom he willeth"; and Surah iii, 139 declares: "It is not given to anyone to die except by permission of Allah written and dated." Hence it is appropriate that Islam, literally meaning "submission (to the will of Allah)," is the name of the Muhammadan faith, and Muslim, meaning "one who has submitted," is the designation of an individual believer.

(2) Angels. While Muhammad repudiated polytheism, he accepted, presumably from pagan, Jewish and Christian influences, belief in demons and angels. He taught that the demons (*jinn*) were created by Allah out of fire (Surah xv, 27), and it is stated (Surah xlvi, 28; cf. lxxii, 1) that he once preached to a band of these spirits.

---

[135] Grace H. Turnbull, *Tongues of Fire, A Bible of Sacred Scriptures of the Pagan World.* 1929, p.403 n.5.
[136] *ibid.*, p.395 n.2.
[137] Wherry, *A Comprehensive Commentary on the Qurán*, ii, p.242 n.181.
[138] D. S. Margoliouth, *Mohammed* (What Did They Teach?). 1939, pp.35f.

The angels were regarded as heavenly beings who sing hymns to Allah and intercede on behalf of men. "The heavens almost split asunder from above while the angels give glory with praise of their Lord, and ask pardon for those upon the earth" (Surah XLII, 3).

Of the angels the foremost was Gabriel, through whom the revelations of the Qur'an were brought to Muhammad. "Whoever is an enemy to Gabriel—verily he hath brought it down upon thy heart with the permission of Allah confirming what was before it, and as guidance and good tidings to the believers" (Surah II, 91). The chief spirit of evil was called Iblis, the name probably being a corruption of the Greek word for Devil (διάβολος).[139] According to Surah II, 32, the evil character of Iblis dates from his refusal to do homage to Adam as commanded by Allah: "We said to the angels: 'Prostrate yourselves to Adam'; they prostrated themselves, with the exception of Iblis; he refused in his pride and became one of the unbelievers." While from this passage Iblis would seem to have once been one of the angels, in another reference (Surah XVIII, 48) to the same act of rebellion it is explicitly stated that he was one of the jinn.

(3) Books. In addition to the book of his own revelations, Muhammad makes mention of the Torah (*Tawrat*) of Moses,[140] the Psalms (*Zabur*) of David,[141] and the Gospel (*Injil*, from εὐαγγέλιον) of Jesus.[142] All these books were sent down by Allah, the Qur'an of course being the last and containing the climactic revelation. "Verily We have sent down the Torah containing guidance and light; by it the prophets who surrendered themselves[143] gave judgment. . . . In their footsteps We caused Jesus, son of Mary, to follow, . . . and We gave him the Evangel, containing guidance and light. . . . To thee also have We sent down the Book with the truth" (Surah V, 48-52).[144]

(4) Messengers. Muhammad recognized a series of apostles who were divinely sent to particular nations or communities, and also numerous prophets who bore witness to the divine message. Of the prophets perhaps two dozen are named in the Qur'an, and of the apostles the following eight: Noah, Lot, Ishmael, Moses, Shu'aib, Hud, Salih, and Jesus. Shu'aib is to be identified with Jethro the Midianite, while Hud and Salih were messengers to Arab tribes.[145]

[139] A. J. Wensinck in EI II, pp.351f.
[140] J. Horovitz in EI IV, pp.706f.
[141] J. Horovitz in EI IV, pp.1184f.
[142] Carra de Vaux in EI II, pp.501-504.   [143] That is, were Muslims.
[144] For the Psalms see Surah XVII, 57: "To David We gave Psalms."
[145] C. R. North, *An Outline of Islâm*. 1934, pp.76f.

Jesus ('Isa)[146] is called the Messiah (Surah III, 40; IV, 169) and "pure" (Surah XIX, 19), and it is stated that "Allah raised him to himself" (Surah IV, 156).

(5) The Last Day. Here is how Muhammad described the day of judgment (Surah LXIX, 13-32):

> So when on the trumpet shall be blown a single blast,
> And the earth and the mountains shall be moved, and shattered at a single blow,
> Then will happen the thing that is to happen,
> The heaven shall be rent asunder, for then it will be weak,
> The angels (will be) on its borders, and above them eight shall then bear the throne of thy Lord.
> That day ye shall be mustered, not one of you concealed;
> As for him who is given his book[147] in his right hand, he will say: "Here, read my book,
> Verily I thought that I should meet my account."
> He shall be in pleasing life,
> In a Garden lofty,
> With clusters near:
> "Eat and drink with relish, for what ye paid in advance in the days gone-by."
> But as for him who is given his book in his left hand, he will say: "Oh, would that I had not been given my book,
> And had not known my account.
> Oh, would that it had been the finish-off![148]
> My wealth has not profited me,
> My authority has gone from me."
> "Take him and bind him,
> Then in the Hot Place roast him,
> Then in a chain of seventy cubits' reach insert him."

Other passages fill in the details concerning the realms of future blessedness and punishment. This is the prospect which awaits faithful Muslims: "Lo, the pious are in Gardens and delight, enjoying what their Lord hath bestowed upon them, and their Lord hath protected them from the punishment of the Hot Place. 'Eat and drink with relish, for what ye have been doing'" (Surah LII, 17-19). "Upon couches set with jewels, on which they recline facing each other, while round them circle boys of perpetual youth, with goblets and jugs, and a cup of flowing (wine), from which they suffer neither headache nor intoxication, and with fruit of their own choice, and

---

[146] D. B. Macdonald in EI II, pp.524-526.

[147] This is the book which contains the record of the man's deeds (cf. Surah XVII, 14f.).

[148] The man wishes that death had been the end.

bird's flesh, of what they desire; and (maidens [*houris*]) with dark, wide eyes, like pearls treasured—a recompense for what they have been doing" (Surah LVI, 15-23). But this is what confronts unbelievers: "Verily We have prepared for the wrong-doers a Fire, the awnings of which have encompassed them, and if they call for aid they will be sprinkled with water like molten metal which will broil their faces; a bad drink, and a bad place to lie in!" (Surah XVIII, 28).

As the discussion and clarification of these doctrines proceeded through the centuries, detailed and lengthy creeds were formulated. Reference to one of these will show how the implications of the Muslim faith were set forth. The creed here selected is the so-called Fiqh Akbar II, which probably originated in the first half of the tenth century A.D. It consists of twenty-nine Articles, the nature of which will be indicated by the following much abbreviated quotations:

1. The heart of the confession of the unity of Allah and the true foundation of faith consist in this obligatory creed: I believe in Allah, his angels, his books, his apostles, the resurrection after death, the decree of Allah the good and the evil thereof, computation of sins, the balance, Paradise and Hell; and that all these are real.

2. Allah the exalted is one, not in the sense of number, but in the sense that he has no partner.

3. The Koran is the speech of Allah.

4. Allah is thing, not as other things but in the sense of positive existence.

5. Allah has not created things from a pre-existent thing.

6. Allah created the creatures free from unbelief and from belief. Allah did not compel any of his creatures to be infidels or faithful. He created them as individuals, and faith and unbelief are the acts of men.

7. All acts of obedience are obligatory on account of Allah's command. All acts of disobedience happen through his knowledge, decision, decree and will; not according to his wish, good pleasure, or command.

8. All the prophets are exempt from sins, yet stumbling and mistakes may happen on their part.

9. Muhammad is his beloved. He did not serve idols, nor was he at any time a polytheist, even for a single moment. And he never committed a light or a grave sin.

10. The most excellent of men after the apostle of Allah is abu Bakr; after him, 'Umar; after him, 'Uthman; after him, 'Ali.

11. We declare no Muslim an infidel on account of any sin.

12. The moistening of the shoes is commendable.[149]

13. Prayer behind every faithful man, be he of good or of bad behavior, is valid.

14. We do not say that sins will do no harm to the faithful.

[149] This refers to sectarian arguments about foot washing.

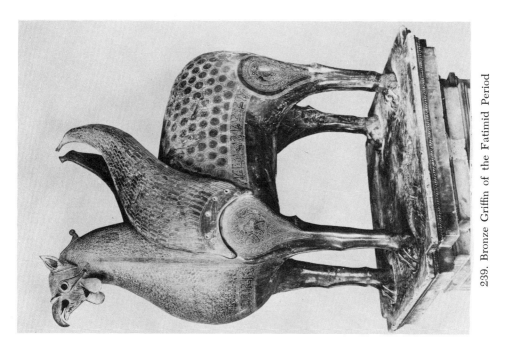

239. Bronze Griffin of the Fatimid Period

238. Fatimid Ewer of Carved Rock Crystal

240. Interior of the Great Mosque of Cordova

242. Inside the Mosque of Qa'it-bay

241. The Mosque of Qa'it-bay

243. The Mosque
at Varamin

244. The Tomb of
Timur at Samarkand

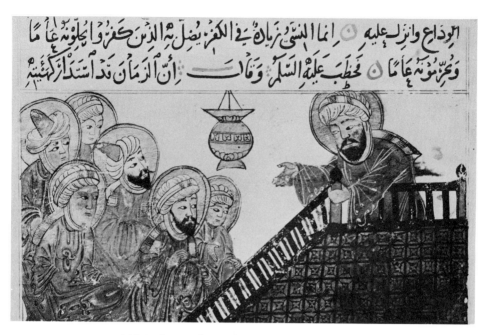

245. Muhammad Preaching His Farewell Sermon

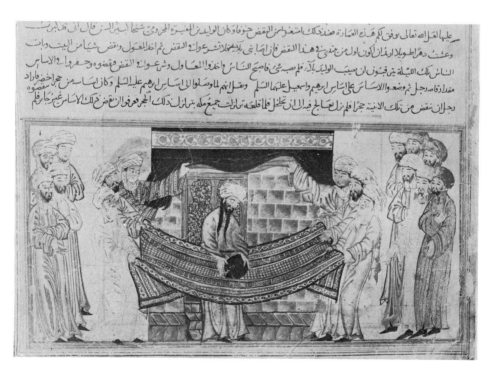

246. Muhammad Replacing the Black Stone in the Ka'bah

247. Muhammad's Visit to Paradise

248. Muhammad Seated among His Companions

249. Dancing Dervishes

15. If any work be mixed with ostentation, its reward is forfeited.

16. The signs of the prophets and the miracles of the saints are a reality.

17. Allah will be seen in the world to come.

18. Faith consists in confessing and believing.

19. We know Allah with adequate knowledge.

20. The intercession of the prophets is a reality.

21. The weighing of works in the balance on the day of resurrection is a reality.

22. Allah guideth whomsoever he pleaseth, by grace, and he leadeth astray whomsoever he pleaseth, by justice.

23. The interrogation of the dead in the tomb by Munkar and Nakir[150] is a reality.

24. It is allowable to follow scholars in expressing the qualities of Allah in Persian, in all instances except in the case of Allah's hand.

25. Allah's being near or far is not to be understood in the sense of a shorter or longer distance. The obedient is near to him, without how, and the disobedient is far from him, without how.

26. The Koran is revealed to the apostle of Allah. The verses are all equal in excellence and greatness.

27. Kasim, Tahir and Ibrahim were the sons of the apostle of Allah. Fatimah, Rukaiya, Zainab and Umm Kulthum were all of them daughters of the apostle of Allah.

28. When a man is uncertain concerning any of the subtleties of theology, it is his duty to cling for the time being to the orthodox faith.

29. The report of the ascension is a reality. The descent of 'Isa from heaven, as well as the other eschatological signs according to the description thereof in authentic tradition, are a reality that will take place. Allah guideth to the straight way whomsoever he willeth.[151]

MECCA AND MEDINA

The two cities which were the chief foci of the life and work of Muhammad have remained virtually inaccessible to the outside world. The prophet himself forbade the visit of unbelievers to Mecca, declaring after his taking of that city: "O ye who have believed, the polytheists are simply filth, so after this present year they shall not approach the Sacred Mosque" (Surah IX, 28); and the interdict has generally been held to apply also to Medina, the sacred burial place of the founder of Islam. Known as al-Haramain, the restricted region has been penetrated by a few western visitors from whose reports it is possible to gain some conception of Islam's two most holy sites.[152]

As seen by Eldon Rutter in 1925-1926, Mecca was "a little old ugly

---

[150] These are two angels.
[151] tr. Wensinck, *The Muslim Creed*, pp.188-197.
[152] Samuel M. Zwemer in *The Moslem World*. 37 (1947), pp.7-15.

Arab town, bare of ornament, but full of fascination."[153] The pilgrim road from Jidda leads in toward the heart of the city and connects through the narrow Zugag es-Suwag with the Suq es-Saghir. The latter is a wadi not infrequently filled with flood water, and at the same time a market street and the main thoroughfare leading to the Sacred Mosque.

The Masjid al-Haram, as the Sacred Mosque is called, is surrounded by a wall with nineteen gates and six minarets. Within the wall are colonnades running around the sides of a large open area. In the center stands the Kaʻbah, a roughly cubical structure, approximately thirty-eight feet long, thirty-one feet wide, and thirty-four feet high. The famous Black Stone is embedded in the southeast corner of the Kaʻbah, about five feet from the ground. Having inspected it carefully, Richard F. Burton was persuaded that it was originally an aerolite.[154] Other structures in the Haram are the building over the well Zamzam, the great pulpit, and two small mosques. A general view of the city and the Sacred Mosque is shown in Fig. 224; a closer view of the Kaʻbah itself in Fig. 225.

As in Mecca, so too in Medina the most sacred shrine stands in the heart of the city. This is the Masjid al-Nebi or Prophet's Mosque, which is the home of Muhammad transformed by successive rebuildings into an actual mosque. This development was natural enough in view of the prophet's use of his courtyard as a place of prayer and of address, and a strong impetus in the same direction came from the fact of his burial there in the apartment (*hujrah*) of ʻAʾishah. Today the mosque is in the form of a large courtyard, marked out with tall minarets at the corners, and surrounded by domed colonnades. In the southeast corner of the mosque there is a rectangular enclosure, within which is a five-sided chamber some twenty feet in height. Surmounting the chamber is a large green dome. This is still called the Hujrah, and is supposed to have once been the apartment of ʻAʾishah. Within the sanctified darkness of this place are said to be the three tombs of Muhammad, Abu Bakr and ʻUmar, while one empty place is traditionally reserved for ʻIsa on his second coming. Adjacent to the Hujrah is a smaller enclosure containing the reputed sepulcher of Fatimah, daughter of Muhammad and Khadi-

153 Eldon Rutter, *The Holy Cities of Arabia*. 1928, i, p.124; cf. C. Snouck Hurgronje, *Bilder aus Mekka, mit kurzem erläuterndem Texte*. 1889.
154 Richard F. Burton, *Personal Narrative of a Pilgrimage to al-Madinah and Meccah*. 1907, ii, p.169.

jah, and wife of 'Ali. The Mosque of the Prophet is illustrated in Fig. 226. The large dome in line with the minaret is that above the grave of the prophet and his successors.[155]

[155] Rutter, *The Holy Cities of Arabia*, II, p.234; John F. Keane, *My Journey to Medinah: Describing a Pilgrimage to Medinah, Performed by the Author Disguised as a Mohammedan.* 1881, pp.108f.; Traugott Mann, *Der Islam einst und jetzt* (Monographien zur Weltgeschichte). 1914. Fig. 25.

5. THE ORTHODOX CALIPHS, A.D. 632-661

As STATED in Article 27 of the creed quoted in the preceding section, Muhammad had several sons, but none of these survived him. Upon his own death, therefore, the leadership of his movement passed in turn to a series of four of his closest associates. These were the "most excellent of men" named in Article 10 of the same creed, and the dates of their rule were as follows: Abu Bakr, A.D. 632-634; 'Umar, 634-644; 'Uthman, 644-656; 'Ali, 656-661. They bore the title of Caliph (*khalifah*)[156] meaning Successor (of Muhammad), and each was chosen to office by a sort of informal election upon the death of his predecessor. Upon the four, Arab historians bestow the designation of "orthodox." The first three ruled at Medina, while 'Ali made his capital at Kufa. Within the period of their rule, Syria, Palestine, Iraq, Persia and Egypt were all subjugated to Islam.

Wherever they went the Muslims fiercely maintained their loyalty to the teachings of Muhammad, and as he had instructed them continued to turn their faces to Mecca in prayer. When they had a formal place of prayer it was known as a mosque, the Arabic word being *masjid*, meaning a place of prostration.[157] The fundamental elements of a mosque were those which we have already seen in Muhammad's home in Medina: a court, a shelter over the worshipers, and a pulpit. There too, it will be remembered, the call to prayer was uttered from the roof. In the fully developed Arab mosque, a tall tower or minaret (*ma'dhana*) provided a vantage point from which to give the call to prayer (*adhan*), while the courtyard not only served as a kind of neutral zone shielding the inner sanctuary from the busy outer world, but also had in its center the fountain where ablutions were performed before prayer. The place of prayer proper was usually an arcaded or colonnaded rectangle, much wider than it was deep; thus it was well qualified to house a congregation which during prayer was like a body of soldiers, arranged in long rows of worshipers and performing certain movements of the body. The direction of prayer (*qibla*) was marked by a *mihrab* or niche in the wall toward which the worshipers faced, and not far away was the *minbar* or pulpit. Genetically connected with the apse in a Christian basilica, the *mihrab* was much different in character.[158] Whereas the

---

[156] Thomas W. Arnold, *The Caliphate*. 1924, pp.19-54; Pringle Kennedy, *Arabian Society at the Time of Muhammad*. 1926, pp.31-100.
[157] J. Pedersen, R. A. Kern and E. Diez in EI III, pp.315-389
[158] E. Diez in EI III, pp.485-490.

basilican apse housed the altar and provided a place for religious pictures in the form of mosaics or paintings, the *mihrab* was left empty and usually only decorated with floral, geometric or epigraphic designs. The ornamentation of the whole mosque was also carried out only in decorative script, usually texts from the Qur'an, and in the intricate patterns known as arabesques.[159] Here too the abstract character of strictly monotheistic Islam is clearly revealed.

In the course of time and in the various lands into which Islam went, Muslim architecture naturally underwent variation. Some mosques were built as tombs, others for the purpose of housing the *madrasa* or religious academy which became so important in Islam. In Persia, the *madrasa*-mosque assumed a distinctive form in that there was a large hall or *iwan* running out from each side of the courtyard, which served as a lecture room for one of the four faculties in Muslim theology and jurisprudence. Characteristic, too, was a lofty dome erected above the *mihrab* or the founder's tomb. In Turkey, Byzantine influence accentuated the importance of the dome, and the Turkish mosque was usually an immense centralized domed building.

At the outset, Islamic expansion involved in many cases the conquest of a town in the Christian world. Here the Muslims might simply arrange to share in the use of one of the churches which was already there, employing some agreed-upon part of it as their own place of devotion; or they might take it over outright and convert it into a mosque. The marks of this process may still be seen at Hama in Syria, for example, where the front of a Christian church of the fifth or sixth century is preserved in the west wall of the Great Mosque.[160]

In the event of the foundation of a new city it was of course necessary to arrange a place of worship from the beginning. The first town so founded was Basra in Mesopotamia, which was settled to some extent in A.D. 635 and permanently occupied from 638 on. At the outset the place of prayer here was simply a marked out area, possibly enclosed by a fence of reeds. Later it was walled with sun-dried bricks and roofed on the Qibla side with brushwood. Similarly at Kufa, founded in A.D. 637, the place of prayer was a square area surrounded by a ditch, perhaps with a roofed colonnade at the south or Qibla side. In Egypt the new Muslim capital was called al-Fustat

[159] E. Diez, *Glaube und Welt des Islam.* 1941, pp.176-179.
[160] CEMA I, p.14.

(from Latin *fossatum* = camp) since it was the place where the conqueror, 'Amr ibn-al-'Asi, made his camp.[161] A mosque was built by 'Amr at the same time that the town was started (A.D. 641/42). It was probably built of mud bricks and covered with a roof of palm branches and mud supported on palm trunk pillars.[162]

Along with Mecca the most holy places of the Muslim world were Medina, sanctified by the later life, death and burial of the prophet, and Jerusalem, rendered more sacred by the traditional visit of Muhammad on his "night-journey." The early Caliphs probably interested themselves in at least limited building works in all three places. In A.D. 638 'Umar went on pilgrimage to Mecca, and finding that the Ka'bah had been washed away by a great flood, rebuilt this sanctuary, enlarging and walling in the surrounding space. At about the same time 'Umar also made enlargements in the former residence of Muhammad at Medina, which was increasingly in use for the purposes of a mosque. The same year (A.D. 638) was the date of the surrender of Jerusalem to the Muslim forces. There the Temple Area had evidently remained in ruins since the time of Titus (A.D. 70). It is probable that 'Umar caused this area to be cleared, and in it constructed a relatively simple, timber-roofed mosque. If this is correct this is the origin of the Aqsa Mosque at Jerusalem, a structure often rebuilt in later centuries.[163] 'Uthman, successor of 'Umar, is known to have carried out further enlargements in the sanctuaries at Medina and Mecca.[164]

[161] This was in the vicinity of modern Cairo.
[162] CEMA I, pp.15-18,28.
[163] It is not to be confused with the Dome of the Rock which will be described later.
[164] CEMA I, pp.19,25,31.

6. THE UMAYYADS OF DAMASCUS, A.D. 661-750

AFTER the four "orthodox" Caliphs there were several great dynasties which held sway in the Islamic world.[165] The first of these was established by Mu'awiyah, who had been governor of Syria and a rival of 'Ali. With his victory, finally accomplished by the murder of 'Ali, Damascus became the capital of the Muslim empire. He was able to hand down his authority to his son, and the hereditary principle thus introduced into the succession was influential from then on. Himself the son of Umayyah, the line which he established was known as that of the Umayyad Caliphs,[166] and it endured from A.D. 661 to 750. In this period the Muslim conquests were extended in the east to the Indus Valley and beyond the Oxus River to the borders of China, and in the west all the way across North Africa and into Spain.

Of the Umayyad Caliphs the two of most interest for our account are 'Abd al-Malik (A.D. 685-705) and his son al-Walid (A.D. 705-715). The former was the builder of the Dome of the Rock at Jerusalem, and the latter of the Great Mosque at Damascus.

THE DOME OF THE ROCK AT JERUSALEM

The authority of 'Abd al-Malik was contested during the early part of his reign by a rival Caliph, Ibn al-Zubayr of Mecca. According to the Arabic historian Ya'qubi (A.D. 874), the latter made a practice of seizing and exploiting Syrian pilgrims to Mecca. Hence 'Abd al-Malik resolved to make the Sacred Rock (as-Sakhra) at Jerusalem, rather than Mecca, the place of pilgrimage for his subjects. This was the ancient rock which formed the highest point in the Temple Area and on which David's altar probably once stood.[167] It was also easily possible to suppose that this was the precise point from which Muhammad had made his miraculous ascent to heaven. So 'Abd al-Malik proceeded as follows, as Ya'qubi relates:

Then 'Abd al-Malik forbade the people of Syria to make the pilgrimage [to Mecca]; and this by reason that 'Abd Allah ibn al-Zubayr was wont to seize on them during the time of the pilgrimage, and force them to pay him allegiance—which, 'Abd al-Malik having knowledge of, forbade the people to journey forth to Mecca. But the people murmured thereat, say-

[165] Philip K. Hitti, *The Arabs, A Short History*. 1946, p.64.
[166] For the genealogical interrelationships of the Umayyads, 'Abbasids and Fatimids, see the table in HHA p.184 n.2.
[167] FLP p.151.

ing, "How dost thou forbid us to make the pilgrimage to Allah's house, seeing that the same is a commandment of Allah upon us?" But the Caliph answered them, "Hath not ibn-Shihab al-Zuhri [a famous student of tradi- tion, d. A.D. 742] told you how the Apostle of Allah did say: *Men shall journey to but three Masjids, al-Masjid Haram [at Mecca], my Masjid [at Medina], and the Masjid of the Holy City [Jerusalem]?* So this last is now appointed for you in lieu of the Masjid al-Haram [of Mecca]. And this Rock, of which it is reported that upon it the Apostle of Allah set his foot when he ascended into heaven, shall be unto you in the place of the Ka'bah." Then 'Abd al-Malik built above the Sakhra a Dome, and hung it around with curtains of brocade, and he instituted door-keepers for the same, and the people took the custom of circumambulating the Rock, even as they had paced round the Ka'bah, and the usage continued thus all the days of the dynasty of the Umayyads.[168]

The structure which 'Abd al-Malik thus erected in Jerusalem was not a mosque (*masjid*) but a shrine (*mashhad*) or "place of witness," that is a sanctuary built over a sacred object, in this case the ancient Rock. Its proper name is the Dome of the Rock (Kubbet as-Sakhra). In its essential structure, a circle of four masonry piers and twelve marble columns encloses the great rock and upholds a drum and lofty timber dome; surrounding this inner circle is an octagonal colonnade and an outer octagonal wall in each face of which are five windows; and in the drum above the roof of the octagon are sixteen windows. The entire impression is one of extraordinary symmetry.[169]

The Dome of the Rock is the oldest existing monument of Muslim architecture, and one of the oldest known Islamic inscriptions is pre- served in the mosaics which run around the octagon. This inscription is written in Kufic script and contains verses from the Qur'an. At the east end of the south face the inscription contains a dedication which begins, "Hath built this dome the servant of Allah," and ends, "In the year two and seventy—Allah accept of him!" The year A.H. 72 is equivalent to A.D. 691 and falls within the reign of 'Abd al-Malik, whose name without doubt stood originally in the middle of the inscription. The name that is there now, however, is that of the 'Ab- basid Caliph al-Ma'mun (A.D. 813-833), who undertook restorations on the Dome of the Rock over a century after its erection. At that

---

[168] Quoted in CEMA I, p.43. Shelomo Dov Goitein questions this account by Ya'qubi and thinks that the building of the Dome of the Rock was motivated primarily by the desire to erect a structure which would rival the splendid Christian churches of the time. See JAOS 70 (1950), pp.104-108.

[169] Ernest T. Richmond, *The Dome of the Rock in Jerusalem, A Description of Its Structure and Decoration.* 1924, pp.7-10.

time he removed the name of 'Abd al-Malik and inserted his own, not, however, remembering to change the date too![170]

The photograph reproduced in Fig. 227 shows a portion of the interior of this structure, particularly revealing the arrangement of the columns and piers which support the drum and dome.[171]

THE GREAT MOSQUE AT DAMASCUS

Al-Walid's most notable architectural work was the Great Mosque at Damascus, a structure which takes rank as perhaps the most famous mosque in Islam and the sanctuary of greatest holiness after Mecca, Medina and Jerusalem. In part at least the motive back of its erection was the desire to provide for the Muslims a place of worship which would rival the churches of the Christians in Syria. This fact is stated by the Arabic geographer al-Muqaddasi (A.D. 985) in the following words: "Now one day I said, speaking to my father's brother, 'O my uncle, verily it was not well of the Caliph al-Walid to expend so much of the wealth of the Muslims on the Mosque at Damascus. Had he expended the same on making roads, or for caravanserais, or in the restoration of the Frontier Fortresses, it would have been more fitting and more excellent of him.' But my uncle said to me in answer, 'O my little son, thou hast not understanding! Verily al-Walid was right, and he was prompted to a worthy work. For he beheld Syria to be a country that had long been occupied by the Christians, and he noted herein the beautiful churches still belonging to them, so enchantingly fair, and so renowned for their splendor, even as are the Qumama [the Church of the Holy Sepulcher at Jerusalem], and the churches of Lydda and Edessa. So he sought to build for the Muslims a mosque that should prevent their regarding these, and that should be unique and a wonder to the world.' "[172]

As made known both by actual remains and by notices of ancient authors, the Great Mosque had an extremely interesting history which is probably to be reconstructed somewhat as follows. The area which the mosque occupies was originally the precinct of a Roman temple, dedicated to Jupiter Damascenus and inscriptionally dated in the third century A.D. At the end of the fourth century under the Emperor Theodosius the Great (A.D. 379-395) the pagan temple became a place of Christian worship. Probably a Christian church

[170] CEMA I, pp.46f.
[171] Richmond, *The Dome of the Rock in Jerusalem*, Fig. 3; see also FLP Figs. 63,64.
[172] Quoted in CEMA I, p.101.

of limited size was built within the western part of the entire temple enclosure. Because the "head" of John the Baptist was transferred here at a later date the church received the name of that personage. When the Muslims first took Damascus (A.D. 635) they shared the large temple enclosure with the Christians and had their place of prayer at one end while the church was at the other. This situation is referred to by the Arab historian Ibn Shakir (d. A.D. 1362) when he says that the Christians and Muslims "entered by the same doorway, which was that of the original temple, placed on the south side where is now the great mihrab. Then the Christians turned to the west towards their church, and the Muslims to the right to reach their mosque."[173] Finally when al-Walid became Caliph, both because of the reason already cited from al-Muqaddasi and because of the large increase in the number of Muslims, the entire area was taken over, the church torn down, and the whole turned into a mosque. Four Roman towers stood at the four corners of the ancient temple enclosure, and these were used for minarets or places from which the call to prayer (*adhan*) was given.[174] Notable mosaics provided the decorations.[175]

As described by the Arab travelers, Ibn Jubayr (last quarter of the twelfth century) and Ibn Batuta (second quarter of the fourteenth century), the Great Mosque at Damascus was a place of much splendor. "I entered Damascus on Thursday 9th Ramadan 726 [August 9, A.D. 1326]," writes Ibn Batuta, "and lodged at the Malikite college called ash-Sharabishiya. Damascus surpasses all other cities in beauty, and no description, however full, can do justice to its charms. Nothing, however, can better the words of Ibn Jubayr in describing it. The Cathedral Mosque, known as the Umayyad Mosque, is the most magnificent mosque in the world, the finest in construction and noblest in beauty, grace and perfection; it is matchless and unequalled."[176]

Several times destroyed and reconstructed in following centuries, a view of this famous mosque is given in Fig. 228.[177]

While the Umayyad capital was at Damascus, these rulers never forgot their Bedouin heritage and lived by preference at camps in

[173] Quoted in CEMA I, p.135.
[174] CEMA I, pp.38f.
[175] Marguerite van Berchem in CEMA I, pp.229-252; AJA 51 (1947), p.194.
[176] tr. H. A. R. Gibb, *Ibn Battúta, Travels in Asia and Africa, 1325-1354, Translated and Selected* (The Argonaut Series). 1929, p.65.
[177] CEMA I, Pl. 38,c.

the desert. There they constructed various residences and forts, the ruins of which still stand. It will suffice to mention two examples of these secular sites.

QUSAYR 'AMRAH

Qusayr 'Amrah, meaning the "little castle of 'Amrah," stands on the edge of a wadi in the desert east of the northern end of the Dead Sea. The site and structure are shown in an air view in Fig. 229. The building, which is made of limestone blocks, comprises a rectangular audience hall with vaulted roof and apsidal rooms at the end, and a bath with two rooms vaulted and one covered by a dome.

The most remarkable feature of Qusayr 'Amrah are the frescoes with which its walls and vaults are painted. In an alcove which was directly opposite the main entrance and which probably served as a throne recess there is a painting of a monarch seated upon a throne and resting his feet upon a footstool. At the south end of the west wall of the main room is a painting showing six royal figures. Accompanying superscriptions in Arabic and Greek lead to the identification of these persons with sovereigns of states overcome by the Umayyads, and make probable a date for the building and its paintings in the reign of al-Walid. Other subjects among the frescoes include figures which symbolize Poesy, History and Philosophy; scenes of the bath, gymnasium, dance and hunt; and a painting, in the dome of the bath, of the signs of the Zodiac.[178]

MSHATTA

Mshatta, located between Qusayr 'Amrah and the Dead Sea, belongs almost certainly to the Umayyad Period and may have been built by al-Walid II who reigned but briefly A.D. 743-744. His death would account for the unfinished state in which the work was left. The ruins consist of a large walled enclosure strengthened with numerous half-round towers, inside which are various courts, halls and rooms. The entrance is in the center of the south side of the enclosure, and here the walls and two half-octagonal towers are decorated with extremely rich carvings.

The nature of this decoration may be seen in Fig. 230 where a portion of the tower flanking the west side of the entrance is shown. The leading motifs are triangles, rosettes and tendrils. Beneath the

---

[178] CEMA I, p.264, Pl. 47,b; Jaussen and Savignac, *Mission archéologique en Arabie*, III, *Les châteaux arabes de Qeṣeir 'Amra, Ḥarâneh et Ṭûba*. 1922, pp.97f.,111; Ernst Diez, *Die Kunst der islamischen Völker* (Handbuch der Kunstwissenschaft). 1917, p.27.

central rosette is a chalice out of which a lion, on the left, and a griffin, on the right, are drinking. Another lion sits in the lower right corner, and some other animal in the lower left corner. Amidst the tendrils around the rosette are a number of birds, and in the rosette are leaves and perhaps a sunflower. The upper parts of the carving are not completely finished.[179]

[179] CEMA I, pp.397f.,403, Pl. 71.

7. THE 'ABBASIDS, A.D. 750-1258

IN THE middle of the eighth century, the 'Abbasids, descendants of an uncle of Muhammad named al-'Abbas, wrested power from the Umayyads. At first they ruled over the whole caliphate, with the exception of Spain; after some time, however, they progressively lost parts of the western regions and eventually ruled only over the eastern part of the Muslim world. The period of their dominion was the golden age of Islamic civilization, and Baghdad, their capital, became a city of fabulous wealth and splendor. Their most famous ruler was the Caliph Harun al-Rashid (A.D. 786-809).

While Baghdad was completely destroyed by the Mongols in A.D. 1258, we learn from descriptions that it was built in circular form, with a surrounding moat and three concentric walls. Four gates placed at equal distances in the walls gave access from the southwest, southeast, northeast and northwest. The distance from one outer gate to the next was said to be seventy-five hundred feet, so that the total circumference of the city was over five and one-half miles. From each of the gates a main thoroughfare led directly to the central circle within the city where were the palace of the Caliph, called the Golden Gate or the Green Dome, and beside it the Great Mosque.[180]

A tremendous intellectual activity unfolded at this time. It was manifest during the first century of the 'Abbasid Period by the translation into Arabic of Persian, Sanskrit, Syriac and Greek writings, and after that by the development of original and notable work in the sciences of medicine, astronomy, geography, mathematics and alchemy leading to chemistry, and in philosophy, history, ethics and literature.[181]

THE SECTS OF ISLAM

Major sectarian divisions also were now fully evident within Islam. According to a tradition cited by the theologian al-Baghdadi (d. A.D. 1037) in the beginning of his work on Muslim schisms and sects, Muhammad himself had prophesied that his followers would form no less than seventy-three groups, surpassing the sectarian separations of both Jews and Christians: "The tradition has come down to us through the following chain of authorities: Abu Sahl

[180] Joseph Hell, *The Arab Civilization.* tr. S. Khuda Bukhsh. 1926, pp.67f.
[181] Hitti, *The Arabs, A Short History*, p.118.

Bishr ibn-Ahmad ibn-Bashshar al-Isfara'ini, 'Abd Allah ibn-Najiyah, Wahb ibn-Bakiyyah, Khalid ibn-'Abdallah, Muhammad ibn-'Amr, Abu Salmah, Abu Hurairah that the last said, the prophet of Allah —peace be unto him—said: 'The Jews are divided into 71 sects, and the Christians are divided into 72 sects, and my people will be divided into 73 sects.'[182]

The two chief groups are those of the Sunnites and the Shi'ites. The Sunnites constitute the orthodox party in Islam, and numerically speaking are greatly in the majority. They are devoted to the *sunnah* or "usage" of Muhammad as embodied in the tradition (*hadith*).[183] The Shi'ites comprise the "following" of 'Ali. This man, it will be remembered, was the cousin of Muhammad and husband of the prophet's daughter Fatimah, and was murdered in the midst of the struggles by which the Umayyad dynasty was established. 'Ali was rightfully succeeded, the Shi'ites believe, by his son al-Hasan, then by his other son al-Husayn, and then by nine descendants of the latter, one after another. These twelve personages are called Imams by the Shi'ites, and regarded as having a divine right of rule.[184] The last of the twelve, a young man named Muhammad, disappeared, they say, in A.D. 878 in the cave of the mosque at Samarra. He is thought to be still alive, but "hidden," and it is believed that he will eventually reappear as the Mahdi or "divinely guided one" to restore the true religion, conquer the world for Islam and reign in a splendid millennium.[185] The chief center of the Shi'ites is in Persia,[186] although this has not at all times been the case; in the tenth to twelfth centuries, for example, Egypt under the Fatimids was the foremost Shi'ite state.

Of the other sects, most interest attaches to the Sufis. These are

---

[182] tr. Kate C. Seelye, *Moslem Schisms and Sects (Al-Farḳ Bain al-Firaḳ), Being the History of the Various Philosophic Systems Developed in Islam, by abū-Manṣūr 'abd-al-Ḳāhir ibn-Ṭāhir al-Baghdādī (d. 1037), Part I, Translated from the Arabic* (Columbia University Oriental Studies, 15). 1919, p.21. Part II of this work is translated by Abraham S. Halkin, 1935.

[183] W. M. Patton in HERE XII, pp.114-119.

[184] HHA pp.440f.; W. M. Patton in HERE XI, pp.453-458; Dwight M. Donaldson, *The Shi'ite Religion, A History of Islam in Persia and Iraḳ.* 1933.

[185] D. B. Macdonald in EI III, pp.111-115; D. S. Margoliouth in HERE VIII, pp.336-340.

[186] It was in Persia in A.D. 1844 that 'Ali Muhammad claimed to be the Bab or "gate" through whom communication could be had with the Hidden Imam. The Bab was put to death only six years after his "manifestation," but in 1863 a new "manifestation" was found in Baha'u'llah or "the Splendor of God" (d. 1892). Known at first as Babism, the religion thus founded is now called Bahaism. Edward G. Browne in HERE II, pp.299-308; Mann, *Der Islam einst und jetzt*, pp.147-150; Mirza Ahmad Sohrab in Vergilius Ferm, ed., *Religion in the Twentieth Century.* 1948, pp.307-314.

the mystics of Islam. Deriving their name from the *suf* or wool of which their white cloaks were made, they have commonly organized themselves in brotherhoods and sought by practices of devotion and contemplation to achieve union with the divine love. Members of the orders are often called Dervishes, this word signifying mendicants and being applicable to ascetic devotees. Philosophically, the Sufis attribute reality to God alone, but teach that through the beatific vision the finite soul of man may attain knowledge of the divine Unity and be absorbed in it. In the words of Von Grunebaum, "Love is the mood of the Sûfî, gnosis his aim, ecstasy his supreme experience."[187]

Orthodoxy and mysticism were combined in the teachings of the man who was probably the greatest theologian ever to arise in Islam and who lived in the period of which we are now speaking. This was al-Ghazzali,[188] who was born at Tus in A.D. 1058, lived as a recluse at Damascus and Jerusalem, taught at Baghdad and Nishapur, and died in Tus in 1111. A single quotation must suffice to suggest the nature of his thought and writing: "Know, therefore, that your companion who never deserts you at home or abroad, when you are asleep or when you are awake, whether you are dead or alive, is your Lord and Master, your Creator and Preserver, and whensoever you remember him he is sitting beside you. For God himself hath said, 'I am the close companion of those who remember me.' And whenever your heart is contrite with sorrow because of your neglect of religion he is your companion who keeps close to you, for God hath said, 'I am with those who are broken-hearted on my account.' And if you only knew him as you ought to know him you would take him as a companion and forsake all men for his sake. But as you are unable to do this at all times, I warn you that you set aside a certain time by night and by day for communion with your Creator that you may delight yourself in him and that he may deliver you from evil."[189]

[187] Gustave E. von Grunebaum, *Medieval Islam, A Study in Cultural Orientation* (An Oriental Institute Essay). 1946, p.133. For the Sufis see pp.133-141 in this work, and also Louis Massignon in EI IV, pp.681-685; Reynold A. Nicholson, *The Mystics of Islam.* 1914; and in HERE XII, pp.10-17; Arthur J. Arberry, *An Introduction to the History of Ṣūfism* (The Sir Abdullah Suhrawardy Lectures for 1942); D. S. Margoliouth in HERE IV, pp.641-643; John P. Brown, *The Darvishes or Oriental Spiritualism.* ed. H. A. Rose. 1927.

[188] Margaret Smith, *Al-Ghazālī the Mystic, A Study of the Life and Personality of Abū Ḥāmid Muḥammad al-Ṭūsī al-Ghazālī, Together with an Account of His Mystical Teaching and an Estimate of His Place in the History of Islamic Mysticism.* 1944; Samuel M. Zwemer, *A Moslem Seeker after God: Showing Islam at Its Best in the Life and Teaching of Al-Ghazali, Mystic and Theologian of the Eleventh Century.* 1920.

[189] tr. Zwemer, *A Moslem Seeker after God,* pp.248f.

SAMARRA

The most impressive extant monuments of the 'Abbasid Period are the ruins of Samarra. This was a city sixty miles up the Tigris River from Baghdad to which the eighth 'Abbasid Caliph, al-Mu'tasim (A.D. 833-842), transferred the seat of government (836) and which remained the capital until 892. The reason for the removal was the unrest created in Baghdad by al-Mu'tasim's introduction of Turkish troops for his bodyguard. This action indeed foreshadowed future events, inasmuch as other Turks eventually assumed the rule, the Seljuqs from A.D. 1037 and the Ottoman Turks from 1299 on.[190]

At Samarra al-Mu'tasim built an enormous palace known as the Jausaq al-Khaqani. Of this, the best preserved portion is the Bab al-'Amma or Hall of Public Audience, the façade of which, consisting of three great arches, still stands to a height of nearly forty feet. Other identified parts of the palace include the throne room, harem, great esplanade, little and great *serdabs*,[191] treasury, barracks and polo ground. As at Qusayr 'Amrah the walls were adorned with paintings, and these include pictures of dancers, hunting scenes, animals and birds.[192]

The second successor of al-Mu'tasim, al-Mutawakkil (A.D. 847-861), built the Great Mosque of Samarra, as is stated in the following words by the geographer al-Ya'qubi (A.D. 891): "He [al-Mutawakkil] built the Great Mosque at the beginning of al-Hair in a broad space beyond the houses and not in contact with the allotments and markets. He made it good and spacious and strong. He placed a fountain in it, which played without ceasing. He provided access to it by means of three great, wide rows coming from the street which leads from the Wadi Ibrahim ibn-Riyah. In each row there were shops containing all sorts of merchandise and [products of] art and trade. The breadth of each row was one hundred black cubits, in order that the approach to the mosque should not be too narrow for the Caliph, when he visited the mosque on Fridays with his troops and followers, cavalry and infantry. From each row there were alleys and passages to the neighboring one, in which were the allotments of a number of common people. The dwellings and houses of the

---

[190] Among other and lesser Turkish dynasties which also found establishment in this period was the one we have already met (p.179) at Ghazni in Afghanistan.

[191] Serdabs, still a feature of houses in southern Mesopotamia, are underground rooms used as retreats from the heat. CEMA II, p.64 n.5.

[192] *Die Ausgrabungen von Samarra* (Forschungen zur islamischen Kunst), III, Ernst Herzfeld, *Die Malereien von Samarra*. 1927.

people had plenty of space, and the people of the markets and crafts-men and artificers had room in their shops and markets, which lay in the rows of the Great Mosque."[193]

The ruins of the Great Mosque are shown in an aerial view in Fig. 231, with the modern walled city of Samarra in the back-ground.[194] As may be clearly seen, the mosque is in the form of an immense rectangle with a spiral minaret outside the walls at one end. The rectangle is walled with kiln-dried bricks, and measures about 787 by 512 feet, which makes it the largest mosque in the world. The main axis runs from northeast to southwest, almost ex-actly in the direction of Mecca. The minaret stands precisely on this line outside the northeast wall, and on the same line in the center of the southwest wall is a rectangular recess (*mihrab*) marking the direction of prayer. The foundations of the twenty-four rows of col-umns which divided the mosque into twenty-five aisles and carried its roof may still be seen, while in the middle of the open court (*sahn*) are the remains of the famous fountain which al-Ya'qubi said played continuously.

The most striking feature of all is the minaret, known as the Mal-wiya or "spiral." It is a helicoidal tower, about one hundred and nine-ty-five feet high, with a ramp running up around it for five complete turns in a counterclockwise direction. This ramp is about seven and one-half feet wide and ascends at a constantly increasing angle, since otherwise the amount of rise would be reduced as the diameter of each turn became smaller. It is almost certainly correct to recog-nize the influence of the ancient Babylonian ziggurat in the construc-tion of this remarkable tower.

According to Yaqut the cost of the Great Mosque at Samarra was a sum equal to nearly two million dollars.[195]

---

[193] tr. in CEMA II, p.254.   [194] CEMA II, Pl. 63,b.
[195] CEMA II, p.261.

8. THE AGHLABIDS (A.D. 800-909), TULUNIDS (A.D. 868-905) AND FATIMIDS (A.D. 909-1171)

EGYPT and North Africa were conquered by the Muslims, it will be remembered, in the days of the Orthodox Caliphs and the Umayyads. In A.D. 800 Harun al-Rashid appointed Ibrahim ibn al-Aghlab governor of what is now Tunisia, and he established a dynasty which ruled in relative independence for a little over a century and dominated most of North Africa and the Middle Mediterranean.

THE GREAT MOSQUE OF QAYRAWAN

The capital of the Aghlabids was at al-Qayrawan (Kairouan). This town is said to have been built originally, with its mosque, in A.D. 674/75 by 'Uqbah ibn-Nafi', a governor sent out by Mu'awiyah. In A.D. 836 the third Aghlabid ruler, Ziyadat-Allah I (817-838), rebuilt the mosque of al-Qayrawan completely. The geographer al-Bakri (A.D. 1068) states that Ziyadat-Allah "had all the mosque demolished, and even ordered the mihrab to be destroyed. People pointed out to him that all his predecessors had abstained from touching this part of the edifice, because 'Uqbah ibn-Nafi' had constructed it; he persisted in his resolution, not wishing that the new building should exhibit the least trace of work that was not his. In order to turn him from his intention, one of the builders proposed that the old mihrab should be enclosed between two walls, in such a way that no part of it was visible from the interior of the mosque. This plan was adopted, and down to our time the mosque of Qayrawan has remained just as Ziyadat-Allah left it. The present mihrab, as well as all that surrounds it, from top to bottom, is constructed of white marble openwork covered with carving. Part of this decoration consists of inscriptions, the rest forms arabesques of various patterns. Round the mihrab are extremely beautiful columns of marble. The two red columns of which we have spoken[196] are placed in front of the mihrab, and serve to support the [semi-]dome of which they form a part. The mosque contains 414 columns, forming seventeen naves. Its length is 220 cubits, and its width 150. The maqsurah was formerly in the interior of the mosque, but as a result of the alterations which Ziyadat-Allah continued to make in this building, it is now only a house on the south side of the mosque which has

---

[196] Al-Bakri had already told how the mosque of 'Uqbah was rebuilt earlier (A.D. 703) by Hassan, and how the latter brought to it from an ancient church "the two red columns spotted with yellow, of which the beauty is unsurpassed."

its entrance in the Fruit Bazaar. It has a second doorway which opens at the side of the pulpit and it is by this one that the Imam enters the mosque, after having stopped in the house to await the hour of prayer. Ziyadat-Allah spent 86,000 *mithqal* for the construction of the mosque."[197]

While Ziyadat-Allah gave to the Great Mosque of Qayrawan the size and shape which it has today, additional work was done on the building by later rulers. Abu Ibrahim Ahmad in A.D. 862/63 decorated the mihrab with marble panels and faïence tiles, made a dome in front of it, and built a magnificent pulpit; Ibrahim II ibn-Ahmad (A.D. 874-902) constructed a beautifully decorated dome at the end of the nave which leads to the mihrab; and al-Mu'izz ibn-Badis, who governed the region in the first half of the eleventh century for the Fatimid Caliph of Egypt, gave the splendid wooden *maqsurah*, or enclosure for the use of the ruler at prayers.[198]

The photograph in Fig. 232 shows the Great Mosque from the northwest, with the massive square minaret in the foreground and the domes above the sanctuary in the background. The central aisle of the sanctuary is pictured in Fig. 233. The mihrab of Ahmad may be seen in the wall straight ahead. It is a recess over six feet wide, flanked by two orange-red marble columns, and lined with carved marble panels, many in openwork. The face of the arch and the rectangular surface surrounding it are adorned with luster tiles, some in monochrome and some in polychrome, featuring varied floral motifs.[199]

To the right of the mihrab is the minbar or pulpit, a side view of which is shown in Fig. 234. Likewise probably erected by Ahmad, it is the oldest and most famous minbar in Islam.[200] Constructed of plane tree wood, it has the usual staircase form with seventeen steps leading up to the speaker's platform. The sides are adorned with openwork panels of remarkable intricacy and beauty. There are geometrical patterns and arabesques employing trees, pine cones, palmettes, acanthus whorls, vine leaves and bunches of grapes. Yet farther to the right of the minbar and partially visible in both of our photographs is the handsome maqsurah of wood with which the mosque was endowed by al-Mu'izz ibn-Badis.

While the Aghlabids were ruling in North Africa, the Tulunid dynasty made itself independent in Egypt. This dynasty was founded

[197] tr. in CEMA II, pp.209,213.
[199] CEMA II, Pls. 46,b; 83,a.
[198] CEMA II, pp.213f.,224.
[200] CEMA II, p.317, Pl. 89,a.

by Ahmad ibn-Tulun (A.D. 868-884), who was sent to Egypt as governor and soon made himself independent, and it endured until A.D. 905. Al-Fustat was still the capital, and here the Mosque of 'Amr, although several times reconstructed, had become too small for the increased numbers of Muslims. Ibn-Tulun consequently built a new mosque which was completed in A.D. 879.

THE MOSQUE OF IBN-TULUN

The Mosque of ibn-Tulun is shown in a general view in Fig. 235. The entire area occupied is a square about five hundred and thirty feet on the side. Within this area there is first an outer court known as a *ziyada* or extension, which once contained places of ablution and subsidiary buildings and which served to separate the mosque proper from its secular surroundings. The wall of the mosque proper is pierced with doors and pointed-arched windows and crested with openwork adornment. In the interior (Fig. 236) the arcades were constructed with brick piers rather than columns, and with pointed arches. Bands of stucco ornamentation adorn the arches, and openwork grilles fill the windows with delicate lacework. Under the ceiling remains a part of a famous Kufic inscription, carved in solid wood, and containing originally about one-fifteenth of the entire Qur'an. The original minaret of the mosque is believed to have resembled that of the Great Mosque of Samarra, which is where ibn-Tulun spent his youth, but the present minaret was probably built by the Mamluk Sultan Lajin (A.D. 1296-1298).[201]

The Fatimids concern us next. They were a Shi'ite dynasty claiming descent from Fatimah and 'Ali through al-Husayn. In A.D. 909 a leader of theirs named 'Abdullah al-Husayn al-Shi'i destroyed the Aghlabid dynasty and began to rule at al-Qayrawan as the Imam 'Ubaydullah al-Mahdi (A.D. 909-934). In A.D. 969 a famous general, Jawhar, took Egypt from the Ikhshidids who had held it briefly, and completed the establishment of the Fatimid empire along the entire southern coast of the Mediterranean. At al-Fustat, Jawhar laid out a new quarter which he named al-Qahirah (the triumphant) after the planet Qahir al-Falak (the triumphant of heaven, Mars) which was then in the ascendant, and in 973 this place, now called Cairo, became the Fatimid capital.[202]

[201] CEMA II, pp.337,354, Pls. 96,99.
[202] HHA p.619.

The first and most famous mosque constructed by the Fatimids was that of al-Azhar, built in al-Qahirah by Jawhar in A.D. 972. Under the Caliph al-'Aziz (A.D. 975-976) this mosque became a place of teaching as well as prayer, and is today the principal university of the Muslim world. The central part of the structure preserves its original form, but otherwise much rebuilding has been done. The photograph in Fig. 237 shows the façade of the mosque from the court. The various minarets are relatively late, dating from the fifteenth to the eighteenth century.[203]

Interestingly enough we possess the very name of al-'Aziz, just mentioned as the inaugurator of the teaching program in the Mosque of al-Azhar, inscribed on the beautiful rock-crystal ewer shown in Fig. 238. Aside from its historical importance in this regard, the object illustrates a high degree of skill in the productions of Muslim artists of the time.[204]

Another striking object of the Fatimid Period, probably of the eleventh century, is the great bronze griffin (Fig. 239) which probably once stood in some royal palace and is now in the Campo Santo at Pisa.[205] The making of such an image as this was in general frowned upon in the Islamic world because it savored of idolatry and might carry an implication of disrespect to the sole creative power of Allah. It will be noted, however, that the body of the griffin is covered with engraved patterns, and that there is a Kufic inscription running around the chest and sides. This decoration has nothing in common with the nature of the animal and serves rather to negate the form of the object. Thus it was shown that the image need not be taken for a living being nor an affront in any wise to the Creator.[206]

[203] Louis Hautecoeur and Gaston Wiet. *Les mosquées du Caire*. 1932, I, pp.218-220; II, Pl. 10; E. T. Richmond, *Moslem Architecture, 623 to 1516, Some Causes and Consequences*. 1926, pp.79-83; Mrs. R. L. Devonshire, *Eighty Mosques and Other Monuments in Cairo*. 1930, pp.97f.

[204] A. H. Christie in Thomas Arnold and Alfred Guillaume, eds., *The Legacy of Islam*. 1931, p.144, Fig. 65.

[205] Gaston Migeon, *Les arts musulmans* (Bibliothèque d'histoire de l'art). 1926, p.32.

[206] Richard Ettinghausen in FAH pp.259f.

9. THE UMAYYADS OF CORDOVA, A.D. 756-1031

WHEN the 'Abbasids overthrew the Umayyads of Damascus (A.D. 750) they destroyed all the members of the house they were able to seize. One youth named 'Abd al-Rahman escaped, however, and ultimately made his way to Spain. There he was able to establish an independent western branch of the Umayyad dynasty which maintained power for two and three-quarters centuries (A.D. 765-1031) and was the chief agency through which the influence of Arab culture was brought to bear upon the western world. 'Abd al-Rahman I and his first successors took only the title of amir, but with the eminent 'Abd al-Rahman III (A.D. 912-961) the title of caliph was assumed.

The capital of the dynasty was at Cordova. Just outside the city 'Abd al-Rahman I built his palace which he named al-Rusafah after the residence of his grandfather Hisham, tenth caliph of Damascus. To a solitary palm tree in the garden, said to be the first imported from Syria, he addressed these verses: "In the midst of Rusafah has appeared to us a palm tree in a Western land far from the home of palm trees. So I said, this resembles me, for I also live in distant exile and separated by a great distance from my children and my family. Thou hast grown up in a foreign land and we are both exiled and far from home."[207]

THE GREAT MOSQUE OF CORDOVA

In A.D. 788, two years before his death, 'Abd al-Rahman I founded the great and famous mosque of Cordova. In its original form, portions of which can still be detected in the present structure, it seems to have consisted of a large court and a sanctuary divided into eleven aisles by ten arcades, each containing twelve arches. Antique columns were used, and in order to gain additional height two tiers of arches were employed to support the ceiling.

At first there was no minaret, but one was added by 'Abd al-Rahman's son and successor, Hisham I (A.D. 788-796); and later an entirely new minaret was erected by 'Abd al-Rahman III. This has been found to still exist inside the present Campanile. Extensive enlargements were also carried out by 'Abd al-Rahman II (A.D. 822-852), al-Hakam II (961-976) and Hisham II (976-1009).[208]

[207] tr. in CEMA II, p.139.
[208] CEMA II, pp.140-145,155; Ernst Kühnel, *Maurische Kunst* (Die Kunst des Ostens,

The building was made into a Christian cathedral in A.D. 1236, and survives today, still being popularly known as La Mezquita or "the mosque." It is an enormous rectangle, measuring about 585 by 410 feet, and comprises an open court and a sanctuary or hall of nineteen aisles. The wonderful vistas through the veritable forest of columns in the interior are suggested by the photograph in Fig. 240.

---

9). 1924, pp.16f.,64; Heinrich Glück and Ernst Diez, *Arte del Islam* (Historia del arte labor, v). 1932, pp.65f.

10. THE MAMLUKS, A.D. 1250-1517

THE high point of Arab expansion was reached in the periods with which we have now dealt. If not in exhaustive recital, at least in selected episodes we have told how the followers of the Arabian prophet carried his religion throughout the Middle East and into northern Africa and western Europe. The halting of Arab expansion and the reducing of Arab power were accomplished by such events as the Christian reconquest of Spain in the west, largely carried out by the middle of the thirteenth century (Cordova fell in 1236); the Crusades in the Near East, launched by the famous speech of Pope Urban II in 1095; and the conquest and destruction of Baghdad (1258) in the Middle East by Hulagu, grandson of Jenghiz Khan.

It was the Mamluks who stopped the Mongols from further progress westward, drove out of Syria and Egypt the last of the Crusaders, and established in the Near East the last and in some respects most remarkable of the medieval Arab dynasties. The name Mamluk means "possessed" and was the common designation for a slave. These rulers were erstwhile slaves who by energetic and ruthless endeavor fought their way to leadership. This domination they maintained from the middle of the thirteenth century until 1517 when the new non-Arab caliphate of the Ottoman Turks was established.[209]

The capitals of the Mamluks were Cairo and Damascus. The title borne by the rulers was Sultan, a designation literally meaning "he with authority" (*al-sultan*) and first borne officially by the Seljuq monarchs.[210] The most famous of the earlier Mamluk Sultans included Baybars (A.D. 1260-1277), distinguished for his campaigns against the Mongols and the Crusaders, Qalawun (1279-1290), specially remembered for the great hospital he built in Cairo, and al-Nasir (1293-1294, 1298-1308, 1309-1340), also a builder of important public works; and of the later Mamluks Qa'it-bay may be singled out, whose reign was relatively long (1468-1495) and successful.

Warlike as the times were, the Mamluk Period was notable for its architectural and artistic activity, and Egypt in particular was adorned with the finest monuments erected there since the times of the Ptolemies and the Pharaohs. Characteristic of the style which prevailed in this climactic period of Arab architecture were a cruciform plan and the use of striped masonry as well as of arabesque decoration and Kufic lettering.

[209] HHA p.671.   [210] HHA pp.464,474.

THE MOSQUE OF QA'IT-BAY

The single structure we select for illustration is the Mosque of Qa'it-bay in Cairo. This remarkable building, a general view of which is shown in Fig. 241, was completed in A.D. 1474 and comprises not only a mosque proper but also a tomb, a school and a fountain. Notable are the fine proportions, the red and white striped masonry, the lofty minaret, and the dome decorated with a lacework of conventionalized foliage and rosettes. Within there is a corresponding richness of exquisite ornamentation as may be seen in Fig. 242, showing the prayer niche and the pulpit.[211]

Of the superb calligraphic art which was lavished upon copies of the Qur'an under the Mamluks we have already given an example (Fig. 223).

---

[211] GCE I, p.231; Heinrich Glück and Ernst Diez, *Die Kunst des Islam* (Propyläen-Kunstgeschichte, v). 3d ed. 1925, p.186, Pl. III.

11. THE IL-KHANS (A.D. 1256-1335) AND THE TIMURIDS (A.D. 1369-1506)

IN THE east, meanwhile, the world had been overrun by the Mongols. Of the fall of 'Abbasid Baghdad to Hulagu, grandson of Jenghiz Khan, in A.D. 1258 we have already spoken. This conqueror took the title Il-Khan, meaning "lord of the tribe," and founded a dynasty which ruled all Iran until about 1335. Then, after a brief feudal period, came Timur Lang, better known as Tamerlane (A.D. 1336-1405). Having become king in Samarkand in A.D. 1369, he went forth on his campaigns, conducted with boundless cruelty, in Iran, Mesopotamia, Russia, India, Syria and Asia Minor. The dynasty which he established ruled Transoxiana and Persia until shortly after A.D. 1500, the approximate date up to which we are carrying this chapter.

The first of the Il-Khans, including Hulagu (A.D. 1256-1265), Abagha (1265-1281) and Arghun (1284-1291), may have shown interest in Buddhism and also in Nestorianism, but the later ones such as Ghazan (1295-1304) and Oljaitu (1304-1316), were converted to Islam. Related as they were to the Yüan dynasty rulers of China (p.376), a strong Chinese influence was felt in their realm. As for Tamerlane, he was a Muslim from the outset.[212]

The architectural monuments of the time and region are massive, mighty structures, expressive of tremendous force, built of brick and surfaced with a ceramic decoration of shimmering color.[213] Two examples are shown here. The first (Fig. 243) is the Masjid-i-Jami' or cathedral mosque built at Varamin, south of Teheran, in A.D. 1325-1326 by Abu Sa'id (A.D. 1316-1335), the last of the Il-Khans. In ruins as it is, the impressive unity of the great building is still manifest, and, on the façade, portions of the original blue faïence remain to give an intimation of its original beauty.[214] The second monument (Fig. 244) is the Gur-i-Mir or Tomb of Timur at Samarkand. This is a cross-formed hall, contained within an octagon and surmounted by a high drum and lofty, swelling dome. Both dome and drum are adorned with blue enameled brickwork, the drum also carrying an inscription in large Kufic characters. Within, the body of the famous conqueror lies beneath a great block of green nephrite.[215]

[212] GCE I, pp.296f.,308f.
[213] Ernst Cohn-Wiener, *Asia, Einführung in die Kunstwelt des Ostens.* 1929, pp.137,139.
[214] PSPA IV, Pl. 405,B.
[215] Ernst Cohn-Wiener, *Turan, islamische Baukunst in Mittelasien.* 1930. pp.30f., 45; PSPA IV, Pl. 419.

PERSIAN PAINTING

Of Muslim architecture, particularly as manifested in imposing mosques, and of calligraphy, as devoted to the production of ornamental inscriptions for the mosques and the making of beautiful copies of the Qur'an, we have had frequent occasion to speak. Alongside these two prime arts of Islam the art of painting also played at least a limited role.

Theologically, this art had long been the object of disapproval, for it was held that the painter who depicted the figure of an animal or a human being was arrogating to himself something of the creative power which belonged alone to Allah. This attitude took form in the traditions in such sayings as the following.[216]

Those who will be most severely punished on the Day of Judgment are the murderer of a prophet, one who has been put to death by a prophet, one who leads men astray without knowledge, and a maker of images or pictures.

A head will thrust itself out of the fire and will ask, Where are those who invented lies against God, or have been the enemies of God, or have made light of God? Then men will ask, Who are these three classes of persons? It will answer, The sorcerer is he who has invented lies against God; the maker of images or pictures is the enemy of God; and he who acts in order to be seen of men, is he that has made light of God.

While this disapprobation served quite universally to keep painted pictures out of the mosques, it did not prevent the art of painting from being practiced and enjoyed in a secular way. At certain times and in certain countries, particularly among the ruling classes, the art asserted itself. Of this we have already encountered examples in the frescoes of Qusayr 'Amrah and Samarra. In the realm and era of the Il-Khans and the Timurids, with which we are now dealing, a notable activity unfolded in the production of miniature illustrations for books. Here, too, in the larger number of cases the books illustrated were of a secular nature, being scientific works on plants, animals, or medicine; collections of poems, or fables; or treatises on history. In the historical works it of course happened not infrequently that persons of religious significance were treated; also manuscripts on religious subjects were sometimes illustrated. In these cases, however, the representations which might be made of Muhammad or other religious leaders remained purely of historical significance; they were not intended as objects of devotion. Thus the

[216] Arnold, *Painting in Islam*, p.6; cf. Hans Much, *Islamik*, 1921, p.8.

miniatures, interesting as they are to us, were only of ephemeral importance in Islamic civilization as a whole.

Turning to this art because of its interest from our historical point of view, we find that the painting may best be described as truly Persian, but influenced by 'Abbasid art on the one side and eventually even more strongly by Chinese on the other.

In A.H. 707 = A.D. 1307/08 a fine illustrated copy was made of The Chronology of Ancient Nations (al-Athar al-Baqiya), a work which was written, it will be remembered, in A.D. 1000 by the scholar al-Biruni. From this manuscript we show in Fig. 245 the painting of Muhammad preaching his farewell sermon on the occasion of his last visit to Mecca. The prophet speaks from upon a minbar, and behind the heads of both himself and his listeners are round halos. The style of the painting is still that of the Arab tradition.[217]

Another historical work of great importance by a Muslim author was the Jami' at-Tawarikh or Universal History of Rashid-al-Din (A.D. c.1247-1318). This historian lived in the city of Tabriz and served as prime minister under the Il-Khans, Ghazan and Oljaitu.[218] An illustrated manuscript of this book made in A.H. 714 = A.D. 1314 contains miniatures showing episodes from the Bible and from Buddhist, Muslim and Chinese history. The picture reproduced in Fig. 246 shows Muhammad replacing the Black Stone in the Ka'bah at Mecca. The story is that the Ka'bah was damaged by a flood and had to be rebuilt. When it came to putting the Black Stone back in its place a dispute arose as to who should have the honor. Muhammad, then about thirty-five years of age, appeared on the scene and was chosen for the purpose. In the painting, Muhammad stands in front of the Ka'bah and takes up the Black Stone which four prominent citizens of Mecca are presenting to him on a long strip of carpet. In other miniatures in the same manuscript, particularly where landscapes are depicted, a definite Chinese influence is to be seen.[219]

Under the favorite son and successor of Timur, Shah Rukh (A.D. 1404-1447), the Timurid capital was established at Herat in Khorasan. Like his father, Shah Rukh was a patron of the arts, and so too was his son, Baysunqur Mirza (A.D. 1397-1433). The last named is said to have employed forty calligraphers and painters in his library, and presumably the staff in his father's establishment was

[217] Arnold, *Painting in Islam*, pp.95f.; GCE I, p.302.
[218] E. Berthels in EI III, pp.1124f.
[219] M. S. Dimand, *A Handbook of Mohammedan Decorative Arts* (The Metropolitan Museum of Art). 1930, p.22.

even larger. With such royal encouragement the school of Herat became the foremost center of Persian painting, and with the experience gained from earlier developments this art now attained its classical form.

A work devoted entirely to religious subject matter provides some of the finest examples of the art. This is a manuscript of an Apocalypse of Muhammad called the Mi'raj Namah, which is wholly occupied with a detailed account of the famous "night-journey" of the prophet through the realms of heaven and hell. The book was copied in Uighur (Eastern Turki) script at Herat by a certain Malik Bakhshi in A.H. 840 = A.D. 1436, that is under Shah Rukh. From the very beautiful miniature paintings with which the manuscript is adorned we reproduce in Fig. 247 the picture of Muhammad's visit to paradise. In accordance with tradition the prophet rides upon the wonderful steed Buraq, and is guided by the archangel Gabriel. Both Muhammad and Gabriel have halos of flame. Paradise is shown as a wonderful garden, and since the day is Friday, the Islamic holiday, the houris are out traveling, visiting and exchanging gifts of flowers.[220]

Continuing to the end of the Timurid Period, the last of the Timurids was Sultan Husayn Bayqara who came to the throne in Herat in A.D. 1468 and died in 1506. His minister was Mir 'Ali Shir Nawa'i (A.D. 1440-1501), himself a talented writer and a patron of men of letters and art.[221] From an illustrated manuscript, dated A.H. 890 = A.D. 1485, containing a work by Nawa'i entitled Nazm al-Jawahir, we reproduce the miniature in Fig. 248. In this we see Muhammad, distinguished by a flame-halo, seated in front of the mihrab of a mosque. The mihrab and surrounding wall are shown decorated with tiles colored in green and blue, above is a green dome, and at one side an ornate minbar. Thus appeared, no doubt, some mosque in Herat or Samarkand with which the painter was familiar, although in the scene the prophet was of course supposed to be in Medina. In front of Muhammad is a brazier from which flames arise vigorously. Gathered around are a number of the companions of the prophet. Seated by the brazier writing at Muhammad's dictation is a secretary, possibly Zayd ibn-Thabit. The man standing at the left is identified by his black face as Bilal, the Abyssinian whom Muhammad chose on account of his stentorian voice to be the first

[220] Basil Gray in *Persian Painting, From Miniatures of the XIII.-XVI. Centuries.* 1940, p.12; Arnold, *Painting in Islam*, p.109 (for Buraq see pp.117-122).

[221] Edward G. Browne, *A History of Persian Literature under Tartar Dominion* (*A.D. 1265-1502*). 1920, pp.390f.,505f.

muezzin.[222] The standing figure at the right is 'Ali, with his famous two-pointed sword.[223]

Among those who enjoyed the patronage of Husayn Bayqara and Mir 'Ali Shir Nawa'i was Kamal al-Din Bihzad, considered the greatest of all Persian painters.[224] Born at Herat about A.D. 1440, he studied under a certain Pir Saiyid Ahmad of Tabriz, worked at Herat throughout the entire reign of Husayn Bayqara, and continued afterward to labor at Tabriz. A contemporary historian, Khwandamir, wrote in his *Habib as-Siyar* (A.D. c.1523) concerning Bihzad: "He sets before us marvelous forms and rarities of art; his draftsmanship which is like the brush of Mani[225] has caused the memorials of all the painters of the world to be obliterated, and his fingers endowed with miraculous qualities have wiped out the pictures of all the artists among the sons of Adam. A hair of his brush, by its mastery, has given life to the lifeless form. My revered master attained to his present eminence through the blessing of the patronage and of the kind favor of the Amir Nizam al-Din 'Ali Shir, and His Majesty the Khan showed him much favor and kindness; and at the present time too this marvel of the age, whose belief is pure, is regarded with benevolence by the kings of the world and is encompassed by the boundless consideration of the rulers of Islam. Without doubt thus will it be for ever."[226]

Famous as he was, Bihzad had many admirers and imitators and the identification of his own originals is not always positive. The picture we choose for illustration (Fig. 249) is certainly in his style, however, and may safely be attributed to either Bihzad or his school and dated around A.D. 1500. It shows a band of dancing dervishes, surrounded by musicians and spectators. Outstanding features are

[222] HHA pp.106,259; Fr. Buhl in EI I, pp.718f.
[223] Arnold, *Painting in Islam*, p.97.
[224] Basil Gray, *Persian Painting*. 1930, pp.57-66.
[225] The founder of Manicheism (cf. above p.115) was himself a famous painter, and his followers practiced the art vigorously, producing many illuminated manuscripts. In A.D. 923 fourteen sacks of Manichean books were burned in Baghdad and trickles of gold and silver ran out of the fire; and in 1092 Mani's own picture-book called *Arzhang* was still in existence in Ghazni. Manichean painting was doubtless one of the influences contributing to the development of the later Persian painting which we are discussing. Arnold, *Painting in Islam*, pp.61f. In modern times portions of actual Manichean manuscripts with pictures dating from around A.D. 750-850, have been recovered at the Oasis of Turfan. A. von Le Coq, *Die buddhistische Spätantike in Mittelasien* (Ergebnisse der kgl. preussischen Turfan-Expeditionen). II, *Die manichaeischen Miniaturen*. 1923.
[226] tr. Thomas W. Arnold and Adolf Grohmann, *The Islamic Book, A Contribution to Its Art and History from the VII-XVIII Century*. 1929, p.75.

the delicacy of execution, gracefulness of the figures, liveliness of the motion, beauty of the landscape, and, in the original, effectiveness of the combination of the colors, pink, vermilion, dark red, brick red, and various shades of yellow, green and blue.[227]

With the adding of painting to calligraphy and mosque architecture the most typical expressions of Islamic art have now come before our view, and this chapter must be closed. Concerning Islam in India, further information will be given in the beginning of the following chapter.[228]

[227] Dimand, *A Handbook of Mohammedan Decorative Arts*, p.36.
[228] For China see Marshall Broomhall, *Islam in China, A Neglected Problem.* 1910.

CHAPTER X

Sikhism

IKHISM is a religion which arose in India around A.D. 1500 and which has today over five million followers. Since it is of comparatively recent origin and since it has neither mythology nor idols, it presents fewer archeological materials than the faiths previously considered. It is properly included in our study, however, both because of its magnitude and because of its significant origin as an effort toward the reconciliation of Hinduism and Islam in India. Even though Sikhism did not accomplish that goal, the story of its early work toward such an end may testify to the growing desire to find a common understanding among the great religions of the modern world.

1. INDIA IN THE MUSLIM PERIOD, A.D. 1206-1857

THE TURKS AND AFGHANS, A.D. 1206-1526

THE period of Sikhism's rise and distinctive development fell within the Muslim Period in Indian history.[1] It will be remembered (p.179) that the Turk Mahmud (A.D. 999-1030), son of Sabuktigin, of Ghazni played an important part in the establishment of Islam in India.[2] This ruler's triumphal tower still stands at Ghazni and is shown in Fig. 250. Later, Qutb-ud-din Aibak, slave and viceroy of the Ghaznavid Muhammad Ghori, occupied Delhi (A.D. 1191) and, upon the death of his master, became sultan (A.D. 1206-1210) and founder of the so-called Slave dynasty. It was in commemoration of the capture of Delhi that Aibak founded in that city the mosque known as Quwwat-ul-Islam or "the might of Islam." An outstanding feature of this mosque was the Qutb Minar (Fig. 251) or "axis-pillar," an imposing tower begun by Aibak and completed by Shams-ud-din Iltutmish (A.D. 1211-1236), probably intended as a minaret for the muezzin but soon regarded as a tower of victory.[3]

[1] For the chronology in the time of the Turks and Afghans see CHI III, p.690; and of the Mughals see CHI IV, p.614.
[2] Murray T. Titus, *Indian Islam, A Religious History of Islam in India* (The Religious Quest of India). 1930, p.6.
[3] John Marshall in CHI III, pp.575-579.

[536]

The dynasty of Qutb-ud-din and his successors held sway in Delhi for some sixty years and then gave way to the house of Balban (A.D. 1266-1290). After that came the dynasty of the Khaljis (A.D. 1290-1320), whose king 'Ala-ud-din (A.D. 1296-1316) subjected Gujarat and the Deccan to Islam. Then the Tughluqs reigned (A.D. 1320-1414), and their king Firuz (A.D. 1351-1388) founded Firuzabad or New Delhi just south of Old Delhi, built four other towns and, it is said, constructed or restored four mosques, thirty palaces, two hundred caravanserais, five reservoirs, five hospitals, one hundred tombs, ten baths, ten monumental pillars and one hundred bridges.[4]

In A.D. 1398 Timur (p.530) invaded India and sacked Delhi, and when Khizr Khan (A.D. 1414-1421), reputed descendant of the prophet Muhammad, established the new Sayyid dynasty (A.D. 1414-1451) at Delhi it was in a position as viceroy to Shah Rukh (p.532), Timur's successor. The Sayyids in turn were displaced by the Lodi dynasty (A.D. 1451-1526), which was founded by Buhlul, an Afghan of the tribe of Lodi. Buhlul ruled from A.D. 1451 to 1489, and fought numerous battles, not always successful, on behalf of the supremacy of Delhi. He was succeeded by his son Sikandar (A.D. 1489-1517), who was the most powerful of the three kings of this house. Sikandar campaigned victoriously and administered his enlarged realms vigorously. In connection with a movement against the district of Gwalior he transferred his capital from Delhi to Agra, a city which attained much importance under the later Mughal (= Mogul) emperors. He was under the strong influence of the theologians of Islam, and displayed his intolerance by the wholesale destruction of Indian temples. Another example of this attitude appeared during a four-year stay in Sambhal, beginning in A.D. 1499. It was reported that a Brahman of Bengal had publicly maintained that the Muslim and Hindu faiths were both true and were but different paths to God. Sikandar had the Brahman brought to his court, and likewise summoned thither Islamic theologians from various parts of his kingdom. Consideration was given to the question of whether it was permissible to preach religious peace as the Brahman had been doing, and the Muslim doctors proposed the following decision. Since the Brahman had admitted the truth of Islam, let him accept it or be put to death. Sikandar agreed with this conclusion, and when the Brahman refused to change his faith the king caused him to be executed.[5]

[4] Wolseley Haig in CHI III, p.175.   [5] Haig in CHI III, p.240.

THE MUGHAL EMPIRE, A.D. 1526-1857

The last of the Lodi kings was Ibrahim who, after a reign of nine years (A.D. 1517-1526), was slain on the battlefield of Panipat by an invader from Kabul named Babur. Babur was the last of the Timurids, being the fifth in descent from the founder of that dynasty, and he attained his own greatest ambition when after the defeat of Ibrahim he entered Delhi and on April 27, 1526, was acclaimed in the Grand Mosque as Emperor of Hindustan. Thus was founded the mighty Mughal (from Mongol) Empire of Delhi which endured until A.D. 1857.

Babur (d. A.D. 1530) was a strong Muslim, and in the year of his victory erected at least two mosques which still survive, the Kabuli Bagh at Panipat and the Jami' Masjid at Sambhal.[6] Neither is of special architectural significance, and indeed Babur did not have any very high opinion of the abilities or achievements of his new subjects in general. He wrote in his *Memoirs*: "Hindustan is a country that has few pleasures to recommend it. The people are not handsome. They have no idea of the charms of friendly society, of frankly mixing together, or of familiar intercourse. They have no genius, no comprehension of mind, no politeness of manner, no kindness or fellow-feeling, no ingenuity or mechanical invention in planning or executing their handicraft works, no skill or knowledge in design or architecture; they have no horses, no good flesh, no grapes or muskmelons, no good fruits, no ice or cold water, no good food or bread in their bazaars, no baths or colleges, no candles, no torches, not a candlestick."[7]

The eldest son and successor of Babur was Humayun, who came to the throne in A.D. 1530 and died by accident in 1556. His reign was not distinguished and he was even driven into exile for a time while Shir Shah, a rebel Afghan of Bengal, ruled Hindustan (A.D. 1538-1545). Shir Shah was a man of culture and a great builder, however, and his splendid island mausoleum at Sasaram is still in existence.[8] Humayun's own tomb, a beautiful structure yet standing at Delhi, was erected by his widow some eight years after his death, when Akbar had fully reestablished Mughal authority throughout the country.

[6] Marshall in CHI III, p.524.

[7] tr. John Leyden and William Erskine, *Memoirs of Zehīr-ed-Dīn Muhammed Bābur, Emperor of Hindustan, Written by Himself, in the Chaghatāi Tūrki*. rev. by Lucas King, 1921. II, p.241.

[8] Percy Brown in CHI IV, pp.526-528; Fergusson, *History of Indian and Eastern Architecture*, II, pp.217-219.

Akbar[9] was the son of Humayun, born while the latter was in exile, but himself destined to become the greatest of all the Mughal emperors. During his reign of nearly fifty years (A.D. 1556-1605), Akbar brought under his own sway more of India than had ever before been ruled by one man, and in the administration of this vast realm displayed much wisdom and inaugurated important financial and military reforms. In religion he was a mystic, and while originally a strict and orthodox Muslim he gradually departed from this belief and proclaimed a doctrine of universal tolerance (*sulh-i-kull*). In his new city of Fatehpur Sikri, Akbar erected a Hall of Worship (*'Ibadat-Khana*) in which not only Muslims but also Hindus, Jains, Zoroastrians and Christians were invited to participate in religious discussions. From his studies in the various religions the emperor at last evolved a composite creed and code of rites on the basis of which he believed all of his subjects could be united in a common faith. The teaching was monotheistic with a tinge of pantheism, and the practice of the cult included the public worship of the sun and the veneration of fire and lights. Known as the Din-i-Ilahi or Divine Faith, the new religion was seriously promulgated with Akbar as its head, but it never attracted more than a few thousand adherents and it ceased to exist after the death of the emperor.[10] The rather beautiful mausoleum of this remarkable ruler was completed by his son, Jahangir, and still stands at Sikandra about five miles from Agra. The entrance gateway of the tomb, with its fine inlaid stonework, is shown in Fig. 252.[11]

Jahangir, son of Akbar, became the next of the Mughal rulers (A.D. 1605-1627). Soon after his accession, he faced a revolt by his own son, Khusrau, but crushed this successfully. After his own death, another son, Shah Jahan, succeeded him upon the throne, although not without a struggle against other contenders. Under the rule of Shah Jahan (A.D. 1628-1658) the Mughal empire attained its greatest magnificence and Mughal architecture achieved its golden age. Buildings of surpassing beauty were erected by the Shah throughout the land. Of these we may recall the imposing Jami' Masjid at Delhi, India's largest and most eminent mosque; and the peerless white marble Taj Mahal at Agra (Fig. 253), the mausoleum of Mumtaz-i-Mahal, the emperor's favorite wife, and at last his own burial place

---

[9] Vincent A. Smith, *Akbar, The Great Mogul, 1542-1605.* 2d ed. 1919.
[10] Haig in CHI IV, pp.119-132.
[11] Brown in CHI IV, pp.549-551; Fergusson, *History of Indian and Eastern Architecture*, II, pp.298-302; Glück and Diez, *Die Kunst des Islam*, p.338.

as well. Religiously, both Jahangir and Shah Jahan were Muslims, but the former manifested a certain tolerance while the latter was intolerant and in particular caused the demolition of many Hindu temples.

The throne of Shah Jahan was seized in A.D. 1658 by his son Aurangzib, and the great emperor spent the rest of his life in imprisonment in the fort of Agra. The son did not even complete the father's own mausoleum, which had been planned as a black marble replica of the Taj Mahal, to stand across the river from the same and be connected with it by a bridge, "an architectural composition which for romance, imagination and magnificence would have had no equal."[12] As for Aurangzib himself, he enjoyed a long reign (A.D. 1658-1707) and made some additional conquests, but was not an outstanding ruler. Actually the decay of the Mughal power had already set in, and art and culture were showing signs of decadence. After his death the decline of the Mughal empire continued, and a series of weak kings held the throne for brief reigns until the last of them was banished in A.D. 1857.

Such in brief outline was the history of India during the time in which the religion of the Sikhs arose.

[12] Brown in CHI IV, p.566.

2. THE SIKH SCRIPTURES

As WE proceed now to speak of Sikhism itself, it will be helpful to describe at the outset the scriptures recognized in this religion.

THE ADI GRANTH

The literary collection which has the place of chief authority is called the Granth, the Granth Sahib, or the Adi Granth.[13] The Sanskrit word *grantha* means "book," "treatise" or "written code," and thus the title of this collection is simply the Book, the Lordly Book, or the First Book. For the most part its contents are composed in Hindi or Hindustani and written in the Gurmukhi script of the Punjab. All together it is a very extensive compilation, comprising not less than 3,384 hymns with 15,575 verses, and it serves the Sikhs as a hymnbook, a prayer book and a book of doctrinal theology. A custodian, reader or expounder of the Granth is known as a *granthi*.

The collecting of the materials of the Adi Granth was done largely by Arjun, the fifth Guru or Teacher of the Sikh religion who was head of the faith from A.D. 1581 to 1606. He is said to have felt the need of recording the exact words of his predecessors and specially of Guru Nanak, the founder of the religion, in order to have a source of authoritative guidance for his disciples. For the purpose of doing this work he took up his abode in a secluded and pleasant place at Amritsar. There, with the assistance of numerous followers and helpers, he gathered materials for the compilation and also composed hymns of his own. When all the texts suitable for inclusion had been determined, Guru Arjun sat in his tent and dictated them to a scribe named Bhai Gur Das who wrote them out in Gurmukhi. After much labor the volume was completed in A.D. 1604, and Arjun wrote these words in conclusion:

Three things have been put into the vessel [the Granth]—truth, patience, and meditation.

The ambrosial name of God the support of all hath also been put therein.

He who eateth and enjoyeth it shall be saved.

This provision should never be abandoned; ever clasp it to your hearts.

[13] Ernest Trumpp, *The Ādi Granth, or the Holy Scriptures of the Sikhs, Translated from the Original Gurmukhī, with Introductory Essays.* 1877; Winternitz, *Geschichte der indischen Litteratur,* III, p.587; Von Glasenapp, *Die Literaturen Indiens von ihren Anfängen bis zur Gegenwart,* p.204.

By embracing God's feet we cross the ocean of darkness; Nanak, every-thing is an extension of God.[14]

While the Granth compiled by Guru Arjun contained the bulk of the materials now found in that work, certain additions were made after his time. It was a third edition which was produced by the last of the Gurus, Gobind Singh (A.D. 1675-1708). In this, some verses of Gobind Singh and some of his father, Teg Bahadur, were added.

In its final form, then, the Adi Granth contained materials from three chief sources. First, there were hymns of the Gurus from Nanak to Arjun, and those of Teg Bahadur and Gobind Singh as well.

Second, there were verses which were composed by various Bha-gats or Devotees, many even earlier than Nanak. The names of these Bhagats follow, with identifications when particulars are known: (1) Beni; (2) Bhikan; (3) Dhanna, said to have been a Jat or culti-vator by caste and a disciple of Ramananda; (4) Shaikh Farid, a famous Muslim saint who died A.D. 1266; (5) Jaidev, a Sanskrit poet who lived at the court of King Lakshmanasena (twelfth century A.D.) of Bengal and wrote the Gitagovinda; (6) Kabir, a later dis-ciple of Ramananda, who probably lived A.D. 1440-1518; (7) Nam-dev, a saint who lived A.D. 1270-1350 and emancipated himself from Hindu idolatry; (8) Parmananda; (9) Pipa, raja in a state called Gagaraungarh, and a disciple of Ramananda; (10) Ramananda, a religious leader of around A.D. 1400 and an adherent of the teachings of Ramanuja who had lived in the eleventh century A.D.; (11) Ravi-das, a leatherworker who lived at Benares at a date not long after Kabir whom he mentions, and who was a disciple of Ramananda; (12) Sadhna, a butcher by trade and a contemporary of Namdev; (13) Sainu, a court barber and disciple of Ramananda; (14) Sur Das, a Brahman born in A.D. 1528 and governor of a province under the Emperor Akbar; (15) Trilochan, a saint of the Vaisya caste and a contemporary of Namdev.

Third, the Granth contained eulogies of the Gurus written by Bhatts or professional bards. These Bhatts presumably lived in the times of the Gurus they praised, and their names were: (1) Bhalhau; (2) Bhika; (3) Dasu; (4) Ganga; (5) Haribans; (6) Jalan; (7) Jalap; (8) Kalu; (9) Kalasu; (10) Kalasahar; (11) Kiratu; (12) Mathura; (13) Nal; (14) Rad; (15) Sal.[15]

[14] Max A. Macauliffe, *The Sikh Religion, Its Gurus, Sacred Writings and Authors.* 1909, III, p.64.

[15] Trumpp, *The Ādi Granth,* pp.cxix-cxx; Macauliffe, *The Sikh Religion,* VI.

As far as its order of arrangement is concerned, the Granth is divided into three parts. The first part is composed of four portions all intended for devotional purposes. These are: (1) the Japji, an introductory book of praise, composed by Nanak, and used in morning worship; (2) the So-daru; (3) the So-purkhu; (4) the So-hila; the last three comprising hymns for use as evening prayers, extracted chiefly from the Rags which will be mentioned next.

The second part of the Granth is the main body of the work, and is made up of a large number of hymns arranged in thirty-one Rags according to the musical measures in which they are sung. The names of these Rags are: (1) Siri; (2) Majh; (3) Gauri; (4) Asa; (5) Gujri; (6) Devgandhari; (7) Bihagra; (8) Vadhansu; (9) Sorathi; (10) Dhanasari; (11) Jaitsiri; (12) Todi; (13) Bairari; (14) Tilang; (15) Suhi; (16) Bilavalu; (17) Gaud; (18) Ramkali; (19) Natnarain; (20) Maligaura; (21) Maru; (22) Tukhari; (23) Kedara; (24) Bhairau; (25) Basantu; (26) Sarang; (27) Malar; (28) Kanara; (29) Kalian; (30) Prabhata; (31) Jaijavanti. Of them all, the first four are the most extensive and contain the most important materials.

The third part of the work serves as conclusion of the whole and is called the Bhog. Here there are many verses or Sloks by various ones of the Gurus, Bhagats and Bhatts. Throughout the entire work there is much repetition and the leading ideas appear again and again in almost endless variations.[16]

THE GRANTH OF THE TENTH GURU

The tenth recognized great teacher of the Sikh religion was Guru Gobind Singh who exercised authority as head of the church from A.D. 1675 to 1708. As we have already noted, at least a small amount of his writing was incorporated in the Adi Granth. All together his literary work was very extensive, however, and in the year 1734 his compositions and translations, as well as those of bards associated with him, were brought together in a large compilation. This was done in Amritsar by Bhai Mani Singh, and the work became known as the Daswan Padshah ka Granth or Granth of the Tenth King, referring to the Guru. It has considerable authority among the Sikhs but certainly much less than that of the Adi Granth.

Its contents include the Japji or psalms of praise; the Akal Ustat or praise of the creator; the Vachitar Natak or wonderful drama,

---

[16] Trumpp, *The Ādi Granth*, pp.cxx-cxxi.

[543]

with an account of Guru Gobind Singh's life and battles, and with hymns in praise of Durga, the goddess of war; the Gyan Parbodh or awakening of knowledge, giving tales of twenty-four Hindu incarnations of deity; the Hazare shabd, quatrains praising God and condemning idolatry; the Shastar Nam Mala, listing weapons used at that time, with special reference to divine attributes; the Tria Charitar, stories illustrating the qualities of women; the Zafarnama, a letter of the Guru to Aurangzib; and some additional metrical narratives.[17]

THE JANAMSAKHIS

In addition to the Adi Granth and the Granth of the Tenth Guru the Sikhs also have a third body of writings to which they attach importance and which are known as the Janamsakhis or Birth Stories. These are for the most part narratives of the life of Guru Nanak, written at various times after his death. In general, these are highly legendary in character, and the later they are the more of the miraculous they contain.[18] We will return to the Janamsakhis when we deal with the life of Nanak.

[17] Macauliffe, *The Sikh Religion*, v, pp.260-331; H. A. Rose in HERE VI, p.390.
[18] Von Glasenapp, *Die Literaturen Indiens von ihren Anfängen bis zur Gegenwart*, p.230.

3. THE FORERUNNERS OF NANAK

IT IS clear from the inclusion of writings of so many different authors in the Adi Granth that the Sikh religion originated out of the work of more than a single teacher. While Guru Nanak ranks properly as the founder of the faith, he was preceded by other leaders whose teachings were enough in harmony with his own to be adjudged worthy of a place in the Sikh Bible. Of these forerunners two were of outstanding importance, Ramananda and Kabir.

RAMANANDA

Ramananda probably lived in the end of the fourteenth and the first half of the fifteenth century. He was originally a follower of the teachings of Ramanuja, an eleventh century Hindu who was devoted to the worship of Vishnu under the form of Narayan, and of Lakshmi, and who inculcated extreme strictness in culinary matters. Ramananda wandered widely throughout India and visited Benares where he came in contact with Muslims. He gradually changed his theological views and founded a sect which worshiped Rama and Sita, and relaxed the strict culinary rules of Ramanuja. He admitted disciples of all castes to this group, and taught that all its members might eat and drink together regardless of birth.

In the hymn of Ramananda found in the Adi Granth, he declines an invitation to attend a religious service of Vishnu and tells how he has learned to recognize the universal God who may be found everywhere.

> Whither shall I go, Sir? I am happy at home.
> My heart will not go with me; it hath become a cripple.
> One day I did have an inclination to go;
> I ground sandal, took distilled aloe wood and many perfumes,
> And was proceeding to worship God in a temple,
> When my spiritual guide showed me God in my heart.
> Wherever I go I find only water or stones.[19]
> But Thou, O God, art equally contained in everything.
> The Vedas and the Puranas all have I seen and searched.
> Go thou thither, if God be not here.
> O true guru, I am a sacrifice unto thee
> Who hast cut away all my perplexities and doubts.
> Ramanand's Lord is the all-pervading God;
> The guru's word cutteth away millions of sins.[20]

[19] i.e., rivers of pilgrimage or idols.
[20] Macauliffe, *The Sikh Religion*, VI, pp.105f.

Among the disciples of Ramananda were Dhanna the cultivator, Pipa the raja, Ravidas the leatherworker, and Sainu the barber, all of whom are represented by hymns in the Adi Granth. The wide variety of their callings attests the broadness of the appeal of Ramananda.

KABIR

Kabir, who probably lived A.D. 1440-1518, was also a disciple of Ramananda. According to a very legendary account of his life,[21] he was born of a widowed mother and left on a blossoming water lily on a lake called Lahar Talao near Benares. A Muslim weaver named Niru found the child there, and took him to his home. In order to find a name for their charge the new foster parents summoned a Kazi or Muslim judge, and a lot was cast with the Qur'an. The Arabic word *kabir*, meaning "great" and employed in the Qur'an as one of the names of Allah, presented itself, and this name was accordingly bestowed upon the child.

Although Kabir grew up in a Muslim home he was still subject to the strong Hindu influences of Benares, and is said to have conversed not only with Muslim but also with Hindu teachers. Then after a time he became a follower of Ramananda. While he continued to work as a weaver, he also did many unusual deeds of kindness to men and even wrought miracles such as curing the Emperor Sikandar Lodi when the latter contracted a fever upon a visit to Benares. Thus Kabir became a great saint, and upon his death the Muslims and Hindus are supposed to have contended for possession of his remains.

In his teachings Kabir transcended caste and separate religions, and called upon all men to worship the one God whom he called Rama, or the True Name, or the True Guru. He was opposed to all formalism in religion, and he declared that idolatry was false and pilgrimages futile. Theistic and mystical in his beliefs, he retained the Hindu conceptions of Karma and transmigration.

So influential was the work of Kabir that he still has some 650,000 followers, known as the Kabirpanthis. They cherish a book containing his teachings, called the Bijak; and, as we have already seen, other of his hymns are preserved in the Adi Granth of the Sikhs. From the texts ascribed to Kabir, Professor John Clark Archer has selected among others the following as giving the gist of his teachings:

[21] Macauliffe, *The Sikh Religion*, vi, pp.122-141; for his hymns, see *ibid.*, pp.142-316.

God is one; there is no second. The One is everywhere.
Search in thy heart; there is His abode.
O men and women, seek the sanctuary of the One.
He pervadeth thy body and the universe as well. . . .

Sacrifice, the rosary, pilgrimage, fasting and alms are cloaks of falsehood.
Why perform so many ceremonies! Of what avail to Hindus to bathe,
and to Moslems to pray at the mosque?
Some pride themselves on the practice of yoga.
Put away suspension of the breath and all the attitudinal in devotion. . . .

Worship God, thou fool!
Renounce family, caste and lineage, lest thou think the Maker thus
distinguished men. . . .
Birth is in accordance with penalties for deeds;
Through wanderings and error man keeps coming to his house
[i.e., the body].
If attention be fixed on God, the dread of and the fact of rebirth are
at an end. . . .

I have met God who dwells within the heart. . . .
Renounce honors, renounce boasting.
They who crave for liquor and incline to drunkenness nowhere find
content. . . .
When thy stewardship is ended, thou must render an account. . . .
Repeat the name of Ram, thou madman!
The ocean of existence is difficult to cross;
The name of God savest him who has tasted of its savour. . . .

I take no thought of sin or virtue; neither go I to a heaven or a hell;
I shall not die as the rest of the world of men.
The soul that is joined with Him is indestructible. . . .[22]

[22] Archer, *The Sikhs in Relation to Hindus, Moslems, Christians, and Ahmadiyyas,*
A Study in Comparative Religion. 1946, pp.53f.

4. THE LIFE AND TEACHINGS OF GURU NANAK

HIS LIFE

IN TELLING of the life of Nanak it may be of interest to follow one of the Janamsakhis or Birth Records. As has already been stated, this type of literature is in general far from trustworthy, being composed without due historical sense and embellished with a great deal of the miraculous. The Janamsakhi here to be cited is relatively early, however, as such literature goes. It is preserved in a manuscript with characters the style of which suggests the time of Guru Arjun or his immediate successor. As compared with yet later accounts, it is at least free of many fantastic details, and even contains points unfavorable to Nanak which are carefully eliminated in versions of a later date. The title of the manuscript is "A Book of Nanak, Referring to His Birth (or Life)."[23]

This manuscript is now in the Commonwealth Relations Office Library, London; its first page is reproduced in Fig. 254. We also show in Fig. 255 a page in a later illuminated Janamsakhi manuscript, likewise in the Commonwealth Relations Office Library.

The account begins: "In Sambat 1526, Baba[24] Nanak was born in the month of Vaisakh; in a moonlight night at an early hour, while yet about a watch of the night was remaining, he was born. Unbeaten sounds were produced at the gate of the Lord. The 33 krores of gods paid homage. The 64 Yoginis, the 52 heroes, the 6 ascetics, the 84 Siddhas, the 9 Naths, paid homage, 'because a great devotee has come to save the world; to him homage should be paid!'"

The date, Sambat 1526, or Year 1526, is reckoned according to the Vikrama Era which began in 58/57 B.C. (p.220); Nanak was born, therefore, in A.D. 1469. The month of Vaisakh is equivalent to the period from the middle of April to the middle of May; other Janamsakhis, however, place Nanak's birth in the month of Katak which falls in October-November.

The record states that the place of Nanak's birth was Talwandi, which was a village, later called Rayapur and now Nankana Sahib, on the Ravi River near Lahore. The name of his father is given as Kalu, and it is said that he was a Khatri, i.e. a Kshatriya by caste; and a Vedi by clan, this being a group which claimed descent from a famous student of the Hindu Vedas, hence the name Vedis.

[23] Trumpp, *The Ādi Granth*, pp.ii-xlv.
[24] A title of respect.

While Nanak was thus of Hindu background, he lived in the time of Muslim supremacy in India, and his home was under the rule of Rai Bular, a convert to Islam and a retainer of the Muslim king of Delhi. It has been estimated that the proportion of Muslims in upper India at this time was ten or fifteen per cent of the total population.[25]

Of Nanak's youth the Janamsakhi says: "When he became big, he began to play with the boys, but the views of the boys and his were different. In his spirit he was occupied with the Lord."

Later he was married and had children, but still spent much time in seclusion and meditation. "Then came the order of the Lord, that in the house of Guru Nanak two sons should be born, Lakhmi Das and Sri Chand. But Nanak's retirement from the world was not given up; Guru Nanak going to trees remained [there] retired from the world."

Then a wonderful event took place. Nanak fell asleep one day in a garden in the shade of a tree. By chance the ruler Rai Bular came by and noticed that while the shadows of all the other trees had moved on around, that of the tree under which Nanak was sleeping had remained stationary. Rai Bular thereupon summoned Kalu, who was known to be displeased by his son's religious preoccupations, and declared to him, "Kalu, thou hast become exalted and I also am exalted, in whose town this one has been born"; but Kalu only made a derogatory remark and went away.

It is further explained that the entire family of Nanak regarded him with displeasure because of his exclusive association with religious mendicants and his neglect of daily work. "Guru Nanak kept company with faqirs, with anyone [else] he did not converse. The whole family was grieved thereby, and said: 'He has become mad.' Then came the mother of Guru Nanak and said to him: 'Son, it does not behoove thee, to sit with faqirs, thou hast a house and family, daughters and sons, do some work! leave off making continually good words! the people laugh at us, that the son of Kalu has become mad.' Such words his mother spoke, but they made no impression whatever on the heart of Nanak. He went away again and fell down. As he had fallen, so he passed four days. When she had ceased rubbing him,[26] the wife of the Baba came to her mother-in-law and said: 'O mother-in-law, how canst thou sit down, whose son has fallen? It is now the fourth day, he does neither eat nor drink.' Then his

[25] Archer, *The Sikhs*, p.65.
[26] i.e., in an attempt to revive him from the swoon.

mother came and said: 'Son, it does not become thee to fall down; eat and drink something and look after thy fields and crops! be a little attentive to thy work! thy whole family is grieved.'"

At last Nanak received his decisive vision and commission. This occurred when he was bathing one day in the river. "As he was doing so, according to the order of the Lord, servants [i.e., angels] took him away to the threshold of the Lord. The servants said: 'Sir, Nanak is present.' Then he obtained a sight of the true court [of God]; the Lord was kind [to him]. . . . Then a cup of nectar was filled and given him by the order [of the Lord]. The command was given: 'Nanak, this nectar is a cup of my name, drink it!' Then Guru Nanak made salutation and drank it. The Lord was kind and said: 'Nanak, I am with thee, I have made thee exalted and who will take thy name, they will all be made exalted by me. Having gone, mutter my name and make also other people mutter it! Remain uncontaminated from the world! Remain in the name, [in giving] alms, in performing ablutions, in worship and remembering [me]! I have given thee my own name, do this work!'"

A servant was with Nanak when he went to bathe, and became greatly alarmed when his master went into the river and did not come out again. The Khan was called and fishermen were set to searching for the presumably lost man, but to no avail. Three days later, however, Nanak returned to his home unharmed. Straightway he gave away his worldly belongings and went forth to his religious work.

Nanak's first public proclamation at this time was the bold and simple affirmation: "There is no Hindu and no Muslim." This attracted much attention, and both Hindus and Muslims began to pay heed to the teachings of this new Guru. As he continued to preach, it was the custom of Nanak to compose and utter verses, and in this he was accompanied by a minstrel named Mardana who played for him upon the rebec. Although not mentioned in this Janamsakhi, other accounts also tell of a certain Bhai Bala who was a prominent disciple and companion of Nanak.

From this time on, Nanak is described as leading a "retired" life, no doubt referring to separation from all worldly concerns and complete devotion to religious work. Five periods follow, according to the Janamsakhi, in each of which Nanak concentrated his efforts in a different geographical area. "First," we read that Nanak "passed his retired life in the East." In this period he visited many places including the great city of Benares, and underwent manifold experiences.

At one time during this period he halted at a village but could find no one who would allow him to stay there. "There was one faqir there, to his hovel he went. That faqir was leprous. The Baba having gone there stood and said: 'O faqir, allow me to remain here during the night!' The faqir said: 'Animals are destroyed, who come near me, but it is the favor of God that a human shape has come again into my sight.' He remained there. The faqir began to lament. . . . The Guru became compassionate and said: 'Mardana, play the rebec!' [Here follow certain verses which Nanak recited to Mardana's accompaniment.] Then in consequence of the interview [with the Guru] the leprosy was removed and his [the faqir's] body was healed. He came and fell down at [Nanak's] feet and became a votary of the name; he began to mutter: 'Guru, Guru!'"

Not long after this, Nanak and Mardana were taken prisoner by an officer of Babur who was then making his conquest of the Lodi kingdom of Delhi. The two were treated as slaves, but when certain wonderful happenings transpired and were reported to the king, he said: "A town in which there are such faqirs should not have been struck." Later Babur visited Nanak in person, and declared: "In the face of this faqir God is coming into sight."

The second period of Nanak's "retired" life was spent in the south, where he visited various places in the Deccan and also went to Ceylon. The third period was passed in the north; the fourth in the west, where he is said to have gone as far as Mecca.

In the fifth and last period of his life, Nanak returned to the banks of the Ravi River to end his days. There he selected a very devoted disciple, Guru Angad, to be his successor, passing over his own two sons who had hoped for the preferment. As the time of his death drew near, "the Hindus and Muslims, who were votaries of the Name, began to say, the Muslims: 'We shall bury him,' and the Hindus: 'We shall burn him.' Then the Baba said: 'Put ye flowers on both sides, on the right side put those of the Hindus and on the left those of the Muslims. If the flowers of the Hindus will remain green tomorrow, then they shall burn me; and if the flowers of Muslims will remain green, then they shall bury me.' Then the Baba ordered the society that they should recite the praises [of God]. [Here follow certain verses, and then there are broken places in the leaf of the manuscript.] . . . he fell asleep. . . . When they lifted up the

[551]

sheet, there was nothing at all. The flowers of both parties had remained green. The Hindus took theirs and went and the Muslims took theirs and went. The whole society fell on their knees. Say: Wahiguru [Hail, Guru]! In Sambat 1595 [A.D. 1538] . . . Baba Nanak was absorbed [i.e., died] in Kartarpur."[27]

HIS TEACHINGS

It is already evident that the teaching of Nanak was in general agreement with that of his predecessor, Kabir, on such points as its transcendence of religious divisions, its opposition to formalism, and its inculcation of devotion to one God.

For his own formulation of his doctrines we may turn to the Japji or book of praise which is found as the introductory section of the Adi Granth. This is a collection of psalms which almost certainly came from Nanak himself. The following quotations, given for the most part in the translation of Professor John Clark Archer, will provide a brief indication of the fundamentals of the message of Nanak in his own words.[28]

> Thinking comprehendeth him not, although there be thoughts by the
> > thousands,
> Silence discovers him not, though it be continuous silence;
> Man is persistently hungry, though he eats of tasty abundance;
> Not one of a hundred thousand artful devices avails him!
> How may the truth be attained, the bonds of falsehood be broken?
> > By obeying the will of God as surely recorded, saith Nanak.
> The Lord is true, glorious forever, his loving kindness infinite;
> To those who crave and seek he gives, gives with full abandon.
> What indeed must he be offered to throw his court wide open?
> What words must lips be uttering to make his love responsive?
> At deathless dawn give Sat Nam [True Name] thought and glory,
> Put on the garb of deeds—and salvation's way is open!
> > Be sure that he himself is fully true, saith Nanak.
> At the place of pilgrimage no bath avails without his favor,
> The whole creation that I see, it came of his exertion,
> Counsel glows like priceless gems, if one harkens to the Guru.
> > Teach me the mystery, O Guru
> > Of the life thou givest—such wisdom may I cherish!
> Truth, knowledge and contentment come by harkening,
> By harkening comes the bathing places' merit,

[27] Kartarpur was a village on the right bank of the Ravi River, opposite the present town of Dehra Baba Nanak. Macauliffe, *The Sikh Religion*, i, p.180.

[28] Archer, *The Sikhs*, pp.120-133; see also Sir Jogendra Singh, *Thus Spoke Guru Nanak, A Collection of the Sayings of Guru Nanak.* 1934.

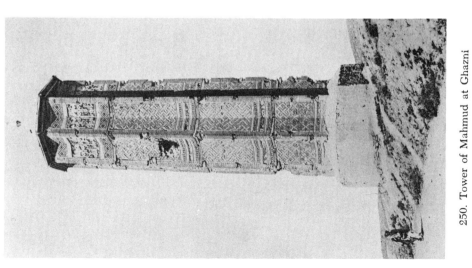

250. Tower of Mahmud at Ghazni

251. The Qutb Minar, Delhi

252. Entrance Gateway of Akbar's Tomb at Sikandra

253. The Taj Mahal, Agra (*Copyright reserved by the Archaeological Survey of India*)

254. A Page in an Early Janamsakhi

255. An Illuminated Janamsakhi Manuscript

256. The Darbar Sahib at Amritsar

257. In the Treasury at Amritsar

258. The Akal Takht at Amritsar

259. The Shrine of Guru Arjun at Lahore

260. The Sikh Temple at Tarn Taran

Honor and the art of reading come by harkening,
And by it the last stage of meditation.
    Devotion leads to happiness, saith Nanak,
    Sins and sorrow are destroyed by harkening.
Wisdom comes and understanding by obedience,
By obedience comes the knowledge of creation,
Slights and slaps are nothing by obedience,
Death's ties are cut asunder by obedience.
The Name is such to him devoid of passion,
Who knows him in his heart by due obedience.
Impressive are the varied forms of beauty,
Who knows the generous bounty of the whole?
How many issues out of one source flowing—
A hundred thousand rivers from one spring.
    What mighty power for man to fix his thought on!
    No self-denial comprehends it all,
    To please thee is a man's best aspiration,
    O thou who art eternal, ever dwelling in repose.

5. THE LATER GURUS

THE adherents of the religion taught by Guru Nanak became known as Sikhs or "learners," and like the founder the following leaders of the church were called Gurus or "teachers." As we have just seen, previous to his death Nanak designated one of the most devoted of his disciples to be his successor, and thus this man, Angad, became the second Guru.

ANGAD

The two chief achievements of Guru Angad (d. A.D. 1552) seem to have been the enlargement of the institution of a public kitchen which Nanak had started, where guests and friends ate with the disciples as a single family regardless of race or religion; and the invention of the Gurmukhi (from Sanskrit *guru*, teacher, and *mukha*, mouth; thus, literally, proceeding from the mouth of the teacher) alphabet in which to write the literature of the faith.[29]

An interesting although perhaps apocryphal story about the same Guru concerns the time when the Emperor Humayun was driven from his throne by Shir Shah. Coming to Lahore, Humayun inquired for some person who could assist him to regain his kingdom. Being told of Angad, the emperor proceeded to the town of Khadur, near Tarn Taran, where the Guru was. Since at the time, however, the Guru was in a trance and his minstrels were playing and singing his hymns, the monarch was kept standing. Angered by such lack of attention, Humayun seized his sword with the intention of striking the Guru, but marvelously enough the weapon would not come out of its sheath. Guru Angad then took notice of the emperor. Addressing him, he reproached him for not having used his sword when he ought against Shir Shah, and then for wishing to draw it against harmless men of religion. "In a cowardly manner hast thou fled from the battle, and now posing as a hero thou wishest to attack a body of men engaged in their devotions." Humayun then expressed his sorrow and begged for the Guru's help. Angad replied: "Hadst thou not put thy hand on the hilt of thy sword, thou shouldst at once have obtained thy kingdom. Thou shalt now proceed for a time to thine own country Persia, and when thou returnest thou shalt recover thy possessions."[30]

[29] Archer, *The Sikhs*, pp.137-139.
[30] Macauliffe, *The Sikh Religion*, II, pp.19f.

AMAR DAS

Guru Angad selected as his successor Guru Amar Das, the latter having been converted to Sikhism through one of his own relatives. Guru Amar Das served as spiritual head of the community from A.D. 1552 until his death in 1574. He made his residence at the village of Goindwal (Govindwal, or Gondwal), in the region of Lahore. He was vigorous in his attacks upon idolatry and polytheism, and also upon the Hindu custom of suttee (*sati*) or widow-burning, which had also continued among the Sikhs.

According to legend, Amar Das, too, had direct contact with the Mughal emperor of his time, in this case none other than Akbar the Great. The story is that the emperor paid a visit of state to the Guru of whose great sanctity he had heard, and brought rich offerings for him. Presenting his gifts, Akbar added, "I will make thee a grant of whatever land thou desirest, and I am ready to perform any other office that may be pleasing to thee." Amar Das, however, replied, "I have obtained lands and rent-free tenures from my Creator. He who cherisheth all existences giveth also unto me. My Sikhs devoutly give me wherewithal to supply my kitchen. Whatever cometh daily is spent daily, and for the morrow my trust is in God." The emperor further urged him to accept the gift of several villages, but the Guru still refused. Akbar then said, "I see thou desirest nothing. From thy treasury and thy kitchen countless beings receive bounties, and I entertain similar hopes. The villages which thou refusest I will grant to thy daughter Bibi Bhani." So the villages were bestowed upon the daughter, and the Guru bade the emperor farewell with appreciation for his pilgrimage.[31]

RAM DAS

Bibi Bhani, the daughter of Amar Das just mentioned, was married to a young man named Jetha who distinguished himself for his devotion and eventually became the fourth Guru under the name Ram Das (d. A.D. 1581). Within the lifetime of Amar Das, Bibi Bhani assigned to her husband the villages she had received from the Emperor Akbar; and Amar Das gave Jetha the following charge: "Search for some place other than Goindwal for the residence of our Sikhs. Go thither, build a great city, and cause it to be inhabited. Thou possessest the lands assigned thee by the emperor. First build a house therein for thyself, and then excavate a pool to the east of it as a place of Sikh pilgrimage."

[31] *ibid.*, p.97.

Jetha found a region some twenty-five miles from Goindwal, built a hut there for himself as did several other people, and began to excavate a pool. Somewhat later Amar Das gave him further instructions: "Cease to construct the rectangular pool thou didst lay out, and on which thou didst perform some work, and give it the name Santokhsar, 'water of joy.' On the low land to the east of it excavate another pool and call it Amritsar, 'water of eternity.' It shall be consolidated with brickwork when there is an opportunity. Go and exert thine efforts to that end."

The location of the Amritsar pool seems to have been on an ancient Hindu property where there was a small sanctuary called Harimandir or "temple of Vishnu." When the new pool was still only partially completed a wonderful occurrence transpired there in the healing of a crippled leper who bathed in its waters. Thereupon he and his faithful wife accepted the Sikh religion and joined in the further efforts toward the completion of the tank.

As the work went on, the hut of Guru Ram Das was enlarged to a better residence, additional accommodations were erected for the laborers as well as for visitors, and eventually a whole city arose. This city was known at first as Ramdaspur, or the city of Ram Das, and later as Amritsar. The residence of Ram Das was called the Guru's Mahal, or palace.[32]

ARJUN

Arjun was the youngest son of Ram Das, and became the fifth Guru, serving as spiritual leader of the Sikhs from A.D. 1581 to 1606. He resided first at Tarn Taran, and then after seven years removed to Amritsar. He did much to make the latter place the real religious capital of the Sikhs. He completed the Santokhsar Pool which had been left unfinished by Ram Das. He rebuilt the former Hindu temple of Harimandir in the midst of the Pool of Amritsar, and renamed it Har Mandir or "everybody's temple." The new Sikh shrine was only a modest structure of burnt brick, but it had doors on all four sides as a symbol of welcome to all worshipers, and when the Adi Granth was compiled the volume was given the central place in the temple. On the bank of the pool he began another shrine, called the Akal Takht or Throne of the Timeless. Also one other pool was excavated by Arjun, its location being in the secluded place where he desired to work on the compilation of the Granth. This pool was called Ramsar.

[32] *ibid.*, pp.141,267-271,276; Archer, *The Sikhs*, pp.141f.

The labor of Arjun in compilation of the Adi Granth has already been described, and this work was doubtless his most important single achievement. Furthermore, under his leadership the organization of Sikhism was much developed, and the movement which had begun as simply the preaching of an inclusive gospel took on more and more the form of a separate church and even of a state. Tithing was instituted to support the Sikh kitchens and sanctuaries and the office of the Guruship, traders were sent as far abroad as Turkestan, and the faith was propagated in an organized way.

A glance at their respective dates will indicate that Guru Arjun was heading the Sikh community during the latter half of the reign of Akbar, which was the time when the emperor was attempting to inaugurate an eclectic religion of his own. As far as we know, however, Akbar took no notice of the proposals of the Sikhs for transcending the differences of Hindus and Muslims, and the two movements went their separate ways. Interestingly enough, while the imperially favored cult perished upon the death of its royal inventor, the humbler and still apparently insignificant church of the Sikhs continued to grow until it became one of India's more important religious groups.

Even if the Sikhs had no connection with Akbar's attempted innovations in religion, they played a relatively prominent part in political affairs immediately after his death. It will be recalled that Jahangir took the throne at that time, but held it only by suppressing a powerful revolt led by his son, Khusrau. In the struggle, Guru Arjun supported Khusrau, making a large financial gift to him and encouraging many of the Sikhs to join the rebel forces. The crucial battle was fought in the region of Lahore, and when Khusrau was defeated Jahangir punished his supporters severely. Guru Arjun was first fined, then apprehended and imprisoned at Lahore where he was tortured and put to death. In the Sikh sources the story is modified to the extent that Arjun is described as walking under prison guard after his tortures to bathe in the Ravi River and there simply disappearing in the waters. Thus he became the first Sikh martyr, and was afterward known as Guru Arjun Deva.[33]

In his time of torture Arjun sent out this message: "I bear all this torture to set an example to the teachers of the True Name, that they may not lose patience or rail at God in affliction. The true test

---

[33] Macauliffe, *The Sikh Religion*, III; Archer, *The Sikhs*, pp.142-171; Richard Burn in CHI IV, p.157.

of faith is the hour of misery." Before he died he addressed his disciples thus: "I have succeeded in effecting the object of my life. Go to my son the holy Har Gobind, and give him from me ample consolation. Bid him not mourn or indulge in unmanly lamentations but sing God's praises. Let him also restrain from grief the other members of my family. Let him sit fully armed on his throne, and maintain an army to the best of his ability. Let him affix the patch of Guruship to his forehead according to ancient custom, and ever treat his Sikhs with the utmost courtesy. Let him . . . in all respects, except the wearing of arms hereby enjoined, adopt the practices of the preceding Gurus. Cremate not my body, but let it flow on the bosom of this river [the Ravi]."[34]

HAR GOBIND

As intimated in the preceding quotation, from this time on a more and more militant spirit was to come into Sikhism. After the martyrdom of Arjun, there was conscious antagonism between the Sikhs and the Muslims, and the sixth Guru, Har Gobind (A.D. 1606-1645), regularly went about with a large armed guard. Concerning his personal arms the new Guru said, "I wear two swords as emblems of spiritual and temporal authority. In the Guru's house religion and worldly enjoyment shall be combined—the caldron to supply the poor and needy and the scimitar to smite oppressors."[35] The chief building enterprises of Guru Har Gobind were the completion of the Akal Takht or Throne of the Timeless, begun by Arjun, and now dedicated to both peace and war; and the construction of two more pools, Kaulsar and Bibeksar, thus bringing to five[36] the total number of sacred tanks in Amritsar.

HAR RAI

The seventh Guru, Har Rai (A.D. 1645-1661), was the grandson of Guru Har Gobind. In his time both the internal solidarity of the Sikhs and their external antagonism to the Delhi regime were increased. Once again the Sikhs supported the loser in a struggle for the imperial throne. This time it was Dara, eldest son of Shah Jahan, to whom Guru Har Rai lent encouragement. As we already know, it was another son, Aurangzib, who actually obtained the throne. The latter slew Dara, and attempted to arrest Har Rai, but was unsuc-

[34] Macauliffe, *The Sikh Religion*, III, pp.94,99.
[35] *ibid.*, IV, p.4.
[36] Santokhsar, Amritsar, Ramsar, Kaulsar, Bibeksar.

cessful in this. Har Rai died in peace, having appointed his own son, Har Kishan, as his successor.[37]

HAR KISHAN

Har Kishan, the eighth Guru, had a relatively brief and uneventful term of leadership of the Sikhs (A.D. 1661-1664). Aurangzib is said to have invited him to Delhi, with a scheme in mind for his destruction. Har Kishan went to the capital, but died there of smallpox rather than by the emperor's intrigue.[38]

TEG BAHADUR

Teg Bahadur, a son of Har Gobind, was the ninth to occupy the exalted but in those days hazardous position of Guru (A.D. 1664-1675). He made his center of residence at Anandpur, a town which he himself founded on the Sutlej River one hundred miles east of Amritsar, but spent much of his time in tours of the surrounding regions. The animosity between the Sikhs and the Muslim government at Delhi continued, and the Guru was eventually arrested and brought to the capital. According to the doubtless apocryphal account of this event, the Emperor Aurangzib said to him: "It is my pleasure that there should be but one religion. Hinduism is false and worthless, and those who profess it will suffer punishment in hell. I pity them and therefore wish to do them a favor. If they of their own accord keep the Id [festival], and fast, and repeat the Muslim creed and prayers, I will reward them with wealth, appointments, land-revenue grants, and lands with irrigating wells. In this case thou, too, shalt have many disciples, and thou shalt become a great priest of Islam. Therefore accept my religion, and thou shalt receive from me whatever thy heart desireth."

To all such invitations Teg Bahadur opposed a steadfast resistance. "Hear, O Aurangzib," he said, "I will never embrace Islam. Thou and I and all creatures are the servants, not the equals of God. The world is subject to him. The prophet of Mecca who originated the religion thou professest, was unable to impose one faith on the world, so how canst thou do so? He was not able to convert even his own uncle to Islam. Of what account art thou? The *aswad* stone [the black stone of Mecca] which the Muslims set up in memory of Adam, and which they call celestial, but which the Hindus call the lingam,

---

[37] Macauliffe, *The Sikh Religion*, IV, pp.275-314.
[38] *ibid.*, pp.315-330.

is worshiped by Muslim pilgrims. Is it anything more than an idol? When Muhammad drove idolatry out of Mecca, the inhabitants formed a design to assassinate him. When he became aware of this, he made his escape at night to Medina, leaving all his property behind, and never returned. Canst thou justly say that he enjoyed God's special favor? Nay, we are all God's people. God alone is master. He can do what he pleaseth. O Aurangzib, who art thou and what power hast thou to convert the whole world to Islam? The Guru hath said, 'Death laugheth over man's head, but the brute knoweth it not.' O king, through pride thou thinkest not that thou too shalt assuredly die. He who practiceth pride shall be utterly extirpated."[39]

When the emperor heard this reply, the Sikh sources relate, he became enraged and delivered the Guru to torture and at last to death. The execution was by beheading, and the head was taken back by the Guru's followers to Anandpur for cremation.

GOBIND SINGH

Teg Bahadur had designated his son, Gobind Rai, as his successor in the Guruship. When word of his father's martyrdom came to this young man he is said to have uttered these words: "You know, my friends, that my father has been murdered at Delhi. I am left alone, but as long as I live I will never cease to avenge his death; should I die in the attempt, it matters not."[40]

The militant note sounded in these words was characteristic of the adventurous career of the tenth Guru who headed the Sikh movement from A.D. 1675 to 1708. He took for himself the name Singh or "lion," and reorganized his followers into a new military theocracy called the Khalsa. Initiation into the order involved a service of communion and baptism, in which sugar was stirred up in water with a two-edged dagger, and the resulting nectar was both sipped by the new members and also sprinkled upon them. Adherence to the movement was also signified by the utterance of the words, Wah Guruji ka Khalsa, Wah Guruji ki Fatah (Hail the Khalsa of the Guru, Hail the triumph of the Guru); and by the wearing of the five *kakkas* or k's: the *kesh*, uncut hair wound into a topknot; the *kangha*, a hair comb; the *kara*, a steel bracelet; the *kachch*, a pair of shorts; and the *kirpan*, a two-edged dagger.

With the establishment of the Khalsa the second period in the development of Sikhism reached its fulfillment. The first period was

[39] *ibid.*, pp.378,380.
[40] W. L. M'Gregor, *The History of the Sikhs.* 1846, I, p.69.

that from the days of Guru Nanak down to the compilation of the Adi Granth under Guru Arjun when the evolution was essentially peaceful; the second took its rise with the martyrdom of Arjun and was marked by an increasing militancy which came to a climax with the inauguration of the new society of sword-bearing men of religion.[41]

The Khalsa was attacked in military force by Emperor Aurangzib, the sons of Gobind Singh were slain, and he himself was driven into hiding in the deserts of Bhatinda south of Amritsar. There, however, he wrote many of the materials which came to make up the Granth of the Tenth Guru; and despite all of their tribulations his followers were welded together more loyally than ever.

With his own sons slain previously, the personal Guruship came to an end upon the death of Gobind Singh. Before he died, he is supposed to have told his disciples that the work of the Gurus was completed, and that from that time on the Khalsa itself, with the Granth Sahib, would represent their spiritual leadership. "I have entrusted you," he said, "to the immortal God. Ever remain under his protection, and trust to none besides. Wherever there are five Sikhs assembled who abide by the Guru's teachings, know that I am in the midst of them. He who serveth them shall obtain the reward thereof—the fulfillment of all his heart's desires. Read the history of your Gurus from the time of Guru Nanak. Henceforth the Guru shall be the Khalsa [or, in the Khalsa] and the Khalsa the Guru [or, in the Guru]. I have infused my mental and bodily spirit into the Granth Sahib and the Khalsa."[42]

At this point we may consider that the story of the development of Sikhism has been carried far enough to exhibit its chief features as a religious movement. In the later years a sort of confederacy of military bands came into being,[43] and under Maharaja Ranjit Singh[44] (A.D. 1780-1839) so powerful a Sikh army was built up that the subsequent British conquest and annexation of the Punjab was only accomplished with very severe fighting. Into these later political events it is not necessary for us to go.[45]

[41] Indubhusan Banerjee, *Evolution of the Khalsa.* i (1936), pp.3f.

[42] Macauliffe, *The Sikh Religion,* v, pp.243f.; C. H. Payne, *A Short History of the Sikhs,* p.43.

[43] Lajwanti Rama Krishna, *Les Sikhs, origine et développement de la communauté jusqu'à nos jours (1469-1930).* 1933, p.183.

[44] Charles Hügel, *Travels in Kashmir and the Panjab, Containing a Particular Account of the Government and Character of the Sikhs.* 1845.

[45] See J. D. Cunningham, *A History of the Sikhs from the Origin of the Nation to the Battles of the Sutlej* (rev. ed. by H. L. O. Garrett). 1918.

6. THE MONUMENTS OF SIKHISM

THE center of the Sikh religion is at Amritsar, the historical importance of which has been apparent in the foregoing narrative. The origin of the chief Sikh shrine at that place has also been indicated. This was the Har Mandir, erected at the end of the sixteenth century by Guru Arjun. In A.D. 1761 this building was demolished by Ahmad Shah (A.D. 1724-1773), Muslim ruler of Afghanistan, on one of his plundering raids into India,[46] but was rebuilt in 1766 on the same site and probably according to the same plan. Finally, when Ranjit Singh took Amritsar in 1802 he adorned and beautified the temple greatly, ornamenting its walls with marble and covering its roof with copper gilt. At this time it became known as the Darbar Sahib or Lordly Court, and now is generally called the Golden Temple.[47]

The Golden Temple (Fig. 256) stands on a small island in the middle of the Pool of Amritsar, a sheet of water perhaps five acres in extent. There are marble pavements around the pool, and from an archway on the west side a marble causeway leads out to the temple. The lower parts of the walls are of white marble, while the upper parts as well as the domes of the roof are encased in gilded copper. There are designs of vines and flowers on the walls, as well as inscribed texts from the Granth Sahib.

On each of the four sides of the building a large doorway, provided with beautiful silver doors, gives access to the interior. In accordance with Sikhism's devotion to one God and opposition to idolatry, there is no idol within. The place of honor is given rather to copies of the sacred Granth.

The archway mentioned above, through which one approaches the causeway to the temple, is part of a larger building which is called the Treasury. Here are kept eight gold doors sometimes used instead of the silver doors on the Darbar Sahib; a jewel-adorned, curved sword of Ranjit Singh; a diadem of diamonds and pearls worn by Ranjit Singh's grandson; ceremonial *chauris* or fly-whisks; and numerous other precious objects used in processions and special observances. A photograph of some of these treasures is reproduced in Fig. 257.

[46] Payne, *A Short History of the Sikhs*, pp.49-58.
[47] Fergusson, *History of Indian and Eastern Architecture*, II, pp.162f.

Also on the bank of the pool stands the Akal Takht or Throne of the Timeless (Fig. 258), built originally by Arjun and Har Gobind, and reconstructed by Gobind Singh. It has a gilded dome and two minarets, and within gives the supreme place to the Granth Sahib. Historical treasures likewise are kept here, including a large sword of Gobind Singh.

LAHORE

As we have also seen, Lahore likewise figured prominently in Sikh history and was specially memorable as the place of death of the first martyr, Guru Arjun. It will be recalled that according to Sikh legend his body was carried away in the waters of the Ravi River. Although this river now flows perhaps a mile away to the west, it once washed the city walls. At the northwest corner of the city stands the Shrine of Guru Arjun (Fig. 259), built by Ranjit Singh to mark the place where the body of the great martyr disappeared in the waters. In this sanctuary, too, the place of honor is given to the Adi Granth, over which attendants wave *chauris* in token of reverence.[48]

TARN TARAN

A third important center of Sikhism is Tarn Taran, fifteen miles south of Amritsar. Here Guru Arjun lived for a number of years. The Sikh temple at this place, built by Maharaja Ranjit Singh, is somewhat reminiscent of the Darbar Sahib at Amritsar. It stands on the east side of a magnificent pool of water, which is filled from the near-by Bari Doab Canal. The temple walls are adorned with flower and vine designs, while other outside walls have paintings of gods and goddesses. A corridor runs around the lower room of the temple, and on the south side of this is the Granth, wrapped in silk and fanned by a functionary with a *chauri*. On the temple roof is a small open pavilion and a fine cupola. Panels at either edge of the roof in front are inscribed with the words in Gurmukhi characters, Satinamu (True Name), and Wahiguru (Hail, Guru).[49] A view of the temple and pool is shown in Fig. 260.

[48] *A Handbook for Travellers in India, Burma and Ceylon* (John Murray), p.352.
[49] Archer, *The Sikhs*, p.30.

[563]

Index

Go-Nishio, 434
Good Thought, *see* Vohu Manah
gopura, 168, 169
Gorakhpur, 257
Go-Reizei, 434
Go-Saga, 434
Go-Sakuramachi, Empress, 434
Gosala, 218
Go-Sanjo, 434
Go-Shirakawa, 434
Gospel, 488, 502
Go-Suzaku, 434
G o t a m a , Gotamas, *see* Gautama, Gautamas
Gotarzes I, 110
Gotarzes II, 110
Gotarzes, the satrap of satrap, *see* Gotarzes I
Gotarzes, the son of Gew, *see* Gotarzes II
Go-Toba, 434
Gotra karma, 211
Go-Tsuchi-mikado, 434
Gottama, *see* Gautama
Go-Uda, 434
Govindwal, *see* Goindwal
Go-Yojo, 434
Grand-Jewel, 429
Grand Mosque at Delhi, 538
Grande Galerie des Fresques, 32
Granth, 556, *see also* Adi Granth
Granth of the Tenth Guru, 561, *see also* Daswan Padshah ka Granth
Granth of the Tenth King, *see* Daswan Padshah ka Granth
Granth Sahib, 561, 562, 5 6 3 , *s e e a l s o* A d i Granth
grantha, 541
granthi, 541
Great Ascetic, *see* Samana
Great Bharata, *see* Mahabharata
Great Bodhisattva, 292
Great Britain, 462
Great Chronicle of Ceylon, *see* Mahavamsa
Great King of the Wo, *see* Ta Wo Wang
Great Lake, *see* Tonle Sap

Great Learning, *see* Ta Hsüeh
Great Monastery, *see* Mahavihara
Great-Mountain-Possessor, 431
Great Mosque at Cordova, 526f.
Great Mosque at Damascus, 511, 513-515
Great Mosque at Hama, 509
Great Mosque at Qayrawan, 522-524
Great Mosque at Samarra, 520f.
Great River, *see* Yangtze Kiang
Great Story, *see* Mahavastu
Great Stupa at Sanchi, 270
Great Vehicle, 288, 289, 294, 306, *see also* Mahayana
Great Wall of China, 305, 362, 364, 366, 367
Greater Imperial Palace, 447
Greco-Bactrians, 107, 108, *see also* Bactrian Greeks
Greco-Buddhist, *see* Gandharan school
Greco-Persian war, 112
Greece, 111
Greek art, 111, 283
Greek deities, 283
Greek elements in the religion of Palmyra, 481
Greek empire, 88
Greek inscription, 114
Greek language, 129
Greek writings, 517
Greeks, 82, 147, 148, 462, 466
Green Dome, *see* Golden Gate
Grihya-Sutras, 160
Grimaldi, 29
Grotto of the Garden, *see* Taq-i-Bustan
Grousset, René, 291
Guardians of the Four Quarters of the World, 309
Guardians of the Religion, *see* Dharmapalas

Guda, 150
Guhasiva, 299
Guiana, 14
Gujarat, 173, 179, 229, 231, 232, 537
Gujri, 543
Gump's, 301
Gunasthanas, 212
Gundaphorus, *see* Gondophares
Gupta, Guptas, 152, 306, 308
Gupta Period, 1 5 8 - 1 6 4 , 224, 288-293, 294, 300
Gupta Temples, 164
Gur, *see* Firuzabad
Gurbaal, 463
Gurgan, *see* Astarabad
Gur-i-Mir, 530
Gurjaras, 173
Gurmukhi, 541, 554, 563
Guru, Gurus, 541, 543, 544, 545, 548-553, 554; Later, 554-561
Guru Arjun Deva, *see* Arjun
Guru's Mahal, 556
Gushasp, 117
Gushtasp, *see* Vishtaspa
Gwalior, 231, 537
Gyan Parbodh, 544
Gyogi, 449

Habib as-Siyar, 534
Hachiman, 449, 451, 452
Hachiman-no-kami, 444, 449, 451, 452
Hadad, 481
Hades, 401, 404
Hadhramaut, 461, 470, *see also* Hadramyta
Hadhramautians, 4 6 6 , 471, 473-475, *see also* Chatramotitae
Hadith, 492f., 494, 518
Hadramyta, 470, 473, *see also* Hadhramaut
Hagar, 495
Hagmatana, 72, *see also* Hamadan
Hahjeenah-dinneh, 51
Hai-den, 456
Hair, al-, 520
Hajar, al-, 471
hajj, 500
Hakam, al- II, 526

Hakhamanish, *see* Achaemenes
Halak'amar, 472
Halebid, 175
Halévy, Joseph, 469
Hall for Prayers, *see* Haiden
Hall of Columns, *see* Apadana of Susa
Hall of One Hundred Columns at Persepolis, 103
Hall of Public Audience, *see* Bab al-'Amma
Hall of Worship, *see* 'Ibadat-Khana
Hama, 509
Hamadan, 72, 109, *see also* Ecbatana, Hagmatana, Hamadhan
Hamadhan, 491
Hamdani, al-, 469, 471, 473, 477
Han art, 368f.
Han dynasty, 335, 348, 377, 381, 398, 402, 407
Han Hsiang, 402
Han Period, 329, 333, 348, 364-369, 372, 393-397; Eastern, *see* Later; Former, 361, 364; Later, 364, 396, 403
Han Wen Kung, 406, 407
Han Yü, 402
Hanazono, 434
Hangchow, 376
Hanif, 488
haniwa, 424
Hansho, *see* Hanzei
Hanuman, 152
Hanzei, 433
Hao, 330, 331
Haoma, 69
Hara, 99
Haram, 506
Har Gobind, 558, 563
Har Kishan, 559
Har Mandir, 556, 562, *see also* Harimandir
Har Rai, 558f.
Haram Bilqis, 471, 476
Haramain, al-, 505
Harappa, 123-125, 130
Hare, 41
Hari Rud, *see* Tejen River
Haribans, 542
Haribhadra, 186
Haridatta, 193

Harimandir, 556, *see also* Har Mandir
Harishena, 216
Harsha Vardhana, 165, 167, 168, 225
Harun al-Rashid, 517, 522
Hasan, al-, 518
Hashjeshjin, 50
hasta, 191
Hastimalla, 189
Hastinapura, 135, 153, *see also* Asandivat
Hastipala, 195, 196
Hathigumpha, 221
Hatshepsut, 462
Haurvatat, 90
Haute Garonne, 34
Hayagriva, 316
Hazare shabd, 544
Heaven, 347, 349, 354, 355, 360, 406, 411, *see also* T'ien
Heaven-Plenty-Earth-Plenty-Heaven's-Sun-Height-Prince-Rice-ear-Ruddy-Plenty, 430, *see also* Prince-Rice-ear-Ruddy-Plenty, Ame-nigi-shi-kuni-nigishi-ama-tsu-hi-daka-hiko-ho-no-ni-nigi-no-mikoto
Heaven-Shining-Great-August-Deity, 429, *see also* Ama-terasu-o-mikami
Heaven-Shining-Great-Deity, 446
Heavenly Avadanas, *see* Divyavadana
Heavenly Rock-Dwelling, *see* Rock-Cave of Heaven
Heavenly-Alarming-Female, 429
Heavenly-Beckoning-Ancestor-Lord, 429, *see also* Ame-no-koyane-no-mikoto
Heavenly-Eternally-Standing-Deity, 427
Heavenly-Hand-Strength-Male-Deity, 429
Heaven's-Sun-Height-Prince-Great-Rice-ears-Lord-Ears, 431, *see also* Ama-tsu-hi-daka-hiko-ho-ho-de-mi-no-mikoto

Heaven's-Sun-Height-Prince-Wave-limit-Brave-Cormorant-Thatch-Meeting-Incompletely, 431, *see also* Ama-tsu-hi-daka-hiko-nagisa-take-u-gaya-fuki-ahezu-no-mikoto
Hebrew, Hebrews, 462, 463, 469, *see also* Jews
Hecatompylos, 107, 109
Hegira, *see* Hijra
Hegr, al-, 481, *see also* Madain Salih
Heian Period, 447-450, 451
Heian-kyo, 447, 448, 449, *see also* Kyoto
Heidelberg, 26
Heijo, 311, 434, *see also* Pyongyang
Hejaz, 461, 482, 483
Heliodorus, 147
Helios, 107, 131, *see also* Mithra
Hellenism, 109, 282, *see also* Greece, Greeks
Hellenistic deities, 151
Hellenistic influence, 284
Helmand swamps, 65
Hemachandra, 186, 188, 197, 204, 219, 225
Heng Shan, 404
Heraclius, 119
Herat, 532, 533, 534
herbad, 81
Herb-Quelling Great Sword, 430, *see also* Kusa-nagi-no-tachi
Hermes, 111
Hermippus, 77
Hermodorus, 77
Herodotus, 72, 83, 84, 100
Herzfeld, Ernst E., 66, 88
Hezekiah, 476
Hidari Jingoro, 457, 458
Hidetada, 456
Higashiyama, 434
High-August-Producing-Wondrous Deity, 427
Hijra, 494
Hill, *see* Ch'iu
Hillqahi, 479
Himalayas, 65, 121, 122, 154, 163, 171, 249, 260, 267
himsa, 209

Jalan, 542
Jalap, 542
Jambhala, 316
Jambuddiva, 185, 203, 219
Jambuddivapannatti, 185
Jambusvami, 214, 218
Jami' at-Tawarikh, 532
Jami' Masjid, 538, 539
Jamshed, *see* Yim
Janaka, 152
Janamsakhis, 544, 548, 549, 550
Japan, 247, 281, 310, 312-314, 419-460; Prehistoric, 420-435
Japanese Analects, *see* Warongo
Japanese Buddhist canon, 247
Japji, 543, 552
Jat, 542
Jataka, Jatakas, 221, 240, 250, 266, 267, 291
Jaugada, 260, 263
Jausaq al-Khaqani, 520
Jaussen, Père, 476
Java, 25, 26, 28, 158, 304f.
Jawhar, 524, 525
Jebel al-Maqla, 461
Jebel Hadhur, 461
Jebel Sham, 461
Jebel Tannur, 481
Jehoram, 463
Jejakabhukti, 173
Jen wu chih, 370
Jenghiz Khan, 376, 413, 528, 530
Jerusalem, 488, 496, 498, 510, 511, 512, 513, 519
Jesuit missionary, 443f., 455, *see also* Francis Xavier, Luis Alameda
Jesus, 494, 502, 503, *see also* 'Isa
Jeta, 268
Jetavana, 263, 268
Jetha, *see* Ram Das
Jethro, *see* Shu'aib
Jewel-Good-Princess, *see* Tamayori-hime-no-mi-koto
Jewish elements in Manichaeism, 115
Jewish influence, 501
Jewish temple, 94

Jewish theory of evil, 76
Jews, 82, 478, 487, 488, 498, 517, 518, *see also* Hebrews, Israelites
Jhelum River, 122
Jidda, 506
Jimmu, 432, 433, 452, *see also* Kamu-yamato-iha-re-biko
Jina, Jinas, 182, 186, 187, 195, 199, 200, 220, 223, 226, 227, 228, 232
Jingo Kogo, 433
jinja, 437
Jinko, 435
jinn, 501
Jito, Empress, 434
jiv, 202
Jiva, Jivas, 202, 207, 208, 209
Jivabhigama, 185
Jivakanda, 187
Jizo, 309, *see also* Kshiti-garbha
Jñanavaraniya karma, 211
Jnatadharmakatha, 185, *see also* Nayadhamma-kahao
Jnatasutra, 232
Jnatri, 194, *see also* Nata, Naya
Jnatriputras, 194, *see also* Nataputtas
Job, 466
Jodhpur, 231
Jodo, 314
John the Baptist, 514
Jomei, 434
Jrimbhikagrama, 195
Jubayr, Ibn, 514
Juchen, 376
Judaea, Judaeans, 466, *see also* Jews
Judah, 463
Judaism, 180, 372, 477, 484, 485, 487
Judas, 258
judge, 81
Judgment, Day of, 531
Juggernaut, 177
Jumada I, 491
Jumna River, 135, 151, 158, 222, 234
Junagadh, 230
Junna, 434
Junnin, 434

Juntoku, 434
Jupiter, 100
Jupiter Damascenus, 513

Ka'bah, 482, 483, 488, 496, 506, 510, 512, 532, *see also* Black Stone
Ka'bah-i-Zardusht, 101, 102
Kabir, 542, 545, 546f., 552
Kabirpanthis, 546
Kabul, 538
Kabul River, 121
Kabuli Bagh, 538
kachch, 560
Kadabat, 479, *see also* Kaddat
Kaddat, 479, *see also* Kadabat
Kadphises I, 149
Kaesong, *see* Songto
Kagu, Mount, 429
K'aifeng, 376
Kaijo, *see* Songto
Kaika, 433
Kai-Kabad, 80
Kai-Kaus, 80, 106
Kai-Khusrov, 80, 106
Kailasa, Mount, 169
Kailasanatha, 169, 179, 226
Kailasanatha temple, 168, 171, 174
Kai-Lorasp, 80
Kairouan, *see* Qayrawan, al-
Kaivalya-Upanishad, 137
Kai-Vishtasp, 80, 81, 105
kakkas, 560
Kalacakra, 204
Kalajambhala, 316
Kalaka, Story of, *see* Kalakacaryakatha
Kalakacaryakatha, 220, 232
Kalasahar, 542
Kalasu, 542
Kalbi, Ibn al-, 483, 484
Kali, 163
Kalian, 543
Kalidasa, 159
Kalinga, Kalingas, 143, 147, 215, 221, 260, 261, 265, 299
Kalki, 162

[595]